Handbook of Fingerprint Recognition

T0180481

Davide Maltoni
Dario Maio
Anil K. Jain
Salil Prabhakar

Second Edition

Handbook of Fingerprint Recognition

 Springer

Davide Maltoni
Biometric Systems Lab (DEIS)
Università di Bologna
Via Sacchi, 3
47023 Cesena, Italy
maltoni@csr.unibo.it

Anil K. Jain
Department of Computer Science
Michigan State University
3115, Engineering Building
East Lansing MI 48823, USA
jain@cse.msu.edu

Dario Maio
Biometric Systems Lab (DEIS)
Università di Bologna
Via Sacchi, 3
47023 Cesena, Italy
dmaio@deis.unibo.it

Salil Prabhakar
DigitalPersona, Inc.
720 Bay Road
Redwood City CA 94063, USA
salilp@digitalpersona.com

Additional material to this book can be downloaded from http:// extras .springer .com .

ISBN 978-1-4471-6106-6   ISBN 978-1-84882-254-2 (eBook)

British Library Cataloguing in Publication Data
A catalogue record for this book is available from the British Library

Printed on acid-free paper

Springer Science+Business Media
springer.com

Contents

Preface

Overview

Biometric recognition, or simply biometrics, refers to the use of distinctive anatomical and behavioral characteristics or identifiers (e.g., fingerprints, face, iris, voice, hand geometry) for automatically recognizing a person. Questions such as "Is this person authorized to enter the facility?", "Is this individual entitled to access the privileged information?", and "Did this person previously apply for a passport?" are routinely asked in a variety of organizations in both public and private sectors. Traditional credential based systems no longer suffice to verify a person's identity. Because biometric identifiers cannot be easily misplaced, forged, or shared, they are considered more reliable for person recognition than traditional token- (e.g., keys or ID cards) or knowledge- (e.g., password or PIN) based methods. Biometric recognition provides better security, higher efficiency, and, in many instances, increased user convenience. It is for these reasons that biometric recognition systems are being increasingly deployed in a large number of government (e.g., border crossing, national ID card, e-passports) and civilian (e.g., computer network logon, mobile phone, Web access, smartcard) applications.

A number of biometric technologies have been developed and several of them have been successfully deployed. Among these, fingerprints, face, iris, voice, and hand geometry are the ones that are most commonly used. Each biometric trait has its strengths and weaknesses and the choice of a particular trait typically depends on the requirements of the application. Various biometric identifiers can also be compared on the following factors; universality, distinctiveness, permanence, collectability, performance, acceptability and circumvention. Because of the well-known distinctiveness (individuality) and persistence properties of fingerprints as well as cost and maturity of products, fingerprints are the most widely deployed biometric characteristics. It is generally believed that the pattern on each finger is unique. Given that there are about 6.5 billion living people on Earth and assuming each person has 10 fingers, there are 65 billion unique fingers! In fact, fingerprints and biometrics are often considered synonyms! Fingerprints were first introduced as a method for person identification over 100 years back. Now, every forensics and law enforcement agency worldwide routinely uses automatic fingerprint identification systems (AFIS). While law enforcement agencies were the earliest adopters of the fingerprint recognition technology, increasing concerns about national security, financial fraud and identity fraud have created a growing need for fingerprint technology for person recognition in a number of non-forensic applications.

Fingerprint recognition system can be viewed as a pattern recognition system. Designing algorithms capable of extracting salient features from fingerprints and matching them in a robust way are quite challenging problems. This is particularly so when the users are uncooperative, the finger surface is dirty or scarred and the resulting fingerprint image quality is poor. There is a popular misconception that automatic fingerprint recognition is a fully solved problem since automatic fingerprint systems have been around for almost 40 years. On the contrary, fingerprint recognition is still a challenging and important pattern recognition problem because of the large intra-class variability and large inter-class similarity in fingerprint patterns.

This book reflects the progress made in automatic techniques for fingerprint recognition over the past 4 decades. We have attempted to organize, classify and present hundreds of existing approaches to feature extraction and matching in a systematic way. We hope this book would be of value to researchers interested in making contributions to this area, and system integrators and experts in different application domains who desire to explore not only the general concepts but also the intricate details of this fascinating technology.

Objectives

The aims and objectives of this book are to:

- Introduce automatic techniques for fingerprint recognition. Introductory material is provided on all components/modules of a fingerprint recognition system.
- Provide an in-depth survey of the state-of-the-art in fingerprint recognition.
- Present in detail recent advances in fingerprint recognition, including sensing, feature extraction, matching and classification techniques, synthetic fingerprint generation, biometric fusion, fingerprint individuality and design of secure fingerprint systems.
- Provide a comprehensive reference book on fingerprint recognition, including an exhaustive bibliography.

Organization and Features

After an introductory chapter, the book chapters are organized logically into four parts: fingerprint sensing (Chapter 2); fingerprint representation, matching and classification (Chapters 3, 4, and 5); advanced topics, including synthetic fingerprint generation, biometric fusion, and fingerprint individuality (Chapters 6, 7, and 8); and fingerprint system security (Chapter 9).

Chapter 1 introduces biometric and fingerprint systems and provides some historical remarks on fingerprints and their adoption in forensic and civilian recognition applications. All the topics that are covered in detail in the successive chapters are introduced here in brief. This will provide the reader an overview of the various book chapters and let her choose a personalized reading path. Other non-technical but important topics such as "applications" and "privacy issues" are also discussed. Some background in image processing and pattern recognition techniques is necessary to fully understand the majority of the book chapters. To facilitate readers who do not have this background, references to basic readings on various topics are provided at the end of Chapter 1.

Chapter 2 surveys the existing fingerprint acquisition techniques: from the traditional "ink technique" to recent optical, capacitive, thermal, and ultrasonic live-scan fingerprint scanners, and discusses the factors that determine the quality of a fingerprint image. Chapter 2 also introduces the compression techniques that are used to efficiently store fingerprint images in a compact form.

Chapters 3, 4, and 5 provide an in-depth treatment of fingerprint feature extraction, matching and classification, respectively. Published techniques (in over 700 technical papers) are divided into various categories to guide the reader through the large number of approaches proposed in the literature. The main approaches are explained in detail to help beginners and practitioners in the field understand the methodology used in building fingerprint systems.

Chapters 6, 7, and 8 are specifically dedicated to the three cutting edge topics: synthetic fingerprint generation, biometric fusion, and fingerprint individuality, respectively. Synthetic fingerprints have been accepted as a reasonable substitute for real fingerprints for the design and benchmarking of fingerprint recognition algorithms. Biometrics fusion techniques (e.g., fusion of fingerprints with iris or fusion of multiple fingers) can be exploited to overcome some of the limitations in the state-of-the-art technology to build practical solutions. Scientific evidence supporting fingerprint individuality is being increasingly demanded, particularly in forensic applications, and this has generated interest in designing accurate fingerprint individuality models.

Finally, Chapter 9 discusses the security issues and countermeasure techniques that are useful in building secure fingerprint recognition systems.

From the First to the Second Edition

This second edition of the "Handbook of Fingerprint Recognition" is not a simple retouch of the first version. While the overall chapter structure has been maintained, a large amount of new information has been included in order to:

- Provide additional details on topics that were only briefly discussed in the first edition.
- Shed light on emerging issues or consolidated trends.
- Organize and generalize the underlying ideas of the approaches published in the literature. Over 500 papers on fingerprint recognition were published in the last 5 years (2003 to 2008) alone! Fingerprint recognition literature is sometimes chaotic and, due

to different (and often cumbersome) notations and conventions followed in the literature, it is not easy to understand the differences among the plethora of published algorithms. Instead of systematically describing every single algorithm, we focused our attention on the contributions that advanced the state-of-the-art. Of course, this is a very difficult task and we apologize for excessive simplification or selectivity that we may have introduced.

The total length of the handbook grew from about 350 to about 500 pages and the number of references increased from about 600 to about 1,200. Several new figures, drawings and tables have been added with the aim of making the presentation illustrative and lucid. The DVD included with the book now also contains the databases used in the 2004 Fingerprint Verification Competition (FVC2004). Table 1 summarizes the new content included in this edition of the Handbook.

Chapter	New content
1	– Improved presentation of need and benefits of fingerprint recognition systems – More comprehensive analysis of system errors and their causes – Application categories – Updated introduction to individual book chapters
2	– New sensing technologies (e.g., multispectral imaging) – Image quality specifications (IQS) – Operational quality of fingerprint scanners – Examples of 1,000 dpi and multi-finger scanners – Examples of commercial single-finger scanners
3	– Level 3 features (pores, incipient ridges, creases) – Wider coverage of the methods for estimating ridge orientations – Learning-based segmentation techniques – Improved methods for singularity detection – Advances in fingerprint enhancement – Minutiae encoding standards – Estimation of fingerprint quality
4	– Advanced correlation filters – Computation of similarity score – Orientation image-based relative pre-alignment – Evolution of two-stage approaches: local structure matching + consolidation – Fingerprint distortion models – Improvements in texture-based matching – Fingerprint comparison based on Level 3 features

	– Fingerprint databases and recent third party evaluations
	– Interoperability of fingerprint recognition algorithms
5	– Improved exclusive classification techniques
	– Advances in continuous classification and fingerprint indexing
	– Performance evaluation on common benchmarks
6	– Physical and statistical models for fingerprint generation
	– Automatic generation of ground truth features corresponding to the synthetic images
	– Testing feature-extractor conformance to standards
7	– Major rewrite of the chapter with systematic presentation of fusion methods
	– More in-depth coverage of fusion methods and published techniques
	– Advances in image, feature, and score fusion techniques
8	– Coverage of the recent finite mixture minutiae placement model
9	– Major rewrite of the chapter with systematic presentation of security techniques
	– Advances in match-on-card (MoC) and system-on-a-chip (SoC)
	– Advances in template protection

Table 1. New content included in the Handbook.

Contents of the DVD

The book includes a DVD that contains the 12 fingerprint databases used in the 2000, 2002 and 2004 Fingerprint Verification Competitions (FVC). The DVD also contains a demonstration version of the SFINGE software that can be used to generate synthetic fingerprint images. These real and synthetic fingerprint images will allow interested readers to evaluate various modules of their own fingerprint recognition systems and to compare their developments with the state-of-the-art algorithms.

Intended Audience

This book will be useful to researchers, practicing engineers, system integrators and students who wish to understand and/or develop fingerprint recognition systems. It would also serve as a reference book for a graduate course on biometrics. For this reason, the book is written in an informal style and the concepts are explained in a simple language. A number of examples and figures are presented to visualize the concepts and methods before giving any mathematical definition. Although the core chapters on fingerprint feature extraction, matching and classification require some background in image processing and pattern recognition, the introduction, sensing and security chapters are accessible to a wider audience (e.g., developers of biometric applications, system integrators, security managers, designers of security systems).

Acknowledgments

A number of individuals helped in making this book a reality. Raffaele Cappelli of the University of Bologna wrote Chapter 6 on synthetic fingerprints, Alexander Ivanisov of Digital Persona Inc. provided invaluable suggestions throughout several revisions of Chapter 9, and Sharath Pankanti of the IBM T. J. Watson Research Center, Arun Ross of West Virginia University, and Abhishek Nagar of Michigan State University provided some portions of text and figures in Chapters 1, 7, and 8. We also thank Wayne Wheeler at Springer, for his encouragement in revising the first edition of this book.

The first edition of the book received many positive feedbacks from readers and colleagues; the book also received the prestigious 2003 PSP award for the "Computer Science" category given by the Association of American Publishers. These accolades motivated us in our efforts to prepare this new edition of the book. One suggestion we received from several readers was to identify and focus on only the most effective algorithms for various stages of a fingerprint recognition system. While this would be very useful, it is not easy to make such a selection. All the evaluation studies on common benchmarks (e.g., FVC databases) are concerned with the accuracy of the entire recognition system. Therefore, it is not possible to determine if the performance improvement is due to a specific matching technique or is in large part due to a minor change to an existing feature extraction method. The only way to objectively compare algorithms is to factor out all the possible difference in the pre- or post- stages. Forthcoming FVC-onGoing (2009) is being organized with such an aim.

This book explores automatic techniques for fingerprint recognition, from the earliest approaches to the current state-of-the-art algorithms. However, with the development of novel sensor technologies, availability of faster processors at lower cost, and emerging applications of fingerprint recognition systems, there continues to be a vigorous activity in the design and development of faster, highly accurate, and robust algorithms. As a result, new algorithms for fingerprint recognition will continue to appear in the literature even after this book goes to press. We hope that the fundamental concepts presented in this book will provide some principled and proven approaches in the rapidly evolving and important field of automatic fingerprint recognition.

April 2009

Davide Maltoni
Dario Maio
Anil K. Jain
Salil Prabhakar

1
Introduction

1.1 Introduction

More than a century has passed since Alphonse Bertillon first conceived and then industriously practiced the idea of using body measurements for solving crimes (Rhodes, 1956). Just as his idea was gaining popularity, it faded into relative obscurity by a far more significant and practical discovery of the distinctiveness of the human fingerprints. In 1893, the Home Ministry Office, UK, accepted that no two individuals have the same fingerprints. Soon after this discovery, many major law enforcement departments saw potential of fingerprints in identifying repeat offenders who used an alias, i.e., changed their names with each arrest to evade the harshest penalties reserved for recidivists in law. The law enforcement departments embraced the idea of "booking" the fingerprints of criminals at the time of arrest, so that their records are readily available for later identification. Fingerprints found an application in forensics. By matching leftover fingerprint smudges (latents) from crime scenes to fingerprints collected during booking, authorities could determine the identity of criminals who have been previously arrested. The law enforcement agencies sponsored a rigorous study of fingerprints, developed scientific methods for visual matching of fingerprints and instituted strong programs/ cultures for training fingerprint experts. They successfully applied the art of fingerprint recognition for nailing down the perpetrators (Scott (1951); Lee and Gaensslen (2001)).

Despite the ingenious methods improvised to increase the efficiency of the manual approach to fingerprint indexing and matching, the ever growing demands on fingerprint recognition quickly became overwhelming. The manual method of fingerprint indexing (based on the Henry system of classification) resulted in a highly skewed distribution of fingerprints into bins (types): most fingerprints fell into a few bins and this did not improve the search efficiency. Fingerprint training procedures were time-intensive and slow. Furthermore, demands imposed by the painstaking attention needed to visually compare two fingerprints of varied qualities, tedium of the monotonous nature of the work, and increasing workloads due to a higher demand on fingerprint recognition services, all prompted the law enforcement agencies to initiate research into acquiring fingerprints through electronic media and automate fingerprint recognition based on the digital representation of fingerprints. These efforts led to the development of *Automatic Fingerprint Identification Systems* (AFIS) over the past 4 decades. Law enforcement agencies were the earliest adopters of the automatic fingerprint recognition technology. More recently, however, increasing concerns about security and identity fraud have created a growing need for fingerprint and other biometric technologies for person recognition in a large number of non-forensic applications.

1.2 Biometric Recognition

As our society has become electronically connected and more mobile, surrogate representations of identity such as passwords (prevalent in electronic access control) and cards (prevalent in banking and government applications) cannot be trusted to establish a person's identity. Cards can be lost or stolen and passwords or PIN can, in most cases, be guessed. Further, passwords and cards can be easily shared and so they do not provide non-repudiation.

Biometric recognition (or simply biometrics) refers to the use of distinctive *anatomical* (e.g., fingerprints, face, iris) and *behavioral* (e.g., speech) characteristics, called *biometric identifiers* or *traits* or *characteristics* for automatically recognizing individuals. Biometrics is becoming an essential component of effective person identification solutions because biometric identifiers cannot be shared or misplaced, and they intrinsically represent the individual's bodily identity. Recognition of a person by their body, then linking that body to an externally established "identity", forms a very powerful tool of identity management with tremendous potential consequences, both positive and negative. Consequently, biometrics is not only a fascinating pattern recognition research problem but, if carefully used, is an enabling technology with the potential to make our society safer, reduce fraud and provide user convenience (user friendly man–machine interface).

The word *biometrics* is derived from the Greek words *bios* (meaning life) and *metron* (meaning measurement); biometric identifiers are measurements from living human body. Perhaps all biometric identifiers are a combination of anatomical and behavioral characteristics and they should not be exclusively classified into either anatomical or behavioral characteristics. For example, fingerprints are anatomical in nature but the usage of the input device (e.g., how a user presents a finger to the fingerprint scanner) depends on the person's behavior. Thus, the input to the recognition engine is a combination of anatomical and behavioral characteristics. Similarly, speech is partly determined by the vocal tract that produces speech and partly by the way a person speaks. Often, a similarity can be noticed among parents, children, and siblings in their speech. The same argument applies to the face: faces of identical twins may be extremely similar at birth but during their growth and development, the faces change based on the person's behavior (e.g., lifestyle differences leading to a difference in bodyweight, etc.).

A number of questions related to a person's identity are asked everyday in a variety of contexts. Is this person authorized to enter the facility? Is this individual entitled to access privileged information? Is this person wanted for a crime? Has this person already received certain benefits? Is the given service being administered exclusively to the enrolled users? Reliable answers to questions such as these are needed by business and government organizations. Because biometric identifiers cannot be easily misplaced, forged, or shared, they are considered more reliable for person recognition than traditional token (ID cards) or knowledge-based (passwords or PIN) methods. The objectives of biometric recognition are user convenience (e.g., money withdrawal at an ATM machine without a card or PIN), better security (e.g., only authorized person can enter a facility), better accountability (e.g., difficult to deny having accessed confidential records), and higher efficiency (e.g., lower overhead than computer password maintenance). The tremendous success of fingerprint-based recognition technology in law enforcement applications, decreasing cost of fingerprint sensing devices, increasing availability of inexpensive computing power, and growing identity fraud/theft have all resulted in increasing use of fingerprint-based person recognition in commercial, government, civilian, and financial domains. In addition to fingerprints, some other traits, primarily hand shape, voice, iris and face have also been successfully deployed.

Thanks to the imaginative and flattering depiction of fingerprint systems in nightly television crime shows (e.g., CSI), the general perception is that automatic fingerprint identification is a foolproof technology! This is not true. There are a number of challenging issues that need to be addressed in order to broaden the scope of niche market for fingerprint recognition systems.

1.3 Biometric Systems

An important issue in designing a practical *biometric system* is to determine how an individual is going to be recognized. Depending on the application context, a biometric system may be called either a *verification* system or an *identification* system:

- A verification system authenticates a person's identity by comparing the captured biometric characteristic with her previously captured (enrolled) biometric reference template pre-stored in the system. It conducts one-to-one comparison to confirm whether the claim of identity by the individual is true. A verification system either rejects or accepts the submitted claim of identity.
- An identification system recognizes an individual by searching the entire enrollment template database for a match. It conducts one-to-many comparisons to establish if the individual is present in the database and if so, returns the identifier of the enrollment reference that matched. In an identification system, the system establishes a subject's identity (or determines that the subject is not enrolled in the system database) without the subject having to claim an identity.

The term *authentication* is also used in the biometric field, sometimes as a synonym for verification; actually, in the information technology language, authenticating a user means to let the system know the identity of the user regardless of the mode (verification or identification). Throughout this book we use the generic term *recognition* where we are not interested in distinguishing between verification and identification.

The block diagrams of verification and identification systems are depicted in Figure 1.1; user enrollment, which is common to both tasks is also graphically illustrated.

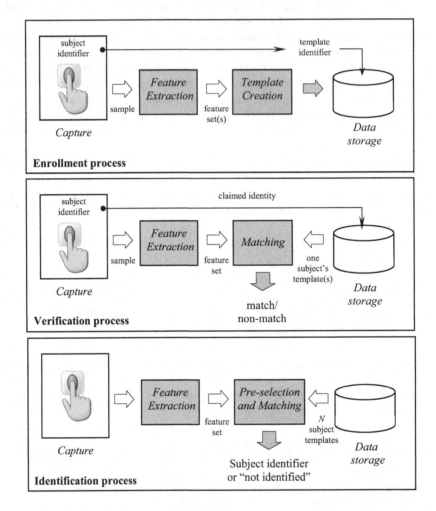

Figure 1.1. Enrollment, verification, and identification processes. These processes use the following modules: capture, feature extraction, template creation, matching, pre-selection, and data storage. In the identification process pre-selection and matching are often combined.

The enrollment, verification, and identification processes involved in user recognition make use of the following system modules:

- *Capture*: a digital representation of biometric characteristic needs to be sensed and captured. A biometric sensor, such as a fingerprint scanner, is one of the central pieces of a biometric capture module. The captured digital representation of the biometric characteristic is often known as a *sample*; for example, in the case of a fingerprint system, the raw digital fingerprint image captured by the fingerprint scanner is the sample. The data capture module may also contain other components (e.g., a keyboard and screen) to capture other (non-biometric) data.
- *Feature extraction*: in order to facilitate matching or comparison, the raw digital representation (sample) is usually further processed by a *feature extractor* to generate a compact but expressive representation, called a *feature set*.
- *Template creation*: the template creation module organizes one or more feature sets into an *enrollment template* that will be saved in some persistent storage. The enrollment template is sometimes also referred to as a *reference*.
- *Pre-selection and matching*: the pre-selection (or filtering) stage is primarily used in an identification system when the number of enrolled templates is large. Its role is to reduce the effective size of the template database so that the input needs to be matched to a relatively small number of templates. The matching (or comparison) stage (also know as a *matcher*) takes a feature set and an enrollment template as inputs and computes the similarity between them in terms of a *matching score*, also known as *similarity score*. The matching score is compared to a *system threshold* to make the final decision; if the match score is higher than the threshold, the person is recognized, otherwise not.
- *Data storage*: is devoted to storing templates and other demographic information about the user. Depending on the application, the template may be stored in internal or external storage devices or be recorded on a smart card issued to the individual.

Using these five modules, three main processes can be performed, namely, enrollment, verification, and identification. A verification system uses the enrollment and verification processes while an identification system uses the enrollment and identification processes. The three processes are:

- *Enrollment*: user enrollment is a process that is responsible for registering individuals in the biometric system storage. During the enrollment process, the biometric characteristic of a subject is first captured by a biometric scanner to produce a sample. A quality check is often performed to ensure that the acquired sample can be reliably processed by successive stages. A feature extraction module is then used to produce a feature set. The template creation module uses the feature set to produce an enrollment template. Some systems collect multiple samples of a user and then either select the best image (or feature set) or fuse multiple images (or feature sets) to create a composite template. The enrollment process then takes the enrollment template and stores it in the system storage together with the demographic information about the user (such as an identifier, name, gender, height, etc.).

- *Verification*: the verification process is responsible for confirming the claim of identity of the subject. During the recognition phase, an identifier of the subject (such as username or PIN [Personal Identification Number]) is provided (e.g., through a keyboard or a keypad or a proximity card) to claim an identity; the biometric scanner captures the characteristic of the subject and converts it to a sample, which is further processed by the feature extraction module to produce a feature set. The resulting feature set is fed to the matcher, where it is compared against the enrollment template(s) of that subject (retrieved from the system storage based on the subject's identifier). The verification process produces a match/non-match decision.

- *Identification*: in the identification process, the subject does not explicitly claim an identity and the system compares the feature set (extracted from the captured biometric sample) against the templates of all (or a subset of) the subjects in the system storage; the output is a *candidate list* that may be empty (if no match is found) or contain one (or more) identifier(s) of matching enrollment templates. Because identification in large databases is computationally expensive, a pre-selection stage is often used to filter the number of enrollment templates that have to be matched against the input feature set.

Depending on the application domain, a biometric system could operate either as an *on-line* system or an *off-line* system. An on-line system requires the recognition to be performed quickly and an immediate response is imposed (e.g., a computer network logon application). On the other hand, an off-line system does not require the recognition to be performed immediately and a relatively longer response delay is allowed (e.g., background check of an applicant). On-line systems are often *fully automatic* and require that the biometric characteristic be captured using a live-scan scanner, the enrollment process be unattended, there be no (manual) quality control, and the matching and decision making be fully automatic. Off-line systems, however, are often *semi-automatic*, where the biometric acquisition could be through an off-line scanner (e.g., scanning a fingerprint image from a latent or inked fingerprint card), the enrollment may be supervised (e.g., when a suspect is "booked," a police officer guides the fingerprint acquisition process), a manual quality check may be performed to ensure good quality acquisition, and the matcher may return a list of candidates which are then manually examined by a forensic expert to arrive at a final decision.

The verification and identification processes differ in whether an identity is claimed or not by the subject. A biometric *claim* (or *claim of identity*) is defined as the implicit or explicit claim that a subject *is* or *is not* the source of a specified or unspecified biometric enrollment template. A claim may be:

- *Positive*: the subject is enrolled.
- *Negative*: the subject is not enrolled.
- *Specific*: the subject is or is not enrolled as a specified biometric enrollee.
- *Non-specific*: the subject is or is not among a set or subset of biometric enrollees.

The application context defines the type of claim. In certain applications, it is in the interest of the subject to make a positive claim of identity. Such applications are typically trying to prevent multiple people from using the same identity. For example, if only Alice is authorized to enter a certain secure area, then it is in the interest of any subject to make a positive claim of identity (of being Alice) to gain access. But the system should grant access only to Alice. If the system fails to match the enrolled template of Alice with the input feature set, access is denied, otherwise, access is granted. In other applications, it is in the interest of the subject to make a negative claim of identity. Such applications are typically trying to prevent a single person from using multiple identities. For example, if Alice has already received certain welfare benefits, it is in her interest to now make a negative claim of identity (that she is not among the people who have already received benefits), so that she can double-dip. The system should establish that Alice's negative claim of identity is false by finding a match between the input feature set of Alice and enrollment templates of all people who have already received the benefits.

The following three types of claims are used depending on the application context:

- *Specific positive claim*: applications such as logical access control (e.g., network-logon) may require a specific positive claim of identity (e.g., through a username or PIN). A verification biometric system is sufficient in this case to confirm whether the specific claim is true or not through a one-to-one comparison.
- *Non-specific positive claim*: applications such as physical access control may assume a non-specific positive claim that the subject is someone who is authorized to access the facility. One of the advantages of this scenario is that the subject does not need to make a specific claim of identity (no need to provide a username, PIN, or any other token), which is quite convenient. However, the disadvantage of this scenario is that an identification biometric system is necessary (which has longer response time and lower accuracy due to one-to-many comparisons).
- *Non-specific negative claim*: applications such as border crossing typically assume a non-specific negative claim, i.e., the subject is not present in a "watch list". Again, an identification system must be used in this scenario. Note that such applications cannot use traditional knowledge-based or possession-based methods of recognition. Surrogates tokens such as passports have been traditionally used in such applications but if passports are forged (or if people obtain duplicate passports under different names), traditional recognition methods cannot solve the problem of duplicate identities or *multiple enrollments*.

1.4 Comparison of Traits

Any human anatomical or behavioral trait can be used as a biometric identifier to recognize a person as long as it satisfies the following requirements:

- *Universality:* each person should possess the biometric trait.
- *Distinctiveness*: any two persons should be sufficiently different in terms of their biometric traits.
- *Permanence*: biometric trait should be invariant (with respect to the matching criterion) over time.
- *Collectability*: biometric trait can be measured quantitatively.

However, in a practical biometric system, there are a number of other issues that should be considered in selecting a trait, including:

- *Performance*: recognition accuracy, speed (throughput), resource requirements, and robustness to operational and environmental factors.
- *Acceptability*: extent to which users are willing to accept the biometric identifier in their daily lives.
- *Circumvention*: ease with which the biometric system can be circumvented by fraudulent methods.

A practical biometric system should have acceptable recognition accuracy and speed with reasonable resource requirements, harmless to the users, accepted by the intended population, and sufficiently robust to various fraudulent methods.

A number of biometric traits are in use in various applications. Each biometric trait has its own strengths and weaknesses and the choice typically depends on the application. No single trait is expected to effectively meet the requirements of all the applications. The match between a biometric trait and an application is determined depending upon the characteristics of the application and the properties of the trait. Some of the issues that need to be addressed in selecting a biometric trait for a particular application are:

- Does the application need a verification or identification system? If an application requires an identification of a subject from a large database, it needs a very distinctive biometric trait (e.g., fingerprints or iris).
- What are the operational characteristics of the application? For example, is the application attended (semi-automatic) or unattended (fully automatic)? Are the users habituated (or willing to become habituated) to the given biometric? Is the application covert or overt? Are subjects cooperative or non-cooperative?
- What is the template storage requirement of the application? For example, an application that performs the recognition on a smart card may require a small template size.
- How stringent are the performance requirements? For example, an application that demands very high accuracy needs a more distinctive biometric.

- What types of biometric traits are acceptable to the target user population? Biometric traits have different degrees of acceptability in different demographic regions depending on the cultural, ethical, social, religious, and hygienic standards. The acceptability of a biometric in an application is often a compromise between the sensitivity of the targeted population to various perceptions or taboos and the value or convenience offered by biometrics-based recognition.

A brief introduction to the most common biometric traits is provided below. We do not cover fingerprints in this list since it is extensively covered in the rest of this book. Figure 1.2 shows several biometric traits that have been either adopted in commercial systems or are being investigated.

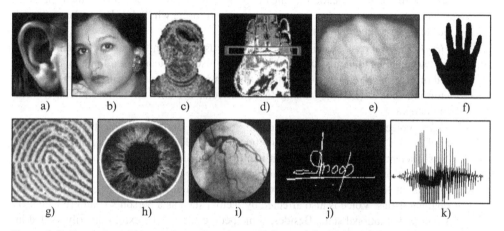

Figure 1.2. Examples of biometrics traits: a) ear, b) face, c) facial thermogram, d) hand thermogram, e) hand vein, f) hand geometry, g) fingerprint, h) iris, i) retina, j) signature, and k) voice.

- *Iris*: visual texture of the human iris is determined by the chaotic morphogenetic processes during embryonic development and is posited to be distinctive for each person and each eye (Daugman, 1999). An iris image is typically captured using a non-contact imaging process. Capturing an iris image often involves cooperation from the user, both to register the image of iris in the central imaging area and to ensure that the iris is at a predetermined distance from the focal plane of the camera. The iris recognition technology has been shown to be extremely accurate and fast on high resolution well-captured iris images.
- *Face*: face is one of the most acceptable biometric traits because it is one of the most common methods of recognition that humans use in their daily visual interactions. In addition, the method of acquiring face images is nonintrusive. Facial disguise is of

concern in unattended recognition applications. It is very challenging to develop face recognition techniques that can tolerate the effects of aging, facial expression, variations in the imaging environment, and facial pose with respect to the camera.

- *Hand and finger geometry*: some features related to the human hand (e.g., length of fingers) are relatively invariant and peculiar (although not very distinctive) to an individual. The image acquisition system requires cooperation of the subject to capture frontal and side view images of the palm flatly placed on a panel with outstretched fingers. The template storage requirements of the hand are very small, which is an attractive feature for bandwidth- and memory-limited systems. Due to its limited distinctiveness, hand geometry-based systems are only used for verification and do not scale well for identification applications. Finger geometry systems (which measure the geometry of at most two fingers as opposed to the whole hand) may be preferred because of their compact size.

- *Hand or finger vein*: near-infrared imaging is used to scan the back of a clenched fist to determine hand vein structure. Veins could also be detected in a finger using infrared or near-infra-red sensing. Systems for vein capture use inexpensive infra-red light emitting diodes (LEDs), leading to commercial systems for hand and finger vein biometrics.

- *Voice*: voice capture is unobtrusive and voice may be the only feasible biometric in applications requiring person recognition over a telephone. Voice is not expected to be sufficiently distinctive to permit identification of an individual from a large database of identities. Moreover, a voice signal available for recognition is typically degraded in quality by the microphone, communication channel, and digitizer characteristics. Voice is also affected by factors such as a person's health (e.g., cold), stress and emotional state. Besides, some people seem to be extraordinarily skilled in mimicking others voice.

- *Signature*: the way a person signs his name is known to be a characteristic of that individual. Signatures have been acceptable in government, legal, and commercial transactions as a method of verification for a long time. Signature is a behavioral biometric that changes over time and is influenced by physical and emotional conditions of the signatories. Signatures of some subjects vary a lot: even successive impressions of their signature are significantly different. Furthermore, professional forgers can reproduce signatures of others to fool the unskilled eye.

The biometric identifiers described above are compared in Table 1.1. Note that fingerprint has a nice balance among all the desirable properties. Every human being possesses fingers (with the exception of hand-related disability) and hence fingerprints. Fingerprints are very distinctive (see Chapter 8) and they are permanent; even if they temporarily change slightly due to cuts and bruises on the skin, the fingerprint reappears after the finger heals. Live-scan fingerprint scanners can easily capture high-quality fingerprint images and unlike face recognition, they do not suffer from the problem of segmenting the fingerprint from the background. However, they are not suitable for covert applications (e.g., surveillance) as live-scan fingerprint scanners cannot capture a fingerprint image from a distance and without the knowledge of the person. The deployed fingerprint recognition systems offer good performance and fingerprint scanners have become quite compact and affordable (see Chapter 2). Because fingerprints have a long history of use in forensic divisions worldwide for criminal investigations, they have some stigma of criminality associated with them. However, this is rapidly changing with the high demand for automatic person recognition to fight identity fraud and security threats. With a layered approach involving fingerprint and other security technologies, fingerprint systems are difficult to circumvent (see Chapter 9). Fingerprint recognition is one of the most mature biometric technologies and is suitable for a large number of recognition applications. This is also reflected in the revenues generated by various biometric technologies (see Figure 1.3).

Biometric identifier	Universality	Distinctiveness	Permanence	Collectability	Performance	Acceptability	Circumvention
Face	H	L	M	H	L	H	H
Fingerprint	M	H	H	M	H	M	M
Hand geometry	M	M	M	H	M	M	M
Hand/finger vein	M	M	M	M	M	M	L
Iris	H	H	H	M	H	L	L
Signature	L	L	L	H	L	H	H
Voice	M	L	L	M	L	H	H

Table 1.1. Comparison of commonly used biometric traits. Entries in the table are based on the perception of the authors. High, Medium, and Low are denoted by H, M, and L, respectively.

1.5 System Errors

The critical promise of the ideal biometric trait is that when a sample is presented to the biometric system, it will offer the correct decision. In practice, a biometric system is a pattern recognition system that inevitably makes some incorrect decisions. Let us first try to understand why a biometric system makes errors and then discuss the various types of errors. We also encouraged the readers to refer to ISO/IEC 19795-2 (2007) and to the other sections of ISO/IEC 19795 for a comprehensive treatment of biometric system errors.

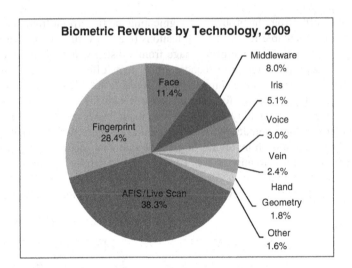

Figure 1.3. Revenue by biometric traits as estimated by International Biometric Group in 2009. Fingerprint-based systems (both forensic and non-forensic applications) continue to be the leading biometric technology in terms of market share, commanding more than 50% of biometric revenue.

1.5.1 Reasons behind system errors

There are three primary reasons that explain the errors made by a biometric system (see Jain et al. (2004b)):

- *Information limitation*: the invariant and distinctive information content in the biometric samples may be inherently limited due to the intrinsic signal capacity (e.g., individuality information) of the biometric identifier. For instance, the distinctive information in hand geometry is less than that in fingerprints. Consequently, hand geometry measurements can differentiate fewer identities than fingerprint even under ideal conditions. Information limitation may also be due to poorly controlled biometric presentation by the users (user interface issue) or inconsistent signal acquisition. Differently acquired measurements of a biometric identifier limit the invariance across different samples of the pattern. For example, information limitation occurs when there is very little overlap between the enrolled and sample fingerprints (e.g., left and right half of the finger). In such situations, even a perfect matcher cannot offer a correct decision. An extreme example of information limitation is when the person does not possess or cannot present the particular biometric needed by the identification system (e.g., amputees with missing hands and fingers).

- *Representation limitation*: the ideal representation scheme should be designed to re-
tain all the invariance as well as discriminatory information in the sensed measurements. Practical feature extraction modules, typically based on simplistic models of
biometric signal, fail to capture the richness of information in a realistic biometric
signal resulting in the inclusion of erroneous features and exclusion of true features.
Consequently, a fraction of legitimate pattern space cannot be handled by the biometric system, resulting in errors.
- *Invariance limitation*: finally, given a representation scheme, the design of an ideal
matcher should perfectly model the invariance relationship among different patterns
from the same class (user), even when imaged under different presentation conditions. Again, in practice (e.g., due to non-availability of sufficient number of training
samples, uncontrolled or unexpected variance in the collection conditions) a matcher
may not correctly model the invariance relationship resulting in matcher errors.

The challenge is to be able to arrive at a realistic and invariant representation of the biometric identifier from a few samples acquired under inconsistent conditions, and then, formally estimate the discriminatory information in the signal from the samples. This is
especially difficult in a large-scale identification system where the number of enrolled users is
huge (e.g., in the millions).

1.5.2 Capture module errors

In a fully automated biometric system, the biometric data is captured without human supervi-
sion and assistance. Such a biometric system typically uses a live-scan device that automatically detects the presence of a biometric characteristic as it appears in the field of view. For
example, a live-scan fingerprint scanner may wait in a low-power-consumption mode, with a
finger detection algorithm continually polling for the approach/presence of a finger. When the
finger detection algorithm detects a finger, the scanner may switch to a finger capture mode to
automatically capture a good quality fingerprint image. The automated biometric capture system can produce two types of errors: *Failure To Detect* (FTD) and *Failure To Capture* (FTC).
Failure to detect error occurs when a finger indeed approaches the fingerprint scanner but the
scanner fails to detect its presence. The failure to capture error occurs when the system knows
that a finger is present but fails to capture a sample. The rate of these two failures is usually
inversely proportions to each other. These failures occur when either the captured image is of
very poor quality (e.g., if the scanner surface is dirty) or when the capture module is used in-
appropriately (e.g., only tip of the finger instead of the central pad of the finger is presented to
the scanner or a finger is moved across on a swipe scanner with dramatically varying speed
and skew).

1.5.3 Feature extraction module errors

After capture the biometric sample is sent to the feature extraction module for processing. If the captured image is of poor quality, the feature extraction algorithm may fail to extract a usable feature set. This error is known as *Failure To Process* (FTP). Since capture module and feature extraction module are common to all the processes (enrollment, verification, and identification), the three types of errors (FTD, FTC, and FTP) mentioned here are often combined into one single measure called the *Failure To Acquire* (FTA). A high FTA rate will affect the throughput of the resulting biometric system and increase user frustration. One way to lower FTA is by increasing the sensitivity of the capture and feature extraction modules. But this will put additional burden on the later modules (such as matching).

1.5.4 Template creation module errors

The template creation module that takes one (or more) feature sets extracted from samples during the enrollment process and produces a template may also fail. Again, this typically happens either when there is not enough discriminatory information present in the feature sets (e.g., too small fingerprint area) or when the fingerprint images are of poor quality and consequently the feature set(s) are very noisy. Since template creation module is used only in the enrollment process and is the most critical part of the enrollment process, the failure of template creation module is known as *Failure To Enroll* (FTE). There is a tradeoff between the FTE rate and the error rates of the matching module discussed below. If the failure to enroll is disabled, then templates can be created from poor quality fingerprints but such noisy templates would result in higher matching errors.

1.5.5 Matching module errors

The result of a fingerprint matching module is typically a matching score (without loss of generality, lying in the interval [0,1]) that quantifies the similarity between the recognition feature set and the enrollment template. The closer the score is to 1, the more certain is the system that the recognition feature set comes from the same finger as the enrollment template. The decision module regulates its decision by using a threshold t; pairs of feature set and template generating scores higher than or equal to t are inferred as *matching pairs* (i.e., belonging to the same finger) and pairs of feature set and template generating scores lower than t are inferred as *non-matching pairs* (i.e., belonging to different fingers).

When the matching module is operating in a one-to-one comparison mode (it compares feature set from one finger with template from one finger), it gives a *match* or *non-match* decision depending on whether the comparison score exceeded the threshold or not, respectively. The matching module, operating in one-to-one comparison mode, can commit two types of errors: (i) mistaking feature set and template from two different fingers to be from the same finger (called *false match*), and (ii) mistaking feature set and template from the same finger to be from two different fingers (called *false non-match*).

It is important to understand the difference between false match and false non-match errors and the more commonly used *false acceptance* and *false rejection* errors. The false match and false non-match are errors of the matching module in one-to-one comparison mode while false acceptance and false rejection are the error rates associated with verification and identification processes and in fact their exact meaning is dependent upon the type of identity claim made by the user. For example, in applications with positive claim of identity (e.g., an access control system) a false match from the matching module results in the false acceptance of an impostor into the system, whereas a false non-match from the matching module causes the false rejection of a genuine user in the system. On the other hand, in an application with negative claim of identity (e.g., preventing users from obtaining welfare benefits under false identities), a false match from the matching module results in rejecting a genuine request, whereas a false non-match from the matching module results in falsely accepting an impostor request. Further, an application may use other criteria for acceptance/rejection in addition to match/non-match decision. The notion of "false match/false non-match" is not application dependent and there-fore, in principle, is more appropriate than "false acceptance/false rejection". However, the use of false acceptance (and False Acceptance Rate, abbreviated as FAR) and false rejection (and False Rejection Rate, abbreviated as FRR) is more popular, especially in the commercial sec-tor. In the rest of this book, while we will try to avoid the use of false acceptance and false rejection, they are synonyms for false match and false non-match, respectively.

When a biometric system operates in the identification mode, matching module works in one-to-many comparison mode. In its simplest form, one-to-many comparison against N templates can be viewed as a series of N one-to-one comparisons. If identification is performed only for subjects who are present in the enrollment database, the identification is known as *closed-set identification*. Closed-set identification always returns a non-empty candidate list. While closed-set identification has been studied extensively by researchers, it is rarely used in practice. In *open-set identification*, some of the identification attempts are made by subjects who are not enrolled. In the rest of this book when we refer to identification we will focus only on the open-set scenario. If the matching module is given a feature set from finger A and a set of templates that includes at least one template of A, and the matching module produces an empty candidate list, the error is called a *false negative identification error*. If the matching module is given a feature set from finger A and a set of templates that does not include any template from A, and the matching module returns a non-empty candidate list, the error is called a *false positive identification error*.

1.5.6 Verification error rates

In the previous section, we defined the errors from the matching module when it operates in one-to-one comparison mode that is typical of the verification process. So the false match and false non-match errors can be considered to be verification errors. Let the stored biometric template of a person be represented as $\mathbf{T}$ and the verification feature set be represented by $\mathbf{I}$. Then the null and alternate hypotheses are:

H_0: $\mathbf{I} \neq \mathbf{T}$, verification feature set does not come from the same finger as the template;
H_1: $\mathbf{I} = \mathbf{T}$, verification feature set comes from the same finger as the template.

The associated decisions are as follows.

D_0: non-match;
D_1: match.

The verification involves matching $\mathbf{T}$ and $\mathbf{I}$ using a similarity measure $s(\mathbf{T},\mathbf{I})$. If the matching score is less than the system threshold t, then we decide D_0, else we decide D_1. The above terminology is borrowed from communication theory, where the goal is to detect a message in the presence of noise. H_0 is the hypothesis that the received signal is noise alone, and H_1 is the hypothesis that the received signal is message plus the noise. Such a hypothesis testing formulation inherently contains two types of errors:

Type I: false match (D_1 is decided when H_0 is true);
Type II: false non-match (D_0 is decided when H_1 is true).

False Match Rate (FMR) is the probability of type I error (also called significance level of the hypothesis test) and *False Non-Match Rate* (FNMR) is the probability of type II error:

FMR = $P(D_1|H_0)$;
FNMR = $P(D_0|H_1)$.

Note that (1 − FNMR) is also called the power of the test.

To evaluate the accuracy of a biometric verification system, one must collect scores generated from a large number of comparisons between feature sets and enrollment templates of the same finger (the distribution $p(s|H_1)$ of such scores is traditionally called the *genuine distribution*), and scores generated from a large number of comparisons between feature sets and enrollment templates from different fingers (the distribution $p(s|H_0)$ of such scores is traditionally called the *impostor distribution*). Figure 1.4 illustrates the computation of FMR and FNMR over genuine and impostor distributions for a given threshold t:

$$\text{FNMR} = \int_0^t p(s \mid H_1)\,ds\,,$$

$$\text{FMR} = \int_t^1 p(s \mid H_0)\,ds\,.$$

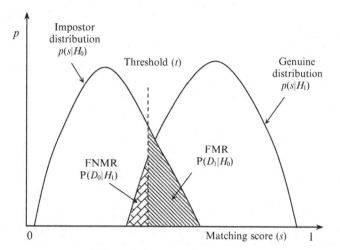

Figure 1.4. FMR and FNMR for a given threshold *t* are displayed over the genuine and impostor score distributions. Note that FMR is the percentage of impostor pairs whose comparison score is greater than or equal to *t*, and FNMR is the percentage of genuine pairs whose comparison score is less than *t*.

There is a strict tradeoff between FMR and FNMR in every biometric system (Golfarelli, Maio, and Maltoni (1997); Bazen and Veldhuis (2004)). In fact, both FMR and FNMR are functions of the system threshold t, and we should, therefore, refer them as FMR(t) and FNMR(t), respectively. If t is decreased to make the system more tolerant with respect to input variations and noise, then FMR(t) increases. On the other hand, if t is raised to make the system more secure, then FNMR(t) increases. A system designer may not know in advance the particular application where the fingerprint system would be deployed. So it is advisable to report system performance at all operating points (threshold, t). This is done by plotting a *Receiver Operating Characteristic* (ROC) curve (or a *Detection-Error Tradeoff* [DET] curve). Both the ROC and the DET curves are threshold independent allowing different fingerprint systems to be compared on a common criterion. The ROC curve is a plot of FMR(t) against $(1 - \text{FNMR}(t))$ for various decision thresholds, t. The DET curve is a plot of FMR(t) against FNMR(t) and provides a more direct view of the error-vs-error tradeoff. Figures 1.5a–c show examples of score distributions, FMR(t) and FNMR(t) curves, and a DET curve, respectively.

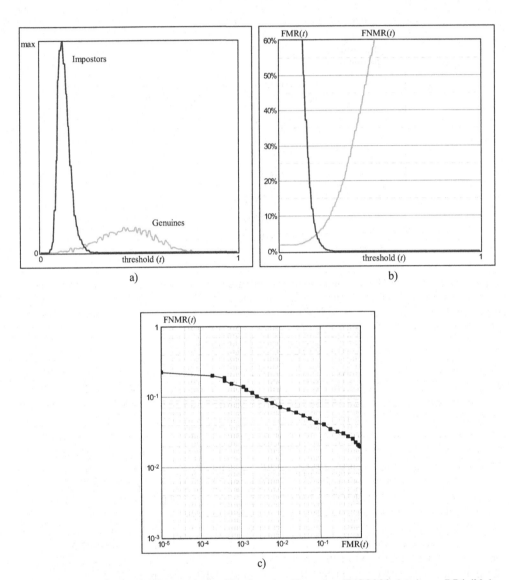

Figure 1.5. Evaluation of a fingerprint verification algorithm over FVC2002 database DB1 (Maio et al., 2002b): a) genuine and impostor distributions were computed from 2800 genuine pairs and 4950 impostor pairs, respectively; b) FMR(t) and FNMR(t) are derived from the score distributions in a); c) DET curve is derived from the FMR(t) and FNMR(t) curves in b).

A few "compact" indices are sometimes used to summarize the accuracy of a verification system but they should be used with caution.

- *Equal-Error Rate* (EER): denotes the error rate at the threshold t for which both false match rate and false non-match rate are identical: $\text{FMR}(t) = \text{FNMR}(t)$ (see Figure 1.6). In practice, because the genuine and impostor score distributions are not continuous (due to the finite number of comparisons and the quantization of the output scores), an exact EER point might not exist. In this case, instead of a single value, an interval is reported (Maio et al., 2000). Although EER is an important indicator, a fingerprint system is rarely used at the operating point corresponding to EER, and often a more stringent threshold is set corresponding to a pre-specified value of FMR.
- *ZeroFNMR*: is defined as the lowest FMR at which no false non-matches occur (see Figure 1.6).
- *ZeroFMR*: is defined as the lowest FNMR at which no false matches occur (see Figure 1.6).

For more formal definitions of errors in a fingerprint verification system, and practical suggestions on how to compute and report them for a given dataset, the reader should refer to ISO/IEC 19795-2 (2007).

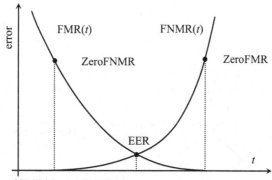

Figure 1.6. An example of FMR(t) and FNMR(t) curves, where the points corresponding to EER, ZeroFNMR, and ZeroFMR are highlighted.

The accuracy requirements of a biometric verification system are very much application dependent. For example, in forensic applications such as criminal identification, it is the false non-match rate that is of more concern than the false match rate: that is, we do not want to miss identifying a criminal even at the risk of manually examining a large number of potential false matches identified by the system. At the other extreme, a very low false match rate may be the most important factor in a highly secure access control application (e.g., physical access to a nuclear facility), where the primary objective is to not let in any impostors. Of course, operating the system at a very low false match rate will potentially lead to inconvenience to legitimate users due to the resulting high false non-match rate. In between these two extremes are several commercial applications, where both false match rate and false non-match rate need to be considered. For example, in applications such as verifying a customer at a bank ATM, a false match means a loss of several hundred dollars whereas a high false non-match rate may upset the genuine customers. Figure 1.7 graphically depict the FMR and FNMR tradeoff preferred by different types of applications.

1.5.7 Identification error rates

We already defined the types of errors that the matching module can make when it operates in one-to-many comparison mode, namely the false positive and false negative identification errors. The rates of these errors, known as *False Negative Identification-error Rate* (FNIR) and *False Positive Identification-error Rate* (FPIR) can be computed in the same way as the FNMR and FMR described above. However, they can also be interpreted from FNMR and FMR under simplifying assumptions.

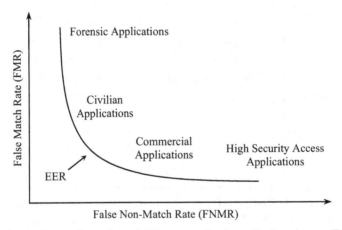

Figure 1.7. Typical operating points of different applications displayed on an ROC curve.

Let us assume that no pre-selection algorithm is available (i.e., the entire database containing N templates is searched), that a single template for each finger is present in the database, and that all imposter matching scores are independent. Since identification error rates are dependent on the number of templates N to be searched, let us denote false negative identification-error rate as $FNIR_N$ and false positive identification-error rate as $FPIR_N$. Then, under the above simplifying assumptions:

- $\text{FNIR}_N = \text{FNMR}$; the probability of false negative error when searching the identification feature set against N templates is the same as the false non-match error in verification mode (except that this expression does not take into account the probability that a false match may occur before the correct template is visited, see Cappelli, Maio, and Maltoni (2000c)).

- $\text{FPIR}_N = 1 - (1 - \text{FMR})^N$; a false positive error occurs when the identification feature set falsely matches one or more templates in the database. FPIR_N is then computed as one minus the probability that no false match is made with any of the database templates. In the above expression $(1 - \text{FMR})$ is the probability that the input does not falsely match a single template, and $(1 - \text{FMR})^N$ is the probability that it does not falsely match any of the database templates. If FMR is very small, then the above expression can be approximated by $\text{FPIR}_N \cong N \cdot \text{FMR}$, and therefore we can state that the probability of false positive errors increases linearly with the size of the database.

This expression for FPIR_N has serious implications for the design of large-scale identification systems. Usually, computation speed is perceived as the bottleneck in scaling an identification application. Actually, accuracy scales even worse than speed. Consider an identification application with 10,000 users. We can certainly find a combination of a fast matching algorithm and an appropriate platform (eventually exploiting parallelism) capable of carrying out an identification in a few seconds. On the other hand, suppose that, for an acceptable FNMR, the FMR of the chosen algorithm is 10^{-5} (i.e., just one false match in 100,000 matches). Then the probability of falsely matching an individual during identification is $\text{FPIR}_N \cong 10\%$, and everyone has a good chance of gaining access to the system by trying to get in with all the 10 fingers in their two hands. Combining multiple fingers and other types of biometric fusion (see Chapter 7) seems to be the only obvious solution to accuracy scalability in large-scale automatic identification.

If the templates in the database have been classified into types (see Section 1.12 and Chapter 5), then a pre-selection algorithm can be used such that only a portion of the database is searched during identification. This results in a different formulation of FPIR_N and FNIR_N under simplifying assumptions:

- $\text{FNIR}_N = \text{PRR} + (1 - \text{PRR}) \cdot \text{FNMR}$, where PRR (PRe-selection error Rate) is the probability that the database template corresponding to the searched finger is wrongly discarded by the pre-selection algorithm. The above expression is obtained using the following argument. In case the template is not correctly retrieved by the pre-selection algorithm (this happens with probability PRR), the system always generates a false negative error, whereas in the case where the pre-selection algorithm returns the right template (this happens with probability $[1 - \text{PRR}]$), the FNIR of the system equals FNMR. Also, this expression is only an approximation as it does not consider the probability of falsely matching an incorrect template before the right one is retrieved (Cappelli, Maio, and Maltoni, 2000c).

- FPIR$_N = 1 - (1 - \text{FMR})^{N \cdot P}$, where P (also called the *Penetration rate*) is the fraction of the database searched during the identification of an input fingerprint.

A detailed analysis of errors in an identification system is derived in Cappelli, Maio, and Maltoni (2000c). The more complex case where the characteristics of the indexing and preselection algorithms are known is also discussed there.

The identification accuracy can also be graphically presented through a ROC curve (plotting FPIR on the x-axis and 1-FNIR on the y-axis) or a DET curve (plotting FPIR on the x-axis and FNIR on the y-axis) for a fixed database size (and fixed size of candidate list returned). If the database is of size 1 (and the candidate list is of size 1), then the ROC and DET curves will show the accuracy performance of verification. In the special case of closed-set identification, or when interested only in the accuracy of the pre-selection algorithm, the performance can be graphically expressed using a Cumulative Match Characteristic (CMC) curve, which plots the rank (order in the candidate list) on the x-axis and the probability of identification at that or better rank on the y-axis. CMC curve is not reported as often as ROC or DET curves because closed-set identification is rarely used in practice.

1.6 System Evaluation

Phillips et al. (2000) define three types of evaluation of biometric systems: *technology evaluation*, *scenario evaluation*, and *operational evaluation*.

- *Technology evaluation*: the goal of a technology evaluation is to compare competing algorithms from a single technology. Only algorithms compliant with a given input/output protocol are tested (sensing devices and application aspects are not taken into account). Testing of all the algorithms is carried out on one or more databases. Although sample data may be made available to prospective participants for algorithm development or parameter tuning purposes prior to the test, the actual testing must be done on data that have not previously been seen by algorithm developers. Because the test database is fixed, the results of technology tests are repeatable. Cappelli et al. (2006) propose a hierarchical taxonomy of technology evaluations: *in-house* and *independent* is the first level dichotomy. In-house evaluations can be carried out on a *self-defined test* or according to an *existing benchmark*; independent evaluations can be classified into *weakly supervised*, *supervised* and *strongly supervised* depending on the amount of control exercised by the tester. Fingerprint Verification Competitions (FVC) in 2000, 2002, 2004, and 2006 (Maio et al. (2002a, b); Cappelli et al. (2006); BioLab (2007)) are examples of strongly supervised technology evaluations of fingerprint verification algorithms. Section 4.7 discusses in more detail the technology evaluation of fingerprint recognition algorithms.
- *Scenario evaluation*: the goal of scenario evaluation is to determine the overall end-to-end system performance in a prototype or simulated application. Testing is

performed on a complete system in an environment that models a real-world target application. Each tested system has its own acquisition device. Data collection across all tested systems has to be carried out in the same environment with the same population. Test results are repeatable only to the extent that the modelled scenario can be carefully controlled (ISO/IEC 19795-1, 2006).

- *Operational evaluation*: the goal of operational testing is to determine the performance of a complete biometric system in a specific application environment with a specific target population. In general, operational test results are not repeatable because of unknown and undocumented differences between operational environments (ISO/IEC 19795-1, 2006).

In scenario and operational evaluations, the accuracy of a biometric system depends heavily on several variables: the composition of the population (e.g., occupation, age, demographics and race), the environment, the system operational mode, and other application-specific constraints. In an ideal situation, one would like to characterize the application-independent performance of a recognition system and be able to predict the real operational performance of the system based on the application. Rigorous and realistic modeling techniques characterizing data acquisition and matching processes are the only way to grasp and extrapolate the performance evaluation results. In the case of fingerprint recognition, the results of fingerprint synthesis (see Chapter 6) exhibit many characteristics of finger appearance that can be exploited for simulations, but there do not exist any formal models for the data acquisition process under different conditions (e.g., different skin conditions, different distortions, different types of cuts and their states of healing, subtle user mischief, and adversarial testing conditions, etc.). Modeling biometrics performance is a daunting task and more effort is needed to address this problem. In the meantime, performing comparative evaluations is the norm. For example, algorithms participating in a particular FVC competition can only be compared with each other within that FVC. In other words, results from one FVC (say FVC2004) cannot be compared with results from another FVC (say FVC2006) due to the vast differences in a large number of factors such as composition of the population (e.g., fraction of male/females, differences in occupations, age, etc.), fingerprint scanner, demographics, ergonomics, environment, etc.

Until many aspects of biometric recognition algorithms and application requirements are clearly understood, the comparative, empirical, application-dependent evaluation techniques will be predominant and the evaluation results obtained using these techniques will be meaningful only for a specific database in a specific test environment and a specific application. The disadvantage of the empirical evaluation is that it is not only expensive to collect the data for each evaluation, but it is also often difficult to objectively compare the evaluation results of two different systems tested under different conditions. Depending upon the data collection protocol, the performance results can vary *significantly* from one test to another. For example, in FVC2004, the fingerprint data was collected by intentionally introducing various types of finger distortion. While this is a good way to compare participating algorithms under a "stress-test", the FVC2004 accuracy performance cannot be compared with FVC2006 where no intentional distortions were introduced. Finally, biometric samples collected in a controlled and laboratory environment provide optimistically biased results that do not generalize well in practice.

For any performance metric to be able to generalize to the entire population of interest, the test data should (i) be *representative* of the population and ii) contain sufficient number of samples from each category of the population (*large sample size*). Furthermore, the collection of samples for enrollment and recognition should be separated in time (e.g., 2 to 3 weeks for fingerprints). Different applications, depending on whether the subjects are cooperative and habituated, or whether the target population is benevolent or subversive, may require a completely different sample set (Wayman, 2001). Size of the sample set is a very important factor in obtaining a reliable estimate of the error rates. The larger the test sample size, more reliable is the test result (smaller confidence interval). Data collection is expensive, so it is desirable to determine the smallest sample size that will result in a given confidence interval. Some efforts have been made to estimate the sample size (Doddington et al. (1998); Wayman (2001); ISO/IEC 19795-1 (2006)).

There are two methods of estimating confidence intervals: parametric and non-parametric. To simplify the estimation, both approaches typically assume independent and identically distributed (i.i.d.) test samples (genuine and imposter match scores). Furthermore, parametric methods make strong assumptions about the form of the (genuine and imposter) match score distributions. A typical parametric approach models the test samples as independent Bernoulli trials and estimates the confidence intervals based on the resulting binomial distribution, inasmuch as a collection of correlated Bernoulli trials is also binomially distributed with a smaller variance (Viveros, Balasubramanian, and Mitas, 1984). Similarly, non-identically distributed test samples can be accommodated within the parametric approach by making some assumptions about the data. Wayman (2001) applied these methods to obtain estimates of accuracies as well as their confidence intervals. A non-parametric approach, such as bootstrap has been used by Bolle, Ratha, and Pankanti (1999) to estimate the error rates as well as their confidence intervals. The non-parametric approaches do not make any assumption about the form of the distributions. In addition, some non-parametric approaches such as bootstrapping techniques are known to be relatively immune to violations of i.i.d. assumptions. Bolle, Ratha, and Pankanti (2004) further explicitly modeled the weak dependence among typical fingerprint test sets by using a *subset bootstrap* technique. This technique obtains a better estimate of the error rate confidence intervals than the techniques that do not take the dependency among the test data into account.

In summary, the performance of a biometric system is determined empirically. The results of these evaluations should be interpreted keeping the test data collection protocol in mind. Fortunately, the biometric standards community is making efforts towards establishing the *best practices* guidelines and standards for biometric performance testing and reporting (ISO/IEC 19795-1, 2006). This will hopefully avoid any egregious mistakes in data collection and allow the test results to be presented in a consistent and descriptive manner.

1.7 Applications of Fingerprint Systems

Fingerprint recognition systems have been deployed in a wide variety of application domains, ranging from forensics to mobile phones. But, the system design depends on the application characteristics that define the application requirements.

1.7.1 Application characteristics

Wayman (1999b) suggests that the application context of a biometric recognition system can be understood by examining the following characteristics:

1. Cooperative versus non-cooperative
2. Habituated versus non-habituated
3. Attended versus non-attended
4. Standard versus non-standard operating environment
5. Public versus private
6. Open versus closed
7. Overt versus covert

Cooperative versus non-cooperative dichotomy refers to the behavior of the impostor in interacting with the fingerprint recognition application. For example, in a positive recognition application (i.e., an application that assumes a positive claim of identity), it is in the best interest of an impostor to cooperate with the system to be accepted as a valid user. On the other hand, in a negative recognition application (i.e., an application that assumes a negative claim of identity), it is in the best interest of the impostor not to cooperate with the system so that the system does not find her matching any of the individuals in the watch list. Electronic banking is an example of a cooperative application whereas an airport application to catch terrorists is an example of a non-cooperative application.

If a subject is aware that she is being recognized by biometrics, the application is categorized as overt. If the subject is unaware, the application is covert. Facial recognition can be used in a covert application (by surveillance cameras) while fingerprint recognition cannot be used in this mode (except for criminal identification based on latent fingerprints). Most commercial applications of biometrics are overt, whereas some government and law enforcement applications are covert. Also, most overt applications need only verification whereas covert applications typically require identification.

Habituated versus non-habituated use of a biometric system refers to how often the users in that application interact with the biometric recognition system. For example, a computer network logon application typically has habituated users (after an initial habituation period) due to their use of the system on a regular basis. However, in a driver's license application, the users are non-habituated since a driver's license is renewed only once in 5 years or so. This is an important consideration when designing a biometric system because the familiarity of users with the system affects its recognition accuracy.

Attended versus non-attended classification refers to whether the process of biometric data acquisition in an application is observed, guided, or supervised by a human (e.g., a security officer). Furthermore, an application may have an attended enrollment but non-attended recognition. For example, a banking application may have a supervised enrollment when an ATM card is issued to a user but the subsequent uses of the biometric system for ATM transactions will be non-attended. Non-cooperative applications generally require attended operation.

Standard versus non-standard environment refers to whether the application is being operated in a controlled environment (such as temperature, pressure, moisture, lighting conditions, etc.). Typically, indoor applications such as computer network logon operate in a controlled environment whereas outdoor applications such as parking lot surveillance operate in a non-standard environment. This classification is also important for the system designer as a more rugged biometric scanner is needed for a non-standard environment. Similarly, infrared face recognition may be preferred over visible-band face recognition for outdoor surveillance at night.

Public or private dichotomy refers to whether the users of the application are customers or employees of the organization deploying the biometric system. For example, a network logon application is used by the employees and managed by the information technology manager of that company. Thus it is a private application. The use of biometric data in conjunction with electronic identity cards is an example of a public application.

Closed versus open application refers to whether a person's biometric template is used for a single or multiple applications. For example, a user may use a fingerprint-based recognition system to enter secure facilities, for computer network logon, electronic banking, and ATM. Should all these applications use separate template storage for each application, or should they all access the same central template storage? A closed application may be based on a proprietary template whereas an open system may need standard biometric data format and compression method to exchange and compare information among different systems (most likely developed by different vendors).

Note that the most popular commercial applications have the following attributes: cooperative, overt, habituated, attended enrollment and non-attended recognition, standard environment, closed, and private. A registered traveler application has the following typical attributes (Wayman, 1999b): cooperative, overt, non-attended, non-habituated, standard environment, public, and closed. A driver license application (to prevent issuance of multiple licenses to the same person) can be characterized by the following attributes: non-cooperative, overt, attended, non-habituated, standard environment, public, open application.

A fingerprint system designer can take advantage of the application characteristics to make sure that the system makes the correct trade-offs. These trade-offs may include recognition accuracy, response time, system integrity, complexity, cost (component price as well as integration and support costs), privacy, government standards, liveness detection, ease of integration, durability, modality of usage, etc. For example, a commercial application that requires the fingerprint recognition system to work for all the people all the time demands a high recognition accuracy which may come at an expense of requiring powerful processors and large memory or specialized biometric capture equipment (for example, large-area fingerprint readers or face recognition booths with controlled lighting). In another example, compliance with certain government standards may facilitate inter-operability but may decrease recognition accuracy.

Fingerprint vendors spend a great deal of effort in optimizing and balancing the various trade-offs for the applications they target. Trade-offs in the commercial applications typically include fingerprint scanner size, scanner cost, scanner ruggedness, recognition accuracy, template size, memory and cache size, security issues, system design, etc. In general, all commercial applications are typically cost sensitive with a strong incentive for being user-friendly. On the other hand, most government applications are typically very large scale with a strong incentive for high data acquisition throughput.

1.7.2 Application categories

The two most popular ways to categorize biometric recognition applications are horizontal categorization and vertical categorization. In horizontal categorization, the categories are applications that have some commonalties in the features that they require from the fingerprint recognition system. The vertical categorization is based on the needs of a particular sector of industry or the government. Horizontal categorization results in the following main categories of biometric applications:

- *Physical access control*: access is restricted to facilities such as nuclear plants, bank vaults, corporate board rooms, and even health-clubs, amusement parks, and lockers.
- *Logical access control*: access to desktop computers or remote servers and databases is restricted to authorized users. Increasingly, access to software applications is also being restricted to only authorized users.
- *Transaction authentication* (or consumer identification): transactions may be executed at ATM site or from remote locations for on-line banking or between banks (e.g., in high-value transactions). Fingerprint recognition systems are used for security of the transaction as well as accountability (so the parties involved in the transaction cannot later deny it).
- *Device access control*: laptops, PDAs, cell phones, and other electronic devices often contain personal and sensitive data. To protect such data, fingerprint recognition systems are used to conduct recognition on the stand-alone device.
- *Time and attendance*: time and attendance systems are used to keep track of employee working hours and to compute payrolls. Use of fingerprint recognition systems in these applications is fairly well received to improve efficiency for employees and also for preventing various types of payroll frauds (e.g., buddy-punching).
- *Civil identification*: in civilian identification application, the most important objective is to prevent multiple enrollments and to find duplicates (e.g., duplicate passport,

driver license, national identification card). The size of the database can be of the order of millions (e.g., the entire population of a country). In some applications (such as border control to prevent suspected terrorists or expellees from entering the country), the identification is not needed to be conducted against the entire population but rather against a "watch-list" database.

- *Forensic identification*: in forensic identification, latent fingerprints lifted from the crime scenes are matched against a criminal database to identify the suspect (and sometimes the victims).

Vertical categorization results in the following main industries that benefit the most from the use of fingerprint systems:

- Health care
- Financial
- Gaming and hospitality (casinos, hotels, etc.)
- Retail
- Education
- Manufacturing
- High technology and telecommunications
- Travel and transport
- Federal, state, municipal, or other governments
- Military
- Law enforcement

Each vertical market may have a need for a number of different horizontal applications. For example, while the most widespread (almost ubiquitous) use of fingerprint recognition systems in law enforcement departments is for criminal investigations, these departments also use computers that contain sensitive data. So, this sector needs solutions for fingerprint-based logical access control. Further, law enforcement departments have laboratories and other restricted physical areas, so they can benefit from fingerprint-based physical access control solutions. Fingerprint-based time and attendance solutions can also be used to manage payroll of law enforcement officers (and other employees of the department).

Table 1.2 shows a categorization that lists applications that are most critical in three major vertical markets. Figure 1.8 shows some applications involving electronic access or transaction where reliable user recognition has become critical. It is not possible to list all the possible applications of fingerprint recognition systems, neither is it possible to list all the industries. New applications continue to emerge. We are also witnessing maturity of products and a range of solutions. Some vendors are now offering products that address multiple horizontal applications with a single solution, for example, a single solution that can manage both the logical access and physical access control in an organization.

Forensic	Government (Civil)	Commercial
Corpse Identification	Social Security	Computer Network Logon
Criminal Investigation	Welfare Disbursement	Electronic Data Security
Missing Children	Border Control	e-Commerce
	Passport Control	Internet Access
	National ID card	ATM, Credit Card
	Driver License	Physical Access Control
	Credentialing	Cellular Phones
		Personal Digital Assistant
		Medical Records Management
		Distance Learning

Table 1.2. Fingerprint recognition applications are divided here into three categories. Traditionally, forensic applications have used forensic experts, government applications have used token-based systems, and commercial applications have used knowledge-based (password) systems. Fingerprint recognition systems are now being increasingly used in all these sectors.

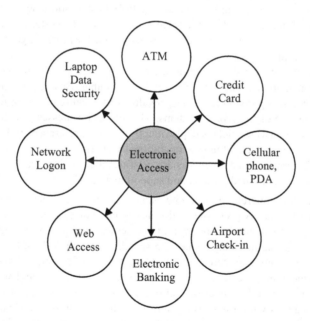

Figure 1.8. Various applications involving electronic access or transaction that require reliable automatic user recognition.

1.7.3 Barriers to adoption

A fingerprint recognition system provides a good balance of security, privacy, convenience, and accountability. While the adoption of these systems is steadily increasing, the rate of adoption has been somewhat slower than anticipated. This is primarily because of lack of awareness about the benefits and capabilities of fingerprint technologies. Another reason is that the business case for fingerprint recognition systems (return on investment analysis) has often proven to be somewhat difficult due to the following reasons:

- The business value of "security" and "deterrence" is difficult to quantify in terms of return on investment, regardless of the technology.
- Fraud rates and the resulting cost of long standing business and government systems (for example, tokens and passwords) are not well understood and quantified.
- Fingerprint recognition systems, being an emerging technology, is sometimes confronted with unrealistic performance expectations and not fairly compared with existing alternatives (for example, tokens and passwords), whose inconvenience and high cost businesses have resigned to tolerate. A successful fingerprint-based solution does not have to be perfect in terms of accuracy and foolproof in terms of security. A particular application simply demands a satisfactory performance justifying the additional investments needed for the fingerprint system. The system designer can exploit the application context to engineer the system to achieve the target performance levels at an acceptable cost.
- The "quality" of available fingerprint technology varies quite dramatically from one application to another and from one vendor to another. Businesses cannot often easily access credible reports on technology evaluations because of a dearth of standardized scenario testing of fingerprint systems. This leaves businesses to either perform their own evaluation (which delays deployment) or rely on references (which could be difficult to obtain because of unique operational scenarios).
- Several fingerprint system vendors are not financially stable, leaving businesses with concerns over continued product and support availability.

In the past, the most concrete return on investment estimates for businesses has come from taking people out of business processes and transactions. For example, forgotten passwords result in helpdesk calls which are expensive to businesses. It is now widely documented that fingerprint systems can significantly reduce the spending on helpdesk calls much beyond the cost of investment. In many commercial applications, the use of fingerprint systems can facilitate businesses to move to a user-friendly self-service model of service and support while providing the same or even higher level of security as the attended model, thus lowering their expenses. In applications with a negative claim of identity, such as background check (often used for "security clearance"), voter registration, and multiple enrollments (duplicate passport, and driver license), there are no alternatives to biometrics. Here, the main barrier to adoption has been public perception and privacy concerns.

Fingerprint recognition systems, when properly implemented, provide more security, convenience and efficiency than any other means of identification. No other technology has the capability to provide non-repudiation or ensure that the person being authenticated is physically present at the point of authentication. Fingerprint-based recognition systems have already replaced passwords and tokens in a large number of applications. In some other applications, they are used to add a layer of security on top of passwords and tokens. The use of fingerprint recognition systems will increasingly reduce identity theft and fraud and protect privacy. As fingerprint recognition technology continues to mature, there will be increasing interaction among markets, technologies, and applications. The emerging interaction is expected to be influenced by the added value of the technology, the sensitivities of the user population, and the credibility of the service provider. It is too early to predict where and how fingerprint technology would evolve and be mated with which applications, but it is certain that fingerprint-based recognition will have a profound influence on the way we will conduct our daily business.

1.8 History of Fingerprints

Human fingerprints have been discovered on a large number of archaeological artifacts and historical items (see Figure 1.9). While these findings provide evidence that ancient people were aware of the individuality of fingerprints, such awareness does not appear to have any scientific basis (Lee and Gaensslen (2001); Moenssens (1971)). It was not until the late sixteenth century that the modern scientific fingerprint technique was first initiated (see Cummins and Midlo (1961); Galton (1892); Lee and Gaensslen (2001)). In 1864, the English plant morphologist, Nehemiah Grew, published the first scientific paper reporting his systematic study on the ridge, furrow, and pore structure in fingerprints (Figure 1.10a) (Lee and Gaensslen, 2001).

The first detailed description of the anatomical formation of fingerprints was made by Mayer in 1788 (Moenssens, 1971) in which a number of fingerprint ridge characteristics were identified and characterized (Figure 1.10b). Starting in 1809, Thomas Bewick started using fingerprint as his trademark (Figure 1.10c), one of the most important milestones in the history of fingerprints (Moenssens, 1971). Purkinje, in 1823, proposed the first fingerprint classification scheme, which classified fingerprints into nine categories according to the ridge configurations (Figure 1.10d) (Moenssens, 1971).

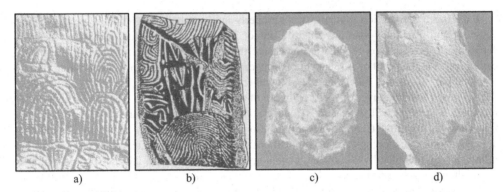

Figure 1.9. Examples of archaeological fingerprint carvings and historic fingerprint impressions: a) Neolithic carvings (Gavrinis Island) (Moenssens, 1971); b) standing stone (Goat Island, 2000 B.C.) (Lee and Gaensslen, 2001); c) a Chinese clay seal (300 B.C.) (Lee and Gaensslen, 2001); d) an impression on a Palestinian lamp (400 A.D.) (Moenssens, 1971). While impressions on the Neolithic carvings and the Goat Island standing stones might not be used to establish identity, there is sufficient evidence to suggest that the Chinese clay seal and impressions on the Palestinian lamp were used to indicate the identity of the fingerprint providers. Figures courtesy of A. Moenssens, R. Gaensslen, and J. Berry.

Henry Fauld, in 1880, first scientifically suggested the individuality of fingerprints based on empirical observations. At the same time, Herschel asserted that he had practiced fingerprint recognition for about 20 years (Lee and Gaensslen (2001); Moenssens (1971)). These findings established the foundation of modern fingerprint recognition. In the late nineteenth century, Sir Francis Galton conducted an extensive study on fingerprints (Galton, 1892). He introduced the minutiae features for comparing fingerprints in 1888.

An important advance in fingerprint recognition was made in 1899 by Edward Henry, who (actually his two assistants from India) established the well-known "Henry system" of fingerprint classification (Lee and Gaensslen, 2001). By the early twentieth century, the formation of fingerprints was well understood. The biological principles of fingerprints (Moenssens, 1971) are summarized below:

1. Individual epidermal ridges and furrows have different characteristics for different fingerprints.
2. The configuration types are individually variable, but they vary within limits that allow for a systematic classification.
3. The configurations and minute details of individual ridges and furrows are permanent and unchanging.

The first principle constitutes the foundation of fingerprint recognition and the second principle constitutes the foundation of fingerprint classification.

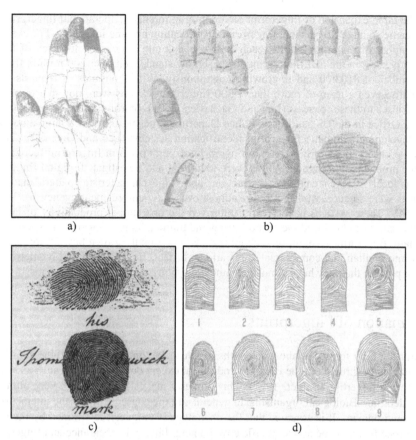

Figure 1.10. a) Dermatoglyphics drawn by Grew (Moenssens, 1971); b) Mayer's drawings of fingerprints (Cummins and Midlo, 1961); c) trademark of Thomas Bewick (Lee and Gaensslen, 2001); d) the nine patterns illustrated in Purkinje's thesis (Moenssens, 1971). Images courtesy of A. Moenssens, R. Gaensslen, and J. Berry.

In the early twentieth century, fingerprint recognition was formally accepted as a valid personal identification method and became a standard routine in forensics (Lee and Gaensslen, 2001). Fingerprint identification agencies were set up worldwide and criminal fingerprint databases were established (Lee and Gaensslen, 2001). Various fingerprint recognition techniques, including latent fingerprint acquisition, fingerprint classification, and fingerprint comparison were developed. For example, the FBI fingerprint identification division was set up in 1924 with a database of 810,000 fingerprint cards (see Federal Bureau of Investigation (1984, 1991)).

With the rapid expansion of fingerprint recognition in forensics, operational fingerprint databases became so huge that manual fingerprint identification became infeasible. For example, the total number of fingerprint cards (each card contains one impression for each of the 10 fingers of a person) in the FBI fingerprint database now stands well over 200 million from its original number of 810,000 and is growing continuously. With thousands of requests being received daily, even a team of more than 1,300 fingerprint experts were not able to provide timely responses to these requests (Lee and Gaensslen, 2001). Starting in the early 1960s, the FBI, Home Office in the UK, and Paris Police Department began to invest a large amount of effort in developing automatic fingerprint identification systems (Lee and Gaensslen, 2001). Based on the observations of how human fingerprint experts perform fingerprint recognition, three major problems in designing AFISs were identified and investigated: digital fingerprint acquisition, local ridge characteristic extraction, and ridge characteristic pattern matching. Their efforts were so successful that today almost every law enforcement agency worldwide uses an AFIS. These systems have greatly improved the operational productivity of law enforcement agencies and reduced the cost of hiring and training human fingerprint experts.

Automatic fingerprint recognition technology has now rapidly grown beyond forensic applications into civilian and commercial applications. In fact, fingerprint-based biometric systems are so popular that they have almost become the synonym for biometric systems.

1.9 Formation of Fingerprints

Fingerprints are fully formed at about 7 months of fetus development. Finger ridge configurations do not change throughout the life of an individual except due to accidents such as bruises and cuts on the fingertips (Babler, 1991). This property makes fingerprints a very attractive biometric identifier. Biological organisms, in general, are the consequence of the interaction of genes and environment. It is assumed that the phenotype is uniquely determined by the interaction of a specific genotype and a specific environment. Physical appearance and fingerprints are, in general, a part of an individual's phenotype. Fingerprint formation is similar to the growth of capillaries and blood vessels in angiogenesis. The general characteristics of the fingerprint emerge as the skin on the fingertip begins to differentiate. The differentiation process is triggered by the growth in size of the volar pads on the palms, fingers, soles, and toes. However, the flow of amniotic fluids around the fetus and its position in the uterus change during the differentiation process. Thus the cells on the fingertip grow in a microenvironment that is slightly different from hand to hand and finger to finger. The finer details of the fingerprints are determined by this changing microenvironment. A small difference in microenvironment is amplified by the differentiation process of the cells. There are so many variations during the formation of fingerprints that it would be virtually impossible for two fingerprints to be exactly alike. But, because the fingerprints are differentiated from the same genes, they are not totally random patterns either.

The extent of variation in a physical trait due to a random development process differs from trait to trait. Typically, most of the physical characteristics such as body type, voice, and face are very similar for identical twins and automatic recognition based on face and hand geometry will most likely fail to distinguish them. Although the minute details in the fingerprints of identical twins are different (Jain, Prabhakar, and Pankanti, 2002), a number of studies have shown significant correlation in the fingerprint class (i.e., whorl, right loop, left loop, arch, tented arch) of identical (monozygotic) twin fingers; correlation based on other generic attributes of the fingerprint such as ridge count, ridge width, ridge separation, and ridge depth has also been found to be significant in identical twins (Lin et al., 1982). In dermatoglyphics studies, the maximum generic difference between fingerprints has been found among individuals of different races. Unrelated persons of the same race have very little generic similarity in their fingerprints, parent and child have some generic similarity as they share half the genes, siblings have more similarity, and the maximum generic similarity is observed in monozygotic (identical) twins, which is the closest genetic relationship (Cummins and Midlo, 1943).

1.10 Individuality of Fingerprints

Although the word "fingerprint" is popularly perceived as synonymous with individuality, uniqueness of fingerprints is not an established fact but an empirical observation. With the stipulation of widespread use of fingerprints, however, there is a rightfully growing public concern about the scientific basis underlying individuality of fingerprints. Lending erroneous legitimacy to these observations will have disastrous consequences, especially if fingerprints will be ubiquitously used to recognize citizens for reasons of efficiency, convenience, and reliability in guarding against security threats and identity fraud. Furthermore, automated fingerprint recognition systems do not appear to use all the available discriminatory information in the fingerprints, but only a parsimonious representation extracted by an automatic feature extraction algorithm.

The amount of distinctive information available in a fingerprint is also being questioned. Simon Cole in "The Myth of Fingerprints," *The New York Times, May 13, 2001*, stated that *"the fingerprints may be unique in the sense that, as Gottfried Wilhelm Leibniz argued, all natural objects can be differentiated if examined in enough detail."* Cole (2001a) further argues that uniqueness may be valid when entire prints are compared but not for prints depicting small portions of a finger; the print size is even more significant in the view of the newer chip-based fingerprint sensors that cover only a small portion of the finger (unlike the nail-to-nail rolled inked fingerprints used in many criminal investigations). Finally, the US Supreme Court Daubert versus. Merrell Dow Pharmaceuticals, Inc. (113 S. Ct. 2786, 1993) hearing started a closer scrutiny of the UK Home Office observation in 1893 that fingerprints are unique. Although the Supreme Court conceded that fingerprints are unique, it subsequently sought (through the United States Department of Justice) to sponsor a systematic study to examine a sound and indisputable scientific basis of fingerprint individuality information. The scientific basis of fingerprint individuality continues to be questioned in the courts of laws in the United States to this day (see Chapter 8). Thus the uniqueness of fingerprints is neither a bygone conclusion nor has it been extensively studied in a systematic fashion.

1.11 Fingerprint Sensing and Storage

Based on the mode of acquisition, a fingerprint image may be classified as off-line or live-scan. An off-line image is typically obtained by smearing ink on the fingertip and creating an inked impression of the fingertip on paper. The inked impression is then digitized by scanning the paper using an optical scanner or a high-quality video camera. A live-scan image, on the other hand, is acquired by sensing the tip of the finger directly, using a sensor that is capable of digitizing the fingerprint on contact. Particular kind of off-line images, extremely important in forensic applications, are the so-called *latent* fingerprints found at crime scenes. The oily nature of the skin results in the impression of a fingerprint being deposited on a surface that is touched by a finger. These latent prints can be "lifted" from the surface by employing certain chemical techniques.

The main parameters characterizing a digital fingerprint image are: resolution, area, number of pixels, geometric accuracy, contrast, and geometric distortion. To maximize compatibility between digital fingerprint images and to ensure good quality of the acquired fingerprint impressions among various AFIS, the US Criminal Justice Information Services (CJIS) released a set of specifications that regulate the quality and the format of both fingerprint images and FBI-compliant off-line/live-scan scanners (Appendix F and Appendix G of CJIS (1999)). More recently, FBI has defined another, less stringent, image quality standard (Nill, 2006) for single-finger capture devices in civilian applications (more specifically for the Personal Identity Verification [PIV] program in the United States). Most of the commercial live-scan devices, designed for the non-AFIS market, do not meet the FBI specifications but, on the other hand, are designed to be compact, and cheap. The operational quality of fingerprint scanners (i.e., the impact of the scanner quality parameters on the fingerprint recognition accuracy) has been the subject of some recent studies (Cappelli, Ferrara, and Maltoni, 2008).

There are a number of live-scan sensing mechanisms (e.g., optical FTIR, capacitive, thermal, pressure-based, ultrasound, etc.) that can be used to detect the ridges and valleys present on the fingertip. Figure 1.11 shows an off-line fingerprint image acquired with the ink technique, a latent fingerprint image, and some live-scan images acquired with different types of commercial live-scan devices. Although optical fingerprint scanners have the longest history, the new solid-state sensors are gaining increasing popularity because of their compact size and the ease with which they can be embedded in consumer products such as laptop computers, cellular phones and PDAs. Figure 1.12 shows some examples of fingerprint sensors embedded in a variety of computer peripherals and other devices.

Chapter 2 of this book discusses fingerprint sensing technologies, provides some characteristics of commercially available fingerprint scanners and shows images acquired with a number of devices in different operating conditions (good quality fingers, poor quality fingers, dry and wet fingers). One of the main causes of accuracy drop in fingerprint recognition systems is the small sensing area. To overcome (or at least to reduce) this problem, mosaicking techniques attempt to build a complete fingerprint representation from several small but partially overlapping images.

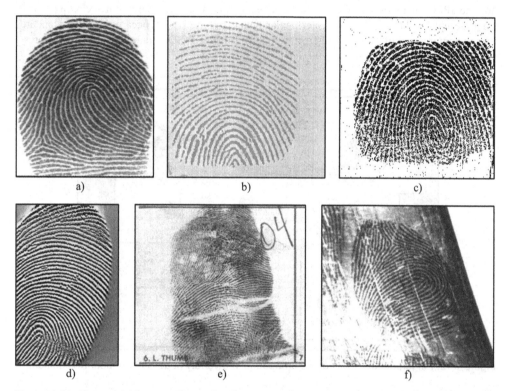

Figure 1.11. Fingerprint images from: a) a live-scan FTIR-based optical scanner; b) a live-scan capacitive scanner; c) a live-scan piezoelectic scanner; d) a live-scan thermal scanner; e) an off-line inked impression; f) a latent fingerprint.

Storing raw fingerprint images may be problematic for large-scale identification systems. In 1995, the size of the FBI fingerprint card archive contained over 200 million items, and archive size was increasing at the rate of 30,000 to 50,000 new cards per day. Although the digitization of fingerprint cards seemed to be the most obvious choice, the resulting digital archive could become extremely large. In fact, each fingerprint card, when digitized at 500 dpi requires about 10 megabytes of storage. A simple multiplication by 200 million yields the massive storage requirement of 2,000 terabytes for the entire archive. An effective compression technique was urgently needed. Unfortunately, neither the well-known lossless methods nor the JPEG methods were found to be satisfactory. A new compression technique (with small acceptable loss), called Wavelet Scalar Quantization (WSQ), became the FBI standard for the compression of 500 dpi fingerprint images. Besides WSQ, a number of other compression techniques (including JPEG2000) have been proposed.

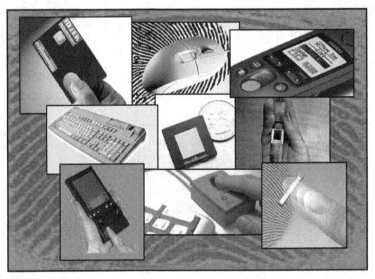

Figure 1.12. Fingerprint sensors can be embedded in a variety of devices for user recognition.

1.12 Fingerprint Representation and Feature Extraction

The representation issue constitutes the essence of fingerprint recognition system design and has far-reaching implications on the matching modules. The pixel intensity values in the fingerprint image are not invariant over time of capture and there is a need to determine salient features of the input fingerprint image that can discriminate between identities as well as remain invariant for a given individual. Thus the problem of representation is to determine a measurement (feature) space in which the fingerprint images belonging to the same finger form a compact cluster (low *intra-class* variations) and those belonging to different fingers occupy different portions of the space (high *inter-class* variations).

A good fingerprint representation should have the following two properties: *saliency* and *suitability*. Saliency means that a representation should contain distinctive information about the fingerprint. Suitability means that the representation can be easily extracted, stored in a compact fashion, and be useful for matching. A salient representation is not necessarily a suitable representation. In addition, in some biometrics applications, storage space is at a premium. For example, only a few kilobytes of storage is typically available in a smartcard. In such situations, the representation also needs to be compact.

Image-based representations, constituted by pixel intensity information, do not perform well due to factors such as brightness variations, image quality variations, scars, and large global distortions present in fingerprint images. Furthermore, an image-based representation requires a considerable amount of storage. On the other hand, an image-based representation preserves the maximum amount of information and makes fewer assumptions about the application domain. For instance, it is extremely difficult to extract any high level features from a (degenerate) finger devoid of any ridge structure.

The fingerprint pattern, when analyzed at different scales, exhibits different types of features.

- *Level* 1: at the global level, the ridge line flow delineates a pattern similar to one of those shown in Figure 1.13. *Singular points*, called loop and delta (denoted as squares and triangles, respectively in Figure 1.13), act as control points around which the ridge lines are "wrapped" (Levi and Sirovich, 1972). Singular points and coarse ridge line shape are useful for fingerprint classification and indexing (see Chapter 5), but their distinctiveness is not sufficient for accurate matching. External fingerprint shape, orientation image, and frequency image also belong to the set of features that can be detected at the global level.

- *Level* 2: at the local level, a total of 150 different local ridge characteristics, called *minute details*, have been identified (Moenssens, 1971). These local ridge characteristics are not evenly distributed. Most of them depend heavily on the impression conditions and quality of fingerprints and are rarely observed in fingerprints. The two most prominent ridge characteristics, called *minutiae* (see Figure 1.14) are: *ridge endings* and *ridge bifurcations*. A ridge ending is defined as the ridge point where a ridge ends abruptly. A ridge bifurcation is defined as the ridge point where a ridge forks or diverges into branch ridges. Minutiae in fingerprints are generally stable and robust to fingerprint impression conditions. Although a minutiae-based representation is characterized by a high saliency, reliable automatic minutiae extraction can be problematic in extremely low-quality fingerprints devoid of any ridge structure.

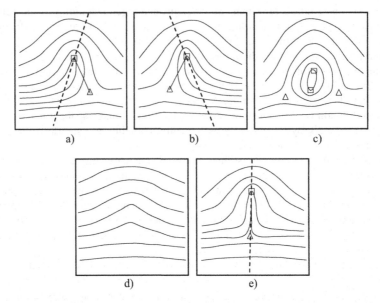

Figure 1.13. Fingerprint patterns as they appear at a coarse level: a) left loop, b) right loop, c) whorl, d) arch, and e) tented arch; squares denote loop-type singular points, and triangles delta-type singular points.

- *Level* 3: at the very-fine level, intra-ridge details can be detected. These include width, shape, curvature, edge contours of ridges as well as other permanent details such as dots and incipient ridges. One of the most important fine-level details is the finger *sweat pores* (see Figure 1.14), whose positions and shapes are considered highly distinctive. However, extracting very-fine details including pores is feasible only in high-resolution (e.g., 1,000 dpi) fingerprint images of good quality and therefore this kind of representation is not practical for non-forensic applications.

Chapter 3 describes fingerprint anatomy and introduces the techniques available for processing fingerprint images and extracting salient features. Specific sections are dedicated to the definition and description of approaches for computing local ridge orientation, local ridge frequency, singular points, and minutiae. Particular emphasis is placed on fingerprint segmentation (i.e., isolation of fingerprint area [foreground] from the background), fingerprint image enhancement, and binarization, which are very important intermediate steps in the extraction of salient features. Algorithms for estimating the quality of fingerprint images are also discussed.

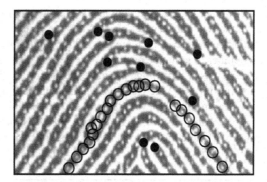

Figure 1.14. Minutiae (black-filled circles) in a portion of fingerprint image; sweat pores (empty circles) on a single ridge line.

1.13 Fingerprint Matching

Reliably matching fingerprints is an extremely difficult problem, mainly due to the large variability in different impressions of the same finger (i.e., large intra-class variations). The main factors responsible for the intra-class variations are: displacement, rotation, partial overlap, non-linear distortion, variable pressure, changing skin condition, noise, and feature extraction errors. Therefore, fingerprints from the same finger may sometimes look quite different whereas fingerprints from different fingers may appear quite similar (see Figure 1.15).

Human fingerprint examiners, in order to claim that two fingerprints are from the same finger, consider several factors: i) global pattern configuration agreement, which means that two fingerprints must be of the same type, ii) qualitative concordance, which requires that the corresponding minute details must be identical, iii) quantitative factor, which specifies that at least a certain number (a minimum of 12 according to the forensic guidelines in the United States) of corresponding minute details must be found, and iv) corresponding minute details, which must be identically inter-related. In practice, complex protocols have been defined for manual fingerprint matching and a detailed flowchart is available to guide fingerprint examiners in manually performing fingerprint matching.

Automatic fingerprint matching does not necessarily follow the same guidelines. In fact, although automatic minutiae-based fingerprint matching is inspired by the manual procedure, a large number of approaches have been designed over the past 40 years, and many of them have been explicitly designed for automation. A (three-class) categorization of fingerprint matching approaches is:

- *Correlation-based matching*: two fingerprint images are superimposed and the correlation between corresponding pixels is computed for different alignments (e.g., various displacements and rotations).

- *Minutiae-based matching*: minutiae are extracted from the two fingerprints and stored as sets of points in the two-dimensional plane. Minutiae matching essentially consists of finding the alignment between the template and the input minutiae sets that results in the maximum number of minutiae pairings.
- *Non-minutiae feature-based matching*: minutiae extraction is difficult in extremely low-quality fingerprint images, whereas other features of the fingerprint ridge pattern (e.g., local orientation and frequency, ridge shape, texture information) may be extracted more reliably than minutiae, even though their distinctiveness is generally lower. The approaches belonging to this family compare fingerprints in term of features extracted from the ridge pattern.

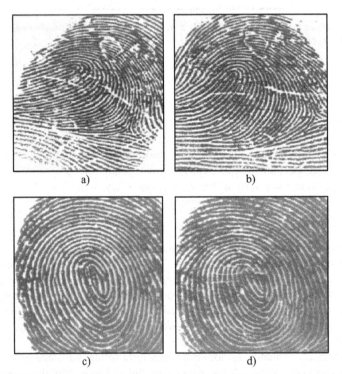

a)   b)

c)   d)

Figure 1.15. Difficulty in fingerprint matching. Fingerprint images in a) and b) look different to an untrained eye but they are impressions of the same finger. Fingerprint images in c) and d) look similar to an untrained eye but they are from different fingers.

Given a complex operating environment, it is critical to identify a set of valid assumptions upon which the fingerprint matcher design could be based. Often there is a tradeoff between whether it is more effective to exert more constraints by incorporating better engineering design to ensure a good representation or to build a more sophisticated matcher for the given representation. For instance, in a fingerprint matcher, one could constrain the elastic distortion altogether and design the matcher based on an assumption of rigid transformation or allow arbitrary distortions and accommodate the variations in the input images using a robust matcher. In light of the operational environments mentioned above, the design of the matching algorithm needs to establish and characterize a realistic model of the expected variations among the representations of mated pairs.

Chapter 4 is dedicated to the fingerprint matching problem. The matching problem is formally presented, the above three classes of matching techniques are discussed, and the related literature is surveyed in detail. Particular emphasis is given to minutiae matching and both global and local minutiae matching algorithms are introduced. The best accuracy versus. efficiency trade-off can be achieved by combining local and global minutiae matching into a two-phase approach where an initial local structure matching is followed by a consolidation step. This technique is extensively discussed in Section 4.4. A separate section is then dedicated to non-linear distortion affecting fingerprint impressions and to the design of distortion-tolerant matchers.

1.14 Fingerprint Classification and Indexing

Large volumes of fingerprints are collected and stored every day in a wide range of applications, particularly in forensics and government applications, e.g., background check of employees. Automatic identification based on fingerprints requires matching the input (query or test) fingerprint against a large number of templates stored in a database. To reduce the search time and computational complexity, it is desirable to classify these fingerprints in an accurate and consistent manner. A fingerprint pre-selection algorithm can then reduce the matching complexity. Fingerprint classification is a technique used to assign a fingerprint to one of the several pre-specified types (see Figure 1.13). Fingerprint classification can be viewed as a coarse-level matching of the fingerprints. An input fingerprint is first classified into one of the pre-specified types and then it is compared to a subset of the database corresponding to that fingerprint type (i.e., the pre-selection algorithm selects a bin to reduce the number of templates to be matched). A well-known classification of fingerprints was proposed by Henry (see Lee and Gaensslen (2001)) that consists of five major classes: whorl, left loop, right loop, arch, and tended arch. If the fingerprint database is binned into these five classes, and a fingerprint classifier outputs two classes (primary and secondary) with extremely high accuracy, then the identification system will only need to search two of the five bins, thus the pre-selection algorithm will decrease (in principle) the search space by 2.5-fold. Unfortunately, the distribution of fingerprints even into these five categories is not uniform, and there are many "ambiguous" fingerprints (see Figure 1.16) that cannot be accurately classified even by human experts. About 17% of the 4000 images in the NIST Special Database 4 (Watson and Wilson, 1992a) have two different ground truth labels! Therefore, in practice, fingerprint classification is not immune to errors and does not offer much selectivity for fingerprint searching in large databases.

To overcome this problem, "continuous classification" or other fingerprint indexing techniques can be used. In continuous classification, fingerprints are not partitioned into non-overlapping classes, but each fingerprint is characterized with a numerical vector summarizing its main features. The continuous features obtained are used for indexing fingerprints through spatial data structures and for retrieving fingerprints by means of spatial queries.

Chapter 5 covers fingerprint classification and indexing techniques and the related pre-selection algorithms (also known as retrieval algorithms). The fingerprint classification literature is surveyed in detail and the proposed methods are categorized into one or more of the following families: rule-based approaches, syntactic approaches, structural approaches, statistical approaches, neural networks-based approaches, and multi-classifier approaches. A separate section introduces the standard metrics and notations used to compute classification performance and compares existing methods on NIST Special Database 4 (Watson and Wilson, 1992a) and NIST Special Database 14 (Watson, 1993a) which are the most commonly used benchmarks for fingerprint classification studies. Fingerprint sub-classification (i.e., a multilevel partitioning strategy) and continuous classification are then discussed and the associated retrieval strategies and pre-selection algorithms are introduced and compared.

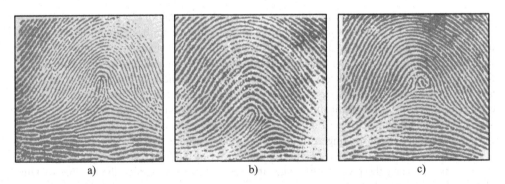

a)   b)   c)

Figure 1.16. Examples of fingerprints that are difficult to classify; a) tented arch; b) a loop; c) a whorl; it appears that all the fingerprints shown here should be in the loop category.

1.15 Synthetic Fingerprints

Performance evaluation of fingerprint recognition systems is data dependent. Therefore, the acquisition conditions, database size, and confidence intervals must be specified when reporting the matching results. Typically, to obtain tight confidence intervals at very low error rates, large databases of representative fingerprint images are required. Moreover, once a fingerprint database has been used for testing and optimizing a system, successive testing cycles require new databases previously unseen by the system.

Collection of large fingerprint database is expensive both in terms of time and money. There are also problems due to data collection errors and of privacy legislation protecting the use and sharing of personal data. In several contexts, a synthetic generation of realistic fingerprint images may alleviate these problems. The most desirable property of such a synthetic fingerprint generator is that it should be able to model the various inter-class and intra-class variations in fingerprint images observed in nature. In particular, multiple "impressions" of the same "virtual finger," should reflect:

- Different touching areas.
- Non-linear distortions produced by non-orthogonal pressure of the finger against the fingerprint scanner.
- Variations in the ridge line thickness given by pressure intensity or by skin dampness.
- Small cuts on the fingertip and other kinds of artifacts.
- Complex background such as those typically observed when the fingerprint scanner surface is dirty.

Chapter 6 describes a synthetic fingerprint generator (Cappelli, Maio, and Maltoni, 2002b) that meets the above requirements and is able to produce realistic-looking examples of fingerprint images (see Figure 1.17). The mathematical models on which the generator is based are introduced, together with the intermediate steps. A validation of the synthetic generator is also presented based on the performance of a fingerprint recognition system on the synthetic as well as real fingerprint images. The software tool, SFINGE, included in the DVD that accompanies this book, can be used to create a synthetic fingerprint step by step, observing the effects of various parameter values on the resulting fingerprint image.

1.16 Biometric Fusion

How can the performance of a fingerprint recognition system be improved? There comes a stage in the development of any biometric recognition system where it becomes increasingly difficult to achieve significantly better performance from a given biometric identifier or a given method. There often is a need to explore other sources and methods for improvement. The *fusion* approach to improve performance can take any number of different forms. One may fuse multiple biometric traits or multiple instances of the same biometric trait or even complimentary feature extraction and matching algorithms for the same instance of a biometric trait. Performance gains have been reported from various such fusion approaches.

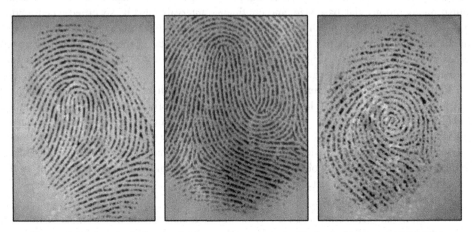

Figure 1.17. Synthetic fingerprint images generated with the software tool SFINGE.

Fusing multiple biometric identifiers can also alleviate several practical problems in biometrics-based personal recognition. For instance, although a biometric identifier is supposed to be *universal* (each person in the target population should possess it), in practice, no biometric identifier is truly universal. Similarly, it is not always possible to sense all the biometric identifiers (non-zero failure to acquire rate). Biometric identifiers are also prone to failure to enroll. That is, there are some users in the target population whose biometric identifiers are not easily quantifiable by the given biometric sensor. Consequently, the recognition system cannot handle these users based on that particular biometric identifier. In highly secure systems, reinforcement of evidence from multiple biometric identifiers offers increasingly irrefutable proof of the identity of the authorized person. It is also extremely difficult for an intruder to fake several different biometric traits of a genuine user in order to circumvent the system. The assumptions of universality, collectability, acceptability, and integrity are more realistically accommodated when person recognition is based on information from several biometric identifiers.

Multiple modalities of biometrics can be combined at the sensor, feature, matcher score, or matcher decision levels (Brooks and Iyengar, 1997). The integration at sensor or feature level assumes a strong interaction among the input measurements and such integration schemes are referred to as *tightly coupled integrations* (Clark and Yuille, 1990). The *loosely coupled integrations*, on the other hand, assume very little or no interaction among the inputs (e.g., face and finger) and the integration occurs at the output of relatively autonomous agents, each agent independently assessing the input from its own perspective.

Focus of most biometric fusion research has been on loosely coupled integration. The loosely coupled integration is not only simpler to implement, it is more feasible in commonly confronted integration scenarios. A typical scenario for integration is two biometric systems (often proprietary) independently acquiring inputs and making an autonomous assessment of the "match" based on their respective identifiers; although the decisions or matching scores of individual biometric systems are available for integration, the features used by one biometric system are usually not accessible to the other biometric system. Decision-level and matcher score-level integration can provably deliver at least as good or better performance than any single constituent biometric (Hong, Jain, and Pankanti, 1999).

Tightly coupled integration is much harder. International Standards Organization (ISO) has introduced standards on interoperability that have led to common formats of fingerprint representations for easy exchange of data among vendors. A limitation of these approaches is that these schemes force vendors to use the least common denomination of the representation as a basis of data sharing (e.g., minutiae) and consequently, there is significant degradation in performance when one vendor is using the features extracted by another vendor (Grother et al., 2006).

Chapter 7 introduces the reader to the various advantages of fusion in biometric systems and presents arguments from the multiclassifier literature in pattern recognition that a (carefully designed) integrated system is expected to result in a significant improvement in recognition accuracy. Fusion of various sources of information (such as multiple biometrics, multiple fingers of the same person, multiple samples of the same finger, multiple representations and matching algorithm) is discussed as well fusion methods at the various information levels (such as image, features, matching score, rank, and decision).

1.17 System Integration and Administration Issues

The major issues in using a fingerprint recognition system in an application include: defining the system working mode (verification or identification), choosing hardware (e.g., fingerprint scanner) and software (e.g., feature extraction and matching algorithms) components and making them work together, dealing with exceptions and poor quality fingerprint images, and defining effective administration and optimization policy. These issues are often left to the application administrator. There are lots of core fingerprint recognition components (scanners and algorithms) available from a variety of vendors. With the advances in interoperability standards, different applications may choose to mix and match such components to achieve the objectives of the application (e.g., the performance versus cost, etc.)

As mentioned in Section 1.3, a fingerprint-based system may operate either in verification or identification mode. As a rule of thumb, when the number of users is large (>1,000) it is recommended that the system designer choose the verification mode unless identification is strictly necessary.[1] This is because the verification system scales very well, i.e., the verification response time, accuracy, and resource consumption (such as system memory and processing power etc.) does not depend on the size of the database. On the other hand, in identification, the response time decreases as the database size increases. Further, the accuracy degrades and more system resources (such as memory and processing power) are required as the database size increases. In case neither binning nor clever indexing/retrieval mechanisms are available, an identification system needs to explore the entire template database to establish an identity. Even if indexing is used, it is doubtful that a one-finger matching can reach the desirable efficiency and accuracy on a large database. As a result, use of multiple fingers is recommended in medium to large scale identification applications.

If the system designer or integrator is also the developer of the feature extraction and matching (and eventually indexing) algorithms, then she certainly has the necessary knowledge to combine all the modules and to select the optimal fingerprint scanner and computing platform. In the biometric field, developers and system integrators are not always the producers of fingerprint scanners and core matching algorithms, and therefore, care must be taken when choosing acquisition scanners and matching algorithms (hardware and software components). The system designer should take into account several factors:

- *Proven technology*: have the hardware and software components been tested by third parties? Are the test results available? Is the vendor available to demonstrate that the claimed performance (accuracy and response time estimates) is true?
- *System interoperability and standards*: is the system compliant with emerging standards? Is the software compliant with all the platforms and operating systems of interest?
- *Cost versus performance tradeoff*: the optimal point in the cost versus performance tradeoff strongly depends on the application requirements. The cheapest solution is not necessarily the best choice; biometrics is not infallible, and the success of an application often depends on how much of the customer expectation is met.
- *Support*: available documentation, examples, etc.

Vendors may supply an SDK (Software Development Kit) in the form of libraries for one or more operating systems. These libraries typically include a series of primitives that allow different tasks to be performed (e.g., fingerprint acquisition, feature extraction, template creation, matching, template storage, etc.). The system designer is usually in charge of developing specific routines for:

---

[1] Applications that assume a negative claim of identity cannot work in verification mode: in fact, the system has to search the entire archive to prove that the query feature set does not have a match in the enrollment database. Sometimes, even in applications that assume positive claim of identity, the system must necessarily work in identification mode, due to the practical difficulty of using an input device to enter a PIN.

- Implementing the enrollment stages.
- Storing and retrieving templates and user information in/from a centralized/ distributed template storage (database).
- Defining the user search order in an identification application. For example, the template of the users most frequently accessing the system may be matched before those of infrequent users.
- Defining policies and administration modules to let the system administration define and control the system behavior. This includes setting the system security options (system threshold, number of trials, alarms, etc.) and logging information about access attempts.

An important point when designing a fingerprint recognition system is to decide from the beginning how to deal with users whose fingerprint quality is extremely poor. Although the percentage of users with "unusable" fingerprints is miniscule, it cannot be ignored, especially in large-scale applications. There are several options to deal with such a problem:

- In the enrollment stage, choose the best quality finger and eventually enroll more fingers or more instances of the same finger.
- Define user-dependent system thresholds. In particular, the system threshold may be relaxed by the system administrator for fingers that are hard to match (to reduce false non-match rate); for other users the threshold is maintained at the default level. Although this has serious security implications, it may be preferable than decreasing the system operating point for all the users, because an impostor who intends to "imitate" an enrolled user usually is not aware of which users have poor quality finger.
- Use an additional biometric (multimodal biometric system).
- Use an additional non-biometric. For example, using a computer-generated difficult password (frequently changed) could be an acceptable authentication alternative for a limited number of users.

System administration and optimization are also very important issues. An administrator (or proper documentation) should briefly instruct users the first time they use the system and, in particular, make them familiar with the use of fingerprint scanner. An attended enrollment is often preferable to check the quality of input, select the best finger, and eventually relax the user-dependent threshold (if this option is available). The administrator is also in charge of setting the global security threshold, controlling the state of the acquisition devices (the live-scan scanners sometimes become dirty over time and therefore, the quality of the input images tends to deteriorate), and to monitor access attempts. In particular, in case some users find it difficult to access the system, the administrator should understand the underlying reasons: a new enrollment could solve the problem in the case of some physical variations in the finger (e.g., a recent injury or scratch); retraining users on how to properly interact with the scanner could be sufficient in several other cases. Monitoring the system log could also be very useful to discover if the system is being subjected to attacks by fraudulent users.

1.18 Securing Fingerprint Systems

Fingerprint recognition systems are security systems and as such they are not foolproof. Despite numerous advantages, fingerprint systems are vulnerable to security breaches and attacks. The system vulnerability depends on the threat model of an application which will use the fingerprint recognition system. The typical threats in a fingerprint recognition system are as follows:

- *Denial-of-service*: an adversary can damage the system to cause a denial-of-service to all the system users.
- *Circumvention* or *intrusion*: an unauthorized user can illegitimately gain access into the system (including, by colluding with the system administrator or by coercing a legitimate authorized user).
- *Function creep*: a wrongful acquisition or use of fingerprint data for a purpose other than intended.
- *Repudiation*: a legitimate user may deny having accessed the system.

The system should be secure in the sense that the hackers should neither be able to obtain fingerprint data from the system nor be able to inject any fingerprint data into the system. Bolle, Connell, and Ratha (2002) and Ratha, Connell, and Bolle (1999, 2001a, 2003) describe an "attack point" model to describe vulnerabilities in biometric systems. Cukic and Bartlow (2005) adopt an "attack tree" model while Jain, Ross, and Pankanti (2006) adopt a "fishbone" model. In Chapter 9, we adopt a slightly different viewpoint in looking at the types of fingerprint system failures, how the failures can be triggered, and discuss some of the techniques that have been developed as countermeasures. It is expected that multiple techniques will be used in building a practical system depending on the application's threat model. For a successful intrusion, a hacker needs to first obtain fingerprint data and then inject it into the authentication system. There are different ways by which a hacker can obtain fingerprint data and different way by which the hacker can inject the data into the system. We will present countermeasures for each.

The most critical user interface of a biometric system is the interaction of the user with the scanner. Of particular interest among the various biometric circumvention measures is that of checking whether the source of the input signal is live and original (i.e., not dead or fake). The premise of a liveness test is that if the finger is live and original, the impression made by it represents the person to whom the finger belongs. One of the approaches of detecting liveness is to measure one or more vital signs (e.g., pulse, temperature) of life in the object being imaged. High-resolution fingerprint scanning can reveal characteristic sweat pore structure of skin (Roddy and Stosz, 1997) that is difficult to replicate in an artificial finger. The skin tone of a live finger turns white or yellow when pressed against a glass platen. This effect can be exploited for detecting a live finger. The blood flow in a live finger and its pulsation can be detected by a careful measurement of light reflected or transmitted through the finger. Difference in action potentials across two specific points on a live fingerprint muscle can also be used to distinguish it from a dead finger. The electrical properties of a live finger are ascertained rather effortlessly in some solid-state fingerprint scanners. Measuring complex impedance of the finger can be a useful attribute to distinguish a live finger from its lifeless counterpart. A live finger generates sweat and this sweating process can be monitored to determine liveness. Any combination of pulse rate, electrocardiographic signals, spectral characteristics of human tissue, percentage of oxygenation of blood, bloodflow, hematocrit, biochemical assays of tissue, electrical plethysmography, transpiration of gases, electrical property of skin, blood pressure, and differential blood volumes can be used to detect a live finger.

A good strategy to secure the modules, communication channels, and template storage of a fingerprint recognition system from the hackers is to design the system such that it is a closed system. A closed system in this context means that the modules of the system trust each other but no one else. We discuss techniques to build a closed system in Chapter 9. In particular, the popular match-on-card, system-on-device, system-on-card, and system-on-a-chip architectures are discussed. Protection of biometric template has received significant attention from the research community. In a knowledge- or token-based system, if the knowledge or token is compromised, it can be changed, but if a biometric template is stolen, it can be used to circumvent the fingerprint system repeatedly as the user cannot change her biometric trait. Template protection techniques are discussed in Chapter 9.

1.19 Privacy Issues

Privacy is the ability to lead one's own life free from intrusions, to remain anonymous, and to control access to one's own personal information. Since privacy deals with personal information, there needs to be an enforceable, objective definition of a person's identity. As the magnitude of identity fraud increases and as we are increasingly being asked to prove our identity to strangers in remote locations, there appears be a tendency to lower the standards of suspecting validity of claimed identity for authorizing transactions. Biometrics such as fingerprints will increasingly come into play for positively recognizing people because of the limitations of the conventional technologies (e.g., knowledge-based or token-based). For instance, US legislation requires the use of strong recognition schemes (such as biometric identifier) for controlling access to sensitive medical records to authorized personnel. Some applications have envisaged using biometrics for anonymous access. For instance, these applications index sensitive individual information without explicitly specifying a name and the access mechanisms (e.g., allow access to medical records if the person's left index fingerprint matches the fingerprint associated with this record). Furthermore, by requiring automated access mechanisms through a secure biometric system, it is hoped that all the accesses to the privileged information can be tracked, thereby increasing the accountability of transactions within the information systems. Thus it is clear that fingerprints will be useful for enhancing the integrity of systems holding personal information.

In spite of the security benefits offered by biometric recognition, there are objections to biometric recognition based on the following arguments. Methods of automatic recognition of individuals based on biometrics may be perceived as undignifying. Religious objections interpret biometric recognition as "the mark of beast" by citing somewhat dubious biblical references.[2] Some potential users have raised concerns about the hygiene of biometric scanners requiring contact. Given that we routinely touch many objects (e.g., money) touched by strangers, this objection may be viewed as a frivolous excuse. There may be negative connotations associated with some biometrics (fingerprint, face, and DNA) due to their prevalent use in criminal investigation.

There are some other stronger criticisms being leveled against the unintended but potentially harmful (to the user) capabilities of biometric identifiers.

- *Unintended functional scope*: because biometric identifiers are based on human anatomy, additional (possibly statistical) personal information may be gleaned from the scanned biometric measurements. For instance, it is known that malformed fingers may be statistically correlated with certain genetic disorders (Babler (1991); Penrose (1965); Mulvhill (1969)). With advancements in human genome research, the fear of inferring personal information from biological measurements may be imminent. Such derived medical information may become a basis for systematic discrimination against the perceived "risky" or "undesirable" sections of population.
- *Unintended application scope*: persons legally maintaining multiple identities (say, for safety reasons under a witness protection program) can be detected based on their fingerprints. By acquiring biometrics identifiers (either covertly or overtly), one has the capacity to track an identified individual. It has been argued that automatically gathering individual information based on biometric identifiers accrues unfair advantage to people in power and reduces the sovereignty of private citizens. In the case of fingerprints, presently there is no technology to automatically capture fingerprints covertly to facilitate effortless tracking.[3] Yet, persons who desire to remain anonymous in any particular situation may be denied their privacy as their fingerprint templates from different systems may be linked together through fingerprint matching.

The possible abuse of biometric information (or their derivatives) and related accountability procedures can be addressed through government legislation (e.g., EU legislation against

---

[2] "He also forced everyone, small and great, rich and poor, free and slave, to receive a mark on his right hand or on his forehead, so that no one could buy or sell unless he had the mark, which is the name of the beast or the number of his name." (Revelation 13:16–17)

[3] Although there is touchless (direct) fingerprint scanning technology available, it is still necessary for the subject to be in the very close proximity of the scanner. There is presently no technology capable of video snooping of fingerprints.

sharing of biometric identifiers and personal information (Woodward, 1999)), assurance of self-regulation by the biometric industry (e.g., self-regulation policies of the International Biometrics Industry Association [IBIA]), and autonomous enforcement by independent regulatory organizations (e.g., a Central Biometric Authority). Until such consensus is reached, there may be reluctance by some users to provide their biometrics measurements. As a result, applications delivering recognition capability in a highly decentralized fashion are likely to be favored.

In verification applications, one way to decentralize a biometric system is by storing the biometric information in a decentralized (encrypted) database over which the individual has complete control. For instance, one could store the fingerprint template in a tamper-resistant smartcard that is issued to the user. The input fingerprint feature set can be directly compared with the template on the smartcard and the decision delivered (possibly in encrypted form) to the application. Thus, the template is never released from the secure storage of the smartcard. Such a smartcard-based system permits all the advantages of biometric recognition without many of the stipulated privacy problems associated with biometrics. Commercial products already exist that implement system-on-a-chip, where the fingerprint scanner is directly connected to the physically secure chip that stores the templates as well as conducts the entire fingerprint processing, from fingerprint acquisition to feature extraction to matching, on the secure chip. See Chapter 9 for a discussion on match-on-card and system-on-a-chip solutions. Chapter 9 also discusses template protection techniques, which have privacy protection and privacy enhancing properties. These methods are currently under intense research and development.

1.20 Summary and Future Prospects

Fingerprint recognition has come a long way since its inception more than 100 years ago. The first primitive live-scan scanners designed by Cornell Aeronautical Lab/North American Aviation, Inc. were unwieldy beasts with many problems as compared to the sleek, inexpensive, and compact scanners available today. Over the past few decades, research and active use of fingerprint matching and indexing have also advanced our understanding of the power as well as limitations of fingerprint recognition. Steady increase in processor power and memory capacity at lower prices, cheap fingerprint scanners, and growing demand for security have lead to the viability of fingerprint matching for routine person recognition tasks.

There is a popular misconception that automatic fingerprint recognition is a fully solved problem. There are still a number of challenges in designing completely automatic and reliable fingerprint recognition algorithms, especially for poor quality fingerprint images. Although state-of-the-art automatic fingerprint systems have impressive performance, they still cannot match the performance of a fingerprint expert in handling poor quality and latent fingerprints. On the other hand, automatic fingerprint recognition systems offer a reliable, rapid, consistent, and cost-effective solution in a number of traditional and emerging applications that require person recognition.

In many pattern recognition applications (e.g., OCR), the state-of-the-art commercial systems often use a combination of representations and matchers. Ongoing work in biometric fusion (Chapter 7), where multiple sources of information (e.g., fingerprint, face and iris) are used to improve the recognition accuracy is addressing this topic. There may be a need for exploring radically different features (see Chapter 4) rich in discriminatory information, robust matching methods, and more ingenious methods for combining fingerprint matching and indexing that are amenable to automation.

Only a few years back, it seemed as though interest in fingerprint matching research was waning. As mentioned earlier, due to a continuing increase in identity fraud, there is a growing need for positive person recognition. Lower fingerprint scanner prices, inexpensive computing power, and our (relatively better) understanding of individuality information in fingerprints (compared to other biometric traits) have attracted a lot of commercial interest in fingerprint-based recognition system. Consequently, market revenue is expected to constantly grow over the next several years (see Figure 1.18a). Embedded application of fingerprint recognition (e.g., in a smartcard or in a cell phone) has already lead to many products in the market. Scientific research on fingerprint recognition is also receiving more attention; evidence of this is the exponentially increasing number of publications on this topic (see Figure 1.18b). Some of the difficult problems in fingerprint recognition will entail solving not only the core pattern recognition challenges but also confronting some challenging system engineering issues related to security and privacy.

Readers interested in additional details on different aspects of fingerprint recognition and biometrics (including forensic practices and AFIS) should consult the following publications: Henry (1900), Pearson (1933), Scott (1951), Trauring (1963), Chapel (1971), Moenssens (1971), Eleccion (1973), Swonger (1973), Shelman and Hodges (1973), Banner and Stock (1974, 1975a, b), Asai et al. (1975), Riganati (1977), Rao (1978), Hoshino et al. (1980), Svigals (1982), Cowger (1983), Misao and Kazuo (1984), Wilson and Woodard (1987), Saviers (1987), Karen (1989), Mehtre and Chatterjee (1991), Federal Bureau of Investigation (1984, 1991), Overton and Richardson (1991), Hollingum (1992), Colins (1992), Miller (1994), NIST (1994), Champod and Margot (1996), Shen and Khanna (1997), Hong et al. (1997), Ashbaugh (1999), Jain, Hong, and Pankanti (2000), Jones (2000), Berry and Stoney (2001), Lee and Gaensslen (2001) and Jain et al. (1999b, 2001).

Following books and articles provide more recent and a more comprehensive introduction: Jain, Bolle, and Pankanti (1999), O'Gorman (1999), Pankanti, Bolle, and Jain (2000), Jain and Pankanti (2000, 2001, 2006), Woodward, Orlans, and Higgins (2002), Bolle et al. (2003), Cole (2004), Champod et al. (2004), Khanna (2004), McCabe (2004), Bhanu and Tan (2004), Prabhakar and Jain (2004), Ratha and Bolle (2004), Shen and Eshera (2004), Wayman et al. (2005), Komarinski (2005), Li and Jain (2005), Ross, Nandakumar, and Jain (2006), Wechsler (2007), Ratha and Govindaraju (2007), Vacca (2007), Jain, Flynn, and Ross (2007), and Wayman (2008).

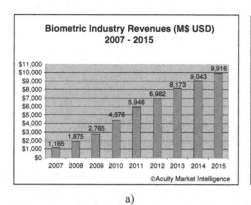
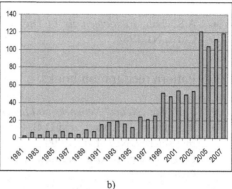

a)   b)

Figure 1.18. a) In a report titled "The future of biometrics: market analysis, segmentation & forecast", Acuity Market Intelligence© predicts that biometrics industry will continue to grow at a healthy rate over the next decade. b) The number of scientific papers published on fingerprint research in the past 30 years shows gaining interest in fingerprint recognition research.

1.21 Image Processing and Pattern Recognition Background

Some background in image processing and pattern recognition techniques is necessary to fully understand a majority of the chapters in this book (especially Chapters 3 to 7). We recommend the following books and periodicals to readers who do not have this background.

1.21.1 Image processing books

- R.C. Gonzalez and R.E. Woods, *Digital Image Processing* (3rd edition), Prentice-Hall, Englewood Cliffs, NJ, 2007.
- J. Bigun, *Vision with Direction: A Systematic Introduction to Image Processing and Computer Vision*, Springer, NY, 2006.
- D.A. Forsyth and J. Ponce, *Computer Vision: A Modern Approach*, Prentice-Hall, Englewood Cliffs, NJ, 2002.
- L.G. Shapiro and G. Stockman, *Computer Vision*, Prentice-Hall, Englewood Cliffs, NJ, 2001.
- R. Bracewell, *The Fourier Transform and Its Applications* (3rd edition), McGraw-Hill, New York, 1999.
- S. Mallat, *A Wavelet Tour of Signal Processing*, Academic, New York, 1997.

- J. Parker, *Algorithms for Image Processing and Computer Vision*, Wiley, New York, 1996.
- A.K. Jain, *Fundamentals of Digital Image Processing*, Prentice-Hall, Englewood Cliffs, NJ, 1988.

1.21.2 Pattern recognition books

- S. Haykin, *Neural Networks and Learning Machines*, Prentice Hall, 2008.
- R.O. Duda, P.E. Hart, and D.G. Stork, *Pattern Classification* (2nd edition), Wiley-Interscience, New York, 2000.
- C.M. Bishop, *Neural Networks for Pattern Recognition*, Oxford University Press, Oxford, 1995.
- A.K. Jain and R.C. Dubes, *Algorithms for Clustering Data*, Prentice-Hall, Englewood Cliffs, NJ, 1988.

1.21.3 Journals

- *IEEE Transactions on Pattern Analysis and Machine Intelligence*
- *IEEE Transactions on Information Forensics and Security*
- *IEEE Transactions on Image Processing*
- *Pattern Recognition*
- *Pattern Recognition Letters*

2
Fingerprint Sensing

2.1 Introduction

Historically, in law enforcement applications, the acquisition of fingerprint images was performed by using the so-called "ink-technique": the subject's fingers were smeared with black ink and pressed or rolled on a paper card; the card was then scanned by using a general purpose scanner, producing a digital image. This kind of acquisition process is referred to as *off-line* fingerprint acquisition or off-line sensing and is briefly discussed in Section 2.2. A particular case of off-line sensing is the acquisition of latent fingerprints from crime scenes (Colins, 1992). Nowadays, most civil and criminal AFIS accept *live-scan* digital images acquired by directly sensing the finger surface with an electronic *fingerprint scanner* (also called *fingerprint reader*). No ink is required in this method, and all that a subject has to do is to present his finger to a live-scan scanner. Although AFIS has greatly benefited from the use of live-scan acquisition techniques, this innovation is undoubtedly more important for a broad range of civil and commercial applications where user acceptance and convenience, low-cost, and reliability are necessary and expected. In civil and commercial applications, certainly, an employee cannot be expected to apply ink to his fingertip every time he has to logon to his personal computer or to carry out a financial transaction; neither could we expect a wide adoption of fingerprint-based biometric techniques if the cost of the acquisition devices was too high.

The general structure of a typical fingerprint scanner is shown in Figure 2.1: a *sensor* reads the ridge pattern on the finger surface and converts the analog reading in the digital form through an A/D (Analog to Digital) converter; an interface module is responsible for communicating (sending images, receiving commands, etc.) with external devices (e.g., a personal computer). Throughout this chapter we use the terms "scanner" and "sensor" with different meanings: with *sensor* we denote the internal active sensing element of a fingerprint scanner that reads the finger surface. The different technologies the sensors are based on (e.g., optical, solid-state, ultrasound, etc.) are surveyed in Section 2.3. In practice, there exist several variants of the schema in Figure 2.1: for example, often the sensor output is already a digital sig-

D. Maltoni et al., *Handbook of Fingerprint Recognition*, 57–95.
© Springer-Verlag London Limited 2009

nal and therefore no separate A/D conversion is necessary; some fingerprint scanners may not have an integrated A/D converter and an external frame grabber would be needed to transform their analog output signal. Furthermore, some embedded System-on-a-Chip devices have been proposed (Anderson et al. (1991); Shigematsu et al. (1999); Jung et al. (1999, 2005)) where, besides the sensor, a processing board is embedded into the chip in order to locally process and/or match the fingerprint data (see Section 9.6.2). The design of secure fingerprint-based biometric systems requires protection/encryption mechanisms to be implemented in the biometric scanners. Chapter 9 discusses the techniques used to protect fingerprint scanners against various attacks and to detect fake fingers presented to the sensors.

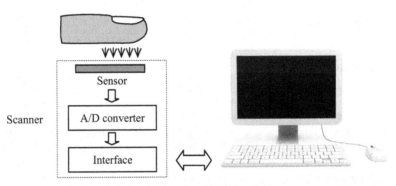

Figure 2.1. Block diagram of a fingerprint scanner.

Existing scanners can be classified into one of the following categories:

- *Multi-finger*: more than one finger can be acquired simultaneously (see Figure 2.2a). Usually the four fingers of one hand (all except the thumb) can be acquired at the same time so that three shots or finger placements are enough to acquire all the 10 fingers in the sequence: four fingers (first hand), four fingers (second hand), and the two thumbs together. The segmentation of a single image containing four fingerprints into four separate single fingerprints is know as *slap segmentation*; this task is generally performed in software (see Figure 2.20): NIST organized a specific evaluation campaign to determine the accuracy of slap segmentation algorithms (Ulery et al., 2005). A typical usage of multi-finger scanners is in forensic and other large-scale civil applications where more than one finger is used to enroll and identify individuals.
- *Single-finger*: only one finger at a time can be acquired (see Figure 2.2b); this type of scanner is most widely used in commercial and personal applications due to its small size, low cost and simplicity of use. Designing compact and cheap scanners is crucial to allow fingerprint scanners to be embedded in low-cost portable devices such as

laptop and mobile phones: sweep sensors (discussed in Section 2.4) are tiny sensing elements that acquire the image of just a small portion of the finger at a time and require the user to sweep the finger over the sensor surface. To achieve reliable fingerprint recognition, fingerprint images should possess certain characteristics. Overly relaxing some of the constraints (e.g., image quality and minimum finger area) may lead to a significant (and sometimes unacceptable) decrease in fingerprint recognition accuracy.

Examples of both multi-finger and single-finger scanners are included in Section 2.8.

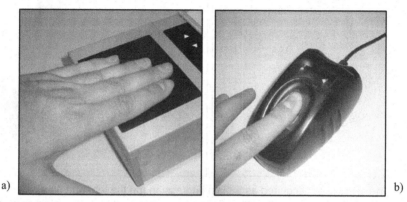

a)   b)

Figure 2.2. Fingerprint scanners. a) simultaneous acquisition of four fingers through a multi-finger scanner; b) acquisition with a single-finger scanner.

Some scanners (either multi-finger or single-finger) can also acquire *rolled impressions*: the user is required to roll a finger "nail-to-nail" on the scanner, thus producing an unwrapped representation of the whole fingerprint pattern which carries more information with respect to a *flat* (also called *dab*, *slapped*, or *plain*) impression (see Figure 2.3). It is often necessary for a trained fingerprint acquisition expert to assist the user in rolling his finger on the sensor. Hardware and software techniques have been introduced (see for example Ratha, Connell, and Bolle, 1998) to enable live-scan fingerprint scanners, operating at proper frame rate, to compose the sequence of images of the rolling finger into a single unwrapped impression.

To maximize the compatibility between fingerprint images acquired by different scanners and ensure good quality of the acquired image, specifications have been released by FBI and other organizations that are involved in large-scale biometric deployments. In fact, as demonstrated by Ross and Jain (2004), Han et al. (2006), Ross and Nadgir (2006, 2008) and Jang, Elliott, and Kim (2007), matching images of the same finger acquired by different scanners, not compliant with given specifications, can lead to a severe drop in fingerprint recognition accuracy. This problem can be partially alleviated with a priori calibration techniques as

shown in Ross and Nadgir (2008) where an average compensation model is a priori determined for two given fingerprint scanners. However, the characteristics of different devices of
exactly the same model/manufacturer can markedly deviate with respect to their nominal values; therefore, a specific compensation would be required for any two pair of devices, and this
is unfeasible in medium-large scale applications.

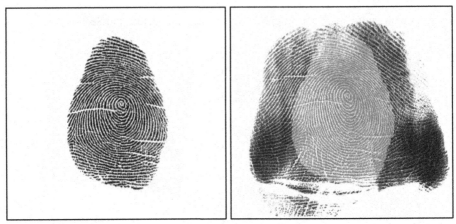

Figure 2.3. The same finger acquired as a plain impression (on the left) and as a rolled impression (on the right): the portion of the rolled fingerprint corresponding to the plain fingerprint is
highlighted.

Section 2.5 introduces the parameters of fingerprint images and Section 2.6 summarizes the
FBI specifications. Section 2.7 defines the scanner quality from an operational point of view
that makes explicit the relationship between the quality parameters of fingerprint scanners and
the performance of fingerprint recognition algorithms.

Matching fingerprints acquired through small area sensors is a difficult task due to the possibility of having too little overlap between different acquisitions of the same finger: Section
2.9 discusses this problem and proposes some techniques that can partially solve it.

Most of the fingerprint recognition systems, especially those in commercial applications,
do not store fingerprint images but only numerical features extracted from the image (see
Chapter 3). However, in certain applications (e.g., law enforcement), it may be necessary to
store the fingerprint images acquired during enrollment in a database so that a trained expert
can verify the matching results output by an AFIS. Storing millions of fingerprint images (as
in a large AFIS), or transmitting these images through low-bandwidth networks, is particularly
demanding in terms of space/time. Hence, several ad hoc compression techniques have been

proposed and one of them, known as Wavelet Scalar Quantization (WSQ), has been adopted as a standard by the FBI; Section 2.10 briefly discusses fingerprint image compression.

2.2 Off-Line Fingerprint Acquisition

Although the first fingerprint scanners were introduced more than 30 years ago, the ink-technique (Reed and Meier (1990); Lee and Gaensslen (2001)) is still used in law enforcement applications. The use of ink-techniques is gradually being replaced as live-scan acquisition techniques are becoming affordable. As a result, the databases that have been built by law enforcement agencies over a long period of time (tens of years) contain fingerprint images acquired by both off-line as well as live-scan scanners. The AFIS fingerprint recognition algorithms are expected to interoperate on these different types of images. In other words, an image acquired using off-line scanner needs to be matched to an image acquired using live-scan scanners without any loss of accuracy. As mentioned earlier, in the ink-technique, the finger skin is first smeared with black ink, finger is pressed or rolled against a paper card and the card is then converted into digital form by means of a paper-scanner. The most commonly used resolution of the scanner/camera is 500 dpi. The ink-technique often produces images that include regions with missing fingerprint information due to excessive or insufficient ink on the finger or excessive or insufficient finger pressure. Figure 2.4 shows two examples of digitized images from fingerprint cards. These images have been taken from the NIST Special Database 14 (Watson, 1993a).

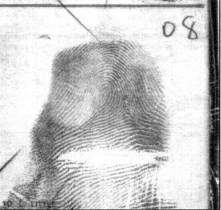

Figure 2.4. Two rolled fingerprint images acquired off-line with the ink technique.

In forensic applications, a special kind of fingerprint image, called *latent fingerprint*, is of great interest. These are partial fingerprint images lifted from a crime scene that are used to apprehend suspects and convict criminals. Constant perspiration exudation of sweat pores on fingerprint ridges and intermittent contact of fingers with other parts of the human body and various objects leaves a film of moisture and/or grease on the surface of the fingers. When touching an object (e.g., a glass surface), the film of moisture and/or grease is transferred from the finger to the object and leaves an impression of the ridges on the object thereon. This type of fingerprint is called a latent fingerprint. In this case, the actual finger that left the impression on the object is not available, so a copy of the latent print needs to be lifted from the surface of the object. Latent fingerprints are not clearly visible and their detection often requires some means of chemical development and enhancement (Figure 2.5). Powder dusting, ninhydrin spraying, iodine fuming, and silver nitrate soaking are the four most commonly used techniques of latent print development (Lee and Gaensslen, 2001). These techniques are quite effective under normal circumstances but are not appropriate in special cases when fingerprints are deposited on certain objects or surfaces (e.g., wet surfaces, untreated wood, human skin, etc.). Better procedures have been developed based on new chemical reagents, instruments, and systematic approaches involving a combination of methods (Lee and Gaensslen (2001); Menzel (2001); Champod et al. (2004); Dinish et al. (2005)) to develop latent fingerprints from such surfaces.

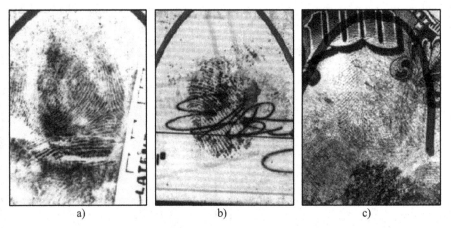

a)   b)   c)

Figure 2.5. Examples of (a) good, (b) bad, and (c) ugly latent fingerprints from NIST Special Database 27 (Garris and McCabe, 2000).

2.3 Live-Scan Fingerprint Sensing

The most important part of a live-scan fingerprint scanner is the sensor (or sensing element), which is the component where the fingerprint image is formed. Almost all the existing sensors belong to one of the following three families: optical, solid-state, and ultrasound.

2.3.1 Optical sensors

- *Frustrated Total Internal Reflection* (*FTIR*): this is the oldest and most commonly used live-scan acquisition technique today (Hase and Shimisu (1984); Bahuguna and Corboline (1996)). As the finger touches the top side of a glass/plastic prism, the ridges are in optical contact with the prism surface, but the valleys remain at a certain distance (see Figure 2.6). The left side of the prism is typically illuminated through a diffused light (a bank of light-emitting diodes [LEDs] or a film of planar light). The light entering the prism is reflected at the valleys, and randomly scattered (absorbed) at the ridges. The lack of reflection allows the ridges (which appear dark in the image) to be discriminated from the valleys (appearing bright). The light rays exit from the right side of the prism and are focused through a lens onto a CCD or CMOS image sensor. Because FTIR devices sense a three-dimensional finger surface, they cannot be easily deceived by presentation of a photograph or printed image of a fingerprint.

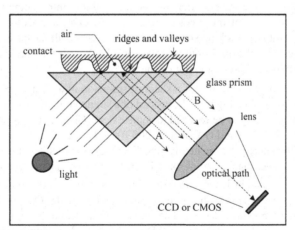

Figure 2.6. FTIR-based fingerprint sensor operation.

The FTIR-based sensor shown in Figure 2.6 often introduces certain geometrical distortions. The most evident one is known as trapezoidal or keystone distortion and is produced by the perspective view of the imaging surface. Since the fingerprint plane is not parallel to the CCD plane, rays A and B in Figure 2.6 have different lengths, resulting in a stretching or compression of the image regions which is a function of their distance from the optical axis. Compensation for this distortion may be optics-based or software-based (i.e., calibration techniques). Some optics-based techniques make use of ad hoc pre-molded plastic lenses or holograms as proposed by Seigo, Shin, and Takashi (1989), Igaki et al. (1992), Drake, Lidd, and Fiddy (1996) and Bahuguna and Corboline (1996) or of a correcting wedge prism as proposed by Rao (2008).

When a finger is very dry, it does not make uniform and consistent contact with the FTIR imaging surface. To improve the formation of fingerprints from dry fingers, whose ridges do not contain sufficient sweat particles, some scanner producers use conformal coating (typically made of silicone), which improves the optical contact of the skin with the prism. With the aim of reducing the cost of the optical devices, plastic is often used instead of glass for prisms and lenses, and CMOS cameras are used instead of the more expensive CCD cameras.

In spite of generally superior image quality and potentially larger sensing areas, FTIR-based fingerprint devices cannot be miniaturized unlike other optical techniques (e.g., optical fibers) or solid-state devices, especially in thickness. In fact, the length of the optical path (i.e., the distance between the prism external surface and the image sensor) cannot be significantly reduced without introducing severe optical distortion at the edges of the image; using one or more intermediate mirrors typically helps in assembling working solutions in reasonably small packages, but even if these are suitable for embedding into a mouse or a keyboard, they are still too large to be integrated into a PDA or a mobile phone.

- *FTIR with a sheet prism*: use of a sheet prism made of a number of "prismlets" adjacent to each other (see Figure 2.7), instead of a single large prism, allows the size of the mechanical assembly to be reduced to some extent (Chen and Kuo (1995); Zhou, Qiao, and Mok (1998); Xia and O'Gorman (2003)): in fact, even if the optical path remains the same, the sheet prism is nearly flat. However, the quality of the acquired images is generally lower than the traditional FTIR techniques that use glass/plastic prisms.

- *Optical fibers*: a significant reduction of the packaging size can be achieved by substituting prism and lens with a fiber–optic platen (Fujieda, Ono, and Sugama (1995); Dowling and Knowlton (1988)). The finger is in direct contact with the upper side of the platen; on the opposite side, a CCD or CMOS, tightly coupled with the platen, receives the finger residual light conveyed through the glass fibers (see Figure 2.8). Unlike the FTIR devices, here the CCD/CMOS is in direct contact with the platen (without any intermediate lens), and therefore its size has to cover the whole sensing area. This may result in a high cost for producing large area sensors. A similar microlens-based sensor has been proposed by Shogenji et al. (2004) based on compound-eye imaging principle.

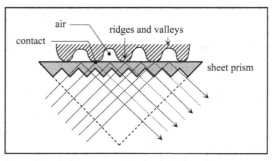

Figure 2.7. The use of a sheet prism in FTIR fingerprint acquisition.

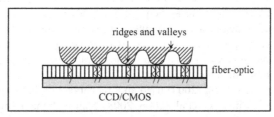

Figure 2.8. A sensor based on optical fibers. Residual light emitted by the finger is conveyed through micro-optical guides to the array of pixels that constitute the CCD/CMOS.

- *Electro-optical*: these devices consist of two main layers; the first layer contains a polymer that, when polarized with the proper voltage, emits light that depends on the potential applied on one side (see Figure 2.9). Since ridges touch the polymer and the valleys do not, the potential is not the same across the surface when a finger is placed on it; the amount of light emitted varies, thus allowing a luminous representation of the fingerprint pattern to be generated. The second layer, strictly coupled with the first one, consists of a photodiode array (embedded in the glass) which is responsible for receiving the light emitted by the polymer and converting it into a digital image (Young et al., 1997). Some commercial sensors use just the first light-emitting layer for the image formation and a standard lens and CMOS for the image acquisition and digitization. In spite of substantial miniaturization, images produced by commercial scanners based on this technology are not comparable with the FTIR images in terms of quality.

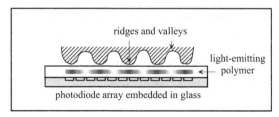

Figure 2.9. Electro-optical fingerprint sensor.

- *Direct reading*: a direct reading device uses a high-quality camera to directly focus on the fingertip. The finger is not in contact with any surface (*touchless acquisition*), but the scanner may be equipped with a mechanical support to facilitate the user in presenting the finger at a uniform distance. Touchless acquisition (Parziale, 2007) may be perceived to be more hygienic and may overcome some problems of touch-based acquisition such as the nonlinear distortion caused by pressing the finger against the sensor platen and the need of periodically cleaning the sensor surface; however, obtaining well-focused and high-contrast images is still quite challenging with the touchless methods.

  Hiew, Teoh, and Pang (2007) used an 8 megapixel digital camera as input device for their system, while Lee et al. (2006, 2008) dealt with the problem of selecting and processing fingerprint images acquired with the camera integrated in a mobile-device. Parziale, Diaz-Santana, and Hauke (2006) proposed an interesting setup where five cameras acquire images from different viewpoints that were then fused into a 3D representation of the finger using a reconstruction algorithm; such a device allows rolled-equivalent impressions to be generated without rotating the finger (Yi et al. (2006); Fatehpuria, Lau, and Hassebrook (2006); Fatehpuria et al. (2007)).

- *Multispectral imaging*: multispectral sensors capture multiple images of the same finger using different wavelengths of light, different illumination orientations, and different polarization conditions (Rowe, Nixon, and Butler, 2007). The resulting data can be processed to generate a single composite fingerprint image. Multispectral imaging is considered more robust than other acquisition techniques when fingerprint images are captured under adverse influences such as suboptimal skin condition and bright ambient light (Rowe and Nixon (2005); Rowe et al. (2007a)). Furthermore, features extracted from multispectral images are better suited in discriminating between real and fake fingers. On the other hand, multispectral imaging devices are more complex and expensive than conventional optical scanners and their adoption is still limited.

2.3.2 Solid-state sensors

Although solid-state sensors (also known as silicon sensors) have been proposed in patent literature since the 1980s, it was not until the middle 1990s that they became commercially viable (Xia and O'Gorman, 2003). Solid-state sensors were designed to overcome the size and cost problems which, at the time seemed to be a barrier against the wide spread deployment of fingerprint recognition systems in various consumer applications. All silicon-based sensors consist of an array of pixels, each pixel being a tiny sensor itself. The user directly touches the surface of the silicon: neither optical components nor external CCD/CMOS image sensors are needed. Four main technologies have been proposed to convert the fingerprint pattern into electrical signals: capacitive, thermal, electric field, and piezoelectric.

- *Capacitive*: this is the most common method used today within the silicon-based sensor arena (Tsikos (1982); Edwards (1984); Knapp (1994); Inglis et al. (1998); Setlak (1999); Lee et al. (1999); Dickinson et al. (2000); Morimura, Shigematsu, and Machida (2000); Hashido et al. (2003)). A capacitive sensor is a two-dimensional array of micro-capacitor plates embedded in a chip (see Figure 2.10).

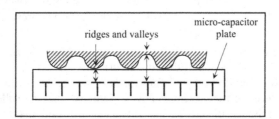

Figure 2.10. Capacitive sensing.

The other plate of each micro-capacitor is the finger skin itself. Small electrical charges are created between the surface of the finger and each of the silicon plates when a finger is placed on the chip. The magnitude of these electrical charges depends on the distance between the fingerprint surface and the capacitance plates (Tartagni and Guerrieri, 1998). Thus fingerprint ridges and valleys result in different capacitance patterns across the plates. An accurate capacitance measurement is quite difficult to make and adjust, and each vendor has its own method to get enough sensitivity to make a difference between the ridges and the valleys. The capacitive sensors, like the optical ones, cannot be easily deceived by presentation of a flat photograph or printed image of a fingerprint since they measure the distances and therefore only a three-dimensional surface can be sensed.

A critical component of capacitive sensors is the surface coating: the silicon chip needs to be protected from chemical substances (e.g., sodium) that are present in finger perspiration. But a coating that is too thick increases the distance between the pixels and the finger, lowering the ability to discriminate between a ridge and a valley, especially for poor quality fingers, where the depth of a valley is in the range of a micron. As a result, the coating must be as thin as possible (a few microns), but not too thin, as it will not be resistant to mechanical abrasions. Yau, Chen, and Morguet (2004) performed stability tests with a capacitive sensor and noted the formation of white blobs in the central part of the image after about 60,000 touches. Also, since the capacitive sensors sense the electrical field, electrostatic discharges (ESD) from the fingertip can cause large electrical fields that could severely damage the device itself. Therefore, proper protection and grounding is necessary to avoid ESD, chemical corrosion, and physical scratches to the sensor surface (Thomas and Bryant (2000); Setlak et al. (2000)).

An interesting property of capacitive sensors is the possibility of adjusting some electrical parameters to deal with non-ideal skin conditions (wet and dry fingers); a drawback is the need for frequently cleaning the surface to prevent the grease and dirt from compromising image quality.

- *Thermal*: these sensors are made of pyro-electric material that generates current based on temperature differentials (Edwards (1984); Mainguet, Pegulu, and Harris (1999); Han and Koshimoto (2008)). The fingerprint ridges, being in contact with the sensor surface, produce a different temperature differential than the valleys, which are at a distance from the sensor surface. The sensors are typically maintained at a high temperature by electrically heating them up, to increase the temperature difference between the sensor surface and the finger ridges. The temperature differential produces an image when contact occurs, but this image soon disappears because the thermal equilibrium is quickly reached and the pixel temperature is stabilized. Hence a sweeping method (as explained in Section 2.4) may be necessary to acquire a stable fingerprint image. On the other hand, thermal sensing has some advantages: it is not sensitive to ESD and it can accept a thick protective coating (10–20 μm) because the thermal information (heat flow) can easily propagate through the coating.

- *Electric field*: in this arrangement (also known as RF imaging), the sensor consists of a drive ring that generates an RF (radio frequency) sinusoidal signal and a matrix of active antennas that receives a very small amplitude signal transmitted by the drive ring and modulated by the derma structure (subsurface of the finger skin). The finger must be simultaneously in contact with both the sensor and the drive ring. To image a fingerprint, the analog response of each (row, column) element in the sensor matrix is amplified, integrated, and digitized (Setlak, 2004).

- *Piezoelectric*: pressure-sensitive sensors have been designed that produce an electrical signal when mechanical stress is applied to them. The sensor surface is made of a non-conducting dielectric material which, on encountering pressure from the finger, generates a small amount of electric current (this effect is called the piezoelectric effect). The strength of the generated current depends on the pressure applied by the finger on the sensor surface. Since ridges and valleys are present at different distances from the sensor surface, they result in different amounts of current. Unfortunately, these materials are typically not sensitive enough to detect the difference and, moreover, the protective coating blurs the resulting image. An alternative solution is to use micro-mechanical switches (a cantilever made of silicon). Coating is still a problem and, in addition, this device delivers a binary image, leading to minimal information about the fingerprint pattern.

2.3.3 Ultrasound sensors

Ultrasound sensing may be viewed as a kind of *echography*. It is based on sending acoustic signals toward the fingertip and capturing the echo signal (see Figure 2.11). The echo signal is used to compute the range (depth) image of the fingerprint and, subsequently, the ridge structure itself.

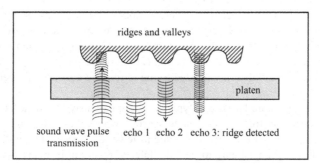

Figure 2.11. The basic principle of the ultrasound technique. A characteristic of sound waves is their ability to penetrate materials, giving a partial echo at each impedance change.

The ultrasound sensor has two main components: a transmitter, which generates short acoustic pulses, and a receiver, which detects the responses obtained when these pulses bounce off the fingerprint surface (Schneider and Wobschall (1991); Bicz et al. (1999); Schneider (2007)). This method images the subsurface of the finger skin (even through thin gloves); therefore, it is resilient to dirt and oil accumulations on the finger. While good quality images may be obtained by this technology, current ultrasound scanners are bulky with mechanical parts and quite expensive (several hundred dollars). Moreover, it takes a few seconds to acquire an image. Hence, this technology is not yet mature enough for large-scale deployment.

2.4 Touch Versus Sweep

Most of the live-scan fingerprint readers available today use the *touch* method: the finger is simply placed on the scanner, without moving it to generate a fingerprint image. The main advantage of this method is its simplicity: very little user training is required. However, in spite of technological innovations, touch sensors still occupy relatively large footprint for embedding in consumer products such as laptops, PDAs, USB drives and mobile phones. Further, the cost of solid state sensors is also a function of the sensor area.

With the aim of reducing the silicon sensor footprint and cost, another sensing method has been proposed which requires the user to *sweep* the finger over the sensor. The size of the swipe sensor ($h \times w$ elements) is much smaller than touch or area sensors, where h is the height of the sensor and w denotes the width of the sensor. As the finger is swept across this sensor, partial images of the finger are formed. Since the sweeping consists of a vertical movement only, the sensor width (w) should be as wide as a finger; on the other hand, in principle, the height of the sensor (h) could be as low as one pixel. In practice, however, since the finger swipe speed is unknown and it can vary during the sweeping, it is necessary to have a certain degree of overlap between the different fingerprint readings (slices) to effectively combine them to generate a full fingerprint image. Alternative solutions have been proposed where the sensor height is just one or a few pixels and: (i) the finger motion is estimated using additional displacement sensors (Vermesan et al. (2003); Clausen (2007)); (ii) a vertically distorted image is acquired and then normalized trying to remove distortion (Lorch, Morguet, and Schroder, 2004).

Touch or area sensors are larger and typically more expensive to manufacture than sweep sensors. This is especially true for solid-state sensors, where the cost mainly depends on the area of the chip die. A larger die costs more due to fewer dies per wafer and lower yield; furthermore, large dies are more likely to include defects, resulting in many discarded chips. A typical capacitive touch sensor has a size of 15 by 15 mm, which is large for a chip. In practice, with the help of sweeping technique, the size of the silicon sensor can be reduced by a factor of 10 with commensurate cost reduction (Xia and O'Gorman, 2003). To explore further cost savings, Mainguet, Gong, and Wang (2004) studied the reduction in the width of a sweeping sensor and its impact on accuracy and found a very high correlation between the two.

At the end of the sweep, a single fingerprint image needs to be reconstructed from the slices. This could be done "on-the-fly" by combining the slices as they are delivered by the sensor (see Figure 2.12). Morguet et al. (2004) proposed matching two fingerprints directly at slice level without any image reconstruction: a pair of slices are matched through normalized correlation and the optimal matching between two complete slice sequences is found by Viterbi search (Viterbi, 1967).

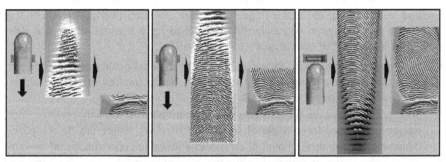

Figure 2.12. As the user sweeps her finger on the sensor, the sensor delivers new image slices, which are combined to form a two-dimensional image.

The sweeping method was initially introduced in conjunction with thermal sensors, because sweeping was necessary to have a working "thermal" device. In fact, as discussed in Section 2.4, the thermal image vanishes very quickly because of the thermal equilibrium between the finger and the sensor. However, the equilibrium is continuously broken during sweeping, as ridges and valleys touch the pixels alternately, introducing a continuous temperature change. Nowadays, both the touch and sweep methods are being used with different sensor technologies. Optical scanners that use the sweeping method are also available (Antonelli et al., 2001).

The most important advantages of the sweep sensors are that they are smaller and typically cheaper. Another advantage is that unlike the touch devices, the sweep sensors are "self cleaning": the finger itself cleans the sensor during usage and no latent fingerprint is left on the sensor. However, there are some drawbacks as well.

- In general, sweeping is less intuitive and natural than using a touch-based device. So, a novice user may encounter some difficulties in performing the sweeping properly (i.e., without sharp speed changes, or discontinuities). This is supported by a noticeable failure to acquire rate of 37.9% (Cappelli et al., 2006) for the sweeping sensor during FVC2004 database collection.
- The reconstruction of full fingerprint image from the slices is time consuming and is prone to errors, especially in the case of poor quality fingerprints and non-uniform sweep speed.

2.4.1 Image reconstruction from slices

The sweep method allows the cost of a sensor to be significantly reduced, but requires a reliable method to reconstruct the entire fingerprint image based on overlapping slices. Figure 2.13 shows the block diagram of an algorithm designed for a thermal sensor that delivers slices of 280×30 pixels. The main stages are as follows.

- *Slice quality computation*: for each slice, a single global quality measure and several local measures are computed by using an image contrast estimator; all successive stages are driven by these measures.
- *Slice pair registration*: for each pair of consecutive slices, the only possible transformation is assumed to be a global translation $[\Delta x, \Delta y]$, where the Δy component is dominant, but a limited amount of Δx is also allowed to cope with lateral movements of the finger during sweeping. Finding the translation vector, or in other words, registering the two slices involves a search over the space of all possible translation vectors.
- *Relaxation*: when the quality of slices is low, the registration may fail and give incorrect translation vectors. Assuming a certain continuity of the finger speed during sweeping allows analogous hypotheses to be generated on the continuity of the translation vectors. The translation vectors' continuity may be obtained through a method called relaxation (Rosenfeld and Kak, 1976) which has the nice property of smoothing the samples without affecting the correct measurements too much.
- *Mosaicking*: the enhanced translation vectors produced by the relaxation stage are used to register and superimpose the slices. Finally, each pixel of the reconstructed output image is generated by performing a weighted sum of the intensities of the corresponding pixels in the slices.

Other approaches to image reconstruction from slices can be found in Lee et al. (1999) and Zhang, Yang, and Wu (2005, 2006a, b). The technique of Zhang, Yang, and Wu (2006a, b) combines consecutive slices by taking elastic distortion into account in addition to translation vectors.

2.5 Fingerprint Images and Their Parameters

A fingerprint image is a digital representation of fingerprint pattern acquired through a scanner. The image sampling and quantization processes cause an alteration of the original pattern: the smaller the alteration, the higher the quality of the fingerprint image in terms of fidelity with respect to the original pattern. It is not easy to precisely define the quality of a fingerprint image, and it is even more difficult to decouple the fingerprint image quality from the intrinsic finger quality or condition of the finger.

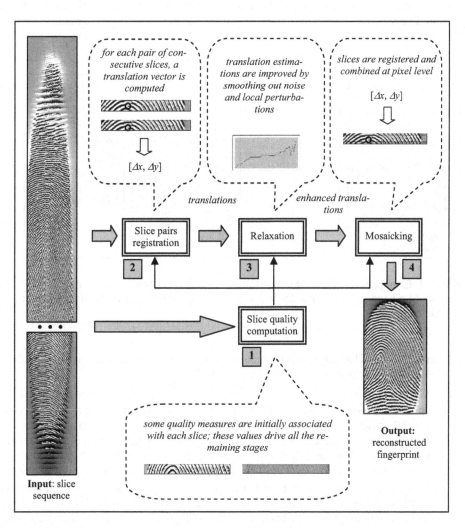

Figure 2.13. An algorithm for fingerprint reconstruction from slices. All the steps are performed sequentially on the set of slices. The output of the slice pair registration is a set of translation estimates that are globally enhanced by the relaxation step. These improved estimates drive the mosaicking phase in order to reconstruct the whole fingerprint image.

In fact, when the ridge prominence is poor (especially for users engaged in heavy manual work and elderly people), the fingers are too moist or too dry, or fingers are improperly placed, most of the scanners produce poor quality images (Figure 2.14). This section focuses on the contribution of the acquisition device to the quality of the image; in Section 3.10, the fingerprint image quality is discussed more in general and independently of scanner- and user-related factors.

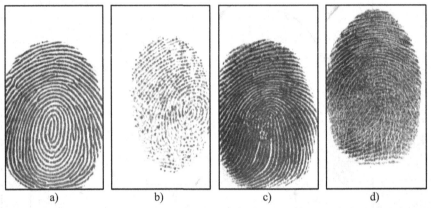

a)   b)   c)   d)

Figure 2.14. Examples of fingerprint images acquired with an optical scanner: a) a good quality fingerprint; b) a fingerprint left by a dry finger; c) a fingerprint left by a wet finger; d) an intrinsically bad fingerprint.

The main parameters characterizing the acquisition of a digital fingerprint image, as defined by the FBI (see Appendix F of CJIS (1999)), are as follows.

- *Resolution*: denotes the number of dots or pixels per inch (*dpi*). A resolution of 500 dpi is the minimum resolution for FBI-compliant scanners and is met by many commercial devices. Figure 2.15 shows the same fingerprint portion sub-sampled at different resolutions; decreasing the resolution results in a greater difficulty in resolving ridges from valleys and isolating minutiae points. A resolution of 250–300 dpi is probably the minimum resolution that allows the fingerprint extraction algorithms to locate the minutiae in fingerprint patterns. Images acquired at 200–300 dpi are often matched through correlation techniques (see Section 4.2) which seem to tolerate lower resolutions better (Wilson, Watson, and Paek, 2000). Finally, 1,000 dpi scanners have started replacing 500-dpi models in forensic applications where analysis of tiny details such as sweat pores, dots, incipient ridges, etc. (see Section 4.6.3) is very important to match small portions of noisy fingerprint images. Figure 2.16 shows the same fingerprint portion acquired at 1,000 dpi and sub-sampled at 500 dpi. Most of the existing specifications for fingerprint scanners distinguish between *native resolution* and *output resolution*: the former is the actual resolution of the sampling process; the latter is the resolution of the output image that can be adjusted by interpolation or re-sampling.

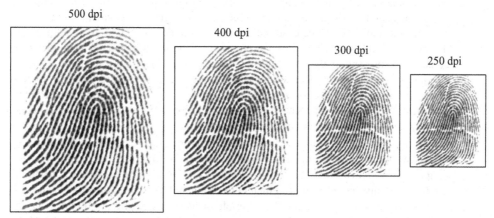

Figure 2.15. The fingerprint on the left, acquired at 500 dpi, is progressively sub-sampled at lower resolutions: 400, 300, and 250 dpi, respectively.

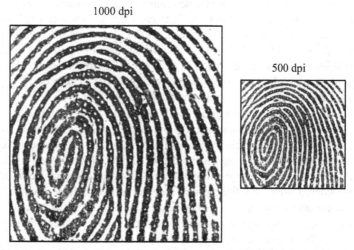

Figure 2.16. The fingerprint portion on the left is acquired at 1000 dpi; sweat pores and other fine details are clearly visible; on the right, the fingerprint portion is sub-sampled at 500 dpi while the fine details are not as clear.

- *Area*: this is the size of the rectangular area sensed by a fingerprint scanner. The acquisition area substantially changes for the two categories of fingerprint scanners introduced in Section 2.1. For multi-finger scanners the area is usually as large as 2×3 inch^2 to allow four fingers to be placed simultaneously; in case of single-finger scanners, an area greater than or equal to 1×1 inch^2 permits a full plain fingerprint impression to be acquired. However, in many commercial single-finger scanners, the area is sacrificed to reduce both the cost and the size of the device. Small-area scanners do not allow the full fingerprint to be captured, and the users encounter difficulties in consistently presenting the same portion of the finger. This may result in a small overlap between different acquisitions of the same finger, leading to false non-match errors. As discussed in Section 2.7, the acquisition area is the most important scanner parameter to maximize the recognition accuracy. Section 2.9 discusses some techniques proposed to deal with small area sensors.
- *Number of pixels*: the number of pixels in a fingerprint image can be simply derived by the resolution and the fingerprint area: a scanner working at R dpi over an area of *height* (h) $\times$ *width* (w) inch^2 has $R \cdot h \times R \cdot w$ pixels. If the area is expressed in mm^2, the formula must include the mm–inch conversion and, therefore, the number of pixels = $R \cdot (h/25.4) \times R \cdot (w/25.4)$. For example, a scanner working at 500 dpi over an area of 20.32×15.24 mm^2 produces images of $500 \cdot (20.32/25.4) \times 500 \cdot (15.24/25.4)$ = 400×300 pixels. The equation is invertible and each value {resolution, area, number of pixels} may be uniquely determined given the other two.
- *Geometric accuracy*: this is usually determined by the maximum geometric distortion introduced by the acquisition device. The geometric distortion can be measured as the absolute value of the difference between the actual distance between two points on a calibrated target and the distance between those same two points as measured on the scanned image of that target. Some of the optical fingerprint scanners introduce geometric distortion which, if not compensated, alters the fingerprint pattern depending on the relative position of the finger on the sensor surface.
- *Gray-level quantization and gray range*: the gray-level quantization denotes the maximum number of gray-levels in the output image and is related to the number of bits used to encode the intensity value of each pixel (e.g., 8 bits per pixel yields 256 levels of gray). The gray-range is the actual number of gray-levels used in an image disregarding the maximum given by the gray-level quantization. Color information is not considered useful for fingerprint recognition, but some researchers have shown that color analysis can be exploited to detect fake fingers (see Section 9.5.1).
- *Gray level uniformity and input/output linearity*: the gray level uniformity is defined as the gray-level homogeneity measured in the image obtained by scanning a uniform dark (or light) gray patch; the Input/Output linearity quantifies the deviation of the

gray levels from a linear mapping when the input pattern is transformed into an output image.

- *Spatial frequency response*: the spatial frequency response denotes the ability of an acquisition device to transfer the details of the original pattern to the output image for different frequencies. It is well-know that the fine details corresponding to the high frequencies tend to be smoothed out when a signal is digitally sampled. Spatial frequency response is usually measured through Modulation Transfer Function (MTF) or Contrast Transfer Function (CTF) as explained in Nill (2005); a specific measure for fingerprint scanners, called Top Sharpening Index (TSI), was introduced by Ferrara, Franco, and Maltoni (2007).

- *Signal-to-noise ratio (SNR)*: the signal to noise ratio quantifies the magnitude of the noise with respect to the magnitude of the signal. The signal magnitude is related to the gray-range in the output image while the noise can be defined as the standard deviation of the gray-levels in uniform gray patches.

Section 2.6 reviews the specifications that FBI has set for two categories of fingerprint scanners; Section 2.7, according to the definition of operational quality, reconsiders the fingerprint image parameters and makes explicit the impact of each of them on the accuracy of automatic fingerprint recognition algorithms.

2.6 Image Quality Specifications for Fingerprint Scanners

In most of the medium- to large-scale biometric applications, the following two requirements are mandatory: (i) the quality of the image must be sufficiently high to guarantee high fingerprint recognition accuracy and (ii) the system must be able to use scanners by different vendors and the fingerprint recognition accuracy should not degrade if the device used for enrolment is different from the one used for recognition. Both these requirements can be fulfilled by enforcing nominal values and tolerances for the parameters defined in Section 2.5.

The FBI established an IAFIS[1] Image Quality Specification (IQS) in order to define the quantitative image quality requirements for IAFIS fingerprint scanners. The IAFIS IQS was defined in Appendix F of the Electronic Fingerprint Transmission Specification (EFTS) (CJIS, 1999), and is also included in the Electronic Biometric Transmission Specification (EBTS) [Department of Defense (US), 2007]; test procedures to verify compliance of fingerprint scanners to the IQS were delineated in Forkert et al. (1994) and have been recently revised and updated in Nill (2005). IAFIS IQS compliant devices typically allow the acquisition of more than one finger at the same time; the minimum sensing area for a plain four-finger scanner is 2.88" × 1.8"

---

[1] IAFIS is the acronym used to denote the FBI's Integrated AFIS.

(see Table 1.1 in Nill (2005)). FBI, supported by MITRE experts, certifies devices compliant with the IAFIS IQS: the list of certified devices is maintained in FBI (2008).

The ISO/IEC 19794-4 (2005) describes the manner in which a fingerprint image must be acquired and stored to maximize interoperability: this document refers to IAFIS IQS as far as the characteristics of fingerprint scanners are concerned. To support the Personal Identity Verification (PIV) program (NIST, 2007), whose goal is to improve the identification and authentication for access to U.S. Federal facilities and information systems, FBI established a PIV IQS (CJIS, 2006), which defines the quantitative image quality requirements for single-finger capture devices suitable for application in the PIV program; these requirements are similar to (but less stringent than) the IAFIS requirements and the corresponding test procedures can be found in Nill (2006).

Table 2.1 summarizes the main IAFIS and PIV IQS requirements. It is worth noting that both IAFIS and PIV specifications have been defined to maximize the fidelity with respect to the original pattern but, as explained in Section 2.7, they do not necessarily constitute the best accuracy/cost trade-off when the aim is to maximize the automatic fingerprint recognition accuracy.

2.7 Operational Quality of Fingerprint Scanners

In Sections 2.5 and 2.6, the scanner quality is defined as "fidelity" in reproducing the original fingerprint pattern. This definition of quality is clearly appropriate to AFIS and other applications where the images may be visually examined by forensic experts. In fact, human experts heavily rely on very fine fingerprint details such as pores, local ridge shape, etc., for which high fidelity of the original pattern is fundamental. On the other hand, the requirement is different in automated fingerprint recognition systems, where: (i) the images are stored but used only for automated comparisons, or (ii) only fingerprint templates consisting of features derived from the image are stored. As discussed in Cappelli, Ferrara, and Maltoni (2008), in these cases it may be more appropriate to define the fingerprint scanner quality as *operational quality*, that is, the ability to acquire images that maximize the accuracy of automated recognition algorithms.

In Cappelli, Ferrara, and Maltoni (2008), the impact on the recognition accuracy of the parameters introduced in Section 2.5 has been separately assessed through systematic experimentations. In particular:

- The main quality parameters and the corresponding requirements defined by FBI have been taken into account.
- For each parameter, an approach has been defined to progressively degrade the quality of fingerprint images, thus simulating scanners compliant with gradually-relaxed requirements. Figure 2.17 shows some examples of degradation simulation for different parameters.

Parameter	Requirement	
	IAFIS IQS (4-finger scanners at 500 dpi)	**PIV IQS** (single-finger scanners)
Area *height (h) × width (w)*	$h \geq 45.7$ mm (1.8") and $w \geq 73.2$ mm (2.88")	$h \geq 16.5$ mm (0.650") and $w \geq 12.8$ mm (0.504")
Native resolution R_N	$R_N \geq 500$ dpi	$R_N \geq 500$ dpi
Output resolution R_O	$R_O = 500$ dpi $\pm 1\%$	$R_O = 500$ dpi $\pm 2\%$
Gray-level quantization	256 gray-levels (8 bit per pixel)	256 gray-levels (8 bit per pixel)
Gray range DR	for at least 80% of the image: $DR \geq 200$ for at least 99% of the image: $DR \geq 128$	for at least 80% of the image: $DR \geq 150$
Geometric accuracy D_{AC} (ACross-bar) D_{AL} (ALong-bar)	for at least 99% of the test: $D_{AC} \leq 1\%$ $D_{AL} \leq 0.016"$	for at least 99% of the test: $D_{AC} \leq 1.8\%$ $D_{AL} \leq 0.027"$
Gray level uniformity[2]	for at least 99% of the cases: $D_{RC}^{dark} \leq 1$; $D_{RC}^{light} \leq 2$ for least for 99.9% of the pixels: $D_{PP}^{dark} \leq 8$; $D_{PP}^{light} \leq 22$ for every two small areas: $D_{SA}^{dark} \leq 3$; $D_{SA}^{light} \leq 12$	for at least 99% of the cases: $D_{RC}^{dark} \leq 1.5$; $D_{RC}^{light} \leq 3$ for at least 99% of the pixels: $D_{PP}^{dark} \leq 8$; $D_{PP}^{light} \leq 22$ for every two small areas: $D_{SA}^{dark} \leq 3$; $D_{SA}^{light} \leq 12$
I/O linearity[3] D_{Lin}	$D_{Lin} \leq 7.65$	No requirements
Spatial frequency response	$\text{MTF}_{\min}(f) \leq \text{MTF}(f) \leq 1.05$ see Nill (2005) for IAFIS $\text{MTF}_{\min}(f)$	$\text{MTF}_{\min}(f) \leq \text{MTF}(f) \leq 1.12$ see Nill (2006) for PIV $\text{MTF}_{\min}(f)$
Signal-to-noise ratio[4] SNR	$SNR \geq 125$	$SNR \geq 70.6$

Table 2.1. A review of IAFIS and PIV IQS. For the parameter definitions, see Section 2.5.

---

[2] defined as the gray-level differences in a uniform dark (or light) gray patch. Gray level uniformity is evaluated by dividing the acquisition area in 0.25"×0.25" regions and measuring the differences between: i) the average gray-levels of adjacent rows/columns D_{RC} ; ii) the average gray-level of any region and the gray-level of each of its pixels D_{PP} ; iii) the average gray-levels of any two regions D_{SA}.

[3] D_{Lin} is measured as the maximum deviation of the output gray levels from a linear least squares regression line fitted between input signal and output gray levels scanning an appropriate target.

[4] actually in PIV IQS this requirement is given by setting the maximum noise standard deviation to 3.5. To make it comparable with the corresponding IAFIS IQS, here this value is transformed to SNR under the hypothesis of a 247 gray-level range (Nill, 2005): SNR = 247/3.5 = 70.6.

- Among the four FVC2006 databases (BioLab, 2007), the database acquired with the wider area optical sensor (DB2) has been selected for assessment.
- Ten best performing algorithms on DB2 from the FVC2006 competition were selected: these algorithms well represent the current state-of-the-art in automated fingerprint recognition technology.
- The correlation between each quality parameter Q and the recognition accuracy was measured by progressively degrading the database images according to Q and analyzing the performance of the 10 algorithms.
- Results are reported in terms of the percentage performance drop: let EER_O be the original equal error rate (without any degradation) and EER_D be the equal error rate measured after applying a degradation D, then the performance drop is computed as $(EER_D - EER_O) / EER_O$.

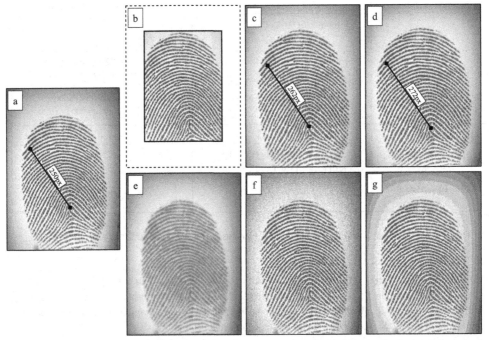

Figure 2.17. Some examples of image degradations: a) original image; b) reduction of area; c) change of resolution; d) barrel distortion; e) reduction of spatial frequency response; f) reduction of SNR; g) reduction of gray-range.

The results of the experiments lead to the following conclusions for single-finger scanners:

- The most critical parameter is the acquisition area: reducing the area to the PIV IQS minimum requirement causes an average performance drop of 73% (see Figure 2.18).
- Output resolution and geometric accuracy are also quite important: setting them to the PIV IQS minimum requirements leads to 20% and 1% performance drop, respectively.
- Other parameters such as signal to noise ratio, and gray-range do not seem to affect the automated recognition considerably: appreciable performance drop can be observed only for very strong degradations (well above PIV IQS requirements).

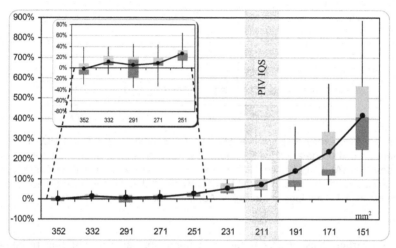

Figure 2.18. Box-plot of the acquisition area experiment: each box graphically shows the descriptive statistics of the test carried out over the ten algorithms. The first five boxes are expanded in the inset graph to better show their statistics. The horizontal axis reports the minimum acquisition area requirements (in square millimeters) and the vertical axis shows the percentage performance drop. The minimum requirement based on the PIV IQS specification is highlighted (211 mm^2).

The simultaneous effect of all the parameters on recognition accuracy has only been briefly addressed in Cappelli, Ferrara, and Maltoni (2008), but it has been investigated in more detail in Alessandroni et al. (2008) with respect to single-finger scanners IQS adopted in certain recent large-scale applications (see Figure 2.19). Their results show that:

- The simultaneous variation causes an average accuracy drop markedly higher than simply summing the individual accuracy drops. The total accuracy drop for PIV IQS is 156%.

- Enforcing "strong" constraints for acquisition area, output resolution and geometric accuracy and "weak" constraints for the rest of parameters are sufficient to assure good accuracy (accuracy drop of only 18%).

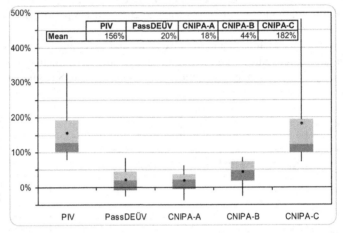

Figure 2.19. Total accuracy drop for five different IQS specifications. PassDEÜV IQS was defined by German BSI (Federal Office for Information Security) for the German passport project and coincides with IAFIS IQS except for the area that can be smaller (20x16 mm^2). CNIPA-A/B/C specifications are being suggested by CNIPA (the Italian National Center for Information and Communication Technology in the Public Administration).

As mentioned earlier, sensing area is the most important parameter of fingerprint sensors. Many different experimental results on sensing area versus accuracy tradeoff have been reported in the tests carried out by Jain, Prabhakar, and Ross (1999), Maio et al. (2002b), Schneider et al. (2003), Ross and Jain (2004), Marcialis and Roli (2004a) and BioLab (2007). In all of these studies, the authors compared the accuracy of one or more fingerprint recognition algorithms on two fingerprint databases acquired under the same conditions except the scanner. The first database is acquired using a large area (usually optical) scanner and the second database is acquired using a small area (usually solid state) scanner. Table 2.2 summarizes the results of these studies and points out the significant accuracy drop observed in each one of them. Although the reported drop in accuracy is largely due to the area reduction, the sensing area is not the only parameter that varies between the two scanners used in the experiments. Hence this accuracy drop is a consequence of a mix of parameter changes. It is worth noting that the accuracy drop reported here is generally higher than that plotted in Figure 2.18, where the impact of the sensing area has been isolated from the other parameters.

Experiment	First scanner	Second scanner	Performance drop
Jain, Prabhakar and Ross (1999)	0.96"×1.0" (500 dpi) Optical, FTIR	0.6"×0.6" (500 dpi) Solid state, Capacitive	220%
Maio et al. (2002b) – FVC2002	0.75"×0.78" (500 dpi) Optical, FTIR	0.6"×0.6" (500 dpi) Solid state, Capacitive	222%
Schneider et al. (2003)	1.2"×0.8" (500 dpi) Ultrasound	0.38"×0.38" (500 dpi) Ultrasound	1200%
Ross and Jain (2004)	0.96"×1.0" (500 dpi) Optical, FTIR	0.6"×0.6" (500 dpi) Solid state, Capacitive	277%
Marcialis and Roli (2004a)	0.98"×0.52" (569 dpi) Optical, FTIR	0.5"×0.5" (500 dpi) Solid state, Capacitive	544%
BioLab (2007) – FVC2006	0.98"×0.7" (569 dpi) Optical, FTIR	0.02"×0.55" (500 dpi) Sweeping, Thermal	3136%
BioLab (2007) – FVC2006	0.98"×0.7" (569 dpi) Optical, FTIR	0.38"×0.38" (250 dpi) Soldid state, Electric field	11832%

Table 2.2. Performance drop in terms of fingerprint verification accuracy obtained on two data-sets collected with two different scanners, where the second scanner area is substantially lower than the first scanner area. In Maio et al. (2002b) and BioLab (2007), the accuracy drop is the average drop over the three best performing matching algorithms.

2.8 Examples of Fingerprint Scanners

Several fingerprint scanners based on the various sensing technologies surveyed in Section 2.3 are commercially available. Certainly, the main characteristics of a fingerprint scanner depend on the specific sensor used in it, which in turn determines the image parameters introduced in Section 2.5 as well as other characteristics such as size, cost, and durability. However, many other features should also be taken into account when choosing a fingerprint scanner for a specific application.

- *I/O Interface*: almost all fingerprint scanners have digital output and they directly interface to an external computer through USB or FireWire interfaces.
- *Frames per second*: indicates the number of images a touch scanner is able to acquire and send to the host in 1 s. A high frame rate (e.g., larger than 5 frames/s) better tolerates movements of the finger on a touch scanner and allows a more friendly interaction with the scanner. It can also provide a natural visual feedback during the acquisition.

- *Automatic finger detection*: some scanners automatically detect the presence of a finger on the acquisition surface, without requiring the host to continually grab and process frames; this allows the acquisition process to be automatically initiated as soon as the user's finger touches the sensor.
- *Encryption*: securing the communication channel between the scanner and the host is an effective way of securing a system against attacks (see Chapter 9). For this purpose, some commercial scanners implement state-of-the-art symmetric and public-key encryption capability.
- *Supported operating systems*: depending on the application and the infrastructure where the fingerprint scanners have to be employed, compatibility with several operating systems, and in particular the support of open-source operating systems such as Linux, could be an important feature.

Tables 2.3 and 2.4 list some multi-finger and single-finger scanners, respectively; the cost of multi-finger scanners is approximately US$5,000; the cost of single-finger large area scanners varies, usually in the range US$50–US$500, according to the size of acquisition area and the quality of the image produced. Cheaper models are generally used for personal or corporate applications such as logon to a PC or a network; high quality and large area (usually at least 1" × 1") models are used in large-scale applications such as border-crossing, e-passports, etc.

Figure 2.20 shows an image acquired with a multi-finger scanner and the result of automatic slap segmentation. Figure 2.21 shows fingerprint images of the same finger acquired with some of the single-finger scanners listed in Table 2.4.

Fingerprint scanners often fail in producing good quality images when the finger skin conditions is overly dry or overly wet. Certain sensing technologies (or certain special coatings applied to the sensor surface) seem to better tolerate certain types of skin conditions. A few studies on the scanner robustness with respect to suboptimal skin conditions can be found in Kang et al. (2003) and Yau, Chen, and Morguet (2004). Figure 2.22 shows images acquired from the same finger under three different skin conditions.

Finally, inherently poor quality fingers, whose ridges are spoiled and damaged by scars and creases, typically produce low quality fingerprint images somewhat independently of the acquisition technology (see Figure 2.23).

	Technology	Company	Model	Dpi	Area (h×w)	IAFIS IQS compliant
Optical	FTIR	Crossmatch www.crossmatch.net	L SCAN 1000	1000	3.0"×3.2"	√
	FTIR	L-1 Identity www.l1id.com	TouchPrint 4100	500	3.0"×3.2"	√
	FTIR	Papillon www.papillon.ru	DS-30	500	3.07"×3.38"	√

Table 2.3. Some examples of multi-finger commercial scanners based on optical FTIR technology. Companies are listed in alphabetical order.

	Technology	Company	Model	Dpi	Area (h×w)	PIV IQS compliant
Optical	FTIR	Biometrika www.biometrika.it	HiScan	500	1"×1"	√
	FTIR	Crossmatch www.crossmatch.net	Verifier 300 LC 2.0	500	1.2"×1.2"	
	FTIR	Digital Persona www.digitalpersona.com	UareU4000	512	0.71"×0.57"	
	FTIR	L-1 Identity www.identix.com	DFR 2100	500	1.05"×1.05"	√
	FTIR	Sagem www.morpho.com	MSO350	500	0.86"×0.86"	√
	FTIR	Secugen www.secugen.com	Hamster IV	500	0.66"×0.51"	√
Solid-state	Capacitive	Upek www.upek.com	TouchChip TCS1	508	0.71"×0.50"	√
	Thermal (sweep)	Atmel www.atmel.com	FingerChip AT77C101B	500	0.02"×0.55"	
	Electric field	Authentec www.authentec.com	AES4000	250	0.38"×0.38"	
	Piezoelectric	BMF www.bm-f.com	BLP-100	406	0.92"×0.63"	

Table 2.4. Commercial scanners grouped by technology. Technologies are presented in the order listed in Section 2.3, and within each technology, companies are listed in alphabetical order. For sweep sensors, the vertical number of pixels varies depending on the length of the sweep, and therefore, cannot be determined a priori.

Figure 2.20. An example of 500 dpi image (1558x1691 pixels) acquired with the multi-finger scanner Papillon DS-30; the four rectangles show the position of the four fingerprints as located by an automatic slap segmentation algorithm.

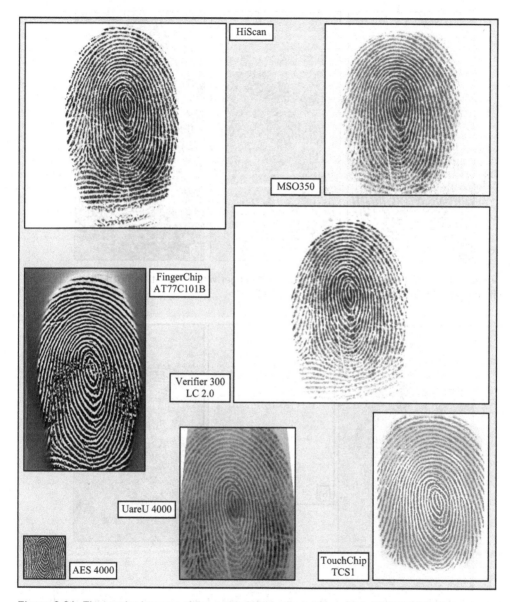

Figure 2.21. Fingerprint images of the same finger acquired by some of the single-finger scanners listed in Table 2.4. Images are shown with true proportions.

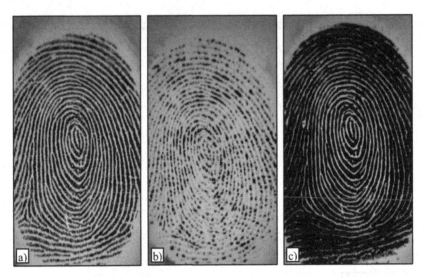

Figure 2.22. Three fingerprint images of the same finger with different skin conditions acquired with an optical FTIR scanner: a) normal, b) dry, c) wet.

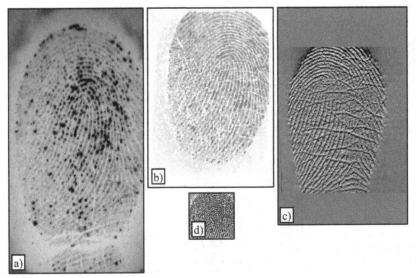

Figure 2.23. Fingerprint images of the same poor quality finger acquired with scanners based on four different sensing technologies: a) Optical FTIR, b) Solid state Capacitive, c) Solid state Thermal, and d) Solid state Electric field.

2.9 Dealing with Small Area Sensors

A low cost good quality scanner will have a wide adoption in fingerprint recognition systems. Sensor manufacturers tend to reduce the sensing area in order to lower the cost of their scanners. For example, sweep scanners are being widely deployed in many commercial applications (e.g., laptops, mobile phones) where a small footprint is essential. However, as shown in Section 2.7, recognizing fingerprints acquired through sensors that capture only a partial fingerprint is difficult due to the possibility of having only a small overlap between different acquisitions of the same finger. For a minutiae-based matching algorithm (see Section 4.3), a small overlap between two fingerprints leads to a small number of minutiae correspondences and thereby a small match score (Yau et al. (2000); Pankanti, Prabhakar, and Jain (2002); Jain and Ross (2002b)). This effect is even more marked on intrinsically poor quality fingers, where only a subset of the minutiae can be reliably extracted and used. A small overlap also affects the reliability of both correlation-based and non-minutiae feature-based matching techniques, since the amount of information available for the matching is reduced.

To deal with small sensing areas, some vendors equip their scanners with mechanical guides with the aim of constraining the finger position so that roughly the same fingerprint portion is captured in different acquisition sessions. In any event, due to the different finger sizes of different users and the difficulty of integrating the guides in certain applications, this solution is not satisfactory.

An interesting alternative is to design an algorithm capable of explicitly dealing with a small sensor area. A feasible approach is sketched in Figure 2.24, where multiple acquisitions of a finger are obtained during the user enrollment, and a "mosaic" is automatically built and stored as a reference fingerprint. This technique is known as fingerprint *mosaicking* which increases the area of the fingerprint in the stored template. At recognition time, the user touches the sensor once, and the small fingerprint area captured is matched against the large reference fingerprint. Although the area of overlap is increased through mosaicking, the fingerprint image acquired at the recognition time is still small that usually leads to lower recognition accuracy as compared to the large area sensors.

Different approaches could be adopted to combine multiple (partially overlapping) fingerprint images into a large fingerprint image (Brown, 1992). A simple idea is to exploit the same algorithm used for matching: in fact, a byproduct of matching two fingerprints is an estimate of the transformation (e.g., displacement and rotation) between the two fingerprints; given this information, fusing more images into a single large image can be accomplished by superimposing the aligned images and by appropriately weighting the intensity of the corresponding pixels. The main difficulty in creating a mosaicked image is that, often, the alignment between the various impressions/pieces cannot be completely recovered.

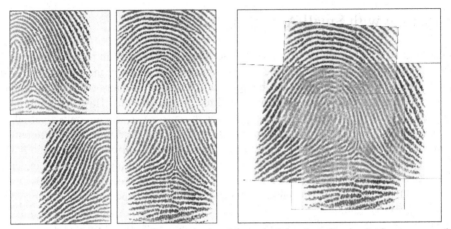

Figure 2.24. A fingerprint mosaic image obtained by combining four fingerprint images acquired with a 0.51 × 0.51 square inch 500 dpi optical sensor.

The mosaicking algorithm of Jain and Ross (2002b) combines two impressions of a finger by first aligning the fingerprint images by using the Iterative Closest Point (ICP) algorithm (Besl and McKay, 1992). A low-pass filter is initially applied to the images and the pixel intensities are sub-sampled to a narrow gray-scale range of [10, 20] to ensure a fairly smooth change in the surface corresponding to the range image of the fingerprints (see Figure 3.8 for an example of surface representation of a fingerprint image). The images are then segmented into foreground and background; an alignment between the two foreground images is estimated using the ICP algorithm, and a composite image is created by taking an average of the corresponding pixel intensities (see Figure 2.25). Jain and Ross (2002b) compared the mosaicking of fingerprints at the gray-scale image representation level with a mosaicking at the minutiae representation level and found the former to outperform the latter. Their results on 320 query images showed an improvement of ~4% in the fingerprint verification accuracy when two impressions of each finger were combined to form a composite template at the gray-scale intensity level.

To compensates for the amount of plastic distortion between two partial images, Lee et al. (2003) and Choi et al. (2007a) use non-rigid alignment transformations such as Chamfer matching (Borgefors, 1988) and Thin-Plate Spline (TPS) model (Ross, Dass, and Jain, 2006). The transform is initially estimated with matched minutiae and then refined by matching ridges. In Choi et al. (2007a) unpaired ridges in the overlapping area between two images are iteratively matched by minimizing the registration error, which consists of the ridge matching error and the inverse consistency error. During the estimation, erroneous correspondences are eliminated by considering the geometric relationship between the correspondences and by checking whether or not the registration error is minimized.

Figure 2.25. Combination of two impressions of a finger (on the left) into one composite finger-print image (on the right) using the Jain and Ross (2002b) method. © IEEE.

Other image mosaicking techniques were proposed by Ratha, Connell, and Bolle (1998) and Zhou et al. (2001) with the aim of obtaining a rolled fingerprint impression from a sequence of flat fingerprint images acquired through a live-scan scanner. In particular, the Ratha, Connell, and Bolle (1998) mosaicking algorithm consists of the following steps: (i) segment finger-print foreground and background areas in each fingerprint image, (ii) use the foreground mask to weight each image's contribution, (iii) stack the weighted gray-scale frames to compute the mosaicked gray-scale image, and (iv) stack the foreground masks to compute a confidence index at each pixel. Because all the fingerprint images to be combined are acquired in a single rolling of a fingerprint, the authors assume that the images are already aligned. Furthermore, the foreground masks are shrunk so that only the central portion of each image with the best contrast and least distortion is used.

For very small area touch sensors, Choi, Choi, and Kim (2005) propose sliding a finger over the sensor surface and mosaicking the pieces into a unique image. The approach is simi-lar to a rolled-from-flat reconstruction (Ratha, Connell, and Bolle, 1998) but due to the finger sliding, the assumption that the images are already aligned does not hold and a more sophisti-cate mosaicking technique is necessary.

For minutiae-based matching algorithms, instead of rebuilding the whole fingerprint im-age, it may be more convenient to build the mosaic at feature level that is, rearranging the mi-nutiae from each fingerprint impression into a single map. Practical implementations of this approach, known in the literature as *template consolidation* or *template improvement* (see Sec-tions 7.6 and 7.7 for more details), are discussed in Yau et al. (2000), Toh et al. (2001), Jain and Ross (2002b), Jiang and Ser (2002), Ramoser, Wachmann, and Bischof (2002), Yeung, Moon, and Chan (2004), Ryu, Han, and Kim (2005), Ryu, Kim, and Jain (2006) and Sha, Zhao, and Tang (2007). In the experiment carried out by Ross, Shah, and Shah (2006), feature level mosaicking outperforms image-based mosaicking. Finally, in Yang and Zhou (2006), different schemes to combine multiple enrolled impressions are comparatively studied. Their experimental results show that a larger improvement can be obtained by using decision fusion scheme rather than feature fusion. However, the experiments have been carried out on databases collected with medium- to large area sensors and it is not clear if they are valid for small area sensors as well.

2.10 Storing and Compressing Fingerprint Images

In many law enforcement and government applications of AFIS, the size of the fingerprint database is large. For example, Hopper, Brislawn, and Bradley (1993) estimated the size of the FBI fingerprint card archive (each card is a paper form containing all ten ink fingerprints from two hands of an individual along with his demographic information) to be over 200 million, occupying an acre of filing cabinets in the J. Edgar Hoover building in Washington, DC. Furthermore, the archive size was increasing at the rate of 30,000–50,000 new cards per day. The digitization of fingerprint cards was an obvious choice, although the size of the resulting digital archive was also problematic. Each fingerprint impression, when digitized at 500 dpi, produces an image with 768×768 pixels at 256 gray-levels. An uncompressed representation of such an image requires 589,824 bytes and about 10 megabytes are necessary to encode a single card (both a dab and rolled impression of each finger are present on the card). A simple multiplication by 200 million yields the massive storage capacity of 2,000 terabytes for the entire archive. Another problem was the long delay involved in transmitting a fingerprint image over a band-limited communication channel: about 3 h were needed for transmitting a single image over a 9,600 baud channel. The need for an effective compression technique was very urgent. Unfortunately, neither the well-known lossless methods nor the JPEG compression method was satisfactory. The former typically provides a compression ratio of 2 when applied to gray-scale fingerprint images and the latter, at the FBI target compression ratio (0.75 bit per pixel, i.e., about 1:10.7), produces block artifacts due to the independent compression through DCT (Discrete Cosine Transform) of single 8×8 image blocks (see Figure 2.26.c).

A new compression technique (with small acceptable loss), called Wavelet Scalar Quantization (WSQ), was then developed on the basis of the work by Hopper and Preston (1991), Bradley, Brislawn, and Hopper (1992), Hopper, Brislawn, and Bradley (1993) and Brislawn et al. (1996). Due to its superiority with respect to other general-purpose compression techniques, WSQ became the FBI standard for the compression of 500 dpi fingerprint images. WSQ is based on adaptive scalar quantization of a discrete wavelet transform (Hopper, Brislawn, and Bradley (1993); Onyshczak and Youssef (2004)). The WSQ encoder performs the following steps:

1. Fingerprint image is decomposed into a number of spatial frequency sub-bands (typically 64) using a Discrete Wavelet Transform (DWT).

2. Resulting DWT coefficients are quantized into discrete values; this is the step that leads to the loss of information and makes it very difficult to invert the process to obtain the exact starting image.
3. Quantized sub-bands are concatenated into several blocks (typically three to eight) and compressed using adaptive entropy encoding (Huffman run-length).

A compressed image can be decoded into the original image (with certain loss) by applying the equivalents of the above steps in reverse order (i.e., Huffman decoding, quantization decoding, and Inverse Discrete Wavelet Transform [IDWT]).

WSQ can compress a fingerprint image by a factor of 10–25 (see Figure 2.26). A typical compression ratio of 10–15 seems to be most appropriate, as higher compression ratios result in an unacceptable degradation of the fingerprint image.

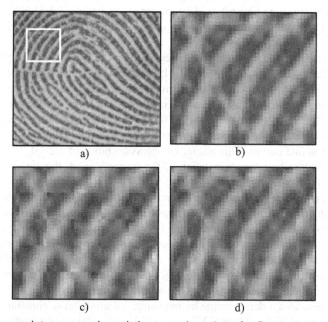

Figure 2.26. Fingerprint compression: a) the central section of a fingerprint image scanned at 500 dpi resolution; b) the marked portion of the image in a); c) the marked portion of the image in a) after the image was compressed using a generic JPEG (www.jpeg.org) image compression algorithm; and d) the marked portion of the image in a) is shown after the image was compressed using the WSQ compression algorithm. Both JPEG and WSQ examples used a compression ratio of 1:12.9; JPEG typically introduces blocky artifacts and obliterates detailed information. Images courtesy of Chris Brislawn, Los Alamos National Laboratory.

Although the common DCT-based JPEG compression is unsatisfactory for highly compressed fingerprint images, an evolution of the same general-purpose image compression, known as JPEG 2000 (Skodras, Christopoulos, and Ebrahimi, 2001), can actually compete with WSQ. Analogously to WSQ, JPEG 2000 is also based on DWT. Since DWT is applied to the whole image and not to separate image blocks, JPEG 2000 compressed images are no longer affected by the undesired blocky artifacts. The differences between WSQ and JPEG 2000 are in the methods used for the decomposition, quantization and entropy encoding (Allinson et al., 2007).

Based on the experimentations carried out until now over different sources and for different compression rates (Lepley (2001); Figueroa-Villanueva, Ratha, and Bolle (2003); Allinson et al. (2007)), it seems than JPEG 2000 is slightly better than WSQ for typical compression rates (e.g., 1:15) and noticeably better for high compression rates (e.g., 1:32). Both WSQ and JPEG 2000 compressions are now allowed by fingerprint standards. ANSI/NIST-ITL 1 (2007) recommends WSQ for 500 dpi images with compression limited to 1:15 and JPEG 2000 (still 1:15) for resolutions higher than 500 dpi.

Some improvements and efficient implementations of the basic WSQ approaches have been proposed (Kasaei, Deriche, and Boashash (1997, 2002); Deriche, Kasaei, and Bouzerdoum (1999)). Alternative approaches have been investigated where the compression relies on explicitly extracting features from fingerprints instead of encoding raw pictorial information (Abdelmalek et al. (1984); Chong et al. (1992)). For example, in Chong et al. (1992), after binarization and thinning of the fingerprint image (see Section 3.7.1), the one-pixel-wide ridges are encoded by B-spline curves. This allows compression ratios of 1:20–1:25 to be achieved, but since only a feature-based representation of the image is used, the gray-scale fingerprint image cannot be reconstructed.

Another compression method based on feature extraction, but which allows the gray-scale image to be reconstructed, was proposed by Gokmen, Ersoy, and Jain (1996) and Ersoy, Ercal, and Gokmen (1999). The binarized and thinned (one-pixel wide) ridges and valleys are encoded through differential chain codes. Gray-scale values along ridges and valleys are also encoded. This allows a sparse representation (e.g., with holes) of the fingerprint image to be obtained. To reconstruct a full gray-scale image, the authors used the Hybrid Image Model (Gokmen and Jain, 1997), which starts from a sparse image (i.e., where not all the pixel values are known) and generates a dense image by imposing the smoothness constraint by means of regularization theory. Finally, Tharna, Nilsson, and Bigun (2003) proposed a lossless compression method where, to maximize redundancy in data and thereby increase the compression rate, the image pixels are not visited row by row but scanned following the ridge lines.

2.11 Summary

Advancements in the area of fingerprint scanners have been fairly rapid. Just 5 years ago, when the first edition of this book was published, there was a remarkable trend towards reducing both the cost and the size of the scanners in order to expand the market of personal and corporate applications: several new companies were founded and new fingerprint image acquisition technologies were developed; some manufacturers went too far and reduced the sensor size and image quality to such an extent that recognition accuracy suffered significantly.

Fingerprint-based authentication is now more mature. Image quality specifications for fingerprint scanners have been introduced to certify the scanners for law enforcement and government applications. Several large-scale applications have been successfully deployed and system integrators are more knowledgeable of the role of scanner quality in determining the overall system accuracy. Consequently, some of the acquisition technologies have been abandoned and the manufactures have concentrated on those that offer the best performance/cost tradeoff for the specific application. However, existing image quality specifications (IQS) are still not perfect and do not cover all the relevant aspects (e.g., the ability of a scanner to acquire dry or wet fingers is not covered by any IQS) so they are "necessary but not sufficient".

For AFIS and large-scale civilian applications, almost all the fingerprint scanners (both multi-finger and single-finger) are based on large area optical FTIR technology that still provide the best image quality. Mid-size area scanners based on different technologies are dominating the market of logical security applications such as logon to a PC or to a network as well as employee physical access control and time and attendance. Small solid state scanners (both touch and sweep models) have found a niche in portable devices or compact access control systems where the sensor size and cost factors are critical.

With the deployment of fingerprint recognition systems in a number of different applications, system integrators are choosing different fingerprint scanners based on the requirements of the specific application. For example, as mentioned earlier, AFIS and large-scale civil applications are using large area optical readers that are compliant with the IAFIS or PIV IQS. Fingerprint readers used in personal verification applications may sacrifice some fingerprint image fidelity and recognition accuracy in favor of small size and lower cost. We believe that the trend of using application-specific fingerprint scanners will continue. However, it is typical that new applications and usage emerge after the hardware has been deployed. These new applications may need higher accuracy from the already-deployed hardware beyond what was envisioned for the first application. In this respect, it is prudent to err on the side of caution and choose the best possible fingerprint scanner envisioning some unforeseen emerging applications.

3
Fingerprint Analysis and Representation

3.1 Introduction

A fingerprint is the reproduction of the exterior appearance of the fingertip epidermis. The most evident structural characteristic of a fingerprint is a pattern of interleaved *ridges* and *valleys* (Ashbaugh, 1999); in a fingerprint image, ridges (also called ridge lines) are dark whereas valleys are bright (see Figure 3.1). Ridges vary in width from 100 μm, for very thin ridges, to 300 μm for thick ridges. Generally, the period of a ridge/valley cycle is about 500 μm. Most injuries to a finger such as superficial burns, abrasions, or cuts do not affect the underlying ridge structure, and the original pattern is duplicated in any new skin that grows.

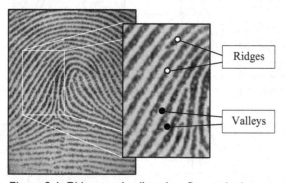

Figure 3.1. Ridges and valleys in a fingerprint image.

Ridge details are generally described in a hierarchical order at three different levels, namely, Level 1 (the overall global ridge flow pattern), Level 2 (minutiae points), and Level 3 (pores, local shape of ridge edges, etc.).

D. Maltoni et al., *Handbook of Fingerprint Recognition*, 97–166.
© Springer-Verlag London Limited 2009

At the global level (Level 1), ridges often run smoothly in parallel but exhibit one or more regions where they assume distinctive shapes (characterized by high curvature, frequent ridge terminations, etc.). These regions, called *singularities* or *singular regions*, may be broadly classified into three typologies: *loop*, *delta*, and *whorl* (see Figure 3.2). Singular regions belonging to loop, delta, and whorl types are typically characterized by ∩, Δ, and O shapes, respectively. Sometimes whorl singularities are not explicitly introduced because a whorl type can be described in terms of two loop singularities facing each other.

Fingerprint matching algorithms can pre-align fingerprint images according to a landmark or a center point, called the *core*. Henry (1900) defined the core point as "the north most point of the innermost ridge line." In practice, the core point corresponds to the center of the north most loop type singularity. For fingerprints that do not contain loop or whorl singularities (e.g., those belonging to the Arch class in Figure 3.3), it is difficult to define the core. In these cases, the core is usually associated with the point of maximum ridge line curvature. Unfortunately, due to the high variability of fingerprint patterns, it is difficult to reliably locate a registration (core) point in all the fingerprint images. Singular regions are commonly used for fingerprint classification (see Figure 3.3), that is assigning a fingerprint to a class among a set of distinct classes, with the aim of simplifying search and retrieval (ref. Chapter 5).

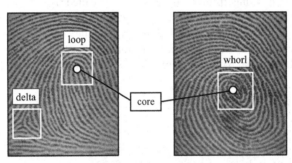

Figure 3.2. Singular regions (white boxes) and core points (small circles) in fingerprint images.

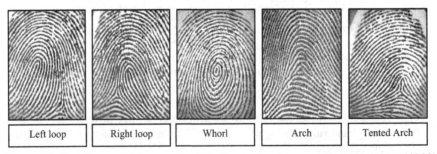

Figure 3.3. One fingerprint from each of the five major classes defined by Henry (1900).

At the local level (Level 2), other important features, called *minutiae* can be found in the fingerprint patterns. Minutia means small detail; in the context of fingerprints, it refers to various ways that the ridges can be discontinuous (see Figure 3.4). For example, a ridge can suddenly come to an end (ridge ending), or can divide into two ridges (bifurcation). Minutiae are the most commonly used features in automatic fingerprint matching. Sir Francis Galton (1822–1911) was the first person to categorize minutiae and to observe that they remain unchanged over an individual's lifetime (Galton, 1892). Minutiae are sometimes called "Galton details" in his honor. In a full fingerprint (i.e., rolled impression) the number of minutiae can be higher than 100; however, as discussed in Chapter 8, the spatial and angular coincidence or correspondence of a small number of minutiae (e.g., 12–15) is sufficient to claim with high confidence that two fingerprint impressions originate from the same finger. Some interesting statistical data on minutiae distribution can be found in Champod et al. (2004) and Stoney and Thornton (1987): in particular, average densities of 0.49 and 0.18 minutiae/mm^2 were estimated by Champod et al. (2004) inside the singular regions and outside the singular regions, respectively. Although several types of minutiae can be considered (the most common types are shown in Figure 3.4), usually only a coarse minutiae classification is adopted to deal with the practical difficulty in automatically discerning the different types with high accuracy. The American National Standards Institute (ANSI/NIST-ITL 1, 2007) proposes a minutiae taxonomy based on four classes: *ridge ending*, *bifurcations*, *compound* (trifurcation or crossovers), and *type undetermined*. The FBI minutiae-coordinate model (McCabe, 2004) considers only ridge endings and bifurcations. In ANSI/NIST-ITL 1 (2007) Type-9 records each minutia is denoted by its class, the *x*- and *y*-coordinates and the angle between the tangent to the ridge line at the minutia position and the horizontal axis (Figure 3.5). In practice, an ambiguity exists between ridge ending and bifurcation minutiae types; depending on the finger pressure against the surface where the fingerprint impression is formed, ridge endings may appear as bifurcations and vice versa. However, thanks to the convention used to define minutiae angle, there is no significant change in the angle if the minutia appears as a ridge ending in one impression and as a bifurcation in another impression of the same finger.

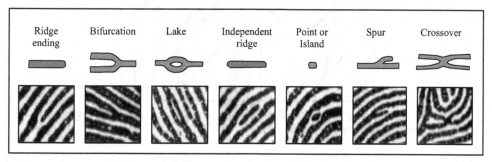

Figure 3.4. Seven most common minutiae types.

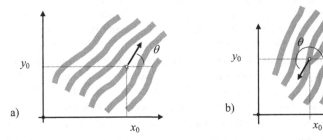

Figure 3.5. a) a ridge ending minutia: $[x_0, y_0]$ are the minutia coordinates; θ is the angle that the minutia tangent forms with the horizontal axis; b) a bifurcation minutia: θ is now defined by means of the ridge ending minutia corresponding to the original bifurcation that exists in the negative image.

With the aim of improving interoperability among minutiae detection algorithms, a few other conventions on minutiae placement and angle, have been adopted in ANSI/INCITS 378 (2004), ISO/IEC 19794-2 (2005) and CDEFFS (2008).

Figure 3.6a shows a portion of the fingerprint image where the ridge lines appear as dark traces on a light background; two ridge endings (1, 2) and one bifurcation (3) are shown. Note that on the negative image (Figure 3.6b) the corresponding minutiae take the same positions, but their type is exchanged: ridge endings now appear as bifurcations and vice versa (this property is known as ridge-ending/bifurcation *duality*). Besides the two coordinates and the angle other attributes can be associated to each minutia: these usually consist in features extracted from the minutia neighbor, and, as discussed in Section 4.4, can be very useful to improve fingerprint matching.

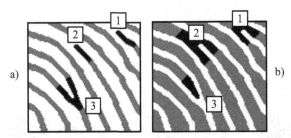

Figure 3.6. The ridge ending/bifurcation duality in a) a binary image and b) its negative image (i.e., dark and bright pixels are swapped).

At the very local level (Level 3), further fine details can be extracted in the fingerprint pattern. They include all dimensional attributes of the ridges such as width, shape, edge contour (Figure 3.7a), pores (Figure 3.7a), incipient ridges (Figure 3.7b), breaks, creases and scars (Figure 3.7c). Each ridge of the epidermis (outer skin) is dotted with *pores* (or *sweat pores*) along its entire length and anchored to the dermis (inner skin) by a double row of peglike protuberances, or papillae (Roddy and Stosz, 1997). Pores may range in size from 60 to 250 μm. It was observed that the number of pores along a centimeter of ridge varies from 9 to 18. It has been claimed that 20–40 pores may be sufficient to determine the identity of a person (Ashbaugh, 1999). Although Level 3 features are highly distinctive and extremely important for latent fingerprint examiners, currently very few automatic matching techniques use them since their reliable detection requires high resolution fingerprint scanners (e.g., 1,000 dpi) and good quality fingerprint images. CDEFFS (2008) is the first effort toward a standard encoding of Level 3 features.

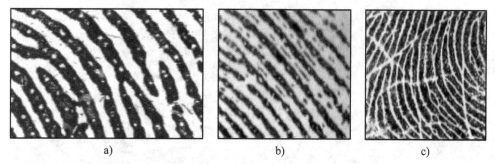

a)   b)   c)

Figure 3.7. a) A fingerprint portion, acquired at 1000 dpi, where pores are well evident. The local variability of the ridge width and shape and the irregularity of the ridge contours is also visible; b) incipient ridges are partially developed ridges that can occur in the valley between normal ridges: they are often fragmented and do not contain pores; c) some creases in a portion of a fingerprint.

Although some fingerprint matching techniques directly compare images through correlation-based methods (see Section 4.2), a representation based on the sensed gray-scale image intensities is not robust. Most of the fingerprint recognition and classification algorithms employ a feature extraction stage for identifying salient features.

The features extracted from fingerprint images often have a direct physical counterpart (e.g., singularities or minutiae), but sometimes they are not directly related to any physical traits (e.g., local orientation image or filter responses). Features may be used either for matching or their computation may serve as an intermediate step for the derivation of other features.

For example, some preprocessing and enhancement steps are often performed to simplify the task of minutiae extraction.

Throughout this book, a fingerprint image is represented as a two-dimensional surface. Let **I** be a gray-scale fingerprint image with g gray-levels, and $\mathbf{I}[x, y]$ be the gray-level of pixel $[x, y]$ in **I**. Let $z = S(x, y) = g-1 - \mathbf{I}[x, y]$ be the discrete surface corresponding to the image **I**. By associating dark pixels with gray-levels close to 0 and bright pixels with gray-levels close to $g-1$, the fingerprint ridge lines (appearing dark in **I**) correspond to surface ridges, and the spaces between the ridge lines (appearing bright in **I**) correspond to surface valleys (Figure 3.8).

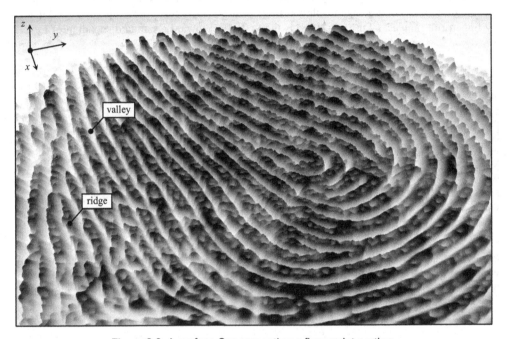

Figure 3.8. A surface S representing a fingerprint portion.

3.2 Local Ridge Orientation

The local ridge orientation at a pixel $[x, y]$ is the angle θ_{xy} that the fingerprint ridges, crossing through an arbitrary small neighborhood centered at $[x, y]$, form with the horizontal axis. Because fingerprint ridges are not directed, θ_{xy} is an unoriented direction lying in $[0 \ldots 180°[$. In the rest of the book we use the term *orientation* to denote an unoriented direction in $[0 \ldots 180°[$, and the term *direction* to indicate an oriented direction in $[0 \ldots 360°[$.

Instead of computing local ridge orientation at each pixel, most of the fingerprint processing and feature extraction methods estimate the local ridge orientation at discrete positions (this reduces computational efforts and still allows estimates at other pixels to be obtained through interpolation). The fingerprint *orientation image* (also called *directional image*), first introduced by Grasselli (1969), is a matrix **D** whose elements encode the local orientation of the fingerprint ridges. Each element θ_{ij}, corresponding to the node $[i,j]$ of a square-meshed grid located over the pixel $[x_i, y_j]$, denotes the average orientation of the fingerprint ridges in a neighborhood of $[x_i, y_i]$ (see Figure 3.9). An additional value r_{ij} is often associated with each element θ_{ij} to denote the reliability (or consistency) of the orientation. The value r_{ij} is low for noisy and seriously corrupted regions and high for good quality regions in the fingerprint image.

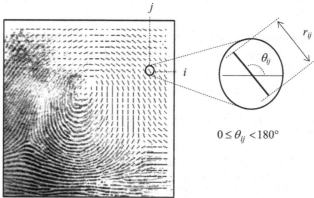

Figure 3.9. A fingerprint image faded into the corresponding orientation image computed over a square-meshed grid of size 16×16. Each element denotes the local orientation of the fingerprint ridges; the element length is proportional to its reliability.

3.2.1 Gradient-based approaches

The simplest and most natural approach for extracting local ridge orientation is based on computation of gradients in the fingerprint image. The gradient $\nabla(x, y)$ at point $[x, y]$ of **I**, is a two-dimensional vector $[\nabla_x(x, y), \nabla_y(x, y)]$, where ∇_x and ∇_y components are the derivatives of **I** at $[x, y]$ with respect to the x and y directions, respectively. It is well known that the gradient phase angle denotes the direction of the maximum intensity change. Therefore, the direction θ

of a hypothetical edge that crosses the region centered at $[x, y]$ is orthogonal to the gradient phase angle at $[x, y]$. This method, although simple and efficient, has some drawbacks. First, using the classical Prewitt or Sobel convolution masks (Gonzales and Woods, 2007) to determine ∇_x and ∇_y components of the gradient, and computing θ as the arctangent of the ∇_y/∇_x ratio, presents problems due to the non-linearity and discontinuity around 90°. Second, a single orientation estimate reflects the ridge–valley orientation at too fine a scale and is generally very sensitive to the noise in the fingerprint image; on the other hand, simply averaging gradient estimates is not meaningful due to the circularity of angles: the average orientation between 5° and 175° is not 90° (as an arithmetic average would suggest) but 0°. Furthermore, the concept of average orientation is not always well defined; consider the two orthogonal orientations 0° and 90°; is the correct average orientation 45° or 135°?

Kass and Witkin (1987) proposed a simple but elegant solution to the above problem, which allows local gradient estimates to be averaged. Their basic idea is to double the angles, so that each single orientation estimate is encoded by the vector:

$$\mathbf{d} = \left[r \cdot cos\left(2\theta\right), r \cdot sin\left(2\theta\right) \right],$$ (1)

where 2θ is used in place of θ to discount the circularity of angles and r is proportional to the orientation estimate strength (e.g., the squared norm of the gradient: $\nabla_x^2 + \nabla_y^2$). Averaging the angles in a local $n \times n$ window W to obtain a more robust estimate $\bar{\mathbf{d}}$, can be performed by separately averaging the two (x and y) components:

$$\bar{\mathbf{d}} = \left[\frac{1}{n^2} \sum_W r \cdot cos(2\theta), \frac{1}{n^2} \sum_W r \cdot sin\left(2\theta\right) \right].$$ (2)

Computing the average between two orthogonal orientations with Equation (2) involves summing two vectors facing each other, and therefore the length of the resulting vector is zero. This indicates that the vector is meaningless, independent of its orientation.

Based on the above idea, an effective method may be derived for computing the fingerprint orientation image (Rao (1990); Ratha, Chen, and Jain (1995); Bazen and Gerez (2002)). For example, Ratha, Chen, and Jain (1995) computed the dominant ridge orientation θ_{ij} by combining multiple gradient estimates within a 17×17 window W centered at $[x_i, y_j]$:

$$\theta_{ij} = 90° + \frac{1}{2} atan2\left(2G_{xy}, G_{xx} - G_{yy}\right),$$ (3)

$$G_{xy} = \sum_{h=-8}^{8} \sum_{k=-8}^{8} \nabla_x\left(x_i + h, y_j + k\right) \cdot \nabla_y\left(x_i + h, y_j + k\right),$$

$$G_{xx} = \sum_{h=-8}^{8} \sum_{k=-8}^{8} \nabla_x\left(x_i + h, y_j + k\right)^2,$$

$$G_{yy} = \sum_{h=-8}^{8} \sum_{k=-8}^{8} \nabla_y\left(x_i + h, y_j + k\right)^2,$$

where ∇_x and ∇_y are the x- and y-gradient components computed through 3×3 Sobel masks, and $atan2(y,x)$ calculates the arctangent of the two variables y and x: it is similar to calculating the arctangent of y/x, except that the signs of both arguments are used to determine the quadrant of the result. An example of local orientation image computed with Equation (3) is shown in Figure 3.10b. Bazen and Gerez (2002) have shown that this method is mathematically equivalent to the principal component analysis of the autocorrelation matrix of the gradient vectors. Another gradient-based method, independently proposed by Donahue and Rokhlin (1993), relies on least-squares minimization to perform the averaging of orientation estimates, and leads to equivalent expressions.

The reliability r of the estimate θ can be derived by the concordance (or coherence) of the orientation vectors $\mathbf{d}$ in the local window W (Kass and Witkin (1987); Bazen and Gerez (2002)). In fact, due to the continuity and smoothness of fingerprint ridges, sharp orientation changes often denote unreliable estimation. Kass and Witkin (1987) define the coherence as the norm of the sum of orientation vectors divided by the sum of their individual norms; this scalar always lies in $[0,1]$: its value is 1 when all the orientations are parallel to each other (maximum coherence) and 0 if they point in opposite directions (minimum coherence):

$$r = coherence(\theta) = \frac{\left| \sum_W \mathbf{d} \right|}{\sum_W |\mathbf{d}|} . \tag{4}$$

An example of local coherence map computed with Equation (4) is shown in Figure 3.10c. For the gradient-based approach corresponding to Equation (3), it can be proved that Equation (4) simplifies to:

$$r_{ij} = coherence(\theta_{ij}) = \frac{\sqrt{(G_{xx} - G_{yy})^2 + 4G_{xy}^2}}{G_{xx} + G_{yy}} . \tag{5}$$

Jain et al. (1997) computed the concordance of the orientations according to their variance in 5×5 neighborhoods whereas Donahue and Rokhlin (1993) computed this according to the residual of the least-square minimization.

The major flaw of gradient-based orientation estimators is their failure in the near-zero gradient regions, namely ridge tops and valley bottoms. In fact, in these regions the small values of both the x and y components of the gradient imply high noise sensitivity. For this reason some authors recommend to look beyond the first-degree derivatives: see Larkin (2005) for a comprehensive review. Using second degree derivatives only partially solves the problem since the high noise sensitivity is moved to the zero crossing regions (i.e., inflexion points) where all the second order derivatives and the Hessian are null. The method by Da Costa et al. (2001) is based on both first- and second-degree derivatives: for each region, a binary decision on which operators to use is taken according to the local coherence of the two operators.

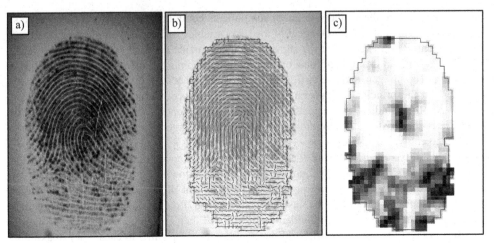

Figure 3.10. A fingerprint image (a), its local orientation (b) computed with Equation (3) and its local coherence (c) computed with Equation (4) over 3x3 blocks.

3.2.2 Slit- and projection-based approaches

The first slit-based approach dates back to 1960s, but some variants have been recently introduced. The basic idea is to define a fixed number (n_S) of reference orientations or slits S_k:

$$S_k = k\frac{\pi}{n_S}, \quad k = 0...n_S - 1$$

and to select the best slit $S_{k_{opt}}$ based on the pixel grey-values along the slits. The local orientation at $[x_i, y_j]$ is the orientation $\theta_{ij} = S_{k_{opt}}$ computed in a local window W centered at $[x_i, y_j]$.

Stock and Swonger (1969) sum the pixel gray-values along eight slits and select the minimum-sum slit or maximum-sum slit for ridge- or valley-pixels, respectively: in fact, for pixels lying on ridges (dark) the sum of gray-values along the ridge orientation is small, whereas for pixel lying on valleys (bright) the sum is high.

Based on the observation that the total fluctuation of the gray-scale is the smallest along the orientation of the ridges and largest in the orthogonal direction, similar methods have been proposed by Mehtre et al. (1987), He et al. (2003a) and Oliveira and Leite (2008). In particular, Oliveira and Leite (2008) compute the standard deviation $stdev(S_k)$ of the gray-scale of the pixels corresponding to each slit S_k, and select the optimal slit according to the maximum standard deviation contrast between a slit and its orthogonal slit (see Figure 3.11):

$$k^* = arg\,\max_k \left| stdev(S_k) - stdev(S_{Orth(k)}) \right|, \;\; Orth(k) = (k + n_S/2) \bmod n_S$$

$$k_{opt} = \begin{cases} k^* & \text{if } stdev(S_{k^*}) < stdev(S_{Orth(k^*)}) \\ Orth(k^*) & \text{otherwise} \end{cases}$$

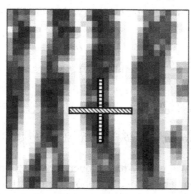

Figure 3.11. A pair of orthogonal slits with high standard deviation contrast is shown for a local region of a fingerprint.

Sherlock (2004) suggests projecting the ridge lines inside a local window along a number of discrete orientations (see Figure 3.14 for an example of gray-scale projection): the projection that exhibits the smallest variation corresponds to the orientation of the ridges within the window. In Ji and Yi (2008) approach, all the ridge lines except the central one are removed from the local window before computing the projections.

The computational complexity of slit- and projection-based approaches is usually higher than gradient-based techniques and quantization might produce a coarser angular resolution. However, these methods allow to assign a probability value to each quantized orientation that can be useful to further process noisy regions. In other words, a gradient-based technique leads to a winner-take-all decision where just the optimal orientation is carried over, whereas in slit- and projection-based methods one can also exploit the probability of the non-winning orientations for subsequent regularization or post processing.

3.2.3 Orientation estimation in the frequency domain

Kamei and Mizoguchi (1995) method (well described in Kamei, 2004a) is based on the application of 16 directional filters in the frequency domain. The optimal orientation at each pixel is then chosen not only according to the highest filter response but also taking local smoothing into consideration. Analogous results can be achieved in the spatial domain by using Gabor-like filters, as proposed by Hong et al. (1996) and Nakamura et al. (2004).

Chikkerur, Cartwright, and Govindaraju (2007) approach is based on Short Time Fourier Transform (STFT) analysis. The image is divided into partially overlapped blocks whose intensity values are cosine tapered moving from the centre toward the borders. For each block the Fourier Transform F(u,v) is computed and its spectrum |F(u,v)| is mapped to polar coordinates |F(r,θ)|. The probability of a given θ value (within the block) is then computed as the marginal density function:

$$p(\theta) = \int_r p(r,\theta) dr, \quad \text{where } p(r,\theta) = \frac{|F(r,\theta)|}{\iint\limits_{r,\theta} |F(r,\theta)| \, dr \, d\theta}$$

The expected value of θ for the block is finally estimated, according to Equation (2), as:

$$E\{\theta\} = 90° + \frac{1}{2} atan2\left(\oint p(\theta)sin(2\theta) d\theta, \oint p(\theta)cos(2\theta) d\theta \right). \qquad (6)$$

Larkin (2005) proposed two energy-based operators that provide uniform and scale-invariant orientation estimation. The second operator, the most robust one, is based on spiral phase quadrature (or Rietz transform). Although both the operators can be applied also in the spatial domain through convolution, the most natural and simpler implementation of these operators is in the frequency domain.

3.2.4 Other approaches

Other techniques for the computation of local ridge orientation (that often are variants of those already discussed) are described in Rao and Balck (1980), Kawagoe and Tojo (1984), Bigun and Granlund (1987), O'Gorman and Nickerson (1989), Srinivasan and Murthy (1992), Beyer, Lake, and Lougheed (1993), Hung (1993), Shumurun et al. (1994), Mardia et al. (1997), Almansa and Lindeberg (2000), Nagaty (2003), Gong (2004), Pattichis and Bovik (2004), Shi and Govindaraju (2006) and Huang, Liu, and Hung (2007).

3.2.5 Orientation image regularization

The orientation image **D**, computed from poor quality fingerprints may contain several unreliable elements due to creases, local scratches or cluttered noise. In this situation, a local smoothing can be very useful in enhancing **D**. This can be done by (re)converting the angles in orientation vectors **d** (Equation (1)) and by averaging them through Equation (2). Figure 3.12 shows an example of orientation image smoothing. However, such a simple averaging has some limitations (Figure 3.12.b):

1. It is ineffective when the incorrect orientations dominate the correct ones.
2. Tends to smooth out high curvature values, especially in singular point regions.
3. Tends to slightly shift the loop singularities.

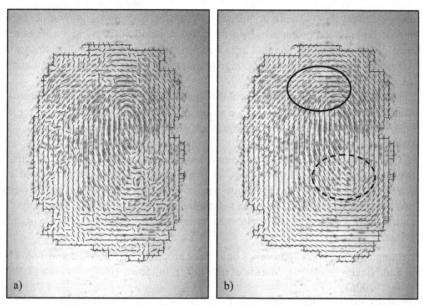

Figure 3.12. a) Estimation of local ridge orientation in a fingerprint through the gradient-based approach corresponding to Equation (3): in the noisy regions the estimation is unreliable; b) two iterations of local (3x3) smoothing are applied, resulting in a more consistent representation; it is worth noting that while the smoothing recovered the correct orientation at several places (e.g., inside the solid circle), it altered the average orientation inside the region denoted by the dashed circle where incorrect orientations were dominating the correct one.

To overcome the undesired effects described above, more elaborate approaches than a simple average have been proposed:

*   Jiang, Liu, and Kot (2004) noted that when a noisy region is smoothed, the local coherence tends to increase. On the other hand, if a high curvature region is smoothed the local coherence remains low. To prevent smoothing out high curvature regions, the size of the smoothing window is then chosen according to a hierarchical coherence analysis.
*   Liu, Jiang, and Kot (2004) also argued that since the noise is often caused by scars and breaks, it can be modelled as an impulse function. To suppress such kind of noise

a simple averaging (i.e., a linear filtering) is not effective and a non linear approach, similar to a median filtering, performs better.

- Zhu et al. (2006) trained a neural network to classify orientation image elements into two classes: correct and incorrect, based on an 11-dimensional feature vector. For each element, the 11 features, including gradient magnitude, gray-scale variance, gray-scale variance projected along the ridge orientation, inter-ridge distance, variance of the peak/valley heights are extracted from the corresponding image block. After classification, the incorrect ridge orientations are corrected using orientation of the neighboring elements.

- Zhang and Yan (2007) define "invalid regions" in the foreground as the sets of connected elements with low coherence value, and use the contours of these regions to build a constrained Delaunay triangulation that is used to correct the orientations through interpolation.

- In Oliveira and Leite (2008) correction is based on multi-scale analysis. In particular, they compute the orientation image at two different scales (fine scale and coarse scale) and correct only the elements whose value substantially differs between the two representations; in case of no substantial difference, the fine scale value is retained; otherwise the coarse scale value is used to correct the fine scale orientation image.

Other interesting regularization approaches have been proposed by Kawagoe and Tojo (1984), O'Gorman and Nickerson (1989), Mardia et al. (1997), Pradenas (1997), Perona (1998) and Chen and Dong (2006).

For very noisy images a local correction based on the above described techniques is often unsatisfactory and only the superimposition of a global model (as those described in the next section) may provide a more effective improvement (Chen et al., 2006b). Lee and Prabhakar (2008) approach computes the orientation image based on an MRF (Markov Random Field) made up of two components; one incorporates a global mixture model of orientation fields learned from training fingerprint examples and the other enforces a smoothness constraint over the orientation image in the neighboring regions. Although Lee and Prabhakar's (2008) current implementation is computationally intensive, it demonstrates the effectiveness of model-based estimation techniques.

3.2.6 Global models of ridge orientations

A global "mathematical" model for ridge orientation can be very useful for several purposes such as orientation image correction, fingerprint data compression, and synthetic fingerprint generation (see Chapter 6).

Sherlock and Monro (1993) proposed a mathematical model to synthesize a fingerprint orientation image from the position of loops and deltas alone. This approach is also known as zero-pole model since it takes a loop as a zero and a delta as a pole in the complex plane. But, the model makes some simplifying assumptions and it does not cover all possible fingerprint patterns (fingerprints with different ridge patterns may present the same singularities at the same locations). Improvements of this method have been proposed by Vizcaya and Gerhardt (1996) and Araque et al. (2002). In particular Vizcaya and Gerhardt (1996) improved the zero-pole model by using a piecewise linear approximation around singularities to adjust the zero and pole's behavior. These new models introduce more degrees of freedom to better cope with fingerprint pattern variability. Vizcaya and Gerhardt (1996) also proposed an optimization technique, based on gradient descent, to determine the model parameters starting from an estimation of the orientation image. More details on Sherlock and Monro (1993) and Vizcaya and Gerhardt (1996) methods can be found in Section 6.4.2 where they are used for the synthetic generation of local orientation images.

In the above mentioned methods the influence of a singularity on the orientation of a given point does not depend on the distance of the point from the singularity; this can cause errors in regions far from singular points. Furthermore, these models cannot deal with fingerprints with no singularities such as Arch type fingerprints. Zhou and Gu (2004b) developed a rational complex model, which generalizes the zero-pole model by adding some pseudozeros and pseudopoles as the control points: the pseudozeros are the roots of the additional polynomial in the numerator and the pseudopoles are the roots of the additional polynomial in the denominator. The model parameters can be derived by Weighted Least Square optimization (WLS) starting from the position of the singularities and estimation of the orientation image. Since the rational complex model does not work well in regions of high curvature and discontinuity, Zhou and Gu (2004a) introduced a combination model which models the real part and the imaginary part of the vector field with two bivariate polynomials, and improved the modelling in the noncontinuous regions around the singular points by imposing a Point-Charge Model for each singular point. Again, the parameters are estimated by WLS. Two simplified (but also less accurate) versions of the rational complex and the combination models, introduced by Gu, Zhou, and Yang (2006), can be used for very low quality images, where singular points extraction is unreliable.

Li, Yau, and Wang (2006a) argued that a good orientation model should not only be accurate in approximating the underlying orientation image, but also should have prediction capability. When the ridge information is not available in the images (e.g., due to excessive noise), the algorithm should still be able to predict the orientation information from known data. The method proposed by Li, Yau, and Wang (2006a), which improves the first version described in Li and Yau (2004), uses a first order phase portrait approach to compute the predicted orientation. This allows a reconstruction of the orientation using the data around the singular points. To increase the prediction accuracy, the initial estimation of the orientation fields (computed through a gradient-based approach) is refined by replacing the unreliable orientations with the predicted orientations. The refined orientation is then used to obtain the final orientation model using a constrained non-linear phase portrait approach. An improved version of this approach was proposed by Li et al. (2007), with the aim of better modelling the cases where singular points are very close to each other. Although this method seems to be able to better predict orientation in noisy regions than other models, it is heavily dependent on the singular points.

Huckemann, Hotz, and Munk (2008) argued that most of the global models proposed after Sherlock and Monro's one are controlled by too many parameters (i.e., too many degrees of freedom) and therefore it can be critical to extract stable parameter values from a given orientation image. Huckemann, Hotz, and Munk (2008) model extends the basic Sherlock and Monro (1993) zero-pole model, by using as control parameters (besides the singularity positions) five values with clear geometric meaning: three parameters control the finger placement with respect to the image (i.e., origin and angle of the reference axes) and the remaining two parameters define the finger horizontal and vertical size. In their experimental results, Huckemann, Hotz, and Munk (2008) compare their method with Sherlock and Monro (1993) and Zhou and Gu (2004b) and conclude that their model better fits real fingerprint data extracted from NIST Special Database 4 (Watson and Wilson, 1992a).

Wang, Hu, and Phillips (2007) proposed a fingerprint orientation model based on 2D Fourier series expansion (FOMFE) that does not require detection of singular points. The model is simpler than previous ones, and can seamlessly summarize global features, including high curvature regions around singularities. However, similar to most existing models, it is closer to an approximation method rather than to a real modelling, since the natural variability of fingerprint patterns is not encoded in the model, and, when a large region is dominated by the noise, the recovery ability is limited.

Dass (2004) proposed an iterative scheme based on a Bayesian formulation for the simultaneous extraction of orientation image and singularities. The orientation image is iteratively updated by taking into account the spatial smoothness in a local neighbourhood, the gradient values, and contributions to the local orientation given by the singularities. Obtaining orientation image and singularity information simultaneously offers the additional advantage of interleaved updating: the orientation image can be dynamically improved based on current singularity information and the singularity extraction can be performed with higher accuracy thanks to the improved orientation image. Unfortunately, the numerical optimization underlying the joint estimation can be very time consuming.

3.3 Local Ridge Frequency

The local ridge frequency (or density) f_{xy} at point $[x, y]$ is the number of ridges per unit length along a hypothetical segment centered at $[x, y]$ and orthogonal to the local ridge orientation θ_{xy}. A frequency image $\mathbf{F}$, analogous to the orientation image $\mathbf{D}$, can be defined if the frequency is estimated at discrete positions and arranged into a matrix.

The local ridge frequency varies across different fingers, and may also noticeably vary across different regions of the same fingerprint (see Figure 3.13).

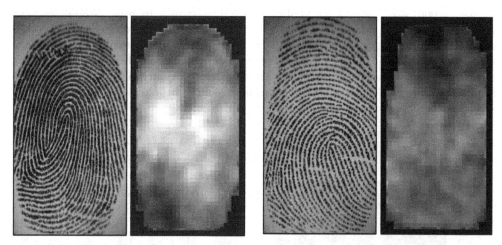

Figure 3.13. Two fingerprint images and the corresponding frequency image computed with the method proposed by Maio and Maltoni (1998a). A local 3 × 3 averaging is performed after frequency estimation to reduce noise. Light blocks denote higher frequencies. It is quite evident that significant changes may characterize different fingerprint regions and different average frequencies may result from different fingers.

Hong, Wan, and Jain (1998) estimate local ridge frequency by counting the average number of pixels between two consecutive peaks of gray-levels along the direction normal to the local ridge orientation (see Figure 3.14). For this purpose, the surface S corresponding to the fingerprint is sectioned with a plane parallel to the z-axis (see Figure 3.8) and orthogonal to local ridge orientation. The frequency f_{ij} at $[x_i, y_j]$ is computed as follows.

1. A 32 × 16 *oriented window* centered at $[x_i, y_j]$ is defined in the ridge coordinate system (i.e., rotated to align the y-axis with the local ridge orientation).
2. The *x-signature* of the gray-levels is obtained by accumulating, for each column x, the gray-levels of the corresponding pixels in the oriented window. This is a sort of averaging that makes the gray-level profile smoother and prevents ridge peaks from being obscured due to small ridge breaks or pores.
3. f_{ij} is determined as the inverse of the average distance between two consecutive peaks of the x-signature.

The method is simple and fast. However, it is difficult to reliably detect consecutive peaks of gray-levels in the spatial domain in noisy fingerprint images. In this case, the authors suggest using interpolation and low-pass filtering. An alternative way to extract ridge distances from the x-signature makes use of a fitting method based on the first and second order derivatives (Yang et al., 2003).

Jiang (2000) also computes the local ridge frequency starting from the x-signatures (see Figure 3.14). However, instead of measuring the distances in the spatial domain, he makes use of a high-order spectrum technique called *mix-spectrum*. The ridge patterns in a fingerprint image are noisy periodic signals; when they deviate from a pure sinusoid shape, their energy is distributed to their fundamental frequency and harmonics. The mix-spectrum technique enhances the fundamental frequency of the signal by exploiting the information contained in the second and third harmonic.

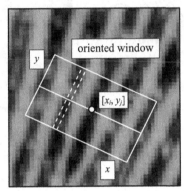
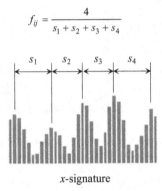

$$f_{ij} = \frac{4}{s_1 + s_2 + s_3 + s_4}$$

Figure 3.14. An oriented window centered at $[x_i, y_j]$; the dashed lines show the pixels whose gray-levels are accumulated for a given column of the x-signature (Hong, Wan, and Jain, 1998). The x-signature on the right clearly exhibits five peaks; the four distances between consecutive peaks are averaged to determine the local ridge frequency.

In the method proposed by Maio and Maltoni (1998a), the ridge pattern is locally modeled as a sinusoidal-shaped surface, and the variation theorem is exploited to estimate the unknown frequency. The variation V of a function h in the interval $[x_1, x_2]$ is the amount of "vertical" change in h:

$$V(h) = \int_{x_1}^{x_2} \left| \frac{dh(x)}{dx} \right| \cdot dx \ .$$

If the function h is periodic at $[x_1, x_2]$ or the amplitude changes within the interval $[x_1, x_2]$ are small, the variation may be expressed as a function of the average amplitude α_m and the average frequency f (see Figure 3.15).

$$V(h) = (x_2 - x_1) \cdot 2\alpha_m \cdot f \ .$$

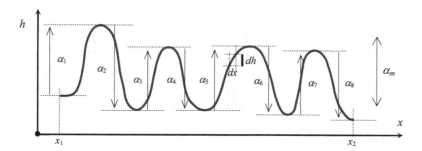

Figure 3.15. The variation of the function h in the interval $[x_1,x_2]$ is the sum of amplitudes α_1, $\alpha_2...\alpha_8$ (Maio and Maltoni, 1998a). If the function is periodic or the function amplitude does not change significantly within the interval of interest, the average amplitude α_m can be used to approximate the individual α values. Then the variation may be expressed as $2\alpha_m$ multiplied by the number of periods of the function over the interval.

Therefore, the unknown frequency can be estimated as

$$f = \frac{V(h)}{2 \cdot (x_2 - x_1) \cdot \alpha_m}. \tag{7}$$

Maio and Maltoni (1998a) proposed a practical method based on the above analysis. The variation and the average amplitude of a two-dimensional ridge pattern are estimated from the first- and second-order partial derivatives and the local ridge frequency is computed from Equation (7). Two examples of frequency images computed using this method are shown in Figure 3.13.

Kovacs-Vajna, Rovatti, and Frazzoni (2000) proposed a two-step procedure: first, the average ridge distance is estimated for each 64×64 sub-block of the image that is of sufficient quality and then this information is propagated, according to a diffusion equation, to the remaining regions. Two methods are considered in the first step: geometric and spectral. In the geometric approach, the central points of the ridges are computed on a regular grid and the ridge distances are measured on straight lines passing through these points. Unlike the x-signature approach, distances are directly measured in the two-dimensional image; several estimates on the same image block are performed to compensate for the noise. The second method is based on a search of the maxima in the Fourier power spectrum of each sub-block. Here too, the method works on two-dimensional signals. The invariance with respect to the local ridge orientations is obtained by performing the maxima search in radial directions: in fact, all the components (harmonics) having the same distance from the origin denote the same frequency.

Almansa and Lindeberg (1997, 2000) use scale space theory to locally estimate ridge width; their approach relies upon combinations of normalized derivatives computed pointwise.

The approach by Chikkerur, Cartwright, and Govindaraju (2007), already discussed in Section 3.2.3 for the estimation of the local ridge orientations, is based on Short Time Fourier Transform (STFT) analysis. The probability of a given r value (corresponding to the average frequency f within the block) is computed as the marginal density function:

$$p(r) = \int_{\theta} p(r, \theta)\, d\theta, \quad \text{where } p(r, \theta) = \frac{|F(r, \theta)|}{\iint_{r, \theta} |F(r, \theta)|\, dr\, d\theta}$$

and the expected value of r for the block is estimated as:

$$E\{r\} = \int_{r} p(r)\, r\, dr. \tag{8}$$

Zhan et al. (2006) compared frequency estimation approaches operating in the spatial domain versus Fourier domain, and concluded that the former can be implemented more efficiently but the latter seems to be more robust to noise.

3.4 Segmentation

The term *segmentation* is generally used to denote the separation of fingerprint area (foreground) from the image background; examples of segmentations are shown in Figures 3.12 and 3.13. Separating the background is useful to avoid extraction of features in noisy areas that is often the background. Some authors use the term segmentation to indicate the transformation of the fingerprint image from gray-scale to black and white; throughout this book the latter processing is referred to as *fingerprint binarization*.

Because fingerprint images are striated patterns, using a global or local thresholding technique (Gonzales and Woods, 2007) does not allow the fingerprint area to be effectively isolated. In fact, what really discriminates foreground and background is not the average image intensity but the presence of a striped and oriented pattern in the foreground and of an isotropic pattern (i.e., which does not have a dominant orientation) in the background. If the image background were always uniform and lighter than the fingerprint area, a simple approach based on local intensity could be effective for discriminating foreground and background; in practice, the presence of noise (such as that produced by dust and grease on the surface of live-scan fingerprint scanners) requires more robust segmentation techniques.

Mehtre et al. (1987) isolated the fingerprint area according to local histograms of ridge orientations. Ridge orientation is estimated at each pixel and a histogram is computed for each 16×16 block. The presence of a significant peak in a histogram denotes an oriented pattern, whereas a flat or near-flat histogram is characteristic of an isotropic signal. The above method fails when a perfectly uniform block is encountered (e.g., a white block in the background) because no local ridge orientation may be found. To deal with this case, Mehtre and Chatterjee

(1989) proposed a composite method that, besides histograms of orientations, computes the gray-scale variance of each block and, in the absence of reliable information from the histograms, assigns the low-variance blocks to the background.

Ratha, Chen, and Jain (1995) assigned each 16×16 block to the foreground or the background according to the variance of gray-levels in the orthogonal direction to the ridge orientation. They also derive a quality index from the block variance (see Figure 3.16); underlying assumption is that the noisy regions have no directional dependence, whereas regions of interest exhibit a very high variance in a direction orthogonal to the orientation of ridges and very low variance along ridges.

Maio and Maltoni (1997) discriminated foreground and background by using the average magnitude of the gradient in each image block (i.e., contrast); in fact, because the fingerprint area is rich in edges due to the ridge/valley alternation, the gradient response is high in the fingerprint area and small in the background. Another method based on gray-scale statistics was proposed by Shi et al. (2004) whose contrast-based segmentation is preceded by a nonlinear histogram manipulation aimed at decreasing the contrast in ambiguous regions.

In the method proposed by Shen, Kot, and Koo (2001), eight Gabor filters (refer to Section 3.6.2) are convolved with each image block, and the variance of the filter responses is used both for fingerprint segmentation and for the classification of the blocks, according to their quality, as "good," "poor," "smudged," or "dry". An improved version of this Gabor-based method was introduced by Alonso-Fernandez, Fierrez-Aguilar, and Ortega-Garcia (2005). Gaussian-Hermite Moments, that have some similarity with Gabor filters, were employed in the context of fingerprint segmentation by Wang, Suo, and Dai (2005).

Ridges and valleys locally exhibit a sinusoidal-shaped plane wave with a well-defined frequency and orientation, whereas background regions are characterized by very little structure and hence very little energy content in the Fourier spectrum. A measure of local energy in the Fourier spectrum was used for fingerprint segmentation by Pais Barreto Marques and Gay Thome (2005) and Chikkerur, Cartwright, and Govindaraju (2007).

Wu, Tulyakov, and Govindaraju (2007) method is based on Harris corner detector (Harris and Stephens, 1988) that can be implemented efficiently by combining first degree partial derivatives. The image points whose response to Harris detector exceeds a given threshold are selected as principal foreground points and the final segmentation is obtained as their convex hull.

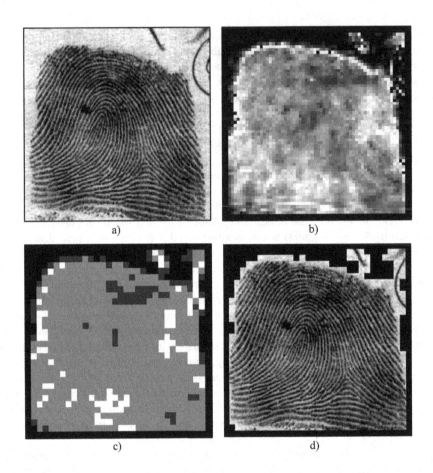

Figure 3.16. Segmentation of a fingerprint image as proposed by Ratha, Chen, and Jain (1995): a) original image; b) variance field; c) quality image derived from the variance field: a quality value "good," "medium," "poor" or "background" is assigned to each block according to its variance; d) segmented image. © Elsevier.

Learning-based segmentation techniques were introduced by Bazen and Gerez (2001b), Chen et al. (2004), Yin, Wang, and Yang (2005) and Zhu et al. (2006); these techniques usually lead to more accurate segmentations with respect to approaches based on feature value thresholding:

- Bazen and Gerez (2001b) proposed a pixel-wise method, where three features (gradient coherence, intensity mean, and intensity variance) are computed for each pixel, and a linear classifier associates the pixel with the background or the foreground. A supervised technique is used to learn the optimal parameters for the linear classifier for each specific fingerprint sensor. A final morphological post-processing step (Gonzales and Woods, 2007) is performed to eliminate holes in both the foreground and background and to regularize the external silhouette of the fingerprint area. Their experimental results showed that this method provides accurate results; however, its computational complexity is markedly higher than most of the previously described block-wise approaches. The same feature vectors were used by Yin, Wang, and Yang (2005) for point-wise segmentation, but adopting a quadratic separation surface (non-linear classifier) instead of a hyperplane (linear classifier) causes a relevant reduction of the pixel classification rate.

- Chen et al. (2004) trained a linear classifier to select foreground blocks based on: (i) the block clusters degree, (ii) the difference of local block intensity mean and global image intensity mean, and (iii) the block variance. The block cluster degree is a measure of clustering of the ridge (dark) and valley (bright) gray-levels. Morphology is then applied during post-processing to regularize the results and reduce the number of classification errors. Some examples of segmentation are shown in Figure 3.17. The authors report a block misclassification error of 2.45% over the four FVC2002 databases (Maio et al., 2002b).

- The basics of Zhu et al. (2006) techniques are discussed in Section 3.2.5 in the context of local orientation correction.

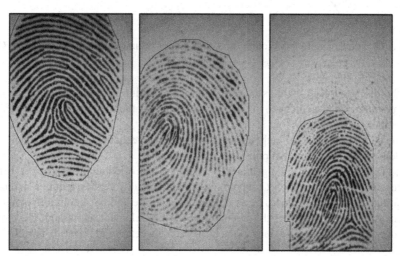

Figure 3.17. Some examples of segmentation with the method proposed by Chen et al. (2004).
© Hindawi.

3.5 Singularity and Core Detection

Most of the approaches proposed in the literature for singularity detection operate on the fingerprint orientation image. In the rest of this section, the main approaches are coarsely classified and a subsection is dedicated to each family of algorithms.

3.5.1 Poincaré index

An elegant and practical method based on the Poincaré index was proposed by Kawagoe and Tojo (1984). Let **G** be a vector field and C be a curve immersed in **G**; then the Poincaré index $P_{G,C}$ is defined as the total rotation of the vectors of **G** along C (see Figure 3.18).

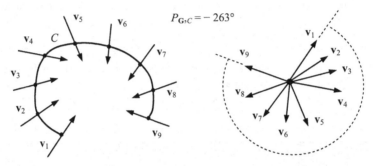

Figure 3.18. The Poincaré index computed over a curve C immersed in a vector field **G**.

Let **G** be the discrete vector field associated with a fingerprint orientation image[1] **D** and let $[i,j]$ be the position of the element θ_{ij} in the orientation image; then the Poincaré index $P_{G,C}(i,j)$ at $[i,j]$ is computed as follows.

- The curve C is a closed path defined as an ordered sequence of some elements of **D**, such that $[i,j]$ is an internal point.
- $P_{G,C}(i,j)$ is computed by algebraically summing the orientation differences between the adjacent elements of C. Summing orientation differences requires a direction (among the two possible) to be associated at each orientation. A solution to this problem is to randomly select the direction of the first element and assign the direction closest to that of the previous element to each successive element. It is well known

---

[1] Note that a fingerprint orientation image is not a true vector field in as much as its elements are unoriented directions.

and can be easily shown that, on closed curves, the Poincaré index assumes only one of the discrete values: $0°, \pm 180°$, and $\pm 360°$. In the case of fingerprint singularities:

$$P_{\mathbf{G},C}(i,j) = \begin{cases} 0° & \text{if } [i,j] \text{ does not belong to any singular region} \\ 360° & \text{if } [i,j] \text{ belongs to a whorl type singular region} \\ 180° & \text{if } [i,j] \text{ belongs to a loop type singular region} \\ -180° & \text{if } [i,j] \text{ belongs to a delta type singular region.} \end{cases}$$

Figure 3.19 shows three portions of orientation image. The path defining C is the ordered sequence of the eight elements $\mathbf{d}_k$ ($k = 0...7$) surrounding $[i,j]$. The direction of the elements $\mathbf{d}_k$ is chosen as follows: $\mathbf{d}_0$ is directed upward; $\mathbf{d}_k$ ($k = 1...7$) is directed so that the absolute value of the angle between $\mathbf{d}_k$ and $\mathbf{d}_{k-1}$ is less than or equal to $90°$. The Poincaré index is then computed as

$$P_{\mathbf{G},C}(i,j) = \sum_{k=0...7} angle\left(\mathbf{d}_k, \mathbf{d}_{(k+1) \bmod 8}\right).$$

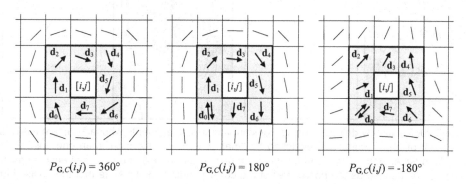

$$P_{\mathbf{G},C}(i,j) = 360° \qquad P_{\mathbf{G},C}(i,j) = 180° \qquad P_{\mathbf{G},C}(i,j) = -180°$$

Figure 3.19. Examples of Poincaré index computation in the 8-neighborhood of points belonging (from left to right) to a whorl, loop, and delta singularity, respectively. Note that, for the loop and delta examples (center and right), the direction of $\mathbf{d}_0$ is first chosen upward (to compute the angle between $\mathbf{d}_0$ and $\mathbf{d}_1$) and then successively downward (when computing the angle between $\mathbf{d}_7$ and $\mathbf{d}_0$).

An example of singularities detected by the above method is shown in Figure 3.20a.

An interesting implementation of the Poincaré method for locating singular points was proposed by Bazen and Gerez (2002): according to Green's theorem, a closed line integral over a vector field can be calculated as a surface integral over the rotation of this vector field; in practice, instead of summing angle differences along a closed path, the authors compute the "rotation" of the orientation image (through a further differentiation) and then perform a local integration (sum) in a small neighborhood of each element. Bazen and Gerez (2002) also provided a method for associating an orientation with each singularity; this is done by comparing the orientation image around each detected singular point with the orientation image of an ideal singularity of the same type.

Singularity detection in noisy or low-quality fingerprints is difficult and the Poincaré method may lead to the detection of false singularities (Figure 3.21). Regularizing the orientation image through a local averaging, as discussed in Section 3.2.5, is often quite effective in preventing the detection of false singularities, even if it can lead to slight displacement of the loop position toward the borders. Wang, Li, and Niu (2007b) propose a posteriori correction of loop location to compensate for the offset introduced by the smoothing.

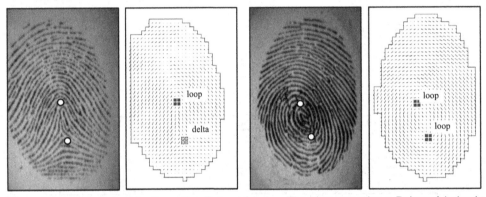

Figure 3.20. Singularity detection using Poincaré index. The elements whose Poincaré index is 180° (loop) or -180° (delta) are enclosed by small boxes. Usually, more than one point (four points in these examples) is found for each singular region: hence, the center of each singular region can be defined as the barycenter of the corresponding points. Note that the position of the loop singularities is slightly moved toward the borders because of the local smoothing of the orientation image.

Based on the observation that only a limited number of singularities can be present in a fingerprint, Karu and Jain (1996) proposed to iteratively smooth the orientation image (through averaging) until a valid number of singularities is detected by the Poincaré index. In fact, a simple analysis of the different fingerprint classes (refer to Chapter 5 for a more detailed discussion) shows that:

- Arch fingerprints do not contain singularities.
- Left loop, right loop, and tented arch fingerprints contain one loop and one delta.
- Whorl fingerprints contain two loops (or one whorl) and two deltas.

The above constraints are nicely demonstrated by Zhou, Gu, and Zhang (2007) who conclude that for each completely captured fingerprint there are the same number of loop and delta. A practical way to enforce this constraint is to compute the Poincaré index along the external boundary of the orientation image and then use the resulting value to limit the number of valid configurations. Another useful suggestion given by Zhou, Gu, and Zhang (2007) is to locally change the path C for the computation of the Poincaré index according to the reliability of the underlying elements; in fact, $P_{\mathbf{G},C}$ being independent of the closed path C, if the eight-neighborhood path (shown in Figure 3.19) includes unreliable elements, C can be progressively enlarged to include more reliable elements. In their approach Zhou, Gu, and Zhang (2007) use the Poincaré index in conjunction with another similar operator, called DORIC, that looks for the presence of a single peak in the sequence of direction differences $\mathbf{d}_k$, $\mathbf{d}_{k+1}$; in Figure 3.19 it can be noted that for loop and delta singularities, there is a single sharp change of direction between $\mathbf{d}_7$ and $\mathbf{d}_0$. After Poincaré-based detection and DORIC-based filtering, Zhou, Gu, and Zhang (2007) select the optimal subset of singular points as the set S that minimizes the difference between the estimated orientation image and a reconstruction of the orientation image through the Sherlock and Monro (1993) model with S as singularities. Zhou, Gu, and Zhang (2007) report a miss detection rate of 14.6% and a false detection rate of 4.8% over a mix of manually labeled databases.

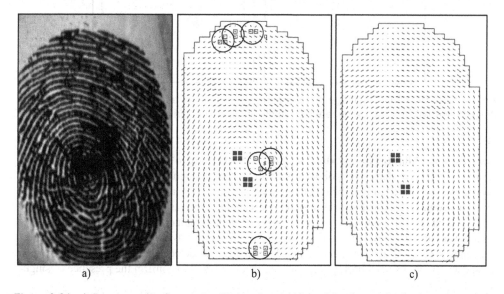

Figure 3.21. a) A poor quality fingerprint; b) the singularities of the fingerprint in a) are extracted through the Poincaré method (circles highlight the false singularities); c) the orientation image has been regularized and the Poincaré method no longer provides false alarms.

3.5.2 Methods based on local characteristics of the orientation image

Some authors have proposed singularity detection approaches where the fundamental idea is to explore the orientation image regions characterized by high irregularity, curvature, or symmetry. In fact, the singularities are the only foreground regions where a dominant orientation does not exist and ridges assume high curvature.

The coherence operator as defined by Equation (4) was used by Cappelli et al. (1999) to coarsely locate singular regions. Figure 3.22 shows an example of coherence map computed over 3×3 neighborhoods.

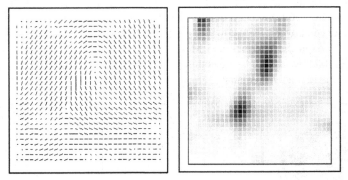

Figure 3.22. An orientation image and the corresponding coherence map that clearly identifies the regions (dark cells ↔ low coherence) containing the singularities.

Srinivasan and Murthy (1992) extract singularities according to the local histogram of the orientation image; in fact, the points where the local histogram does not exhibit a well-pronounced peak are likely to belong to singular regions. By analyzing the predominant orientation in some predefined sectors around the candidate points, the Srinivasan and Murthy method is able to discriminate between loop and delta singularities. Another rule-based approach was proposed by Park et al. (2006): the orientation of any two horizontally adjacent elements is checked against a set of pre-defined rules to detect candidate regions; for each candidate region, its neighboring elements are then analyzed to confirm the presence of singularities.

The Local Axial Symmetry (LAS) introduced by Liu, Zhang, and Hao (2006b) is a pixel-wise feature, derived from the orientation image that denotes the symmetry of the orientations inside circular regions centered at each pixel. Based on the observation that there are two regions with lower LAS value on the two opposite sides of each loop type singularity, a simple binarization scheme is proposed to isolate these two regions and locate the loop(s) as midpoint(s) of their barycenters. A similar symmetry-based technique was used by Liu, Hao, and

Zhang (2005) to check the validity of singular points (both loop and delta) initially detected through the Poincaré index approach.

Some researchers argued that multi-resolution analysis is an effective tool for singularity detection since it allows: (i) to increase robustness against the noise; (ii) to locate singular points with sub-block accuracy, and (iii) to reduce computational costs:

- Koo and Kot (2001) approach allows to detect the singularities with single pixel accuracy. At each resolution, they derive from the orientation image a curvature image whose blocks indicate the local degree of ridge curvature. High-curvature blocks, which denote singularities, are retained and analyzed at finer resolutions. The block-resolution pyramid consists of four levels: 11×11, 7×7, 3×3 and 1×1. At the finest resolution, the neighborhood of each detected singular point is further analyzed to discriminate between loop and delta singularities.

- Nilsson and Bigun (2002a, b, 2003) multi-resolution analysis is based on the convolution of the orientation field with two complex filters tuned to detect points of rotational symmetry. The two filters (one for loop type singularity and one for delta-type singularity) are convolved with orientation image and the points where the response of any one filter is high are retained and analyzed at finer resolution (see Figure 3.23). Orientation of the detected singularities can also be estimated from the argument of the complex filter responses. This technique can be implemented in an efficient way thanks to the separability of the filters used. An improved version of this approach is described in Chikkerur and Ratha (2005).

- Liu, Jiang, and Kot's (2004) approach iteratively checks for the existence of singularities and refines their position over a sequence of resolutions, based on local features such as Poincaré index and orientation variance.

- Wang, Li, and Niu's (2007b) multi-resolution approach is based on harmonic relationships between the orientation of a singular point and its neighbours.

3.5.3 Partitioning-based methods

Some authors noted that partitioning the orientation image in regions characterized by homogeneous orientation implicitly reveals the position of singularities. Hung and Huang (1996) and Huang, Liu, and Hung (2007) coarsely discretize the orientation image by using a very small number of orientation values. Each orientation value determines a region. The borderline between two adjacent regions is called a fault-line. By noting that fault lines converge towards loop singularities and diverge from deltas, the authors define a geometrical method for determining the convergence and divergence points. In Maio and Maltoni (1996) and Cappelli et al. (1999), the orientation image is partitioned by using an iterative clustering algorithm and a set of dynamic masks, respectively (Figure 3.24). Ohtsuka and Takahashi (2005) and Ohtsuka and Kondo (2005) derive the position of singularities from the extended relational graphs modelling the orientation image. Rämö et al. (2001) and Kryszczuk and Drygajlo (2006) implicitly partition the orientation image in correspondence with the points where the x- and y-orientation components (refer to Equation (1)) change sign: efficient methods are then introduced to extract singularities based on the contemporary zero crossings of both orientation components.

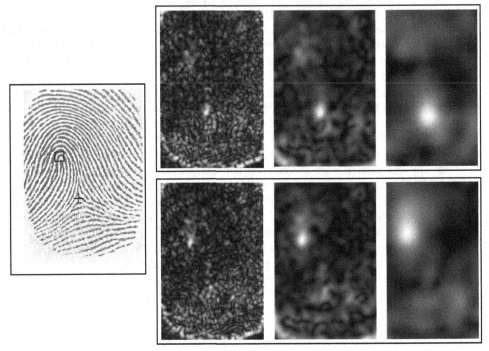

Figure 3.23. An example of the Nilsson and Bigun (2003) approach. A fingerprint image and its responses of the loop filter (bottom row) and delta filter (top row) at three different scales are shown. Images courtesy of J. Bigun.

3.5.4 Methods based on a global model of the orientation image

An effective strategy to improve robustness is to exploit a global model of the orientation image (see Section 3.2.6):

- Wu and Zhou (2004) used the zero-pole model and the Hough transform to detect the position of singularities starting from the orientation image. In the zero-pole model the orientation around each singularity is not much influenced by the other singularities, and therefore within a local window the singularities position and the surrounding orientations are bound by simple linear equations. This makes it possible to implement the voting scheme which is the basis of the Hough transform. An initial location of the singularities is performed with the Poincaré approach; each singularity is then checked and its location refined through the Hough transform.

- Fan et al. (2008) approach is also based on the zero-pole model and the Hough transform. The robustness of this method to identify a single dominant loop (or delta) for a given fingerprint area is demonstrated for real fingerprint images (including noisy samples). However, to refine the position of singularities and to deal with the presence of more loops/deltas other heuristics based on Poincaré index and ridge tracing are used in conjunction with the zero-pole model and the Hough transform. See Figure 3.25 for an example.

- Dass (2004) used the simultaneous computation of orientation image and singularities that is briefly discussed in Section 3.2.6.

- Wang, Hu, and Phillips (2007) exploited their global model (FOMFE) to obtain an analytical expression of the local orientation topology: in particular the classification of each point as {normal point, loop or delta} is determined by the sign of the determinant of a 2×2 matrix, called the characteristic matrix. The computation of additional information such as the local curl and divergence assists in implementing effective rules for the removal of false singular points (Wang and Hu, 2008).

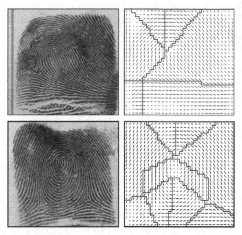

Figure 3.24. Orientation image partitioning with the MASK approach (Cappelli et al., 1999). The intersections between region border lines denote fingerprint singularities. © IEEE.

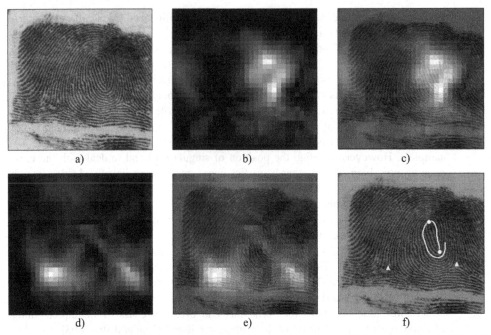

Figure 3.25. An example of singularity detection with Fan et al. (2008) approach. a) Original image; b) Hough space (loop); c) Hough space (loop) superimposed over the original image; d) Hough space (delta); e) Hough space (delta) superimposed over the original image; f) detected loops (circle) and deltas (triangle), ridge-tracing is also shown. © IEEE.

3.5.5 Core detection and registration

Once the singularities have been extracted, the core position may be simply defined as the location of the northern most loop. Some problems arise with the arch type fingerprints that do not have singularities; for these fingerprints, the estimated flow field is flat and no core position can be located. When the core point is detected with the aim of registering fingerprint images (thus obtaining invariance with respect to (x, y) displacement), its location may be quite critical and an error at this stage often leads to a failure of subsequent processing steps (e.g., matching). On the other hand, if the core has to be used only for fingerprint registration, it is not important to find the northern most loop exactly and any stable point in the fingerprint pattern is suitable.

One of the first automatic methods for fingerprint registration was proposed by Wegstein (1982). This method, known as R92, searches for a core point independently of the other singularities. The core is searched by scanning (row by row) the orientation image to find *well-formed arches*; a well-formed arch is denoted by a sextet (set of six) of adjacent elements whose orientations comply with several rules controlled by many parameters. One sextet is chosen among the valid sextets by evaluating the orientation of the elements in adjacent rows. The exact core position is then located through interpolation (Figure 3.26). Even though R92 is quite complicated and heuristic in nature, it usually gives good results and is able to localize the core point with sub-block accuracy. This algorithm was a fundamental component of the fingerprint identification systems used by the FBI and is still extensively used by other authors (e.g., Candela et al. (1995)).

Figure 3.26. The core point "+" located on the chosen sextet.

Several other ideas for the location of stable registration points have been proposed. Novikov and Kot (1998) define the core as the crossing point of the lines normal to the ridges (Figure 3.27) and used the Hough transform (Ballard, 1981) to determine its coordinates. Similarly, Rerkrai and Areekul (2000) define the *focal point* as the point where pairs of straight lines normal to the ridges intersect. Because the ridges do not draw perfect concentric circumferences around the core, the normal lines (dashed lines in Figure 3.27) do not exactly cross at a single point and a sort of average point has to be defined as the center of curvature. Novikov and Kot (1998) compute this average point in a least squares sense, whereas Rerkrai and Areekul (2000) compute the barycenter of the crossing between pairs of normals.

Figure 3.27. The straight lines normal to the ridges identify a valid registration point that corresponds to the center of curvature.

Although the focal point (or the center of curvature) does not necessarily correspond to the core point, it has been experimentally demonstrated to be quite stable with respect to fingerprint variation (displacement, rotation, distortion, etc.). Therefore, it can be reliably used for fingerprint registration. The main problem of these methods is in isolating a fingerprint region characterized by a single center of curvature. In fact, if the selected fingerprint region contains more than one singularity, the result may be unpredictable. To solve this problem, Areekul, Suppasriwasuseth, and Jirachawang (2006) proposed an algorithm that separately determines a focal point for each neighbor of a high curvature point and then tries to reach a consensus.

Jain et al. (2000) proposed a multi-resolution approach for locating the north most loop type singularities (core) based on integration of sine components in two adjacent regions R_I and R_{II} (Figure 3.28). The geometry of the two regions is designed to capture the maximum curvature in concave ridges. At each scale and for each candidate position $[x, y]$, the sine components of the orientation image are integrated over the two regions resulting in the values SR_I and SR_{II}. The points $[x, y]$ that maximize the quantity $(SR_I - SR_{II})$ are retained as candidate positions and analyzed at a finer resolution. Another interesting multi-resolution approach, designed by Jiang, Liu, and Kot (2004), performs the core localization by means of a hierarchical analysis of orientation coherence: the core is chosen as the point having local minimum coherence at both large and fine scales. This approach was able to correctly locate the core position in about 95% of the FVC2000 DB2 fingerprint images (Maio et al., 2002a).

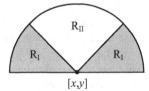

Figure 3.28. Regions of integration of the sine components in the method proposed by Jain et al. (2000).

3.5.6 Miscellanea

Other approaches for singularity or core detection, besides those already described, have been proposed by Tou and Hankley (1968), Levi and Sirovich (1972), Aushermann et al. (1973), Rao, Prasad, and Sharma (1974), Rao and Balck (1978, 1980), Chang (1980), Drets and Liljenstrom (1998), Tico and Kuosmanen (1999b), Cho et al. (2000), Sha, Zhao, and Tang (2003) and Wang et al. (2004).

3.6 Enhancement

The performance of minutiae extraction algorithms and other fingerprint recognition techniques relies heavily on the quality of the input fingerprint images. In an ideal fingerprint image, ridges and valleys alternate and flow in a locally constant direction. In such situations, the ridges can be easily detected and minutiae can be precisely located in the image. Figure 3.29a shows an example of a good quality fingerprint image. However, in practice, due to skin conditions (e.g., wet or dry, cuts, and bruises), sensor noise, incorrect finger pressure, and inherently low-quality fingers (e.g., elderly people, manual workers), a significant percentage of fingerprint images (approximately 10%, according to our experience) is of poor quality like those in Figures 3.29b, c. In many cases, a single fingerprint image contains regions of good, medium, and poor quality where the ridge pattern is very noisy and corrupted (Figure 3.30). In general, there are several types of degradation associated with fingerprint images:

1. The ridges are not strictly continuous; that is, the ridges have small breaks (gaps).
2. Parallel ridges are not well separated. This is due to the presence of noise which links parallel ridges, resulting in their poor separation.
3. Cuts, creases, and bruises on the finger.

These three types of degradation make ridge extraction extremely difficult in the highly corrupted regions. This leads to the following problems in minutiae extraction: (i) a significant number of spurious minutiae are extracted, (ii) a large number of genuine minutiae are missed, and (iii) large errors in the location (position and orientation) of minutiae are introduced. In order to ensure good performance of the ridge and minutiae extraction algorithms in poor quality fingerprint images, an enhancement algorithm to improve the clarity of the ridge structure is necessary.

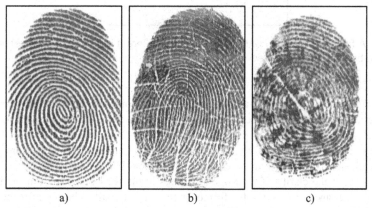

a)   b)   c)

Figure 3.29. a) A good quality fingerprint; b) a medium quality fingerprint characterized by scratches and ridge breaks; c) a poor quality fingerprint containing a lot of noise.

A fingerprint expert is often able to correctly identify the minutiae by using various visual clues such as local ridge orientation, ridge continuity, ridge tendency, and so on. In theory, it is possible to develop an enhancement algorithm that exploits these visual clues to improve image quality. Generally, for a given fingerprint image, the fingerprint areas resulting from the segmentation step may be divided into three categories (Figure 3.30):

- *Well-defined region*: ridges can be clearly differentiated from each another.
- *Recoverable region*: ridges are corrupted by a small amount of gaps, creases, smudges, links, and the like, but they are still visible and the neighboring regions provide sufficient information about their true structure.
- *Unrecoverable region*: ridges are corrupted by such a severe amount of noise and distortion that no ridges are visible and the neighboring regions do not allow them to be reconstructed.

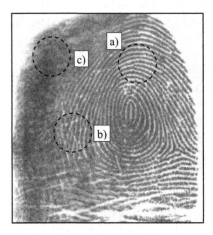

Figure 3.30. A fingerprint image containing regions of different quality: a) a well-defined region; b) a recoverable region; c) an unrecoverable region.

Good quality regions, recoverable, and unrecoverable regions may be identified according to several criteria; in general, image contrast, orientation consistency, ridge frequency, and other local features may be combined to define a quality index. Since the estimation of fingerprint quality is central for a number of algorithms and practical applications, a section devoted to quality computation is provided at the end of this chapter. The goal of an enhancement algorithm is to improve the clarity of the ridge structures in the recoverable regions and mark the unrecoverable regions as too noisy for further processing. Usually, the input of the enhancement algorithm is a gray-scale image. The output may either be a gray-scale or a binary image, depending on the algorithm and goal.

3.6.1 Pixel-wise enhancement

In a pixel-wise image processing operation the new value of each pixel only depends on its previous value and some global parameters (but not on the value of the neighboring pixels). Pixel-wise techniques do not produce satisfying and definitive results for fingerprint image enhancement. However, contrast stretching, histogram manipulation, normalization (Hong, Wan, and Jain, 1998), and Wiener filtering (Greenberg et al., 2000) have been shown to be effective as initial processing steps in a more sophisticated fingerprint enhancement algorithm.

The normalization approach used by Hong, Wan, and Jain (1998) determines the new intensity value of each pixel in an image as

$$\mathbf{I}'[x,y] = \begin{cases} m_0 + \sqrt{(\mathbf{I}[x,y]-m)^2 \cdot v_0 / v} & \text{if } \mathbf{I}[x,y] > m \\ m_0 - \sqrt{(\mathbf{I}[x,y]-m)^2 \cdot v_0 / v} & \text{otherwise,} \end{cases} \tag{9}$$

where m and v are the image mean and variance and m_0 and v_0 are the desired mean and variance after the normalization. Figure 3.31 shows an example. Since the mean and variance can change in different regions of a fingerprint image, the above global technique can be implemented in a local fashion: Kim and Park (2002) introduced a block-wise implementation of Equation (9) where m and v are the block mean and variance, respectively, and m_0 and v_0 are adjusted for each block according to the block features. A similar adaptive normalization was proposed by Zhixin and Govindaraju (2006). However, this kind of normalization involves pixel-wise operations and does not change the ridge and valley structures. In particular, it is not able to fill small ridge breaks, fill intra-ridge holes, or separate parallel touching ridges.

Figure 3.31. An example of normalization with the method described in Hong, Wan, and Jain (1998) using (m_0 = 100, v_0 = 100). © IEEE.

3.6.2 Contextual filtering

The most widely used technique for fingerprint image enhancement is based on *contextual filters*. In conventional image filtering, only a single filter is used for convolution throughout the image. In contextual filtering, the filter characteristics change according to the local context. Usually, a set of filters is pre-computed and one of them is selected for each image region. In fingerprint enhancement, the context is often defined by the local ridge orientation and local ridge frequency. In fact, the sinusoidal-shaped wave of ridges and valleys is mainly defined by a local orientation and frequency that varies slowly across the fingerprint area. An appropriate filter that is tuned to the local ridge frequency and orientation can efficiently remove the undesired noise and preserve the true ridge and valley structure.

Several types of contextual filters have been proposed in the literature for fingerprint enhancement. Although they have different definitions, the intended behavior is almost the same: (1) provide a low-pass (averaging) effect along the ridge direction with the aim of linking small gaps and filling impurities due to pores or noise; (2) perform a bandpass (differentiating) effect in the direction orthogonal to the ridges to increase the discrimination between ridges and valleys and to separate parallel linked ridges.

The method proposed by O'Gorman and Nickerson (1988, 1989) was one of the first to use contextual filtering for fingerprint enhancement; the authors defined a mother filter based on four main parameters of fingerprint images at a given resolution: minimum and maximum ridge width, and minimum and maximum valley width. The filter is bell-shaped (see Figure 3.32), elongated along the ridge direction, and cosine tapered in the direction normal to the ridges. The local ridge frequency is assumed constant and therefore, the context is defined only by the local ridge orientation. Once the mother filter has been generated, a set of 16 rotated versions (in steps of 22.5°) is derived. The image enhancement is performed by convolving each point of the image with the filter in the set whose orientation best matches the local ridge orientation. Depending on some input parameters, the output image may be gray-scale or binary. Examples of image binarization using this technique are shown in Figures 3.39b and 3.42a.

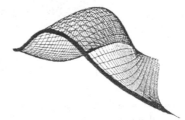

Figure 3.32. The shape of the filter proposed by O'Gorman and Nickerson (1989). © Elsevier.

Sherlock, Monro, and Millard (1992, 1994) performed contextual filtering in the Fourier domain; in fact, it is well-known that a convolution in the spatial domain corresponds to a point-by-point complex multiplication in the Fourier domain (Gonzales and Woods, 2007). The filter is defined in the frequency domain by the function:

$$H(\rho,\theta) = H_{radial}(\rho) \cdot H_{angle}(\theta), \tag{10}$$

where H_{radial} depends only on the local ridge spacing $\rho = 1/f$ and H_{angle} depends only on the local ridge orientation θ. Both H_{radial} and H_{angle} are defined as bandpass filters and are characterized by a mean value and a bandwidth. A set of n discrete filters is derived by their analytical definition. Actually, in the experiments, to reduce the number of filters, only a single value is used for the local ridge frequency and, therefore, the context is determined only by the orientation. The Fourier transform $\mathbf{P}_i$, $i = 1 \ldots n$ of the filters is pre-computed and stored. Filtering an input fingerprint image $\mathbf{I}$ is performed as follows (see Figure 3.33).

- The FFT (Fast Fourier Transform) $\mathbf{F}$ of $\mathbf{I}$ is computed.
- Each filter $\mathbf{P}_i$ is point-by-point multiplied by $\mathbf{F}$, thus obtaining n filtered image transforms $\mathbf{PF}_i$, $i = 1 \ldots n$ (in the frequency domain).
- Inverse FFT is computed for each $\mathbf{PF}_i$ resulting in n filtered images $\mathbf{PI}_i$, $i = 1 \ldots n$ (in the spatial domain).

The enhanced image $\mathbf{I}_{enh}$ is obtained by setting, for each pixel $[x, y]$, $\mathbf{I}_{enh}[x, y] = \mathbf{PI}_k[x, y]$, where k is the index of the filter whose orientation is the closest to θ_{xy}.

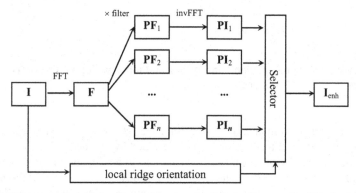

Figure 3.33. Enhancement of the fingerprint image **I** according to the Sherlock, Monro, and Millard (1994) method.

Hong, Wan, and Jain (1998) proposed an effective method based on Gabor filters. Gabor filters have both frequency-selective and orientation-selective properties and have optimal joint resolution in both spatial and frequency domains (Daugman (1985); Jain and Farrokhnia (1991)). As shown in Figure 3.34, a Gabor filter is defined by a sinusoidal plane wave (the second term of

Equation (11)) tapered by a Gaussian (the first term in Equation (11)). The even symmetric two-dimensional Gabor filter has the following form.

$$g(x, y : \theta, f) = exp\left\{-\frac{1}{2}\left[\frac{x_\theta^2}{\sigma_x^2} + \frac{y_\theta^2}{\sigma_y^2}\right]\right\} \cdot cos(2\pi f \cdot x_\theta),\tag{11}$$

where θ is the orientation of the filter, and $[x_\theta, y_\theta]$ are the coordinates of $[x, y]$ after a clockwise rotation of the Cartesian axes by an angle of $(90° - \theta)$.

$$\begin{bmatrix} x_\theta \\ y_\theta \end{bmatrix} = \begin{bmatrix} cos(90° - \theta) & sin(90° - \theta) \\ -sin(90° - \theta) & cos(90° - \theta) \end{bmatrix} \begin{bmatrix} x \\ y \end{bmatrix} = \begin{bmatrix} sin\,\theta & cos\,\theta \\ -cos\,\theta & sin\,\theta \end{bmatrix} \begin{bmatrix} x \\ y \end{bmatrix}.$$

In the above expressions, f is the frequency of a sinusoidal plane wave, and σ_x and σ_y are the standard deviations of the Gaussian envelope along the x- and y-axes, respectively.

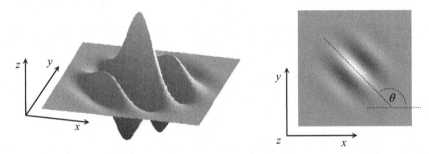

Figure 3.34. Graphical representation (lateral view and top view) of the Gabor filter defined by the parameters $\theta = 135°$, $f = 1/5$, and $\sigma_x = \sigma_y = 3$.

To apply Gabor filters to an image, the four parameters $(\theta, f, \sigma_x, \sigma_y)$ must be specified. Obviously, the frequency of the filter is completely determined by the local ridge frequency and the orientation is determined by the local ridge orientation. The selection of the values σ_x and σ_y involves a tradeoff. The larger the values, the more robust the filters are to the noise in the fingerprint image, but they are also more likely to create spurious ridges and valleys. On the other hand, the smaller the values, the less likely the filters are to introduce spurious ridges and valleys but then they will be less effective in removing the noise. In fact, from the Modulation Transfer Function (MTF) of the Gabor filter, it can be shown that increasing σ_x and σ_y decreases the bandwidth of the filter and vice versa. Based on empirical data, Hong, Wan, and Jain (1998) set $\sigma_x = \sigma_y = 4$. To make the enhancement faster, instead of computing the best-suited contextual filter for each pixel "on the fly," a set $\{g_{ij}(x, y)| \ i = 1...n_o, j = 1...n_f\}$ of filters are a priori created and stored, where n_o is the number of discrete orientations $\{\theta_i | i = 1...n_o\}$ and n_f the number of discrete frequencies $\{f_j | j = 1...n_f\}$. Then each pixel $[x, y]$ of the image is convolved, in the spatial domain, with the filter $g_{ij}(x, y)$ such that θ_i is the discretized orientation closest to θ_{xy} and f_j is the discretized frequency closest to f_{xy}. Figure 3.35 shows an example of the filter set for $n_o = 8$ and $n_f = 3$. Figure 3.36 shows the application of Gabor-based contextual filtering on medium and poor quality images.

$$\theta_i$$

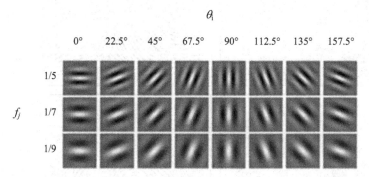

Figure 3.35. A graphical representation of a bank of 24 ($n_o = 8$ and $n_f = 3$) Gabor filters where $\sigma_x = \sigma_y = 4$.

Greenberg et al. (2000) noted that by reducing the value of σ_x with respect to σ_y, the filtering creates fewer spurious ridges and is more robust to noise. In practice, reducing σ_x results in increasing the frequency bandwidth, independently of the angular bandwidth which remains unchanged; this allows the filter to better tolerate errors in local frequency estimates. Analogously, one could decrease σ_y in order to increase the angular bandwidth as pointed out by Sherlock, Monro, and Millard (1994). Their method increases the angular bandwidth near the singularities where the ridges are characterized by higher curvatures and the orientation changes rapidly. The methods by Erol, Halici, and Ongun (1999) and Wu and Govindaraju (2006) relate the filter bandwidth to the local orientation coherence, whereas the Bernard et al. (2002) approach reduces the filter bandwidth if none of the responses to an initial set of filters exceeds a certain threshold. Yang et al. (2003) argue that the fingerprint ridge and valley pattern does not always resemble a pure sinusoidal pattern, mainly because of the different values of ridge and valley width in some regions (see Figure 3.37). Therefore they propose Gabor-like filters whose positive and negative peaks can have different periods and contextually adjust the two periods based on the local ridge width and local valley width, respectively. Zhu, Yin, and Zhang (2004) note that implementing Gabor-based contextual filtering with squared mask can lead to artifacts that can be removed if the mask support is circular.

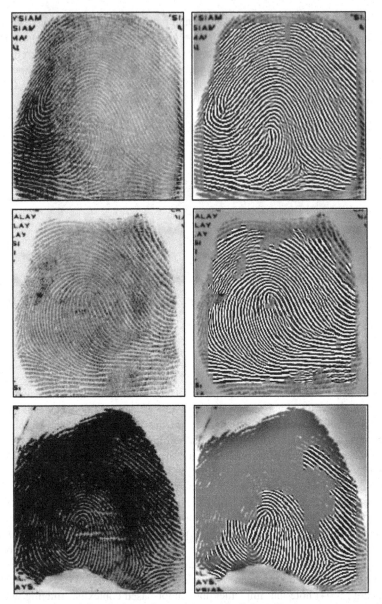

Figure 3.36. Examples of fingerprint enhancement with Gabor filtering as proposed by Hong, Wan, and Jain (1998). On the right, the enhanced recoverable regions are superimposed on the corresponding input images. © IEEE.

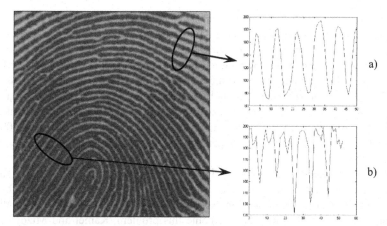

Figure 3.37. Two examples of fingerprint regions where the local ridge-valley pattern conforms to (a), and deviates from (b) a sinusoidal pattern. © Elsevier.

Wang et al. (2008) suggest replacing standard Gabor filter with Log-Gabor filter to overcome the drawbacks that the maximum bandwidth of a Gabor filter is limited to approximately one octave and Gabor filters are not optimal if one is seeking broad spectral information with maximal spatial localization.

For low-cost and computation-limited fingerprint systems (e.g., embedded systems), the 2D convolution of an image with a Gabor filter pre-computed over a discrete mask (e.g., 15 × 15) can be too time consuming. The computational complexity can be reduced by using separable Gabor filters (Areekul et al., 2005) or masks with sparse coefficients (Jang et al., 2006).

Chikkerur, Cartwright, and Govindaraju (2007) proposed an efficient implementation of contextual filtering based on short-time Fourier transform (STFT) that requires partitioning the image into small overlapping blocks and performing Fourier analysis separately on each block. The orientation and frequency of each block are probabilistically determined through Equations (7) and (8), and the orientation coherence is computed similar to Equation (4). Each block is then filtered (by complex multiplication in the Fourier domain) with a filter equivalent to Equation (10) except for the angular bandwidth which is adjusted according to the orientation coherence; in Sherlock, Monro, and Millard (1994) the angular bandwidth is related to the distance from the closest singular point. Since singular point estimation is less robust than coherence estimation, Chikkerur, Cartwright, and Govindaraju (2007) bandwidth adjustment seems to be more effective than the approach by Sherlock, Monro, and Millard (1994).

An approach similar to that of Chikkerur, Cartwright, and Govindaraju (2007) was introduced by Jirachaweng and Areekul (2007), but their block-wise contextual information computation and filtering is performed in the DCT (Discrete Cosine Transform) domain instead of in the Fourier domain.

The output of a contextual fingerprint enhancement can be a gray-scale, near-binary, or binary image, depending on the filter parameters chosen. When selecting the appropriate set of filters and tuning their parameters, one should keep in mind that the goal is not to produce a good visual appearance of the image but to facilitate robustness of the successive feature extraction steps. If the filters are tuned to increase the contrast and suppress the noise, the estimation of the local context (orientation and frequency) may be erroneous in poor quality areas and the filtering is likely to produce spurious structures (Jiang, 2001). For example, an iterative application of Gabor filters has been used by Cappelli, Maio, and Maltoni (2000b) (refer to Chapter 6) to generate a synthetic fingerprint pattern; in this case the filters generate non-existent ridge patterns.

The need of an effective enhancement is particularly important in poor quality fingerprints where only the recoverable regions carry information necessary for matching. On the other hand, computing local information (context) with sufficient reliability in poor quality fingerprint images is very challenging. To overcome this problem, Kamei and Mizoguchi (1995), Hong et al. (1996), Bernard et al. (2002) and Nakamura et al. (2004) proposed to apply all the filters of a given set at each point in the image (as in Figure 3.33). A "selector" then chooses the best response from all the filter responses:

- In the method by Kamei and Mizoguchi (1995), the selection is performed by minimizing an energy function that includes terms that require orientation and frequency to be locally smooth.
- Hong et al. (1996) and Nakamura et al. (2004) base their selection on the analysis of local ridges extracted form the filtered images. In particular, Nakamura et al. (2004) enforce orientations that are consistent with a ridge parallelism model.
- Bernard et al. (2002) make the selection according to the maximum response. However, unlike most of the Gabor-based methods, phase information coming from the real and the imaginary part of Gabor filters is also used for the final image enhancement.

As expected, approaches that require convolution of an image with a large number of filters are computationally expensive, and it is difficult to obtain efficient implementations. This problem can be partially alleviated by exploiting steerable filter (Freeman and Adelson, 1991) which filters the image with a reduced number of basis filters and derives the remaining filter responses by a linear combination.

Another interesting technique that is able to perform a sort of contextual filtering without explicitly computing local ridge orientation and frequency was proposed by Watson, Candela, and Grother (1994) and Willis and Myers (2001). Each 32×32 image block is enhanced separately; the Fourier transform of the block is multiplied by its power spectrum raised to a power k:

$$\mathrm{I}_{enh}[x, y] = F^{-1}\left\{F\left(\mathrm{I}[x, y]\right) \times \left| F\left(\mathrm{I}[x, y]\right)\right|^{k}\right\}.$$

The power spectrum contains information about the underlying dominant ridge orientation and frequency and the multiplication has the effect of enhancing the block accordingly. Watson, Candela, and Grother (1994) set $k = 0.6$ whereas Willis and Myers (2001) proposed a more aggressive value of $k = 1.4$. Unfortunately, to avoid discontinuities at the edges between adjacent blocks, a large amount of overlap between the neighboring blocks (e.g., 24 pixels) is necessary and this significantly increases the enhancement time.

3.6.3 Multi-resolution enhancement

Multi-resolution analysis has been proposed to remove noise from fingerprint images. Decomposing the image into different frequency bands (or sub-images) allows us to compensate for different noise components at different scales: in particular, at higher levels (low and intermediate frequency bands) the rough ridge-valley flow is cleaned and gaps are closed, whereas at the lower levels (higher frequencies) the finer details are preserved. The enhanced image bands are then recombined to obtain the final image.

- Almansa and Lindeberg (2000) technique performs shape-adapted smoothing based on second moment descriptors and automatic scale selection (over a number of scales) based on normalized derivatives. The smoothing operation is adapted according to the local ridge structures, allowing interrupted ridges to be joined. The scale selection procedure estimates local ridge width and adapts the amount of smoothing to the local noise.
- In Hsieh, Lai, and Wang (2003) the multi-resolution representation is based on wavelet decomposition (Mallat, 1989). Each sub-image is processed through both textural and directional filtering to suppress spectral noise and to close the gaps produced by creases and scars.
- Cheng and Tian (2004) method is based on dyadic space scale and the decomposition depth is determined according to the average ridge width in the image; the noise reduction relies on smoothing the differential images between successive scales (i.e., the details that are lost passing from one scale to the successive one).
- Fronthaler, Kollreider, and Bigun (2007, 2008) use a Laplacian like image-scale pyramid to decompose the original fingerprint into three smaller images corresponding to different frequency bands. Each image is then processed through contextual filtering.

3.6.4 Crease detection and removal

Some fingerprints (the incidence is higher in elderly people) are affected by the presence of a large number of creases (see Figure 3.7c). The presence of creases adversely influences the computation of orientation image and can lead to the detection of false ridge-ending minutiae.

Provided that contextual information (i.e., local orientation and frequency) has been correctly estimated, contextual filtering techniques are usually capable of filling the small ridge-gap produced by creases: however if the image is very noisy or the creases are too wide, contextual filtering can fail. Furthermore, in some cases creases themselves could be used as features to drive or improve the fingerprint matching and therefore their deletion during enhancement may be undesirable.

To explicitly detect (and optionally remove) creases, some ad-hoc techniques have been proposed:

- Vernon (1993) argued that creases are characterized by collinear terminations on ridges and proposed a detection approach based on the analysis of the Hough transform space derived from the ridge ending minutiae. The Hough transform (Ballard, 1981) is in fact a simple but powerful technique aimed to detect lines in noisy data.
- Wu et al. (2003) and Zhou et al. (2004) modelled a crease by using a parameterized rectangle, followed by a multi-channel filtering framework to detect creases at different orientations. Principal Component Analysis is applied to estimate the crease orientation, length and width. Figure 3.38 shows some examples of crease detection.
- Oliveira and Leite (2008) identify crease points by looking at the discordance between local orientations computed at two different scales. In fact, when computed at fine scale (i.e. on a small neighbourhood) the local orientation within a crease markedly deviates from the overall underlying ridgeline orientation that can be estimated at coarse scale (i.e. on a large neighbourhood). An approach based on Watershed transform is then proposed to remove the creases.

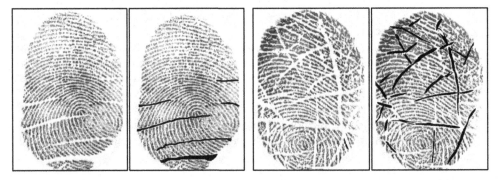

Figure 3.38. Two examples of crease detection (in black) by Wu et al. (2003) approach. © IEEE.

3.6.5 Miscellanea

Other fingerprint enhancement approaches can be found in Asai et al. (1975), Berdan and Chiralo (1978), Nakamura, Nagaoka, and Minami (1986), Danielsson and Ye (1988), Sasakawa, Isogai, and Ikebata (1990), Kaymaz and Mitra (1993), Mehtre (1993), Bergengruen (1994), Sherstinsky and Picard (1994, 1996), Szu et al. (1995), Almansa and Lindeberg (1997), Pradenas (1997), Park and Smith (2000), Greenberg et al. (2000), Ghosal et al. (2000a, b), Simon-Zorita et al. (2001a, b), Cheng, Tian, and Zhang (2002), Connell, Ratha, and Bolle (2002), Kim, Kim, and Park (2002), Cheng et al. (2003), Pattichis and Bovik (2004), Wu, Shi, and Govindaraju (2004), Bal, El-Saba, and Alam (2005a), Greenberg and Kogan (2005), Chen and Dong (2006), Chen et al. (2006b) and Rahmes et al. (2007).

3.7 Minutiae Detection

Most automatic systems for fingerprint comparison are based on minutiae matching (see Chapter 4); hence, reliable minutiae extraction is an extremely important task and a substantial amount of research has been devoted to this topic. Most of the proposed methods require the fingerprint gray-scale image to be converted into a binary image. Some binarization processes greatly benefit from an a priori enhancement (see Section 3.6); on the other hand, some enhancement algorithms directly produce a binary output, and therefore the distinction between enhancement and binarization is sometimes faded. The binary images are usually submitted to a thinning stage which allows for the ridge line thickness to be reduced to one pixel, resulting in a skeleton image (Figure 3.39). A simple image scan then allows the detection of pixels that correspond to minutiae.

Some authors have proposed minutiae extraction approaches that work directly on the gray-scale images without binarization and thinning. This choice is motivated by the following considerations:

- A significant amount of information may be lost during the binarization process.
- Binarization and thinning are time consuming; thinning may introduce a large number of spurious minutiae.
- In the absence of an a priori enhancement step, most of the binarization techniques do not provide satisfactory results when applied to low-quality images.

3.7.1 Binarization-based methods

The general problem of image binarization has been widely studied in the fields of image processing and pattern recognition (Trier and Jain, 1995). The simplest approach uses a *global threshold t* and works by setting the pixels whose gray-level is lower than *t* to 0 and the remaining pixels to 1.

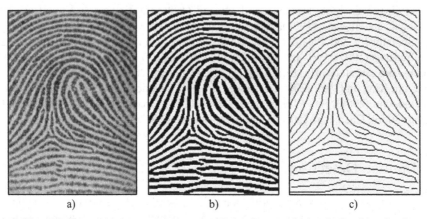

Figure 3.39. a) A fingerprint gray-scale image; b) the image obtained after binarization of the image in a); c) skeleton image obtained after a thinning of the image in b). Reprinted with permission from Maio and Maltoni (1997). © IEEE.

In general, different portions of an image may be characterized by different contrast and intensity and, consequently, a single threshold for the entire image is not sufficient for a correct binarization. For this reason, the *local threshold* technique changes *t* locally, by adapting its value to the average local intensity. In the specific case of fingerprint images, which are sometimes of very poor quality, a local threshold method cannot always guarantee acceptable results and more effective fingerprint-specific solutions are necessary. In the rest of this section, the commonly used binarization methods used for fingerprints are briefly summarized.

The FBI "minutiae reader" designed by Stock and Swonger (1969) (see also Stock, 1977) binarizes the image through a composite approach based on a local threshold and a "slit comparison" formula that compares pixel alignment along eight discrete directions. In fact, it is observed that for each pixel that belongs to a ridge line, there exists an orientation (the ridge line orientation) whose average local intensity is higher than those of the remaining orientations (which cross different ridges and valleys).

Moayer and Fu (1986) proposed a binarization technique based on an iterative application of a Laplacian operator and a pair of dynamic thresholds. At each iteration, the image is convolved through a Laplacian operator and the pixels whose intensity lies outside the range bounded by the two thresholds are set to 0 and 1, respectively. The thresholds are progressively moved towards a unique value so that a guaranteed convergence is obtained. A similar method was proposed by Xiao and Raafat (1991a, b) who, after the convolution step, employed a local threshold to deal with regions with different contrast.

A fuzzy approach to image enhancement proposed by Verma, Majumdar, and Chatterjee (1987) that uses an adaptive threshold to preserve the same number of 1 and 0 pixels for each neighborhood forms the basis of their binarization technique. The image is initially partitioned in small regions and each region is processed separately. Each region is submitted to the following steps: smoothing, fuzzy coding of the pixel intensities, contrast enhancement, binarization, 1s and 0s counting, fuzzy decoding, and parameter adjusting. This sequence is repeated until the number of 1s approximately equals the number of 0s.

Coetzee and Botha (1993) presented a binarization technique based on the use of edges in conjunction with the gray-scale image. Edge extraction is performed by using the standard Marr and Hildreth (1980) algorithm. Then, the ridges are tracked by two local windows: one in the gray-scale image and the other in the edge image; in the gray-scale domain, the binarization is performed with a local threshold, whereas in the edge-image, a blob-coloring routine is used to fill the area delimited by the two ridge edges. The resulting binary image is the logical OR of the two individual binary images.

Ratha, Chen, and Jain (1995) introduced a binarization approach based on peak detection in the gray-level profiles along sections orthogonal to the ridge orientation (see Figure 3.40). A 16×16 oriented window is centered around each pixel $[x, y]$. The gray-level profile is obtained by projection of the pixel intensities onto the central section. The profile is smoothed through local averaging; the peaks and the two neighboring pixels on either side of each peak constitute the foreground of the resulting binary image (see Figure 3.41).

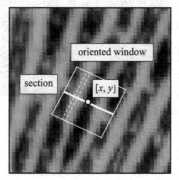
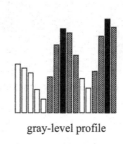

gray-level profile

Figure 3.40. An example of a gray-level profile obtained through projection of pixel intensities on the segment centered at $[x,y]$ and normal to the local ridge orientation θ_{xy}.

Sherstinsky and Picard (1996) designed a method for fingerprint binarization that employs a dynamic non-linear system called "M–lattice." This method is based on the reaction-diffusion model first proposed by Turing in 1952 to explain the formation of texture patterns such as zebra stripes.

Domeniconi, Tari, and Liang (1998) modeled fingerprint ridges and valleys as sequences of local maxima and saddle points. Maxima and saddle points are detected by evaluating the gradient ∇ and the Hessian matrix $\mathbf{H}$ at each point. The Hessian of a two-dimensional surface $S(x, y)$ is a 2×2 symmetric matrix whose elements are the second-order derivatives of S with respect to x^2, xy, and y^2. The eigenvectors of $\mathbf{H}$ are the directions along which the curvature of S is extremized. Let $\mathbf{p}$ be a stationary point (i.e., a point such that ∇ in $\mathbf{p}$ is $\mathbf{0}$) and let λ_1 and λ_2 be the eigenvalues of $\mathbf{H}$ in $\mathbf{p}$. Then $\mathbf{p}$ is a local maximum if $\lambda_1 \leq \lambda_2 < 0$ and is a saddle point if $(\lambda_1 \cdot \lambda_2) < 0$. Since ridges may gradually change their intensity values along the ridge direction, causing the surface to have either positive or negative slope, the algorithm also considers non-stationary points $\mathbf{p}$ such that the gradient directions φ_1 and φ_2 at two neighboring points $\mathbf{p}_1$ and $\mathbf{p}_2$ (located along the normal to the ridge) face each other: $angle(\varphi_1, \varphi_2) \cong 180°$. The authors also proposed an edge-linking algorithm to connect the ridge pixels detected in the first stage.

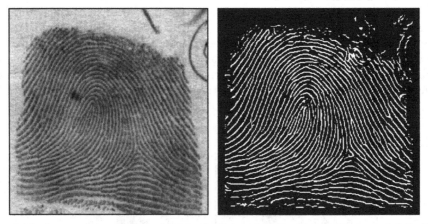

Figure 3.41. An example of fingerprint binarization using the Ratha, Chen, and Jain (1995) method. © Elsevier.

A slightly different topological approach was proposed by Tico and Kuosmanen (1999a) who treated a fingerprint image as a noisy sampling of the underlying continuous surface (Figure 3.8) and approximated it by orthogonal Chebyshev polynomials. Ridge and valley regions are discriminated by the sign of the maximal normal curvature of this continuous surface (Wang and Pavlidis, 1993). The maximal normal curvature along a given direction $\mathbf{d}$ may be computed as $\mathbf{d}^T \mathbf{H} \mathbf{d}$, where $\mathbf{H}$ is the Hessian matrix; this means that the second-order derivatives have to be estimated at each point.

Other binarization approaches can be found in Abutaleb and Kamel (1999), Govindaraju, Shi, and Schneider (2003), Mieloch, Mihailescu, and Munk (2005) and Zhang and Xiao (2006).

Most of the enhancement algorithms based on contextual filtering (discussed in Section 3.6.2) may produce a clear binary image for appropriately chosen parameters. In any case, even when the output of the contextual filtering is a gray-scale image, a simple local thresholding technique often results in satisfactory binarization. Examples of binary images obtained through the O'Gorman and Nickerson (1989) approach are shown in Figures 3.39b and 3.42a. Analogous results may be obtained through the contextual filtering techniques proposed by Donahue and Rokhlin (1993), Mehtre (1993), Sherlock, Monro, and Millard (1992, 1994), Watson, Candela, and Grother (1994) and Hong, Wan, and Jain (1998). Figure 3.42 shows the results obtained by binarizing a portion of a good quality fingerprint image through some of the methods described in this section; contextual filtering-based methods (a) and (d) produced the most regular binary ridge patterns.

Minutiae detection from binary images is usually performed after an intermediate thinning step that reduces the width of the ridges to one pixel. Unfortunately, thinning algorithms are rather critical and the aberrations and irregularity of the binary-ridge boundaries have an adverse effect on the *skeletons* (i.e., the one-pixel-width ridge structure), resulting in "hairy" growths (spikes) that lead to the detection of spurious minutiae. With the aim of improving the quality of the binary images before the thinning step, some researchers have introduced regularization techniques which usually work by filling holes (see Figure 3.43), removing small breaks, eliminating bridges between ridges, and other artifacts. For this purpose, Coetzee and Botha (1993) identify holes and gaps by tracking the ridge line edges through adaptive windows and removing them using a simple blob-coloring algorithm. Hung (1993) uses an adaptive filtering technique to equalize the width of the ridges; narrow ridges in under-saturated regions are expanded and thick ridges in over-saturated regions are shrunk. Wahab, Chin, and Tan (1998) correct the binary image at locations where orientation estimates deviate from their neighboring estimates. This correction is performed by substituting the noisy pixels according to some oriented templates. Luo and Tian (2000) implement a two-step method, where the skeleton extracted at the end of the first step is used to improve the quality of the binary image based on a set of structural rules; a new skeleton is then extracted from the improved binary image.

Mathematical morphology (Gonzales and Woods, 2007) is a powerful and elegant tool of digital topology that allows a regularization of the shape of binary objects. Some authors propose morphology-based techniques for regularizing binary fingerprint images:

- Fitz and Green's (1996) and Ikeda et al. (2002) remove small lines and dots both in the ridges and valleys of binary images through the application of morphological operators.
- To remove the spikes that often characterize the thinned binary images, Ratha, Chen, and Jain (1995) implement a morphological "open" operator whose structuring element is a small box oriented according to the local ridge orientation.

- Liang and Asano (2006a) recommend using Generalized Morphology Operators (GMO) that may increase the robustness of the algorithms to noise and small intrusions, especially when medium size structuring elements are used. An efficient implementation of GMO-based techniques for removing salt and pepper noise and small islands is proposed based on the distance transform (Gonzales and Woods, 2007) and the integral image (Viola and Jones, 2001).

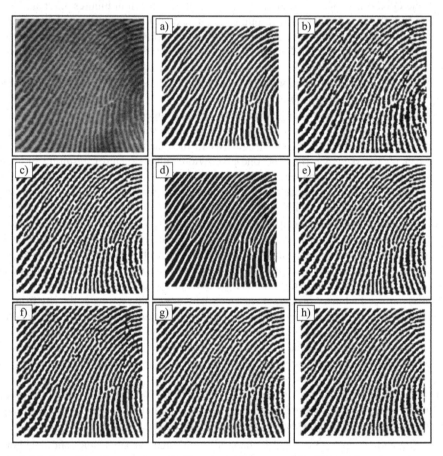

Figure 3.42. A portion of a good quality fingerprint image and its binarization through some of the methods discussed in this section: a) O'Gorman and Nickerson (1989); b) Verma, Majumdar, and Chatterjee (1987); c) local threshold approach; d) Sherlock, Monro, and Millard (1994); e) Xiao and Raafat (1991b); f) Moayer and Fu (1986); g) Stock and Swonger (1969); h) Watson, Candela, and Grother (1994).

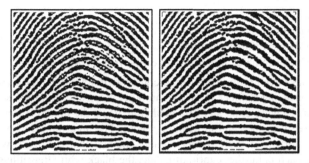

Figure 3.43. The result of eliminating small holes from both the ridges and valleys of the binary image; input image is shown on the left and the output is shown on the right. The filtering is performed by computing the connected components of the image and by removing the components whose area (number of pixels) is smaller than a given threshold.

As far as thinning techniques are concerned (Lam, Lee, and Suen, 1992), a large number of approaches are available in the literature due to the central role of this processing step in many pattern recognition applications: character recognition, document analysis, and map and drawing vectorization. Hung (1993) used the algorithm by Arcelli and Baja (1984); Ratha, Chen, and Jain (1995) adopted a technique included in the HIPS library (Landy, Cohen, and Sperling, 1984), Mehtre (1993) employed the parallel algorithm described in Tamura (1978) and Coetzee and Botha (1993) used the method by Baruch (1988). In Ji et al. (2007) the skeleton is computed through a constrained PCNN (Pulse Coupled Neural Network) where the orientation image is used to constrain the thinning direction of PCNN thus allowing to reduce bothersome artifacts such as the short spikes that conventional thinning algorithms often produce. Sudiro, Paindavoine, and Kusuma (2007) noted that in the binarized image, valleys are often thinner than ridges, and since the time taken by a thinning algorithm increases with the initial thickness of the objects, they propose extracting minutiae from valleys to reduce the computation time.

Once a binary skeleton has been obtained, a simple image scan allows the pixels corresponding to minutiae to be detected according to the ANSI/NIST-ITL 1 (2007) coordinate models shown in Figure 3.5: in fact the pixels corresponding to minutiae are characterized by a *crossing number* different from 2. The crossing number $cn(\mathbf{p})$ of a pixel $\mathbf{p}$ in a binary image is defined (Arcelli and Baja, 1984) as half the sum of the differences between pairs of adjacent pixels in the 8-neighborhood of $\mathbf{p}$:

$$cn(\mathbf{p}) = \frac{1}{2} \sum_{i=1\ldots8} \left| val(\mathbf{p}_{i \bmod 8}) - val(\mathbf{p}_{i-1}) \right|,$$

where $\mathbf{p}_0$, $\mathbf{p}_1$, ...$\mathbf{p}_7$ are the pixels belonging to an ordered sequence of pixels defining the eight-neighborhood of $\mathbf{p}$ and $val(\mathbf{p}) \in \{0,1\}$ is the pixel value. It is simple to note (Figure 3.44) that a pixel $\mathbf{p}$ with $val(\mathbf{p}) = 1$:

- Is an intermediate ridge point if $cn(\mathbf{p}) = 2$.
- Corresponds to a ridge ending minutia if $cn(\mathbf{p}) = 1$.
- Corresponds to a bifurcation minutia if $cn(\mathbf{p}) = 3$.
- Defines a more complex minutia (e.g., crossover) if $cn(\mathbf{p}) > 3$.

Some techniques have been proposed in the literature to extract minutiae from binary images without using the crossing number to check the pixel connectivity on the skeleton resulting from a thinning step: Leung et al.'s (1991) method extracts the minutiae from thinned binary images using a three-layer perceptron neural network. The algorithm by Gamassi, Piuri, and Scotti (2005) is a variant of the crossing number method that can work with thick binary ridges: in fact, for each point the algorithm counts the black-white transitions along a square path centered at that point and large enough to touch two ridges. Approaches by Weber (1992), Govindaraju, Shi, and Schneider (2003) and Shi and Govindaraju (2006) work on thick binary ridges and exploit special ridge tracking algorithms. Shin, Hwang, and Chien (2006) encode thick binary ridges with Run Length Code (RLC), and extract minutiae by searching for the termination or bifurcation points of ridges in the RLC. Miao, Tang, and Fu (2007) encode the skeleton by means of principal curves extracted through the principal graph algorithms; principal curves are self-consistent smooth curves that are suitable to approximate noisy data. Finally, the foundation of the method developed by Székely and Székely (1993) lies in the use of a divergence operator capable of discerning fingerprint pattern discontinuities that correspond to minutiae.

Minutiae direction θ (see Figure 3.5), in addition to the minutiae coordinates, is used by most of the matching algorithms, to enforce minutiae pairing. A simple way to determine the minutiae direction is to start from the local ridge orientation at the minutia origin and to convert this orientation into a direction (i.e., deciding the quadrant) by looking at the departing ridge(s).

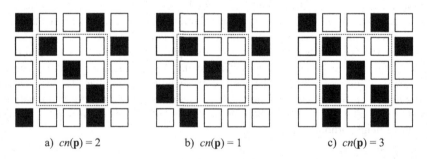

a) $cn(\mathbf{p}) = 2$ b) $cn(\mathbf{p}) = 1$ c) $cn(\mathbf{p}) = 3$

Figure 3.44. a) intra-ridge pixel; b) ridge ending minutia; c) bifurcation minutia.

3.7.2 Direct gray-scale extraction

With the aim of overcoming some of the problems related to fingerprint image binarization and thinning (e.g., the presence of spurious minutiae in the case of irregular ridge edges), some authors have proposed direct gray-scale extraction methods.

Maio and Maltoni (1997) proposed a direct gray-scale minutiae extraction technique, whose basic idea is to track the ridge lines in the gray-scale image, by "sailing" according to the local orientation of the ridge pattern. From a mathematical point of view, a ridge line is defined as a set of points that are local maxima along one direction. The ridge line extraction algorithm attempts to locate, at each step, a local maximum relative to a section orthogonal to the ridge direction. By connecting the consecutive maxima, a polygonal approximation of the ridge line can be obtained.

Given a starting point $[x_c, y_c]$ and a starting direction θ_c, the *ridge line following* algorithm (see Figure 3.45) computes a new point $[x_t, y_t]$ at each step by moving μ pixels from the current point $[x_c, y_c]$ along direction θ_c. Then it computes the *section set* Ω as the set of points belonging to the section segment lying on the xy-plane with a median point $[x_t, y_t]$, direction orthogonal to θ_c and length $2\sigma + 1$. A new point $[x_n, y_n]$, belonging to the ridge line, is chosen among the local maxima of an enhanced version of the set Ω. The point $[x_n, y_n]$ becomes the current point $[x_c, y_c]$ and a new direction θ_c is computed (Figure 3.45).

The optimal value of the parameters μ and σ can be determined according to the average thickness of the ridge lines. The algorithm runs until one of the four stopping criteria becomes true. In particular, when a ridge line terminates or intersects another ridge line (location of a minutia), the algorithm stops and returns the characteristics (type, coordinates and direction) of the detected minutia. The ridge line following algorithm extracts a ridge line, given a starting point and a direction. By exploiting such an algorithm, it is possible to define a schema for extracting all the ridge lines in an image and, consequently, detect all the minutiae. The main problems arise from the difficulty of examining each ridge line only once and locating the intersections with the ridge lines already extracted. For this purpose, an auxiliary image $\mathbf{T}$ of the same dimension as $\mathbf{I}$ is used. $\mathbf{T}$ is initialized by setting its pixel values to 0; each time a new ridge line is extracted from $\mathbf{I}$, the pixels of $\mathbf{T}$ corresponding to the ridge line are labeled. The pixels of $\mathbf{T}$ corresponding to a ridge line are the pixels belonging to the ε-pixel thick polygonal chain, which links the consecutive maximum points $[x_n, y_n]$ located by the ridge line following algorithm (Figure 3.46).

Let $\mathbf{G}$ be a regular square-meshed grid superimposed on the image $\mathbf{I}$. For each node of $\mathbf{G}$, the minutiae detection algorithm searches the nearest ridge line and tracks it by means of the ridge line following routine. Because the initial point can be anywhere in the middle of a ridge line, the tracking is executed alternately in both directions. The auxiliary image $\mathbf{T}$, which is updated after each ridge line following, provides a simple and effective way to discover ridge line intersections and to avoid multiple trackings.

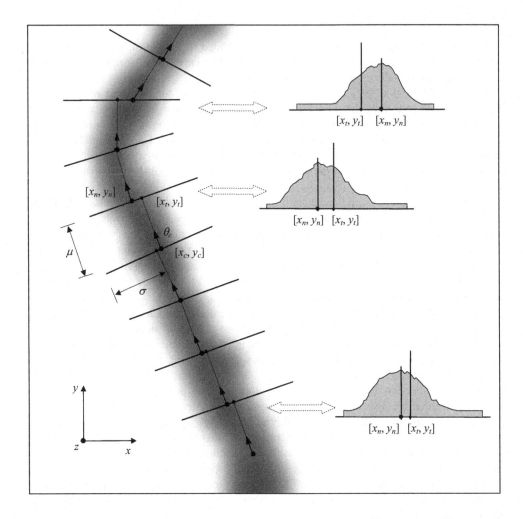

Figure 3.45. Some ridge line following steps (Maio and Maltoni, 1997). On the right, some sections of the ridge line are shown. © IEEE.

Figure 3.47 shows the results obtained by applying the minutiae detection algorithm to a sample fingerprint. Maio and Maltoni (1997) compared their method with four binarization thinning-based approaches and concluded that direct gray-scale extraction can significantly reduce processing time as well as the number of spurious minutiae resulting from thinning algorithms.

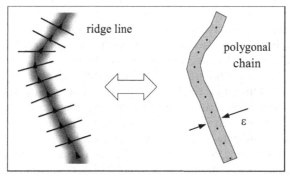

Figure 3.46. A ridge line and the corresponding ε-pixel thick polygonal chain (Maio and Maltoni, 1997). © IEEE.

Figure 3.47. Minutiae detection on a sample fingerprint by using the Maio and Maltoni (1997) method. Contextual filtering is performed on "touched" pixels during ridge line following. The ridge lines are represented through the corresponding polylines of **T**. Ridge ending minutiae are denoted by gray boxes and bifurcation minutiae are denoted by black boxes.

Jiang, Yau, and Ser (1999, 2001) proposed a variant of the Maio and Maltoni (1997) method, where the ridge following step μ is dynamically adapted to the change of ridge contrast and bending level. Referring to Figure 3.45, a long step is executed if there is little variation in the gray-level intensity along the segment $[x_c, y_c]$ $[x_t, y_t]$, and the ridge bending is low. On the other hand, high bending level of the ridge (possibly facing a ridge bifurcation) or large intensity variations (possibly facing a ridge ending) will result in a short step. Using a dynamic step speeds up the tracing while maintaining good precision.

Liu, Huang, and Chan (2000) introduced another modification of the Maio and Maltoni (1997) method. Instead of tracking a single ridge, the algorithm simultaneously tracks a central ridge and the two surrounding valleys. For this purpose, they search a central maximum and two adjacent minima in each section Ω. Minutiae are detected where the configuration < minimum, maximum, minimum > is no longer valid. Here too, the ridge following step μ is dynamically adjusted according to the distances between lateral minima from the central maximum. This approach does not need an a priori setting of some parameters such as the maximum bending angle (which determines a stopping criterion in the original algorithm) and the step value μ.

The Chang and Fan (2001) approach is aimed at discriminating the true ridge maxima in the sections Ω obtained during ridge line following. Two thresholds are initially determined based on the gray-level histogram decomposition. The histogram is modeled as a sum of three Gaussian contributions associated with the background, valleys, and ridges, respectively. The mean, variance, and probability of each Gaussian is estimated and two thresholds are derived for successive characterization of maxima and minima of the section Ω. A set of rules is employed to discriminate real ridge points from background noise and intra-ridge variations.

Finally, an efficient integer-arithmetic version of Maio and Maltoni (1997) algorithm has been developed by Canyellas et al. (2005) whose main aim was to port it to low cost hardware.

Minutiae extraction from gray-scale images is not necessarily based on ridge-line tracking. In fact, the presence of a minutia in local windows can be checked through a classifier:

- Leung, Engeler, and Frank (1990) and Wahab, Tan, and Jonatan (2004) introduced neural network-based approaches. In Leung, Engeler, and Frank (1990) a multi-layer perceptron analyzes the output of a rank of Gabor filters applied to the gray-scale image. The image is first transformed into the frequency domain where the filtering takes place; the resultant magnitude and phase signals constitute the input to a neural network composed of six sub-networks, each of which is responsible for detecting minutiae at a specific orientation; a final classifier is employed to combine the intermediate responses.

- Nilsson and Bigun (2001) proposed using Linear Symmetry (LS) properties computed by spatial filtering (Bigun and Granlund, 1987) via separable Gaussian filters and Gaussian derivative filters. Minutiae are identified in the gray-scale image as points characterized by the lack of symmetry. In fact, whereas a non-minutia point is characterized by a direction (i.e., the minutiae angle) along which an infinitesimal translation leaves the pattern least variant, minutiae are local discontinuities in the LS vector field.

- Fronthaler, Kollreider, and Bigun (2008) used both Linear Symmetry (LS) and Parabolic Symmetry (PS) to detect minutiae. Near a minutia point the response to a parabolic symmetry filter is high while the response to a linear symmetry filter is low: hence, the expression PS·(1−|LS|) allows to detect minutiae more reliably than PS or LS alone. Figure 3.48 shows an example.

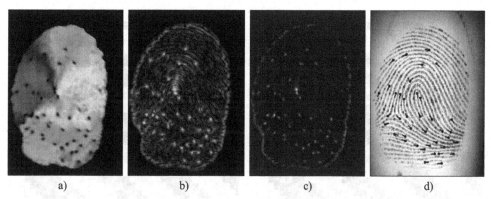

Figure 3.48. Application of the minutiae detection method proposed by Fronthaler, Kollreider, and Bigun (2008) to the fingerprint image d). a) Linear Simmetry (LS), b) Parabolic Symmetry (PS), c) PS·(1−|LS|), d) minutiae detected as local maxima of c) superimposed to the original fingerprint image. Images courtesy of J. Bigun.

Bolle et al. (2002) addressed the problem of precisely and consistently locating the minutiae points in the gray-scale fingerprint pattern. In fact, different feature extraction algorithms tend to locate the minutiae at slightly different positions (depending on their operational definition of minutia and the intermediate processing steps) and this may lead to interoperability problems. Bolle et al. (2002) provided a formal definition of minutia based on the gray-scale image that allows the location and orientation of an existing minutia to be more precisely determined. However, this approach is ignored by current standards that usually define the minutiae location on the basis of binary skeletons as discussed in the following subsection.

3.7.3 Minutiae encoding standards

Standards have been introduced to define the way minutiae information should be encoded. Unfortunately, the simple minutiae coordinate model adopted by ANSI/NIST-ITL 1 (2007) is different from those adopted by other standards such as ANSI/INCITS 378 (2004), ISO/IEC 19794-2 (2005) and CDEFFS (2008), see Figure 3.49. For example, ISO/IEC 19794-2 (2005) requires to extract both the ridge and the valley skeletons and to place: (i) bifurcation minutiae in correspondence with the ridge skeleton bifurcations (i.e., pixels **p** with $cn(\mathbf{p}) = 3$), and (ii) ridge ending minutiae in correspondence with the valley skeleton bifurcations (this exploits the ridge-ending/bifurcation duality shown in Figure 3.6); the minutia direction θ is computed in both the cases (ridge ending and bifurcation) as the bisector of the two angularly closest branches departing from **p**.

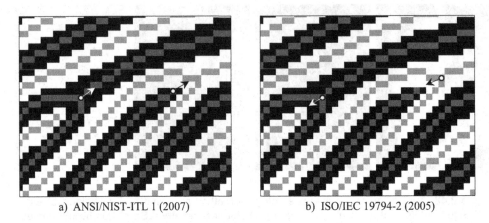

a) ANSI/NIST-ITL 1 (2007)   b) ISO/IEC 19794-2 (2005)

Figure 3.49. In the figure ridges are black, valleys are white and ridge and valley skeletons are gray. a) ridge-ending (black arrow) and bifurcation (white arrow) placement on ridge skeleton according to ANSI/NIST-ITL 1 (2007); b) ridge-ending (black arrow) placement on valley skeleton and bifurcation (white arrow) placement on ridge skeleton according to ISO/IEC 19794-2 (2005); note that the direction of the minutiae in ANSI/NIST-ITL 1 (2007) and ISO/IEC 19794-2 (2005) is opposite to each other and the placement of ridge-ending is slightly different.

The main aim of the standards is to achieve interoperability among minutiae templates extracted by different approaches and so for this purpose clear and unambiguous rules should be given; unfortunately none of the current standards is sufficiently clear and exhaustive and new efforts are being made to improve them. The interoperability evaluation conducted in the MINEX (Grother et al. (2006); Wu and Garris (2007)) and MTIT (Bazin and Mansfield, 2007) projects have clearly pointed out such limits. The main problems are:

- Minutiae position is often defined resorting to the skeleton of a binary fingerprint image, but the skeleton itself depends on enhancement, binarization and thinning algorithms.
- Some criteria are given to validate minutiae and filter out spurious minutiae (e.g., if one of the branches departing from a minutia cannot be tracked for more than a given

length, then the minutia is invalid), but the iterative unordered application of these rules can also lead to unintended deletion of valid minutiae.
- No specific rules are given to define how to deal with very noisy regions and with high curvature regions (i.e., singularities) where minutiae tend to cluster.

3.8 Minutiae Filtering

A post-processing stage is often useful in removing the spurious minutiae detected in highly corrupted fingerprint regions or introduced by preceding processing steps (e.g., thinning). Two main post-processing types have been proposed:
- Structural post-processing
- Minutiae filtering in the gray-scale domain

3.8.1 Structural post-processing

Simple structural rules may be used to detect many of the false minutiae that usually affect thinned binary fingerprint images. Xiao and Raafat (1991b) identified the most common false minutiae structures and introduced an ad hoc approach to remove them (Figure 3.50). Their algorithm is rule-based and requires some numerical characteristics associated with the minutiae as input: the length of the associated ridge(s), the minutia angle, and the number of facing minutiae in a neighborhood. As shown in Figure 3.50, the algorithm connects facing endpoints (a), (b), removes bifurcations facing with endpoints (c) or with other bifurcations (d), and removes spurs (e), bridges (f), triangles (g), and ladder structures (h).

Hung (1993) and Zhao and Tang (2007) exploited the minutiae duality (Figure 3.6) to purify false minutiae extracted from binary thinned images.
- In Hung (1993) both ridge and valley skeletons are extracted and only ridge minutiae having a counterpart (of complementary type) in the valley skeleton are retained. A graph is defined for both ridge and valley skeletons by assigning a vertex to each ridge ending and bifurcation and by assigning an edge to each ridge. Each edge is characterized by the length of the corresponding ridge, and the degree of a vertex is given by the number of converging edges. Spurs (i.e., very short edges) and holes (i.e., loops with a very small diameter) are first removed by considering some property of the ridge graph. Bridges between adjacent ridges are then removed by exploiting their relation with breaks in the dual space.
- Zhao and Tang (2007) argue that for most of the false minutiae there is at least a bridge structure: referring to Figure 3.50 this is true for bridges (f), triangles (g) and ladders (h) in the ridge skeleton but also for breaks (a) in the valley skeleton. An H-point is defined as a bridge structure in one of the two (ridge or valley) skeletons and its corresponding break in the dual skeleton; a simple rule is then defined to detect

and remove H-points thereby eliminating many false minutiae. However, to avoid cancellation of genuine structures the H-point removal must be embedded within an ordered sequence of deletion steps: short breaks, spurs, H-points, close minutiae and border minutiae.

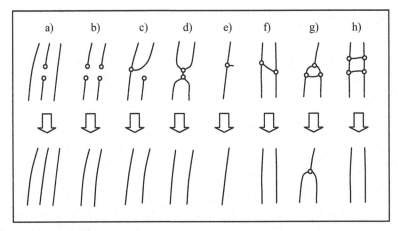

Figure 3.50. The most common false-minutiae structures (on the top row) and the structural changes resulting from their removal (bottom row).

In the approach by Farina, Kovacs-Vajna, and Leone (1999) spurs and bridges are removed based on the observation that in a "spurious" bifurcation, only two branches are generally aligned whereas the third one is almost orthogonal to the other two. Short ridges are removed on the basis of the relationship between the ridge length and the average distance between ridges. Ridge endings and bifurcations are then topologically validated; they are: (i) removed if topological requirements are not satisfied; (ii) classified as less reliable if the requirements are not fully satisfied; (iii) considered as highly reliable minutiae, otherwise. An example is shown in Figure 3.51.

A slightly different implementation of spurious minutiae removal was proposed by Kim, Lee, and Kim (2001). In their work, local orientation and flow of ridges are key factors for post-processing to avoid eliminating true minutiae. Bhowmick et al. (2002) assign a score to each minutia based on clarity of ridge and valley flow and the noise level in the locality of the minutia; Kim (2005) and Chen, Chan, and Moon (2007) also assign scores to the minutiae based on local ridge connectivity, interspacing and symmetry. The scores can then be used either for immediate filtering or minutiae weighting during matching.

The filtering method of Bhanu, Boshra, and Tan (2000) verifies each minutia, detected from the thinned binary image, through correlation with logical templates (i.e., template matching) adapted to the local ridge orientation. In Bhanu and Tan (2001b), an evolution of the above method is proposed where templates are not static, but are learned in a supervised manner from examples.

3.8.2 Minutiae filtering in the gray-scale domain

A direct gray-scale minutiae filtering technique reexamines the gray-scale image in the spatial neighborhood of a detected minutia with the aim of verifying the presence of a real minutia.

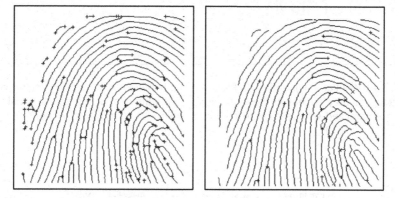

Figure 3.51. Minutiae post-processing according to Farina, Kovacs-Vajna, and Leone (1999). On the right, most of the false minutiae present in the thinned binary image (on the left) have been removed. © Elsevier.

Maio and Maltoni (1998b) used a shared-weights neural network to verify the minutiae detected by their gray-scale algorithm (Maio and Maltoni, 1997). The minutiae neighborhoods in the original gray-scale image are normalized, with respect to their angle and the local ridge frequency, before passing them to a neural network classifier, which classifies them as ridge ending, bifurcation, and non-minutia. Figure 3.52b shows the same minutiae neighborhoods of Figure 3.52a after the normalization. To take advantage of the ridge-ending/bifurcation duality, both the original neighborhood and its negative version constitute the input to the neural network classifier. Additionally, to avoid the problems related to training large networks, the dimensionality of the normalized neighborhoods is reduced through the Karhunen–Loeve transform (Jolliffe, 1986). A typical three-layer neural network architecture has been adopted, where a partial weight sharing allows the ridge-ending/bifurcation duality to be exploited (Figure 3.53). In fact, the weight sharing requires the same type of processing to be performed by the first layer of neurons both on the positive and the negative neighborhoods. This network has more degrees of freedom with respect to a three-layer (26–10–2) perceptron trained both on the positive and the negative versions of the same neighborhood, and used twice for each classification.

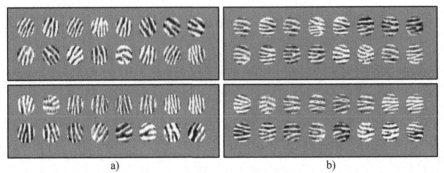

a)   b)

Figure 3.52. a) Minutiae neighborhoods (ridge ending minutiae at the top, bifurcation minutiae at the bottom) as they appear in the original gray-scale images; b) the same neighborhoods have been normalized with respect to minutiae angle and local ridge frequency (Maio and Maltoni, 1998b). © IEEE.

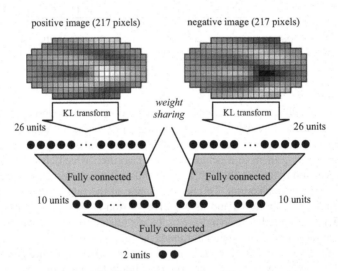

Figure 3.53. The neural network architecture to classify gray-scale minutiae neighborhoods into ridge ending, bifurcation, and non-minutiae (Maio and Maltoni, 1998b). © IEEE.

In this case, both the positive and negative images convey contemporary information to the third layer, which acts as the final decision maker. Experimental results showed that this filtering method, in spite of a certain increase in missed minutiae, provides significant reduction in false minutiae and misclassified minutiae (i.e., a ridge ending detected as bifurcation and vice versa) errors.

The minutiae verifier of Prabhakar, Jain, and Pankanti (2003) operates on the gray-scale neighborhoods extracted from the original image after enhancement through Gabor filtering (Hong, Wan, and Jain, 1998). Minutiae neighborhoods are normalized with respect to minutiae angle and local ridge frequency. The resulting patterns are classified through a Learning Vector Quantizer (Kohonen et al., 1992) trained in a supervised fashion to discriminate between minutiae and non-minutiae. The authors obtained a classification accuracy of 87% and a reduction of about 4% fingerprint matching error when their minutiae verification algorithm was embedded into the minutiae-based fingerprint verification system described in Jain et al. (1997).

Chikkerur et al. (2005) proposed two minutiae verifiers:

- First one is based on the response of the minutiae neighborhood to a bank of steerable wedge filters. The response is fed to a feedforward back propagation network to classify the inputs as either minutiae or non minutiae neighborhood.
- Second (and more accurate) one encodes the minutiae neighborhoods as a linear sum of basis images made up of multi-resolution Gabor elementary functions. A parametric Bayesian classification is then applied. The authors report minutiae verification accuracy of 98%.

3.9 Estimation of Ridge Count

Absolute position, direction, and type of minutiae (e.g., ridge ending or bifurcation) are not the only features that may be used for fingerprint recognition. In fact, forensic experts and latent fingerprint examiners have often used *ridge count* to increase the reliability of their analysis (Henry, 1900). Ridge count is an abstract measurement of the distances between any two points in a fingerprint image (Lin and Dubes, 1983). Let **a** and **b** be two points in a fingerprint; then the ridge count between **a** and **b** is the number of ridges intersected by segment **ab** (Figure 3.54).

Ridge count has been typically used in forensic matching because of the difficulty of human experts to work in the Euclidean space. However, because the early automatic systems were developed from an intuitive design geared towards duplicating the performance of human experts in matching fingerprints, ridge counts have been used in the AFIS systems. With an increased interest in improving the performance of fingerprint recognition systems in commercial applications, several authors have proposed ridge counts as features.

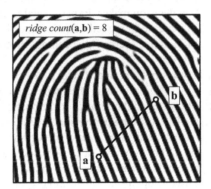

Figure 3.54. In this example the number of ridges intersected by segment **ab** (ridge count between **a** and **b**) is 8.

Although the general definition of ridge count includes measuring the number of ridges between any two points in the fingerprint images, typically, **a** and **b** (refer to Figure 3.54) coincide with some well defined points in the fingerprint pattern (e.g., position of the singularities or position of the minutiae). For example, in forensic AFIS it is common to count the ridges between core and delta.

There exist two main approaches for counting the number of ridges between points **a** and **b** in a fingerprint image:

- Determine the number of (0–1) transitions along the segment **ab** in a binarized image.
- Determine the number of local maxima in the section **ab** of a gray-scale image. Refer to the x-signature method (Figure 3.14) for an example of a possible implementation.

In both cases, the estimation of ridge count may be problematic in noisy areas, near singularities, near minutiae, and when the segment orientation is close to the underlying ridge orientation. Sha, Zhao, and Tang (2006) suggest using only a subset of highly reliable ridge-counts and propose a labeling-based algorithm for their extraction. Kovacs-Vajna (2000) matched the ridge profiles between pairs of minutiae using the dynamic time warping technique. This method is conceptually similar to ridge counting, even if it cannot be directly used to estimate the ridge count but only to verify that the ridge–valley profiles between two pairs of corresponding points are similar.

3.10 Estimation of Fingerprint Quality

Many different meanings could be associated with the term quality. However, most of the researchers have focused only on the *operational* definition of quality, that is, estimate of quality must be predictive of the utility of features and/or "matchability" of the fingerprint images.

In general, fingerprint quality can be estimated at a *global* level (i.e., a single quality value is derived for the whole image) or at a *local* level (i.e., a distinct value is estimated for each block/pixel of the image). Of course the availability of local estimates is preferable since it is more descriptive and in any case, one could compute the global quality from the statistics of the local estimates. Estimating fingerprint quality is important since it enables:

- To reject very low-quality samples during enrollment or/and to select the best sample(s).
- To isolate unrecoverable regions (see Section 3.6) where fingerprint enhancement is counterproductive as it leads to the detection of several spurious features.
- To adapt the matching strategy to the quality of fingerprints.
- To assign weights to features (at matching stage) according to the quality.

Some studies (Young and Elliott, 2007) have shown that, on the average, (i) fingerprint images from index and middle fingers exhibit better quality than images taken from ring and little fingers; (ii) Whorl is the fingerprint class containing the largest proportion of good quality fingerprint images, whereas Arch is at the opposite side of quality scale. This knowledge, when available, could be useful as a prior probability to quality estimation approaches.

In the following, a brief summary of the existing global and local approaches for estimating fingerprint image quality is reported. A more comprehensive (and comparative) review can be found in Alonso-Fernandez et al. (2007).

3.10.1 Global quality estimation

The most popular approach to estimate global fingerprint quality has been proposed by Tabassi, Wilson, and Watson (2004) and is known as NFIQ (NIST Fingerprint Image Quality). NFIQ defines the quality as a prediction of a matcher performance: good quality fingerprints are likely to produce high match scores. An important advantage of this method is that it does not require a ground truth provided by a human expert; in fact, defining the ground truth by visual inspection is quite complicated, could lead to subjective evaluations, and is not necessarily the best approach when the focus is on automatic matching algorithms. Let T be a training set containing n fingers and a pair of image samples (x_i, x_i') for each finger $i = 1...n$. The normalized matching score of x_i is defined according to the separation of the x_i genuine matching score from the x_i impostor scores:

$$normscore(x_i) = \frac{score(x_i, x_i') - avg_{j=1...n, j \neq i}(score(x_i, x_j))}{stdev_{j=1...n, j \neq i}(score(x_i, x_j))},$$

where $score(a, b)$ returns the matching score between the two fingerprints a and b according to a given automatic matcher, $avg()$ is the average value and $stdev()$ the standard deviation. The quality $q(x_i)$ of fingerprint image x_i is then defined as the prediction of its normalized matching score $normscore(x_i)$. Given a feature vector $\mathbf{v}_i$ extracted from x_i, a mapping between $\mathbf{v}_i$ and $q(x_i)$ can be found by regression over T by considering the pairs $<\mathbf{v}_i, normscore(x_i) >$, $i = 1...n$. Tabassi, Wilson, and Watson (2004) preferred to formulate the problem as a classification problem (instead of as a regression problem) in order to quantize the fingerprint quality into just 5 values; to this purpose a neural network classifier is trained to classify the feature vector into one of the five predefined quality classes (where class 1 means top quality and class five the worst quality). Each feature vector is constituted by 11 features as reported in Table 3.1. To extract these features, the method calculates a quality map of the foreground according to the consistency of local orientation, the local contrast and the curvature. Minutiae detection is then performed and the reliability of each detected minutia point is computed according to simple pixel intensity statistics (mean and standard deviation) within the immediate neighborhood of the minutia point. The minutiae reliability is then combined with the local quality at the minutiae location (from the quality map) to produce a quality measure for each minutia.

Number	Feature
1	number of blocks that have quality 1 or better
2	number of total minutiae found in the fingerprint
3	number of minutiae that have quality 0.5 or better
4	number of minutiae that have quality 0.6 or better
5	number of minutiae that have quality 0.75 or better
6	number of minutiae that have quality 0.8 or better
7	number of minutiae that have quality 0.9 or better
8	percentage of the foreground blocks of quality map with quality = 1
9	percentage of the foreground blocks of quality map with quality = 2
10	percentage of the foreground blocks of quality map with quality = 3
11	percentage of the foreground blocks of quality map with quality = 4

Table 3.1. Features used in NFIQ

Qi et al. (2005b) combine local and global features already available in the literature, but among the global features the authors suggest taking into account the size of the foreground area, the foreground centering with respect to the image centre and the presence of detectable singularities.

A good quality fingerprint image exhibits a ring around the origin of the frequency coordinate in the Fourier spectrum, because the ridge-valley patterns are quasi-periodic structures and present a dominant frequency in most directions with an almost uniform modulus. The implementation of ad-hoc ring detectors allows an estimate of the overall fingerprint image quality: see Uchida (2004), Chen, Dass, and Jain (2005) and Lee, Moon, and Kim (2005).

3.10.2 Local quality estimation

A number of methods have been proposed to estimate block-wise fingerprint quality. Most of them estimate the local quality according to the local orientation reliability (see Section 3.2.1): Shen, Kot, and Koo (2001), Lim, Jiang, and Yau (2002), Chen, Jiang, and Yau (2004), Yao, Pankanti, and Hass (2004), Chen, Dass, and Jain (2005) and Zhu et al. (2005). The way the reliability of a single orientation is obtained depends on the orientation computation method, but is usually related to the coherence of a set of orientation estimations in a given neighborhood (see Equation (4) and Figure 3.10c). Although orientation coherence is a very powerful feature to measure quality, it fails near the singularities: in fact, singularities are characterized by high curvatures which results in low coherence (see Figure 3.22). The use of linear and parabolic symmetry operators (see Fronthaler, Kollreider, and Bigun (2006, 2008); Fronthaler et al. (2008)) overcomes this problem. In fact, the orientations in good quality regions highly correlate with: (i) linear symmetry filters outside singularities; (ii) parabolic symmetry filters near the singularities, whereas low quality regions weakly respond to both type of filters.
Other features can be used to characterize local quality:

- Statistics derived from pixel intensities (e.g., mean, variance, contrast, gradient magnitude, histogram properties, etc.) as proposed by Shi et al. (2004), Uchida (2004), Chen, Jiang, and Yau (2004), Lim et al. (2004), Hwang (2004), Qi et al. (2005a) and Zhu et al. (2005).
- Ridge frequency, ridge thickness and ridge-to-valley thickness (Lim, Jiang, and Yau, 2002; Zhu et al., 2005); a substantial deviation of these values from their typical range is alarming and can be exploited to detect unreliable regions.
- The presence of dominant frequencies in the Fourier spectrum of a local region (Lim et al., 2004) and the local resemblance to an ideal sinusoidal wave pattern in the spatial domain (Lee, Lee, and Kim, 2006).

3.11 Summary

Most of the early work in fingerprint analysis was based on general-purpose image processing techniques, and therefore the resulting matching performance was often inadequate. Subsequently, several special purpose (domain specific) algorithms have been designed for processing fingerprint images, exploiting the peculiarity of fingerprint patterns: an example is contextual enhancement. Today, fingerprint image processing and feature extraction is undoubtedly a more mature field and effective algorithms are available for most of the problems at hand: local orientation and local frequency estimation, foreground segmentation, image enhancement, singularity and minutiae extraction, etc. However, robust feature extraction in poor quality fingerprint images, particularly latent prints (lifted from the crime scenes) remains a challenging problem and the accuracy gap between a computer and human-based feature analysis remains substantial in such images. New methods for computation (or restoration) of the orientation image and the frequency image in very low-quality images are highly desirable, because these features are central for most of the successive feature extraction and matching steps. The knowledge of the global fingerprint structure and its variability has only been partially embedded into the feature extraction techniques, and modern learning-based methods, such as cascades of classifiers that proved to be very efficient and effective in other fields (see the Viola and Jones (2001) approach to face location), have not been fully evaluated to detect features in fingerprints.

For the near future we foresee two trends: (i) consolidation and emergence of some of the existent techniques from the plethora of proposed approaches. This will be facilitated by the increasing interest in comparative evaluation such as FVC-onGoing (2009) that will concentrate not only on the evaluation of the complete fingerprint verification systems but also on the assessment of feature extraction algorithms; (ii) introduction of new robust approaches that fully exploit the available domain knowledge and cues to come close to the capability of human experts, particularly for poor quality fingerprints.

4
Fingerprint Matching

4.1 Introduction

A fingerprint matching algorithm compares two given fingerprints and returns either a degree of similarity (without loss of generality, a score between 0 and 1) or a binary decision (mated/non-mated). Only a few matching algorithms operate directly on grayscale fingerprint images; most of them require that an intermediate fingerprint representation be derived through a feature extraction stage (refer to Chapter 3). Without loss of generality, hereafter we denote the representation of the fingerprint acquired during enrollment as the *template* ($\mathbf{T}$) and the representation of the fingerprint to be matched as the *input* ($\mathbf{I}$). In case no feature extraction is performed, the fingerprint representation coincides with the grayscale fingerprint image itself; hence, throughout this chapter, we denote both raw fingerprint images and fingerprint feature vectors (e.g., minutiae) with $\mathbf{T}$ and $\mathbf{I}$.

The fingerprint feature extraction and matching algorithms are usually quite similar for both fingerprint verification and identification problems. This is because the fingerprint identification problem (i.e., searching for an input fingerprint in a database of N fingerprints) can be implemented as a sequential execution of N one-to-one comparisons (verifications) between pairs of fingerprints. The fingerprint classification and indexing techniques are usually exploited to speed up the search (refer to Chapter 5) in fingerprint identification problems.

Matching fingerprint images is a very difficult problem, mainly due to the large variability in different impressions of the same finger (i.e., large *intra-class* variations). The main factors responsible for intra-class variations are summarized below.

- *Displacement*: the same finger may be placed at different locations on a touch sensor during different acquisitions resulting in a (global) translation of the fingerprint area. A finger displacement of just 2 mm (imperceptible to the user) results in a translation of about 40 pixels in a fingerprint image scanned at a resolution of 500 dpi.
- *Rotation*: the same finger may be rotated at different angles with respect to the sensor surface during different acquisitions. In spite of the finger "guide" mounted in certain

D. Maltoni et al., *Handbook of Fingerprint Recognition*, 167–233.
© Springer-Verlag London Limited 2009

commercial scanners, involuntary finger rotations of up to ±20° with respect to vertical orientation can be observed in practice.

- *Partial overlap*: finger displacement and rotation often cause part of the fingerprint area to fall outside the sensor's "field of view," resulting in a smaller overlap between the foreground areas of the template and the input fingerprints. This problem is particularly serious for small-area touch sensors (see Section 2.7).

- *Non-linear distortion*: the act of sensing maps the three-dimensional shape of a finger onto the two-dimensional surface of the sensor. This mapping results in a non-linear distortion in successive acquisitions of the same finger due to skin plasticity. Often, fingerprint matching algorithms disregard the characteristic of such a mapping, and consider a fingerprint image as non-distorted by assuming that it was produced by a correct finger placement; a finger placement is correct when: (i) the trajectory of the finger approaching the sensor is orthogonal to the sensor surface; (ii) once the finger touches the sensor surface, the user does not apply traction or torsion. However, due to skin plasticity, the components of the force that are non-orthogonal to the sensor surface produce non-linear distortions (compression or stretching) in the acquired fingerprints. Distortion results in the inability to match fingerprints as rigid patterns.

- *Pressure and skin condition*: the ridge structure of a finger would be accurately captured if ridges of the part of the finger being imaged were in uniform contact with the sensor surface. However, finger pressure, dryness of the skin, skin disease, sweat, dirt, grease, and humidity in the air all confound the situation, resulting in a non-uniform contact. As a consequence, the acquired fingerprint images are very noisy and the noise strongly varies in successive acquisitions of the same finger depending on the magnitude of the above cited causes.

- *Noise*: it is mainly introduced by the fingerprint sensing system; for example, residues are left over on the glass platen from the previous fingerprint capture.

- *Feature extraction errors*: the feature extraction algorithms are imperfect and often introduce measurement errors. Errors may be made during any of the feature extraction stages (e.g., estimation of orientation and frequency images, detection of the number, type, and position of the singularities, segmentation of the fingerprint area from the background, etc.). Aggressive enhancement algorithms may introduce inconsistent biases that perturb the location and orientation of the reported minutiae from their gray-scale counterparts. In low-quality fingerprint images, the minutiae extraction process may introduce a large number of spurious minutiae and may not be able to detect all the true minutiae.

The pairs of images in Figure 4.1 visually show the high variability (large *intra-class* variations) that can characterize two different impressions of the same finger.

Figure 4.1. Each row shows a pair of impressions of the same finger, taken from the FVC2002 DB1 (Maio et al., 2002b), which were falsely non-matched by most of the algorithms submitted to FVC2002. The main cause of difficulty is a very small overlap in the first row, high non-linear distortion in the second row, and very different skin conditions in the third row.

On the other hand, as evident from Figure 4.2, fingerprint images from different fingers may sometimes appear quite similar (small *inter-class* variations), especially in terms of global structure (position of the singularity, local ridge orientation, etc.). Although the probability that a large number of minutiae from impressions of two different fingers will match is extremely small (refer to Chapter 8), fingerprint matchers aim to find the "best" alignment. They often tend to declare that a pair of the minutiae "match" even when they are not perfectly coincident.

Figure 4.2. Each row shows a pair of impressions of different fingers, taken from the FVC2002 databases (Maio et al., 2002b) which were falsely matched by some of the algorithms submitted to FVC2002.

A large number of automatic fingerprint matching algorithms have been proposed in the literature. Most of these algorithms have no difficulty in matching good quality fingerprint images. However, fingerprint matching remains a challenging problem to date due to the difficulty in matching low-quality and partial latent fingerprints. In the case of human-assisted AFIS, a quality-checking algorithm can be used to acquire and insert only good quality fingerprints into the enrollment database. Furthermore, the processing of "difficult" latent fingerprints can be supervised. However, human intervention is not feasible in unattended on-line fingerprint recognition systems, which are being increasingly deployed in commercial applications.

A coarse analysis of the false non-match errors produced by the various fingerprint matching algorithms that participated in FVC2000 showed that most errors were made on about 20% poor quality fingerprints. In other words, typically, 20% of the database is responsible for about 80% of the false non-match errors (Maio et al., 2002b). Advances in state-of-the-art of fingerprint recognition technology was perceived throughout the different editions of the Fingerprint Verification Competition (BioLab, 2007). Although a direct comparison across the different competitions is not possible due to the use of databases of unequal difficulty, the performance of the top algorithms on database DB2 of FVC2006 (which was collected under realistic operating conditions with a large area sensor) are extremely good (EER $\cong 0.05\%$, see Section 4.7.2). However, there is still a need to continually develop more robust systems capable of properly processing and comparing poor quality fingerprint images; this is particularly important when dealing with large scale applications or when small area and relatively inexpensive low quality sensors are employed.

Approaches to fingerprint matching can be coarsely classified into three families.

- *Correlation-based matching*: two fingerprint images are superimposed and the correlation between the corresponding pixels is computed for different alignments (e.g., various displacements and rotations). Correlation-based techniques are described in Section 4.2.
- *Minutiae-based matching*: this is the most popular and widely used technique, being the basis of the fingerprint comparison made by fingerprint examiners. Minutiae are extracted from the two fingerprints and stored as sets of points in the two-dimensional plane. Minutiae-based matching essentially consists of finding the alignment between the template and the input minutiae feature sets that result in the maximum number of minutiae pairings. Sections 4.3 and 4.4 are dedicated to minutiae matching techniques.
- *Non-Minutiae feature-based matching*: minutiae extraction is difficult in extremely low-quality fingerprint images. While some other features of the fingerprint ridge pattern (e.g., local orientation and frequency, ridge shape, texture information) may be extracted more reliably than minutiae, their distinctiveness as well as persistence is generally lower. The approaches belonging to this family compare fingerprints in term of features extracted from the ridge pattern. In principle, correlation-based matching could be conceived of as a subfamily of non-minutiae feature-based matching, inasmuch as the pixel intensity are themselves features of the finger pattern; throughout this book we address them separately, and in Section 4.6 we discuss only

those matching techniques that use neither minutiae nor pixel intensity as their main fingerprint representation.

Many other techniques have also been proposed in the literature that, in principle, could be associated with one of the above three families according to the features used, but we prefer to categorize them separately on the basis of the matching technique. These include the neural network-based approaches (Sjogaard (1992); Baldi and Chauvin (1993); Quek, Tan, and Sagar (2001); Coetzee and Botha (1990); Melin, Bravo, and Castillo (2005)) and the attempts made to carry out fingerprint matching using parallel processors or with other dedicated architectures (Gowrishankar (1989); Ratha, Rover, and Jain (1996); Prabhakar and Rao (1989)).

Finally, to provide a more complete panorama of the techniques proposed in the past, we cite some early studies presented in AFIS, academic, and commercial environments: Banner and Stock (1974, 1975a, b), Millard (1975, 1983), Singh, Gyergyek, and Pavesic (1977), Hoshino et al. (1980), Liu et al. (1982), Li and Zhang (1984) and Sparrow and Sparrow (1985a, b).

4.2 Correlation-Based Techniques

Let $\mathbf{T}$ and $\mathbf{I}$ be the two fingerprint images corresponding to the template and the input fingerprint, respectively. Then an intuitive measure of their diversity is the sum of squared differences (*SSD*) between the intensities of the corresponding pixels:

$$SSD(\mathbf{T},\mathbf{I}) = \|\mathbf{T}-\mathbf{I}\|^2 = (\mathbf{T}-\mathbf{I})^{\mathrm{T}}(\mathbf{T}-\mathbf{I}) = \|\mathbf{T}\|^2 + \|\mathbf{I}\|^2 - 2\mathbf{T}^{\mathrm{T}}\mathbf{I}, \tag{1}$$

where the superscript "T" denotes the transpose of a vector. If the terms $\|\mathbf{T}\|^2$ and $\|\mathbf{I}\|^2$ are constant, the diversity between the two images is minimized when the cross-correlation (*CC*) between $\mathbf{T}$ and $\mathbf{I}$ is maximized:

$$CC(\mathbf{T},\mathbf{I}) = \mathbf{T}^{\mathrm{T}}\mathbf{I}. \tag{2}$$

Note that the quantity $-2 \times CC(\mathbf{T},\mathbf{I})$ appears as the third term in Equation (1). The cross-correlation (or simply correlation) is then a measure of the image similarity. Due to the displacement and rotation that unavoidably characterize two impressions of a given finger, their similarity cannot be simply computed by superimposing $\mathbf{T}$ and $\mathbf{I}$ and applying Equation (2).

Let $\mathbf{I}^{(\Delta x,\,\Delta y,\,\theta)}$ represent a rotation of the input image $\mathbf{I}$ by an angle θ around the origin (usually the image center) and shifted by Δx and Δy pixels in directions x and y, respectively; then the similarity between the two fingerprint images $\mathbf{T}$ and $\mathbf{I}$ can be measured as

$$S(\mathbf{T},\mathbf{I}) = \max_{\Delta x, \Delta y, \theta} CC\left(\mathbf{T},\mathbf{I}^{(\Delta x, \Delta y, \theta)}\right). \tag{3}$$

A direct application of Equation (3) rarely leads to acceptable results (see Figure 4.3a) mainly due to the following problems.

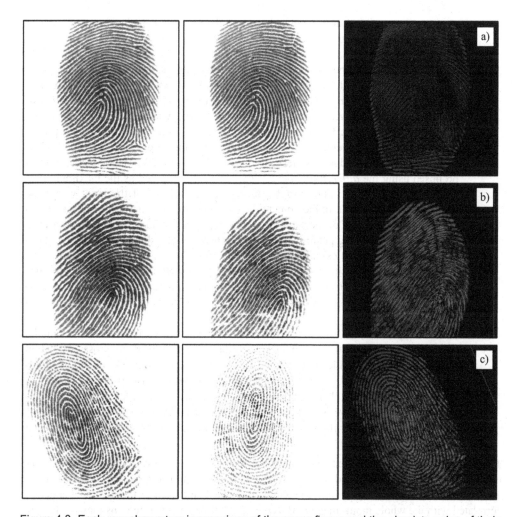

Figure 4.3. Each row shows two impressions of the same finger and the absolute value of their difference (residual) for the best alignment (i.e., that maximize correlation). In the first row, a) the two impressions are very similar and their images correlate well (the residual is very small). In the second row, b), and third row, c), due to high distortion and skin condition, respectively, the residuals are high and the global correlation methods fail.

1. Non-linear distortion makes impressions of the same finger significantly different in terms of global structure; in particular, the elastic distortion does not significantly

alter the fingerprint pattern locally, but since the effects of distortion get integrated in image space, two global fingerprint patterns cannot be reliably correlated (see Figure 4.3b).

2. Skin condition and finger pressure cause image brightness, contrast, and ridge thickness to vary significantly across different impressions (see Figure 4.3c). The use of more sophisticated correlation measures such as the *normalized cross-correlation* or the *zero-mean normalized cross-correlation* (Crouzil, Massip-Pailhes, and Castan, 1996) may compensate for contrast and brightness variations and applying a proper combination of enhancement, binarization, and thinning steps (performed on both **T** and **I**) may limit the ridge thickness problem (Kobayashi, 1992). Hatano et al. (2002) proposed using the *differential correlation*, which is computed as the maximum correlation minus the minimum correlation, in a neighborhood of the point where the correlation is maximum. In fact, due to the cyclic nature of fingerprint patterns, if two corresponding portions of the same fingerprint are slightly misaligned with respect to their optimum matching position, the correlation value falls sharply whereas two non-corresponding portions exhibit a flatter correlation value in the neighborhood of the optimum matching position. Hatano et al. (2002) reported a significant accuracy improvement with respect to the conventional correlation method. A very similar technique is known as Peak-to-Sidelobe-Ratio (PSR), see Venkataramani, Keskinoz, and Kumar (2005).

3. A direct application of Equation (3) is computationally very expensive. For example, consider two 400 × 400 pixel images; then the computation of the cross-correlation (Equation (2)) for a single value of the $(\Delta x, \Delta y, \theta)$ triplet would require 160,000 multiplications and 160,000 summations (neglecting border effects). If $\Delta x, \Delta y$ were both sampled with a one-pixel step in the range [−200,200], and θ with a step size of 1° in the range [−30°,30°] we would have to compute 401 × 401 × 61 cross-correlations, resulting in about 1.5 trillion multiplications and summations (i.e., about 2.6 min on a 10,000 MIPS computer).

The fingerprint distortion problem (point 1 in the above list) is usually addressed by computing the correlation locally instead of globally: a set of local regions (whose typical size may be 24 × 24 or 32 × 32) is extracted from the template image **T** and each of them is independently correlated with the whole input image **I** (Bazen et al., 2000). The local regions may be defined in several ways:

- Their union completely covers **T** and their intersection is null (full coverage without any overlap).
- Their union completely covers **T** and they locally overlap (full coverage with overlap).
- Only certain "interesting" regions are selected from **T**. For example, Yahagi, Igaki, and Yamagishi (1990), Kovacs-Vajna (2000), and Beleznai et al. (2001) select small windows around the minutiae, whereas Bazen et al. (2000) consider selective regions

that are distinctively localized in the input image (i.e., which fit well at the right location, but do not fit at other locations). Three different criteria are given by Bazen
et al. (2000) to identify such selective regions in the template image: regions around
minutiae, regions where ridges have a high curvature, and regions that exhibit a low
(auto)correlation at other locations in the template image itself.

When fingerprint correlation is carried out locally, the correlation estimates at different regions may be simply combined to obtain a similarity measure (e.g., the number of estimates
exceeding a certain threshold divided by the total number of estimates). In addition to the values of the correlation, the coordinates of the points where each region has maximum correlation can be exploited to strengthen the matching (*consolidation* step): in fact, the spatial
relationship (distances, angles, etc.) between the regions in the template and their mates in the
input image is required to be preserved (Bazen et al., 2000). In any case, there is no guarantee
that using such a consolidation step is really advantageous.

As to the computational complexity of the correlation technique, smart approaches may be
exploited to achieve efficient implementations.

- The correlation theorem (Gonzales and Woods, 2007) states that computing the correlation in the spatial domain (operator $\otimes$) is equivalent to performing a point-wise
  multiplication in the Fourier domain; in particular,

$$\mathbf{T} \otimes \mathbf{I} = F^{-1}\big(F^*(\mathbf{T}) \times F(\mathbf{I})\big), \tag{4}$$

  where $F(\ )$ is the Fourier transform of an image, $F^{-1}(\ )$ is the inverse Fourier transform, "*" denotes the complex conjugate, and "×" denotes the point-by-point multiplication of two vectors. The result of Equation (4) is a correlation image whose value
  at the pixel $[x,y]$ denotes the correlation between $\mathbf{T}$ and $\mathbf{I}$ when the displacement is
  $\Delta x = x$ and $\Delta y = y$. However the output of Equation (4) is dependent on the image energy and the correlation peak (corresponding to the optimal registration) can be small.
  The Symmetric Phase Only Filter (SPOF) often provides better results (Equation (5)):

$$\mathbf{T} \otimes_{\text{SPOF}} \mathbf{I} = F^{-1}\left(\frac{F^*(\mathbf{T})}{|F(\mathbf{T})|} \times \frac{F(\mathbf{I})}{|F(\mathbf{I})|} \right). \tag{5}$$

  To reduce the effect of noise Ito et al. (2005, 2006) and Shuai, Zhang, and Hao (2007)
  suggest restricting the SPOF domain to the frequency range characterizing a fingerprint image: this can be simply dealt with through band-pass filtering in the Fourier
  space. Equations (4) and (5) do not take into account rotation, which has to be dealt
  with separately; in any case, the computational saving is very high when correlation
  is performed globally (Coetzee and Botha, 1993) and considerable when it is performed locally by using medium-size regions.

- Computing the maximum correlation need not necessarily be done in a sequential,
  exhaustive manner; multi-resolution approaches, space-searching techniques (e.g.,
  gradient descent), and other heuristics can be adopted to reduce the number of

evaluations. For example, Lindoso et al. (2007) propose to coarsely pre-align the two fingerprints based on their orientation images.

- The Fourier–Mellin transform (Sujan and Mulqueen, 2002) may be used instead of the Fourier transform to achieve rotation invariance in addition to translation invariance; on the other hand, some additional steps (such as the log–polar coordinate transformation) have to be performed, that can reduce the accuracy of this solution. Ouyang et al. (2006) method computes the Fourier–Mellin descriptors locally and uses SPOF to determine the similarity between any two image portions.

- The approach proposed by Wilson, Watson, and Paek (1997) partitions both **T** and **I** into local regions and computes the maximum correlation (in the Fourier domain) between any pair of regions. This method suffers from "border effects" because of the partial overlapping between the different blocks, but can considerably speed up the whole matching process.

More sophisticated correlation techniques make use of advanced correlation filters (Kumar et al. 2004), where the template **T** is not just a single image but is obtained as a linear combination of several fingerprint images of the same finger; the combination coefficients are determined through an optimization approach (e.g., maximize the correlation peak for fingerprints from the same finger and minimize the correlation peak for fingerprints from other fingers). A preliminary work in this direction was proposed by He, Kohno, and Imai (1993). Roberge, Soutar, and Kumar (1999), Venkataramani and Kumar (2003, 2004) and Watson and Casasent (2004a, b) tested different types of advanced correlation filters for matching distorted fingerprints: the results of their experiments show that these techniques, in case a sufficient number of training set images is available and these images can be properly pre-aligned, are quite robust and can effectively work with resolutions lower than 500 dpi.

Finally, it is well known that correlation between two signals can be computed by an optical system that uses lenses to derive the Fourier transform of the images and a joint transform correlator for their matching. Several systems have been proposed in the literature for optical fingerprint matching: McMahon et al. (1975), Fielding, Homer, and Makekau (1991), Grycewicz (1995, 1996, 1999), Rodolfo, Rajbenbach, and Huignard (1995), Grycewicz and Javidi (1996), Petillot, Guibert, and De Bougrenet (1996), Soifer et al. (1996), Gamble, Frye, and Grieser (1992), Wilson, Watson, and Paek (1997), Kobayashi and Toyoda (1999), Lal, Zang, and Millerd (1999), Stoianov, Soutar, and Graham (1999), Watson, Grother, and Casasent (2000) and Bal, El-Saba, and Alam (2005b). However, these optical systems usually suffer from rotation and distortion variations and the hardware/optical components are complex and expensive; therefore efforts in this direction have been pretty much abandoned.

4.3 Minutiae-Based Methods

Minutiae matching is certainly the most well-known and most widely used method for fingerprint matching, thanks to its strict analogy with the way forensic experts compare fingerprints
and its acceptance as a proof of identity in the courts of law in almost all countries around the
world.

4.3.1 Problem formulation

Let $\mathbf{T}$ and $\mathbf{I}$ be the representation of the template and input fingerprint, respectively. Unlike in
correlation-based techniques, where the fingerprint representation coincides with the fingerprint image, here the representation is a feature vector (of variable length) whose elements are
the fingerprint minutiae. Each minutia may be described by a number of attributes, including
its location in the fingerprint image, orientation, type (e.g., ridge ending or ridge bifurcation),
a weight based on the quality of the fingerprint image in the neighborhood of the minutia, and
so on. Most common minutiae matching algorithms consider each minutia as a triplet
$\mathbf{m} = \{x, y, \theta\}$ that indicates the x, y minutia location coordinates and the minutia angle θ:

$$\mathbf{T} = \{\mathbf{m}_1, \mathbf{m}_2, \ldots \mathbf{m}_m\}, \quad \mathbf{m}_i = \{x_i, y_i, \theta_i\}, \quad i = 1 \ldots m$$
$$\mathbf{I} = \{\mathbf{m}'_1, \mathbf{m}'_2, \ldots \mathbf{m}'_n\}, \quad \mathbf{m}'_j = \{x'_j, y'_j, \theta'_j\}, \quad j = 1 \ldots n,$$

where m and n denote the number of minutiae in $\mathbf{T}$ and $\mathbf{I}$, respectively.

A minutia $\mathbf{m}'_j$ in $\mathbf{I}$ and a minutia $\mathbf{m}_i$ in $\mathbf{T}$ are considered "matching," if the *spatial dis-*
tance (*sd*) between them is smaller than a given tolerance r_0 and the *direction difference* (*dd*)
between them is smaller than an angular tolerance θ_0:

$$sd(\mathbf{m}'_j, \mathbf{m}_i) = \sqrt{(x'_j - x_i)^2 + (y'_j - y_i)^2} \leq r_0, \text{ and} \tag{6}$$

$$dd(\mathbf{m}'_j, \mathbf{m}_i) = min\left(\left|\theta'_j - \theta_i\right|, 360° - \left|\theta'_j - \theta_i\right|\right) \leq \theta_0. \tag{7}$$

Equation (7) takes the minimum of $\left|\theta'_j - \theta_i\right|$ and $360° - \left|\theta'_j - \theta_i\right|$ because of the circularity of
angles (the difference between angles of 2° and 358° is only 4°). The *tolerance boxes* (or hy-
per-spheres) defined by r_0 and θ_0 are necessary to compensate for the unavoidable errors made
by feature extraction algorithms and to account for the small plastic distortions that cause the
minutiae positions to change.

Aligning the two fingerprints is a mandatory step in order to maximize the number of
matching minutiae. Correctly aligning two fingerprints certainly requires *displacement* (in x
and y) and *rotation* (θ) to be recovered, and likely involves compensating for other geometrical transformations:

- *Scale* has to be considered when the resolution of the two fingerprints may vary (e.g., the two fingerprint images have been taken by scanners operating at different resolutions).
- Other *distortion-tolerant* geometrical transformations could be useful to match minutiae in case one or both of the fingerprints is affected by severe distortions.

In any case, tolerating more geometric transformations beyond translation and rotation results in additional degrees of freedom to the minutiae matcher: when a matcher is designed, this issue needs to be carefully evaluated, as each degree of freedom results in a huge number of new possible alignments which significantly increases the chance of incorrectly matching two fingerprints from different fingers.

Let *map*( ) be the function that maps a minutia $\mathbf{m}'_j$ (from $\mathbf{I}$) into $\mathbf{m}''_j$ according to a given geometrical transformation; for example, by considering a displacement of $[\Delta x, \Delta y]$ and a counterclockwise rotation θ around the origin[1]:

$$map_{\Delta x, \Delta y, \theta}\left(\mathbf{m}'_j = \{x'_j, y'_j, \theta'_j\}\right) = \mathbf{m}''_j = \{x''_j, y''_j, \theta'_j + \theta\}, \text{ where}$$

$$\begin{bmatrix} x''_j \\ y''_j \end{bmatrix} = \begin{bmatrix} \cos\theta & -\sin\theta \\ \sin\theta & \cos\theta \end{bmatrix} \begin{bmatrix} x'_j \\ y'_j \end{bmatrix} + \begin{bmatrix} \Delta x \\ \Delta y \end{bmatrix}.$$

Let *mm*( ) be an indicator function that returns 1 in the case where the minutiae $\mathbf{m}''_j$ and $\mathbf{m}_i$ match according to Equations (6) and (7):

$$mm\left(\mathbf{m}''_j, \mathbf{m}_i\right) = \begin{cases} 1 & sd\left(\mathbf{m}''_j, \mathbf{m}_i\right) \le r_0 \text{ and } dd\left(\mathbf{m}''_j, \mathbf{m}_i\right) \le \theta_0 \\ 0 & \text{otherwise.} \end{cases}$$

Then, the matching problem can be formulated as

$$\underset{\Delta x, \Delta y, \theta, P}{\text{maximize}} \sum_{i=1}^{m} mm\left(map_{\Delta x, \Delta y, \theta}\left(\mathbf{m}'_{P(i)}\right), \mathbf{m}_i\right), \tag{8}$$

where $P(i)$ is an unknown function that determines the *pairing* between $\mathbf{I}$ and $\mathbf{T}$ minutiae; in particular, each minutia has either exactly one mate in the other fingerprint or has no mate at all:

1. $P(i) = j$ indicates that the mate of the $\mathbf{m}_i$ in $\mathbf{T}$ is the minutia $\mathbf{m}'_j$ in $\mathbf{I}$.
2. $P(i) = $ null indicates that minutia $\mathbf{m}_i$ in $\mathbf{T}$ has no mate in $\mathbf{I}$.
3. A minutia $\mathbf{m}'_j$ in $\mathbf{I}$, has no mate in $\mathbf{T}$ if $P(i) \ne j \ \forall\ i = 1...m$.

---

[1] The origin is usually selected as the minutiae centroid (i.e., the average point); before the matching step, minutiae coordinates are adjusted by subtracting the centroid coordinates.

4. $\forall\ i = 1...m,\ k = 1...m,\ i \neq k \Rightarrow P(i) \neq P(k)$ or $P(i) = P(k) =$ null (this means that each minutia in **I** is associated with a maximum of one minutia in **T**, that is P is a bijective function).

Note that, in general, $P(i) = j$ does not necessarily mean that minutiae $\mathbf{m}'_j$ and $\mathbf{m}_i$ match in the sense of Equations (6) and (7) but only that they are the most likely pair under the current transformation.

Expression (8) requires that the number of minutiae mates be maximized, independently of how strict these mates are; in other words, if two minutiae comply with Equations (6) and (7), then their contribution to expression (8) is made independently of their spatial distance and of their direction difference. Alternatives to expression (8) may be introduced where the residual (i.e., the spatial distance and the direction difference between minutiae) for the optimal alignment is also taken into account.

Solving the minutiae matching problem (expression (8)) is trivial when the correct alignment (Δx, Δy, θ) is known; in fact, the pairing (i.e., the function P) can be determined by setting for each $i = 1...m$:

- $P(i) = j$ if $\mathbf{m}''_j = map_{\Delta x, \Delta y, \theta}\!\left(\mathbf{m}'_j\right)$ is closest to $\mathbf{m}_i$ among the minutiae $\left\{\ \mathbf{m}''_k = map_{\Delta x, \Delta y, \theta}\!\left(\mathbf{m}'_k\right) \mid k = 1...n,\ \ mm\!\left(\mathbf{m}''_k, \mathbf{m}_i\right) = 1\ \right\}$.

- $P(i) = $ null if $\forall\ k = 1...n,\ mm\!\left(map_{\Delta x, \Delta y, \theta}\!\left(\mathbf{m}'_k\right), \mathbf{m}_i\right) = 0$.

To comply with constraint (4) above, each minutia $\mathbf{m}''_j$ already mated has to be marked, to avoid mating it twice or more. Figure 4.4 shows an example of minutiae pairing given a fingerprint alignment.

To achieve the optimum pairing (according to Equation (8)), a slightly more complicated scheme should be adopted: in fact, in the case when a minutia of **I** falls within the tolerance hyper-sphere of more than one minutia of **T**, the optimum assignment is that which maximizes the number of mates (refer to Figure 4.5 for a simple example). Hungarian assignment algorithm (see Ahuja, Magnanti, and Orlin, 1993) with polynomial time complexity has been used for this purpose (see also Jea and Govindaraju (2005); Wang et al. (2006b)).

The maximization in (8) can be easily solved if the function P (minutiae correspondence) is known; in this case, the unknown alignment (Δx, Δy, θ) can be determined in the least square sense (Umeyama (1991); Chang et al. (1997)). Unfortunately, in practice, neither the alignment parameters nor the correspondence function P are known a priori and, therefore, solving the matching problem is hard. A brute force approach, that is, evaluating all the possible solutions (correspondences and alignments) is prohibitive as the number of possible solutions is exponential in the number of minutiae (the function P is more than a permutation due to the possible null values). A few brute force approaches have also been proposed in the literature; for example, Huvanandana, Kim, and Hwang (2000) proposed coarsely quantizing the minutiae locations and performing an exhaustive search to find the optimum alignment. He et al.

(2003b) suggested a coarse-to-fine search of the discretized parameter space to determine the alignment, and used Hausdorff distance to evaluate minutiae correspondences.

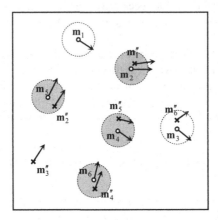

Figure 4.4. Minutiae of I mapped into T coordinates for a given alignment. Minutiae of T are denoted by os, whereas I minutiae are denoted by xs. Note that I minutiae are referred to as m″, because what is shown in the figure is their mapping into T coordinates. Pairing is performed according to the minimum distance. The dashed circles indicate the maximum spatial distance. The gray circles denote successfully mated minutiae; minutia m_1 of T and minutia m_3'' of I have no mates, minutiae m_3 and m_6'' cannot be mated due to their large direction difference (Kryszczuk, Drygajlo, and Morier, 2004).

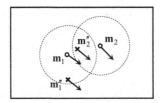

Figure 4.5. In this example, if m_1 was mated with m_2'' (the closest minutia), m_2 would remain unmated; however, pairing m_1 with m_1'', allows m_2 to be mated with m_2'', thus maximizing Equation (8).

4.3.2 Similarity score

Unlike in manual matching performed by forensic experts where the number of matching minutiae is itself the main output of the comparison, automatic matching systems must convert this number into a similarity score. This is often performed by simply normalizing the number of matching minutiae (here denoted by k) by the average number $(m + n)/2$ of minutiae in $\mathbf{T}$ and $\mathbf{I}$:

$$score = \frac{k}{(n+m)/2} .$$ (9)

However, further information can be exploited, especially in case of noisy images and limited overlap between $\mathbf{T}$ and $\mathbf{I}$, to compute a more reliable score; in fact:

- Minutiae quality can be used to weight differently reliable and unreliable minutiae pairs: the contribution from a pair of reliable minutiae should be higher than that from a pair where at least one the two minutiae is of low quality (Chen, Chan, and Moon, 2007). The quality of a minutia (and of a minutia pair) can be defined according to the fingerprint quality in the region where the minutia lies (see Section 3.10.2) and/or by keeping into account other local information (see Section 3.8.1).
- The normalization in Equation (9) tends to excessively penalize fingerprint pairs with partial overlap; a more effective normalization considers the number or minutiae belonging to the intersection of the two fingerprints after the optimal alignment has been determined (Jea and Govindaraju, 2005).

In general, the definition of optimal rules for combining various similarity contributions into a single score can be complex; some researchers (Jea and Govindaraju (2005); Srinivasan et al. (2006); Jia et al. (2007b); Feng (2008); Lumini and Nanni (2008)) propose to apply learning-based techniques where the rule and its parameters are optimized to best separate genuine from impostor scores. Supervised classification is central also in the method proposed by Mansukhani, Tulyakov, and Govindaraju (2007) and by Mansukhani and Govindaraju (2008) where an SVM is trained to distinguish between genuine and false minutiae pairs. Finally, methods based on the computation of the likelihood ratio to assess the evidential value of comparisons with an arbitrary number of minutiae are quite popular in forensic identification (see Neumann et al. (2006); Bazen and Veldhuis (2004)).

4.3.3 Point pattern matching

The minutiae matching problem can also be viewed as a *point pattern matching* problem. Because of its central role in many pattern recognition and computer vision tasks (e.g., object matching, remote sensing, camera calibration, motion estimation), point pattern matching has been extensively studied yielding families of approaches known as *algebraic geometry*, *Hough transform*, *relaxation*, *Operations Research solutions*, *energy-minimization*, and so on.

- *Algebraic geometry*: several methods have been proposed in the literature for different versions of the problem: $n = m$ or $n \le m$, exact or inexact point matching; see Brass and Knauer (2002) and Bishnu et al. (2006) for a survey. Bishnu et al. (2006) proposed an algorithm to perform an inexact partial point pattern matching with $O(m^2 \times n^2 \times log\ m)$ time complexity. However, this algorithm makes some simplifying assumptions that are not always fulfilled by minutiae points; in fact, the algorithm requires that: (i) all the points in **I** have a mate in **T**, even if some points in **T** can have no mate in **I**, and (ii) the tolerance boxes around the points do not intersect each other or, equivalently, that the points in **T** are not too close to each other. Since, general purpose algebraic geometry methods do not fit the peculiarity of minutiae matching, some ad-hoc algorithms have been designed for fingerprints: some examples are presented below.
- *Hough transform*: the generalized Hough transform-based approach (Ballard (1981); Stockman, Kopstein, and Benett (1982)) converts point pattern matching to the problem of detecting peaks in the Hough space of transformation parameters. It discretizes the parameter space and accumulates evidence in the discretized space by deriving transformation parameters that relate two sets of points using a substructure of the feature matching technique. A hierarchical Hough transform-based algorithm may be used to reduce the size of the accumulator array by using a multi-resolution approach. Hough transform-based approaches, also known as "voting-based approaches" are quite popular for minutiae matching; a more in-depth analysis of this method is provided below.
- *Relaxation*: the relaxation approach (e.g., Rosenfeld and Kak (1976); Ranade and Rosenfeld (1993)) iteratively adjusts the confidence level of each corresponding pair of points based on its consistency with other pairs until a certain criterion is satisfied. At each iteration r, the method computes $m \times n$ probabilities p_{ij} (probability that point i corresponds to point j):

$$p_{ij}^{(r+1)} = \frac{1}{m} \sum_{h=1}^{m} \left[\max_{k=1...n} \left\{ c(i,j;h,k) \cdot p_{ij}^{(r)} \right\} \right], \quad i = 1...m, \quad j = 1...n, \quad (10)$$

where $c(i,j;h,k)$ is a compatibility measure between the pairing (i,j) and (h,k), which can be defined according to the consistency of the alignments necessary to map point j into i and point k into h. Equation (10) increases the probability of those pairs that receive substantial support by other pairs, and decreases the probability of the remaining ones. At convergence, each point i may be associated with the point j such that $p_{ij} = \max_s\{p_{is}\}$, where s is any other point in the set. Although a number of modified versions of this algorithm have been proposed to reduce the matching complexity (Ton and Jain, 1989), these methods are inherently slow due to their iterative nature.

- *Operations Research solutions*: tree-pruning approaches attempt to find the correspondence between the two point sets by searching over a tree of possible matches while employing different tree-pruning methods (e.g., branch and bound) to reduce the search space (Baird, 1984). To prune the tree of possible matches efficiently, this approach tends to impose a number of requirements on the input point sets, such as an equal number of points ($n = m$) and no outliers (points without correspondence). These requirements are difficult to satisfy in practice, especially in fingerprint minutiae matching. Solutions to point pattern matching may also be derived from some problems which are known in the field of Operations Research as assignment problems, bipartite graph matching (Murty (1992); Gold and Rangarajan (1996)). A minutiae matching algorithm based on minimum spanning tree matching was proposed by Oh and Ryu (2004).

- *Energy minimization*: these methods define a function that associates an *energy* or *fitness* with each solution of the problem. Optimal solutions are then derived by minimizing the energy function (or maximizing fitness) by using a stochastic algorithm such as the Genetic algorithm (Ansari, Chen, and Hou (1992); Zhang, Xu, and Chang (2003)) or simulated annealing (Starink and Backer, 1995). Le, Cheung, and Nguyen (2001) and Tan and Bhanu (2006) provided specific Genetic algorithm implementations for global minutiae matching. It has been shown that pure Genetic Algorithms are not well suited to fine-tuning the search in complex search spaces, and that hybridization with other local-searches techniques (called Memetic algorithms) can improve their efficiency. A Memetic algorithm for minutiae matching has been recently proposed by Sheng et al. (2007). In general, the methods belonging to this category tend to be slow and are unsuitable for real-time minutiae matching.

4.3.4 Some simple algebraic geometry methods

An interesting approach based on algebraic geometry was introduced by Udupa, Garg, and Sharma (2001) who significantly improved an idea earlier published by Weber (1992). No scale change is allowed (rigid transformation) and the algorithm is simpler than Hough transform-based methods. The main steps are:

1. The segments identified by pairs of minutiae $\overline{\mathbf{m}_{i2}\mathbf{m}_{i1}}$ in $\mathbf{T}$ and $\overline{\mathbf{m}'_{j2}\mathbf{m}'_{j1}}$ in $\mathbf{I}$ are considered, and from each pair of segments that have approximately the same length (remember that the transformation is rigid), the alignment parameters $(\Delta x, \Delta y, \theta)$ are derived.

2. For each alignment $(\Delta x, \Delta y, \theta)$ obtained in Step 1, $\mathbf{T}$ and $\mathbf{I}$ are superimposed and the pairing between the remaining minutiae is determined by using tolerance boxes, resulting in a number of mated pairs.

3. The top 10 alignments (i.e., those giving the 10 largest number of mates) are checked for consistency; in case of matching fingerprints, a majority of these alignments are mutually consistent, whereas for non-matching fingerprints they are not. A score is computed based on the fraction of mutually consistent transformations.

The final score is determined by combining the maximum number of mated pairs, the fraction of mutually consistent alignments, and the topological correspondence (i.e., minutiae direction and ridge counts) for the top 10 alignments. Even if the Hough transform is not explicitly used here, the consistency check made in Step 3 is, in principle, very similar to the accumulation of evidence which characterizes the Hough transform. To reduce the computational complexity of their methods, Udupa, Garg, and Sharma (2001) suggest to consider only segments whose lengths lie in a given range, and to filter out most of the candidate alignments in Step 1 early on according to the consistency of minutiae directions and of the ridge counts along the two segments.

Carvalho and Yehia (2004), in order to further speed-up Udupa, Garg, and Sharma (2001) algorithm, proposed to independently pre-sort the minutiae in **T** and **I**, by using the probability of the lengths formed by minutiae pairs as a key to the sorting operation. This increases the chance that corresponding line segments in two fingerprints are tested in the early iterations. Bhowmick and Bhattacharya (2004) approach also relies on the above Steps 1 and 2, but the authors make use of spatial data structures such as AVL and Kd-Tree to efficiently search and match distances and points, and consider minutiae quality during matching.

Another simple method relying on the combination of multiple alignments was proposed by Wang, Li, and Chen (2006). For every minutiae pair $\mathbf{m}_i$, $\mathbf{m}'_j$, a trivial alignment between **T** and **I** is achieved by superimposing the minutiae origin and by rotating the Cartesian axis according to the minutiae direction. A support $S(i,j)$ is then obtained by counting the number of pairs $\mathbf{m}_a$, $\mathbf{m}''_b$ that spatially match under the $\mathbf{m}_i$, $\mathbf{m}'_j$ alignment. However, the single minutiae pair receiving the highest support and its corresponding alignment are not robust enough for the final global matching and therefore the fusion (through averaging) of the parameters of the top few alignments is performed.

4.3.5 Hough transform-based approaches for minutiae matching

Ratha et al. (1996) proposed a generalized Hough transform-based minutiae matching approach, whose underlying alignment transformation, besides displacement and rotation, also includes scale. The space of transformations consists of quadruples $(\Delta x, \Delta y, \theta, s)$, where each parameter is discretized (denoted by the symbol [+]) into a finite set of values:

$$\Delta x^+ \in \left\{ \Delta x_1^+, \Delta x_2^+, \ldots \Delta x_a^+ \right\}, \quad \Delta y^+ \in \left\{ \Delta y_1^+, \Delta y_2^+, \ldots \Delta y_b^+ \right\},$$
$$\theta^+ \in \left\{ \theta_1^+, \theta_2^+, \ldots \theta_c^+ \right\}, \quad s^+ \in \left\{ s_1^+, s_2^+, \ldots s_d^+ \right\}.$$

A four-dimensional array **A**, with one entry for each of the parameter discretizations, is initially reset and the following algorithm is used to accumulate evidence/votes:

for each $\mathbf{m}_i$, $i = 1 \ldots m$

for each $\mathbf{m}'_j$, $j = 1 \ldots n$

  for each $\theta^+ \in \left\{ \theta_1^+, \theta_2^+, \ldots \theta_c^+ \right\}$

  if $dd\left(\theta'_j + \theta^+, \theta_i \right) < \theta_0$ // the minutiae directions after the rotation are sufficiently close as per Equation (7)

    for each $s^+ \in \left\{ s_1^+, s_2^+, \ldots s_d^+ \right\}$

$$\left\{ \begin{bmatrix} \Delta x \\ \Delta y \end{bmatrix} = \begin{bmatrix} x_i \\ y_i \end{bmatrix} - s^+ \cdot \begin{bmatrix} \cos\theta^+ & -\sin\theta^+ \\ \sin\theta^+ & \cos\theta^+ \end{bmatrix} \begin{bmatrix} x'_j \\ y'_j \end{bmatrix} \quad \text{// the } map \text{ function including scale}$$

$\Delta x^+, \Delta y^+$ = quantization of Δx, Δy to the nearest bin

$\mathbf{A}[\Delta x^+, \Delta y^+, \theta^+, s^+] = \mathbf{A}[\Delta x^+, \Delta y^+, \theta^+, s^+] + 1\}$

At the end of the accumulation process, the best alignment transformation $(\Delta x^*, \Delta y^*, \theta^*, s^*)$ is obtained as

$$\left(\Delta x^*, \Delta y^*, \theta^*, s^* \right) = arg \max_{\Delta x^+, \Delta y^+, \theta^+, s^+} \mathbf{A}\left[\Delta x^+, \Delta y^+, \theta^+, s^+ \right]$$

and the minutiae pairing is performed as previously explained (in Section 4.3.1). To increase robustness of the Hough transform, it is common to cast a vote not only in the discretized bin, but also in its nearest neighbors; hence, in the above pseudo-code, the accumulator update can be substituted by a simple procedure that updates all the entries in the neighborhood of the selected bin.

    An efficient parallel implementation of the above algorithm, whose complexity is $O(m \times n \times c \times d)$, was introduced by Ratha, Rover, and Jain (1995), where dedicated hardware consisting of a Field Programmable Gate Array (FPGA)-based point pattern matching processor was designed.

    An alternative approach to point pattern matching, as proposed by Chang et al. (1997) consists of the following main steps:

1. Detect the minutiae pair (called the *principal pair*) that receives the maximum *Matching Pair Support* (MPS) and the alignment parameters (θ, s) that can match most minutiae between **T** and **I**. The principal pair that has the maximum MPS is determined through a Hough transform-based voting process.

2. The remaining minutiae mates (i.e., the function P) are then determined once the two fingerprints have been registered to superimpose the minutiae constituting the principal pair.

3.   The exact alignment is computed in the least square sense once the correspondence function is known.

To accomplish Step 1, which is at the core of this approach, the algorithm considers segments defined by pairs of minutiae $\overline{\mathbf{m}_{i2}\mathbf{m}_{i1}}$ in $\mathbf{T}$ and $\overline{\mathbf{m}'_{j2}\mathbf{m}'_{j1}}$ in $\mathbf{I}$ and derives, from each pair of segments, the parameters θ and s simply as

$$\theta = angle\left(\overline{\mathbf{m}_{i2}\mathbf{m}_{i1}}\right) - angle\left(\overline{\mathbf{m}'_{j2}\mathbf{m}'_{j1}}\right), \tag{11}$$

$$s = \frac{length\left(\overline{\mathbf{m}_{i2}\mathbf{m}_{i1}}\right)}{length\left(\overline{\mathbf{m}'_{j2}\mathbf{m}'_{j1}}\right)}. \tag{12}$$

A transformation $(\Delta x, \Delta y, \theta, s)$, which aligns the two segments, must necessarily involve a scale change by an amount given by the ratio of the two segment lengths, and a rotation by an angle equal to the difference between the two segment angles (see Figure 4.6).
The principal pair and the parameters (θ^*, s^*) are determined as

$maxMPS = 0$ // maximum Matching Pair Support
for each $\mathbf{m}_{i1}$, $i1 = 1...m$

for each $\mathbf{m}'_{j1}$, $j1 = 1...n$ // $\mathbf{m}_{i1}, \mathbf{m}'_{j1}$ is the current pair for which MPS has be to estimated

   { Reset $\mathbf{A}$ // the accumulator array
     for each $\mathbf{m}_{i2}$, $i2 = 1...m$, $i2 \neq i1$

     for each $\mathbf{m}'_{j2}$, $j2 = 1...n$, $j2 \neq j1$

       { θ, s are computed from $\overline{\mathbf{m}_{i2}\mathbf{m}_{i1}}$, $\overline{\mathbf{m}'_{j2}\mathbf{m}'_{j1}}$ according to Equations (11) and (12)

       θ^+, s^+ = quantization of θ, s to the nearest bins
       $\mathbf{A}[\theta^+, s^+] = \mathbf{A}[\theta^+, s^+] + 1$ }
   $MPS = \max_{\theta^+, s^+} \mathbf{A}\left[\theta^+, s^+\right]$

   if $MPS \geq maxMPS$
   { $maxMPS = MPS$

    $\left(\theta^*, s^*\right) = arg \max_{\theta^+, s^+} \mathbf{A}\left[\theta^+, s^+\right]$

    Principal pair = ($\mathbf{m}_{i1}$, $\mathbf{m}'_{j1}$)

   }

}

Some heuristics were introduced by Chang et al. (1997) to reduce the number of segments considered and therefore, to limit the computational complexity. An example of minutiae matching by the above method is shown in Figure 4.7.

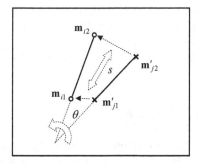

Figure 4.6. The transformation that aligns the two segments involves a rotation and a scale change as defined by Equations (11) and (12).

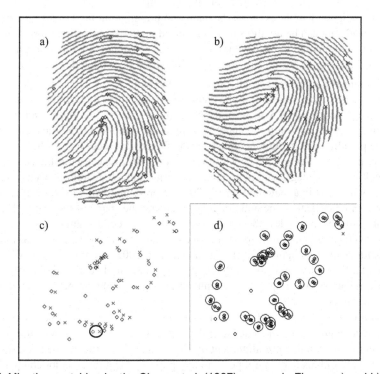

Figure 4.7. Minutiae matching by the Chang et al. (1997) approach. Figures a) and b) show the minutiae extracted from the template and the input fingerprint, respectively; c) the minutiae are coarsely superimposed and the principal pair is marked with an ellipse; d) each circle denotes a pair of minutiae as mated by the Step 3 of the algorithm.

Liu, Xia, and Li (2004) proposed a hierarchical Hough transform implementation aimed at improving efficiency and accuracy of the conventional Hough approach. The discretization of the transformation parameters is done hierarchically (coarse to fine) and specific mechanisms are adopted to avoid: (i) loosing minutiae pairs due to quantization errors, and (ii) matching each minutia more than once.

4.3.6 Minutiae matching with pre-alignment

Embedding fingerprint alignment into the minutiae matching stage (as the methods presented in the previous section do), certainly leads to the design of robust algorithms, which are often able to operate with noisy and incomplete data. On the other hand, the computational complexity of such methods does not provide a high matching throughput (e.g., 10,000 or more matches per second), as required by AFIS or civil systems.

Storing pre-aligned templates in the database and pre-aligning the input fingerprint before the minutiae matching can be a valid solution to speed up the 1:N identification. In theory, if a perfect pre-alignment could be achieved, the minutiae matching could be reduced to a simple pairing. Two main approaches for pre-alignment have been investigated.

- *Absolute pre-alignment*: each fingerprint template is pre-aligned, independently of the others, before storing it in the database. Matching an input fingerprint **I** with a set of templates requires **I** to be independently registered just once, and the resulting aligned representation to be matched with all the templates. The most common absolute pre-alignment technique translates the fingerprint according to the position of the core point (see Section 3.5.5). Unfortunately, reliable detection of the core is very difficult in noisy images and in arch type patterns, and a registration error at this level is likely to result in a matching error. Absolute pre-alignment with respect to rotation is even more critical; some authors proposed using the shape of the external fingerprint silhouette (if available), the orientation of the core delta segment (if a delta exists), the average orientation in some regions around the core (Wegstein, 1982), or the orientations of the singularities (Bazen and Gerez, 2002). In any case, no definite solution has been proposed for a reliable pre-alignment to date and, therefore, the design of a robust system requires the minutiae matcher to tolerate pre-alignment errors to some extent.

- *Relative pre-alignment*: the input fingerprint **I** has to be pre-aligned with respect to each template **T** in the database; 1:N identification requires N independent pre-alignments. Relative pre-alignment may determine a significant speed up with respect to the algorithms that do not perform any pre-alignment, but cannot compete in terms of efficiency with absolute pre-alignment. However, relative pre-alignment is in general more effective (in terms of accuracy) than absolute pre-alignment, because the features of the template **T** may be used to drive the registration process.

The M82 method, developed for minutiae-based fingerprint matching in the AFIS community (Wegstein (1972, 1982); Wegstein and Rafferty (1978), performs a coarse absolute pre-alignment according to the core position (detected through the R92 method; ref. Section 3.5.5) and the average orientation of the two regions on the two sides of the core (see Figure 4.8).

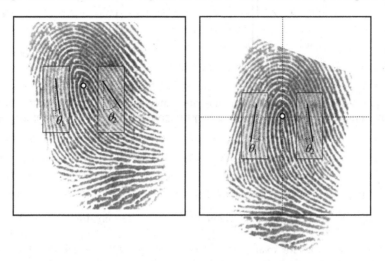

Figure 4.8. The fingerprint on the right has been translated to move the core point to the image center and rotated to minimize the difference between the angles θ_1 and θ_2.

After the coarse pre-alignment of both **T** and **I** minutiae, M82 determines a list of candidate minutiae pairs by considering the minutiae that are closer than a given distance (this relies on the assumption of a correct coarse pre-alignment); the matching degree of each candidate pair is consolidated according to the compatibility with other pairs. The list is sorted with respect to the degree of matching; the top pair is selected as the principal pair and all the remaining minutiae are translated accordingly. In the second stage, a deformation tensor, which allows the matching to tolerate small linear distortion and rotations, is determined (see Figure 4.9).

Relative pre-alignment may be performed in several ways; for example:

- By superimposing the singularities.
- By correlating the orientation images.
- By comparing ridge features (e.g., length and orientation of the ridges).

Yager and Amin (2006a) proved that relative pre-alignment of fingerprints based on a dynamic selection among different registration techniques lead to significant improvement over single alignment approaches.

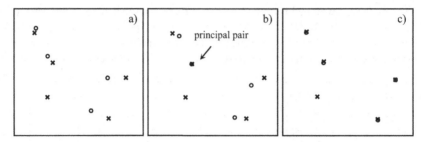

Figure 4.9. a) An example of minutiae matching as performed by M82, starting from a coarse absolute pre-alignment; b) the two minutiae sets after alignment with respect to the principal pair; c) the final result obtained after applying the correction given by the deformation/rotation tensor.

Singularity-based relative pre-alignment

Assuming that the core location and orientation can be determined for the two fingerprint images, the transformation leading to a proper pre-alignment is straightforward. Some recent methods rely on it: see for example Nilsson and Bigun (2002b, 2003), Zhang and Wang (2002), Bigun, Bigun, and Nilsson (2004), Chan, Moon, and Cheng (2004), Chikkerur and Ratha (2005) and Jie et al. (2006). A smart exploitation of core point is suggested by Chikkerur and Ratha (2005) who have shown that by incorporating a core-based pre-alignment into a (graph-based) minutiae matching algorithm yields a 43% efficiency improvement without compromising accuracy. To avoid losing accuracy, the pre-alignment is performed only on fingerprints where singularities detection is reliable; in fact their technique can work (even if less efficiently) without any pre-alignment.

Orientation image-based relative pre-alignment

A basic implementation requires computing the similarity between the orientation image of $\mathbf{T}$ (here denoted by $\mathbf{D_T}$) with every possible transformation $\mathbf{D_I}^{(\Delta x, \Delta y, \theta)}$ of the orientation image of $\mathbf{I}$, where $\Delta x, \Delta y$ denote the translation and θ the rotation, respectively. This is similar to correlating images at intensity level (refer to Section 4.2) even if the block-wise definition of the orientation image and the nature of the orientations require some adjustments; in particular, the similarity among angles must be defined by keeping into account angle circularity and rotating/shifting $\mathbf{D_I}$ may require the use of resampling techniques to avoid loosing accuracy. Unlike classical definition based on angular differences, Liu et al. (2006) define the similarity between orientation images by means of the Mutual Information (Guiasu, 1977).

To determine the optimal alignment, the space of possible transformations is usually discretized and the single transformation leading to the highest similarity is selected: see for example Lindoso et al. (2007). To improve efficiency, instead of performing an exhaustive evaluation of all the transformations:

- Yager and Amin (2004, 2006b) suggest using local optimization techniques such as the steepest descent.
- Nilsson and Bigun (2005) focus on 1D projections of orientation images.
- Liu et al. (2006) implement a two stage coarse-to-fine search strategy.

Finally, Yager and Amin (2006b), besides the orientation image, also use ridge frequency and ridge curvature images.

Ridge-based relative pre-alignment

An interesting minutiae matching approach that exploits ridge features for relative pre-alignment was proposed by Jain, Hong, and Bolle (1997); see also Hong and Jain (1996) and Jain et al. (1997). The relative pre-alignment is based on the observation that minutiae registration can be performed by registering the corresponding ridges. In fact, each minutia in a fingerprint is associated with a ridge; during the minutiae extraction stage, when a minutia is detected and recorded, the ridge on which it resides is also recorded. The ridge is represented as a planar curve, with its origin coincident with the minutia and its x-coordinate being in the same direction as the minutia direction. Also, this planar curve is normalized (in scale) with respect to the average ridge frequency. By matching these ridges (see Figure 4.10) the parameters $(\Delta x, \Delta y, \theta)$ may be recovered. The ridge matching task proceeds by iteratively matching pairs of ridges until a pair is found whose matching degree exceeds a certain threshold. The pair found is then used for relative pre-alignment.

To tolerate local distortion and minutiae extraction errors (i.e., false and missing minutiae, location errors) Jain, Hong, and Bolle (1997), instead of using the classical pairing based on tolerance boxes, propose an adaptive elastic matching algorithm:

1. Each minutia in **T** and **I** is converted to a polar coordinate system with respect to the reference minutia in its set (the reference minutia is the one associated with the ridge selected during pre-alignment).
2. Both **T** and **I** are transformed into symbolic strings by concatenating each minutia in the increasing order of radial angle.

The two strings are matched with a dynamic programming technique (Cormen, Leiserson, and Rivest, 1990) to find their *edit distance*. The edit distance between two strings is the minimum cost of transformations (symbol insertion, symbol deletion, symbol exchange) necessary to make the two strings coincident (Bunke, 1993). Matching minutiae representations by their edit distance tolerates missing and spurious minutiae as these are dealt with as symbol insertion and deletion. Radial and angular minutiae errors are handled by defining the cost of symbol exchange proportional to the position difference. However, some problems are due to "order flips" possibly inserted in Step 2, which could be solved by exhaustive reordering and matching within a local angular window. Figure 4.11 shows an example of minutiae matching by the Jain, Hong, and Bolle (1997) approach.

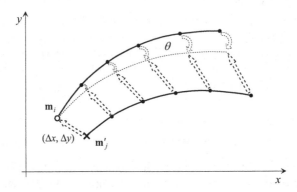

Figure 4.10. Matching of the two ridges associated with minutiae $\mathbf{m}_i$ of $\mathbf{T}$ and $\mathbf{m}'_j$ of $\mathbf{I}$. Both ridges are sampled with step size equal to the average inter-ridge distance (sampling points are denoted by small black dots in the figure) and the matching is carried out by correlating the y-coordinates of the sampling points.

A variant of the above method was proposed by Luo, Tian, and Wu (2000), where ridge matching was performed in a slightly different manner: instead of correlating the y-coordinates of the sampled points along the two ridges, the authors matched distances and relative angles of the sampled points. The minutiae matching stage also deviated at some points: ridge information was fused into the computation of the edit distance and variable bounding boxes were introduced to deal with distortion. Other implementations of ridge-based alignment can be found in Hao, Tan, and Wang (2002), He et al. (2003a), Cheng, Tian, and Chen (2004) and Feng and Cai (2006a).

4.3.7 Avoiding alignment

Fingerprint alignment is certainly a critical and time-consuming step. To overcome problems involved in alignment, and to better cope with local distortions, some authors perform minutiae matching locally (as discussed in Section 4.4).

A few other attempts have been proposed that try to globally match minutiae without requiring explicit recovery of the parameters of the transformation. Bazen and Gerez (2001a) introduced an *intrinsic coordinate system* (ICS) whose axes run along hypothetical lines defined by the local orientation of the fingerprint pattern. First, the fingerprint is partitioned in regular regions (i.e., regions that do not contain singular points). In each regular region, the ICS is defined by the orientation field. When using intrinsic coordinates instead of pixel coordinates, minutiae are defined with respect to their position in the orientation field (Figure 4.12). Translation, displacement, and distortion move minutiae with the orientation field they are immersed in and therefore do not change their intrinsic coordinates. On the other hand, some practical problems such as reliably partitioning the fingerprint in regular regions and unambiguously defining intrinsic coordinate axes in low-quality fingerprints still remain to be solved.

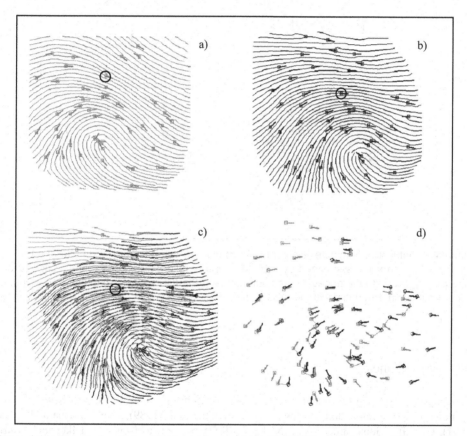

Figure 4.11. Result of applying the Jain, Hong, and Bolle (1997) matching algorithm to an input fingerprint b) and a template fingerprint a). c) Pre-alignment result based on the minutiae marked with circles and the associated ridges; ridges and minutiae of I and T are gray and black, respectively. d) Matching result where paired minutiae are connected by gray lines. © IEEE.

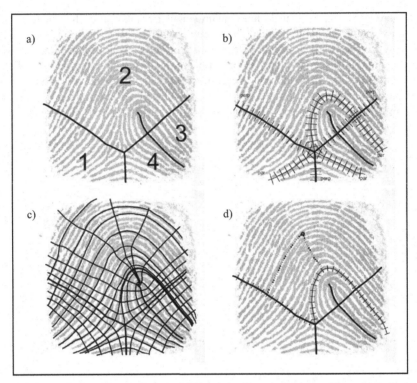

Figure 4.12. Intrinsic Coordinate System (ICS): a) the fingerprint is partitioned into four regular regions; b) each region is spanned by two axes, one parallel to the ridge orientation, and the other perpendicular to the ridges; c) iso-coordinates in the ICS spaces; d) intrinsic coordinates of a given minutia. Reprinted with permission from Bazen and Gerez (2001). © Springer-Verlag.

4.3.8 Miscellanea

Other algorithms based on global minutiae matching are described in Pernus, Kovacic, and Gyergyek (1980), Mehtre and Murthy (1986), Xuening et al. (1989), Gunawardena and Sagar (1991), Costello, Gunawardena, and Nadiadi (1994), Sasakawa, Isogai, and Ikebata (1990), Johannesen et al. (1996), Jea et al. (2004), Kim and Yoo (2005), Park et al. (2005), Zhu, Yin, and Zhang (2005), Jie et al. (2006) and Liang and Asano (2006b).

4.4 Global Versus Local Minutiae Matching

Local minutiae matching consists of comparing two fingerprints according to local minutiae structures; local structures are characterized by attributes that are invariant with respect to global transformation (e.g., translation, rotation, etc.) and therefore are suitable for matching without any a priori global alignment. Matching fingerprints based only on local minutiae arrangements relaxes global spatial relationships which are highly distinctive and therefore reduce the amount of information available for discriminating fingerprints. Global versus local matching is a tradeoff among simplicity, low computational complexity, and high distortion-tolerance (local matching), and high distinctiveness on the other hand (global matching). Actually, the benefits of both local and global matching can be obtained by implementing hybrid strategies that perform a *local structure matching* followed by a *consolidation* stage. The local structure matching allows to quickly and robustly determine pairs of minutiae that match locally (i.e., whose neighboring features are compatible) and derive from them one or more candidate alignments for **T** and **I**. The consolidation is aimed at verifying if and to what extent local matches hold at global level. It is worth noting that the consolidation step is not mandatory and a score can be derived directly from the local structure matching. The local matching itself can also lead to an early rejection in case of very different fingerprints.

Local minutiae matching algorithms evolved through three generations of methods: (i) the earlier approaches whose local structures were typically formed by counting the number of minutiae falling inside some regions and no global consolidation were performed; (ii) the approaches by Jiang and Yau (2000) and Ratha et al. (2000) who first encoded the relationship between a minutia and its neighboring minutiae in term of invariant distances and angles and proposed global consolidation; (iii) the plethora of variants and evolutions of Jiang and Yau (2000) and Ratha et al. (2000) methods.

4.4.1 The earlier approaches

Hrechak and McHugh (1990) associated an eight-dimensional feature vector $\mathbf{v}_i = [v_{i1}, v_{i2}, \dots v_{i8}]$ to each minutia $\mathbf{m}_i$, where v_{ij} is the number of occurrences of minutiae of type j in a neighborhood of the minutia $\mathbf{m}_i$. The minutiae types considered are dots, ridge endings, bifurcations, island, spurs, crossovers, bridges, and short ridges (ref. Section 3.1). These vectors are invariant with respect to fingerprint alignment and can be easily matched; however, the difficulty of automatically discriminating various minutiae types with sufficient reliability diminishes the practical applicability of this method.

Chen and Kuo (1991) and Wahab, Chin, and Tan (1998) enriched the local structures initially proposed by Hrechak and McHugh (1990) by including in the feature vectors: (i) the distance and (ii) the ridge count between the central minutia and each surrounding minutia, (iii) the relative orientation of each surrounding minutia with respect to the central one, and (iv) the angle between the orientation of the central minutia and the direction of the segment connecting the surrounding minutia to the central one. Local structures are then compared by correlation or tree-matching.

Finally, Fan, Liu, and Wang (2000) performed a geometric clustering of minutiae points. Each cluster is represented by the rectangular bounding box enclosing all the minutiae associated with it. During the matching stage, search for an optimal assignment between clusters of **T** and **I** is made by using a fuzzy bipartite weighted graph matching, where the clusters of **T** are the right nodes of a fuzzy bipartite weighted graph and the **I** clusters are the left nodes of the graph. Willis and Myers (2001) also group minutiae, by counting the number of minutiae falling inside the cells of a "dart board" pattern of wedges and rings; fixed-length feature vectors are obtained from the groupings which are partially invariant with respect to rotation and translation.

4.4.2 Local structure matching through invariant distances and angles

In Jiang and Yau (2000) local structures are formed by a central minutia and its two nearest-neighbor minutiae; the feature vector v_i associated with the minutia m_i, whose nearest neighbors are minutiae m_j (the closest to m_i) and m_k (the second closest) is:

$$v_i = [d_{ij}, d_{ik}, \theta_{ij}, \theta_{ik}, \varphi_{ij}, \varphi_{ik}, n_{ij}, n_{ik}, t_i, t_j, t_k],$$

where d_{ab} is the distance between minutiae m_a and m_b, θ_{ab} is the direction difference between the angles θ_a and θ_b of m_a and m_b, φ_{ab} is the direction difference between the angle θ_a of m_a and the direction of the edge connecting m_a to m_b, n_{ab} is the ridge count between m_a and m_b, and t_a is the minutia type of m_a (Figure 4.13).

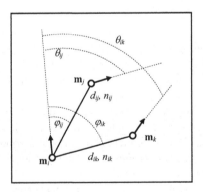

Figure 4.13. Features of the local structures used by Jiang and Yau (2000).

Local minutiae matching is performed by computing, for each pair of minutiae $\mathbf{m}_i$ and $\mathbf{m}'_j$, $i = 1\ldots m$, $j = 1\ldots n$, a weighted Euclidean distance between their vectors $\mathbf{v}_i$ and $\mathbf{v}'_j$. The computation of the $m \times n$ distances is very fast and an overall similarity score between $\mathbf{T}$ and $\mathbf{I}$ can be directly derived by the TOP matching (i.e., less distant) structure pairs. However, to improve accuracy, Jiang and Yau (2000) suggested implementing a consolidation step as described in Section 4.4.4.

Ratha et al. (2000) defined the concept of local structure by using graph notation. The *star* associated with the minutia $\mathbf{m}_i$ for a given distance $d_{\max}$ is the graph $S_i = (V_i, E_i)$ consisting of:

- The set of vertices V_i containing all the minutiae $\mathbf{m}_j$ whose spatial distance $sd(\ )$ from $\mathbf{m}_i$ is less than or equal to $d_{\max}$: $V_i = \{\ \mathbf{m}_j \mid sd(\mathbf{m}_i, \mathbf{m}_j) \le d_{\max}\ \}$.
- The set of edges $E_i = \{\mathbf{e}_{ij}\}$, where $\mathbf{e}_{ij}$ is the edge connecting minutia $\mathbf{m}_i$ with minutia $\mathbf{m}_j$ in V_i; $\mathbf{e}_{ij}$ is labeled with a 5-tuple $(i, j, sd(\mathbf{m}_i, \mathbf{m}_j), rc(\mathbf{m}_i, \mathbf{m}_j), \varphi_{ij})$, where $rc(\mathbf{m}_i, \mathbf{m}_j)$ is the ridge count between $\mathbf{m}_i$ and $\mathbf{m}_j$ and φ_{ij} is the angle subtended by the edge with the x-axis.

Figure 4.14 shows the star of a given minutia for two different values of $d_{\max}$.

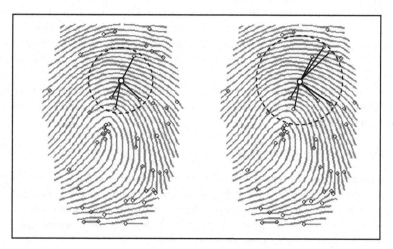

Figure 4.14. The stars of a given minutia for $d_{\max} = 70$ (left) and $d_{\max} = 100$ (right) (Ratha et al., 2000).

During local minutiae matching, each star from $\mathbf{I}$ is matched against each star from $\mathbf{T}$. The matching between two stars $S_a = (V_a, E_a)$ from $\mathbf{T}$ and $S_b = (V_b, E_b)$ from $\mathbf{I}$ is performed as follows: given a starting pair of edges $\mathbf{e}_{aj} \in E_a$ and $\mathbf{e}_{bk} \in E_b$, a clockwise traversing of the two set of edges E_a and E_b is executed in increasing order of radial angles φ and a score is obtained by accumulating the similarities between pairs of corresponding edges. The traversing is repeated by using every pairs of edges as starting pair, and the maximum score is returned. It is worth noting that Ratha et al. (2000) did not encode the angles φ as relative angles with respect to the direction of central minutia; for this reason the stars are not rotation invariant and the matching between two stars is not straightforward. Ratha et al. (2000) also recommended a consolidation step (see Section 4.4.4).

4.4.3 Evolution of local structure matching

The matching of local structures invariant with respect to translation and rotation, forms the basis of most of the minutiae matching algorithms proposed after the year 2000. Unfortunately, the related literature is quite chaotic and, due to different (and often cumbersome) notations and conventions, it is sometimes difficult to understand the differences among the tens of algorithms published. Instead of systematically describing individual approaches we prefer to focus attention on the main ideas that lead to evolutions with respect to the "root methods" described in Section 4.4.2. Of course, this is a very difficult task and we apologize for the excessive simplification that we may introduce.

Local structures can be classified into nearest neighbor-based and fixed radius-based. In the former family (whose archetype is Jiang and Yau (2000)), the neighbors of the central minutia are formed by its K spatially closest minutiae. This leads to fixed-length descriptors that can be usually matched very efficiently. In the latter (whose archetype is Ratha et al. (2000)), the neighbors are defined as all the minutiae that are closer than a given radius R from the central minutia. The descriptor length is variable and depends on the local minutiae density; this can lead to a more complex local matching; however, in principle, missing and spurious minutiae can be better tolerated.

Nearest neighbour-based structures

Jea and Govindaraju (2005) argue that a critical point of Jiang and Yau (2000) descriptors is the possibility of exchanging the nearest neighbour minutia with the second nearest neighbour in case the two distances are similar. Such a minutiae flip would lead to a failure of local matching: hence, Jea and Govindaraju (2005) propose choosing the minutiae order based on the angular relationships, which are usually more stable.

In Chikkerur, Cartwright, and Govindaraju (2006) local structures (called K-plet) are formed by the K nearest neighbor minutiae. To avoid reducing the neighborhood size too much (this can happen for high minutiae density), a constraint can be added to ensure that the K nearest neighbors are equally distributed in the four quadrants around the minutia. Similarly, Kwon et al. (2006) subdivide the plane around a minutia into K angular sectors and take the nearest neighbour minutia for each sector. The comparison of two K-plets is performed by Chikkerur, Cartwright, and Govindaraju (2006) by computing the edit distance between the two strings obtained by concatenating the K neighboring minutiae sorted by their radial distance by the central minutia; in spite of an higher matching complexity, this approach can tolerate, to some extent, missing and spurious minutiae.

In the method proposed by Deng and Huo (2005) the nearest neighbour minutiae are not directly selected based on Euclidean distance, but from the Delaunay triangulation of the entire minutiae set; in particular a local structure is constructed around each minutia by labelling with invariant features (the same used by Jiang and Yau (2000)) the edges that connect it with the neighbouring minutiae in the Delaunay triangulation. This results in a variable length descriptors. A similar neighbouring relationship was used in the method by Yu, Na, and Choi (2005).

Fixed radius-based structures

One drawback of Ratha et al. (2000) approach is the absolute encoding of angles φ_{ij}. Most of the variants of this method encode this angle as relative to the central minutia direction; this makes the resulting feature invariant to rotation and the local structure comparison simpler. Another useful feature that was not considered for local structure matching by Ratha et al. (2000) is the direction difference between the central minutia and the neighbouring ones (these are denoted by the symbol θ in Figure 4.13).

Matching fixed radius-based structures can lead to border errors: in particular, minutiae which are close to the local region border in one of the two fingerprints can be mismatched because of different local distortion or location inaccuracy that cause the same minutiae to move out of the local region in the second fingerprint. To overcome this problem Chen, Tian, and Yang (2006) proposed matching local structures in two steps: in the first step local structures of **T** with radius R are matched with local structures of **I** with radius $R+r$, where r is a small offset; in the second step, **T** local structures with radius $R+r$ are matched with **I** local structures of radius R. Feng (2008) suggests labelling a subset of minutiae which fall within the fixed-radius local structures as *should-be matching*; in particular, the above constraint is not enforced for: unreliable (i.e., low quality), occluded (i.e., out of the foreground area) and close-to-the-border minutiae.

Minutiae triangles

Minutiae triangles (or triplets) were first introduced in the context of fingerprint indexing by Germain, Califano, and Colville (1997), as explained in Chapter 5. Although minutiae triangles still represent today one of the most interesting approaches for indexing, some researchers have also demonstrated their potential for local structure matching for fingerprint verification; see for example: Tan and Bhanu (2003a, 2006), Parziale and Niel (2004), Yin, Zhang, and Yang (2005), Chen et al. (2006a), Zhao, Su, and Cai (2006) and Xu, Chen, and Feng (2007). Several features invariant with respect to translation, rotation (and sometimes scale) can be extracted from triangles whose vertices coincide with minutiae:

- Germain, Califano, and Colville (1997) used the length of each side, the angles that the ridges make with respect to the x-axis of the reference frame, and the ridge count between each pair of vertices.
- Tan and Bhanu (2003a) selected the triangle features according to some stability analysis. They finally choose: triangle handedness, triangle type, triangle direction, maximum side, minimum and median angle, minutiae density in a local area and ridge counts along the three sides.
- Chen et al. (2006a) also record, for each triangle vertex, the average deviation of the local orientations in a neighbourhood.

The similarity between any two triangles can be defined according to a weighted distance between the triangles features or, as proposed by Tan and Bhanu (2003a), by counting the number of minutiae that can be matched once the two fingerprints are aligned with the transformation aligning the two triangles. Chen et al. (2006a) proposed a fuzzy similarity measure between triangles where a learning process is performed off-line to learn the genuine similarity (i.e., the typical similarity among corresponding triangles in genuine matches). When combining the triangle similarities into a single matching score, Chen et al. (2006a) assign higher weights to triangles closer to the centre of the fingerprint and to triangles whose area is similar to a desired one. For local structures centred into a single minutia, as that proposed by Jiang and Yau (2000), the number of local structures is the same as the number of minutiae; on the other hand, the number of possible minutiae triangles equals the combination of three minutiae from a set of n minutiae, that is potentially very large (e.g., 19,600 triangles for $n = 50$). Some rules and constraints are then utilized to limit the number of triplets and at the same time to select the most discriminating triangles (e.g., collinear or near collinear triplets are excluded and the triangle sides must have a minimum length). Parziale and Niel (2004), Yin, Zhang, and Yang (2005) and Xu, Chen, and Feng (2007) suggested using only the triangles resulting from the Delaunay triangulation of the minutiae set; in fact the Delaunay triangulation was found to have the best structural stability under random positional perturbations (Bebis, Deaconu, and Georgiopoulos, 1999). To further improve tolerance to perturbation, Liang, Bishnu, and Asano (2007) suggest using both 0-order and 1-order Delaunay triangles.

Texture-based local structures

Tico and Kuosmanen (2003) proposed to create minutiae-centred local structures by using invariant information not directly related to the neighbouring minutiae. Their local descriptors include orientation information taken at some sampling points around a minutia **m** (see Figure 4.15). Each orientation is recorded as relative angle with respect to the minutia angle θ, and therefore it is invariant with respect to the minutia location and direction. The sampling points **p** are located along L concentric circles of radii r_l, ($1 \leq l \leq L$): the first sampling point along each circle has a zero angular displacement with respect to the minutia direction; the rest of the K_l sampling points are uniformly distributed; note that the number of sampling points varies for the different circles. Tico and Kuosmanen (2003) proposed the relation

$K_l = \lceil 172 \cdot r_l / R \rceil$, where R is the fingerprint resolution in dpi. The similarity between two descriptors can be simply computed as the average angular difference between corresponding orientation information. It is worth noting that using local structures not encoding the inter-minutiae relationships can better tolerate missing and false minutiae; however a subsequent consolidation step is, in this case, mandatory to exploit the discriminability given by the minutiae location and angles.

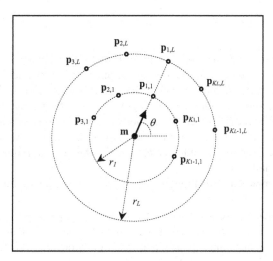

Figure 4.15. The sampling point $\mathbf{p}_{i,j}$, $j=1...L$, $i=1...K_j$ around a minutia $\mathbf{m}$ with direction θ as proposed by Tico and Kuosmanen (2003).

Several variants of Tico and Kuosmanen descriptors have been proposed; the main differences can be summarized as:

- Diverse definitions of the sampling pattern; see for example: Qi and Wang (2005), Zhu, Yin, and Zhang (2005).
- The use of average local orientation over blocks (Wang, Li, and Niu, 2007) instead of point-wise orientations.
- Sampling (at each point **p**) of further information, such as the local ridge frequency (Feng, 2008), the Linear Symmetry (Nilsson and Bigun, 2001), the gray-scale variance (He et al. (2006, 2007)), the gray-scale images encoded through Gabor expansion (Chikkerur et al., 2006) and FingerCode like texture features (Benhammadi et al., 2007a).
- Combination with classical structures based on minutiae inter-relationship such as Jiang and Yau (2000); see for example: Wei, Guo, and Ou (2006) and Feng (2008).

- Combination with local ridge information such as distances and relative angles sampled at different points along the ridge originating at each minutia, and different kinds of ridge-counts (e.g., between minutiae or between minutiae and ridges): Ng et al. (2004), Sha and Tang (2004b), Tong et al. (2005), Sha, Zhao, and Tang (2006), Feng, Ouyang, and Cai (2006), He et al. (2006, 2007), Wang, Li, and Niu (2007a) and Zhang et al. (2007b).

4.4.4 Consolidation

Although the scores obtained from the comparison of local structures can directly lead to a final matching decision, usually a further consolidation stage is implemented to check whether the local similarity holds at the global level. In fact, some minutiae-based local configurations could coincide in fingerprints from different fingers, but the chance that their spatial relationships are coherent is markedly lower. Even though different consolidation techniques have been proposed in conjunction with a specific local structure matching, we believe that most of the underlying ideas can be cross-implemented, and for this reason in this section we concentrate only on the consolidation step.

A conceptually simple consolidation approach is to use a global minutiae matching technique (e.g., a Hough transform based method such as Chang et al. (1997)) where the minutiae pairs ($\mathbf{m}_i$, $\mathbf{m}'_j$) considered are restricted to those obtaining a sufficient score at local level. This can significantly reduce the search space and make the entire matching very efficient. However, if the global matching algorithm is not distortion tolerant, such a consolidation could reduce the overall robustness of the approach.

Single transformation

The simplest consolidation approach relies on the alignment of **T** and **I** minutiae based on the *best transformation* resulting from the local structure matching:

- In Jiang and Yau (2000) the best transformation is that obtained by aligning the central minutiae of the two local structures receiving the highest matching score: the translation vector is the displacement between the minutiae origin and the rotation is the angular difference between the minutiae directions.
- In Tong et al. (2005) the best transformation is determined by the simultaneous local matching of two minutiae in **T** with two minutiae in **I**. This is computationally more demanding but can lead to a more robust alignment.

Once **T** and **I** minutiae have been aligned, the pairing can be computed by using tolerance boxes.

Multiple transformations

Using a single (the best) transformation for the alignment can lead to unsatisfactory results on low-quality and distorted fingerprints. In fact, even for genuine pair of fingerprints, the best transformation originating by local structures matching is not necessarily the best transformation that maximizes pairing at the global level. Therefore several authors have proposed to adopt multiple candidate transformations for the alignments and:

- Select the final transformation according to the highest score achieved (i.e., max. rule) in the final pairing stage; see for example: Parziale and Niel (2004), Deng and Huo (2005), Wei, Guo, and Ou (2006), Zhang et al. (2007b), He et al. (2007), Wang, Li, and Niu (2007a) and Feng (2008).
- Restrict the global matching to regions close to the each reference pair (Lee, Choi, and Kim, 2002) and/or fuse the results of multiple registrations (Sha, Zhao, and Tang, 2006). More details on methods by Sha, Zhao, and Tang (2006) can be found in Section 4.5.3.

Consensus of transformations

The aim is to compute to what extent the individual transformations resulting from the local structure matching are consistent and/or to extract a maximal subset of cross-consistent transformations. This can be obtained by binning (or clustering) the transformation space. Ratha et al.'s (2000) consolidation checks whether the TOP matching local structures are consistent: a pair of local structures is consistent if their spatial relationships (distance and ridge count) with a minimum fraction of the remaining structures in TOP are consistent. Other examples can be found in Chen, Tian, and Yang (2003), Jea and Govindaraju (2005) and Kwon et al. (2006).

Zhang et al. (2003) and He et al. (2006) create a histogram starting from the scores of the local structures and the corresponding transformations and selected the optimum alignment in correspondence with the histogram peak. The histogram technique is conceptually not much different from the voting process underlying a Hough transform-based approach. A similar but more elegant approach, based on Parzen Window estimation, was proposed by He et al. (2007).

Feng et al. (2006) proposed an interesting approach to consolidate local structure compatibility. Their method is based on a relaxation process (see Equation (10)), that iteratively updates the matching scores of any two local structures based on the scores of neighbouring local structures. If A and B are two neighbouring local structures in **T** and C and D are two local structures in **I**, then the compatibility coefficient $c(A,C,B,D)$, that is the support given by B,D to the pair A,C is determined according to the compatibility of the two transformations aligning B,D and A,C. After a number of iterations, the scores of the genuine local structure pairs, which are consistent with their neighbours, are substantially incremented and can be more easily discriminated from the impostor pairs that obtained an initial high score by chance.

Incremental consolidation

Chikkerur, Cartwright, and Govindaraju (2006) arrange their local structures (see *K*-plet definition in the Section 4.4.3) into a directed graph, whose nodes are the *K*-plets and whose connectivity (i.e., edges) encode the *K* nearest neighbour relationships between the nodes (see Figure 4.16). The matching between two graphs is performed through a dual graph traversal algorithm, that, starting from a given pair of nodes <**u**, **v**> (**u** from **T** and **v** from **I**), propagates the visit to neighbouring nodes (in the *K*-plet) in a breadth-first fashion; if two nodes cannot be locally matched, the visit along the corresponding branch is terminated. At the end of the visit, the algorithm returns the number of matched nodes. Since no point correspondence is known a-priori, the whole dual graph traversal is repeated for every pair <**u**, **v**> of nodes and the best solution (i.e. the maximum number of matched nodes) is finally chosen. A similar approach is described in Jain et al. (2006).

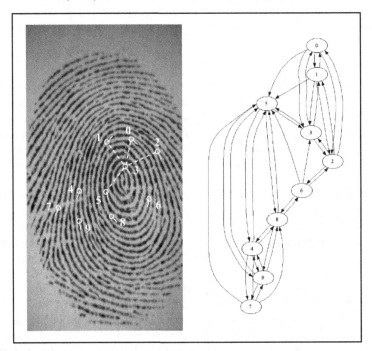

Figure 4.16. Chikkerur, Cartwright, and Govindaraju (2006): the graphs built from the *K*-plets of a fingerprint image; the *K*-plet of the node 3 is highlighted over the fingerprint image. © Springer.

Xu, Chen, and Feng (2007) method uses triangles as local structures, and its consolidation is then based on the following steps: (i) a *growing region* is built around each triangle by extending it with neighbouring triangles; (ii) for each pair of triangles (one from **T** and the other from **I**) the matching score (called *credibility*) is consolidated according to the number of matching minutiae in the two corresponding growing regions; (iii) all growing regions are fused into a *fusion region*: the fusion process is driven by a majority voting with competition strategy, in which every pair of minutiae structures votes for the other and only the minutiae structure pairs that accumulated enough votes survive and are finally fused. The strength of the votes depends on the compatibility between the structures and the credibility of the voter.

4.4.5 Asymmetrical local matching

Two quite atypical fingerprint matching approaches, that can be considered as local minutiae matching, were introduced by Maio and Maltoni (1995) and Kovacs-Vajna (2000). Both these techniques operate asymmetrically; fingerprint enhancement and accurate minutiae extraction (which are time-consuming tasks) are performed only on the template fingerprint at enrollment time, resulting in the minutiae set **T**. During verification, the existence of a correspondence for each minutia in **T** is checked by locally searching the input fingerprint **I**; this allows fingerprint verification to be executed very quickly.

Maio and Maltoni (1995) verified the minutiae existence by using their gray-scale-based minutiae detection algorithm (ref. Section 3.7.2); for each minutia in **T**, a neighborhood of the expected position in the input fingerprint **I** is searched by tracking the ridge(s) in an attempt to establish a correspondence.

The Kovacs-Vajna (2000) method can be sketched as follows.

- The 16×16 gray-scale neighborhood of each minutia $\mathbf{m}_i$ of **T** is correlated with the gray-scale image **I** at all possible positions, and a list of *candidate positions* (i.e., those producing a very high correlation) is recorded.
- A triangular matching is carried out, where minutiae from **T** are incrementally matched with candidate positions from **I**. The matching starts by associating two minutiae from **T** with two candidate positions, and at each step, it is expanded by adding a pair (minutia, candidate position) that is compliant with the already created structure (Figure 4.17).
- The pairing obtained at the end of the above step is consolidated by checking the correspondence of gray-scale profiles between every pair of minutiae from **T** and the corresponding positions in **I**. Instead of explicitly computing the ridge count, Kovacs-Vajna (2000) matches gray-scale profiles via a dynamic time warping algorithm which is able to tolerate perturbations and small location errors.

Similar to Kovacs-Vajna (2000), the Xie et al. (2004) method progressively expands small sets of minutiae, called *seeds*. Each seed initially consists of three minutiae of **I**, each having at least one matching minutia in **T**. Seeds are then expanded by iteratively trying to add spatially close minutiae. A seed fusion step is then performed to improve minutiae pairing uniqueness (i.e., each **I** minutia should be paired to only one **T** minutia), before computing the final score.

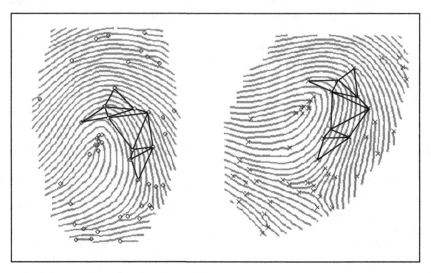

Figure 4.17. An example of partial triangular matching as proposed by Kovacs-Vajna (2000).

4.5 Dealing with Distortion

Non-linear distortion introduced during fingerprint sensing is certainly one of the most critical intra-class variability. NIST Special Database 24 (Watson, 1998) contains videos of live-scan fingerprint data that clearly show the effect of distortion produced by users deliberately moving their fingers on the scanner surface once they are in contact.

Ratha and Bolle (1998) demonstrated that equipping a fingerprint scanner with a mechanical force sensor may help in controlling fingerprint acquisition and guiding the users toward a correct interaction with the sensor. Dorai, Ratha, and Bolle (2000, 2004) proposed an automatic method for detecting the presence of distortion from compressed fingerprint videos and rejecting the distorted frames. Unfortunately, most of the commercial acquisition devices do not mount force sensors and are not able to deliver images at a high frame rate and, therefore, the need for distortion-tolerant matchers is apparent.

Some of the matching algorithms discussed earlier incorporate ad hoc countermeasures to deal with distortion; in particular, local structure matching (see Section 4.4) is itself a valid strategy to control the effects of distortion: for example, methods such as Chen et al. (2006a) and Chen, Tian, and Yang (2006) achieved very good results on FVC2004 databases whose images are markedly affected by distortion.

Throughout the rest of this section we will review the techniques that were explicitly introduced to address the problem of fingerprint matching under non-linear distortion. Once again, we attempt to consistently group them according to the underlying ideas.

4.5.1 Tolerance boxes

Distortion is dealt with by relaxing the spatial relationships between minutiae: in particular, parameters r_0 and θ_0 in Equations (6) and (7) are increased, thus making the pairing constraints less stringent.

In global minutiae matching, distortion may significantly alter the relative distance of two minutiae far away from the principal pair (i.e., the pair used for registration) because of the spatial integration of the skin stretching/compression, and therefore large tolerance boxes need to be used. As a consequence, the probability of falsely matching fingerprints from different fingers increases. In local minutia matching the tolerance box technique is usually more effective; however, particular care must be taken in the consolidation phase to avoid diminishing this advantage.

Tolerance boxes are defined in polar coordinates (sectors of circular annuluses) in the approaches by Jain et al. (1997) and Luo, Tian, and Wu (2000), where edit distance is used for matching pre-aligned minutiae. The size of the tolerance boxes is incrementally increased moving from the center towards the borders of the fingerprint area in order to compensate for the effect of distortion. Jea and Govindaraju (2005) and Chen, Tian, and Yang (2006) suggest that, unlike the radial tolerance, the angular tolerance must decrease with the distance from the centre. Zheng, Wang, and Zhao (2007) argue that a larger tolerance box can be used to match the subsets of ARM (Absolutely Reliable Minutiae) in **T** and **I**, since the risk of matching by chance markedly reduces.

Hao, Tan, and Wang (2002) method not only increases the tolerance with the radius but also implements an iterative error propagation algorithm, where tolerance boxes of the unmatched minutiae are iteratively adapted according to the actual positional errors of the spatially close (already) matched minutiae. A similar idea is exploited by Tong et al. (2008), who define the Relative Location Error (RLE) between two corresponding minutiae according to the location error of neighbouring minutiae. A rigid alignment with large tolerance boxes is initially performed to determine minutiae correspondences. Let $\mathbf{m}_i, \mathbf{m}'_s$ be a pair of corresponding minutiae (i.e., $P(i) = s$), then their relative location error RLE_{is} is defined as:

$$\text{RLE}_{is} = \min_{j,t}\left\{\left|sd\left(\mathbf{m}_i,\mathbf{m}_s''\right)-sd\left(\mathbf{m}_j,\mathbf{m}_t''\right)\right|\right\}$$

where $\mathbf{m}_j,\mathbf{m}_t'$ is another pair of corresponding minutiae (i.e., $P(j) = t$), $\mathbf{m}_j$ lies in the neighborhood of $\mathbf{m}_i$ and $\mathbf{m}_t'$ lies in the neighborhood of $\mathbf{m}_s'$. Using tolerance boxes in RLE instead of an "absolute" location error allows to cope with local distortion, and, at the same time, to tighten the thresholds, thus reducing the probability of matching imposter by chance.

4.5.2 Warping

These techniques explicitly address the fingerprint distortion problem, by allowing one of the two fingerprints to be locally warped to maximize the number of matching minutiae. In general these methods start from a solution determined under the rigid-matching constraint that is relaxed in the second stage: this allows to deal with the large number of degrees of freedom and to improve efficiency.

Bazen and Gerez (2003) attempt to find a smoothed mapping between the template and the input minutiae feature set. Minutiae pairing is initially computed through a local approach and a consolidation step; then the size of the tolerance boxes is reduced and a thin-plate spline (TPS) model is used to deal with the non-linear distortions. Through an iterative procedure, which starts from the initial pairing, the minutiae in the input fingerprint are locally moved (according to the model smoothness constraints) to best fit the template minutiae. The authors report that they obtained a significant improvement when the distortion-tolerant matcher was used instead of the rigid matcher. Some researchers have suggested replacing TPS with other interpolation techniques:

- Novikov and Ushmaev (2004) warping technique relies on the elasticity theory in solid state mechanics, and defines the elastic distortion as a solution of Navier linear Partial Differential Equations (PDE). The registration of elastic distortion between two fingerprints, when a set of mated minutiae is known, can be done using the numerical solution of Navier PDE by Finite Elements Method (FEM). Novikov and Ushmaev (2004) claim that this method is more robust than TPS-based warping when only a small number of reliable mated minutiae is available. A simplification of the initial constraints leads to a computationally simpler implementation based on the convolution with pulse responses.
- Liang and Asano (2006b) used multi-quadratic base functions in conjunction with Radial Basis Function (RBF) interpolation. This allows to better control the range of influence of each control point (i.e., minutia pair); a consequence is that the distortion correction is softer where control points are widely spaced and stronger where they are closer together.
- Meenen, Ashrafi, and Adhami (2006) warping is implemented through a two-dimensional Taylor series expansion truncated at the second degree.

Ross, Dass, and Jain (2005, 2006) proposed two techniques for computing the *average deformation model* of a fingerprint impression by using the TPS warping technique. Given several impressions of a finger, they estimate the average deformation of each impression by comparing it with the rest of the impressions of that finger. The average deformation is developed using TPS warping and is based on minutiae correspondences in Ross, Dass, and Jain (2005) and on ridge curve correspondences in Ross, Dass, and Jain (2006). The estimated average deformation is then utilized to pre-distort the minutiae points in **T** image before matching with **I**. Experimental results show that the use of an average deformation model leads to a better alignment between minutiae resulting in higher matching accuracy. Ross, Dass, and Jain (2006) argue that modeling the distortion using ridge curve correspondences offers several advantages over minutiae correspondences, resulting in improved matching performance (see Figure 4.18). Unlike minutiae points, which can be sparsely distributed in certain regions of a fingerprint image, ridge curves are present all over the image domain, thereby permitting a more reliable estimate of the distortion. The spatial continuity of ridge curves enables sampling of a large number of points on the ridges for establishing correspondences, including points in the vicinity of undetected minutiae points.

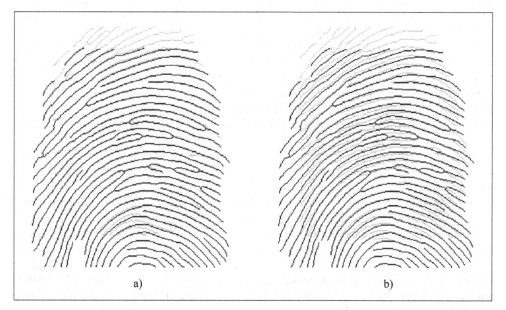

a)   b)

Figure 4.18. (a) Alignment of two fingerprint images using the ridge curve correspondences proposed by Ross, Dass, and Jain (2006); (b) The same fingerprints are aligned using minutiae minutiae correspondences. Both use the TPS warping model. © IEEE.

Almansa and Cohen (2000) introduced a 2D warping algorithm controlled by an energy function that has to be minimized in order to find the optimal mapping. The first term of the energy function requires the two minutiae sets to spatially coincide, whereas the second term introduces a penalty that increases with the irregularity of the warping. Unfortunately, energy minimization is performed with a two-step iterative algorithm whose convergence may be critical and whose time complexity is high. A computationally more efficient energy minimization technique was introduced by Kwon, Yun, and Lee (2007) whose distortion correction is based on a triangular mesh model. A gradient-based optimization technique is used to control the distortion of the mesh by minimizing a two-term energy function: the first term induces the minutiae to be spatially close and the second term favors regular meshes. From their experiments Kwon, Yun, and Lee (2007) conclude that this approach is more robust than TPS for outliers (i.e., false minutiae, or wrong minutiae correspondence).

4.5.3 Multiple-registration and clustering

When two distorted fingerprints are matched using a global approach, the result is that, for different alignments, different subsets of minutiae are matched. Restricting the matching to subgroups (i.e., clusters) of minutiae could alleviate the distortion effects and, at the same time, preserve the distinctiveness of global matching.

Sha, Zhao, and Tang (2006) suggest a multiple transformation-based consolidation where the subsets of minutiae corresponding to the top alignments, i.e., those individually leading to the maximum number of matching minutiae, are fused. Two subsets of matched minutiae can be fused if they share at least three minutiae. During the fusion ambiguous minutiae (i.e., those having inconsistent mates throughout the subsets) are eliminated. Sha, Zhao, and Tang (2006) experimentally determined that subset fusion is more effective than 2D warping to deal with distorted fingerprints.

In the approach by Zhao, Su, and Cai (2006), minutiae are a-priori clustered and global matching is performed among clusters starting from the set of plausible alignments resulting from local matching.

Chen, Tian, and Yang (2003), after globally registering **T** and **I** by using a variant of Jiang and Yau (2000) method, perform a tessellation of the overlap portion of **I** into seven non-overlapping hexagonal regions with fixed radius. Then, they compute the optimal alignment parameters of **T** with respect to each hexagonal region of **I**. A *Registration Pattern* (RP) between **T** and **I** is defined as the concatenation of the seven alignment parameter groups. The authors show that RP for genuine matches is usually quite different from RP of impostor matches (see Figure 4.19); so they learn the genuine RP space off-line by using samples from the NIST Special Database 24. For every new match they perform the following steps: (i) early discard the two fingerprints if the current RP is too far from the genuine RP space, and (ii) use the regions alignment in the computation of the final match score.

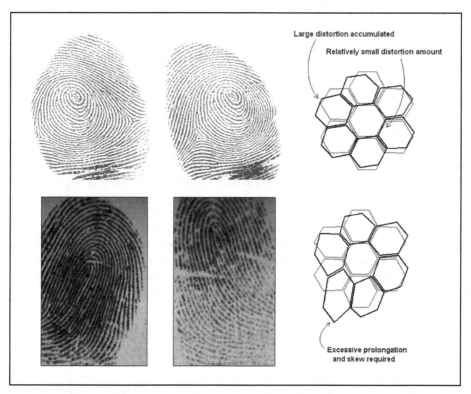

Figure 4.19. An example of Registration Pattern (RP) for a genuine (top row) and an impostor (bottom row) match from Chen, Tian, and Yang (2003). © Springer.

4.5.4 Triangulation and incremental expansion

The local triangular matching proposed by Kovacs-Vajna (2000) (see Section 4.4.5) allows only small local distortion but can tolerate large global distortion; in fact, the geometric aspect of the minutiae triangles that are incrementally constructed may differ only by a small percentage, but the spatial accumulation of small differences may result in a large correction.

Other triangulation-based techniques were proposed by Qi and Wang (2005) and Feng et al. (2006). Minutiae are initially matched with strict tolerance boxes and, as a consequence, some genuine minutiae pairs are not matched. In the second extension stage, for each unmatched minutia $\mathbf{m}_i$ of $\mathbf{T}$, two neighboring matched minutiae, $\mathbf{m}_j$ and $\mathbf{m}_k$ are selected from

T; the mates $\mathbf{m}'_{P(j)}$ and $\mathbf{m}'_{P(k)}$ of $\mathbf{m}_j$ and $\mathbf{m}_k$ are retrieved from **I** and a minutia $\mathbf{m}'_s$ is searched in **I** such that the triangle formed by minutiae $<\mathbf{m}'_s, \mathbf{m}'_{P(j)}, \mathbf{m}'_{P(k)}>$ is sufficiently similar to the triangle $<\mathbf{m}_i, \mathbf{m}_j, \mathbf{m}_k>$; if a similar triangle is found then the pair $\mathbf{m}_i, \mathbf{m}'_s$ is added to the list of matched minutiae (i.e., $P(i) = s$). The process continues until no more (unmatched) minutiae can be added.

4.5.5 Normalization

The idea consists of a-priori correction for distortion from fingerprint samples so that a conventional matcher using rigid alignment can work properly even on distorted fingerprints. The most evident effect of distortion is the local compression/stretching of the fingerprint ridges and valley. To eliminate the undesired effects of distortion, Senior and Bolle (2001) proposed normalizing the fingerprint image to a *canonical* form by deriving a fingerprint representation where all the ridges are equally spaced. The fingerprint images are binarized and thinned, and ridge lines are approximated by spline curves. The average inter-ridge distance is then determined and two ridge dilatation maps are computed that encode the local deviation of the inter-ridge distance from the average one. Transformation into a canonical form is then performed by integration according to the two dilatation maps (Figure 4.20).

Figure 4.20. Transformation of a fingerprint skeleton (left) into canonical form (right) (Senior and Bolle, 2001). © IEICE.

While such a normalization can effectively deal with a cross-ridge stretching/compression compensation, it cannot handle along-ridge distortion component very well, because ridge spacing is not useful for this purpose. Furthermore, even though this approach can be adequate for a proprietary solution, such a canonical representation conflicts with efforts in establishing standard and interoperable fingerprint templates.

Ross and Nadgir (2008) proposed a TPS-based calibration technique to compensate for the variability introduced in the fingerprint images of an individual due to the deployment of different fingerprint scanners. In particular starting from two small sets of manually annotated fingerprint images taken with two given scanners, they derive an average distortion model that can be successfully used to normalize the position of the minutiae. Normalization through distortion removal from images produced by sweep sensor has been investigated by Lorch, Morguet, and Schroder (2004); however, in this specific case distortion is limited to the overall vertical scaling and shear components that can be detected by looking at distance statistics (e.g., ridge distances) or through FFT analysis.

A different normalization technique was proposed by Lee, Choi, and Kim (2002) and Bhowmick and Bhattacharya (2004). They normalized the minutiae distance during the matching stage instead of computing a canonical representation of the fingerprint. In particular, the distance between any two minutiae is normalized according to the local ridge frequency. Suppose that a portion of a fingerprint is distorted by a traction force that increases the distance between two minutiae. Then the local ridge frequency decreases accordingly, and therefore a simple normalization of the distance by the frequency results in a sort of distortion-tolerant distance. Lee, Choi, and Kim (2002) used normalized distances only for matching local minutiae arrangements; in fact, reliably estimating the ridge frequency profile between two minutiae that are far apart might introduce distance errors higher than those made by neglecting the effect of distortion.

4.5.6 Fingerprint distortion models

Distortion models have been proposed with the aim of mathematically describing how a fingerprint pattern can be modified when a finger touches a rigid flat surface. Understanding such mechanisms not only can lead to the design of more robust matchers, but also allows simulating distortion for fingerprint synthesis (see Chapter 6).

Cappelli, Maio, and Maltoni (2001a) explicitly modelled skin distortion caused by nonorthogonal pressure of the finger against the sensor surface. By noting that the finger pressure against the sensor is not uniform but decreases from the center towards the borders, their distortion model defined three distinct regions (see Figure 4.21):

1. A close-contact region (*a*), where the high pressure and the surface friction do not allow any skin slippage.
2. An external region (*c*), whose boundary delimits the fingerprint visible area, where the small pressure allows the finger skin to be dragged by the finger movement.

3. A transitional region (*b*) where an elastic distortion is produced to smoothly combine regions *a* and *c*. The skin compression and stretching is restricted to region *b*, as points in *a* remain almost fixed and points in *c* rigidly move together with the rest of the finger.

The distortion model is defined by a mapping $\Re^2 \rightarrow \Re^2$ that can be viewed as an affine transformation (with no scale change) which is progressively "braked" as it moves from *c* towards *a*. Each point **v** is mapped into *distortion*(**v**) such that:

$$distortion(\mathbf{v}) = \mathbf{v} + \Delta(\mathbf{v}) \cdot brake(shapedist_a(\mathbf{v}), k), \tag{13}$$

where $\Delta(\ )$ specifies the affine transformation of a point in the external region *c*; $shapedist_a(\ )$ is a shape function describing the boundary of region *a*; *brake* is a monotonically increasing function that controls the gradual transition from region *a* towards region *c*; the input parameter *k* regulates the skin plasticity. Figure 4.21b shows some examples of distortion by varying the parameters.

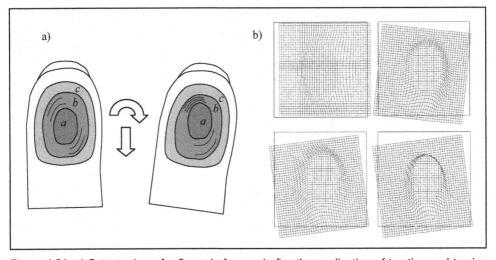

Figure 4.21. a) Bottom view of a finger before and after the application of traction and torsion forces. In both cases the fingerprint area detected by the sensor (i.e., the finger touching area) is delimited by the external boundary of region *c*. b) Distortions of a square mesh obtained by applying the above model with different parameter settings. The black square denotes the initial mesh position and its movement with respect to the mesh boundary indicating the amount of displacement and rotation that occurred. In the first row, two different transformations are shown: from left to right: a horizontal displacement ($\Delta x = 18$) and a combined displacement and rotation ($\Delta x = -6$, $\Delta y = 27$, $\theta = -6°$); the second row shows the effect of varying the skin plasticity coefficient *k* from 1.0 (left) and 0.5 (right) for a given transformation. Reprinted with permission from Cappelli, Maio, and Maltoni (2001). © Springer-Verlag.

Figure 4.22 shows an example of distortion recovery applied to fingerprint images; in the left column two distorted fingerprint images are shown and both their minutiae (denoted by small squares) and the corresponding minutiae (small circles) extracted from previous undistorted frames are superimposed. A displacement between pairs of corresponding minutiae is evident. In the central column, the same frames are shown, but now the minutiae from the non-distorted frames have been remapped by applying the distortion transformation. The good spatial minutiae matching obtained shows that the model is capable of dealing with such deformations. The model parameters have been manually adjusted and do not necessarily constitute the best choice. The corresponding mesh distortion is plotted in the third column and shows that, in the former case, the deformation is mainly caused by a vertical (downward) traction producing a compression at the top, whereas, in the latter, a (counterclockwise) torsion is the most evident cause. In this example, the 10 parameters controlling the distortion model were manually adjusted to achieve optimal distortion recovery. The study of an effective and efficient optimization technique (eventually embedded into a minutiae matcher), which is capable of automatically deriving the deformation parameters, still remains a challenging research task.

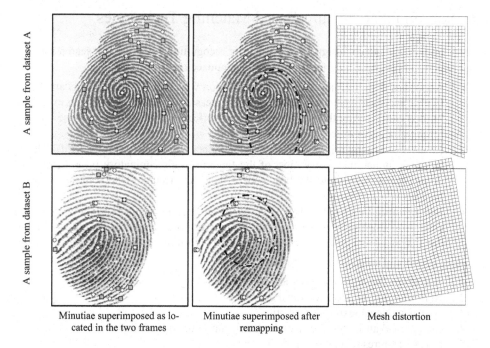

A sample from dataset A

A sample from dataset B

| Minutiae superimposed as located in the two frames | Minutiae superimposed after remapping | Mesh distortion |

Figure 4.22. Minutiae correspondence before (first column) and after (second column) the distortion mapping. The third column shows the corresponding mesh distortion. Reprinted with permission from Cappelli, Maio, and Maltoni (2001). © Springer-Verlag.

Another distortion model, similar to that proposed by Cappelli, Maio, and Maltoni (2001a), was introduced by Novikov and Ushmaev (2004). This model is based on the solution of a set of Navier linear partial differential equations (see Section 4.5.2) and it does not explicitly define an immobile region (a) or a transitional area (b); however, the output is very similar to the typical deformation shown in Figure 4.21 and demonstrates the existence of an ellipse-like quasi un-deformable region. Novikov and Ushmaev (2005) also studied the principal deformation of fingerprints, that is, the typical way a fingerprint distorts. The analysis is performed by reducing (through PCA) the dimensionality of the displacement vectors obtained by registering the elastic distortion in fingerprint pairs with the method described in Novikov and Ushmaev (2004). With fingerprints being pre-aligned with respect to rigid transformations, the main eigenvectors just encode the principal modes of variation of the distortion with respect to a neutral print. Test performed over FVC2002 databases reveal that torsion and traction along the two axes are among the few principal distortions of fingerprints; the experiments also confirm the presence of a quasi un-deformable region.

4.6 Non-minutiae Feature-Based Matching Techniques

Three main reasons induce designers of fingerprint recognition techniques to search for additional fingerprint distinguishing features, beyond minutiae:

- Additional features may be used in conjunction with minutiae (and not as an alternative) to increase system accuracy and robustness (see feature level fusion in Chapter 7). It is worth noting that several non-minutiae feature based techniques use minutiae for pre-alignment or to define anchor points.
- Reliably extracting minutiae from extremely poor quality fingerprints is difficult. Although minutiae may carry most of the fingerprint discriminatory information, they do not always constitute the best tradeoff between accuracy and robustness for the poor quality fingerprints.
- Non-minutiae-based methods may perform better than minutiae-based methods when the area of fingerprint sensor is small. In fingerprints with small area, only 4–5 minutiae may exist and in that case minutiae-based algorithm do not behave satisfactorily.

The more commonly used non-minutiae features are

1. Size of the fingerprint and shape of the external fingerprint silhouette.
2. Number, type, and position of singularities.
3. Global and local texture information.
4. Geometrical attributes and spatial relationship of the ridge lines.
5. Level 3 features (e.g., sweat pores).
6. Other features: fractal features (Polikarpova, 1996), shape features derived from the one-dimensional projection of the two dimensional fingerprint image (Takeda et al., 1990; Ceguerra and Koprinska, 2002a, b).

Features listed in (1) and (2) above are, in general, very unstable, and they vary depending on which part of the finger touches the sensor. Features (3), (4) and (5) have been shown to be particularly useful in the context of automatic fingerprint matching: a separate section is provided for each of them in the following.

4.6.1 Global and local texture information

Global and local texture information sources are important alternatives to minutiae, and texture-based fingerprint matching is an active area of research. Image texture is defined by spatial repetition of basic elements, and are characterized by properties such as scale, orientation, frequency, symmetry, isotropy, and so on. Fingerprint ridge lines (as discussed in Chapter 3) are mainly described by smooth ridge orientation and frequency, except in singular regions. These singular regions are discontinuities in a basically regular pattern and include the loop(s) and the delta(s) at a coarse resolution and the minutiae points at a high resolution.

Coetzee and Botha (1993) and Willis and Myers (2001) proposed analyzing fingerprint texture in the Fourier domain. Although ridges in the spatial domain transform to a fairly constant frequency (in the frequency domain), the distinguishing characteristics of a fingerprint such as the specific ridge orientation and the minutiae manifest themselves as small deviations from the dominant spatial frequency of the ridges. A "wedge-ring detector" is then used to perform the analysis in the frequency domain; the harmonics in each of the individual regions of the detector are accumulated, resulting in a fixed-length feature vector that is translation, rotation, and scale invariant.

Global texture analysis fuses contributions from different characteristic regions into a global measurement and, as a result, most of the available spatial information is lost. Local texture analysis has proved to be more effective than global feature analysis. We already pointed out in Section 4.4.3, the relevance of texture-based local structures in the evolution of local structure matching.

We know that most of the local texture information is contained in the orientation and frequency images (ref. Sections 3.2 and 3.3). Several methods have been proposed where a similarity score is derived from the correlation between the aligned orientation images of the two fingerprints: Qi and Wang (2005), Cheng, Tian, and Chen (2004), Yager and Amin (2004), Kulkarni, Patil, and Holambe (2006), Zhang et al. (2007b), and Zheng, Wang, and Zhao (2007). The alignment can be based on the orientation image alone (see Section 4.3.6) or delegated to a further minutiae matching stage. Gu, Zhou, and Yang (2006) also used orientation image in their hybrid matching technique, but unlike other researchers they used a model-based approximation of the orientation image (see Section 3.2.6). Their experimental results show that, not only this allows to reduce the template size (in fact only the model parameters have to be stored), but also improve accuracy due to the robustness of the model to local perturbation of the orientation image. Wan and Zhou (2006) used frequency image correlation in conjunction with minutiae matching to produce a final score. Since the frequency images directly computed from the fingerprints may lack in robustness against noise and distortion, a polynomial model is proposed to approximate the coarse frequency map, thus making the resulting feature more robust.

The most popular technique to match fingerprints based on texture information remains the FingerCode approach by Jain et al. (2000). The fingerprint area of interest is tessellated with respect to the core point (see Figure 4.23). A feature vector is composed of an ordered enumeration of the features extracted from the local information contained in each sector specified by the tessellation. Thus the feature elements capture the local texture information and the ordered enumeration of the tessellation captures the global relationship among the local contributions. The local texture information in each sector is decomposed into separate channels by using a Gabor filterbank (ref. Section 3.6.2); in fact, the Gabor filterbank is a well-known technique for capturing useful texture information in specific bandpass channels as well as decomposing this information into biorthogonal components in terms of spatial frequencies. In their experimentation, Jain et al. (2000) obtained good results by tessellating the area of interest into 80 cells (five bands and 16 sectors), and by using a bank of eight Gabor filters (eight orientations, 1 scale = 1/10 for 500 dpi fingerprint images). Therefore, each fingerprint is represented by a $80 \times 8 = 640$ fixed-size feature vector, called the *FingerCode*. The generic element V_{ij} of the vector ($i = 1...80$ is the cell index, $j = 1...8$ is the filter index) denotes the energy revealed by the filter j in cell i, and is computed as the average absolute deviation (AAD) from the mean of the responses of the filter j over all the pixels of the cell i:

$$V_{ij} = \frac{1}{n_i}\left(\sum_{C_i}\left|g(x,y:\theta_j,1/10) - \overline{g_i}\right|\right),$$

where C_i is the ith cell of the tessellation, n_i is the number of pixels in C_i, the Gabor filter expression $g(\ )$ is defined by Equation (11) in Section 3.6.2 and $\overline{g_i}$ is the mean value of g over the cell C_i. Matching two fingerprints is then translated into matching their respective FingerCodes, which is simply performed by computing the Euclidean distance between two FingerCodes.

From experimentation results over two fingerprint databases, Jain et al. (2000) concluded that although FingerCodes are not as distinctive as minutiae, they carry complementary information which, as they explicitly demonstrated, can be combined with minutiae to improve the overall matching accuracy.

One critical point in the above approach is the alignment of the grid defining the tessellation with respect to the core point. When the core point cannot be reliably detected, or it is close to the border of the fingerprint area, the FingerCode of the input fingerprint may be incomplete or incompatible with respect to the template. Jain, Ross, and Prabhakar (2001) and Ross, Jain, and Reisman (2003) propose variants of the above method, suitable for small-area capacitive sensors, where tessellation is performed over a square mesh grid after the two fingerprints have been aligned by using minutiae. The score obtained by minutiae matching is fused with that produced by FingerCode matching to improve accuracy. A different way to overcome the critical core-based alignment is to use a feature-space correlation technique to simultaneously align and match the FingerCodes (Ross, Reisman, and Jain, 2002).

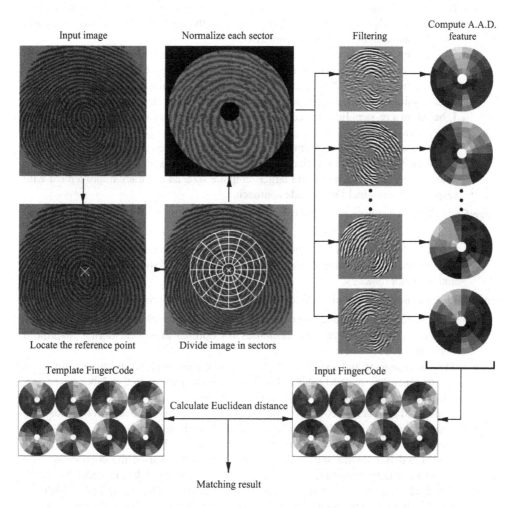

Figure 4.23. System diagram of Jain et al.'s (2000) FingerCode approach. © IEEE.

Several variants of the Jain et al. (2000) have been introduced:

- In Lee and Wang (1999), instead of convolving the Gabor filters with all the pixels of each cell, the authors performed a sub-sampling at block level with the aim of improving efficiency.
- In Lee and Wang (2001), instead of recording the response of each filter at each sampling point, only the index of the filter that gives the highest response was stored and used for subsequent fingerprint comparison.
- Sha, Zhao, and Tang (2003) extend FingerCode features by adding to each AAD value the dominant orientation inside the corresponding block. Sha, Zhao, and Tang (2005) introduced an efficient implementation of Ross, Jain, and Reisman (2003) approach suitable for identification; in fact, in their version the FingerCode features of **I**, based on a re-sampling procedure, do not need to be recomputed for every template **T** in the database.
- Benhammadi et al. (2007) extract FingerCode like features around each minutia and then locally match these invariant representations. Their experimental results show, in spite of a higher complexity and larger template size, an accuracy improvement with respect to the original FingerCode approach.

FingerCode like features were also used by:

- Hui et al. (2004) and Hui and Li (2004) to train an ANFIS (Adaptive Neuro-Fuzzy Inference System) based classifier to perform fingerprint recognition.
- Lumini and Nanni (2006) to train an SVM classifier to distinguish between genuine and impostor matches.

Finally, other techniques based on local texture analysis have been proposed as follows.

- Hamamoto (1999) applied Gabor filters at nine fixed positions around the core and used correlation between filter responses for optimal alignment during fingerprint matching.
- Tico, Kuosmanen, and Saarinen (2001) suggested using wavelet domain features, and claimed that their method achieved performance comparable to the Gabor-based one, but had the advantage of avoiding any pre-processing such as core point detection. Huang and Aviyente (2004a, b) work focuses on choosing the best wavelets basis for fingerprint matching. Multi-resolution approaches based on the Discrete Wavelet Transform (DWT) were also introduced by Chebira et al. (2007), Nanni and Lumini (2007) and Bouchaffra and Amira (2008). Rowe (2007) used the coefficients of a wavelet decomposition to match the large amount of textural data provided by a multispectral imaging fingerprint scanner. Amornraksa and Tachaphetpiboon (2006) report that in their experiments Discrete Cosine Transform (DCT) coefficients provided better accuracy with respect to DWT coefficients.
- Nanni and Lumini (2008), after a minutiae-based alignment, decompose the image into several overlapping blocks, and for each block: (i) apply a bank of Gabor filters, (ii) extract LBP (Local Binary Pattern) features; (iii) use Euclidean distance to compare LBP histograms. LBP features (Zhang et al., 2004) are grayscale invariant statis-

tics that can be computed as the difference between the gray value of a central pixel and the average gray value over its circular neighborhood.

- Park, Pankanti, and Jain (2008) adopted Scale Invariant Feature Transformation (SIFT). SIFT extracts repeatable characteristic feature points from an image and generates descriptors representing the texture around the feature points.

4.6.2 Geometrical attributes and spatial relationship of the ridge lines

The use of spatial relationship of ridges forms the basis of the earlier methods proposed by Moayer and Fu (1986) and Isenor and Zaky (1986). In the former, tree grammars are introduced to classify ridge line patterns after they are binarized and thinned. In the latter, incremental graph matching was carried out to compare a set of ridges arranged in graph structures (ridges are the graph nodes and arches are defined according to ridge adjacency and visibility). More recently other researchers focused on techniques relying (at least partially) on ridge matching. The ridges representation is usually obtained by sampling points (at fixed intervals) along each thinned ridge.

In Chen, Tian, and Yang (2006) ridge information is associated with the minutiae they originate from; once the minutiae are paired with a local structure based algorithm, the computation of the final score is consolidated by taking into account the spatial matching of the ridge points; experimental results show that the contribution by the ridge sampling is significant.

Xie, Su, and Cai (2006a), Feng, Ouyang, and Cai (2006) and Feng and Cai (2006) explicitly exploit ridge relationships: for each sampled point they annotate the labels of the two neighboring ridges. More details are given below:

- In Xie, Su, and Cai (2006) ridge-matching is performed by comparing neighboring information for all the pre-matched pairs of ridges: two ridges (one from **T** and one from **I**) are pre-matched if they have similar length and curvature. The ridge matching implementation outperforms a minutiae matching implementation of the same authors over the four FVC2000 databases.
- In Feng, Ouyang, and Cai (2006), the ridge and minutiae matching is performed incrementally, starting from a local structure based alignment.
- Feng and Cai (2006a) encode the geometric relationships among points sampled over ridges based on RCS (Ridge Coordinate System); an RCS is defined for every ridge R by using a minutia to define the origin and the direction of the reference axes and the ridge count as a metric for measuring distances. The RCS coordinates of the points of all the ridges (except R) form the feature vector associated to R. These feature vectors, which are invariant under translation and rotation, are used for alignment and matching through a greedy algorithm.

Zhang et al. (2007b) overcome the problems introduced by the ambiguity between ridge ending and bifurcation minutiae by sampling both the ridge and valley on the two sides of each minutia. Feng, Ouyang and Cai (2006) simplify the successive ridge matching, by implementing a post-processing stage where the ridge pattern is regularized by: (i) disconnecting closed ridges (i.e. loops), (ii) splitting into three parts the ridges associated with bifurcations, and (iii) removing short ridges.

Other techniques can be found in Xiao and Bian (1986), Kaymaz and Mitra (1992), He et al. (2003a), Cheng, Tian, and Chen (2004) and Fang et al. (2007).

4.6.3 Level 3 features

Arrangement of sweat pores along fingerprint ridges is undoubtedly highly discriminant but, as pointed out by several researchers, reliable detection of sweat pores requires high-resolution scanners and robust extraction algorithms. Stosz and Alyea (1994) argued that a resolution of at least 800 dpi is required to detect small pores.

Stosz and Alyea (1994) proposed a skeletonization-based pore extraction and matching algorithm. Specifically, the locations of all end points (with at most one neighbor) and branch points (with exactly three neighbors) in the skeleton image are extracted and each end point is used as a starting location for tracking the skeleton. The tracking algorithm advances one element at a time until one of the following stopping criteria is encountered: (1) another end point is detected, (2) a branch point is detected, and (3) the path length exceeds a maximum allowed value. Condition (1) implies that the tracked segment is a *closed pore*, while Condition (2) implies an *open pore*. Finally, skeleton artifacts resulting from scars and wrinkles are corrected and pores from reconnected skeletons are removed. An example of pore extraction is shown in Figure 4.24.

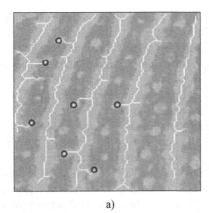 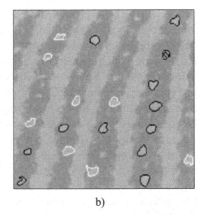

a)   b)

Figure 4.24. Examples from Stosz and Alyea (1994): a) detection of open pores from the skeleton; b) extraction of open pores (white) and closed pores (black). Images courtesy of K. Kryszczuk.

The pore matching is performed (in a human-assisted or semi-automatic mode) by: (i) subdividing the images in small regions and retaining only discriminant regions; (ii) pre-aligning the regions through intensity correlation; (iii) counting the numbers of spatially coincident pores for each pair of regions. The experiments conducted over a database of 258 fingerprints from 137 individuals (images were acquired at an average resolution of 1,835 dpi) showed that by combining minutia and pore information a reduction of 6.96% in the FNMR can be achieved at a FMR of 0.04% (the FNMR for minutiae alone was 31%).

Based on the above algorithm, Roddy and Stosz (1997) later conducted a statistical analysis of pores and presented a model to predict the upper bound on performance of a pore-based automated fingerprint system. For example, they demonstrated that the probability of occurrence of a particular combination of 20 ridge-independent pores is 5.186×10^{-8}.

Kryszczuk, Morier, and Drygajlo (2004) studied the distinctiveness of minutiae and pore features in fragmentary fingerprint comparison by using images acquired at about 2,000 dpi. For this purpose they also implemented a skeletonization-based pore detection algorithm with more anatomical constraints with respect to Stosz and Alyea (1994) algorithm. Kryszczuk, Morier, and Drygajlo (2004) concluded that the use of pores can offer at least a comparable recognition potential from a small area fingerprint fragment, as minutiae features offer for fragments of larger area.

Jain, Chen, and Demirkus (2007) conducted a systematic study to determine how much performance gain one can achieve by introducing Level 3 features in AFIS. They noted that skeletonization is effective for pore extraction only when the image quality is very good and the image resolution is very high. Hence, unlike in previous studies, Level 3 features, including pores and ridge contours, were extracted using Gabor filters and wavelet transform: see Figure 4.25 for some details of a pore extraction process. Level 1 (orientation images), Level 2 (minutiae) and Level 3 (pores and ridge contours) features are then hierarchically matched, leading to early rejection in case of very low similarity. Pores and ridge contours are locally matched (in the neighbourhoods of the already paired minutiae) using the Iterative Closest Point (ICP) algorithm. Jain, Chen, and Demirkus (2007) evaluated their approach over a database acquired with a 1,000 dpi commercial scanner and showed that Level 3 features carry significant discriminatory information. There is a relative reduction of 20% in the EER of the matching system when Level 3 features were employed in combination with Level 1 and 2 features. The performance gain is consistently observed across various quality fingerprint images.

Chen and Jain (2007) proposed an algorithm, based on local phase symmetry, to extract other Level 3 features such as dots and incipient ridges. According to some latent examiners these features are often more valuable and reproducible than pores for the purpose of partial latent fingerprint matching. Dots and incipients were added to the minutiae set and matched as they were normal minutiae (the origin of an incipient ridge is placed in its midpoint). This led to a significant accuracy improvement when matching partial fingerprints.

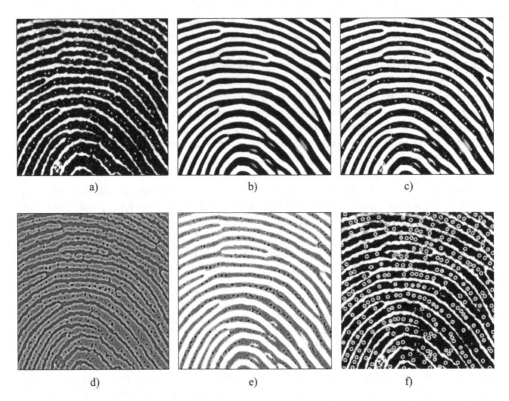

Figure 4.25. Pores extraction in Jain, Chen, and Demirkus (2007): a) a partial fingerprint image at 1,000 ppi; b) enhancement of the image shown in a) using a Gabor filter-based contextual technique. c) a linear combination of a) and b); d) wavelet band-pass filtering of the image in a) that exhibits small dark blob in correspondence of the pores; e) a linear combination of d) and b); f) extracted pores (white circles) after thresholding the image in e). © IEEE.

4.7 Comparing the Performance of Matching Algorithms

Within the biometric recognition context a benchmark is defined by a database and an associated testing protocol. The protocol defines the subsets of images that can be used for training and testing, the pair of images that have to be compared, the performance metrics to be used and how they must be computed. Collecting fingerprint databases is expensive and prone to human errors. Chapter 6 addresses this problem in more details and introduces synthetic fingerprint generation as a viable solution for fingerprint algorithm testing. Using exactly the same benchmark is essential to compare the performance of different algorithms.

4.7.1 Fingerprint database

Before the organization of the first fingerprint verification competitions FVC2000, the only large public domain fingerprint datasets were the National Institute of Standards and Technology (NIST) databases. Although these NIST databases constitute an excellent benchmark for AFIS development (Shen and Khanna, 1994) and fingerprint classification studies (ref. Chapter 5), they are not well suited for the evaluation of algorithms operating on live-scan (dab) images. In fact:

- NIST DB 4 (Watson and Wilson, 1992a), NIST DB 9 (Watson and Wilson, 1992b), NIST DB 10 (Watson, 1993a), and NIST DB 14 (Watson, 1993a) contain thousands of images scanned from rolled inked impressions on cards, which are quite different from live-scan dab images.
- NIST DB 24 (Watson, 1998) contains 100 live sequences (capture video) from 10 individuals. In principle, static frames could be extracted from the videos and used for performance evaluation; on the other hand, most of the videos have been taken under particular conditions to study the effect of finger rotation and plastic distortion, and therefore are not well suited for overall system evaluations.
- NIST DB 27 (Garris and McCabe, 2000) was released to test the performance of latent fingerprint identification. Latent fingerprint images of varying quality were provided together with their corresponding rolled impressions taken from cards. Minutiae data manually extracted by human experts were also provided. NIST DB 27 is a valuable source of information for studying the difficult problems of latent fingerprint enhancement and matching.

FVC campaigns (2000, 2002, 2004 and 2006) were organized with the aim of providing fingerprint databases to any interested researcher and to track performance of the state-of-the-art fingerprint matching algorithms. Fortunately, most of the authors now report the results of their experiments on one or more of these databases according to the proposed protocol, thus producing results that can be compared across the whole scientific community. It is hoped that this will become a common practice for all the scientists and practitioners in the field. For this purpose, we have included the complete FVC2000, FVC2002 and FVC2004 databases in the DVD accompanying this book. FVC2006 can be obtained upon request following the instruction in BioLab (2007). Readers are invited to consult the FVC reports (also included in the DVD) where they will find all the details necessary to set up a test session identical to that performed in the competitions. Table 4.1 provides a brief summary of FVC databases. The difficulty of each database (as reported in the note field) depends on several factors: the population, the perturbations voluntarily introduced, the quality of the scanner, etc.; the difficulty reported in Table 4.1 derives from an a-posteriori analysis of the results achieved by top performing participants (see also Table 4.3). In general FVC databases should not be used to infer or compare the scanner quality; in fact, except for FVC2006, the protocol and volunteers were not the same for the different scanners; furthermore, other indicators such as the Failure To Enroll should be taken into account to perform a fair scanner comparison.

While future FVC initiatives will converge in FVC-onGoing (2009), for now we recommend scientists and practitioners to continue testing their systems according to the scenarios reported in Table 4.2.

Competition	Number of databases	Size of each Database: A - Evaluation set B - Trainin set	Notes
FVC2000 Maio et al. (2002a)	4	A: 100×8 B: 10×8	- Volunteers are mainly unhabituated students. - Two sessions, no quality check. - Low/Medium difficulty (DB1, DB2, DB4); Medium/High difficulty (DB3).
FVC2002 Maio et al. (2002b)	4	A: 100×8 B: 10×8	- Volunteers are mainly unhabituated students. - Three sessions, no quality check. - Voluntarily exaggerated perturbations: displacement, rotation, wetness and dryness. - Low difficulty (DB1, DB2, DB3, DB4).
FVC2004 Maio et al. (2004) Cappelli et al. (2006)	4	A: 100×8 B: 10×8	- Volunteers are mainly unhabituated students. - Three sessions, no quality check. - Voluntarily exaggerated perturbations: distortion, wetness and dryness. - Medium difficulty (DB1, DB2, DB3, DB4).
FVC2006 BioLab (2007)	4	A: 140×12 B: 10×12	- Heterogeneous population also includes unhabituated manual workers and elderly people. No quality check. - The final datasets were selected from a larger database by choosing the most difficult fingerprints according to a quality index. - High difficulty (DB1), Medium difficulty (DB3), Low difficulty (DB2, DB4).

Table 4.1. A summary of FVC databases. In the database size the notation MxN, denotes M fingers and N samples per finger. In all the competitions the first three databases were acquired by selecting commercial scanners of different types, including large-area optical, small area optical, solid state capacitive and thermal sweep. The fourth database was synthetically generated by using the SFinGe tool (see Chapter 6).

Scenario	Benchmark
Algorithms optimized to work with large-area touch sensors (e.g., AFIS, government applications).	FVC2000 – DB3 FVC2002 – DB1, DB2 FVC2004 – DB1 FVC2006 – DB2
Algorithms designed to work with large-, medium- and small-area touch sensors	FVC2000 – DB1, DB2, DB3, DB4 FVC2002 – DB1, DB2, DB3, DB4 FVC2004 – DB1, DB2, DB4 FVC2006 – DB1, DB2, DB4
Algorithms to be used with sweep sensors	FVC2004 – DB3 FVC2006 – DB3
Test aimed at showing the algorithms robustness with respect to plastic distorsion	FVC2004 – DB1, DB2, DB3, DB4

Table 4.2. Recommended benchmarks for the evaluation of algorithms in different contexts: performance should be reported on the largest subset of databases listed for the scenario of interest.

Besides NIST and FVC databases, other fingerprint collections can be used for testing fingerprint algorithms. The following ones are recommended for the design and test of multimodal systems since they provide not only fingerprints, but also other biometric characteristics of the same group of subjects.

- *MCYT Bimodal Database* (Ortega-Garcia et al. (2003); Simon-Zorita et al. (2003b)): fingerprint and signature modalities from 330 subjects.
- *BIOMET Multimodal Database* (Garcia-Salicetti et al., 2003): speech, face, hand, fingerprint and signature from 91 subjects.
- *BioSec Multimodal Database* (Fierrez-Aguilar et al., 2007): face, speech, fingerprint and iris from 250 subjects. FVC2006 DB1, DB2 and DB3 are subsets of this database.
- *BioSecure Multimodal Database* (BioSecure, 2008) is composed of three parts; DB1: speech and face from 1,000 subjects acquired over the Internet under unsupervised conditions; DB2: speech, face, signature, fingerprint, hand and iris from 700 subjects acquired in a standard office environment; DB3: speech, face, signature and fingerprint from 700 subjects acquired using mobile hand-held devices under two acquisition conditions (controlled/indoor and uncontrolled/outdoor).

4.7.2 Fingerprint evaluation campaigns

The most important evaluation campaigns for fingerprint recognition are the NIST Fingerprint Vendor Technology Evaluation (FpVTE2003) (Wilson et al., 2004) and the four Fingerprint Verification Competitions (FVC), which took place in 2000, 2002, 2004 and 2006. A comparative summary of the performances obtained in the four FVC campaigns is given in Table 4.3 while a comparison between FVC2006 and FpVTE2003 is provided in Table 4.4.

	DB1	DB2	DB3	DB4
FVC2000	2.30%	1.39%	4.34%	3.38%
FVC2002	0.20%	0.17%	0.63%	0.16%
FVC2004	1.61%	2.32%	1.34%	0.81%
FVC2006	5.88%	0.05%	1.59%	0.39%

Table 4.3. Average accuracy (EER) of the three best performing algorithms over the different FVC databases. A direct comparison across the different competitions is not possible due to the use of databases of unequal difficulty.

Another interesting "on-going" evaluation campaign is NIST Proprietary Fingerprint Template (PFT) Testing (NIST, 2008). The results of the first round of test performed over a number of large sequestered databases are reported in Watson et al. (2005a): considering the two most accurate systems, the average FNMR at a FMR of 0.01% was lower than 2% while the worst FNMR at a FMR of 0.01% was about 6%. Further analysis has been carried out to measure the accuracy of a two-finger system (Watson et al., 2005b). Updates are periodically published (NIST, 2008) focusing only on the accuracy of two finger systems measured over four sequestered databases of large size. As of May 2, 2008 the average EER of the three best algorithms over the four databases are: 0.34%, 0.05%, 0.04% and 0.03%. Note that performance on the first database is markedly lower; this is due to the relatively low quality of the images in this database that includes DHS (US Department of Homeland Security) recidivist cases.

4.7.3 Interoperability of fingerprint recognition algorithms

As already discussed in Section 3.7.3, standards have been recently released to specify the format of fingerprint templates, paving the way for interoperability of algorithms designed by different developers (e.g., the template created with vendor A's feature extractor must be matched with vendor B's matcher). The minutiae-based standard ISO/IEC 19794–2 (2005) is the most important one, due to the wide diffusion of minutiae-based systems.

FVC2006 BioLab (2007)	**FpVTE 2003** Wilson et al. (2004)
Databases - Population: data collected in 2 European countries by 4 organizations. - Low-cost commercial scanners (including small area & sweep sensors). - New databases collected and then made publicly available after the competition. - Four databases of small/medium size: 1,680 images each.	**Databases** - Operational fingerprint data from a variety of U.S. Government sources, including poor-quality fingers and low-quality sources. - Mainly AFIS-compliant scanners. - Existing databases not made available after the competition. - Large databases. MST database (whose test is the most similar to FVC) contains 10,000 images.
Evaluation procedure - Data collection is strongly supervised (evaluator's hardware). - Verification time (efficiency), template size and memory usage are reported.	**Evaluation procedure** - Data collection is supervised (testee's hardware). - Cannot avoid template consolidation, score normalization.
Participants - 53 (13 academic, 13 independent developers, 27 commercial). - Anonymous participation allowed (31 decided to remain anonymous).	**Participants** - 18 (commercial). - Anonymous participation not allowed.
Accuracy - The average EER among the three most accurate algorithms on DB2 database (whose scanner is the most similar to those used in FpVTE) is 0.049%	**Accuracy** - The average EER among the three most accurate algorithms on MST subtest (whose test is the most similar to FVC) is 0.55%

Table 4.4. A comparison between FVC2006 and FpVTE2003.

The purpose of the NIST Minutiae Interoperability Exchange Test (MINEX) (Grother et al., 2006) was to quantify the impact of the minutiae template standard on the verification accuracy. Actually, the template format used was ANSI/INCITS 378 (2004) which is slightly different compared to ISO/IEC 19794–2 (2005). As expected, the results obtained demonstrated that:

- Standard templates lead to lower verification performance than proprietary templates even if the feature extractor and matcher are provided by the same vendor; the most accurate systems tested in MINEX nearly doubled their FNMR error for FMR = 1% (see Table 4.5), and increased their FMR error about 10 times for FNMR = 1%. We have pointed out already how many features can be used in conjunction with minutiae to improve accuracy and robustness; unfortunately, these non-minutia features extracted and stored in a proprietary format cannot currently be used in an interoperable scenario.

- In a typical interoperability scenario (where vendor A extracts the first standard template T_A to be matched and vendor B extracts the second standard template T_B and provides the matching algorithm to compare T_A against T_B) the FNMR error at FMR = 1% is about 2.5 higher with respect to the standard template scenario and about 5.4 times higher with respect to proprietary template scenario (see Table 4.5).
- The reduced accuracy obtained using standard templates compared to proprietary templates can be compensated for by using two fingers for all authentication attempts (see Chapter 7). In such a case the performance gain is about one order of magnitude. However, using two fingers is not as convenient for the user and, in general, it results in a longer transaction time; hence it is not feasible for many applications.

Within the scope of the PIV (Personal Identity Verification) project (NIST, 2007), for single finger verification, NIST has set the maximum error (both FMR and FNMR) to 1% that an algorithm can exhibit when interoperating with every other algorithm (in a group of existing interoperable algorithms) in order to be declared interoperable.

	Proprietary template scenario	Standard template scenario	Interoperability scenario
Vendor 1	0.47%	1.29%	4.28%
Vendor 2	0.89%	1.36%	3.26%
Vendor 3	0.89%	1.40%	3.08%

Table 4.5. Some MINEX results: the table reports values of FNMR for FMR =1% for the three most accurate algorithms. In the "proprietary template" scenario the vendor provided both feature extraction and matching algorithms and used its proprietary format for the template. In the "standard template" scenario the vendor provided both feature extraction and matching but used a standard format for the template. Finally, in the "interoperability" scenario the vendor extracted a standard template from the first image and matched it (with its own matcher) against the standard template extracted from the second image by any another vendor participating in MINEX.

Another evaluation campaign was organized within the European Project MTIT to explicitly investigate ISO/IEC 19794-2 (2005) interoperability (Bazin and Mansfield, 2007). While the results are in-line with MINEX outcomes, MTIT attempted to analyze in depth underlying factors for the performance loss, in order to give developers useful advise to make their technology more interoperable. As explained in Section 3.7.3, the principal reasons are the different definitions of minutiae origin and the use of diverse criteria for placing (or not) minutiae in noisy regions or near singularities. On the other hand, it seems that the specific formats and rules (e.g., data quantization) that the minutiae-based standards impose, do not cause an accuracy drop with respect to proprietary encoding of the same feature. Since ISO/IEC 19794–2 (2005) allows to embed "proprietary data" within a standard template, we recommend developers to use standard templates and to enrich them with proprietary data. This enables (at least partially) interoperability and, at the same time, does not degrade the accuracy when the entire processing is done through a single developer's technology.

Further standards have been defined to encode fingerprint features beyond minutiae:

- ISO/IEC 19794–3 (2006) named "*Finger pattern spectral data*" to provide flexibility in the choice of spectral representation in that spectral components may be based on quantized cosinusoidal triplets, Discrete Fourier Transforms or Gabor filters. This enables data representations in a form that is more compact than storage of the entire fingerprint image.
- ISO/IEC 19794–8 (2006) named "*Finger pattern skeletal data*" encodes the directions of the skeleton line elements. The start and end points of the skeleton ridge lines are marked as minutiae. The line from start to end point is encoded by successive direction changes.

Unfortunately the application of these standards is still very limited and no large-scale interoperability study has been performed.

4.7.4 Further notes on performance evaluation

Readers interested in measuring the performance of a biometric system, including fingerprints, in an operational environment or specific application (see Section 1.5) should read the document "Best Practices in Testing and Reporting Performance of Biometric Devices" by UKBWG (2002) and consult the standards focusing on biometric system testing: ISO/IEC 19795–1 (2006), ISO/IEC 19795–2 (2007), ISO/IEC TR 19795–3 (2007) and ISO/IEC 19795–4 (2008). In fact, volunteer or subject selection, operational conditions, and several other issues have to be taken into consideration when a test is performed in a laboratory or in the field. FVC data collection and protocol comply with the above cited standards. Other interesting readings on biometric system performance evaluation include Bradley (1981), Golfarelli, Maio, and Maltoni (1997), Jain, Prabhakar, and Ross (1999), Wayman (1999a, c, 2001), Phillips et al. (2000), Bolle, Ratha, and Pankanti (1999, 2000), Pankanti, Ratha, and Bolle (2002), Snelick et al. (2005), Wu and Wilson (2006, 2007), Cappelli et al. (2006), Dass, Zhu, and Jain (2006), Modi et al. (2007) and Wang and Bhanu (2007).

To conclude this section, we caution practitioners against these common mistakes in evaluating the performance of their matching algorithms, giving the following suggestions:

- Avoid using the same dataset for training, validating, and testing an algorithm.
- Do not compute performance on a very small dataset, and in particular abstain from claiming that a system has a very low error rate when the errors have been measured over a small dataset; if possible, report statistical significance of the results (e.g., confidence intervals).

- Avoid "cleaning" the database by removing samples that are either "rejected" or misclassified by the system; in principle, by iteratively removing the fastidious samples, one could reach any desired level of accuracy.
- Do not conclude that the accuracy of a system is better than that of a competing system when they were evaluated over different datasets.
- Do not hide the weak points of an algorithm, but document its failures.

4.8 Summary

Throughout this chapter several techniques for fingerprint matching have been surveyed and the pros and cons of different approaches have been highlighted. However, an explicit answer has not been provided to the question: what is the best algorithm for matching fingerprints? The main reasons why it is difficult to assess the relative performance of the various matching algorithms are as follows.

- The performance of a fingerprint recognition method involves a tradeoff among different indicators: accuracy (e.g., FMR and FNMR), efficiency (enrollment time, verification time), scalability to 1:N identification, template size, memory requirement, and so on. Different applications have different performance requirements. For example, an application may prefer a fingerprint matching algorithm that is lower in accuracy but has a small template size over an algorithm that is more accurate but requires a large template size; specific constraints are also imposed by system security related issues (see Chapter 9).
- Although several papers published after the year 2002 report experimental results on FVC databases (with FVC protocol), this is not always the case. The performance measured is clearly related to the "difficulty" of the benchmark, and it is extremely difficult to extrapolate results in case of heterogeneous benchmarks.
- Let us consider matching algorithms tested on FVC2002 databases. Since results are always reported as FMR/FNMR values of the entire fingerprint recognition system developed, it is practically impossible to understand if an advancement in performance is due to a specific matching technique or is in large part due to a minor change in an existing feature extraction method. The only way to objectively compare fingerprint matchers is to start from the same set of features (i.e., the set of minutiae for minutiae based matchers). Forthcoming FVC-onGoing (2009) is being organized with such an aim.

Most of the fingerprint matching approaches introduced in the last 4 decades are minutiae-based. One of the reasons to expect minutiae-based algorithms to perform well is the sheer amount of research done on this approach. Non-minutiae features are now receiving substantial interest: new methods based on local texture, ridge geometry, ridge spatial relationship and pores have been proposed in conjunction with minutiae matching. The integration of approaches relying on different features seems to be the most promising way to significantly improve the accuracy of fingerprint recognition systems.

Global (and rigid) minutiae matching which was the main approach in the past, is being often replaced by two-phase approaches, that initially matches local portions of the fingerprint (e.g., local minutiae structures) and then consolidates the matching at global level. This allows a reduction in the computational complexity, and if the consolidation stage is designed appropriately, it also reduces the adverse effects of distortion. However, robust alignment remains a difficult task in fingerprints as compared to other biometrics such as iris or face.

The world-wide large scale deployment of fingerprint systems demands a new generation of accurate and highly interoperable algorithms; therefore the development of minutiae-only matching algorithms (i.e., compliant with ISO/IEC 19794–2 (2005) and its future evolution) will not be abandoned for a long time.

5
Fingerprint Classification and Indexing

5.1 Introduction

The identification of a person requires a comparison of her fingerprint with all the fingerprints in a database. This database may be very large (e.g., several million fingerprints) in many forensic and civilian applications. In such cases, the identification typically has an unacceptably long response time. The identification process can be speeded up by reducing the number of comparisons that are required to be performed. Sometimes, information about sex, race, age, and other data related to the individual are available and the portion of the database to be searched can be significantly reduced; however, this information is not always accessible (e.g., criminal identification based on latent fingerprints) and, in the general case, information intrinsic to the biometric samples has to be used for an efficient retrieval. A common strategy to speed up the search is to divide the fingerprint database into a number of bins (based on some predefined classes). A fingerprint to be identified is then required to be compared only to the fingerprints in a single bin of the database based on its class.

Fingerprint classification refers to the problem of assigning a fingerprint to a class in a consistent and reliable way. Although fingerprint matching is usually performed according to local features (e.g., minutiae), fingerprint classification is generally based on global features, such as global ridge structure and singularities.

The first fingerprint classification rules were proposed in 1823 by Purkinje (Moenssens, 1971), who classified fingerprints into nine categories (transverse curve, central longitudinal stria, oblique stripe, oblique loop, almond whorl, spiral whorl, ellipse, circle, and double whorl) according to the global ridge configurations. The first in-depth scientific study on fingerprint classification was made by Francis Galton, who divided the fingerprints into three major classes (arch, loop, and whorl) and further divided each category into subcategories (Galton, 1892). Around the same time, Juan Vucetich, an Argentine police official, developed a different system of classification; the Vucetich classification system is still used in many Spanish-speaking countries. Vucetich was also the first to make a fingerprint identification of a suspect in 1892. Ten years later, Edward Henry refined Galton's classification by increasing

D. Maltoni et al., *Handbook of Fingerprint Recognition*, 235–269.
© Springer-Verlag London Limited 2009

the number of classes (Henry, 1900); the Galton–Henry classification scheme was adopted in several countries: in fact, most of the classification schemes currently used by law enforcement agencies worldwide are variants of the Galton–Henry classification scheme. Figure 5.1 shows the five most common classes of the Galton–Henry classification scheme (*arch, tented arch, left loop, right loop*, and *whorl*):

- An arch fingerprint has ridges that enter from one side, rise to a small bump, and go out the opposite side from which they entered. Arches do not have loops or deltas.
- A tented arch fingerprint is similar to the (plain) arch, except that at least one ridge exhibits a high curvature and one loop and one delta are present.
- A loop fingerprint has one or more ridges that enter from one side, curve back, and go out the same side they entered. A loop and a delta singularities are present; the delta is assumed to be south of the loop. Loops can be further subdivided: loops that have ridges that enter and leave from the left side are called left loops and loops that have ridges that enter and leave from the right side are called right loops.
- A whorl fingerprint contains at least one ridge that makes a complete 360° path around the center of the fingerprint. Two loops (or a whorl) and two deltas can be found in whorl fingerprints. The whorl class is quite complex and in some classification schemes, it is further divided into two categories: twin loop (or double loop) and plain whorl (see Figure 5.1).

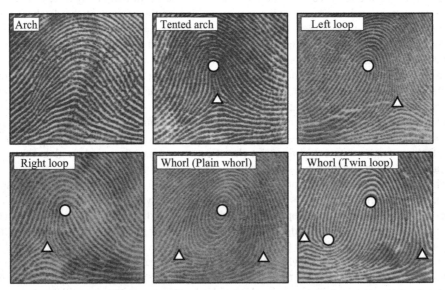

Figure 5.1. The five commonly used fingerprint classes: two whorl fingerprints are shown (a plain whorl and a twin loop, respectively).

Fingerprint classification is a difficult pattern recognition problem due to the small inter-class variability and the large intra-class variability in the fingerprint patterns (Figure 5.2). Moreover, fingerprint images often contain noise, which makes the classification task even more difficult (Figure 5.3). Several methods have been proposed for automatic fingerprint classification: Section 5.2 presents a survey of the main approaches in the literature; in Section 5.3, the performance of several classification approaches on some publicly available databases is summarized.

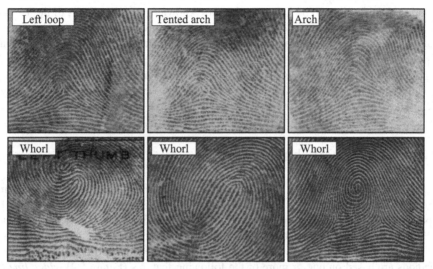

Figure 5.2. Top row: three fingerprints belonging to different classes that have similar appearance (small inter-class variability). Bottom row: three fingerprints belonging to the same class that have very different characteristics (large intra-class variability).

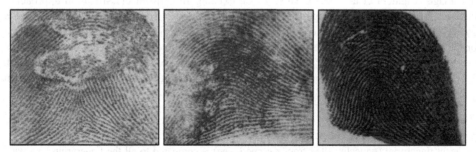

Figure 5.3. Examples of noisy fingerprint images.

The selectivity of classification-based techniques strongly depends on the number of classes and the natural distribution of fingerprints in these classes. Unfortunately, the number of classes used is often small and the fingerprints are non-uniformly distributed in these classes. For example, most automatic systems use five classes (i.e., arch, tented arch, left loop, right loop, and whorl) and the natural proportion of fingerprints in these classes is 3.7%, 2.9%, 33.8%, 31.7% and 27.9%, respectively (Wilson, Candela, and Watson, 1994). Furthermore, there are many "ambiguous" fingerprints, whose exclusive membership cannot be reliably stated even by human experts. Nevertheless, exclusive classification allows the efficiency of the 10-print identification[1] to be improved, because knowledge of the classes of the 10 fingerprints can be used as a code for reducing the number of comparisons at minutiae level. On the other hand, a fingerprint classification approach does not offer sufficient selectivity for latent fingerprint searching.[2]

For applications where there is no need to comply with an existing classification schema, some authors have proposed methods based on "continuous classification" or on other indexing techniques; these approaches are addressed in Section 5.4.

5.2 Classification Techniques

Fingerprint classification problem has attracted a significant amount of interest in the scientific community due to its importance and intrinsic difficulty, and a large number of papers have been published on this topic during the last 30 years. Although a wide variety of classification algorithms has been developed for this problem, a relatively small number of features extracted from fingerprint images have been used by most of the authors. In particular, almost all the methods are based on one or more of the following features (Figure 5.4): *ridge line flow*, *orientation image*, *singular points*, and *Gabor filter responses*. The ridge line flow is usually represented as a set of curves running parallel to the ridge lines; these curves do not necessarily coincide with the fingerprint ridges and valleys, but they exhibit the same local orientation. The ridge line flow can be traced by drawing curves locally oriented according to the orientation image (Candela et al., 1995). Most of the existing fingerprint classification approaches make use of the orientation image (see Table 5.1). This is not surprising inasmuch as such a feature, if computed with sufficient accuracy and detail, contains all the information required for the classification. Usually the orientation image is registered with respect to the core point (see Section 3.5) before being processed further. Furthermore, some authors (Cappelli et al. (1999); Candela et al. (1995)) proposed specific enhancement techniques for the orientation

---

[1] Fingerprints from the ten fingers of an individual are compared with the corresponding fingerprints from known individuals (e.g., convicted criminals).

[2] A latent fingerprint (typically lifted from a crime scene) is compared to all the fingerprints in a database.

image **D**, which allow higher accuracy to be achieved in the successive classification stages; these techniques work by strengthening the orientation elements located in the most distinctive regions of the fingerprint image.

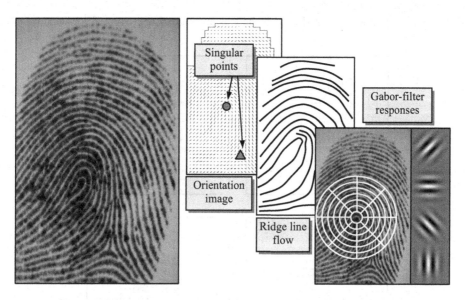

Figure 5.4. Most frequently used features for fingerprint classification.

In Cappelli et al. (1999), the enhancement is performed in two steps (Figure 5.5): the effects of noise (which affects the border elements significantly) is reduced through the application of a Gaussian-like attenuation function (*att*), which progressively reduces the magnitude of the elements **d** of **D** moving from the center towards the borders, thus obtaining the new elements **d**′:

$$\mathbf{d}' = \mathbf{d} \cdot att(\mathbf{d},\sigma_1), \qquad \text{where} \quad att(\mathbf{d},\sigma) = \frac{1}{\sqrt{2\pi}\cdot\sigma}\,e^{-\left(distc(\mathbf{d})^2 / 2\sigma^2\right)}; \qquad (1)$$

distc(**v**) returns the distance of **d** from the center of the image and σ is the scale of the Gaussian function. Then, to increase the significance of the distinctive elements, the elements located in the irregular regions are strengthened by calculating, for each **d**′:

$$str_{\mathbf{d}'} = 1 - \left| \sum_{\mathbf{d}'\in W_{5\times5}}\mathbf{d}' \right| / \sum_{\mathbf{d}'\in W_{5\times5}}\left|\mathbf{d}'\right|. \qquad (2)$$

$str_{\mathbf{d}'}$ is a measure of irregularity of the 5×5 neighborhood of $\mathbf{d}'$ (denoted by $W_{5 \times 5}$). The final enhanced orientation image is made up of vectors $\mathbf{d}''$ such that:

$$\mathbf{d}'' = \mathbf{d}' \cdot \left(1 + R_m \cdot \overline{str_{\mathbf{d}'}} \cdot att(\mathbf{d}', \sigma_2)\right), \tag{3}$$

where R_m is a weighting factor and $\overline{str_{\mathbf{d}'}}$ is the local average of $str_{\mathbf{d}'}$ over a 3×3 window.

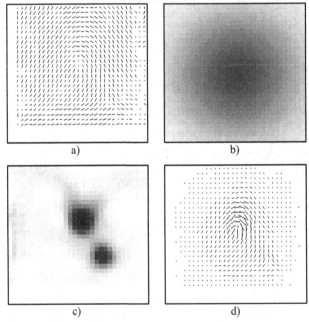

a)   b)   c)   d)

Figure 5.5. Enhancement of the orientation image as described in Cappelli et al. (1999): a) orientation image; b) Gaussian map obtained by applying the function *att*; c) irregularity map $str_{\mathbf{d}'}$; d) enhanced orientation image.

Most of the existing fingerprint classification methods can be coarsely assigned to one of these categories: *rule-based, syntactic, structural, statistical, neural network-based* and *multi-classifier* approaches. Table 5.1 highlights the features used and the classification strategy adopted by fingerprint classification methods published over the last 30 years. Fingerprint classification is one of the most representative pattern recognition problems; by observing the table, one can retrace the last 3 decades of research in the pattern recognition field: the interest in syntactical approaches in the 1970s/1980s, and the success of neural networks in the 1990s and of multiple classifier systems in recent years.

Fingerprint classification approach	Features				Classifier					
	O	S	R	G	Rb	Sy	Str	Sta	Nn	Mc
Moayer and Fu (1975)	√					√				
Moayer and Fu (1976)	√					√				
Rao and Balck (1980)	√					√				
Kawagoe and Tojo (1984)		√	√		√					
Hughes and Green (1991)	√								√	
Bowen (1992)	√	√							√	
Kamijo, Mieno, and Kojima (1992)	√								√	
Kamijo (1993)	√								√	
Moscinska and Tyma (1993)	√				√				√	
Wilson, Candela, and Watson (1994)	√								√	
Candela et al. (1995)	√		√		√				√	√
Omidvar, Blue, and Wilson (1995)	√								√	
Halici and Ongun (1996)	√								√	
Karu and Jain (1996)		√			√					
Maio and Maltoni (1996)	√						√			
Ballan, Sakarya, and Evans (1997)		√			√					
Chong et al. (1997)			√		√					
Senior (1997)			√				√			
Wei, Yuan, and Jie (1998)	√				√				√	√
Cappelli et al. (1999)	√						√			
Cappelli, Maio, and Maltoni (1999)	√							√		
Hong and Jain (1999)		√	√		√					√
Jain, Prabhakar, and Hong (1999)				√				√	√	√
Lumini, Maio, and Maltoni (1999)	√						√			
Cappelli, Maio, and Maltoni (2000a)	√							√		√
Cho et al. (2000)		√			√					
Bartesaghi, Fernández, and Gómez (2001)		√			√					
Bernard et al. (2001)	√								√	
Marcialis, Roli, and Frasconi (2001)	√			√			√	√	√	√
Pattichis et al. (2001)	√				√				√	√
Senior (2001)	√		√		√		√		√	√
Yao, Frasconi, and Pontil (2001)				√				√		√
Cappelli, Maio, and Maltoni (2002a)	√							√		√
Jain and Minut (2002)			√		√					
Cappelli et al. (2003)	√							√		√
Yao et al. (2003)	√			√			√	√	√	√

Fingerprint classification approach	Features				Classifier					
	O	S	R	G	Rb	Sy	Str	Sta	Nn	Mc
Cappelli and Maio (2004)	√							√		√
Klimanee and Nguyen (2004)	√	√			√					
Senior and Bolle (2004)	√		√		√		√		√	√
Shah and Sastry (2004)								√	√	√
Wang and Xie (2004)	√	√	√		√					
Zhang and Yan (2004)	√	√	√		√					
Park and Park (2005)	√							√		
Neuhaus and Bunke (2005)	√						√			
Tan, Bhanu, and Lin (2005)	√							√		
Min, Hong, and Cho (2006)				√				√		√
Kristensen, Borthen, and Fyllingsnes (2007)				√					√	
Wang and Dai (2007)	√	√			√					
Hong et al. (2008)	√	√		√				√		√
Li, Yau, and Wang (2008)	√	√						√		

Table 5.1. A chronological review of several fingerprint classification methods: each work is labeled according to the features used (**O** = orientation image, **S** = singularities, **R** = ridge flow, **G** = Gabor) and the classification technique (**Rb** = rule-based, **Sy** = syntactic, **Str** = structural, **Sta** = statistical, **Nn** = neural network, **Mc** = multiple classifiers).

5.2.1 Rule-based approaches

A fingerprint can be simply classified according to the number and the position of the singularities (see Table 5.2 and Figure 5.1); this is the approach commonly used by human experts for manual classification, therefore several authors proposed to adopt the same technique for automatic classification.

Fingerprint class	Singular points
Arch	No singular points
Tented arch, Left loop, Right loop	One loop and one delta
Whorl	Two loops (or a whorl) and two deltas

Table 5.2. Singular points in the five fingerprint classes.

In Kawagoe and Tojo (1984), the Poincaré index (see Section 3.5.1) is exploited to find type and position of the singular points and a coarse classification (according to Table 5.2) is derived. Then, a finer classification is obtained by tracing the ridge line flow. Discrimination among tented arch, left loop, and right loop is performed according to the inclination of the central trace (Figure 5.6). The authors also try to distinguish between plain whorl and twin loop; for this purpose, two parameters (*twinness* and *flatness*) are calculated (see Figure 5.6) and an empirical rule is adopted to make the final decision.

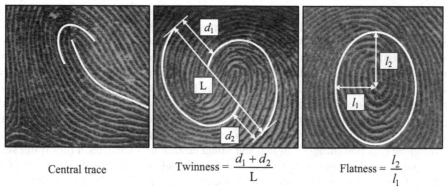

$$\text{Central trace} \qquad \text{Twinness} = \frac{d_1 + d_2}{L} \qquad \text{Flatness} = \frac{l_2}{l_1}$$

Figure 5.6. Central trace, twinness, and flatness as defined by Kawagoe and Tojo (1984).

Although singularity-based methods are attractive for their simplicity, some problems arise in the presence of noisy or partial fingerprints, where singularity detection can be extremely difficult. In Karu and Jain (1996) an iterative regularization (by smoothing the orientation image with a 3×3 box filter) is carried out until a valid number of singular points are detected; this allows reducing noise and consequently improving classification accuracy. The criterion used to discriminate tented arches from loops consists of connecting the two singularities with a straight line and measuring the average difference between the local orientations along the line and the slope of the line itself. A fingerprint is classified as a tented arch if:

$$\frac{1}{n} \sum_{i=1}^{n} sin(\alpha_i - \beta) \le 0.2 , \qquad (4)$$

where β is the slope of the line and α_i, $i = 1...n$, are the local orientations of elements lying along the straight line. Further discrimination between right and left loops is performed according to the relative position of the delta singularity with respect to the loop singularity.

Other classification strategies similar to the two described above can be found in Ratha et al. (1996), Ballan, Sakarya, and Evans (1997), Bartesaghi, Fernández, and Gómez (2001), Wang and Xie (2004), and Klimanee and Nguyen (2004). More robust techniques are proposed in Hong and Jain (1999), Zhang and Yan (2004) and Wang and Dai (2007). Hong and Jain (1999) introduce a rule-based classification algorithm that uses the number of singularities together with the number of recurring ridges found in the image; Zhang and Yan (2004), and Wang and Dai (2007) use a pseudo-ridge tracing algorithm to classify the fingerprint when only one singularity (a loop or a delta) is found. In both Hong and Jain (1999) and Wang and Dai (2007), the combination of these two distinct features leads to a performance better than Karu and Jain (1996).

A further problem with the singularity-based approaches is that, although they may work reasonably well on *rolled* (nail-to-nail) fingerprint impressions scanned from cards, they are not suitable to be used on *dab* (live-scan) fingerprint images, because delta points are often missing in these types of images. Cho et al. (2000) propose a method that uses only the loop points and classifies fingerprints according to the curvature and orientation of the fingerprint area near the loop. Chong et al. (1997) and Jain and Minut (2002) propose rule-based approaches that do not search for any singularity: the classification is based on the geometrical shape of the ridge lines. In Chong et al. (1997), B-spline curves (Bartels, Beatty, and Barsky, 1987) are used to model fingerprint ridge lines, adjacent curves are merged to limit noise artifacts, and the classification is performed by tracing the resulting curves in order to detect turns (i.e., complete direction changes). In Jain and Minut (2002), for each class, a fingerprint kernel (which models the shape of fingerprints in that class) is defined; the classification is then performed by finding the kernel that best fits the orientation image of the given fingerprint.

5.2.2 Syntactic approaches

A syntactic method describes patterns by means of terminal symbols and production rules; a grammar is defined for each class and a parsing process is responsible for classifying each new pattern (Fu and Booth, 1986a, b).

Syntactic approaches were proposed by Tou and Hankley (1968) and Grasselli (1969), whose methods were based on context-free grammars and by Verma and Chatterjee (1989), who adopted regular grammars.

In Moayer and Fu (1973) the authors proposed a syntactic approach where terminal symbols are associated with small groups of orientation elements within the fingerprint orientation image; a class of context-free grammars is used to describe the fingerprint patterns, which are divided into seven classes (see also Moayer and Fu (1975)). The same authors also experimented with other types of grammars: stochastic grammars (Moayer and Fu, 1976) and tree grammars (Moayer and Fu, 1986).

The approach introduced by Rao and Balck (1980) is based on the analysis of ridge line flow, which is represented by a set of connected lines (Figure 5.7). These lines are labeled according to the direction changes, thus obtaining a set of strings that are processed through ad hoc grammars or string-matching techniques to derive the final classification (Figure 5.7).

In general, due to the great diversity of fingerprint patterns, syntactic approaches require very complex grammars whose inference requires complicated and unstable approaches; for this reason, the use of syntactic methods for fingerprint classification has been almost abandoned, with a few exceptions (Chang and Fan, 2002).

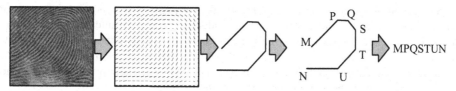

Figure 5.7. A schema of the string-construction approach in Rao and Balck (1980).

5.2.3 Structural approaches

Structural approaches are based on the relational organization of low-level features into higher-level structures. This relational organization is represented by means of symbolic data structures, such as trees and graphs, which allow a hierarchical organization of the information (Bunke, 1993).

The orientation image is well suited for structural representation: in fact, it can be partitioned into connected regions that are characterized by "homogeneous" orientations; these regions and the relations among them contain information useful for classification. This is the basic idea of the method proposed by Maio and Maltoni (1996): the orientation image is partitioned into regions by minimizing a cost function that takes into account the variance of the element orientations within each region (Figure 5.8). An inexact graph matching technique is then used to compare the relational graphs with class-prototype graphs (see also Lumini, Maio, and Maltoni, 1999). A similar structural representation is also adopted by Yao et al. (2003) to train a recursive neural network that is combined with a Support Vector Machine classifier (see Section 5.2.6). Another approach based on relational graphs, but created starting from different features, is proposed by Neuhaus and Bunke (2005): regions that are relevant for the classification are extracted from the fingerprint orientation image through a directional variance filter that selects potential singular points and regions characterized by vertical orientations; the resulting structures are converted into attributed graphs and the classification is finally performed with a graph edit distance algorithm.

Although relational graph approaches have interesting properties (such as invariance to rotation and displacement, and the possibility of handling partial fingerprints), it is not easy to robustly partition the orientation image into homogeneous regions, especially in poor quality fingerprints. In Cappelli et al. (1999), a template-based matching is performed to guide the partitioning of the orientation images (Figure 5.9): the main advantage of the approach is that, because it relies only on global structural information, it is able to deal with partial finger-prints, where sometimes, singular points are not available, and it can also work on very noisy images.

Senior (1997) adopted a Hidden Markov Model (HMM) classifier for fingerprint classifi-cation; the input features are the measurements taken at the intersection points between some horizontal and vertical "fiducial lines" and the ridge lines. At each intersection, the features extracted are: the local orientation of the ridge lines, the distance and the change in orientation since the last intersection, and the curvature of the ridge line at the intersection. Since HMM are inherently one-dimensional, the two-dimensional fingerprint pattern is linearized by nest-ing its rows, thus obtaining a unique sequence of observations.

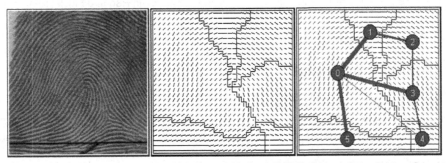

Figure 5.8. Classification approach of Maio and Maltoni (1996): from left to right: a fingerprint image, the partitioning of its orientation image, and the corresponding relational graph. © IEEE.

5.2.4 Statistical approaches

In statistical approaches, a fixed-size numerical feature vector is derived from each fingerprint and a general-purpose statistical classifier is used for the classification. Some of the most widely adopted statistical classifiers (Jain, Duin, and Mao, 2000) are: Bayes decision rule, k-nearest neighbor, and Support Vector Machines (SVM). Examples of their application can be found in several fingerprint-classification approaches, for instance:

- The Bayes decision rule is adopted by Tan, Bhanu, and Lin (2005) to classify features learned by a genetic algorithm starting from the orientation image, and by Hong et al. (2008) to dynamically organize a set of SVM classifiers.
- The k-nearest neighbor is exploited in Fitz and Green (1996), where wedge-ring fea-tures obtained from the hexagonal Fourier transform are used as input, and in Jain, Prabhakar, and Hong (1999), where the first step of a two-stage classification tech-nique is performed by means of the k-nearest neighbor rule (see Section 5.2.6).

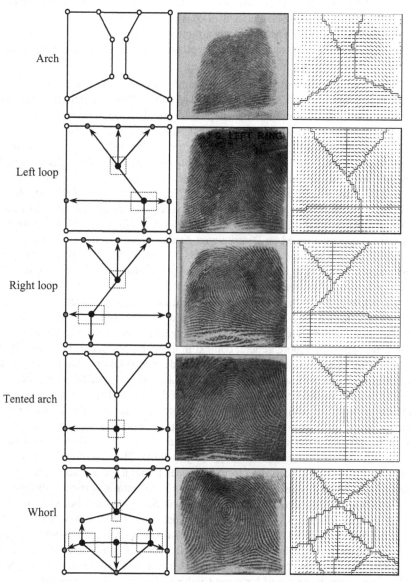

Figure 5.9. Classification scheme of Cappelli et al. (1999): the templates corresponding to the five classes and an example of application of each template to the orientation image of a fingerprint belonging to the corresponding class. © IEEE.

- SVM classifiers are used by Li, Yau, and Wang (2008) to classify feature vectors obtained from the coefficients of a constrained nonlinear phase orientation model (see Section 3.2.6); SVM classifiers are often combined with other classifiers to improve the performance, such as in Yao et al. (2003), Min, Hong, and Cho (2006), and Hong et al. (2008), see Section 5.2.6.

Many approaches directly use the orientation image as a feature vector, by simply nesting its rows (see, for instance, Cappelli, Maio, and Maltoni (1999); Candela et al. (1995)). By encoding each element of the orientation image with the two components $[r \cdot cos(2\theta), r \cdot sin(2\theta)]$ (see Equation (1) in Section 3.2.1), a typical 30×30 orientation image results in a vector of 1,800 elements. Training a classifier with such high-dimensional vectors would require large amounts of training data, memory, and computation time. For this reason, statistical dimensionality reduction techniques are often applied to reduce the dimensionality of the feature vector. The Karhunen–Loève (KL) transform (Jolliffe, 1986) is usually adopted for this purpose, as it guarantees a good preservation of Euclidean distances between vectors (see, for instance, Wilson, Candela, and Watson (1994); Halici and Ongun (1996)). Another possibility is to apply an approach based on Discriminant Analysis (Jain, Duin, and Mao, 2000) to extract a more discriminant reduced feature vector; for instance Park and Park (2005) apply Nonlinear Discriminant Analysis to the orientation image and classify the feature vectors in the reduced space through a simple nearest-centroid rule.

The KL transform, besides being used for dimensionality reduction, can also be adopted for the classification itself. In Cappelli, Maio, and Maltoni (1999), Cappelli, Maio, and Maltoni (2000a) and Cappelli and Maio (2004), a generalization of the KL transform called MKL (which was given in a more general context in Cappelli, Maio, and Maltoni, 2001b) was used for representing and classifying feature vectors derived from orientation images. The underlying idea of the approach was to find, for each class, one or more KL subspaces that were well suited to represent the fingerprints belonging to that class. These subspaces were created according to an optimization criterion that attempted to minimize the average mean square reconstruction error over a representative training set (Figure 5.10). The number of subspaces for each class was fixed a priori according to the class "complexity"; in particular, more subspaces were created for complex classes (e.g., whorl). The classification of an unknown fingerprint was performed according to its distances from all the KL subspaces. For example, in Figure 5.10, three KL subspaces (S_1, S_2, S_3) have been computed from a training set containing elements from the two classes A and B: subspaces S_1 and S_2 have been obtained from the elements in A, and S_3 has been obtained from those in B. Given a new vector $\mathbf{x}$, the distances from the three subspaces (d_1, d_2, and d_3) contain useful information for its classification. In Cappelli, Maio, and Maltoni (1999) the classification was simply performed according to the minimum distance from the MKL subspaces, whereas in Cappelli and Maio (2004) the results of both minimum distance and k-nearest neighbor classifiers were reported.

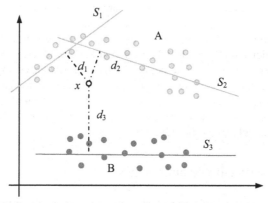

Figure 5.10. A two-dimensional example of the MKL transform (Cappelli, Maio, and Maltoni, 2001b), where two subspaces (S_1, S_2) and one subspace (S_3) are used to represent classes A and B, respectively.

5.2.5 Neural network-based approaches

Most of the proposed neural network approaches are based on multilayer perceptrons and use the elements of the orientation image as input features (Hughes and Green (1991); Bowen (1992); Kamijo, Mieno, and Kojima (1992); Kamijo (1993); Pal and Mitra (1996); Shah and Sastry (2004)). Kamijo (1993) presents a pyramidal architecture constituted of several multilayer perceptrons, each of which is trained to recognize fingerprints belonging to a different class. In Bowen (1992), the location of the singularities is used together with a 20 × 20 orientation image for the training of two disjoint neural networks, whose outputs are passed to a third one, which produces the final classification. Jain, Prabhakar, and Hong (1999) train 10 feed-forward neural networks to distinguish between each possible pair of classes (this method is described in more detail in the Section 5.2.6).

One of the best-known neural network approaches to fingerprint classification was proposed by NIST researchers (Wilson, Candela, and Watson, 1994). This work was the result of previous studies aimed at: comparing different types of classifiers for fingerprint classification (Candela and Chellappa (1993); Blue et al. (1993)), evaluating different fingerprint enhancement techniques (Watson, Candela, and Grother, 1994) and improving classification accuracy (Wilson et al., 1992). In Wilson, Candela, and Watson (1994) a multilayer perceptron is used for classification after reducing the dimensionality of the feature vector as explained in the previous section. Improved versions of this method are presented in Omidvar, Blue, and Wilson

(1995), where specific changes and optimizations are introduced in the network architecture, and in Candela et al. (1995), which is described in Section 5.2.6.

Finally, some researchers proposed the use of self-organizing neural networks: Moscinska and Tyma (1993), Halici and Ongun (1996) and Bernard et al. (2001). In Moscinska and Tyma (1993), a Kohonen map is trained to find delta points, and a rule-based approach is applied for the final classification; in Halici and Ongun (1996) a multilayer self-organizing map provides the classification. A comparison of the performance of different neural network architectures for fingerprint classification (including multilayer perceptrons and Kohonen maps) is reported in Kristensen, Borthen, and Fyllingsnes (2007).

5.2.6 Multiple classifier-based approaches

Different classifiers potentially offer complementary information about the patterns to be classified, which may be exploited to improve performance; in fact, in a number of pattern classification studies, it has been observed that different classifiers often misclassify different patterns (see Section 7.2 for an introduction to multiple classifiers). This motivates the recent interest in combining different approaches for the fingerprint classification task.

Several choices are possible for the selection of the component classifiers (e.g., different classifiers trained on the same data, the same classifier trained on different data, different input features) and for the combination strategy (from simple heuristic criteria of majority vote rule to more complex techniques that involve training an additional classifier for the final decision). Table 5.3 compares some fingerprint classification approaches that adopt different combination techniques.

Candela et al. (1995) introduced PCASYS (Pattern-level Classification Automation SYStem): a complete fingerprint classification system based on the evolution of the methods proposed in Wilson, Candela, and Watson, (1994). Figure 5.11 shows a functional schema of PCASYS: a probabilistic neural network (which replaced the multilayer perceptron used in Wilson, Candela, and Watson (1994)) is coupled with an auxiliary ridge tracing module, which determines the ridge flow in the bottom part of the fingerprint; this module is specifically designed to detect whorl fingerprints. PCASYS was a milestone for successive fingerprint classification studies thanks to the availability of open source code and because it was one of the first studies that reported precise and reproducible results on publicly available databases (see Section 5.3). Wei, Yuan, and Jie (1998) proposed a feedback method based on a genetic algorithm to automatically select the best input parameters for PCASYS and achieved better accuracy. In Pattichis et al. (2001), a feature extraction method was adopted to improve PCASYS performance. Senior (2001) combined PCASYS with two other classifiers: the hidden Markov model classifier introduced in Senior (1997) and an approach based on ridge shape features classified by means of a decision tree.

	Distinct features	Distinct classi-fiers	Distinct training sets	Combination strategy
Candela et al. (1995)	Yes	Yes	No	Rule-based
Jain, Prabhakar, and Hong (1999)	No	Yes	No	Sequential (two stages)
Cappelli, Maio, and Maltoni (2000a)	No	Yes	Yes	Majority vote rule
Senior (2001)	Yes	Yes	No	Neural network
Marcialis, Roli, and Frasconi (2001)	Yes	Yes	No	k-nearest neighbor
Yao et al. (2003)	Yes	Yes	No	k-nearest neighbor
Cappelli et al. (2003)	No	Yes	No	Sequential (two stages)
Shah and Sastry (2004)	Yes	Yes	No	Sequential (two stages)
Hong et al. (2008)	Yes	Yes	No	Bayes rule

Table 5.3. Some approaches based on multiple classifiers.

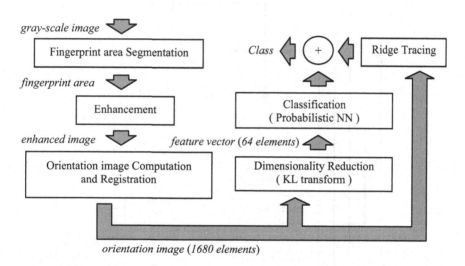

Figure 5.11. A functional scheme of PCASYS (Candela et al., 1995). Reprinted with permission from Cappelli et al. (1999). © IEEE.

Jain, Prabhakar, and Hong (1999) adopt a two-stage classification strategy: a *k*-nearest neighbor classifier is used to find the two most likely classes from a FingerCode feature vector (see Section 4.6.1); then a specific neural network, trained to distinguish between the two classes, is exploited to obtain the final decision. A total of 10 neural networks is trained to distinguish between each possible pair of classes. In Figure 5.12, a graphical scheme of this sequential classification strategy is reported. A similar strategy is proposed by Cappelli et al. (2003), starting from different features (the orientation image) and using an MKL-based classifier to find the two most likely classes and one among 10 subspace-based classifiers for the final decision; very good results were reported by Cappelli et al. (2003) on a publicly available database (see Section 5.3). Shah and Sastry (2004) propose another two-stage classification strategy: at the first stage, a classifier separates arch and tented arch classes from loop and whorl, at the second stage a classifier is trained to discriminate between arch and tented arch and three classifiers to deal with left loop, right loop and whorl classes in a one-versus-all fashion; the authors report results obtained using this strategy with various types of classifiers (SVM, nearest neighbor and neural network).

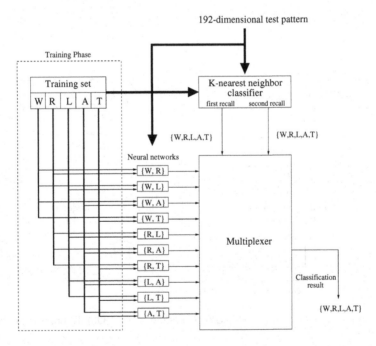

Figure 5.12. The classifier combination scheme proposed by Jain, Prabhakar, and Hong (1999). © IEEE.

Cappelli and Maio (2004) trained two different types of classifiers (see Section 5.2.4) on three disjoint training sets, thus obtaining a total of six classifiers that the authors combined using a majority vote rule, see also Cappelli, Maio, and Maltoni (2000a, 2002a).

Hong et al. (2008) train five SVM classifiers on FingerCode features with a one-versus-all approach and use a Bayes classifier trained on singularities and pseudo ridges features to dynamically select the sequence of SVMs to be used for classifying a given fingerprint.

Other attempts at fingerprint classifier combinations can be found in Uchida et al. (1998), Marcialis, Roli, and Frasconi (2001), Yao, Frasconi, and Pontil (2001), Marcialis, Roli, and Serrau (2003), Yao et al. (2003) and Min, Hong, and Cho (2006). In Marcialis, Roli, and Frasconi (2001) a structural approach similar to Maio and Maltoni (1996) is combined with a neural network classifier that uses FingerCode feature vectors; Yao et al. (2003) combine the same structural approach with a SVM; Yao, Frasconi, and Pontil (2001) combine multiple SVM trained to classify FingerCode feature vectors.

5.2.7 Miscellanea

Other approaches for fingerprint classification, in addition to those already described, were proposed by Shelman and Hodges (1973), Rao, Prasad, and Sharma (1974), Millard (1975), Rao (1976, 1978), Shelman (1976), Singh, Gyergyek, and Pavesic (1977), Shizume and Hefner (1978), Rabinowitz (1980), Lindh, Ford, and Boudreaux (1981), Nakamura, Goto, and Minami (1982), Fjetland and Robbins (1989), Geng and Shen (1997), Sarbadhikari et al. (1998), Shen and Khanna (1994) and Khanna (2004).

5.3 Performance of Fingerprint Classification Techniques

The performance of a fingerprint classification system is usually measured in terms of *error rate* or *accuracy*. The error rate is computed as the ratio between the number of misclassified fingerprints and the total number of samples in the test set; the accuracy is simply the percentage of correctly classified fingerprints:

$$\text{error rate} = \frac{\text{number of misclassified fingerprints} \times 100}{\text{total number of fingerprints}} \% \qquad (5)$$

$$\text{accuracy} = 100\% - \text{error rate}. \qquad (6)$$

The error rate of a classification system is generally reported as a function of the percentage of the database that the system has to search; this percentage is called *penetration rate* and can be simply computed as

$$\text{penetration rate} = \frac{\text{number of accessed fingerprints} \times 100}{\text{total number of fingerprints in the database}} \% . \qquad (7)$$

A more detailed analysis of the behavior of a classifier can be obtained by examining the *confusion matrix*. This matrix has a row for each true class and a column for each hypothesized class; each cell at row r and column c reports how many fingerprints belonging to class r are assigned to class c. Table 5.5 shows two examples of confusion matrix.

Fingerprint images of poor quality are often difficult to classify, even for a human expert: in many applications it is desirable that a fingerprint classification algorithm rejects such images because this would be less damaging than a wrong decision. For this reason, several classification approaches include a rejection mechanism, which improves the accuracy at the cost of discarding some fingerprints (i.e., classifying them as "unknown"). A confidence value is usually assigned to the classifier decision or to the fingerprint itself: the rejection simply consists of discarding fingerprints whose confidence is lower than a fixed threshold. By taking into account the rejection rate, the performance of a fingerprint classifier can be described by a graph with the rejection rate on one axis and the error rate (or the accuracy) on the other (see Figure 5.13).

The early fingerprint classification systems proposed in the literature (years 1970–1990) were tested on small databases, usually collected by the authors themselves. Although the results reported on these internal databases provided an initial glimpse regarding the difficulty of the classification problem, a comparison among the various techniques was impossible and the results were not useful for tracking advances in the field. For example, in Moayer and Fu (1975) and Bowen (1992), the test sets used were two internally collected databases of 92 and 47 fingerprints, respectively: it is very difficult to deduce any conclusions from results reported on such small datasets.

In 1992 and 1993, NIST released two fingerprint databases well suited for development and testing of fingerprint classification systems: NIST Special Database 4 (Watson and Wilson, 1992a) and NIST Special Database 14 (Watson, 1993a), hereinafter named DB4 and DB14, respectively. Both databases consist of 8-bit grey-level images of rolled fingerprint impressions scanned from cards; two different fingerprint instances (F and S) are present for each finger. Each fingerprint was manually analyzed by a human expert and assigned to one of the five classes: Arch (A), Left loop (L), Right loop (R), Tented arch (T), and Whorl (W). Actually, in DB4, some ambiguous fingerprints (about 17%) have an additional reference to a "secondary" class and in DB14, there are a few fingerprints that the human expert was not able to classify. DB4 contains 2,000 fingerprint pairs, uniformly distributed in the five classes; the images are numbered from F0001 to F2000 and from S0001 to S2000. DB14 contains 27,000 fingerprint pairs whose class distribution resembles natural fingerprint distribution: the images are numbered from F00001 to F27000 and from S00001 to S27000. NIST DB4 and DB14 became de facto standard benchmarks for fingerprint classification and most of the algorithms published in the last decade were tested on one of these databases. Sections 5.3.1 and 5.3.2 report the performance of the main fingerprint classification approaches for which results on DB4 or DB14 are available.

Although DB4 and DB14 constitute very useful benchmarks for studies on fingerprint classification, they are not well suited for testing pre-selection approaches using live-scan images. In fact, on-line impressions rarely contain all the fingerprint singularities (usually they do not cover the entire fingerprint area) and this may cause problems for methods using a global description of fingerprints (e.g., orientation image).

5.3.1 Results on NIST DB4

Table 5.4 reports the error rates on DB4 of 10 different approaches: most of them were obtained by using the 2,000 images from the first 1,000 fingers (F0001 to F1000 and S0001 to S1000) for the training and the remaining 2,000 images for testing the system. Some rule-based methods (such as Karu and Jain (1996); Hong and Jain (1999); Jain and Minut (2002)) were tested on the whole database; Senior (1997) reports results on 542 randomly selected fingerprints. All the results are reported at 0% rejection rate, with the exception of the approaches based on FingerCode feature vectors, where 1.8% fingerprints are rejected during the feature extraction stage. As to the ambiguous fingerprints with two class labels, the result is usually assumed correct if the class hypothesized by the classifier matches any of the two labels. Some authors, by noting that many errors are due to the misclassification of some tented arch fingerprints as arch (e.g., see the confusion matrix in Table 5.5) and considering that these two classes are not very common in nature (see Section 5.1), proposed to merge these two classes into a single class (four-class problem). When available, results of both the five-class and four-class problems are reported in Table 5.4. Furthermore, since DB4 contains an equal number of fingerprints for each class, some authors prefer to weight the results according to the natural class distribution (see Section 5.1): weighted results, when published by the authors themselves or derivable from the confusion matrices, are reported in Table 5.4 for both the five-class and four-class cases.

5.3.2 Results on NIST DB14

Table 5.6 reports the error rates on DB14 of three published approaches; all the results were obtained using the last 2,700 fingerprints (S24301 to S27000) as the test set.

The graph in Figure 5.13 shows how the accuracy of two of these approaches can be improved by including a rejection option. Two curves are drawn for the classifier proposed in Candela et al. (1995), to show the performance of the Probabilistic Neural Network alone (PNN only) and combined with the auxiliary Pseudo Ridge Tracing module (PNN + PRT). According to FBI specialists, the target error rate for automatic classification is 1% at a 20% rejection rate (Karu and Jain, 1996): the region where this requirement is met is displayed in gray in the graph.

Method	Test set	5 classes		4 classes	
		%	Weighted (%)	%	Weighted (%)
Candela et al. (1995)	Second half	–	–	11.4	6.1
Karu and Jain (1996)	Whole DB	14.6	11.9	8.6	9.4
Senior (1997)	Random 542	–	–	–	8.4
Cappelli, Maio, and Maltoni (1999)	Second half	7.9	6.5	5.5	–
Hong and Jain (1999)	Whole DB	12.5	10.6	7.7	–
Jain, Prabhakar, and Hong (1999)	Second half [*]	10.0	7.0	5.2	–
Marcialis, Roli, and Frasconi (2001)	Second half [*]	12.1	9.6	–	–
Senior (2001)	Second half	–	–	–	5.1
Yao, Frasconi, and Pontil (2001)	Second half [*]	10.7	9.0	6.9	–
Jain and Minut (2002)	Whole DB	–	–	8.8	9.3
Cappelli et al. (2003)	Second half	4.8	3.7	3.7	3.4
Yao et al. (2003)	Second half [*]	10.0	8.1	-	-
Cappelli and Maio (2004)	Second half	7.0	5.9	4.7	5.4
Wang and Xie (2004)	Whole DB	-	-	18.0	-
Zhang and Yan (2004)	Whole DB	15.7	11.0	7.3	8.3
Neuhaus and Bunke (2005)	Second half	19.8	-	-	-
Park and Park (2005)	Second half	9.3	7.9	6.0	-
Tan, Bhanu, and Lin (2005)	Second half	8.4	8.0	6.7	7.5
Min, Hong, and Cho (2006)	Second half [*]	9.6	7.2	-	-
Wang and Dai (2007)	Whole DB	11.5	9.4	-	-
Hong et al. (2008)	Second half [*]	9.2	6.2	5.1	-
Li, Yau, and Wang (2008)	Second half	6.5	7.0	5.0	-

Table 5.4. Error rates on NIST DB4. The results of the PCASYS system presented in Candela et al. (1995) were not reported in that work, but in Senior (2001). The (*) denotes approaches based on FingerCode feature vectors, where 1.8% fingerprints are rejected during the feature extraction stage (all the other results are reported at 0% rejection rate).

True class	Hypothesized class				
	A	L	R	W	T
A	420	6	3	1	11
L	3	376	3	9	11
R	5	1	392	6	16
W	2	5	14	377	1
T	33	18	9	0	278

True class	Hypothesized class			
	A+T	L	R	W
A+T	782	10	17	6
L	6	373	2	4
R	7	1	381	9
W	0	4	7	391

Table 5.5. Confusion matrices of the results on DB4 for the approach proposed in Cappelli et al. (2003): five-class problem (on the left) and four-class problem (on the right).

Method	Error rate (%)
Candela et al. (1995)	7.8
Wei, Yuan, and Jie (1998)	6.0
Cappelli, Maio, and Maltoni (2000a)	5.6

Table 5.6. Error rates on NIST DB14.

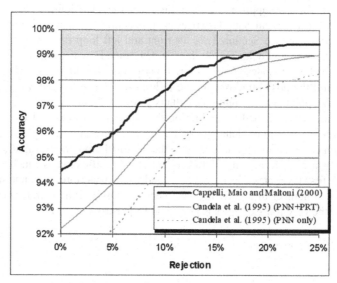

Figure 5.13. Accuracy versus rejection curves. PCASYS performance was manually sampled from the graph reported by Candela et al. (1995). The gray area denotes the target accuracy of automatic classification set by the FBI.

5.4 Fingerprint Indexing and Retrieval

The main problem of the classification schemes discussed in the previous sections (and of all the other commonly used schemes) is that the number of classes is small and fingerprints are unevenly distributed among them: more than 90% of the fingerprints belong to only three classes (right loop, left loop, and whorl). In 10-print identification (where an individual has to be identified using information from all of his 10 fingers) this does not compromise the efficiency too much, inasmuch as the knowledge of the classes of all the fingerprints can be used as a distinctive code for reducing the number of comparisons; on the other hand, when a single fingerprint has to be searched in a large database, the classification stage is not able to sufficiently narrow down the search. Furthermore, when classification is performed automatically, errors and rejected fingerprints are required to be handled gracefully. This problem can be addressed with various pre-selection approaches, such as: *sub-classification*, *continuous classification* and other *indexing* techniques.

5.4.1 Fingerprint sub-classification

The goal of sub-classification is to further divide some of the classes into more specific categories. This approach has been typically adopted by human experts to perform manual fingerprint searching in forensic applications. For instance, the FBI defined (Federal Bureau of Investigation, 1984) a manual sub-classification procedure for loop and whorl fingerprints based on ridge counting (see Section 3.9); for right and left loop fingerprints, the number of ridges between the loop and delta singularities is determined: two sub-classes are defined according to the number of ridges. As to whorl fingerprints, the ridge just below the leftmost delta is traced until the position closest to the rightmost delta is reached; then the number of ridges between that point and the rightmost delta is counted (Figure 5.14).

Three sub-classes are defined depending on the number of ridges and whether the traced ridge passes over the rightmost delta. Actually, the rules are quite complicated because the sub-classification criteria also vary according to the finger (thumb, index, middle, …).

Implementing a reliable automated fingerprint sub-classification is much more difficult than realizing a first-level classification into five classes. Therefore, it is not surprising that only a very limited number of algorithms have been proposed in the literature to address this problem (one of the very few examples is Drets and Liljenstrom (1998)).

 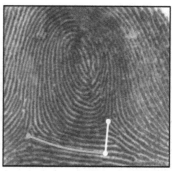

Figure 5.14. Left: ridge counting for loop sub-classification (the number of ridges between loop and delta is 16). Right: ridge tracing and counting for whorl sub-classification (the closest point is below the rightmost delta and number of the ridges is 5).

5.4.2 Continuous classification and other indexing techniques

The intrinsic difficulties in automating fingerprint classification and sub-classification led some researchers to investigate fingerprint retrieval systems that are not based on human defined classes. In fact, for applications where there is no need to adhere to the Henry's classification scheme, and where the goal is purely to minimize the number of comparisons during fingerprint pre-selection, any technique able to characterize each fingerprint in a robust and stable manner (among different impressions of the same finger) may, in principle, be used.

An interesting approach is so-called "continuous classification" (Lumini, Maio, and Maltoni, 1997): in continuous classification, fingerprints are not partitioned into disjoint classes, but associated with numerical vectors summarizing their main features. These feature vectors are created through a similarity-preserving transformation, so that similar fingerprints are mapped into close points (vectors) in the multidimensional space. The retrieval is performed by matching the input fingerprint with those in the database whose corresponding vectors are close to the searched one. Spatial data structures (Samet, 1990) can be used for indexing very large databases. A continuous classification approach allows the problem of exclusive membership of ambiguous fingerprints to be avoided and the system efficiency and accuracy to be balanced by adjusting the size of the neighborhood considered (see the Section 5.4.3). Most of the continuous classification techniques proposed in the literature use the orientation image as an initial feature, but differ in the transformation adopted to create the final vectors and in the distance measure. In Lumini, Maio, and Maltoni (1997) and in Kamei and Mizoguchi (1998), the orientation image is aligned with respect to the core and treated as a single vector (by concatenating its rows); a dimensionality reduction (KL transform) is then performed to compute the final vectors. The similarity between two vectors is calculated with the Euclidean distance in Lumini, Maio, and Maltoni (1997) and with an approach that also takes into account a quality index, in Kamei and Mizoguchi (1998) (see also Kamei (2004b)). In some works, the orientation image is coupled with ridge-line frequency information: in Lee, Kim, and Park (2005) a block-based local frequency is used, whereas in Jiang, Liu, and Kot (2006), and in Liu, Jiang, and Kot (2007), a single value summarizing the dominant ridge-line frequency of the whole fingerprint is computed; in fact, Jiang, Liu, and Kot noted from their experiments that the local ridge-line frequency is much less stable than the local orientation, while a single scalar value encoding the dominant frequency is stable enough and has a good discriminant power. Finally, a more sophisticated approach is proposed by Wang, Hu, and Phillips (2007): the authors use the coefficients of their FOMFE orientation model (see Section 3.2.6) as feature vectors for the continuous classification and report performance improvements with respect to feature vectors based on the raw orientation image.

In Cappelli et al. (1999), the templates corresponding to the five classes (see Section 5.2) are used to create a numerical vector for continuous classification; the cost of the adaptation of each template to a given fingerprint is calculated and a five-dimensional vector is assembled by using the five normalized costs. The main advantage of this approach is that the orientation images do not need to be aligned with respect to a fixed point. In Cappelli, Maio, and Maltoni (2000a), the vector adopted for continuous classification is created by using the distances of the orientation image from all the MKL subspaces (see description of Cappelli, Maio, and Maltoni (2002a) in Section 5.2).

Some researchers proposed to index fingerprints using minutiae points (Germain, Califano, and Colville, 1997): exploiting the same feature for matching and indexing fingerprints is attractive, but care must be taken to construct an extremely redundant representation, inasmuch as only a subset of all the minutiae is always present in different impressions of the same finger. The algorithm proposed by Germain, Califano, and Colville (1997) first identifies all the minutiae triplets in a fingerprint. Each triplet defines a triangle whose geometric features are extracted: length of each side, the angles, and the ridge count between each pair of vertices. The similarity between two fingerprints is defined by the number of corresponding minutiae triplets that can be found under a rigid transformation; this method of defining fingerprint similarity has strong analogies with local minutiae-based matching described in Section 4.4.3. Instead of explicitly comparing the similarity between the input fingerprint and all the fingerprints in the database (which would be very time consuming), the authors use a geometric hashing technique: a hash table is built by quantizing all the possible triplets and, for each quantized triplet, a list of pointers (ID) to the fingerprints in the database containing that specific triplet is maintained. When a new fingerprint is inserted in the database, its triplets are extracted, and the hash table is updated by adding the fingerprint ID in the cell corresponding to the fingerprint triplets (Figure 5.15). At retrieval time, the triplets of the input fingerprint are computed and quantized and, for each triplet, the list of fingerprint IDs in which that triplet is present is retrieved together with the coordinate transformations that best map the input fingerprint into the database fingerprints. Intuitively, if the same fingerprint ID is hit by more triplets in the input (under consistent coordinate transformations), then it is more likely that the corresponding fingerprint is the searched one. A voting technique is then applied to obtain a final ranking, which is used for visiting the database in a convenient order (Figure 5.15).

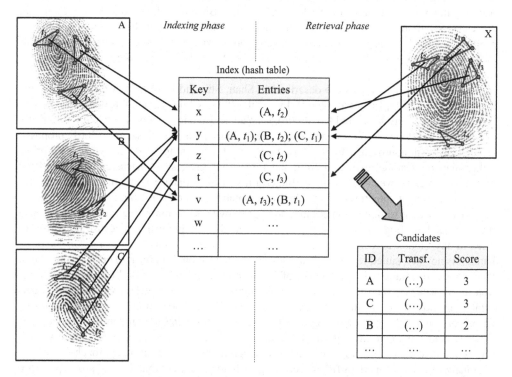

Figure 5.15. An example of the approach proposed by Germain, Califano, and Colville (1997). During the indexing phase (on the left), the extracted features from each fingerprint in the database are used to generate the key values (x, y, z, ... in the figure) for the hash table; for each key value, the index maintains the list of fingerprint IDs (A, B, C) and the corresponding triplets (t_1, t_2, ...). During the retrieval phase, the triplets of the input fingerprint X are computed and the list of fingerprint IDs in which that triplet is present is retrieved, together with the coordinate transformations that best map X into the database fingerprints.

Some variants of the above-described technique are presented in Bhanu and Tan (2001), Tan and Bhanu (2003a), Bhanu and Tan (2003) and Choi et al. (2003), where more robust features are extracted from the minutiae triplets and geometric constraints are introduced to more effectively filter the database. Bebis, Deaconu, and Georgiopoulos (1999) suggest the use of the

Delaunay triangulation for selecting minutiae triplets: assuming an average number of m minutiae per fingerprint, this allows to consider only $O(m)$ minutiae triplets during indexing, thus saving memory and improving efficiency. The same technique is adopted in Ross and Mukherjee (2007), with the addition of information on ridge curvature to the minutiae triplets, resulting in an improved indexing performance. Liang, Bishnu, and Asano (2007) observe that the Delaunay triangulation is not tolerant enough to skin distortion that often affect fingerprints and show how an algorithm that consider both order-0 and order-1 Delaunay triangles (see Gudmundsso, Hammar, and Van Kreveld (2002)) can be more stable and robust against distortion.

Other indexing techniques are described in Shan, Shi, and Li (1994), Maeda, Matsushita, and Sasakawa (2001), Ren et al. (2002), Liu et al. (2005), Chikkerur et al. (2006), Liu, Zhang, and Hao (2006a), Liu, Jiang, and Kot (2006), Li, Yau, and Wang (2006b), Feng and Cai (2006b), and Becker and Potts (2007). In particular, Maeda, Matsushita, and Sasakawa (2001) proposed a rather different approach, which is based only on the matching scores between fingerprints rather than on features extracted from the fingerprint images: a matrix containing all the matching scores between each pair of fingerprints in the database is maintained. During retrieval, as the input fingerprint is matched with database fingerprints, the resulting scores are incrementally used to find the maximum correlation with a column of the matrix and to select the next database fingerprint to be matched. The method is interesting, because it can be applied to any biometric identifier, inasmuch as it only relies on matching scores; on the other hand, it is not well suited for large databases (e.g., one million fingerprints) because the size of the matrix is quadratic with the number of fingerprints in the database and for each new insertion in the database (enrollment), the new fingerprint has to be matched with all the fingerprints currently stored in the database. Becker and Potts (2007) propose another approach based only on matching scores, where a set of *fiduciary templates* are randomly selected in the database and the input fingerprint is compared against all those templates. The matching scores obtained are used as a feature vector for a continuous classification approach.

Finally, in some papers, different indexing techniques are combined to improve performance. In Cappelli, Maio, and Maltoni (2000a), the continuous classification technique proposed in Cappelli et al. (1999) is combined with an MKL-based approach: the distance measures produced by the two methods are fused by registering the different values according to their statistical distributions. In De Boer, Bazen, and Gerez (2001), two continuous classification techniques (the former similar to Lumini, Maio, and Maltoni (1997) and the latter using FingerCode feature vectors Jain, Prabhakar, and Hong (1999)) are combined with a simplified version of the minutiae-triplet approach proposed by Germain, Califano, and Colville (1997). In Sha and Tang (2004a), continuous classification approaches are combined to exclusive classification techniques.

5.4.3 Retrieval strategies

Choosing an indexing technique alone is usually not sufficient: a retrieval strategy should also be defined according to the application requirements such as the desired accuracy and efficiency, the matching algorithm used to compare fingerprints, the presence of a human supervisor, and so on. In general, different pre-selection strategies may be defined for the same indexing mechanism: for instance, the search may be stopped when a fixed portion of the database has been explored, or as soon as a matching fingerprint is found (in AFIS, this requires the presence of a human expert who visually examines the fingerprints that are considered sufficiently similar by the minutiae matcher and terminates the search when a true correspondence is found).

If an exclusive classification technique is used for indexing, these retrieval strategies can be used:

- *Hypothesized class only*: only fingerprints belonging to the class to which the input fingerprint has been assigned, are retrieved. The search may be stopped as soon as a matching fingerprint is found, or extended to all the fingerprints of that class in the database.

- *Fixed search order*: the search continues until a match is found, or the whole database has been explored; if a correspondence is not found within the hypothesized class, the search continues in another class, and so on. The optimal class visiting order can be a priori determined from the confusion matrix of a given fingerprint classifier (Lumini, Maio, and Maltoni, 1997). For example, if the input fingerprint is assigned to the arch class, the order could be: arch, tented arch, left loop, right loop, and whorl.

- *Variable search order*: the different classes are visited according to the class likelihoods produced by the classifier for the input fingerprint. The search may be stopped as soon as a match is found, or when the likelihood ratio between the current class and the next to be visited is less than a fixed threshold, see Senior (2001) or Senior and Bolle (2004).

Obviously, the first strategy (hypothesized class only) assumes no classification errors, which is quite unlikely for state-of-the-art automatic classifiers (see Section 5.3); the other strategies are more complex, but allow adjusting the accuracy of the system at the cost of speed. Each of the above three strategies may be combined with a rejection mechanism (see Section 5.3): if the input fingerprint is rejected by the automatic classifier, it has to be either manually classified, or compared with all the fingerprints in the database.

If a continuous classification technique is used for indexing the database, these retrieval strategies may be used (Lumini, Maio, and Maltoni, 1997):

- *Fixed radius*: given a prefixed tolerance ρ, the fingerprints considered are those whose corresponding vectors are inside the hypersphere with radius ρ centered at the point associated with the input fingerprint; the search may be halted as soon as a match is found, or when the whole portion of the database enclosed by the hypersphere has been explored.

• *Incremental search*: fingerprints are visited according to the distance between their associated vectors and the input point; the search continues until a match is found (in the worst case, it is extended to the whole database).

Figure 5.16 shows an example of the above two strategies. The incremental search allows the corresponding fingerprint to be found in any case (if present), even if the indexing technique fails; on the other hand, it does not guarantee an upper bound on the retrieval time. Obviously, an intermediate approach is also possible, where fingerprints are incrementally searched until a match is found or a prefixed distance (or portion of the database) has been explored (Cappelli, Maio, and Maltoni, 2000c).

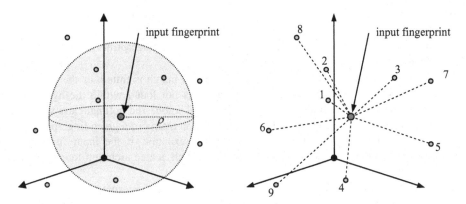

Figure 5.16. Retrieval strategies for continuous classification. On the left: the fingerprints whose corresponding vectors are inside the hypersphere are considered (*fixed radius*); on the right: the fingerprints are incrementally retrieved according to the distance of the corresponding vectors from the input point (*incremental search*).

Another retrieval strategy, which is often used in practice, is the application of cascaded filtering based on different techniques: the basic idea is to set up a sequential approach that progressively refines the search when a large database has to be explored (Wilson, Garris, and Watson (2004); Jarosz, Founder, and Dupre (2005)). In principle, both exclusive and continuous classification techniques may be adopted as filters, as well as other indexing techniques (e.g., based on minutiae triplets). Generally, the order of the filters is chosen such that the first filters are those with lower computational complexity and greater robustness, in spite of a limited selectivity; the ideal filters for the first steps of such a cascading strategy are able to quickly remove those fingerprints that significantly differ from the searched one, while avoiding to eliminate genuine candidates.

5.4.4 Performance of fingerprint retrieval techniques

In Lumini, Maio, and Maltoni (1997) and Cappelli et al. (1999) the performance of different retrieval strategies was measured both for continuous and exclusive classifications on the following benchmarks:

- One thousand two hundred and four fingerprint pairs from NIST Special Database 4 (see Section 5.3) obtained, from the 2,000 fingerprint pairs in the database, by reducing the cardinality of the less frequent classes in nature, in order to resemble the natural distribution (see Section 5.1); continuous classification results on this dataset were reported also by Jiang, Liu, and Kot (2006).
- The last 2,700 fingerprint pairs of NIST Special Database 14 (see Section 5.3); continuous classification results on this dataset were reported also by Cappelli, Maio, and Maltoni (2000a, 2002a).

The graphs in Figure 5.17 show the performance of three continuous and one exclusive classification approach on each dataset, for strategies where retrieval errors are possible (i.e., where the fingerprint corresponding to the input may not be found): *fixed radius* and *hypothesized class* only. In both the graphs, the performance of the exclusive classification approach is denoted by a single point, whereas performances of continuous classification approaches are reported for different operating points, as the speed/accuracy tradeoff depends on the chosen radius (ρ). For all the approaches, the search was not halted as soon as the corresponding fingerprint was found, but the whole portion of the database considered was explored.

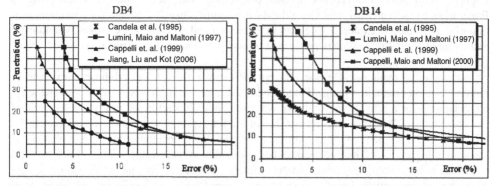

Figure 5.17. *Fixed radius* strategy: tradeoff between the average portion of database searched and the average retrieval error by varying the radius ρ. In each graph, the point marked with "*" denotes the performance of an exclusive classification technique using the *hypothesized class only* strategy.

Table 5.7 reports the performance of the same approaches using strategies that do not allow any retrieval errors (i.e., the search can be extended to the whole database): *incremental search* and *fixed search order*. The advantage of continuous classification approaches is well evident: in the exclusive case, even if the hypothesized class is correct, half of the fingerprints belonging to that class have to be visited on average, whereas in the continuous case, if the features used are sufficiently selective, the portion of the database searched can be very small.

Average penetration rate (%)		
Indexing approach	*DB4*	*DB14*
Candela et al. (1995)	17.2	18.9
Lumini, Maio, and Maltoni (1997)	6.9	7.1
Cappelli et al. (1999)	5.2	6.4
Cappelli, Maio, and Maltoni (2000a)	-	3.7
Jiang, Liu, and Kot (2006)	2.9	-

Table 5.7. Average penetration rate using the fixed search order strategy for the exclusive classification approach (Candela et al., 1995) and the incremental search strategy for the continuous classification approaches (Lumini, Maio, and Maltoni (1997), Cappelli et al. (1999), Cappelli, Maio, and Maltoni (2000a, 2002a) and Jiang, Liu, and Kot (2006)).

Other results have been published in the literature, where instead of using the NIST databases, the authors studied the effects of indexing/retrieval in the case of "smaller" live-scan dab images. Cappelli, Maio, and Maltoni (2000c) and De Boer, Bazen, and Gerez (2001) tested their retrieval systems on the second database (DB2) from FVC2000 (Maio et al., 2002a). The Cappelli, Maio, and Maltoni (2000c) method is based on MKL (see Section 5.2.4) and retrieves fingerprints by incrementally searching the database until a match is found or a maximum portion of the database is explored. The feature extraction and indexing are completely automatic and no manual quality control is performed. Figure 5.18 shows the retrieval error rate versus penetration rate graph.

As previously explained, De Boer, Bazen, and Gerez (2001) evaluated three indexing techniques based on orientation image, FingerCode, and minutiae triplets. Core detection (which is a crucial step for a reliable registration), was automatically performed but manually verified and corrected in 13% of the fingerprints; 1% of the fingerprints were also rejected because the core point could not be found. The retrieval error rate versus penetration rate graph obtained is reported in Figure 5.19. The two methods based on orientation image and FingerCode perform significantly better than that using minutiae triplets, and the performance of the minutiae triplet method is substantially lower than those reported by Bhanu and Tan (2001). Actually:

- The authors implemented a simplified version of the original triplet-based indexing (as introduced by Germain, Califano, and Colville (1997)), where the consistency of coordinate transformations was not taken into account in the computation of the final ranking

- The semi-automatic core extraction significantly helps orientation image- and FingerCode-based methods, and it is influential for the triplet-based method, which does not require any registration.

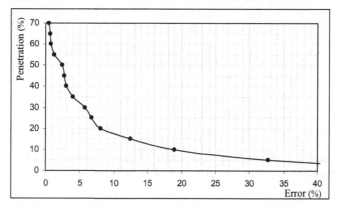

Figure 5.18. Retrieval error rate versus penetration rate graph of the automatic indexing/retrieval method proposed by Cappelli, Maio, and Maltoni (2000c).

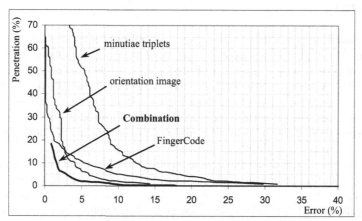

Figure 5.19. Retrieval error rate versus penetration rate graph of the different indexing/retrieval approaches evaluated by De Boer, Bazen, and Gerez (2001). These results are not directly comparable with those in Figure 5.18 because De Boer, Bazen, and Gerez (2001) manually assisted in the core detection stage.

When combining the three methods at rank level, De Boer, Bazen, and Gerez (2001) obtained a significant improvement, as shown in Figure 5.19. The main advantage is due to the combination of the first two features (i.e., orientation image and FingerCode) and adding minutiae triplets does not seem to improve the performance significantly. This is somewhat unexpected, because of the relatively high correlation between orientation image and FingerCode, and the low correlation between minutiae arrangements and texture information carried by the orientation image and FingerCode. The average portion of the database explored to find the query fingerprint for the three methods and their best combination is shown in Table 5.8.

Average penetration rate (%)	
Orientation image	2.58
FingerCode	2.40
Minutiae triplets	7.27
Combination	1.34

Table 5.8. Average penetration rate (with the incremental search strategy) in the indexing/retrieval approaches evaluated by De Boer, Bazen, and Gerez (2001).

5.5 Summary

Fingerprint classification has been the subject of several pattern recognition studies over the last 3 decades. Different solutions have been proposed and it is now possible to design classification systems that are able to meet the FBI requirement of 99% accuracy with a maximum rejection of 20%. However, it is unlikely that exclusive classification would make it possible to significantly reduce the effort of searching for a single fingerprint in the absence of other information (e.g., sex, age, race, etc.). Pre-selection strategies based on features extracted from fingerprints seem to be more promising alternatives for efficient implementations of the identification task in a variety of applications.

In AFIS and other semi-automatic civilian applications, the enrollment is supervised, the quality of the input fingerprint can be checked, and manual intervention is possible to correct feature extraction errors: this allows to design indexing/retrieval mechanisms that achieve a relatively small retrieval error and a good penetration rate. On the other hand, the identification task in a completely automatic system, working with live-scan dab images, has more severe constraints: database templates and input fingerprint images are often low quality and provide only a partial impression of the finger, and the system response is usually expected within a few seconds. The development of such an automatic fingerprint-based identification system for large databases is a challenging task, due to both accuracy and speed issues. Multimodal systems (see Chapter 7) seem to be the most promising way to improve accuracy (De Boer, Bazen, and Gerez, 2001), and to derive sequential approaches that progressively refine the search when a large database has to be explored.

6
Synthetic Fingerprint Generation[*]

6.1 Introduction

Significant efforts are continuously being made in designing new fingerprint recognition algorithms both in academic and industrial institutions. However, the accuracy of each algorithm is usually evaluated on relatively small databases. An evaluation on small databases makes the accuracy estimates highly data dependent; as a result, they do not generalize well on fingerprint images captured in different applications and different environments. Furthermore, when the databases are proprietary, the accuracy of various matching algorithms cannot be compared directly. A sharable large database of fingerprints (thousands or tens of thousands of images) is required to evaluate and compare various fingerprint recognition algorithms due to the very small error rates that have to be estimated. Unfortunately, collecting large databases of fingerprint images is: (i) expensive both in terms of money and time; and (ii) tedious for both the data collection technicians and for the subjects providing the data. Even if one is able to collect such a large fingerprint database, it is difficult to share it with others due to privacy legislations that often protect such personal data. Finally, publicly available databases of real fingerprints, such as those used in FVC technology evaluations (Maio et al., 2002a, b, 2004), Cappelli et al. (2006), do not constitute lasting solutions for evaluating and comparing different algorithms because they expire once "used," and new databases have to be collected for future evaluations. In other words, once an evaluation database is released, algorithm developers can "train" their algorithm to perform well on this specific database.

A potential alternative to collecting large fingerprint databases is fingerprint sample synthesis, i.e., generating images similar to human fingerprints, through parametric models that encode the salient characteristics of such images and their modes of variation. This chapter describes SFinGe, a synthetic fingerprint generation approach developed by Cappelli, Maio, and Maltoni (2000a, b, 2004); see also Maltoni (2004). SFinGe can be used to automatically create large databases of fingerprints, thus allowing fingerprint recognition algorithms to be effectively trained, tested, optimized, and compared. The artificial fingerprints emulate images acquired with electronic fingerprint scanners, because most commercial applications require

---

[*] Invited Chapter by Raffaele Cappelli, University of Bologna

D. Maltoni et al., *Handbook of Fingerprint Recognition*, 271–302.
© Springer-Verlag London Limited 2009

on-line acquisition. It is also possible to generate impressions similar to those acquired by the traditional "ink-technique" with relatively minor changes in the algorithm.

This chapter is organized as follows. Section 6.2 reviews synthetic fingerprint generation techniques proposed in the literature, classifying them according to the underlying generation model (physical or statistical). Section 6.3 introduces the basic schema of the SFinGe approach, including the different steps involved in the generation of a *master fingerprint* and its derived *fingerprint impressions*. A master fingerprint is a pattern that encodes the unique and immutable characteristics of a "synthetic finger" independently of the variations (displacement, rotation, pressure, skin condition, distortion, noise, etc.), that make the successive acquisitions different from each other. Sections 6.4 and 6.5 present the details of the generation of a master fingerprint and the derivation of fingerprint impressions, respectively. Section 6.6 introduces the evaluation performed to validate SFinGe; Section 6.7 discusses the possibility of associating ground-truth features to each synthetic fingerprint. Section 6.8 briefly describes a software tool (whose demo version is included in the DVD that accompanies this book) that implements the SFinGe approach; finally, Section 6.9 provides some concluding remarks.

6.2 Background

Existing studies on synthetic fingerprint generation can be grouped into two main categories: those based on *physical models* and those based on *statistical models* (see Buettner and Orlans (2005); Yanushkevich et al. (2005)).

Physical ridge pattern models rely on some hypothesized physical mechanisms of fingerprint formation during embryogenesis. In Sherstinsky and Picard (1994), a complex method which employs a dynamic non-linear system called "M-lattice" is introduced with the aim of binarizing a gray-scale fingerprint image. The method is based on the reaction–diffusion model first proposed by Turing (1952) to explain the formation of various patterns observed on animal skin such as zebra stripes. Although Sherstinsky and Picard do not address fingerprint synthesis, the ridge line model they proposed could be used as a basis for synthetic fingerprint generation. Penrose hypothesized that fingerprint patterns such as loops, whorls, etc. are formed by ridges corresponding to the lines of curvature of the skin of the embryo at the time when the ridges were being formed (Penrose, 1965). Under this hypothesis, Mardia, Li, and Hainsworth (1992) demonstrated that fingerprint patterns can be modeled by differential equations having exact solution. An interesting model was proposed by Kücken and Newell (2004), based on the following hypotheses: (i) fingerprint patterns are created by forces that are induced by differential growth of the epidermis' basal layer (as argued by Cummins (1926) from the observed dependency of the fingerprint pattern class on the fingertip geometry); (ii) non-uniform growth of the epidermis' basal layer results in compressive stress that leads to buckling, creating the primary ridges (see Bonnevie, 1924). Computer simulations have shown that an almost periodic pattern very similar to human fingerprints can be generated by applying Kücken's model: the three main fingerprint classes can be simulated and minutiae are present in regions where ridge patches with different directions and/or wavelength meet (Kücken, 2007). It is interesting to note that the formation of minutiae according to Kücken's method has strong analogies with minutiae genesis in SFinGe (see Section 6.5), although the two approaches have been developed starting from totally different hypotheses.

Statistical ridge pattern models are aimed at reproducing realistic-looking fingerprints without starting from embryological hypothesis. Such models are based on the empirical analysis of real fingerprints, from which statistical data about the main characteristics of the patterns are derived and parameterized into appropriate equations or synthesis algorithms. Novikov and Glushchenko (1998) proposed a ridge generation technique operating in the frequency domain. For each pixel $[x,y]$ of an initial random image, the 2D Fourier spectrum of a local window, centered in $[x,y]$, is computed. The highest-energy harmonic (i.e., a pure two-dimensional sinusoid in the spatial domain) is chosen from the Fourier spectrum along the normal to the local ridge orientation at $[x,y]$ (according to an a priori artificially generated orientation image). All the sinusoids are summed and the result is binarized; the procedure is iteratively repeated until a sufficiently smooth image is obtained. This method has some analogies with the iterative application of Gabor filters in the spatial domain discussed in Section 6.4; in fact, the MTF of a Gabor filter is characterized by two symmetric peaks along the normal to the filter orientation (see Section 3.6.2). Kosz (1999) published some results concerning synthetic fingerprint generation based on a mathematical model of ridge patterns and minutiae; further details on this technique have been provided online by Bicz (2003). According to this model, a fingerprint can be described by a wave pattern whose phase is determined by a function that can be decomposed into two parts: one explains the global "shape" of the ridge lines and the other describes the minutiae. This model was described also in Larkin and Fletcher (2007), who suggested its possible application to the compression of fingerprint images. A constructive approach was proposed by Hill (2001) where a fingerprint pattern is generated starting from a given set of minutiae points; the work is aimed at proving that a masquerade attack can be carried out against a fingerprint-based biometric system, by "fraudulently" accessing and deciphering the content of a stored template and by recreating an artificial clone (either digital or synthetic). Unfortunately, the algorithm proposed to draw ridge patterns (starting from minutiae positions and then iteratively filling empty spaces) produces images that are visually non-realistic. A more effective ridge reconstruction approach was introduced by Rahmes et al. (2007), with the aim of improving latent fingerprint comparison by automatically restoring low quality or missing regions in ridge line patterns; however this approach is only suited to reconstruct a few missing areas in a real fingerprint and cannot be used to create a whole new fingerprint pattern. Reconstruction of realistic fingerprint images from stored templates was shown by Cappelli et al. (2007) and by Franco and Maltoni (2007), using techniques based on the SFinGe ridge-pattern generation models. Araque et al. (2002) introduced a synthetic fingerprint generation technique whose main steps are similar to SFinGe, but with following main differences: (i) the orientation image synthesis is based on a new second-order model controlled by up to 11 complex coefficients, whose distributions are inferred from real data; (ii) the filters used for ridge pattern generation are simple binary masks instead of the Gabor filters used by SFinGe. Finally, Cho, Hong, and Cho (2007) proposed a genetic algorithm-based approach that is able to synthesize new impressions from a given dataset of fingerprints, by selecting a set of filters for simulating different acquisition conditions. This approach may be an alternative to (or used in conjunction with) SFinGe to derive synthetic impressions from a given master fingerprint (see Section 6.5).

6.3 The SFinGe Method

A typical fingerprint matching algorithm processes a fingerprint as summarized in Figure 6.1: (i) fingerprint is first segmented from the background, (ii) the local frequency and orientation maps are estimated, and (iii) this information is exploited to enhance the ridge pattern and find the minutiae. In order to generate fingerprint images, SFinGe "inverts" some of the above operations (see Figure 6.2): a fingerprint area, an orientation image, and a frequency image, generated independently of each other, are the inputs to a ridge generation process; the resulting binary ridge pattern is then rendered by adding fingerprint-specific noise.

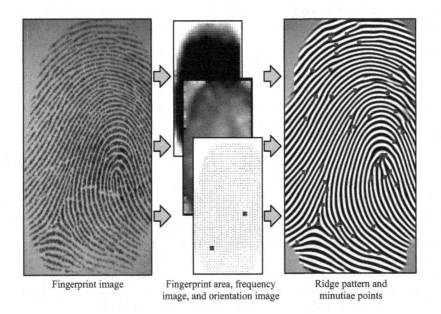

| Fingerprint image | Fingerprint area, frequency image, and orientation image | Ridge pattern and minutiae points |

Figure 6.1. A typical fingerprint feature extraction process.

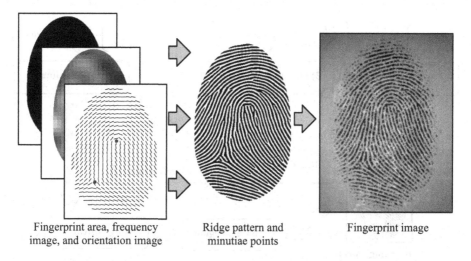

Fingerprint area, frequency   Ridge pattern and   Fingerprint image
image, and orientation image   minutiae points

Figure 6.2. The basic idea of the fingerprint generation method.

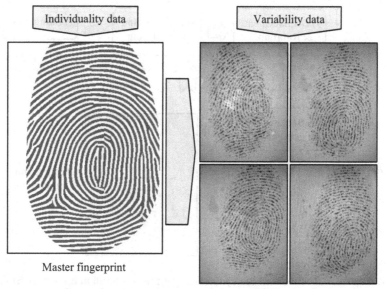

Master fingerprint

Figure 6.3. Starting from a set of parameters that represent the unique and immutable features of a "synthetic finger" (individuality data), SFinGe creates a master fingerprint; then a number of fingerprint impressions can be generated by changing several parameters that control the fingerprint appearance (variability data).

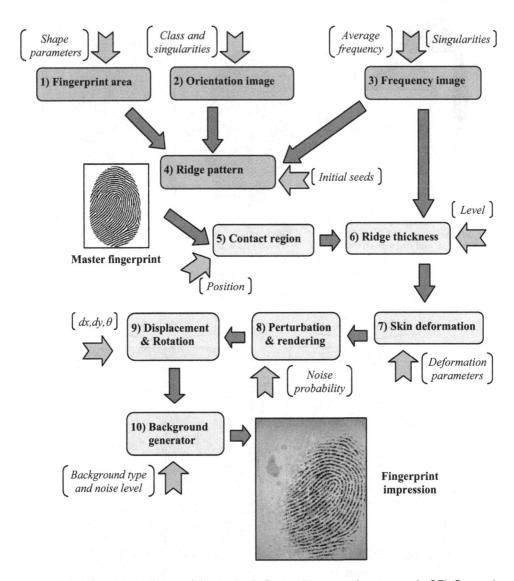

Figure 6.4. A functional schema of the synthetic fingerprint generation approach, SFinGe: each rounded box represents a generation step; the main input parameters that control each step are reported between brackets. Steps 1 to 4 create a master fingerprint; Steps 5 to 10 derive a fingerprint impression from the master fingerprint and can be iterated to produce multiple impressions of the same finger.

In order to generate multiple impressions of the same "synthetic finger," a more complicated schema needs to be introduced: a *master fingerprint* (i.e., a ridge pattern that represents the unique and immutable characteristics of a "synthetic finger") is first generated; then several synthetic impressions can be derived from the master fingerprint by explicitly tuning displacement, rotation, distortion, skin condition, and noise (see Figure 6.3). Figure 6.4 shows the complete generation process: Steps 1 to 4 create a master fingerprint; Steps 5 to 10 are performed for each fingerprint impression derived from the master fingerprint.

6.4 Generation of a Master Fingerprint

Creating a master fingerprint involves the following steps:

1. Fingerprint area generation
2. Orientation image generation
3. Frequency image generation
4. Ridge pattern generation

Step 1 defines the external silhouette of the fingerprint; Step 2 starts from the positions of loop and delta singularities and exploits a mathematical flow model to generate a consistent orientation image. Step 3 creates a frequency image on the basis of some heuristic criteria inferred by visual inspection of a large number of real fingerprints. In Step 4, the ridge line pattern and the minutiae are created through a contextual iterative filtering; the output is a near-binary fingerprint image. A separate section is dedicated to the explanation of each of the above steps.

6.4.1 Fingerprint area generation

Depending on the finger size, position, and pressure against the acquisition sensor, the fingerprint images have different sizes and external shapes (Figure 6.5).

Figure 6.5. Examples of fingerprint images with different size and shape.

A visual examination of a large number of fingerprint images suggested that a simple model, based on four elliptical arcs and a rectangle and controlled by five parameters (see Figure 6.6), can handle most of the variations present in fingerprint shape. Figure 6.6 shows some examples of fingerprint shapes generated by this model by varying the five parameters.

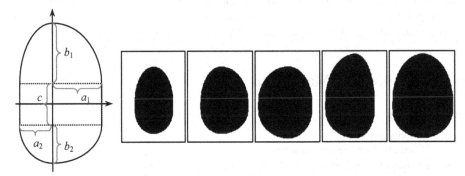

Figure 6.6. The fingerprint shape model (on the left) and some examples of fingerprint silhouettes generated by this model (on the right).

6.4.2 Orientation image generation

The orientation model proposed by Sherlock and Monro (1993) allows a consistent orientation image to be computed from the knowledge of the position of fingerprint singularities (loops and deltas) alone. In this model, the image is located in the complex plane and the local ridge orientation is the phase of the square root of a complex rational function whose singularities (poles and zeros) are located at the same place as the fingerprint singularities (loops and deltas). Let $\mathbf{ls}_i$, $i = 1...n_c$ and $\mathbf{ds}_i$, $i = 1...n_d$ be the coordinates of the loops and deltas, respectively. The orientation θ at each point $\mathbf{z} = [x,y]$ is calculated as

$$\theta = \frac{1}{2}\left[\sum_{i=1}^{n_d} arg(\mathbf{z} - \mathbf{ds}_i) - \sum_{i=1}^{n_c} arg(\mathbf{z} - \mathbf{ls}_i)\right], \tag{1}$$

where the function $arg(\mathbf{c})$ returns the phase angle of the complex number $\mathbf{c}$ (see Figure 6.7).

Sherlock and Monro's model may be exploited for generating synthetic orientation images as follows. First a fingerprint class is randomly chosen and then the positions of the singularities are randomly selected according to class-specific constraints (for instance, in a left loop, the delta must be on the right side of the loop). Figure 6.8 shows some examples of orientation images generated by this model. Unfortunately, the generation of synthetic orientation images for arch type patterns that do not contain any singularities is not supported by this model, and it must be considered separately. However, this does not pose a serious problem inasmuch as arch orientation image generation is straightforward, and a simple sinusoidal function (whose frequency and amplitude are tuned to control the arch curvature and aspect) adequately approximates this pattern.

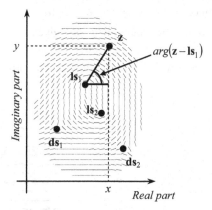

Figure 6.7. Each element of the orientation image is considered as a complex number (Sherlock and Monro, 1993).

The ridge line flow in a real fingerprint image cannot be completely determined by the singularity type and position. Hence, although the Sherlock and Monro model is a good starting point, it is not satisfactory. Figure 6.8e shows a fingerprint image (belonging to the left loop class) and the orientation image generated by the Sherlock and Monro model, with the same position of loop and delta. Clear differences exist among the real ridge line orientations and the corresponding elements in the orientation image: in particular, the regions above the loop and between the loop and the delta are not well modeled.

Vizcaya and Gerhardt (1996) proposed a variant of the Sherlock and Monro model that introduces more degrees of freedom to cope with the orientation variability that may characterize orientation images with coincident singularities. The orientation θ at each point $\mathbf{z}$ is calculated as

$$\theta = \frac{1}{2}\left[\sum_{i=1}^{n_d} g_{\mathbf{ds}_i}\left(arg(\mathbf{z}-\mathbf{ds}_i)\right) - \sum_{i=1}^{n_c} g_{\mathbf{ls}_i}\left(arg(\mathbf{z}-\mathbf{ls}_i)\right)\right], \tag{2}$$

where $g_k(\alpha)$, for $k \in \left\{\mathbf{ls}_1,\dots\mathbf{ls}_{n_c},\mathbf{ds}_1,\dots\mathbf{ds}_{n_d}\right\}$, are piecewise linear functions capable of locally correcting the orientation image with respect to the value given by the Sherlock and Monroe model:

$$g_k(\alpha) = \bar{g}_k(\alpha_i) + \frac{\alpha - \alpha_i}{2\pi/L}\left(\bar{g}_k(\alpha_{i+1}) - \bar{g}_k(\alpha_i)\right), \tag{3}$$

for $\alpha_i \le \alpha \le \alpha_{i+1}$, $\alpha_i = -\pi + \dfrac{2\pi i}{L}$.

Each function $g_k(\alpha)$ is defined by the set of values $\left\{\bar{g}_k(\alpha_i)\middle| i = 0...L-1\right\}$, where each value is the amount of correction of the orientation image at a given angle (in a set of L angles uniformly distributed between $-\pi$ and π). If $\bar{g}_k(\alpha_i) = \alpha_i \ \forall i \in \{0...L-1\}$ (i.e., $g_k(\alpha)$ is the identity function), the model coincides with that of Sherlock and Monro (see Figure 6.9).

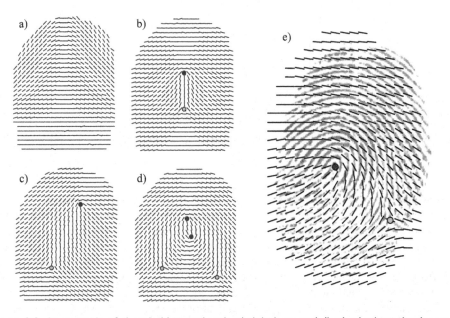

Figure 6.8. An example of a) arch, b) tented arch, c) right loop and d) whorl orientation image as generated by the Sherlock and Monro model. e) An example of a left loop orientation image superimposed over a left loop fingerprint with coincident singularity positions.

The aim of the Vizcaya and Gerhardt (1996) work is to approximate a real orientation image, given a specific fingerprint, and so the authors derive the values $\bar{g}_k(\alpha_i)$ through an optimization procedure. In SFinGe, the Vizcaya and Gerhardt model is not used to approximate the orientation image of a given fingerprint but instead, the additional degrees of freedom given by the Vizcaya and Gerhardt model are exploited to provide more variations. From the analysis of real fingerprints, Cappelli, Maio, and Maltoni (2000b) found that $L = 8$ is a reasonable value and derived appropriate ranges for the parameters $\overline{g}_k(\alpha_i)$ for each fingerprint class: during the orientation-image generation, random values are selected within such ranges. Actually, in order to produce realistic results, for each singularity k, only $\overline{g}_k(\alpha_0)$ and $\overline{g}_k(\alpha_4)$ are randomly selected: the other values are determined so that a smooth mapping function $g_k(\alpha)$ is obtained. Figure 6.10 shows the effect of changing the parameter $\overline{g}_{ls_1}(\alpha_4)$ in a right loop fingerprint: the changes with respect to the Sherlock and Monro formulation (see Figure 6.9) are highlighted in the corresponding orientation image.

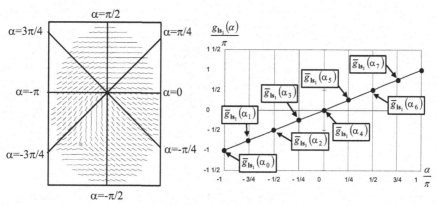

Figure 6.9. Definition of a function $g_k(\alpha)$ for the loop singularity of a right loop orientation image (Vizcaya and Gerhardt, 1996). In this case, $g_k(\alpha)$ is the identity function and the model coincides with that of Sherlock and Monro (1993).

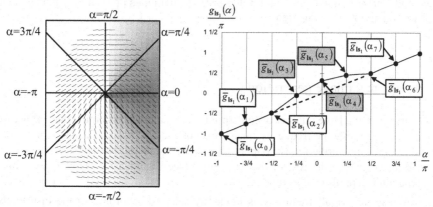

Figure 6.10. The effects of modifying the parameters that control a mapping function $g_k(\alpha)$ are highlighted in the corresponding orientation image (Vizcaya and Gerhardt, 1996).

Figure 6.11a and b show two examples of orientation images generated according to the Vizcaya and Gerhardt model; these images appear to be more realistic than those in Figure 6.8. The superiority of the Vizcaya and Gerhardt model in approximating real ridge patterns is also evident from the comparison between Figure 6.11c and d.

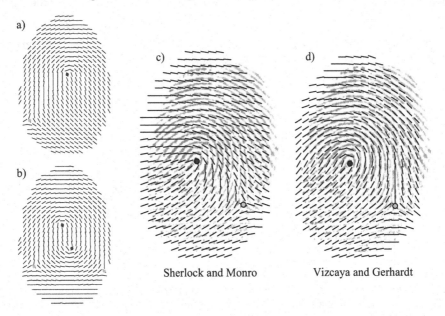

Sherlock and Monro   Vizcaya and Gerhardt

Figure 6.11. An example of a) right loop and b) whorl orientation images, as generated by the Vizcaya and Gerhardt model. In c) and d) the orientation images produced by the two models, for a given fingerprint, are compared.

6.4.3 Frequency image generation

Visual inspection of a large number of fingerprint images allows us to immediately discard the possibility of generating the frequency image in a completely random fashion. Quite often, in the regions above the northernmost loop and below the southernmost delta, the ridge line frequency is lower than in the rest of the fingerprint (see Figure 6.12). Therefore, frequency-image generation is performed as follows:

1. A feasible overall frequency is randomly selected according to the distribution of ridge line frequency in real fingerprints; an average ridge/valley period of nine pixels is used. This simulates a 500 dpi sensor.

2. The frequency in the above-described regions is slightly decreased according to the positions of the singularities.
3. The frequency image is randomly perturbed to improve its appearance.
4. A local smoothing by a 3×3 averaging box filter is performed.

Figure 6.13 shows some examples of synthetically generated frequency images.

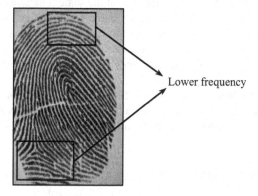

Lower frequency

Figure 6.12. An example of a right loop fingerprint, where the ridge line frequency is lower in the regions above the loop and below the delta.

Figure 6.13. Some examples of synthesized frequency images: light blocks denote higher frequencies.

6.4.4 Ridge pattern generation

Given an orientation image and a frequency image as an input, a deterministic generation of a ridge line pattern, including consistent minutiae, is not an easy task. One could try to fix a priori the number, the type, and the location of the minutiae, and by means of an explicit model, generate the gray-scale fingerprint image starting from the minutiae neighborhoods and expanding to connect different regions until the whole image is covered. Such a constructive approach would require several complex rules and heuristics to be implemented in order to deal with the complexity of fingerprint ridge line patterns. A more elegant solution could be based on the use of a syntactic approach that generates fingerprints according to some starting symbols and a set of production rules.

The method used by SFinGe is very simple and at the same time powerful: an initial image is created by randomly placing a few black points into a white image; then, by iteratively enhancing this initial image through Gabor filters (adjusted according to the local ridge orientation and frequency), a consistent and very realistic ridge line pattern gradually appears; in particular, fingerprint minutiae of different types (endings, bifurcations, islands, etc.) are automatically generated at random positions.

Gabor filters were introduced in Section 3.6.2 as an effective tool for fingerprint enhancement; with respect to Equation (11) in Section 3.6.2, SFinGe uses equal values for the standard deviations of the Gaussian envelope along the x- and y-axes:

$$\sigma_x = \sigma_y = \sigma .$$

The filter applied at each pixel has the form:

$$g(x, y : \theta, f) = e^{-\left((x^2 + y^2)/2\sigma^2\right)} \cdot \cos\left[2\pi \cdot f \cdot (x \cdot \sin\theta + y \cdot \cos\theta)\right], \tag{4}$$

where θ and f are the corresponding local orientation and frequency, respectively. The parameter σ, which determines the bandwidth of the filter, is adjusted according to the local frequency so that the filter does not contain more than three effective peaks (as in Figure 3.28). In particular, the value of σ is determined by the solution to the following equation.

$$e^{-\left(\left(\frac{3}{2f}\right)^2 / 2\sigma^2\right)} = 10^{-3} . \tag{5}$$

Although one could reasonably expect that iteratively applying "striped" filters to random images would simply produce striped images, very realistic minutiae are generated at random positions. Based on their experiments, Cappelli, Maio, and Maltoni (2000b) argue that minutiae primarily originate from the ridge line disparity produced by local convergence/divergence of the orientation image and by frequency changes. Figures 6.14 and 6.15 show some examples of the iterative ridge line generation process. Cappelli, Maio, and Maltoni (2000b) experimentally found that increasing the number of initial points provides a more irregular ridge pattern richer in minutiae (see Figure 6.14). This is not surprising, because expanding distinct image regions causes interference where regions merge, thus favoring the creation of minutiae (see Figure 6.16).

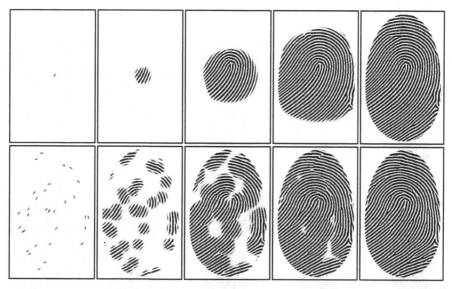

Figure 6.14. Some intermediate steps of a fingerprint generation process starting from a single central point (top row) and from a number of randomly located points (bottom row). Usually, increasing the number of initial points provides a more irregular ridge pattern richer in minutiae.

6.5 Generation of Synthetic Fingerprint Impressions

Several factors contribute to intra-fingerprint variability (making the impressions of a given finger substantially different) when captured by a live-scan scanner (see Chapter 2):

- Displacement in the x- and y-directions and rotation.
- Different finger portions touching the sensor.
- Non-linear distortion produced by the non-orthogonal pressure of the finger against the sensor.
- Variations in the ridge line thickness due to pressure intensity or by skin dampness (wet or dry).
- Small cuts or abrasions on the fingertip.
- Background noise and other sources of noise.

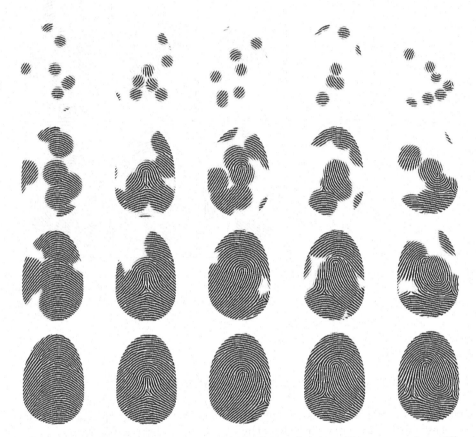

Figure 6.15. Each column shows an example of a fingerprint generation process for a different fingerprint class; from left to right: arch, tented arch, left loop, right loop, and whorl.

Figure 6.16. Genesis of a minutia point during the fusion of two regions created by two different initial points.

For each fingerprint impression to be generated from a given master fingerprint, SFinGe sequentially performs the following steps (the numbering continues from Section 6.5 according to Figure 6.4):

5. Definition of the fingerprint portion that is in contact with the sensor (this is simply performed by shifting the fingerprint pattern with respect to the fixed external silhouette).
6. Variation in the average thickness of the ridge (skin condition).
7. Distortion.
8. Perturbation.
9. Global translation/rotation.
10. Background generation.

6.5.1 Variation in ridge thickness

Skin dampness and finger pressure against the sensor platen have similar effects on the acquired images: when the skin is dry or the pressure is low, ridges appear thinner, whereas when the skin is wet or the pressure is high, ridges appear thicker (see Figure 6.17).

Figure 6.17. Three impressions of the same real finger as captured when the finger is dry, normal, and wet, respectively. Reprinted with permission from Cappelli, Maio, and Maltoni (2002b). © IEEE.

Morphological operators (Gonzales and Woods, 2007) are applied to the master fingerprint to simulate different degrees of dampness/pressure. In particular, the erosion operator is applied to simulate low pressure or dry skin, and the dilation operator is adopted to simulate high pressure or wet skin (see Figure 6.18). The structuring element used is a square box whose size varies from 2×2 to 4×4, to modulate the magnitude of the ridge thickness variation.

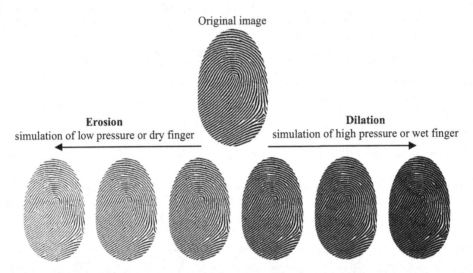

Figure 6.18. Application of different levels of erosion/dilation to the same master fingerprint. Reprinted with permission from Cappelli, Maio, and Maltoni (2002b). © IEEE.

6.5.2 Fingerprint distortion

One of the main characteristics that distinguishes different impressions of the same finger is the presence of non-linear distortions, mainly due to skin deformations according to different finger placements over the sensing element (see Figure 6.19). In fact due to skin plasticity, the application of force, some of whose components are not orthogonal to the sensor surface, produces non-linear distortions (compression or stretching) in the acquired fingerprints (see Chapter 4).

SFinGe exploits the skin-distortion model introduced in Cappelli, Maio, and Maltoni (2001). Unlike in fingerprint matching, where the function *distortion*( ) (see Section 4.5.6) is applied to re-map minutiae points in order to improve fingerprint matching, here the mapping is applied to the whole image, in order to simulate realistic distorted impressions. For this purpose, Lagrangian interpolation is employed to obtain smoothed gray-scale deformed images. Performing Lagrangian interpolation requires the inverse mapping function *distortion*$^{-1}$( ) to be computed, but unfortunately, this function cannot be analytically expressed. Therefore, for each pixel involved in the mapping, the Newton–Raphson method (Press et al., 1992) is used for numerically calculating the inverse. Figure 6.20 shows a master fingerprint and its distorted impression.

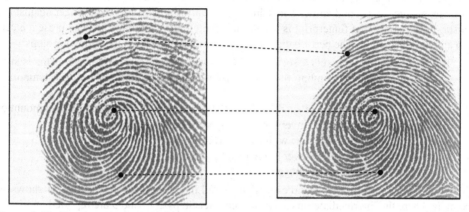

Figure 6.19. Two impressions of the same real finger where a few corresponding minutiae are marked to highlight the distortion. Reprinted with permission from Cappelli, Maio, and Maltoni (2002b). © IEEE.

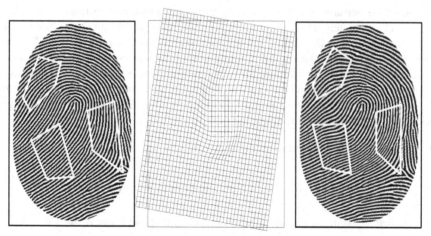

Figure 6.20. A master fingerprint (on the left) and a distorted impression (on the right); the equivalent distortion of a square mesh is shown in the middle. To better highlight the non-linear deformations, a few corresponding minutiae are connected by white segments in the two images.

6.5.3 Perturbation and global translation/rotation

During fingerprint acquisition, several factors contribute to the deterioration of the true image, thus producing a noisy gray-scale image: irregularity of the ridges and their different contact with the sensor surface, presence of small pores within the ridges, presence of very small prominent ridges, gaps, and clutter noise due to non-uniform pressure of the finger against the sensor. Furthermore, the fingerprint is usually not centered in the image and can present a certain amount of rotation. The perturbation phase sequentially performs the following steps:

1. Isolate the white pixels associated with the valleys into a separate layer. This is simply performed by copying the pixels brighter than a fixed threshold to a temporary image.
2. Add noise in the form of small white blobs of variable size and shape. The amount of noise increases with the inverse of the fingerprint border distance.
3. Smooth the resulting image with a 3×3 averaging box filter.
4. Superimpose the valley layer to the resulting image.
5. Rotate and translate the image.

Steps 1 and 4 are necessary to avoid excessive overall image smoothing. Figure 6.21 shows an example where the intermediate images produced after Steps 2, 4, and 5 are reported.

6.5.4 Background generation

The output of the perturbation phase is a fingerprint image that appears realistic, but the background is still completely white. In order to generate backgrounds similar to those of fingerprint images acquired with a given sensor, a statistical model based on the KL transform (Jolliffe, 1986) is adopted. The model requires a set of background-only images as a training set (see Figure 6.22): a linear subspace that represents the main variations in the training background images is calculated and then used to randomly generate new backgrounds. Formally, let B = {$\mathbf{b}_1$, $\mathbf{b}_2$,...$\mathbf{b}_m$} be a set of m n-dimensional vectors (obtained from the background images by concatenating their rows) and let:

* $\bar{\mathbf{b}} = \dfrac{1}{m}\sum_{b \in B} \mathbf{b}$ be their mean vector

* $\mathbf{C} = \dfrac{1}{m}\sum_{b \in B} (\mathbf{b} - \bar{\mathbf{b}})(\mathbf{b} - \bar{\mathbf{b}})^T$ be their covariance matrix

* $\mathbf{\Phi} \in \Re^{n \times n}$ be the orthonormal matrix that diagonalizes $\mathbf{C}$; that is, $\mathbf{\Phi}^T \mathbf{C} \mathbf{\Phi} = \mathbf{\Lambda}$,

    $\mathbf{\Lambda} = Diag(\lambda_1, \lambda_2, ... \lambda_n)$, $\mathbf{\Phi} = [\boldsymbol{\varphi}_1, \boldsymbol{\varphi}_2, ... \boldsymbol{\varphi}_n]$

    where λ_i and $\boldsymbol{\varphi}_i$, $i = 1...n$ are the eigenvalues and the eigenvectors of $\mathbf{C}$, respectively.

Then, given a parameter k, $0 < k < \min(n,m)$, the k-dimensional subspace S_B is identified by the mean vector $\overline{\mathbf{b}}$ and by the projection matrix $\mathbf{\Phi}_k \in \mathfrak{R}^{n \times k}$, whose columns are the k columns of $\mathbf{\Phi}$ corresponding to the k largest eigenvalues:

$$\mathbf{\Phi}_k = \left[\boldsymbol{\varphi}_{i_1}, \boldsymbol{\varphi}_{i_2}, \ldots \boldsymbol{\varphi}_{i_k} \right] \quad \text{with} \quad \lambda_{i_1} \geq \lambda_{i_2} \geq \ldots \lambda_{i_k} \geq \ldots \lambda_{i_n}.$$

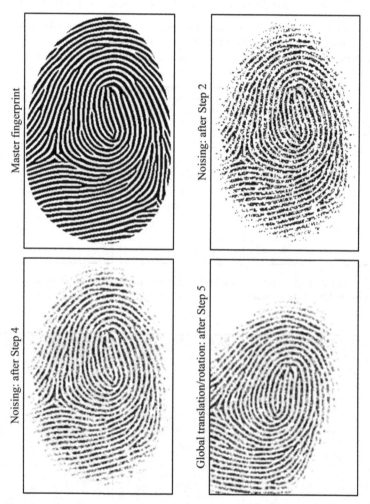

Figure 6.21. An example of perturbation and global translation/rotation, where the intermediate images produced after Steps 2, 4, and 5 are reported.

The generation of a new background is performed by selecting a point in the subspace S_B and by back projecting it in the original n-dimensional space:

1.   A k-dimensional vector $\mathbf{y} = [y_1, y_2, ... y_k]$ is randomly generated according to k normal distributions: $y_j = N\left(0, \lambda_{i_j}^{1/2}\right)$, $j = 1...k$

2.   The corresponding n-dimensional vector $\mathbf{b}$ is obtained as: $\mathbf{b} = \mathbf{\Phi}_k \mathbf{y} + \overline{\mathbf{b}}$.

Figure 6.22 shows some examples of the background images (obtained from an optical scanner) used as a training set for the background generation step; Figure 6.23 reports three synthetic fingerprints with backgrounds generated according to the above model.

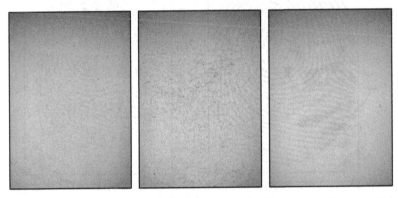

Figure 6.22. Examples of background-only images (acquired from an optical scanner) used for training the background generator.

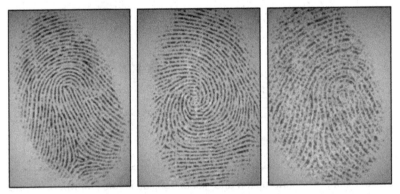

Figure 6.23. Three synthetic images with backgrounds generated according to the model (the parameters used for training are $m = 65$ and $k = 8$).

6.6 Validation of the Synthetic Generator

The fingerprint images generated by SFinGe appear very realistic (Figures 6.24 and 6.25 show some examples), but an in-depth analysis is necessary to understand if they can be a valid substitute for real fingerprints for testing and training fingerprint recognition algorithms. Some of the experiments that have been carried out to validate the images produced by SFinGe are described in the following.

Figure 6.24. Two synthetic fingerprint images (first row) are compared with two real fingerprints captured with a live-scan scanner (second row).

The first test was an experiment to determine if the synthetic fingerprints appeared visually similar to the real fingerprints. This test was performed during the Fifteenth International Conference on Pattern Recognition (September 2000), when about 90 participants, most of them with some background in fingerprint analysis, were asked to find a synthetic fingerprint image when presented with four images (three of which were real fingerprints). Only 23% of subjects (refer to Figure 6.26 and Table 6.1) could correctly identify the synthetic image.

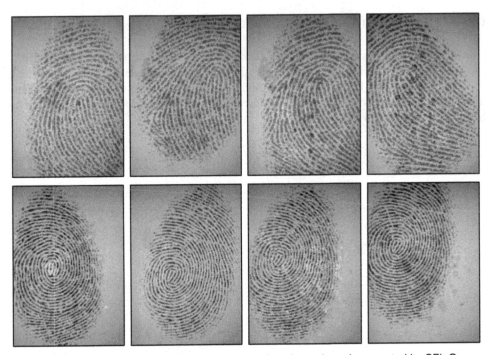

Figure 6.25. Two sets of fingerprint impressions (one in each row) generated by SFinGe.

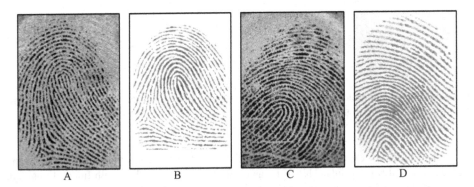

Figure 6.26. Three real fingerprints (B, C, and D), acquired with different sensors and a synthetic fingerprint (A).

Survey results (%)	
A	23
B	27
C	21
D	29

Table 6.1. Percentage of subjects (out of 90) that chose each of the four fingerprints in Figure 6.26 as synthetically generated fingerprint.

Extensive tests were performed in conjunction with the first two International Fingerprint Verification Competitions (FVC2000, Maio et al. (2002a) and FVC2002, Maio et al. (2002b)). In both the contests, four fingerprint databases were used. Three of the databases (DB1, DB2, and DB3) were acquired from real fingers through various live-scan scanners, and fingerprints in the fourth database (DB4) were synthetically generated by SFinGe. Not only did the participating algorithms exhibit very similar performance on DB4 as on the other databases, but the genuine/impostor distributions and the FMR/FNMR curves were also surprisingly close. Figure 6.27 shows the performance of one of the participating algorithm, PA15, over the four databases of FVC2002. It is worth noting here that the graph computed on the synthetic database has a trend very similar to the other three graphs. This means that fingerprints generated by SFinGe are realistic from the point of view of the matching algorithm PA15.

In order to better support this claim and to consider all the algorithms evaluated in FVC2002, an analysis of the ranking distributions among all the participating algorithms over the four FVC2002 databases was performed. Let $R_{ik}^{(j)}$ be the ranking of algorithm i over database k according to the performance indicator j (in FVC2002, the number of participants was 31 and four accuracy indicators were used to compare their performance: EER, ZeroFMR, FMR1000, and FMR100; see Section 1.5.6); let $RRD_i^{(j)}$ and $SRD_i^{(j)}$ be the average ranking difference of participant i according to indicator j, among the three real databases and between the synthetic database and each of the real ones, respectively:

$$RRD_i^{(j)} = \frac{\left|R_{i1}^{(j)} - R_{i2}^{(j)}\right| + \left|R_{i1}^{(j)} - R_{i3}^{(j)}\right| + \left|R_{i2}^{(j)} - R_{i3}^{(j)}\right|}{3} \tag{6}$$

$$SRD_i^{(j)} = \frac{\left|R_{i4}^{(j)} - R_{i1}^{(j)}\right| + \left|R_{i4}^{(j)} - R_{i2}^{(j)}\right| + \left|R_{i4}^{(j)} - R_{i3}^{(j)}\right|}{3} . \tag{7}$$

$RRD_i^{(j)}$ indicates how stable is the performance of participant i (according to indicator j) over the three databases; $SRD_i^{(j)}$ denotes the amount of variation between synthetic and real databases. Table 6.2 reports, for each indicator $j = 1...4$, a summary of the distribution of $RRD_i^{(j)}$

and $SRD_i^{(j)}$ for $i = 1...31$; the results are somewhat unexpected: the ranking difference $SRD^{(j)}$ is often even lower than the corresponding $RRD^{(j)}$, indicating that the difference between the synthetic database and the real databases is even smaller than the inter-difference among the three real databases; this shows that a database of synthetic fingerprints generated by SFinGe can be successfully used to measure the performance of matching algorithms.

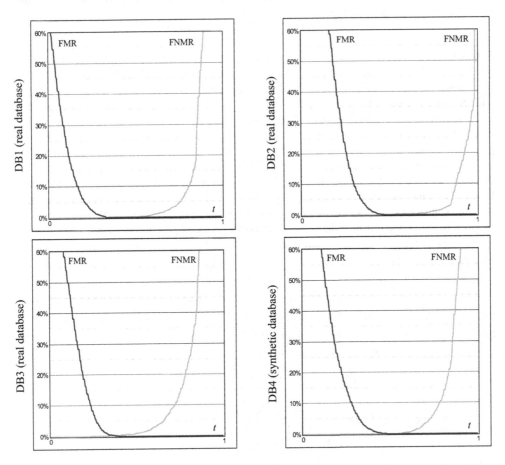

Figure 6.27. FVC2002: FMR versus FNMR graphs for the algorithm PA15 on the four databases.

	$RRD_i^{(1)}$	$SRD_i^{(1)}$	$RRD_i^{(2)}$	$SRD_i^{(2)}$	$RRD_i^{(3)}$	$SRD_i^{(3)}$	$RRD_i^{(4)}$	$SRD_i^{(4)}$
Average	2.84	2.65	3.14	2.74	2.58	2.58	2.69	2.59
Max	8.67	11.33	11.33	7.67	7.33	5.67	8.00	10.67
Min	0.00	0.00	0.67	0.33	0.00	0.33	0.00	0.33
St. Dev.	2.51	2.43	2.35	1.76	1.94	1.45	2.15	2.36

Table 6.2. Distributions of $RRD_i^{(j)}$ and $SRD_i^{(j)}$ over all the FVC2002 participating algorithms: average, maximum, minimum values, and the standard deviations are reported for each indicator j.

6.7 Automatic Generation of Ground Truth Features

Synthetic generation of fingerprint patterns allows us to easily obtain the ground truth about relevant features, such as the orientation image, the local ridge-line frequency, and the minutiae. The availability of ground-truth is very useful for the development, optimization and evaluation of feature extraction algorithms, especially for learning-based techniques that usually need large amount of labeled data. For instance, creation of minutiae ground truth can be performed in parallel with the fingerprint generation (Figure 6.28): the standard minutiae extraction rules defined in ISO/IEC 19794–2 (2005) are applied to the master fingerprint, then all the relevant transformations executed on the pattern are applied to the minutiae (e.g. translation, rotation, distortion). This approach has some clear advantages:

- The features can be reliably extracted through simple algorithms, since the extraction occurs in a binary image without any noise.
- The ground truth is always unique and accurate, even when the quality of the final image is relatively low (see Figure 6.29).

Generation of other ground truth features can be performed in a similar fashion; for instance, all the relevant transformations can be applied to the orientation image calculated at Step 2 (Section 6.3), thereby obtaining the true orientation image of the final synthetic fingerprint impression.

6.8 SFinGe Software Tool

Biometric Systems Lab, University of Bologna, Cesena, Italy has developed an automated software tool for generating synthetic fingerprint images according to the SFinGe method described in this chapter. A demo version of this tool is included in the DVD that accompanies this book. Figures 6.30 through 6.32 show the user interface of the software: for each step of the generation method, the user can adjust the main parameters and observe the corresponding effects on the resulting synthetic fingerprint (Figure 6.32).

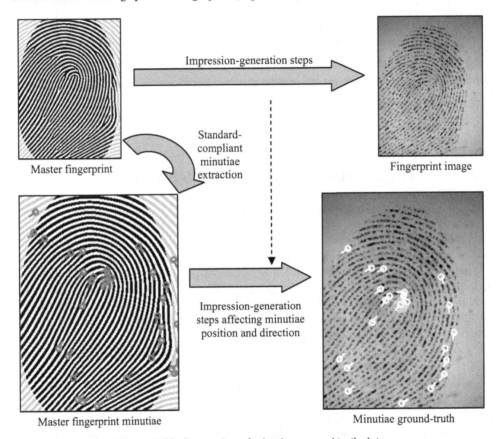

Figure 6.28. Generation of minutiae ground truth data.

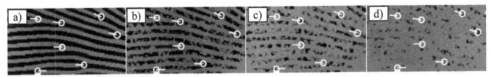

Figure 6.29. Minutiae ground truth as generated by SFinGe for the same fingerprint portion at different levels of noise: low noise (a), medium noise (b, c), and high noise (d).

Figure 6.30. Main window of the SFinGe software tool.

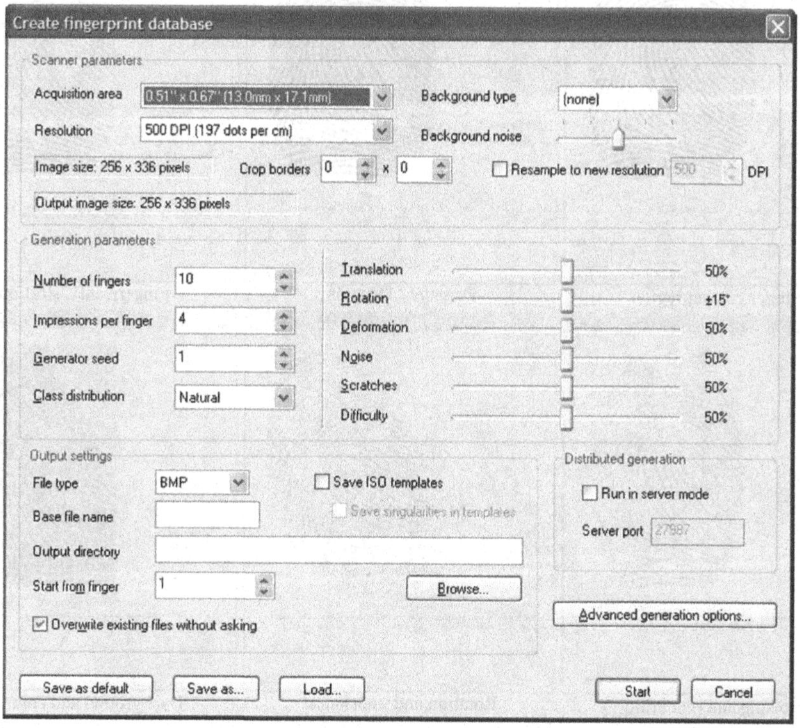

Figure 6.31. Batch generation options.

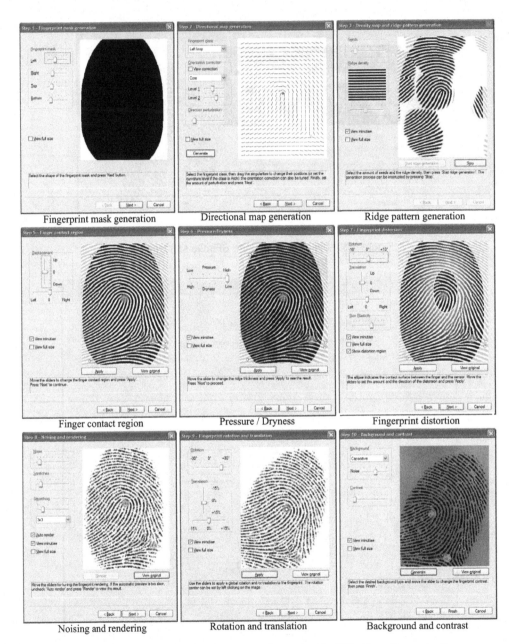

Fingerprint mask generation — Directional map generation — Ridge pattern generation

Finger contact region — Pressure / Dryness — Fingerprint distortion

Noising and rendering — Rotation and translation — Background and contrast

Figure 6.32. Main steps in fingerprint generation, using the SFinGe software tool.

The software also allows a database of synthetic fingerprints to be generated in a batch mode, given a relatively small set of input parameters (see Figure 6.31): number of fingers, impressions per finger, image size and resolution, seed for the random number generator, maximum amount of translation/rotation, maximum amount of perturbation or noise, maximum amount of deformation, and global database difficulty.

The generation of a fingerprint database (including ground-truth data) can be executed in a parallel mode, since each master fingerprint (with its impressions) is independent of the others; this makes it possible to distribute the process on many computers. For instance, using 10 3GHz PCs in a network, a database of 100,000 fingerprints (10,000 fingers, 10 impressions per finger) can be generated in less than 2 h. Thus a large database of synthetic fingerprints can be generated in a short amount of time without any subject and cost! Furthermore, by using this software, two identical databases can be generated at different places by specifying the same pseudo random number and parameters; this allows the same test to be reproduced without exchanging huge amounts of test data.

6.9 Summary

Synthetic fingerprint generation is an effective technique to overcome the problem of collecting large fingerprint databases for test purposes. Obviously, synthetic fingerprints are not a substitute for real fingerprint databases, especially when the performance has to be measured with respect to a given application environment and demographics of the user population; on the other hand, synthetic fingerprints have been shown to be well suited for technology evaluations like FVC2000–FVC2006 (Maio et al., 2002a, b, 2004), Cappelli et al. (2006). The use of synthetic fingerprints is not only limited to the problem of performance evaluation. It can also be used for the following tasks:

- Many classifiers and pattern recognition techniques (i.e., neural networks, principal component analysis, Support Vector Machines, etc.) require a large training set for their learning stage. Synthetic fingerprint images, automatically annotated with ground-truth features, are very well suited for this purpose: in fact, the generator parameters allow explicit control of the type and features of the synthetic fingerprints (e.g., fingerprint type, type of noise, distortion, etc.) and this can be exploited in conjunction with boosting techniques (Schapire (1990); Freund and Schapire (1996)) to drive the learning process. For example, in Cappelli, Maio, and Maltoni (2000c), a large synthetic training set (generated by SFinGe) was successfully used to derive optimal MKL subspaces for fingerprint indexing.

- The synthetic fingerprints generated by SFinGe can be used to test the robustness of fingerprint verification systems against "Trojan horse" attacks at the sensor or the feature extractor module (see Section 9.4). SFinGe allows us to generate large sets of fingerprints whose features (e.g., minutiae distribution) can be varied independently of other fingerprint characteristics (e.g., orientation image) and, therefore, it is well suited to study the robustness against "hill-climbing" types of Trojan horse attacks and against template reverse engineering (Cappelli et al., 2007).

- Interoperability tests, such as MINEX (Grother et al., 2006) and MTIT (Bazin and Mansfield, 2007), have shown that the location, direction, and type of minutiae extracted by different minutiae extraction algorithms from the same finger image tend to be different. Algorithms *syntactically compliant* to standards such as ISO/IEC 19794–2 (2005), are often not *semantically compliant* (that is, they adopt different rules and conventions to define minutiae placement and direction) and this creates huge interoperability problems. Unfortunately, testing semantic conformance to a minutiae extraction standard is not easy, since it requires a lot of data with manually-labeled minutiae points (ground-truth); furthermore, in low-quality image areas, even manual labeling of minutiae points is not reliable. The automatic generation of ground-truth data for synthetic fingerprint images provided by SFinGe is an effective way to carry out semantic conformance and interoperability studies.

The SFinGe method described here, however, has some limitations:

- The ridge thickness in synthetic images is constant throughout the fingerprint image; this is not true in nature, where this feature may vary across the same fingerprint.
- SFinGe distributes the noise uniformly over the entire fingerprint area (except for the borders where it gradually increases); in real fingerprints, the noise tends to be clustered in certain regions; both high quality and poor quality regions can be found in the same fingerprint (see Chapter 3); a first step to solve this limitation has been done in Cappelli, Maio, and Maltoni (2004), where a new noise model based on the function defined by Perlin (1985) was introduced.
- Intra-ridge noise, which in nature is partially produced by finger pores, is randomly generated by SFinGe. Although this is not a problem when generating fingerprints from different fingers, this is not very realistic for impressions of the same finger, where a certain correlation among these impressions should be taken into account.

Finally, further investigations are necessary to better understand how similar the synthetic fingerprints are to the real ones from an "individuality" point of view (ref. Chapter 8). Some experimentation in this direction has been performed to measure the intra-class and inter-class variations of the various fingerprint features (e.g., orientation image, frequency image, minutiae), showing that the parameters of the generator can be tuned to properly emulate the variations in real fingerprints. However, a more in-depth analysis is necessary to determine whether SFinGe is capable of generating different types of minutiae with the corresponding frequencies observed in nature.

7
Biometric Fusion

7.1 Introduction

In this chapter we will discuss fusion (i.e., combination) of multiple sources of information with the goal of improving the performance of fingerprint systems. This topic is also known as multibiometrics or multimodal biometrics. Biometric fusion is a very important topic that has already been in use in law enforcement for some time (e.g., fusion of 10 rolled fingerprints in AFIS), but the challenge is to determine which information sources to combine and which combination strategies to use. Answers to these questions are application specific. Our intention is not to make specific recommendation, but rather to discuss the tools available to system designers to make informed decision and implementation. A large body of literature exists on information fusion in many different fields, including data mining, pattern recognition and computer vision. Fusion in biometric (Ross, Nandakumar, and Jain, 2006), and fingerprint systems in particular, is an instance of information fusion (Dasarathy, 1994). A strong theoretical base as well as numerous empirical studies has been documented that support the advantages of fusion in fingerprint systems. The main advantage of fusion in the context of biometrics is an improvement in the overall matching accuracy.

Not surprisingly, the improvement in matching accuracy due to fusion also comes at a cost. For example, the multibiometric system may require many sensors and thus will be more expensive. Further, such a system may also increase the user inconvenience as the user needs to interact with more than one sensor, increasing both the enrollment and verification times. For example, in a multibiometric system that requires both fingerprint and iris images of a person, a user will not only need to touch the fingerprint scanner, but will also need to interact with an iris imaging system. Such a system may also require more computational power and storage.

It is quite popular to combine fingerprints with non-biometric information such as passwords and tokens in many logical and physical access control applications. This is commonly known as multifactor authentication and is considered more secure than using fingerprints alone as these other "factors" have some of their own strengths. However, they also reintroduce certain of their own weaknesses – for example, passwords and tokens can be lost, stolen,

D. Maltoni et al., *Handbook of Fingerprint Recognition*, 303–339.
© Springer-Verlag London Limited 2009

or forgotten. Some applications require that only one of the two or three factors match. In this case, the application is focusing on convenience and taking advantages of the strengths of all the factors. However, such a system is not as secure.

Combining fingerprints with other biometric traits offers several advantages. For example, one of the important factors in selecting a biometric identifier is the universality property, but arguably, no single biometric is truly universal. For example, fingerprints are supposedly universal, but there is a small fraction of the population that does not possess all the fingerprints due to hand-related disabilities such as missing digits etc., and yet another small fraction of the population (such as manual workers) that has very poor quality fingerprints. Furthermore, fingerprint sensors have difficulties in acquiring good quality images from fingers that are oily, dry, or devoid of well defined ridge structures. This results in non-zero failure to acquire (FTA) and failure to enroll (FTE) errors. Figure 7.1 shows an example of fingerprint images where a fingerprint sensor does not acquire good quality image from a dry finger.

Figure 7.1. Three impressions of a subject's finger are shown in which a fingerprint sensor is unable to obtain good quality fingerprints from a dry finger.

Combining fingerprint with other biometric traits is likely to produce a system that is usable by a larger population and thus will be perceived as more user friendly. Figure 7.2 shows some examples of different biometric traits that can be considered for fusion. Combining fingerprints with other biometric traits also has the advantage of the system being more robust to impostor attacks. For example, a system that combines fingerprint and voice not only leads to higher recognition accuracy, but it is also more difficult to circumvent. In such a multimodal biometric system, the fingerprint subsystem provides high accuracy whereas the challenge-response-based (i.e., question answer) property of voice verification subsystem (Campbell, 1997) ensures higher protection from attacks. In addition, a multimodal system can request a user to present a subset of biometric traits in a random order to ensure that a "live" person is indeed present at the point of data acquisition. For example, a 10 finger-based biometric system may ask users to select a specific sequence of fingers at the time of enrollment. Suppose a user chooses to present three of his fingers in the following order: left index, right middle, right index. At the time of verification, this user will be required to present his fingerprints in the same order. To fool this system, a hacker will not only need the three fingerprints of the enrolled user, but also knowledge of the correct sequence of finger placement on the fingerprint scanner. An arbitrarily long sequence of the 10 fingerprints of a person can be used to make the system increasingly difficult to circumvent and extremely accurate, although at the expense of user convenience. In other schemes, a fingerprint recognition system may enroll all the fingers of a user and prompt the user during the verification to present all or a subset of her fingerprints in an order that is randomly generated for each verification attempt. This is also known as the challenge-response process.

A system based on a combination of fingerprints with other biometric traits may also be viewed as fault-tolerant as it may continue to operate even when certain biometric sources become unreliable due to scanner or software malfunction, or deliberate user manipulation. The notion of fault tolerance is especially useful in systems handling a large number of users (e.g., border control system).

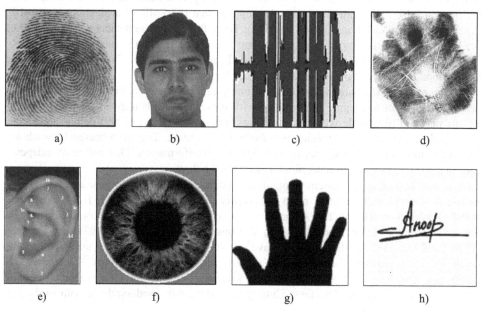

Figure 7.2. Examples of different biometric traits that can be fused together. a) fingerprint, b) face, c) voice, d) palmprint, e) ear, f) iris, g) hand geometry, and h) signature.

7.2 Performance Improvement from Fusion

Individual biometric identifiers, including fingerprints, have limited discriminatory information. Golfarelli, Maio, and Maltoni (1997) have shown that the *information content* (number of distinguishable patterns) in commonly used representations of hand geometry and face are only of the order of 10^5 and 10^3, respectively. Based on this analysis, hand geometry and face recognition systems are not expected to discriminate a large number of users in an identification scenario (one-to-many matching). In addition, although fingerprint and iris inherently possess a significantly higher information content (see Chapter 8), automatic recognition systems are not able to use all of the available discriminatory information due to limitations such as poor image quality and errors in feature extraction and matching stages.

The limitation of information content and effects of noisy signal is more apparent if the automated system has to operate in the identification mode. As discussed in Section 1.5.7, the false positive identification-error rate (FPIR_N) increases linearly with the number of users, N, in the database since $\text{FPIR}_N \cong N \cdot \text{FMR}$ (under simplifying assumptions), where FMR is the verification false match rate. For example, suppose that the FMR of a given system is 10^{-5} (i.e., just one false match in 100,000 matches). Then, for a template database of size 10^4 (i.e., $N = 10,000$), the probability of falsely matching a template with an impostor input is $\text{FPIR}_N = 10\%$. This suggests that an impostor has a good chance of "breaking" the security provided by the biometric system by using all 10 fingers of her two hands.

Fusion can also alleviate the problems of noisy data more effectively. For example, when one acquired biometric signal is corrupted with noise, the availability of other (less noisy) signals may aid in reliable recognition. Hong, Jain, and Pankanti (1999) demonstrated that fusion indeed can improve accuracy in a multimodal system. The main reason for such improvement in recognition accuracy is *independence* of information. This notion of independence in the context of pattern recognition is explained below.

It is well known in the pattern recognition literature that different classifiers[1] with essentially the same overall accuracy often misclassify different patterns (Ho, Hull, and Srihari (1994); Kittler et al. (1998)). This suggests that these classifiers offer rather complementary information about a given classification task. Toussaint (1971), Cover (1974, 1977), Fang (1979), and Oh, Lee, and Suen (1999) have shown that a classifier using statistically independent features performs better than a classifier using correlated features. Kuncheva et al. (2000) and Kuncheva and Whitaker (2003) further showed that the same reasoning is valid when combining different classifiers. Kuncheva et al. (2000) used synthetic data to demon-

---

[1] Fingerprint verification and identification tasks are essentially *pattern classification* problems. In fingerprint verification, the matcher classifies the input fingerprint feature vector into one of two classes ("genuine" and "impostor"). In fingerprint identification, the matcher classifies the input fingerprint feature vector into one of $N + 1$ classes ("user 1", "user 2",…"user N", and the (N+1)th class of "impostor").

strate that the best improvement through classifier combination is achieved when the component classifiers are negatively correlated (i.e., when one classifier is wrong, but the other is
correct, and vice versa) and the amount of improvement is directly proportional to the degree
of the negative correlation.

Consider a two-class classification problem and a multi-classifier system consisting of NC
component classifiers (assume NC is odd); the majority vote rule classifies an input pattern as
belonging to the class that obtains at least $K = (NC + 1)/2$ votes (this and other combination
methods will be explained in detail later in the chapter). If p is the probability that a single
classifier performs correctly, then the probability that the multi-classifier system correctly
classifies the input is given by the binomial equation

$$P_{correct}(NC) = \sum_{m=K}^{NC} \binom{NC}{m} p^m (1 - p)^{NC-m}. \tag{1}$$

If $p = 0.80$ (i.e., each individual classifier has a 20% error), then we obtain the following performance of the multi-classifier system for several different values of NC.

$NC = 3$ $(K = 2) \rightarrow P_{correct} = 0.896,$
$NC = 5$ $(K = 3) \rightarrow P_{correct} = 0.942,$
$NC = 7$ $(K = 4) \rightarrow P_{correct} = 0.966,$
$NC = 9$ $(K = 5) \rightarrow P_{correct} = 0.980,$
$NC = 15$ $(K = 8) \rightarrow P_{correct} = 0.995,$
$NC = 21$ $(K = 11) \rightarrow P_{correct} = 0.999.$

The above formulation assumes that the classifiers themselves are statistically independent,
which is not easy to justify in practice. Nevertheless, this analysis shows that a combination of
multiple classifiers should be explored. In practice, accuracy can be improved even if the classifiers are highly correlated. Prabhakar and Jain (2002) demonstrated the improvement in
matching accuracy from a combination of four highly correlated fingerprint matchers.

According to Jain, Duin, and Mao (2000), there are several reasons why different classifiers
may convey complementary information for a given classification task:

- Different classifiers may be developed in different contexts for the same classification problem; for example, fingerprint and face information can be combined to establish the identity of a person.
- When a classifier is trained on a small, often proprietary, training set collected at a
certain time and in a certain environment, it may not generalize well on another data
set collected at a different time and in a different environment.
- Different classifiers trained on the same data differ in their performance in local regions as well as globally in the feature space.
- Many classifiers provide different results with different (parameter) initializations. As
an example, multilayer neural networks result in different output decisions when
trained with different initializations.

- Multiple representations of the same biometric characteristic would lead to different matchers. For example, fingerprint matchers can be designed based on minutiae representation or texture features.

In summary, different feature sets, different training sets, different classification methods, or different training sessions result in classifiers that misclassify different test patterns. With a suitable combination of the outputs from all these classifiers, the overall recognition accuracy can be improved.

It may appear to be counterintuitive, but an improper combination of classifiers (or biometric matchers) may even degrade the classification accuracy or increase the matching error. Combining classifiers that are highly (positively) correlated may actually result in performance degradation, because the additional discriminatory information available may not compensate for the estimation errors. This is related to the phenomenon of the "curse of dimensionality" (Jain and Chandrasekaran, 1982). To ensure that biometric fusion indeed results in performance improvement, Prabhakar and Jain (2002) stressed that an automatic classifier selection (similar to feature selection methods proposed by Toussaint (1971) and Oh, Lee, and Suen (1999)) be first performed to eliminate highly correlated matchers. Typically, a fusion scheme is designed based on certain assumptions (e.g., many schemes assume that the component classifiers are independent and identically distributed or the impostor and genuine distributions are "known"). A violation of these assumptions may result in the fusion scheme actually degrading the system performance. Furthermore, a fusion scheme may be sound from a theoretical point of view, but the training data may either be not representative or not sufficient (Jain and Chandrasekaran (1982); Raudys and Jain (1991)). If the fusion method is trained on a small sample size, it is not expected to generalize well.

7.3 Application-specific Considerations

Given the surmounting evidence from the literature in pattern recognition and information fusion, one could expect to significantly improve the recognition accuracy by carefully fusing information in biometric systems. Before discussing the fusion methods, there are a few architectural considerations that need to be understood in the context of the biometric applications.

Let us take the "voter registration" application of biometric systems. In this application, the goal is to find (and prevent) duplicate voters in a national election. The voting population of a country could be extremely large, say, of the order of tens or even hundreds of millions. The system accuracy requirements for such a large scale and critical identification application would be so stringent that it may be necessary to combine as many independent biometric traits as feasible. However, it may be infeasible to acquire many biometric traits because the acquisition process would then be too slow and too expensive. While a prudent choice may be to combine all 10 fingers of a person, two irises, and face, such a multimodal system would not be too acceptable, both in terms of cost and throughput. So, the policymakers may choose to acquire only the 10 fingers or a subset of the fingers; fingerprint systems are not only accurate, but multiple fingers can be efficiently acquired using multi-finger fingerprint scanners. In general, the following design considerations should be made within the context of the application.

- User interface of an application may determine acquisition throughput and the cost. To lower the cost, acquisition of multiple traits may need to be done in a single interaction with the user. Face and iris information may be simultaneously collected as can be face, voice, and lip movement by utilizing a video camera (Frischholz and Dieckmann, 2000). Fingerprint, palmprint and hand geometry can also be acquired simultaneously (see Figure 7.3 and Rowe et al. (2007b)). Alternatively, certain biometric traits may need to be collected sequentially, for example, fingerprint and iris. This may lower the acquisition throughput but increase the recognition accuracy as both iris and fingerprints systems are highly accurate and independent.

- If limited processing power is available, the individual biometric systems can be combined in a *serial* (i.e., *cascade*) mode. The cascade scheme can improve user convenience as well since a user may not be required to provide all the biometric traits if the decision can be made using only a subset of them. Further, if the system is faced with the task of identifying the user from a large database, it can utilize the outcome of matching each trait to successively prune the database, thereby making the search faster and more efficient. For example, face matching can be used first to reduce the database size for the subsequent fingerprint search. If there are no constraints on the processing requirements, the biometric information can be processed in a *parallel* mode. In this mode, each biometric subsystem processes its information independently at the same time and the processed information is combined using an appropriate fusion scheme.

The application requirements may impose what *sources of information* are available. Further, it may also impose the *level of detail* of the available information. Are the biometric samples (raw signal or image) available? Is the output of feature extractor available? Are matching scores available or is only a decision (yes/no or rank) available from the component recognition systems? In principle, a fusion at a more detailed level of information (e.g., samples) is more beneficial than a fusion at a higher level of detail (e.g., decisions) as information content is lost in the processing of the biometric sample. However, most multibiometric systems conduct fusion at a higher level of information (e.g., matching score or decision). This is because of two reasons. Firstly, signal level and feature level information may not be compatible and thus harder to combine. Secondly, designers of fusion system are often not the same as those who design and develop the individual component biometric systems. For example, a system integrator may purchase commercial off-the-shelf biometric systems for individual modalities and then combine them per the requirements of the application. Off-the-shelf systems are proprietary in nature and do not provide access to biometric sample and the feature vectors used in them.

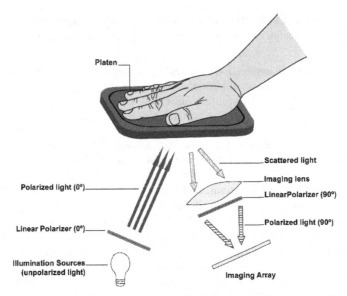

Figure 7.3. Layout of a prototype multispectral whole-hand imaging system that can capture multiple fingerprints, palmprint, and hand geometry in a single acquisition. © IEEE.

7.4 Sources of Information

Biometric fusion involving fingerprints can be performed in one of the following scenarios (see Figure 7.4) depending upon the information sources used.

1. *Multiple traits*: fingerprints can be combined with some other trait such as iris or face.
2. *Multiple fingers of the same person*: fingerprints from two or more fingers of a person may be combined.
3. *Multiple samples of the same finger acquired using different sensors*: information obtained from different sensing technologies for the same finger is combined.
4. *Multiple samples of the same finger*: multiple impressions of the same finger are combined.
5. *Multiple representations and matching algorithms*: this involves combining different approaches to feature extraction and/or matching of fingerprints.

Scenarios 1 and 2 combine highly independent information sources and are expected to result in better improvement in accuracy than scenarios 3, 4, and 5. Finally, a combination of more than one of these scenarios may also be used. The choice of the specific scenario depends on the requirements of the particular application and the related cost-benefit analysis.

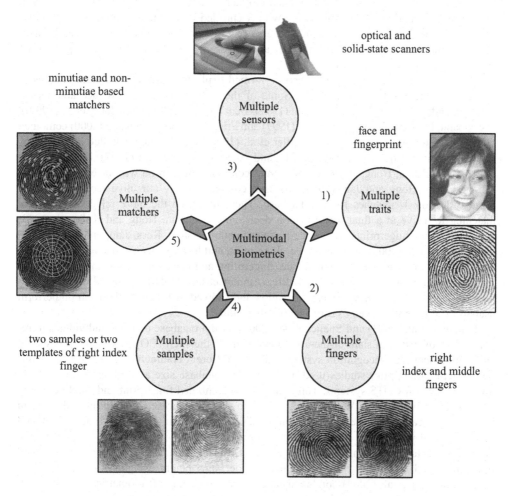

Figure 7.4. Various scenarios of fusion in a fingerprint system.

7.4.1 Fusion of multiple traits

When fusing fingerprints with other biometric traits, use of multiple biometric sensors is necessary. Some new sensors under development, such as the whole hand sensor (Rowe et al., 2007b), provide all five fingerprints, palmprint and hand geometry in a single presentation of a hand. In a verification system, the additional biometrics may be used to improve the verification accuracy. In an identification system with N enrolled users, the matching speed can also be improved with a proper combination scheme (e.g., one of the traits, say face, can be used first to retrieve the top M [$M<<N$] matches and fingerprint can be used for making the final accurate identification decision).

A large number of studies have been performed exploring fusion of different sources of biometric information (see Table 7.1). Some of the early work combined face and speech (Brunelli and Falavigna (1995); Duc et al. (1997); Ben-Yacoub (1999); Choudhury et al. (1999)). Dieckmann, Plankensteiner, and Wagner (1997) and Frischholz and Dieckmann (2000) combined face, voice, and lip movement while Kittler et al. (1998) and Verlinde, Chollet, and Acheroy (2000) combined frontal face, face profile, and voice. Hong and Jain (1997), Hong and Jain (1998a, b) and Jain, Hong, and Kulkarni (1998) combined fingerprint with face in an identification system. Hong and Jain (1998a, b) used computationally attractive face matching to retrieve the top M matches from a database. Then they used the more reliable fingerprint matching to arrive at a final identification decision. Later, Jain, Hong and Kulkarni (1999) combined faces, fingerprints, and voice in a verification system. Ross, Jain, and Qian (2001) and Ross and Jain (2003) combined face, fingerprint, and hand geometry in a verification system. Jain and Ross (2002a) combined face, fingerprint, and hand geometry using user-specific weights and user-specific thresholds. Fierrez-Aguilar et al. (2005b) combined on-line signature and fingerprints using Bayesian adaptation and showed that their method can outperform user-specific weights as well as user-specific thresholds.

Indovina et al. (2003) and Snelick et al. (2005) used a database of 1,000 individuals to report results of fusion of state-of-the-art commercial off-the-shelf (COTS) systems. They used one commercial face recognition system and three different commercial fingerprint recognition systems. Most prior studies used much smaller database size as well as combined only low-accuracy non-COTS systems. Toh et al. (2003) combined fingerprint and hand geometry in verification mode while Wang, Wang, and Tan (2004) combined fingerprint and voice in both the verification and the identification modes. Toh and Yau (2004, 2005) also combined fingerprint and voice. Patra and Das (2008) combined face and fingerprint by first enhancing the face algorithm through prior knowledge. Jain, Dass, and Nandakumar (2004a, b) combined fingerprints and soft biometric traits such as gender, age, height, weight, ethnicity, and eye color while Jain et al. (2004) combined face, fingerprint, and soft biometrics. Ailisto et al. (2006) combined fingerprint with soft biometrics such as body weight and fat percentage. Ribaric and Fratric (2005) combined fingerprint and palmprint. Kumar and Zhang (2006) combined fingerprint, palmprint, and hand geometry in a verification system; the advantage of combining these three specific characteristics is that they all come from the human hand and thus may be acquired in a single presentation of the hand. Bouchaffra and Amira (2008) combined fingerprint and face. While Sim et al. (2007) also combined fingerprint and face, they proposed continuous verification, i.e., the fusion is not only across multiple modalities but also across time. The authors also proposed new performance metrics that take the time into account.

Authors	Modalities Fused
Brunelli and Falavigna (1995), Duc et al. (1997), Ben-Yacoub (1999), Choudhury et al. (1999), Kittler et al. (1998), Verlinde, Chollet, and Acheroy (2000)	Face and speech
Dieckmann, Plankensteiner, and Wagner (1997), Frischholz and Dieckmann (2000)	Face, voice, and lip movement
Hong and Jain (1997), Hong and Jain (1998, 1998b), Jain, Hong, and Kulkarni (1998), Indovina et al. (2003), Snelick et al. (2005), Bouchaffra and Amira (2008), Sim et al. (2007), Patra and Das (2008)	Face and fingerprint
Jain, Hong, and Kulkarni (1999)	Face, fingerprint, and speech
Ross, Jain, and Qian (2001), Ross and Jain (2003), Ross and Jain (2002)	Face, fingerprint, and hand geometry
Fierrez-Aguilar et al. (2005b)	Online-signature and fingerprints
Toh et al. (2003)	Fingerprint and hand geometry
Wang, Wang, and Tan (2004), Toh and Yau (2004, 2005)	Fingerprint and voice
Jain, Dass, and Nandakumar (2004, 2004b), Ailisto et al. (2006)	Fingerprint and soft biometrics (e.g., gender, age, height, weight, ethnicity, and eye color)
Jain et al. (2004)	Face, fingerprint, and soft biometrics
Ribaric and Fratric (2005)	Fingerprint and palmprint
Kumar and Zhang (2006)	Fingerprint, palmprint, and hand geometry

Table 7.1. Some of the studies on the fusion of multiple biometric traits.

Fusion of systems based on different biometric traits continues to be very popular. A number of systems deployed in the field have adopted multibiometric systems. However, due to the additional inconvenience and cost, the adoption of these systems remains restricted to government applications such as border control. Since systems for different biometric traits use different representations, the fusion is typically performed at the rank or the score level (see Sections 7.7 and 7.8). Table 7.2 shows some examples of different fusion levels and methods used in various studies; we cover them in detail later in this chapter.

Modalities Fused	Authors	Level of Fusion	Fusion Method
Face and voice	Brunelli and Falavigna (1995)	Score, rank	Geometric weighted average, HyperBF
	Kitler et al. (1998)	Score	Sum, product, min, max and median rules
	Ben-Yacoub et al. (1999)	Score	SVM, multilayer perceptron, C4.5 decision tree, Fisher's linear discriminant, Bayesian classifier
	Bigun et al. (1997)	Score	Statistical model based on Bayesian theory
Face, voice and lip movement	Frischholz and Deckmann (2000)	Score, decision	Weighted sum rule, majority voting
Face and fingerprint	Hong and Jain (1998)	Score	Product rule
	Snelick et al. (2005)	Score	Sum rule, weighted sum rule
Face, fingerprint and hand geometry	Ross and Jain (2003)	Score	Sum rule, decision tree, linear discriminant function
Face, fingerprint and voice	Jain et al. (1999)	Score	Likelihood ratio
Fingerprint and hand geometry	Toh et al. (2003)	Score	Reduced multivariate polynomial model
Fingerprint and voice	Toh and Yau (2005)	Score	Functional link network
Fingerprint and signature	Fierrez-Aguilar et al. (2005)	Score	SVM in which quality measures are incorporated
Fingerprint and face	Patra and Das (2008)	Score	Sum, product, max, min, decision template, Dempster-Shafer theory

Table 7.2. Fusion techniques involving multiple biometric traits.

7.4.2 Multi-finger fusion

These systems do not require different types of sensors as fusion involves only fingerprint images and are thus generally cheaper than the multiple sensor systems. The acquisition throughput may be poor in case the fingers are captured sequentially, but can be sped-up by using a multi-finger fingerprint scanner that can capture all four fingers of a hand (except the thumb) in a single acquisition (see Chapter 2). There are also touchless fingerprint scanners under development that are expected to capture all five or even all 10 fingers of both the hands in a single acquisition.

Multi-finger systems are very popular in large scale identification applications such as law enforcement, border control, background checks, etc. as they strike the right balance between information content, accuracy, cost, and acquisition throughputs. National Institute of Standards and Technology (NIST) conducted benchmarks of fingerprint recognition algorithms in 2003 and 2005. The benchmark in 2003 was known as FpVTE 2003 (Wilson et al., 2004) and the benchmark in 2005 was known as NIST Proprietary Fingerprint Template (PTE) Testing (Watson et al., 2005b). In both the cases, an increase in the number of fingers resulted in an increase in accuracy. The accuracy of searches using four or more fingers was better than the accuracy of two-finger searches, which was better than the accuracy of single-finger searches. With each doubling of the number of fingers, the FNMR decreased by about a factor of 5. In NIST's MINEX benchmark, Grother et al. (2006) illustrate that the standard minutiae templates increase the FNMR about two times compared to using proprietary minutiae templates. However, a combination of two fingers can adequately compensate for the increase in FNMR due to standard templates. Ulery et al. (2006) performed an experimental evaluation of various types of fusion and reported that combining two fingers reduced the FNMR by 48–90% at the same FMR. Prabhakar and Jain (2002) and Ushmaev and Novikov (2004) also document significant improvement in FNMR from combination of multiple fingers. Lee et al. (2004) and Lee et al. (2005a) collected two fingerprint images (one from each of the two fingers) of the user but then use a quality checker algorithm to select the better quality fingerprint image and use it for recognition. The authors report a good improvement in recognition accuracy.

Wayman (2004) studied the correlation between the images of multiple fingers of a user and empirically evaluated the penetration rates and binning rates for two, four, and eight fingers. While the fusion of multiple fingers is possible at the feature level (e.g., minutiae), rank or score level fusion is used most often (see Sections 7.7 and 7.8).

7.4.3 Fusion of multiple samples of a finger: different sensors

In fusing multiple samples of the same finger that are acquired using different sensing technologies, it is the same physical finger that is acquired multiple times, each time on a different sensor. For example, optical, solid-state, and ultrasound scanners are available to capture fingerprints. Optical scanners may work better with certain finger conditions (e.g., wet) while solid-state scanners may capture better quality image with different type of finger conditions (e.g., dry). Marcialis and Roli (2004a, b) discuss the benefits of fusing fingerprint information from an optical (FTIR) and a solid-state (capacitive) scanner. The authors conclude that the two sensing technologies provide complementary information thereby resulting in better matching accuracy. They also suggest the possibility of employing a dynamic scanner selection scheme wherein, based on the nature of the image obtained from the two scanners, the information from only one of the scanner may be used to perform recognition. However, the use of two different scanners increases not only the hardware cost but also the acquisition time and thus poses more inconvenience to the user.

Fingerprint scanners can be designed such that the same sensor (or more sensors within the same scanner) captures different information from a single acquisition. One such example is the combination of multispectral and frustrated total internal reflection (FTIR) sensing technologies in an optical fingerprint scanner (Rowe, Nixon, and Butler, 2007). Similarly, FTIR and direct reading can also be combined in a single fingerprint scanner. These scanners will likely still be more expensive than a scanner based on a single sensing technology but will provide much better acquisition throughput.

7.4.4 Fusion of multiple samples of a finger: same sensor

A fingerprint scanner equipped with a small area sensor may acquire multiple fingerprint images of an individual's finger in order to obtain images of various regions of the finger. A mosaicking scheme may then be used to stitch the multiple impressions and create a composite as discussed in Section 2.9. Even if the multiple impressions captured the same region of the finger, the signal-to-noise ratio can be improved by combining the information from multiple impressions. It is more popular to use multiple samples during enrollment than during recognition. This typically achieves the right balance between information content and recognition throughput.

Combination of multiple impressions of the same finger has been proposed in several studies. For example, Prabhakar and Jain (2002) combined multiple impressions of a finger in a verification system and showed good improvement in recognition accuracy. This idea was further developed by Simon-Zorita et al. (2003a) who proposed to store three impressions of a finger during enrollment. During verification, the image is compared with all the three enrollment impressions and the maximum score is considered the fused score. The authors show that their method improved the recognition accuracy. Jain, Uludag, and Ross (2003) proposed to acquire multiple impressions of a finger during enrollment but then select the most salient subset. The fusion of matching scores is performed during verification.

Multiple impressions of a finger can be fused at the image level or at the feature level during enrollment (known as image mosaicking or template consolidation). Many approaches have been proposed in Jain and Ross (2002b), Jain, Uludag, and Ross (2003), Shogenji et al. (2004), Ryu, Kim, and Jain (2006), Yager and Amin (2006a), Sha, Zhao, and Tang (2007). The fusion can also be performed during verification to update the enrollment template (known as template adaptation) (Yin, Zhao, and Yang, 2005). We discuss these methods further in Sections 7.5 and 7.6. Instead of fusing several impressions of a finger, selection of a subset of the most suitable impressions could be performed. Uludag, Ross, and Jain (2004) propose to either select the most similar subset or the most dissimilar subset. The authors first obtain matching scores by matching the available impressions among themselves and then use clustering techniques on the matching scores to select the appropriate subset.

7.4.5 Fusion of multiple representation and matching algorithms

Here, the fusion involves different types of processing and matching on the same image. Such a fusion strategy can be used either for verification or for indexing in an identification system. For example, a texture-based representation can be combined with a minutiae-based representation to yield matching accuracy better than either of the component algorithms (Ross, Jain, and Reisman, 2003). This does not require the use of different scanners and is thus cost effective. Furthermore the user is not required to interact with multiple scanners thereby not affecting throughput and user convenience. However, use of multiple representations and matching algorithms does increase the computational requirements of the system.

Fusion of multiple representations and matching algorithms for the same fingerprint sample has been proposed by several researchers. Jain et al. (1999) fuse the evidence of two different fingerprint matchers to determine the similarity between the minutiae sets. Jain, Prabhakar, and Chen (1999) fuse three different fingerprint matchers while Nanni and Lumini (2008b) fuse fingerprint matchers selected from as many as 41 different fingerprint matchers. The three minutiae matchers combined by Jain et al. (1999) are based on the Hough transform, one-dimensional string matching, and two-dimensional dynamic programming. They observe that the matching performance of the combined algorithm is better than the individual constituent algorithms. However, they also observe that the matching accuracy obtained by combining two of the three matchers is comparable to combining all the three matchers. They recommend carefully selecting the constituent algorithms to combine. Although the improvement reported by the authors was modest, the performance improvement was more pronounced when they combined a non-minutiae-based algorithm with a minutiae-based algorithm (Jain et al., 2000). Also see Section 4.6.

Marcialis and Roli (2003, 2005) also document the improvement in verification accuracy from combining multiple fingerprint matchers. Fierrez-Aguilar et al. (2006) and Fronthaler et al. (2008) take the quality of fingerprint image into account when combining multiple matchers. Ito et al. (2006) combine a phase-based fingerprint matching system with a minutiae-based fingerprint matching system. In Yager and Amin (2006), instead of combining disparate fingerprint matching algorithms at the score-level, the authors propose to combine them at the alignment stage, i.e., multiple alignment hypotheses between the input and template are generated using different fingerprint matching algorithms, followed by a selection of the most likely alignment. The matching score is then computed using the selected alignment.

7.5 Level of Detail of Information in Fusion

In a pattern recognition system, the amount of information available to the system gets compressed as the information travels through the pattern recognition system from the sensor to the final decision stage. For example, a typical sensed fingerprint image is 120 KB. A fingerprint template or feature set is typically less than 2 KB, the matching score can typically be represented as an integer (4 bytes), while the final recognition decision is a single bit (i.e. Yes/No) in the case of a verification system. Based on the difference in the level of detail of available information, different methods of fusion are needed. The five levels of detail are:

- *Image*: a fusion at this level is typically referred to as: signal-level fusion, sample-level fusion, image-level fusion, sensor-level fusion or measurement-level fusion (see Figure 7.5a).
- *Feature*: a fusion at this level is typically referred to as feature-level fusion. Such fusion is performed after feature extraction but before matching (see Figure 7.5b).
- *Matching (similarity) score*: a fusion at this level is typically referred to as score-level or confidence-level fusion. Such fusion is performed after the matching stage (see Figure 7.5c).
- *Rank*: an identification system typically outputs a ranking or a candidate list instead of a match score. In other words, the similarity in this case is not explicitly coded into a score but rather is implicitly coded in the ranking. So, rank 1 template is more similar to the input pattern than rank 2 template, and so forth (see Figure 7.5c).
- *Decision*: a fusion at this level of information is typically referred to as decision-level or abstract label-level fusion (Dasarathy, 1994). In a verification system, the decision is of the form Yes/No. On the other hand, in an identification system the decision is typically "identified" (present in the database) or "not identified"; in some cases, an identification system can output a "candidate list" with no particular ordering/ranking of the candidates. Strictly speaking, decision-level fusion does not have access to any type of confidence on the matcher output (see Figure 7.5d).

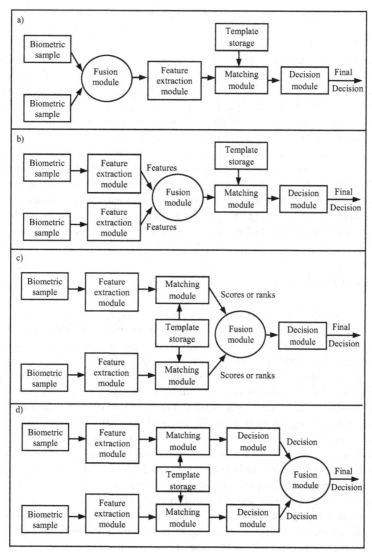

Figure 7.5. Different levels of fusion: a) fusion at the image level; b) fusion at the feature level; c) fusion at the score level or the rank level; d) fusion at the decision level. In all the four cases the final decision is "match" or "no match" when the biometric system is operating in the verification mode and the identity of the best matched user when operating in the identification mode. In d), the intermediate decisions could be "match" or "non-match" in a verification system or a "candidate list" (i.e., the retrieved subset of identities) in an identification system.

Each of these levels of fusion has its own advantages and disadvantages. Further, applicability of a certain level of fusion will depend upon the requirements of the application and the availability of the level of detail of information. For example, image-level fusion can only be implemented in the case when the multiple sources represent samples of the same finger obtained using a single sensor (or different but compatible sensors). Similarly, the feature sets need to be available (for example, a system integrator performing the fusion may not have access to the proprietary feature sets of third-party feature extraction algorithms) and the feature sets need to be compatible for feature-level fusion. Some commercial biometric algorithms do not output matching scores and the system integrator may have access only to the final decisions. In this case, even though it may be more accurate to combine matching scores, the specifics of the application and availability of the details of information prohibit the practical feasibility of fusion at this level. In practice, the score-level fusion is most commonly used as it strikes the right balance between the detail and availability of the information as well as ease and robustness of the fusion. In the following sections we will discuss fusion at all these levels of information but we will put special emphasis on score-level fusion and present it in more detail.

7.6 Image-Level Fusion

In practice it is possible to combine only "compatible images". Therefore, in the context of fingerprints, image level combination is used only to combine multiple images of the same finger. Fingerprint images first need to be registered with each other before fusion. In case fingerprint images from multiple sensors are combined, the sensors must be pre-registered (calibrated). For example, a multispectral fingerprint scanner developed by Lumidigm (Rowe, Nixon, and Butler, 2007) internally acquires multiple images by using different wavelengths, polarization conditions, and optical geometries. The objective of such a fusion is to improve the quality of acquired fingerprint images. The basis of the improvement is that the useful signal in the fingerprint images captured with different sensing technologies will be independent because different imaging conditions capture different surface and subsurface properties of the skin. Rowe, Nixon, and Butler (2007) combine the multiple sensed images into a single composite fingerprint image. They first decompose each component image into its wavelet coefficients using a dual-tree complex wavelet transform. Then, for each pixel, the coefficient that has the maximum absolute magnitude is selected. The inverse wavelet transform is performed using only the selected coefficients. This results in a single composite image. Such a fused image has higher quality, especially in the case of poor quality skin condition.

Another reason to conduct an image-level fusion of fingerprint images is to increase the acquired fingerprint area wherein each individual image has captured only a portion of the finger. For example, a small area fingerprint sensor may have been used to capture several impressions of a person's fingerprint which can then be fused to create a composite image that represents a larger area of the finger than any of the individual images. This process is known as *mosaicking* and it is particularly useful in small-area silicon sensors (Xia and O'Gorman, 2003).

Jain and Ross (2002b) proposed a mosaicking scheme that first performs a minutiae extraction on the component images. Then it uses a minutiae matching algorithm to approximately register two images using a simple affine transformation followed by a refinement of the alignment. The pixel intensities in the two images are smoothed using a low-pass filter and normalized such that the pixel intensities and contrast between the two images are compatible. The mosaic is then created by concatenating the two registered images. The authors showed that the recognition accuracy using the mosaicked images was much better than that of the individual component images. Figure 7.6 shows the intermediate results of the abovementioned mosaicking algorithm.

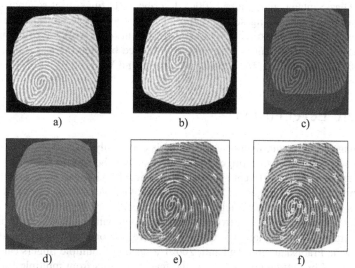

Figure 7.6. Fingerprint mosaicking. a) first impression, b) second impression, c) coarse alignment, d) fine alignment, e) minutiae extracted from mosaicked fingerprint, and f) minutiae extracted from individual fingerprint overlaid over mosaicked fingerprint.

Mosaicking is also extensively used in sweep-based fingerprint scanners. Sweep fingerprint scanners capture only small horizontal slices of a finger as it slides over the sensor. The mosaicking algorithm in this case is commonly known as fingerprint image reconstruction (see Chapter 2). Successive image slices are registered by determining the translation offset between them. The fingerprint scanner interface is designed in such a way as to avoid rotational offsets between slices thus reducing the complexity associated with the fingerprint image registration procedure. More complex fingerprint image reconstruction algorithms account for rotation and skew as well.

In forensic and government applications, rolled fingerprints have been historically acquired. A rolled fingerprint image from a live-scan fingerprint scanner is generated from the multiple frames in a video acquired when a finger is rolled on the surface of the fingerprint scanner. Ratha, Connell, and Bolle (1998) describe such a mosaicking scheme to fuse multiple snapshots of a fingerprint. Since the multiple fingerprint images to be combined are from a video, they imposed a specified temporal order on the image frames when constructing the composite rolled image. The authors investigated five different blending algorithms to construct the composite image from the individual images. They evaluated these five schemes by observing the size of the mosaicked print as well as its quality (in terms of the number of valid minutiae points detected).

Parziale, Diaz-Santana, and Hauke (2006) describe a 3D fingerprint scanner that captures multiple views of a finger using several calibrated cameras. These multiple views are combined together to yield a single nail-to-nail fingerprint, in other words, a rolled image. Other approaches to fingerprint mosaicking have been discussed by Moon et al. (2004), Choi, Choi, and Kim (2005), Choi et al. (2007a), and Zhang, Yang, and Wu (2005).

7.7 Feature-Level Fusion

Similar to image-level fusion, feature-level fusion is commonly used only for combining multiple feature sets from the same finger irrespective of whether the multiple impressions are acquired using the same or different sensors. Feature-level fusion can conceptually be used to combine prints of different fingers or fingerprint with other biometrics. The difficulty in coming up with a method to perform such a fusion is immediately apparent when one considers the fingerprint minutiae, which is a two-dimensional point pattern. However, if one considers rotation and translation invariant fixed-length feature vector based representation such as FingerCode (Jain, Prabhakar, and Pankanti, 2000), a fusion of multiple fingers can be achieved at the feature level by simply concatenating the feature vectors from multiple fingers. In fact, such concatenation of feature vectors (after normalization but before feature selection) has been proposed by Ross and Govindarajan (2005) for hand and face biometrics. Rattani et al. (2007) combine face and fingerprint at the feature level by concatenating point-based features from both face and fingerprint. The authors use scale invariant features transform (SIFT)-based point features for face and minutiae-based point features for fingerprints. Feature selection is performed using k-means clustering to reduce the number of features (points). The point-pattern-based matching uses the concatenated feature set and finds the correspondence among points without having to establish any global alignment.

Feature-level fusion is used to combine multiple impressions of a finger with many of the same goals as image-level fusion of multiple impressions of a finger: (i) it is expected that noise will not be highly repeatable in the multiple acquisitions of a finger and thus it can be cancelled in the combination, and (ii) the fingerprint area represented in the image can be increased. However, feature-level fusion may be preferred because features are more compact than image, leading to efficient fusion algorithms. Further, many commercial fingerprint recognition systems do not store fingerprint images during fingerprint enrollment, either due to privacy reasons or to reduce the amount of stored data. Finally, the images have to be typically registered very precisely to be combined while the feature sets may be combined less precisely.

The most commonly used feature-level fusion in fingerprint recognition is performed for the fingerprint enrollment template. Many commercial fingerprint recognition systems acquire multiple impressions of the same finger (between 3 and 5) during enrollment. These impressions are then combined at the feature level to produce a single enrollment template. This is known as *template consolidation*. Certain systems continue to perform the feature-level fusion within a template when additional impressions of the same finger become available at a later time during recognition (fusion is performed only when the fingerprint recognition confirms that the new impression is from the same finger). This is known as template learning or *template adaptation*.

Many techniques have been proposed for template consolidation and template adaptation. Yau et al. (2000) proposed taking a union of minutiae points from multiple feature sets after aligning the various feature sets with each other. The authors assume a fingerprint feature extraction algorithm that does not find many false minutiae but often misses genuine minutiae. So by taking a union of the minutiae from multiple impressions, the missing minutiae are recovered (since they will hopefully be found in at least one of the impressions) as well as the finger area represented by the consolidated template is increased. Ramoser, Wachmann, and Bischof (2002) also proposed to simply compute a union of the minutiae points after a random sample consensus (RANSAC)-based alignment has been established. Jiang and Ser (2002) extended Yau et al.'s (2000) approach by taking minutiae reliability into account and proposed that the templates be adapted over time. They updated the minutia reliability measure as matching minutiae are encountered in the newly available recognition feature set at verification; the parameters of the minutiae points (i.e., the minutiae locations and orientations and type) are updated by a weighted average measure. Template consolidation/adaptation is applicable only when the new fingerprint feature set is accurately aligned with the stored one. Jiang and Ser (2002) showed that their scheme resulted in (i) elimination of spurious minutiae points, (ii) addition of missed minutiae points, (iii) relabeling of incorrect minutiae types, and (iv) an overall improvement in matching accuracy.

Toh et al. (2001) specifically targeted small area solid-state fingerprint scanners and proposed a template consolidation approach with low storage requirement and computational complexity. The authors experimented with several different alignment models and empirically determined that the affine alignment was the best. Yin, Zhao, and Yang (2005) proposed a template adaptation algorithm which includes deleting pseudo minutiae, restoring lost genuine minutiae, and updating the position and directions of minutiae. In Ryu, Han, and Kim (2005), the credibility/reliability of each minutia is updated by applying a successive Bayesian estimation to a sequence of minutiae feature sets obtained from multiple impressions of a finger. Ryu, Kim, and Jain (2006) use not only minutia but also local fingerprint quality information to estimate the credibility of minutiae from successive Bayesian estimation. Moon et al. (2004) studied and compared image mosaicking and template consolidation using iterative closest point (ICP)-based alignment. They conclude that template consolidation is more suitable for larger fingerprint images while image mosaicking is more suitable for small fingerprint images (e.g., from small area scanners). Ross, Shah, and Shah (2006) compare image-level mosaicking and feature-level template consolidation and show that while both methods improve the accuracy, feature-level template consolidation outperforms image-level mosaicking. Yang and Zhou (2006) performed a comparative study of combining multiple enrolled samples for fingerprint verification. The authors study both the fusion of feature sets and a combination of scores. While both the techniques improve the accuracy, the authors find that a larger improvement can be obtained by fusing scores than by fusing feature sets. This is somewhat surprising but plausible given the sensitivity of feature set fusion to alignment computation. If alignment cannot be robustly and accurately estimated, the fusion of feature set can be misleading. The authors demonstrate that by fusing both the feature sets as well as the scores, the accuracy is even better. Sha, Zhao, and Tang (2007) also use both the feature-level fusion as well as the score-level fusion to combine multiple impressions of a finger. Their matching algorithm compares the query feature set with each template impression and then performs a feature-level fusion based on subset combination. The individual comparison scores are then fused to yield the final score for decision making. Uz et al. (2007) fuse multiple impressions of a finger based on hierarchical Delaunay triangulations. In addition to increasing the image area, restoration of missing minutiae, and deletion of spurious minutiae, the minutiae in the composite enrollment template are assigned a weight based on their frequency of occurrence. These weights serve as minutiae quality measure and are useful in matching.

7.8 Rank-Level Fusion

Rank-level fusion is used only in identification systems and is applicable when the matcher output is a ranking of the "candidates" in the template database. The system is expected to assign a higher rank to a template that is more similar to the query. Most identification systems actually provide the matching score associated with the candidates. So, while the rank level fusion is widely used in other fields such as pattern recognition and data mining, we will not dwell deeply on the subject within the biometric identification context and cover only the basic methodologies presented in Ho, Hull, and Srihari (1994).

Let us assume that there are N identities enrolled in the template database and there are R biometric matchers. Let $r_{j,k}$ be the rank assigned to the user k by the jth matcher. Let s_k be a statistic computed from identity k such that the lowest value of s is the best, just like the lowest rank value assigned by a matcher is the best (most similar to the pattern being searched).

One method to define s is to assign, for each identity k, the minimum of the ranks generated by the R matchers. That is,

$$s_k = \min_{j=1}^{R} r_{j,k}. \tag{2}$$

This is called the *highest rank* method. This method has the problem that it produces lots of ties, especially if the number of identities is small. The ties have to be broken by a random process since no other information is available. On the other hand, this method works well when strong matcher(s) are combined with weak matcher(s) as the strong matcher's ranking will win.

Another method, known as *Borda count*, uses the sum of the ranks assigned by the individual matchers. This method is popular in determining a winner in a political voting system, where the voters are asked to provide only a ranking of their selection of each candidate. The statistic s for the identity k is computed as:

$$s_k = \sum_{j=1}^{R} r_{j,k}. \tag{3}$$

The Borda count, represented by s_k, is a measure of agreement among the outcomes of multiple matchers for the kth user. The Borda count method assumes that the ranks assigned to the identity by the matchers are statistically independent and all the matchers perform equally well. While this is a valid assumption in a political voting system, it is often violated in biometric identification. An extension and generalization to the Borda count method would be to compute a weighted sum instead of a straight sum. The weighted Borda count leads to:

$$s_k = \sum_{j=1}^{R} w_j r_{j,k}. \tag{4}$$

Ho et al. (1994) determined the weights using logistic regression and hence called this method as logistic regression method of rank-level fusion. Melnik, Vardi, and Zhang (2004) presented a so called *mixed group ranks* method which unifies the framework of rank-level fusion; the methods discussed above are extreme cases of this framework. Lee et al. (2005c) explored a naïve Bayes approach referred to as *Bayes fuse* to combine ranks. Nandakumar (2008) proposed a related Bayesian approach to rank-level fusion by estimating rank distribution from the marginal genuine and imposter distributions and assuming independence among the individual matchers. An iterative approach to rank-level fusion is presented by Bhatanagar, Kumar, and Sagar (2007).

7.9 Score-Level Fusion

Score-level fusion is widely recognized to offer the best tradeoff between the effectiveness of fusion and the ease of fusion. While the information contained in matching scores is not as rich as in images or features, it is much richer than ranks and decisions. Further, while score-level fusion is not as easy or intuitive as rank-level or decision-level fusion, it is easier to study and implement than image-level and feature-level fusion. It can also be used in all types of biometric fusion scenarios, i.e., combining fingerprints with other biometric traits, combining multiple fingers, combining multiple impressions of the same finger (whether acquired using the same sensor or different sensors), and combining multiple feature extraction and matching algorithms. Finally, most, if not all, of the commercial systems output either raw scores or quantized scores or probability of a false match (which is typically the raw score transformed into false match rates using the imposter distribution). As a result, scores are typically more accessible and available than images or features. These reasons have made score-level fusion very popular in biometric fusion.

Fusion at the score level requires some care. The main difficulties emanate from non-homogeneity of scores from different matchers (e.g., one score could be in the range of 1 to 100, while the other score could be in the range of 1,000 to 6,000), differences in the distributions of scores, correlation among the scores, and differences in the accuracies of different matchers. Let us first consider the methods to solve the non-homogeneity of scores.

7.9.1 Score normalization methods

In some score-level fusion scenarios, the scores output by different matchers are homogenous and do not need to be normalized. For example, if two (or more) fingers of the same person or two (or more) impressions of the same finger are being combined, it is very likely that the scores do not need to be normalized. In case different fingers of the same person are not equally distinctive or reliable (e.g., due to their different quality), it may be desirable to weight the scores appropriately, but in general, score normalization would not be needed. However, when different matching algorithms are used, even on the same finger, the scores are not homogeneous. This is especially true when fingerprint match scores are combined with other biometric matchers such as iris.

The simplest method of normalizing the scores is to remap them to a common range. This method is sometimes referred to as *min–max normalization* method. The range of a score may be already known or learned from training data. Given a set of matching scores $\{s_k\}$, $k = 1, 2, \ldots n$, the normalized scores are given by:

$$s'_k = \frac{s_k - min}{max - min},$$

(5)

where the minimum (*min*) and maximum (*max*) values are estimated from training data. Min-max normalization retains the original distribution of scores except for a scaling factor and transforms all the scores into a common range of [0, 1]. In case one score is on a linear scale while the other one is on an exponential scale, *decimal scaling* can be applied:

$$s_k' = \frac{s_k}{10^n}, \tag{6}$$

where $n = log_{10}(max)$. This is based on the assumption that the relation between the different scores is strictly logarithmic, which may not be a valid assumption. Both of the above normalizations are sensitive to outliers. One way to overcome the problem with outliers is to scale the scores such that they have the unit variance; this is based on the assumption that scores follow a Gaussian distribution

$$s_k' = \frac{s_k - \mu}{\sigma^2}, \tag{7}$$

where μ is the mean of the scores and σ^2 is their variance. This normalizes the scores to zero mean and unit variance and is commonly known as *z-normalization*. In case, the Gaussian distribution assumption is not valid, this method does not preserve the original distribution of scores and is not very robust. Surely, mean and variance are less sensitive to outliers than minimum and maximum. By replacing mean with median and by replacing variance with the median absolute deviation (*MAD*), the z-normalization method can be made even more robust to outliers:

$$s_k' = \frac{s_k - \text{median}}{MAD}. \tag{8}$$

Although more robust to outliers, this method still assumes that the score distributions are Gaussian.

So far we have discussed only linear normalization schemes. These methods are fairly simple and require very simple training. However, they rely on certain assumptions and when the assumptions are violated, the normalization may not be very robust. There is another class of normalization methods that are essentially based on applying a non-linear mapping to the scores. The common non-linear functions are *sigmoid* (a type of logistic function), and *hyperbolic tangent*. Many other non-linear functions or combinations of multiple functions can be used. These methods require some parameters to be tuned and therefore require more training. With large amount of training data and careful training, these methods can overcome the limitations of linear methods and lead to better performance.

Cappelli, Maio, and Maltoni (2000a) used a *double-sigmoid* function. The normalized scores are given by:

$$s_k' = \begin{cases} \dfrac{1}{1 + \exp\left(-2(t - s_k)/r_1\right)} & \text{if } s_k < t \\[3mm] \dfrac{1}{1 + \exp\left(-2(s_k - t)/r_2\right)} & \text{otherwise} \end{cases}, \tag{9}$$

where t is the reference operating point (a score $s_k = t$ is mapped to 0.5) and r_1 and r_2 denote the left and right edges of the region in which the function is near-linear. As a result, this function exhibits near-linear characteristics in the interval $(t - r_1, t + r_2)$, and robustly remaps the outliers falling out of this range (see Figure 7.7). An effective way for choosing appropriate values for t, r_1, r_2, is to select anchor points over the curve denoting the genuine score distribution: for example t can be placed close to the peak of the distribution, r_1 can be chosen such that just 5% of the scores are lower than $t - r_1$ and r_2 can be chosen such that only 5% of the scores are higher than $t + r_2$. The authors show that the method provides very good accuracy. However, as mentioned earlier, it requires careful tuning of the parameters.

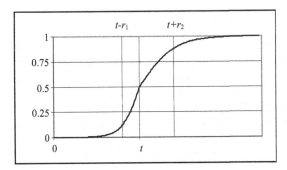

Figure 7.7. Double-sigmoid function used in Cappelli, Maio, and Maltoni (2000a).

Hampel et al. (1986) introduced the *tanh-estimator* for score normalization. This method turns out to be fairly robust and efficient. However, similar to the sigmoid method, it has many parameters that need to be carefully tuned. The tanh normalization is given by:

$$s'_k = \frac{1}{2} \left\{ tanh\left(0.01\left(\frac{s_k - \mu_{GH}}{\sigma_{GH}} \right)\right) + 1 \right\}, \tag{10}$$

where μ_{GH} and σ_{GH} are the mean and standard deviation estimates, respectively, of the genuine score distribution as given by Hampel estimators. Hampel estimators are based on the following influence function:

$$\psi(u) = \begin{cases} u & 0 \leq |u| < a, \\ a\, sign(u) & a \leq |u| < b, \\ a\, sign(u)\left(\dfrac{c - |u|}{c - b} \right) & b \leq |u| < c, \\ 0 & |u| \geq c. \end{cases} \tag{11}$$

The function ψ is used to reduce the influence of the points at the tails of the distribution (identified by a, b, and c) during the estimation of the mean and standard deviation. Let m be the median score, then a reasonable way to choose values for the parameters is to set a, b and c such that 70%, 85% and 95% of the scores fall in the range $(m - a, m + a)$, $(m - b, m + b)$ and $(m - c, m + c)$, respectively. As a result of reducing the influence at the tails, this method is not very sensitive to outliers (which represent the tails of the distributions).

It is to be noted that no single score normalization method has been found to be universally the best. This should be expected since each method makes certain assumptions (e.g., about distributions of scores) and are dependent on the quantity of training data and the training procedure. Jain, Nandakumar, and Ross (2005) studied the performance of different normalization techniques used with many different fusion rules in the context of a multimodal biometric system based on face, fingerprint and hand-geometry traits. Their empirical results showed that min–max normalization, z-normalization and tanh normalization work fairly well. Their experimental results also confirmed that min–max normalization and z-normalization methods are sensitive to outliers and as a result, they suggest the use of tanh normalization as it is more robust and efficient.

7.9.2 Bayesian framework for score fusion

Let us now assume that the scores are either homogenous (as output by the individual matchers) or have been suitably normalized. The next step is to combine these scores. One could simply take the sum (or equivalently, an average), product, maximum, minimum, or the median of the scores. In fact, Kittler et al. (1998) showed that all these "rules" are special cases of a unified framework based on the Bayesian decision theory. None of these rules, however, are optimal as they are marginalized from the general theoretical framework under specific assumptions. Consider a verification system, where each matcher outputs a score; the available scores are s_1, s_2, … s_R. The pattern X is to be assigned to one of the two classes: $w_{genuine} \equiv$ *match* or $w_{imposter} \equiv$ *non-match*. Each class w_k has an associated probability density function $p(s_j|w_k)$ and a prior probability of occurrence $P(w_k)$. According to the Bayesian decision theory, given the vector X, assign it to the class w_r that maximizes the a posteriori probability, i.e.,

Assign $X \rightarrow$ *match* if

$$P\left(w_{genuine} \mid s_1, s_2, \dots s_R\right) \geq P\left(w_{imposter} \mid s_1, s_2, \dots s_R\right), \tag{12}$$

else

Assign $X \rightarrow$ *non-match*.

The a posteriori probabilities can be expressed in terms of the conditional joint probability densities, $p(s_1, s_2, \dots s_R|w_i)$, by using the Bayes rule as follows:

$$P\left(w_{genuine} \mid s_1, s_2, \ldots s_R\right) =$$

$$\frac{p\left(s_1, s_2, \ldots s_R \mid w_{genuine}\right) P\left(w_{genuine}\right)}{p\left(s_1, s_2, \ldots s_R \mid w_{genuine}\right) P\left(w_{genuine}\right) + p\left(s_1, s_2, \ldots s_R \mid w_{imposter}\right) P\left(w_{imposter}\right)}, \tag{13}$$

$$P\left(w_{imposter} \mid s_1, s_2, \ldots s_R\right) =$$

$$\frac{p\left(s_1, s_2, \ldots s_R \mid w_{imposter}\right) P\left(w_{imposter}\right)}{p\left(s_1, s_2, \ldots s_R \mid w_{genuine}\right) P\left(w_{genuine}\right) + p\left(s_1, s_2, \ldots s_R \mid w_{imposter}\right) P\left(w_{imposter}\right)}. \tag{14}$$

Kittler et al. (1998) made several approximations to simplify the computation of the a posteriori probabilities. Each approximation results in one of the combination rules mentioned above (sum, product, minimum, maximum, and median). The first assumption is the statistical independence of the R scores. Under this assumption, the density $p(s_1, s_2, \ldots s_R \mid w_k)$ can be expressed as the product of the marginals, i.e.,

$$p\left(s_1, s_2, \ldots s_R \mid w_k\right) = \prod_{j=1}^{R} p\left(s_j \mid w_k\right), \tag{15}$$

where $k = genuine, imposter$. While in certain situations, such as combining multiple fingers of a user, the independence assumption holds quite well, in many other cases, the independence assumption does not hold (e.g., multiple impressions of the same finger of a user are not independent). Still, the resulting fusion rules appear to be robust to the independence assumption.

The *product rule* is a direct implication of the statistical independence assumption; it can be stated as:

Assign $X \rightarrow match$ if

$$P\left(w_{genuine}\right) \prod_{j=1}^{R} p\left(s_j \mid w_{genuine}\right) \geq P\left(w_{imposter}\right) \prod_{j=1}^{R} p\left(s_j \mid w_{imposter}\right). \tag{16}$$

Under the assumption that priors are equal, i.e., $P(w_{genuine}) = P(w_{imposter})$, the product rule can be expressed in terms of a posteriori probabilities:

Assign $X \rightarrow match$ if

$$\prod_{j=1}^{R} P\left(w_{genuine} \mid s_j\right) \geq \prod_{j=1}^{R} P\left(w_{imposter} \mid s_j\right). \tag{17}$$

If the scores have been normalized such that $s_j \in [0,1]$, the score itself can be considered as an estimate of the a posteriori probability of a genuine match, that is,

$$s_j \approx P\left(w_{genuine} \mid s_j\right). \tag{18}$$

The a posteriori probability of imposter is then $1-s_j$. The product rule can be stated as:
Assign $X \rightarrow$ *match* if

$$\prod_{j=1}^{R} s_j \geq \prod_{j=1}^{R} (1 - s_j). \tag{19}$$

The above equation considers a *zero-one* loss function in the Bayesian framework, i.e., there is no loss for a correct decision and there is a unit loss for a wrong decision (a false match or a false non-match). In case of a weighted loss function, the final decision is essentially based upon some threshold, i.e.:

$$\prod_{j=1}^{R} s_j \geq T, \tag{20}$$

where T is a threshold whose value depends on the loss function. In practice, product rule is not very effective because it is very sensitive to errors, i.e., if even one of the matcher in the combination is incorrect (small matching score), it will pull the product significantly lower, which would lead to errors.

The *sum rule* avoids the above mentioned limitation of the product rule. It is particularly effective when the match scores tend to be noisy, that is, the estimates of the a posteriori probabilities are noisy. In such a scenario, we can assume that the a posteriori probabilities do not deviate significantly from the prior probabilities, i.e.,

$$P\left(w_{genuine} \mid s_j\right) = P\left(w_{genuine}\right)\left(1 + \delta_{genuine,j}\right) \text{ and }$$

$$P\left(w_{imposter} \mid s_j\right) = P\left(w_{imposter}\right)\left(1 + \delta_{imposter,j}\right) \tag{21}$$

where $\delta_{genuine,j}$ and $\delta_{imposter,j}$ are small deviations ($\ll 1$), $j = 1, 2, \ldots R$. Assuming equal priors, and non-zero loss function, the sum rule can be stated as:
Assign $X \rightarrow$ *match* if

$$\sum_{j=1}^{R} s_j \geq T. \tag{22}$$

This combination rule is also known as mean or average rule. Kittler et al. (1998) showed that the sum rule works quite well in practice. It has become the most commonly used rule to combine the normalized matching scores.

The *maximum rule* approximates the mean of the a posteriori probabilities by their maximum value, i.e.:

$$\frac{1}{R} \sum_{j=1}^{R} P\left(w_{genuine} \mid s_j\right) \approx \max_{j=1}^{R} P\left(w_{genuine} \mid s_j\right)$$

$$\frac{1}{R}\sum_{j=1}^{R}P\left(w_{imposter}\mid s_j\right)\approx \max_{j=1}^{R}P\left(w_{imposter}\mid s_j\right). \tag{23}$$

Under the assumption of equal priors and non zero-one loss function, the maximum rule results in:

Assign $X \rightarrow$ *match* if

$$\max_{j=1}^{R}s_j \geq T . \tag{24}$$

The *minimum rule* is derived under the well known inequality that the product of probabilities is always less than or equal to the minimum value of probability in the product. Hence,

$$\prod_{j=1}^{R}P\left(w_{genuine}\mid s_j\right)\leq \min_{j=1}^{R}P\left(w_{genuine}\mid s_j\right) \text{ and}$$

$$\prod_{j=1}^{R}P\left(w_{imposter}\mid s_j\right)\leq \min_{j=1}^{R}P\left(w_{imposter}\mid s_j\right). \tag{25}$$

Under the assumption of equal priors and non zero-one loss function, this leads to:

Assign $X \rightarrow$ *match* if

$$\min_{j=1}^{R}s_j \geq T . \tag{26}$$

Since the average a posteriori probabilities are somewhat sensitive to outliers, the mean rule can be converted to median rule. So under the same assumptions as above, the median rule becomes:

Assign $X \rightarrow w_{genuine}$ if

$$\operatorname*{median}_{j=1}^{R}s_j \geq T . \tag{27}$$

The above mentioned combination rules, that is, product, sum, maximum, minimum, and median are all very commonly used in combining matching scores that are either compatible or normalized to be compatible. The sum rule in particular has received significant attention due to its superior performance and simplicity. We have illustrated these rules assuming a two-class ($w_{genuine}$ and $w_{imposter}$) verification problem but the rules are extensible to multi-class identification problem. Given the training data to estimate the relative accuracies of the component scores, the scores can be appropriately weighted before combining them with the above mentioned combination rules.

7.9.3 Density-based methods

Let us consider the Bayesian framework given in Equations (12) to (15). Under the assumption of equal priors, we have:

$$\frac{P\left(w_{genuine} \mid s_1, s_2, \ldots s_R\right)}{P\left(w_{imposter} \mid s_1, s_2, \ldots s_R\right)} = \frac{p\left(s_1, s_2, \ldots s_R \mid w_{genuine}\right)}{p\left(s_1, s_2, \ldots s_R \mid w_{imposter}\right)}. \tag{28}$$

The right hand side in Equation (28) is known as the likelihood ratio. The Neyman–Pearson theorem (Duda, Hart, and Stork, 2000) states that the optimal test for deciding whether a matching score vector $\mathbf{s} = [s_1, s_2, \ldots s_R]$ corresponds to a genuine or imposter match is the likelihood ratio test. The Neyman–Pearson (NP) decision rule is optimal in the sense that for any specified false match rate (FMR), there is no other decision rule that will result in a lower false non-match rate (FNMR) than the likelihood ratio test. The NP decision rule is given by:

Assign $X \rightarrow match$ if

$$\frac{p\left(s_1, s_2, \ldots s_R \mid w_{genuine}\right)}{p\left(s_1, s_2, \ldots s_R \mid w_{imposter}\right)} \geq \eta, \tag{29}$$

where η is the threshold value that achieves the specified value of FMR. The above rule is optimal only when the underlying class conditional densities, i.e., $p(s_1, s_2, \ldots s_R \mid w_{genuine})$ and $p(s_1, s_2, \ldots s_R \mid w_{imposter})$, are known (see Figure 7.8).

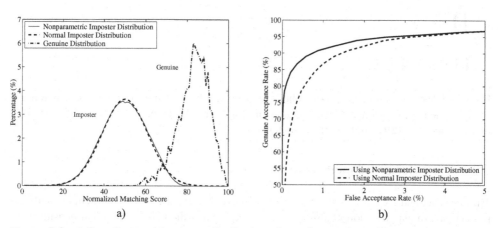

a)   b)

Figure 7.8. a) Genuine and impostor distributions for a fingerprint verification system (Jain et al., 2000) and a Normal approximation for the impostor distribution. Visually, the Normal approximation seems to be good, but causes significant decrease in performance compared to the non-parametric estimate as shown in the ROCs in b), where FMR is referred to as FAR (False Acceptance Rate) and (1-FNMR) as Genuine Acceptance Rate. © Elsevier.

In practice, class conditional densities are estimated using either parametric methods or nonparametric methods (Duda, Hart, and Stork, 2000). In the parametric density estimation, the general form or shape of the density is assumed to be known and only the parameters of the density function are estimated. For example, it is common to assume a Gaussian density function, where only the mean and the standard deviation parameters that characterize the Gaussian density are estimated. However, it is well known that the Gaussian assumption is usually not appropriate for genuine and imposter scores of a biometric matcher. For this reason, nonparametric methods need to be used to estimate the score densities.

Prabhakar and Jain (2002) estimated the multivariate impostor and genuine densities using the Parzen window-based nonparametric method in combining multiple fingerprint matchers (see Figure 7.9) and showed that the Neyman–Pearson fusion method is superior in accuracy to both the sum rule and the product rule. Nandakumar et al. (2008) used finite Gaussian mixture model (GMM) to estimate the multivariate class conditional densities.

One of the practical limitations in taking full advantage of the optimality of the Neyman–Pearson likelihood ratio test is the requirement of huge amounts of training data to accurately estimate the impostor and genuine densities. As a result, it is very common to reduce the sample size requirements by assuming independence among the scores output by different matchers. While this assumption is not strictly true in practice, the performance in practice is not hampered. Under this assumption, the multivariate densities can be approximated by a product of the univariate marginal densities. Equation (29) reduces to:

Assign $X \to$ *match* if

$$\frac{\prod\limits_{j=1}^{R} p\left(s_j \mid w_{genuine}\right)}{\prod\limits_{j=1}^{R} p\left(s_j \mid w_{imposter}\right)} \geq \eta . \tag{30}$$

Dass, Nandakumar, and Jain (2005) obtained good results by using a univariate generalized marginal densities (estimated using nonparametric methods) to combine two different face matchers and two different fingerprint matchers.

7.9.4 Classifier-based methods

The Bayesian and Neyman-Pearson methods discussed above are two-class (genuine and impostor) pattern classification algorithms that are optimal if the class-conditional densities are either known or can be accurately estimated from large amounts of training data. In practice, with limited training data, it is possible that other classification algorithms may perform better than Bayesian methods. Examples of these classification algorithms are linear and quadratic discriminant functions, logistic regression, neural networks, k-nearest neighbor, decision trees, support vector machines, etc. (Duda, Hart, and Stork, 2000). Other fusion methods, well known in the pattern recognition literature, such as generalized ensemble, adaptive weighting (Tresp and Taniguchi, 1995), stacking, mixture of local experts (MLE) (Jacobs et al., 1991), hierarchical MLE (Jordan and Jacobs, 1994), bagging and boosting have also been used in the context of fusion in biometric systems. It is well known that no single classifier performs best on all classification problems; classifier performance depends greatly on the characteristic of the data to be classified as well as the amount and nature of training data.

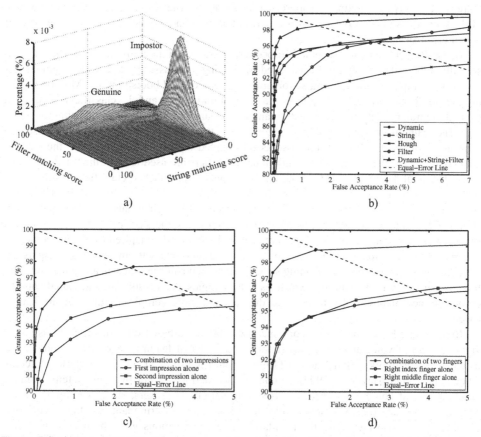

Figure 7.9 a) Two dimensional genuine and impostor densities estimated from training data using the Parzen window estimator. The ROCs in b), c), and d) show the improvement in verification performance from a combination of four fingerprint matching algorithms, a combination of two impressions per finger, and a combination of two fingers, respectively, using the Neyman-Pearson method (Prabhakar and Jain, 2002). In the graphics, FMR is referred to as FAR (False Acceptance Rate) and (1−FNMR) as Genuine Acceptance Rate. © Elsevier.

Any of the classification algorithms mentioned above can be used for fusing matching scores. In this case, the individual matching scores are viewed as features constituting a feature vector, which must be classified into "match" and "non-match" in the case of a verification system. The classifier is trained on the training data (a set of representative feature vectors together with the true class labels) to learn a decision boundary between the two classes. The resulting decision boundary could be quite simple, for example a hyperplane in the case of a linear classifier, or fairly complex, for example in the case of kernel-based classifiers. While there is flexibility in selecting the appropriate pattern classifier for specific combinations, one of the limitations of this approach is that it is not easy to operate the system at a fixed rate of one of the error type (say FMR).

A classifier combination scheme is especially useful when the individual classifiers are essentially independent. This can be achieved by training the classifier on different training sets or various samples of the training set obtained by rotation and bootstrapping. Modified training sets are formed by resampling from the original training set and the classifiers constructed using these training sets are combined. Examples are stacking, bagging and boosting (or ARC-ing). The main difference among these algorithms is the type of resampling technique used. In stacking (Wolpert, 1992), the training set is subsampled with replacement to train the individual classifiers and the outputs of the individual classifiers are used to train the "stacked" classifier. The final decision is made based on the outputs of the stacked classifier in conjunction with the outputs of individual classifiers. In bagging (Breiman, 1996), different datasets called bootstrapped sets are created by randomly subsampling the original dataset with replacement. A classifier is trained on each bootstrap set and various classifiers are combined using a fixed rule such as averaging. Boosting (Schapire (1990); Freund and Schapire (1996)) is another resampling technique for generating a sequence of training data sets. In boosting, weights are attached to each element of the training set and the subsequent training sets are generated from the original set by re-weighting the misclassified samples. As a result, the individual classifiers are trained hierarchically to learn to discriminate more complex regions in the feature space.

Brunelli and Falavigna (1995) combined two classifiers based on acoustic features (static and dynamic) of voice and three classifiers based on facial features (eyes, nose, and mouth) using neural networks. Ben-Yacoub (1999), Ben-Yacoub et al. (1999) and Ben-Yacoub, Abdeljaoued, and Mayoraz (1999) combined face and voice verification systems using a large number of combination schemes based on various classifiers, such as Support Vector Machines, tree classifiers, neural networks, the Fisher linear discriminant, and the naïve Bayes classifier. They also compared the results of these combinations with the maximum, minimum, median, average, and product rules. The best performance was achieved using a Bayesian classifier on a database of 295 subjects. Choudhury et al. (1999) also reported an improvement in performance from a combination of face and voice verification systems using the Bayes classifier. Bigun et al. (1997) used synthetic data to demonstrate fusion using the Bayesian approach.

Dieckmann, Plankensteiner, and Wagner (1997) and Frischholz and Dieckmann (2000) combined face, voice and lip movement for their verification system using a "2 out of 3" (voting) and a weighted sum rule. Verlinde, Chollet, and Acheroy (2000) combined frontal face, face profile and voice verification systems using a large number of classifiers that included the maximum likelihood method, naïve Bayes classifier, logistic regression, quadratic classifier, linear classifier, voting rule (AND and OR), k-nearest neighbor using vector quantization, and binary decision tree. The validation results showed that the naïve Bayes and logistic regression classifiers yielded the best improvement in performance.

In conclusion, a large number of classifiers and fusion methods are available to system designers. A priori, it is not well understood which one of them works better than the others and if so, under what circumstances. Traditionally, selection of a particular fusion method is based on either human intuition or on an empirical evaluation. The fusion method with the best classification accuracy over a given set of test samples is finally chosen.

7.10 Decision-Level Fusion

Decision-level fusion is not as popular as score-level or rank-level fusion. Still, it may be the only feasible approach if the commercial biometric systems involved in fusion provide only the final match decision. Similar to the rank-level and score-level fusions, decision-level fusion is conducted at a high level, so it does not matter which entities are being combined (different biometric traits, different fingers, different impression of the same finger, or different feature extraction and matching algorithms). So, we will use the term "matcher" to refer to the systems that are generating the individual decisions.

In a verification system, since each component system returns either a "match" or a "non-match" binary decision, the obvious decision-level fusion methods are AND and OR (Daugman, 2000), majority voting (Lam and Suen, 1997), and weighted majority voting (Kuncheva, 2004). One major advantage of AND, OR, and majority voting methods is that they are very intuitive and thus easy to explain and understand. The AND method outputs a "match" decision only if each one of component decision in fusion is a "match". In the OR method the combined decision is a "match" as long as at least one of the component systems generate a "match" output. The AND and OR decision-level fusions are duals of each other. AND results in lowering the FMR but increases the FNMR whereas OR results in lowering the FNMR but increases the FMR. The magnitude of change in the error rates due to fusion is highly dependent on the independence among the component systems. Further, as Daugman (2000) has shown, these methods could actually result in worse performance than the best of the individual components. This would happen if the individual matchers do not have comparable accuracy. That is, while a combination of all weak matchers or all strong matchers is expected to improve the accuracy, a combination of some weak matchers with some strong matchers may actually degrade the overall performance. As a result, in practice, these methods are used only when combining multiple fingers of a person or multiple impressions of a finger.

The AND and OR methods can be generalized into a single framework of "k out of R" method, where k is the number of "match" decisions and R is the total number of matchers; "k out of R" means that the combined decision is a "match" if at least k individual decisions are "match". When k is equal to R, the method is essentially the AND method and when k is equal to 1, the fusion method is essentially the OR method. When k is larger than 1 but less than $R/2$, the resulting fusion method is similar to OR but seeks some agreement among matchers; when k is larger than $R/2$, the resulting fusion method is more similar to AND but some disagreement among individual matchers is allowed. Similar to AND and OR methods, their generalized versions also work well only when the individual matchers have comparable performance.

With the availability of training data, the majority voting method can be improved. For example, the contribution of individual matchers can be weighted based on the relative accuracy of the matcher. A number of other methods model the probability, belief, etc. of identities/matchers through training (see Bayesian theory-based fusion and Dempster-Shafer theory-based fusion by Xu, Krzyzac, and Suen (1992); and behavior knowledge space-based fusion by Huang and Suen (1995)).

We have explained AND, OR, majority voting and weighted majority voting in the context of a verification system, but these methods can also be adopted to work for an identification system by considering voting among the returned identities or candidates instead of "match"/ "non-match" binary decisions.

7.11 Summary

Fusion in biometric systems is gaining popularity among system designers due to its proven capability in improving system accuracy. Numerous techniques for fusion have been proposed by researches in the context of fingerprint systems at the image, feature, score, rank, and decision levels (Table 7.3). With such widespread interest, there is a need for common databases for benchmarking fusion studies in biometrics. Some benchmark databases have been recently collected and made available to the research community: Garcia-Salicetti et al. (2003), Ortega-Garcia et al. (2003), NIST (2004), Fierrez-Aguilar et al. (2007), BioSecure (2008); refer to Section 4.7.1 for further details. New evaluation campaigns are currently underway (see Phillips (2008)).

Fusion in a verification system is typically used to improve the system accuracy, whereas fusion in an identification system is used to improve system speed (throughput) as well. Multiple modalities that are combined in a verification system are chosen based on their verification accuracies and they are typically combined in parallel. On the other hand, in an identification system, the first modality selected is typically based on the matching speed rather than its accuracy and is combined in serial fashion with subsequent modalities that are relatively slower but more accurate.

Information level	Fusion method
Image	Image mosaicking, image compositing
Feature	Feature concatenation, template consolidation, template adaptation
Score	Sum, mean, median, product, min, max
	Linear discriminant function, logistic regression, neural networks, quadratic classifiers, k-nearest neighbor, decision trees, support vector machines
	Generalized ensemble, adaptive weighting, stacking, mixture of local experts (MLE), bagging, boosting, random subspace
Rank	Highest rank, Borda count, weighted Borda count, Dempster-Shafer
Decision	AND, OR, voting, weighted voting

Table 7.3. A summary of fusion methods classified according to the information level of fusion.

It is well known that the independence among biometric systems plays a very important role in the amount of improvement from fusion. A fusion of uncorrelated systems (e.g., fingerprint and face, two fingers of a person, etc.) is expected to result in a better improvement in performance than a fusion of correlated systems (e.g., different impressions of the same finger, different fingerprint feature extraction and matching algorithms, etc.). Furthermore, a fusion of uncorrelated systems has the additional advantages of reducing the failure to enroll rate and enhancing system security. Some fusion methods may require the users to interact with different scanners or multiple times with the same scanner, which not only increases the enrollment and verification times, but also leads to user inconvenience. Cost remains the single biggest barrier in multibiometric systems that need different scanners. Many government and civilian applications that require user identification against millions of identities are rapidly adopting multibiometric systems. These applications are somewhat more tolerant to the cost of scanners and user inconvenience but need to achieve acceptable levels of accuracy. New scanners are being designed so that the biometric acquisition system can capture multiple body measurements in a single interaction with the user. We anticipate that high security physical access control applications and large-scale identification systems will increasingly adopt multibiometric systems while the personal low-cost commercial applications will probably continue to use unimodal systems.

8
Fingerprint Individuality[1]

8.1 Introduction

Expert testimony based on forensic evidence (such as handwriting, fingerprint, hair, bite marks, etc.) is routinely collected and presented in courtrooms. Among the various sources of evidence, fingerprints have been used in courts of law for almost 100 years and the testimony based on fingerprints carries substantial credibility and weight. The use of fingerprint evidence involves comparing salient features of a latent print lifted from a crime scene with those of rolled (full) impressions taken either from the known defendant or the entire criminal database. A reasonably high degree of match between the salient features leads the latent experts to testify irrefutably that the owner of the latent print and the defendant are one and the same person. For decades, the testimonies provided by latent print experts were almost never excluded from these cases, and on cross-examination, the foundations and basis of such testimonies were rarely questioned (Cole (2001a, b)). Central to establishing an identity based on fingerprint evidence is the assumption of discernible uniqueness; salient features of different individuals are observably different, and therefore, when two prints share many common features, the experts conclude that the owner of the two different prints is one and the same person. The assumption of discernible uniqueness (Saks and Koehler, 2005), although lacking sound theoretical and empirical foundations, allows forensic experts to offer unquestionable proof towards the defendant's guilt, and to make matters worse, these experts are never questioned on the uncertainty associated with their testimonials (that is, how frequently would an observable match between a pair of prints lead to errors in the identification of individuals; see Haber and Haber (2004)). Thus, discernible uniqueness precludes the opportunity to establish error rates which would be known from collecting population samples, analyzing the inherent feature variability, and reporting the corresponding probability of two different persons sharing a set of common fingerprint features.

---

[1] Portions reprinted with permission from *IEEE Transactions on Pattern Analysis and Machine Intelligence*, vol. 24, no. 8, pp. 1010–1025, 2002. © 2002 IEEE.

D. Maltoni et al., *Handbook of Fingerprint Recognition*, 341–370.
© Springer-Verlag London Limited 2009

A significant break from this trend occurred in the 1993 case of Daubert v. Merrell Dow Pharmaceuticals (113 S. Ct. 2786) where the U.S. Supreme Court ruled that in order for expert forensic testimony to be allowed in a court case, it had to be subject to three main criteria of scientific validation, that is, whether the particular tool or methodology in question (i) has been tested, (ii) has been subjected to peer-review, and (iii) possesses known error rates. Following Daubert, fingerprint identification was first challenged in the 1999 case of U.S. v. Byron Mitchell (Criminal Action No. 96-407, US District Court for the Eastern District of Pennsylvania) under the premise that the uniqueness of fingerprints has not been objectively tested and matching error rates are unknown (also see Newman (2001)). Based on the outcome of U.S. v. Byron Mitchell, fingerprint based identification has been challenged in more than 20 court cases in the United States (for example, U.S. v. Llera Plaza [179 F Supp 2d 492 ED Pa 2002 and 188 F Supp 2d 549 Ed Pa 2002] and U.S. v. Crisp [324 F 3d 261 4th Cir 2003]). Cole (2006) has compiled a list of 22 known exposed cases of erroneous fingerprint identifications made by forensic experts.

In December 2005, the Massachusetts Supreme Judicial Court barred key fingerprint evidence obtained from several latent prints in the case of Terry L. Patterson (Saltzman (2005a, b)). As recently as October 2007, in the case of State of Maryland v. Bryan Rose (Circuit Court, case number K06-0545), judge Susan Souder ruled to exclude fingerprint evidence "because the State did not prove in this case that opinion testimony by experts regarding the ACE-V (Analysis, Comparison, Evaluation, and Verification) method of latent print identification rests on a reliable factual foundation as required by MD Rule 5-702". In making this ruling, the judge heavily relied on the case of an Oregon lawyer who was mistakenly linked through fingerprint analysis to the 2004 Madrid train bombings. These court rulings demonstrate both the awareness and the need to develop measures that reflect the confidence in a match when fingerprints are used as evidence in the courts of law. Fingerprint individuality deals with the problem of quantifying the extent of uniqueness of a fingerprint. How similar should two fingerprints be before we can conclude with high confidence that they are from the same finger? What are the measures of fingerprint individuality that reflect the extent of uncertainty in the observed match?

The main challenge in studying fingerprint individuality is to develop statistical models that adequately describe the variability of fingerprint features in a target population. These models can, in turn, be used to derive the probability of a random match between two different fingerprints picked arbitrarily from the target population. Eliciting candidate models for representing the variability of fingerprint features is not an easy task due to the complex nature of this variability. Candidate models should satisfy two important requirements, namely, (i) flexibility, that is, the models can represent a wide range of distributional characteristics of fingerprint features in the population, and (ii) associated confidence measures can be easily obtained from these models.

The fingerprint individuality problem can be formulated in many different ways, depending on which one of the following aspects of the problem is under examination: (i) the individuality problem may be cast as determining the probability that any two or more individuals may have sufficiently similar fingerprints in a given target population; (ii) given a sample fingerprint, determine the probability of finding a sufficiently similar fingerprint in a target population; (iii) given two fingerprints from two different fingers, determine the probability that they are sufficiently similar (*probability of a random correspondence*). When the comparison is made by an automatic system (AFIS), the probability of random correspondence coincides with the false match rate (FMR). Formulation (iii) is more general as its solution would also provide solutions to the other two formulations (Rice, 1995). A reliable statistical estimate of the matching error in fingerprint comparison can determine the admissibility of fingerprint recognition in the courts of law as an evidence of identity. Furthermore, it can establish an upper bound on the performance of automatic fingerprint recognition systems.

In order to solve the individuality problem, one needs to define a priori the representation of the fingerprint. Fingerprints can be represented by several different features, including the overall ridge flow pattern, ridge frequency, number and position of singularities (loops and deltas), type, direction, and location of minutiae points, ridge counts between pairs of minutiae, and location of pores. All these features contribute to fingerprint individuality. In this chapter, we have focused only on minutiae representation of the fingerprints (refer to Chapter 3) because it is the most common feature utilized by forensic experts, it has been demonstrated to be highly stable, and it has been adopted by most of the commercially available automatic fingerprint matching systems. Note that latent experts use several other features in addition to minutiae when matching fingerprints. Moreover, neither the minutiae-based representation nor the simple similarity metric model considered in this chapter completely captures the complexity of the fingerprint expert matching process. Perhaps the individuality estimates are a reasonable first-order approximation of most of the discriminatory information that is consistently available to the experts across the impressions.

Given a representation scheme and a similarity metric, there are two approaches for determining the individuality of the fingerprints. In the empirical approach, representative samples of fingerprints are collected and, using a typical fingerprint matcher (automatic or human), the accuracy of the matcher is calculated which provides an indication of the uniqueness of the fingerprint with respect to the matcher. Instead of collecting representative samples of the entire population, one could instead get an upper bound of matching accuracy by matching most genetically similar fingerprints, i.e., from identical twins (Lin et al. (1982); Jain, Prabhakar, and Pankanti (2001, 2002)). There are known problems (and costs) associated with collection of the representative sample of fingerprints. In addition, even if a large database of fingerprints such as the IAFIS database (maintained by FBI) which contains over 200 million fingerprints is used for an empirical evaluation of fingerprint individuality, it would take approximately 634 years to match all the fingerprints in the database with each other using a processor with a speed of one million matches per second $((200 \times 10^6)^2/2)/(10^6 \times 60 \times 60 \times 24 \times 365) \cong 634$! On the other hand, in a theoretical approach to individuality estimation, one needs to model all realistic phenomena affecting inter-class and intra-class fingerprint pattern variations. Given the similarity metric, one could then theoretically estimate the probability of a random correspondence. Theoretical approaches are often limited by the extent to which the assumed models conform to reality. In this chapter, we give a brief survey of the existing work on fingerprint individuality. Two individuality models introduced by Pankanti, Prabhakar, and Jain (2001, 2002) and Dass, Zhu, and Jain (2005) and Zhu, Dass, and Jain (2006, 2007) are described in detail. We also juxtapose the probabilities obtained from these individuality models with the empirical results obtained using a specific automatic fingerprint matcher (Jain et al., 1997).

One could think of using the total number of degrees-of-freedom of the minutiae configuration space as a measure of the discriminability of different fingers. But, the effective estimation of discriminatory information can only be achieved by taking into account intra-pattern variations. There are several sources of variability in the multiple impressions of a finger (see Section 4.1). This variability in multiple impressions of a finger manifests itself into (i) detection of spurious minutiae or missing genuine minutiae, (ii) displacement/disorientation (also called deformation) of the genuine minutiae, and (iii) transformation of the type of minutiae (connective ambiguity). This entails designing a similarity metric (matcher) that accommodates these intra-class variations.

Most of the early approaches to fingerprint individuality do not explicitly account for these sources of intra-class variability in their models (see Stoney and Thornton (1986) for a critical review of several early models) and, therefore, overestimate fingerprint individuality (give a smaller probability of random correspondence). Furthermore, because most of the early models of individuality do not address the problems associated with the occurrence of spurious minutiae or missing genuine minutiae, they do not provide a systematic framework to address issues related to a partial representational match between two fingerprints (e.g., what is the probability of finding seven matched minutiae between two fingerprints that have 18 and 37 minutiae, respectively?). This is a very important issue in an automatic fingerprint matching system where the feature extraction algorithms do not always provide the true minutiae and in matching latent prints to full prints. Although the likelihood of detecting false minutiae is significantly smaller in a manual fingerprint matching procedure than in an automatic system, the manual procedure suffers from lack of consistency. The approaches described in Pankanti, Prabhakar, and Jain (2002) and Zhu, Dass, and Jain (2007) not only explicitly model the situation of partial representational match, but also incorporate constraints on the configuration space imposed by intra-class variations (e.g., number of minutiae, minutiae position/orientation, image area) based on empirical estimates derived from the ground truth data marked by an expert on fingerprints obtained in a realistic environment.

8.2 Background

Fingerprint individuality studies have typically focused on minutiae-based representations; some studies explicitly factored in fingerprint class (e.g., right loop, left loop, whorl, arch, tented arch, etc.) information. The type, direction, and location of minutiae are the most commonly used features in these individuality studies. See Table 8.1 for a comparison of the features used in various fingerprint individuality models.

Author	Fingerprint features
Galton (1892)	Ridges, minutiae types
Pearson (1930, 1933)	Ridges, minutiae types
Henry (1900)	Minutiae locations, types, core-to-delta ridge count
Balthazard (1911) (cf. Stoney and Thornton, 1986)	Minutiae locations, two types, and two directions
Bose (1917) (cf. Stoney and Thornton, 1986)	Minutiae locations and three types
Wentworth and Wilder (1918)	Minutiae locations
Cummins and Midlo (1943)	Minutiae locations and types, core-to-delta ridge count
Gupta (1968)	Minutiae locations and types, fingerprint types, ridge count
Roxburgh (1933)	Minutiae locations, two minutiae types, two orientations, fingerprint and core types, number of positionings, area, fingerprint quality
Amy (1948) (cf. Stoney and Thornton, 1986)	Minutiae locations, number, types, and orientation
Trauring (1963)	Minutiae locations, two types, and two orientations
Kingston (1964)	Minutiae locations, number, and types
Osterburg et al. (1977)	Minutiae locations and types
Stoney and Thornton (1986)	Minutiae locations, distribution, orientation, and types, variation among prints from the same source, ridge counts, and number of alignments
Pankanti, Prabhakar, and Jain (2002)	Minutiae locations, number, and direction
Zhu, Dass, and Jain (2007)	Minutiae locations, number, and direction

Table 8.1. Fingerprint features used in different individuality models.

The use of the types of minutiae vary from one study to another: some studies used two minutiae types (ridge ending and bifurcation) whereas others (e.g., Osterburg (1964); Osterburg et al. (1977)) used as many as 13 types of events (empty cell, ridge ending, ridge bifurcation, island, dot, broken ridge, bridge, spur, enclosure, delta, double bifurcation, trifurcation and multiple events). Some models included additional features (e.g., ridge counts Stoney (1985) or sweat pores Roddy and Stosz (1997)) to determine the probability of occurrence of a particular fingerprint configuration. Most of the early individuality studies examined the distinctiveness of a portion/feature of the fingerprint. By assuming that events (e.g., placement of minutiae) are independent and identically distributed, these studies estimated the distinctiveness of the entire fingerprint (total pattern variation) by collating the distinctiveness in the features extracted from fingerprints (total feature variation). We refer to these total pattern variation-based fingerprint individuality estimates as the *probability of a fingerprint configuration*. A summary of these studies is presented in Table 8.1.

The fingerprint individuality problem was first addressed by Galton in 1892 (Galton, 1892), who considered a square region spanning six-ridges in a given fingerprint. He assumed that, on average, a full fingerprint can be covered by 24 such six-ridge wide independent square regions. Galton estimated that he could correctly reconstruct any of the regions with a probability of 1/2, by looking at the surrounding ridges (see Figure 8.1). Accordingly, the probability of a specific fingerprint configuration, given the surrounding ridges, is $(1/2)^{24}$. Galton multiplied this conditional (on surrounding ridges) probability with the probability of finding the surrounding ridges to obtain the probability of occurrence of a fingerprint as

$$\text{P(Fingerprint Configuration)} = \frac{1}{16} \times \frac{1}{256} \times \left(\frac{1}{2}\right)^{24} = 1.45 \times 10^{-11}, \tag{1}$$

where 1/16 is the probability of occurrence of a specific fingerprint type (such as arch, tented arch, left loop, right loop, double loop, whorl, etc.) and 1/256 is the probability of occurrence of the correct number of ridges entering and exiting each of the 24 regions. Equation (1) gives the probability that a particular fingerprint configuration in an average size fingerprint (containing 24 regions defined by Galton) will be observed in nature.

Roxburgh (1933), Pearson (1930, 1933), and Kingston (1964) objected to Galton's assumption that the probability of occurrence of any particular ridge configuration in a six-ridge square is 1/2 and claimed that Equation (1) grossly underestimates fingerprint individuality (i.e., overestimates the probability of occurrence). Pearson (1930, 1933) argued that there could be 36 (6 × 6) possible minutiae locations within one of Galton's six-ridge-square regions, leading to a probability of occurrence of a particular fingerprint configuration of

$$\text{P(Fingerprint Configuration)} = \frac{1}{16} \times \frac{1}{256} \times \left(\frac{1}{36}\right)^{24} = 1.09 \times 10^{-41}. \tag{2}$$

A number of subsequent models (Henry (1900); Balthazard (1911) (cf. Stoney and Thornton, 1986); Bose (1917) (cf. Stoney and Thornton, 1986); Wentworth and Wilder (1918); Cummins and Midlo (1943); Gupta (1968)) are interrelated and are based on a fixed probability p for the occurrence of a minutia. They compute the probability of a particular n-minutiae fingerprint configuration as

$$\text{P(Fingerprint Configuration)} = p^n. \tag{3}$$

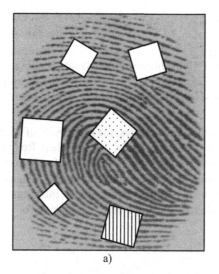 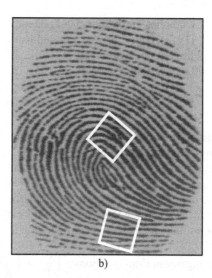

a)   b)

Figure 8.1. Example of Galton's method of individuality estimation. Galton laid out enlargements of the fingerprints on the floor. He then dropped different sized squares such that they fell randomly on the enlarged fingerprint. Galton sought that size of paper square where he could correctly guess the ridge structure hidden underneath with a probability of 1/2. For example, one can easily guess the ridges hidden by the six-ridge wide square marked with dots in a) by looking at the surrounding ridges around the square. On the other hand, one cannot correctly guess the ridge structure hidden by the six-ridge wide square marked with vertical stripes in a). The hidden areas for these two squares are shown in b).

In the following, we provide the values of p used in these studies. In most cases, the authors do not present any details on how they arrived at their choice of p.

- Henry (1900) chose $p = 1/4$ and added two to the number of minutiae n if the fingerprint type and core-to-delta ridge count could be determined from the given (latent) fingerprint.
- Balthazard (1911) (cf. Stoney and Toronton, 1986) also set $p = 1/4$, under the assumption that there are four types of equally likely minutiae events: bifurcation to the right, bifurcation to the left, termination to the right, and termination to the left.
- Bose (1917) (cf. Stoney and Thornton, 1986) adopted $p=1/4$, under the assumption that there are four possibilities in each square region of one ridge interval width in a fingerprint: a dot, a bifurcation, a ridge ending, and a continuous ridge.
- Wentworth and Wilder (1918) chose 1/50 as the value of p.

- Cummins and Midlo (1943) adopted the same value of p as Wentworth and Wilder (1918), but introduced a multiplicative constant of 1/31 to account for the variation in fingerprint pattern type.
- Gupta (1968) estimated the value of p as 1/10 for bifurcations and ridge endings, and 1/100 for the less commonly occurring minutiae types, based on 1,000 fingerprints. He also used a fingerprint type factor of 1/10 and correspondence in ridge count factor of 1/10.

Because of the widely varying values of p used in the above studies, the probability of a given fingerprint configuration also dramatically varies from one model to the other. Roxburgh (1933) proposed a more comprehensive analysis to compute the probability of a fingerprint configuration. His analysis was based on considering a fingerprint as a pattern with concentric circles, one ridge interval apart, in a polar coordinate system. Roxburgh also incorporated a quality measure of the fingerprint into his calculations. He computed the probability of a particular n-minutiae fingerprint configuration to be:

$$P(\text{Fingerprint Configuration}) = \left(\frac{C}{P}\right) \times \left(\frac{Q}{R \times T}\right)^n \tag{4}$$

where P is the probability of encountering a particular fingerprint type and core type, Q is a measure of quality ($Q = 1.5$ for an average quality print, and $Q = 3.0$ for a poor quality print), R is the number of semicircular ridges in a fingerprint ($R = 10$), T is the corrected number of minutiae types ($T = 2.412$), and C is the number of possible positions for the configuration ($C = 1$). Amy (1948) (cf. Stoney and Thornton, 1986) considered the variability in minutiae type, number, and position in his model for computing the probability of a fingerprint configuration. He further recognized that K multiple comparisons of the fingerprint pair (e.g., each hypothesized orientation alignment and each reference point correspondence) increase the possibility of false association which is given by

$$P(\text{False Association}) = 1 - \left(1 - P(\text{Fingerprint Configuration})\right)^K . \tag{5}$$

Kingston's (1964) model, which is very similar to Amy's model, computes the probability of a fingerprint configuration based on the probabilities of the observed number of minutiae, observed positions of minutiae, and observed minutiae types as follows

$$P(\text{Fingerprint Configuration}) = \left(e^{-y}\right)\left(y^n / n!\right)\left(P_1\right)\prod_{i=2}^{n}\left(P_i\right)\frac{(0.082)}{[S-(i-1)(0.082)]} , \tag{6}$$

where y is the expected number of minutiae in a region of given size S (in mm^2) and P_i is the probability of occurrence of a particular minutiae type in the ith minutia.

Most of the models discussed above implicitly assume that fingerprints are being matched manually. The probability of observing a given fingerprint feature is estimated by manually extracting the features from a small number of fingerprint images. Champod and Margot (1996) used an AFIS to extract minutiae from 977 fingerprint images scanned at a relatively high resolution of 800 dpi. They generated frequencies of minutiae occurrence and minutiae densities after manually verifying the thinned ridges produced by the AFIS to ensure that the feature extraction algorithm did not introduce errors. They considered minutiae only in concentric bands (five ridges wide) above the core and acknowledged that their individuality estimates were conservative (i.e., provided an upper bound). As an example, they estimated the probability of occurrence of a seven-minutia cluster configuration (five ridge endings and two bifurcations) as 2.25×10^{-5}.

Osterburg et al. (1977) divided fingerprints into discrete cells of size 1×1 mm. They computed the frequencies of 13 types of minutiae events (including an empty cell) from 39 fingerprints (8591 cells) and estimated the probability that 12 ridge endings will match between two fingerprints based on an average fingerprint area of 72 mm^2 as 1.25×10^{-20}. Sclove (1979) modified Osterburg et al.'s model by incorporating the observed dependence of minutiae occurrence in cells and came up with an estimate of probability of fingerprint configuration that is slightly higher than that obtained by Osterburg et al.; Stoney and Thornton (1986) criticized Osterburg et al.'s and Sclove's models because these models did not consider the fingerprint ridge structure, distortions, and the uncertainty in the positioning of the grid. Stoney and Thornton (1986) critically reviewed earlier fingerprint individuality models and proposed a detailed set of fingerprint features that should be taken into consideration. These features included ridge structure and description of minutiae location, ridge counts between pairs of minutiae, description of minutiae distribution, orientation of minutiae, variation in minutiae type, variation among fingerprints from the same source, number of positions (different translations and rotations of the input fingerprint), and number of comparisons performed with other fingerprints for identification.

Stoney's (1985) model is different from other models in that it attempts to characterize a significant component of pair-wise minutiae dependence. Stoney (1985) and Stoney and Thornton (1986) studied probabilities of occurrences of various types of minutiae, their orientation, number of neighboring minutiae, and distances/ridge counts to the neighboring minutiae. Given a minutiae set, they calculated the probability of a minutiae configuration by conjoining the probabilities of the individual events in the configuration. For instance, they proposed a linear ordering of minutiae in a minutiae configuration and recursively estimated the probability of an n-minutiae configuration from the probability of an $(n-1)$-minutiae configuration and the occurrence of a new minutia of certain type/orientation at a particular distance/ridge counts from its nearest minutia within the $(n-1)$-minutiae configuration. The model also incorporated constraints due to connective ambiguity and due to minutiae-free areas. The model corrected for the probability of false association by accounting for the various possible linear orderings that could initiate/drive the search for correspondence. A sample calculation for computing the probability of a false association using Stoney's model is given below.

$$P(\text{False Association}) = 1 - \left(1 - 0.6 \times \left(0.5 \times 10^{-3}\right)^{(n-1)}\right)^{\lfloor n/5 \rfloor}$$
$$\approx \frac{n}{5} \times 0.6 \times \left(0.5 \times 10^{-3}\right)^{(n-1)}. \tag{7}$$

For the sake of simplicity, we have considered only a rudimentary version of Stoney's model for the above computation; it is arbitrarily assumed that the probability of a typical *starting* minutia is 0.6, a typical neighboring minutia places an additional constraint on the probability, and there are no constraints due to connective ambiguity, minutiae-free areas, or minutiae-free borders. Finally, it is (arbitrarily) assumed that one in every five minutiae can potentially serve as a starting point for a new search. Stoney and Thornton identified weaknesses in their model and acknowledged that one of the most critical requirements (i.e., consideration of variation among prints from the same finger) was not sufficiently addressed. Their tolerances for minutiae position were derived from successive printings under ideal conditions and are far too low to be applicable in practical fingerprint comparisons.

The models discussed above (including Amy's model of false association due to multiple comparisons) focused mainly on measuring the amount of detail in a single fingerprint (i.e., estimation of the probability of a fingerprint configuration). These models did not emphasize the intra-class variations in multiple impressions of a finger. We refer to the quantifications of fingerprint individuality that explicitly consider the intra-class variations as the probability of a random correspondence. Trauring (1963) was the first to concentrate explicitly on measuring the amount of detail needed to establish a correspondence between two prints from the same finger (intra-class variation) using an AFIS and observed that corresponding fingerprint features in impressions of the same finger could be displaced from each other by as much as 1.5 times the inter-ridge distance. He further assumed that (i) minutiae are distributed randomly, (ii) there are only two types of minutiae (ridge ending and bifurcation), (iii) the two types of minutiae are equally likely, (iv) the two possible orientations of minutiae are equally likely, and (v) minutiae type, orientation, and position are independent variables. Trauring computed the probability of a coincidental correspondence of n minutiae between two fingerprints from different fingers to be:

$$P(\text{Random Correspondence}) = \left(0.1944\right)^{n}. \tag{8}$$

Stoney and Thornton's (1986) criticism of the Trauring model is that he did not consider ridge count, connective ambiguity, and correlation among minutiae location. Furthermore, they claim that Trauring's assumption that the minutiae types and orientations are equally probable is not correct. The probabilities of observing a particular minutiae configuration from different models are compared in Table 8.2.

Author	P(Fingerprint Configuration)	Probability values for $n=36$, $G=24$, $B=72$ $(n=12, G=8, B=24)$
Galton (1892)	$(1/16)\times(1/256)\times(1/2)^G$	1.45×10^{-11} (9.54×10^{-7})
Pearson (1930, 1933)	$(1/16)\times(1/256)\times(1/36)^G$	1.09×10^{-41} (8.65×10^{-17})
Henry (1900)	$(1/4)^{n+2}$	1.32×10^{-23} (3.72×10^{-9})
Balthazard (1911) (cf. Stoney and Thornton, 1986)	$(1/4)^n$	2.12×10^{-22} (5.96×10^{-8})
Bose (1917) (cf. Stoney and Thornton, 1986)	$(1/4)^n$	2.12×10^{-22} (5.96×10^{-8})
Wentworth and Wilder (1918)	$(1/50)^n$	6.87×10^{-62} (4.10×10^{-22})
Cummins and Midlo (1943)	$(1/31)\times(1/50)^n$	2.22×10^{-63} (1.32×10^{-22})
Gupta (1968)	$(1/10)\times(1/10)\times(1/10)^n$	1.00×10^{-38} (1.00×10^{-14})
Roxburgh (1933)	$(1/1000)\times(1.5/24.12)^n$	3.75×10^{-47} (3.35×10^{-18})
Trauring (1963)	$(0.1944)^n$	2.47×10^{-26} (2.91×10^{-9})
Osterburg et al. (1977)	$(0.766)^{B-n}(0.234)^n$	1.33×10^{-27} (1.10×10^{-9})
Stoney (1985)	$(n/5)\times0.6\times(0.5\times10^{-3})^{n-1}$	1.20×10^{-80} (3.50×10^{-26})

Table 8.2. A comparison of the probability of a particular fingerprint configuration using different models. For a fair comparison, we do not distinguish between minutiae types. By assuming that an average size fingerprint has 24 regions ($G = 24$) as defined by Galton, 72 regions ($B = 72$) as defined by Osterburg et al., and has 36 minutiae on average ($n = 36$), we compute the probability of observing a given fingerprint configuration in the last column of the table. The probability of observing a fingerprint configuration with $n = 12$ and, equivalently, $G = 8$ and $B = 24$, is also given in braces in the third column. Note that all probabilities represent a full (n minutiae) match as opposed to a partial match (see Table 8.3).

There have been few studies that empirically estimate the probability of finding a fingerprint in a large database that successfully matches the input fingerprint. Meagher et al. (1999) matched about 50,000 rolled fingerprints belonging to the same fingerprint class (left loop) with each other, to compute the impostor distribution. However, the genuine distribution was computed by matching each fingerprint image with itself; this ignores the variability present in different impressions of the same finger, namely, the intra-class variability. Furthermore, they assumed that the impostor and the genuine distributions follow a Gaussian distribution and computed the probability of a random correspondence to be 10^{-97}. This model grossly underestimates the probability of a random correspondence because it does not consider realistic intraclass variations in impressions of a finger.

Daugman (1999) analyzed the probability of a false match in an iris recognition system based on an empirical impostor distribution of the IrisCode matching scores from 340 irises. Under the assumption that the impostor and the genuine distributions follow a binomial distribution, he concluded that irises are extremely unique (false match rate of 10^{-12} at false non-match rate of 8.5×10^{-5}). Golfarelli, Maio, and Maltoni (1997) formulated the optimum Bayesian decision criterion for a biometric verification system; assuming the data distributions to be multinormals, they derived two statistical expressions for theoretically calculating the false match and false non-match rates. By inferring the model parameters from real prototypes, they obtained a theoretical equal error rate of 1.31×10^{-5} for a hand-geometry-based verification system and of 2×10^{-3} for a face-based verification system.

8.3 Uniform Minutiae Placement Model

Pankanti, Prabhakar, and Jain (2002) developed a simple fingerprint individuality model in an attempt to estimate the probability of a random correspondence between fingerprints. To make the model tractable, they made the following simplifying assumptions:

1. Only ridge endings and ridge bifurcation minutiae features are considered, because the occurrence of other minutiae types such as islands, dots, enclosures, bridges, double bifurcations, trifurcations, and so on is relatively rare. Because minutiae can reside only on ridges that follow certain overall patterns in a fingerprint, the minutiae directions are not completely independent of the minutiae locations. The statistical dependence between minutiae directions and locations is implicitly modeled.

2. A uniform distribution of minutiae in a fingerprint is assumed with the restriction that two minutiae cannot be very close to each other. Although minutiae locations are not uniformly distributed, this assumption approximates the slightly over-dispersed uniform distribution found by Stoney (1988).

3. Correspondence of a minutiae pair is an independent event and each correspondence is equally important. It is possible to assign a higher weight to spatially diverse correspondences compared to correspondences localized in a narrow spatial neighborhood.

4. Fingerprint image quality is not explicitly taken into account in the individuality determination. It is very difficult to reliably assign a quality index to a fingerprint because image quality is a subjective concept.

5. Ridge widths are assumed to be the same across the population and spatially uniform in the same finger. This assumption is justified because pressure variations could make non-uniform ridge variations uniform and vice versa.

6. The analysis of matching results of different impressions of the same finger binds the parameters of the probability of matching minutiae in two fingerprints from different fingers.

7. It is assumed that there exists one and only one (correct) alignment between the template and the input minutiae sets. It is assumed that a reasonable *alignment* has been established between the template and the input.

8.3.1 The model

Given an input fingerprint containing n minutiae, Pankanti, Prabhakar, and Jain (2002) computed the probability that an arbitrary fingerprint (i.e., a template in the database) containing m minutiae will have exactly q corresponding minutiae with the input. The fingerprint minutiae are defined by their location, $[x,y]$ coordinates, and by the angle of the ridge on which they reside, θ. The template and the input minutiae sets **T** and **I**, respectively, were defined as

$$\mathbf{T} = \{\{x_1, y_1, \theta_1\}, \{x_2, y_2, \theta_2\}, \ldots \{x_m, y_m, \theta_m\}\}, \tag{9}$$

$$\mathbf{I} = \{\{x_1', y_1', \theta_1'\}, \{x_2', y_2', \theta_2'\}, \ldots \{x_n', y_n', \theta_n'\}\}. \tag{10}$$

Under this simple model, a minutia i in the input fingerprint is considered as "corresponding" or "matching" to the minutia j in the template, if and only if

$$\sqrt{(x_i' - x_j)^2 + (y_i' - y_j)^2} \le r_0, \quad \text{and} \tag{11}$$

$$min\left(|\theta_i' - \theta_j|, \; 360° - |\theta_i' - \theta_j|\right) \le \theta_0, \tag{12}$$

where r_0 is the tolerance in distance and θ_0 is the tolerance in angle. Both manual and automatic fingerprint matches are based on some tolerance in minutiae location and angle to account for the variations in different impressions of the same finger (see Section 4.3.1). Equation (12) computes the minimum of $|\theta_i' - \theta_j|$ and $360° - |\theta_i' - \theta_j|$ because the angles are mod 360° (the difference between angles of 2° and 358° is only 4°).

Let A be the total area of overlap between the input and the template fingerprints after a reasonable alignment has been achieved (see Figure 8.2). The probabilities that an arbitrary minutia in the input will match an arbitrary minutia in the template, only in terms of location, and only in terms of direction, are given by Equations (13) and (14), respectively. Equation (13) assumes that $[x,y]$ and $[x',y']$ are independent and Equation (14) assumes that θ and θ' are independent.

$$P\left(\sqrt{(x' - x)^2 + (y' - y)^2} \le r_0\right) = \frac{\text{area of tolerance}}{\text{total area of overlap}} = \frac{\pi r_0^2}{A} = \frac{C}{A}, \tag{13}$$

$$P\left(min\left(|\theta' - \theta|, 360 - |\theta' - \theta|\right) \le \theta_0\right) = \frac{\text{angle of tolerance}}{\text{total angle}} = \frac{2\theta_0}{360}. \tag{14}$$

First consider the scenario when only minutiae locations are matched; minutiae angles are introduced later in the formulation. If the template contains m minutiae, the probability that one minutia in the input will correspond to any of the m template minutiae is given by mC/A. Note that this and the subsequent location-based probability estimates are based on the assumption that the minutiae in fingerprints follow a slightly over-dispersed uniform distribution (Stoney, 1988); that is, only one template and one input minutia can occur in a single tolerance area (C). If this assumption is violated, the model becomes brittle and mC/A could actually become greater than one.

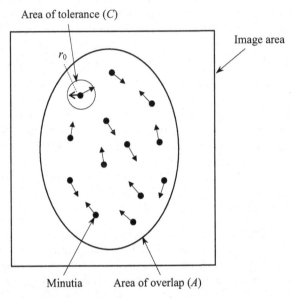

Figure 8.2. The area of the input fingerprint image that overlaps with the template and the input minutiae within the overlap area are shown. In addition, tolerance (in area) for minutia matching for one particular minutia is illustrated.

Now, given two input minutiae, the probability that only the first one corresponds to one of the m template minutiae is the product of the probabilities that the first input minutia has a correspondence (mC/A) and the second minutia does not have a correspondence $(A - mC)/(A - C)$. Thus the probability that exactly one of the two input minutiae matches any of the m template minutiae is $2 \times (mC/A) \times (A - mC)/(A - C)$, as either the first input minutia alone may have a correspondence or the second input minutia alone may have a correspondence. If the input fingerprint has n minutiae, the probability that exactly one input minutia matches one of the m template minutiae is

$$p(A,C,m,n) = \binom{n}{1}\left(\frac{mC}{A}\right)\left(\frac{A-mC}{A-C}\right).$$

(15)

The probability that there are exactly ρ corresponding minutiae, given n input minutiae, m template minutiae, the area of overlap (A), and area of tolerance (C) is:

$$p(\rho \mid A,C,m,n) = \binom{n}{\rho} \underbrace{\left(\frac{mC}{A}\right)\left(\frac{(m-1)C}{A-C}\right)\cdots\left(\frac{(m-\rho-1)C}{A-(\rho-1)C}\right)}_{\rho \text{ terms}} \times$$

$$\underbrace{\left(\frac{A-mC}{A-\rho C}\right)\left(\frac{A-(m-1)C}{A-(\rho+1)C}\right)\cdots\left(\frac{A-(m-(n-\rho+1)C}{A-(n-1)C}\right)}_{n-\rho \text{ terms}}. \tag{16}$$

The first ρ terms in Equation (16) denote the probability of matching ρ minutiae between the template and the input, and remaining $(n-\rho)$ terms express the probability that $(n-\rho)$ minutiae in the input do not match any minutiae in the template. Dividing the numerator and denominator of each term in Equation (16) by C, replacing A/C with M, and assuming that M is an integer (which is a realistic assumption because A is much greater than C), one can write the above equation in a compact form as (Rice, 1995)

$$p(\rho \mid M,m,n) = \frac{\binom{m}{\rho}\binom{M-m}{n-\rho}}{\binom{M}{n}}. \tag{17}$$

Equation (17) defines a hyper-geometric distribution of ρ with parameters m, M, and n (Rice, 1995). To get an intuitive understanding of the probability model for the minutiae correspondence in two fingerprints, imagine that the overlapping area of the template and the input fingerprints is divided into M non-overlapping cells. The shape of the individual cells does not matter, just the number of cells. Now consider a deck of cards containing M distinct cards. Each card represents a cell in the overlapping area. There is one such deck of M cards for the template fingerprint and an identical deck of M cards for the input fingerprint. If m cards are drawn from the first (template) deck without replacement, and n cards are drawn from the second (input) deck without replacement, the probability of matching exactly ρ cards among the cards drawn is given by the hyper-geometric distribution in Equation (17) (Rice, 1995).

The above analysis considers a minutiae correspondence based solely on the minutiae location. Since minutiae patterns are generated by the underlying fingerprints which are smoothly flowing oriented textures, the orientations of neighboring minutiae points are strongly correlated. Further, the orientations of minutiae points are also correlated with their locations depending on the fingerprint type. Thus the configuration space spanned by the minutiae pattern is smaller than that spanned by a pattern of (directed) random points. This typically implies that the probability of finding sufficiently similar prints from two different fingers is higher than that of finding sufficiently similar sets of random (directed) point patterns.

To account for the dependence between two minutiae with orientations θ and θ', let l be such that $P(min(|\theta' - \theta|, 360° - |\theta' - \theta|) \le \theta_0) = l$ in Equation (14). Given n input and m template minutiae, the probability of minutiae falling into *similar* positions can be estimated by

Equation (17). Once p minutiae positions are matched, the probability that q $(q \leq p)$ minutiae among them have similar directions is given by

$$\binom{p}{q}(l)^q(1-l)^{p-q},$$

where l is the probability of two position-matched minutiae having a similar direction and $1 - l$ is the probability of two position-matched minutiae taking different directions. This analysis assumes that the ridge direction information/uncertainty can be completely captured by $P(min(|\theta' - \theta|, 360° - |\theta' - \theta|) \leq \theta_0)$. Therefore, the probability of matching q minutiae in both position as well as direction, given M, m, and n is:

$$p(q \mid M, m, n) = \sum_{\rho=q}^{min(m,n)} \left(\frac{\binom{m}{\rho}\binom{M-m}{n-\rho}}{\binom{M}{n}} \times \binom{\rho}{q}(l)^q(1-l)^{\rho-q} \right). \tag{18}$$

The above formulation has assumed that the minutiae locations are uniformly distributed within the *entire* fingerprint area. Since A is the area of overlap between the template and the input fingerprints, the ridges occupy approximately $A/2$ of the area with the other half occupied by the valleys. It is assumed that the number (or the area) of ridges across all fingerprint types is the same. Because the minutiae can lie only on ridges (i.e., along a curve of length A/w, where w is the ridge period), the value of M in Equation (18) should, therefore, be changed from $M = A/C$ to $M = (A/w)/2r_0$, where $2r_0$ is the length tolerance in minutiae location (see Figure 8.3).

8.3.2 Parameter estimation

The individuality model of Pankanti, Prabhakar, and Jain (2002) has several parameters, namely, r_0, l, w, A, m, n, and q. The value of l further depends on θ_0. These parameters (r_0, θ_0, l, and w) further depend on the fingerprint scanner resolution. To compare the probabilities obtained from the theoretical model with the empirical results, the values of A, m, and n were estimated from two different databases as described in the next section.

Pankanti, Prabhakar, and Jain (2002) estimated the value of r_0 to account for the variations in different impressions of the same finger (intra-class variation). However, given that the spatial tolerance is dependent upon the scale at which the fingerprint images are scanned, r_0 should be estimated for a specific fingerprint scanner resolution. For this, a database (called GT) consisting of 450 mated pairs of fingerprints using a high-quality optical scanner, manufactured by Identicator, at a resolution of 500 dpi was used.

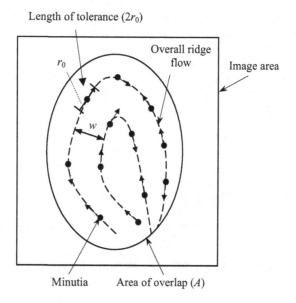

Figure 8.3. The area of the input fingerprint image that overlaps with the template and the input minutiae within the overlap area are shown. In addition, the overall ridge flow is shown and the tolerance (in length) for minutia matching for one particular minutia is illustrated.

The second print in the mated pair in the GT database was acquired at least one week after the first print. The minutiae were manually extracted from the prints by a fingerprint expert. The expert also determined the correspondence for each minutia in the mated print. Using the ground truth minutiae correspondence information, a rigid transformation between the mated pair was determined. The overall rigid transformation between the mated fingerprint pair was determined using a least square approximation of the candidate rigid transformations estimated from each duplex pair of the corresponding minutiae. After aligning a given mated pair of fingerprints using the overall transformation, the spatial difference $(x' - x, y' - y)$ for each corresponding minutiae pair was computed; distances between all minutiae pairs in all mated fingerprint pairs were pooled to obtain an empirical distribution (see Figure 8.4). The smallest value of r_0 is sought for which:

$$P\left(\sqrt{(x' - x)^2 + (y' - y)^2} \le r_0 \right) \ge 0.975,$$

that is, the value of r_0 that accounts for at least 97.5% of variation in the minutiae position of genuine fingerprint matches. Thus r_0 is determined from the distribution shown in Figure 8.4 and is found to be 15 pixels for fingerprint images scanned at 500 dpi resolution under the assumption that the matcher uses a rigid transformation. Note that if the matcher can correctly model the non-linear distortion in fingerprints, the value of r_0 may be smaller (Bazen and Gerez, 2003).

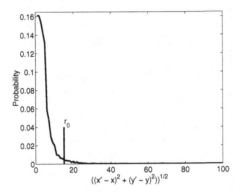

Figure 8.4. Distribution of minutia distance differences for the genuine fingerprint pairs in the GT database.

To estimate the value of l, Pankanti, Prabhakar, and Jain (2002) first estimated the value of θ_0 using the GT database. After aligning a given mated pair of fingerprints using the overall transformation, that value of θ_0 is sought that accounts for 97.5% variation in the minutiae angles in the genuine fingerprint matches; that is, find the value of θ_0 for which $P(min(|\theta' - \theta|, 360° - |\theta' - \theta|) \leq \theta_0) \geq 0.975$. The distribution $P(min(|\theta' - \theta|, 360° - |\theta' - \theta|))$ for the genuine fingerprint matches in the GT database is shown in Figure 8.5a. The smallest value of θ_0 for which $P(min(|\theta' - \theta|, 360° - |\theta' - \theta|) \leq \theta_0) \geq 0.975$ is found to be $\theta_0 = 22.5°$. In the second step, the distribution $P(min(|\theta' - \theta|, 360° - |\theta' - \theta|))$ for the impostor fingerprint matches is determined. Because the GT database does not have correspondences marked by an expert between impostor fingerprint pairs, an automatic fingerprint matcher (Jain et al., 1997) is used to establish correspondences between minutiae in impostor pairs. Thus, the estimation of l depends on the automatic fingerprint matcher used. The distribution $P(min(|\theta' - \theta|, 360° - |\theta' - \theta|))$ estimated by using this matcher on the GT database is shown in Figure 8.5b from which it is determined that $P(min(|\theta' - \theta|, 360° - |\theta' - \theta|) \leq 22.5°) = 0.267$; that is, $l = 0.267$. Note that under the assumption that minutiae directions are uniformly distributed and the directions for the minutiae that match in their location (θ' and θ) are independent, $l = (2 \times 22.5)/360 = 0.125$. If minutiae orientations were considered instead of directions, the estimated value of l would be 0.417 as opposed to a value of $(2 \times 22.5)/180 = 0.25$ determined under the assumption stated above.

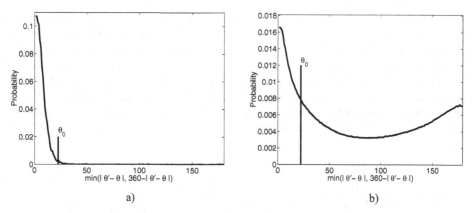

a)   b)

Figure 8.5. Distribution of minutiae angle differences for the a) genuine fingerprint pairs using the ground truth and b) impostor matches using the automatic fingerprint matcher.

Pankanti, Prabhakar, and Jain (2002) used the same value of w as reported by Stoney (1988). Stoney estimated the value of the ridge period as 0.463 mm/ridge from a database of 412 fingerprints. For fingerprint scanners with a resolution of 500 dpi, the ridge period converts to ~9.1 pixels/ridge. Thus $w \sim 9.1$. This value is also in close agreement with the values reported by Cummins, Waits, and McQuitty (1941), Cummins and Midlo (1961) and Kingston (1964).

8.3.3 Experimental evaluation

In order to evaluate their individuality model, Pankanti, Prabhakar, and Jain (2002) used two fingerprint databases (called MSU_DBI and MSU_VERIDICOM). The MSU_DBI database contains fingerprint images of 167 subjects using an optical fingerprint scanner manufactured by Digital Biometrics, Inc. (image size = 508 × 480, resolution = 500 dpi). Four impressions of the right index, right middle, left index, and left middle fingers for each subject are available that were captured over an interval of 6 weeks. The database contains a total of 2,672 (167 × 4 × 4) fingerprint images. The MSU_VERIDICOM database was collected following the same protocol, but using a solid-state capacitive fingerprint scanner manufactured by Veridicom, Inc. (image size = 300 × 300, resolution = 500 dpi).

A large number of impostor matches (over 4,000,000) were generated using the automatic fingerprint matcher of Jain et al. (1997). The mean values of m and n for impostor matches were estimated as 46 for the MSU_DBI database and as 26 for the MSU_VERIDICOM database from the distributions of m and n (Figure 8.6a, b). The average values of A for the MSU_DBI and the MSU_VERIDICOM databases are 67,415 pixels and 28,383 pixels, respectively. Pankanti, Prabhakar, and Jain (2002) estimated the value of the overall effective area A in the following fashion. After the template and the input fingerprints were aligned using the estimated transformation, a bounding box A_i of all the corresponding minutiae in the input fingerprint was computed in a common coordinate system. Similarly, a bounding box A_t of all the corresponding minutiae in the template fingerprint was also computed in the common coordinate system. The intersection A of these two bounding boxes A_i and A_t for each matching was then estimated. The estimates of A for all the matches performed in the database were pooled to obtain a distribution for A (see Figure 8.7a, b). An arithmetic mean of the distribution was used to arrive at an estimate of A.

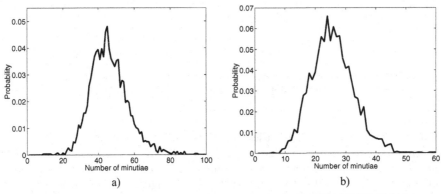

Figure 8.6. Distributions of m and n for a) MSU_DBI database, b) MSU_VERIDICOM database.

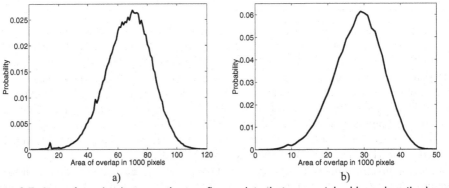

Figure 8.7. Area of overlap between the two fingerprints that are matched based on the bounding boxes of the minutiae features for a) MSU_DBI database, b) MSU_VERIDICOM database.

The probabilities of a random correspondence obtained for the different values of M, m, n, and q are given in Table 8.3. The values shown in Table 8.3 obtained based on the model of Pankanti, Prabhakar, and Jain (2002) can be compared with values obtained from the other models in Table 8.2 for $m = 36$, $n = 36$, and $q = 36$, 12.

M, n, m, q	P(Fingerprint Correspondence)
104, 26, 26, 26	5.27×10^{-40}
104, 26, 26, 12	3.87×10^{-9}
176, 36, 36, 36	5.47×10^{-59}
176, 36, 36, 12	6.10×10^{-8}
248, 46, 46, 46	1.33×10^{-77}
248, 46, 46, 12	5.86×10^{-7}
70, 12, 12, 12	1.22×10^{-20}

Table 8.3. Probabilities of a random correspondence obtained from the individuality model of Pankanti, Prabhakar, and Jain (2002) for different sizes of fingerprint images containing 26, 36, or 46 minutiae. The entry (70, 12, 12, 12) corresponds to the 12-point guideline. The value of M for this entry was computed by estimating typical fingerprint area manifesting 12 minutiae in a 500 dpi optical fingerprint scan.

Typically, a match consisting of 12 minutiae points (the 12-*point guideline*) is considered as sufficient evidence in many courts of law. Assuming that an expert can correctly glean all the minutiae in a latent, a 12-point match with the full-print template (see the first row, last column entry in Table 8.4) is an overwhelming amount of evidence, provided that there is no contradictory minutiae evidence in the overlapping area. The value of A was computed for 500 dpi fingerprint images from the minutiae density of 0.246 minutiae/mm^2 estimated by Kingston (1964) from 100 fingerprints; thus $M = 70$ was used for all the entries in Table 8.4. Because latent prints are typically of very poor quality, minutiae detection and matching errors are frequent. The effect of such errors on the probability of a random correspondence can be severe. For instance, two incorrect minutiae matches increases the probability of a random correspondence from 1.22×10^{-20} (entry $n = 12$, $q = 12$ in Table 8.4) to 1.96×10^{-14} (entry $n = 12$, $q = 10$ in Table 8.4) and ignoring two genuine minutiae present in the input (latent) print increases the probability from 1.22×10^{-20} (entry $n = 12$, $q = 12$ in Table 8.4) to 1.11×10^{-18} (entry $n = 14$, $q = 12$ in Table 8.4). Thus a false minutiae match has significantly more impact than that of missing genuine minutiae in the input latent print.

				q		
		8	9	10	11	12
	12	6.19×10^{-10}	4.88×10^{-12}	1.96×10^{-14}	3.21×10^{-17}	$\mathbf{1.22\times10^{-20}}$
	13	1.58×10^{-9}	1.56×10^{-11}	8.42×10^{-14}	2.08×10^{-16}	1.58×10^{-19}
n	14	3.62×10^{-9}	4.32×10^{-11}	2.92×10^{-13}	9.66×10^{-16}	1.11×10^{-18}
	15	7.63×10^{-9}	1.06×10^{-10}	8.68×10^{-13}	3.60×10^{-15}	5.53×10^{-18}
	16	1.50×10^{-8}	2.40×10^{-10}	2.30×10^{-12}	1.45×10^{-14}	2.21×10^{-17}

Table 8.4. Effects of the fingerprint expert/matcher misjudgments in using the 12-point guideline. The source of error could be in underestimating the number of actual minutiae in the latent print (n) or overestimating the number of matched minutiae (q). The value of m is 12 for all entries in this table. The entry ($n = 12$, $q = 12$) represents the probability of a random correspondence when the 12-point guideline is correctly applied by a fingerprint examiner. Except for the ($n = 12$, $q = 12$) entry, all other entries represent incorrect judgments by the fingerprint expert to arrive at a decision that exactly 12 minutiae in the latent print matched 12 corresponding minutiae in the template print. For instance, the entry ($n = 14$, $q = 8$) in the table represents an estimate of probability of a random correspondence due to two misjudgments by the examiner: the fingerprint examiner detected 12 minutiae in the latent print although there were in fact 14 minutiae in the latent print; that is, the examiner overlooked 2 latent print minutiae; furthermore, although he associated all 12 minutiae he detected in the latent print to the 12 minutiae in the template print, only 8 of those correspondences were indeed genuine correspondences (4 incorrect minutiae match judgments).

Figure 8.8a, b show the distributions of the number of matching minutiae computed from the MSU_DBI and MSU_VERIDICOM databases using the matcher of Jain et al. (1997), respectively. These figures also show the theoretical distributions obtained from the model of Pankanti, Prabhakar, and Jain (2002), described in Section 8.3.1, for the average values of M, m, and n computed from the databases. The empirical distribution is to the right of the theoretical distribution. This is because the theoretical model deviates from the Jain et al.'s (1997) matcher at several places. First, the theoretical model assumes that the "true" alignment between the input and the template is known although the matcher estimates the alignment between the two fingerprints based on the minutiae information alone. For example, if there is only one minutia in the input fingerprint, the matcher will establish an alignment such that this minutia matches with a minutia in the template with a probability of 1. Thus the theoretical probability estimate of (mC/A) for $n = 1$ is a gross underestimate for this matcher. In addition, the matcher seeks that alignment which maximizes the number of minutiae correspondences. Thus it may find an alignment that is wrong but results in a large number of minutiae correspondences. Moreover, the matcher tests a large number of alignment hypotheses and, consequently, the probability of a random correspondence increases significantly according to Equation (5). Second, the theoretical model assumes that two minutiae cannot be closer than the tolerance distance of $2r_0$ both in the input and the template fingerprints. However, the automatic matcher does not enforce this requirement and both the input and the template mi-nutiae sets contain minutiae that are closer than the tolerance. This difference between the theoretical model and the automatic matcher becomes larger in the case of poor quality finger-print images where the matcher detects clusters of spurious minutiae. Finally, as explained in Table 8.4, any spurious minutia detected by the matcher increases the probability of a random correspondence.

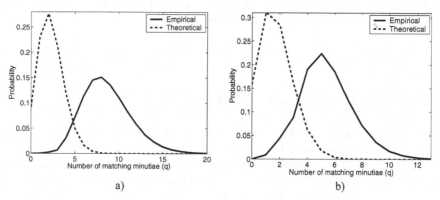

Figure 8.8. Comparison of experimental and theoretical probabilities of random correspon-dence: a) MSU_DBI database, b) MSU_VERIDICOM database.

Table 8.5 shows the empirical probabilities of matching 10 and 15 minutiae in the MSU_VERIDICOM and MSU_DBI databases, respectively. The typical values of m and n were estimated from their distributions by computing the arithmetic means. The probabilities of a random correspondence for these values of m, n, and q are reported in the third column of Table 8.5 (note that Table 8.5 reports the probabilities of matching exactly q minutiae). The probabilities for matching "q or more" minutiae are 3.0×10^{-2} and 3.2×10^{-2} for the MSU_VERIDICOM and MSU_DBI databases, respectively; that is, they are of the same order of magnitude. The probabilities of false match (FMR) obtained on these databases are consistent with those obtained on similar databases by several other automatic fingerprint verification systems reported in the FVC2002 fingerprint verification competition (Maio et al., 2002b). On the other hand, the performance claims by several fingerprint vendors vary over a large range (a false match rate of 10^{-9} to 10^{-3}) due to the different characteristics of the databases they use. The probabilities of a random correspondence from Pankanti, Prabhakar, and Jain's (2002) theoretical model obtained for different values of M, m, n, and q given in Table 8.3 are several orders of magnitude lower than the corresponding empirical probabilities given in Table 8.5.

Database	m, n, q	P(Random Correspondence)
MSU_VERIDICOM	26, 26, 10	1.7×10^{-2}
MSU_DBI	46, 46, 15	1.4×10^{-2}

Table 8.5. Probabilities of a random correspondence obtained from matching impostor finger-prints using an automatic matcher (Jain et al., 1997) for the MSU_VERIDICOM and MSU_DBI databases. The probabilities given in the table are for matching "exactly q" minutiae. The average values for A, m, and n are 28,383, 26, and 26 for the MSU_VERIDICOM database and 67,415, 46, and 46 for the MSU_DBI database, respectively.

8.4 Finite Mixture Minutiae Placement Model

Pankanti, Prabhakar, and Jain (2002) assumed a uniform distribution as the model on minutiae locations and directions to derive the probability of a random correspondence between a pair of fingerprints. The uniform model on fingerprint minutiae has several drawbacks. It is well known that fingerprint minutiae form clusters (see, for example, Stoney (1986)). Further, minu-tiae locations in different regions of the fingerprint domain are observed to be associated with different region-specific minutiae directions. Also, minutiae that are spatially close tend to have similar direction values to each other. Empirical observations such as these need to be taken into account when eliciting reliable statistical models on fingerprint features. For the reasons mentioned above, Pankanti, Prabhakar, and Jain (2002)'s model underestimates the probability of a random correspondence. To alleviate the problem with the uniform distribu-tion, a family of finite mixture models was developed to represent minutiae clusters in Zhu, Dass, and Jain (2007).

8.4.1 The model

In this section we will use a different notation than the one used in the previous sections. The notation used here is consistent with Zhu, Dass, and Jain (2007) so that the readers can refer to the original work for details.

Let X denote a generic random minutia location and D denote its corresponding direction. Let $S \subseteq \mathbf{R}^2$ denote the subset of the plane representing the fingerprint domain. Then, the set of all possible configurations for X is the subset $s \equiv \{(x, y) \in S\}$ of coordinate points in S. The mi-nutiae direction D takes values in $[0, 2\pi]$. Denoting the total number of minutiae in a finger-print image by k, the authors developed a joint distribution model for the k pairs of minutiae features $(X,D): \{(X_j, D_j), j=1,2,\ldots k\}$ that accounts for:

1. Clustering tendencies (nonuniformity) of minutiae.
2. The dependence between minutiae location and direction (X_j and D_j) in different regions of S.

The joint distribution model is based on a mixture consisting of G components or clusters. Let c_j be the cluster label of the j-th minutia $\left(X_j, D_j\right)$, $c_j \in \{1, 2, ... G\}, j = 1, 2, ... k$. The labels c_j are independently distributed according to a single multinomial distribution with G classes and class probabilities $\tau_1, \tau_2, , \tau_G$ such that $\tau_j \geq 0$ and $\sum_{j=1}^{G} \tau_j = 1$. Given label $c_j = g$, the minutiae locations X_j is distributed according to the density

$$f_g^X\left(s \mid \mu_g, \Sigma_g\right) = \phi_2\left(s \mid \mu_g, \Sigma_g\right), \tag{19}$$

where ϕ_2 is the bivariate Gaussian density with mean μ_g and covariance matrix Σ_g. Equation (19) states that the minutiae locations arising from the g-th cluster follow a 2-D Gaussian with mean μ_g and covariance matrix Σ_g. The Von-Mises distribution (Mardia, 1972) is a typical distribution used to model angular random variables, such as minutiae directions. The distribution of j-th minutiae direction, D_j, belonging to the g-th cluster follows the density

$$f_g^D\left(\theta \mid v_g, \kappa_g, p_g\right) = p_g \cdot v(\theta) \cdot I\{0 \leq \theta < \pi\} + \left(1 - p_g\right) \cdot v(\theta - \pi) \cdot I\{\pi \leq \theta < 2\pi\}, \tag{20}$$

where $I\{A\}$ is the indicator function of the set A (i.e., $I(A) = 1$ if A is true, and 0, otherwise), p_g is a real number between 0 and 1, and $v(\theta)$ is the Von-Mises distribution given by

$$v(\theta) \equiv \frac{2}{I_0(\kappa_g)} exp\{\kappa_g \, cos \, 2(\theta - v_g)\}, \tag{21}$$

with $I_0(\kappa_g)$ defined as

$$I_0(\kappa_g) = \int_0^{2\pi} exp\{\kappa_g \, cos \, 2(\theta - v_g)\} \cdot d\theta . \tag{22}$$

In (21) and (22), v_g and κ_g represent the mean angle and the precision (inverse of the variance) of the Von-Mises distribution, respectively. The density f_g^D in (20) can be interpreted in the following way: the ridge flow orientation O is assumed to follow the Von-Mises distribution (21) with mean v_g and precision κ_g. Subsequently, minutiae arising from the g-th component have the direction that is either O or $O + \pi$ with probabilities p_g and $1 - p_g$, respectively.

Combining the distributions of the minutiae location (X) and the direction (D), it follows that each (X, D) is distributed according to the mixture density

$$f(s, \theta \mid \Theta_G) = \sum_{g=1}^{G} \tau_g f_g^X\left(s \mid \mu_g, \Sigma_g\right) \cdot f_g^D\left(\theta \mid v_g, \kappa_g, p_g\right), \tag{23}$$

where $f_g^X(\ )$ and $f_g^D(\ )$ are defined as in (19) and (20), respectively. In (23), Θ_G denotes all of the unknown parameters in the mixture model which include the total number of mixture components G, the mixture probabilities τ_g, $g = 1,2,\ldots G$, the component mean and covariance matrices of f_g^X's given by $\mu_G \equiv \{\mu_1 , \mu_2 ,\ldots \mu_G\}$, and $\{\Sigma_1, \Sigma_2,\ldots \Sigma_G\}$, the component mean angles and precisions of f_g^D's given by $v_G \equiv \{v_1 , v_2 ,\ldots v_G\}$, and $\{\kappa_1, \kappa_2,\ldots \kappa_G\}$, and the mixing probabilities $p_g \equiv \{p_1, p_2, \ldots p_G\}$. The model in (23) allows for (i) different clustering tendencies in the minutiae locations and directions via G different clusters, and (ii) incorporates dependence between minutiae location and direction since if X_j is known to come from the g-th component, then it follows that the direction D_j also comes from the same mixture component.

The mixture density given in (23) is defined on the entire plane $\mathbf{R}^2$ and is not restricted to the fingerprint domain S. This can be corrected by defining the mixture model on the fingerprint area $A \subset S$ as

$$f_A(s,\theta \mid \Theta_G) = \frac{f(s,\theta \mid \Theta_G)}{\int_{s \in A} \int_{\theta=0}^{2\pi} f(s,\theta \mid \Theta_G) \cdot d\theta \cdot ds} . \tag{24}$$

If most of the fingerprint area A encompasses the entire rectangular sensing area S (i.e., $A \approx S$), then

$$f_A(s,\theta \mid \Theta_G) = f(s,\theta \mid \Theta_G), \tag{25}$$

since the denominator in (24)

$$\int_{s \in A} \int_{\theta=0}^{2\pi} f(s,\theta \mid \Theta_G) \cdot d\theta \cdot ds \approx 1 .$$

8.4.2 Model fitting

Zhu, Dass, and Jain (2007) developed a model fitting technique, based on the EM algorithm, to estimate the parameters for a given fingerprint and demonstrated a good fit between the model and the observations.

Let us now consider the computation of the Probability of a Random Correspondence (PRC) between two given fingerprints Q and T that do not come from the same finger. Let m be the number of minutiae in Q, n be the number of minutiae in T, and w be the number of matching minutiae between the two (the matching is based on the same criteria as given in Section 8.3, see Equations (11) and (12)). The authors assume that Q and T minutiae are distributed independently according to the mixture densities (24):

$$f_Q(X^Q, D^Q) = f(X^Q, D^Q \mid \Theta_G^Q), \tag{26}$$

and

$$f_T(X^T, D^T) = f(X^T, D^T \mid \Theta_G^T), \tag{27}$$

respectively. The probability of a random correspondence with exactly w minutiae matches, given that there are m and n minutiae in Q and T, respectively, is given by:

$$PRC(w; Q,T) = \frac{e^{-\lambda(Q,T)}\lambda(Q,T)^w}{w!}, \tag{28}$$

for large m and n. Equation (28) corresponds to the Poisson probability mass function with mean $\lambda(Q,T)$ given by

$$\lambda(Q,T) = m \cdot n \cdot p(Q,T), \tag{29}$$

where

$$p(Q,T) = P\left(\left|X^Q - X^T\right|_s \le r_0 \ and \ \left|D^Q - D^T\right|_a \le d_0\right), \tag{30}$$

denotes the probability of a match when (X^Q, D^Q) and (X^T, D^T) are random minutiae from (26) and (27), respectively. The parameters r_0 and d_0 are the matching tolerance of minutiae directions and distances, the value of which are the same as in Section 8.3; $|\ |_s$ and $|\ |_a$ denote the location distance and the angular distance as defined by Equations (11) and (12), respectively. The mean parameter $\lambda(Q,T)$ can be interpreted as the expected number of matches from the total $m{\times}n$ possible pairings between m minutiae in Q and n minutiae in T with the probability of each match being $p(Q,T)$.

To compute an "average" PRC using this model, one needs to fit a separate mixture model to each fingerprint from a target population. This is an important difference from the previous work described in Sections 8.3 in that Zhu, Dass, and Jain (2007) fit mixture models to each finger whereas the previous studies assumed a common distribution for all fingerprints. Assuming a common minutiae distribution for all fingerprint impressions has a drawback, namely, that the true distribution of minutiae may not be modeled well. For example, it is well known that the five major fingerprint classes in the Henry system of classification (i.e., right loop, left loop, whorl, arch, and tented arch) have different class-specific minutiae distributions and the proportion of fingerprints in the Henry classes is highly unbalanced (see Section 5.1). Thus, using one common minutiae distribution may smooth out important clusters in the different fingerprint classes, whereas by fitting a separate mixture model to each finger ensures that the composition of a target population is correctly represented.

Instead of fitting a mixture model to each single fingerprint impression, the authors fuse multiple impressions of each finger by performing a consolidation of minutiae points. Each impression of fingerprint contains only a certain (partial) area of the finger; the consolidation process creates a mosaic of the minutiae that effectively represents a larger area of the finger than any individual impression. Further, it leads to a more reliable fit of the mixture model and the assumption of large m and n required for computing the individuality estimates is satisfied. Finally, since the consolidation process involves averaging the location and direction of the same minutiae obtained from the multiple impressions, it helps smooth out some of the nonlinear distortion that can affect the estimate of fingerprint individuality.

In order to compute the average PRC over a given fingerprint database, Zhu, Dass, and Jain (2007) proceed as follows:

- Fit the mixture model of Equation (24) to each consolidated fingerprint.
- Derive the mean parameter λ (Equation (29)) for each pair of consolidated fingerprints Q and T coming from different fingers (i.e., impostor pair), and use the Poisson approximation (28).
- Compute the average probability of a random correspondence as the average of the PRCs over all the impostor pairs.

The average PRC depends on the choice of bounding boxes that determine a minutiae match. Larger bounding boxes yield higher spurious matches and thereby increase the probability of a random correspondence. Better matching techniques that reduce the number of spurious matches will decrease the magnitude of the probabilities of a random correspondence.

8.4.3 Experimental evaluation

Zhu, Dass, and Jain (2007) compared their model with Pankanti, Prabhakar, and Jain (2002) model, on three different databases using the same values of parameters (e.g., size of bounding boxes, etc). The fingerprint individuality estimates using the mixture models are a few orders of magnitude higher compared to the Pankanti, Prabhakar, and Jain (2002) model. The reason for this is that when minutiae from the query and template have similar clustering tendencies, a larger number of random matches are observed compared to the predictions by Pankanti, Prabhakar, and Jain (2002) model. Table 8.6 compares the average PRC obtained by the uniform model, finite mixture model and empirical evaluation for the same values of m, n, area of overlap, and w.

Database	m, n, w	a. Empirical		b. Zhu, Dass, and Jain (2007)		c. Pankanti, Prabhakar, and Jain (2002)	
		Mean no. of matches	PRC	Mean λ	Average PRC	Mean λ	Average PRC
NIST 4	52, 52, 12	7.1	3.9×10^{-3}	3.1	4.4×10^{-3}	1.2	4.3×10^{-8}
FVC2002 DB1	51, 51, 12	8.0	2.9×10^{-2}	4.9	1.1×10^{-2}	2.4	4.1×10^{-6}
FVC2002 DB2	63, 63, 12	8.6	6.5×10^{-2}	5.9	1.1×10^{-2}	2.5	4.3×10^{-6}

Table 8.6. A comparison between fingerprint individuality estimates using (a) an empirical test based on a given automatic matcher; (b) mixture model of Zhu, Dass, and Jain (2007) and, (c) uniform model of Pankanti, Prabhakar, and Jain (2002).

8.5 Other Recent Approaches

A few other techniques have been proposed for estimation of fingerprint individuality. Ratha, Connell, and Bolle (2001a) present a simple individuality model in the context of assessing the information content in fingerprints. Chen and Moon (2006, 2007, 2008) extend the Pankanti, Prabhakar, and Jain (2002) model. They assume that the minutiae locations follow complete spatial randomness and the minutiae directions follow a certain specific distribution. Tan and Bhanu (2003b) compute the probability of a random correspondence by including ridge counts in addition to minutiae location and direction and Fang, Srihari, and Srinivasan (2008) further include other properties of the ridge structure. Neumann et al. (2006, 2007) model considers minutiae locations, directions, type, and relative spatial relationships.

8.6 Summary

Estimating fingerprint individuality essentially involves determining the discriminatory information in fingerprint images to distinguish different individuals. The empirical and theoretical methods of estimating individuality serve complementary goals. Empirical observations lead us to characterize the constraints on the discriminatory information across different fingers as well as the invariant information among the different impressions of the same finger; the theoretical modeling/generalization of these constraints permits prediction of the bounds on the performance and facilitates development of constructive methods for an independent empirical validation. Historically, there has been a disconnection in the performance evaluation of practical fingerprint systems and theoretical performance predictions. Furthermore, results of the data-dependent empirical performance evaluations themselves have varied quite dramatically.

Although the minutiae-based individuality estimates based on the models of Pankanti, Prabhakar, and Jain (2002) and Zhu, Dass, and Jain (2007) are lower than the previous estimates, they indicate that the likelihood of an adversary guessing someone's fingerprint pattern (e.g., requiring matching 20 or more minutiae from a total of 36) is significantly lower than a hacker being able to guess a six-character alphanumeric case-sensitive (most probably weak) password by social engineering techniques (most common passwords are based on users' birthday, spouse's name, etc. that can be easily guessed) or by brute force methods (the probability of guessing such a password in a single attempt is $(1 / (26 + 26 + 10))^6 = 1.76 \times 10^{-11}$). Obviously, more stringent conditions on matching will provide better cryptographic strength at the risk of increasing the false non-match error rate.

Although there is a huge amount of "inherent" discriminatory information available in minutiae representation, the observed matching performance of the state-of-the art automatic matching systems is often significantly lower than the theoretical performance because of the noise in sensing fingerprints, errors in locating minutiae, and brittleness of the matching algorithms. In addition, present understanding of fingerprint feature (minutiae) detection and invariance as implemented in automatic fingerprint matching systems is too simplistic to accomplish significantly better accuracies. If a typical full dab fingerprint contains approximately 50 minutiae, it provides an overwhelming amount of information for manual recognition. However, an automatic system that makes its decision based on 12 minutiae correspondences is utilizing only limited information. Given this liberal operating point of an automatic matcher, it may be desirable to explore additional complementary representations of fingerprints for automatic matching as well as more accurate fingerprint comparison techniques (see Chapters 4 and 5).

9
Securing Fingerprint Systems

9.1 Introduction

Consider that a facility is secured with a lock. Usually, the sturdier the lock, the higher is the perceived level of security. However, even if a facility is equipped with the strongest possible lock, it is still possible to break into the facility. For example, instead of trying to break the lock, a burglar may break the door, make a big hole in the wall, smash windows, or rob the owner at gunpoint to gain entry. Thus a stronger lock does not necessarily mean better security. In fact, irrespective of the installed security system, no system is absolutely secure or foolproof. Given the right opportunity and plenty of time and resources, any security system can be broken.

This is not to say that a system designer should not try his best to guard against all possible security threats. What it implies is that the type of security needed depends upon the requirements of the application. A *threat model* for an application can be defined based on what needs to be protected and from whom. Threat models are almost always tied to the expected attacks (e.g., resources available, intent, and expertise of the attacker). Unless a threat model is clearly defined for a system, it is very difficult to decide if the proposed security solution is adequate. Depending upon the threat model of an application, an intruder may invest varying degree of time and resources in launching an attack. For example, in a remote and unattended application that requires recognition from a remote server, a hacker may have the opportunity and plenty of time to make a number of attacks or even physically violate the integrity of a client system.

Anderson (1994) illustrates the vulnerabilities of general cryptosystems and authentication systems. He studied the technical aspects of fraud involved in using ATMs and found that most of the failures were due to poor design and system administration. Schneier (1998b) listed a number of system vulnerabilities due to errors in system design, implementation, and installation. He commented that "strong cryptography is very powerful when it is done right, but it is not a panacea. Focusing on cryptographic algorithms while ignoring other aspects of security is like defending your house not by building a fence around it, but by putting an

D. Maltoni et al., *Handbook of Fingerprint Recognition*, 371–416.
© Springer-Verlag London Limited 2009

immense stake in the ground and hoping that your adversary runs right into it." This is true for any security systems, including biometrics and fingerprints.

In this chapter, we will focus our discussion only on those security issues and solutions that are specific and peculiar to fingerprint recognition systems. Ideally, a holistic view of system security is essential but due to the vast differences in application contexts and threat models, we will take a step by step approach in our discussion. That is, we will discuss many important security issues, specific vulnerabilities in fingerprint systems, and techniques that have been developed to address them. It is expected that one or more of these technological components will be useful in preparing a holistic security solution for a practical application with a given threat model.

We refer the readers to the literature which presents vulnerabilities in fingerprint systems from different viewpoints. Ratha, Connell, and Bolle (1999, 2001b, 2003), and Bolle, Connell, and Ratha (2002), looked at the architectural diagram of a biometric system and identified a number of *points of attack* (see Figure 9.1). Cukic and Bartlow (2005) adopted Schneier's (1999b) *attack tree* model for biometric systems and identified 20 potential attack points with 22 vulnerability possibilities. This model integrates threats and therefore it depends on the threat model of an application. Roberts (2007) presented a simpler and more practical model to analyze the risk of attacks on biometric systems based on three main dimensions of system attacks: (i) threat agents, (ii) threat vectors, and (iii) system vulnerabilities. Jain, Ross, and Pankanti (2006) and Jain, Nandakumar, and Nagar (2008) used a compact *fishbone* model to summarize the biometric system vulnerabilities (see Figure 9.2). Fish-bone model captures the relationship between causes and effects of failures. They listed four causes, namely, intrinsic, non-secure infrastructure, administrative abuse, and biometric overtness and two effects, namely, denial of service and intrusion. Other useful discussions on system threats, vulnerabilities, and countermeasures have been presented in Jain and Uludag (2004), Dimitriadis and Polemi (2004), Buhan and Hartel (2005), Jain, Ross, and Uludag (2005) and Adler (2005).

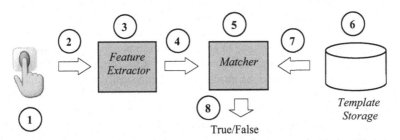

Figure 9.1. Architecture of a fingerprint recognition system that illustrates the eight possible attack points identified by Ratha, Connell, and Bolle (1999, 2001b, 2003).

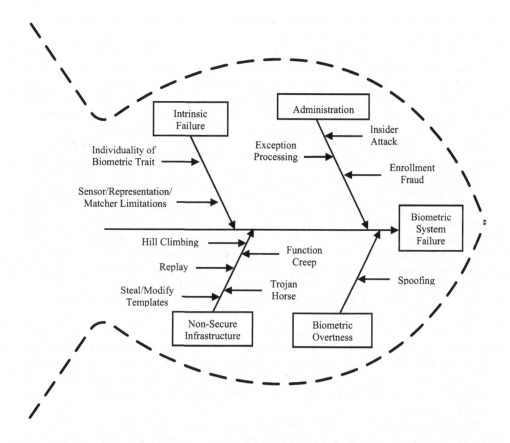

Figure 9.2. The fish-bone model of fingerprint system illustrates the cause-effect relationships of system failures as identified by Jain, Ross, and Pankanti (2006) and Jain, Nandakumar, and Nagar (2008).

In this chapter, we will adopt a slightly different viewpoint in looking at the types of fingerprint system failures, how the failures can be triggered, and discuss some of the techniques that have been developed as countermeasures. We expect that multiple techniques will be used in building a practical system depending on the application's threat model.

Let us first revisit some of the advantages of fingerprint-based authentication so that its benefit (and necessity) is not lost on the readers as we go through the vulnerabilities specific to the fingerprint or any other biometric systems. Traditionally, surrogate representations of identity, such as passwords and tokens, have been used for person recognition. Most users set their passwords based on words or numbers that they can easily remember, such as names and birthdays of family members, favorite movie or music star, and dictionary words. This makes the passwords easy to crack by guessing or a simple brute force dictionary attack. Although it is advisable to keep different passwords for different applications, most people use the same password across multiple applications. If a single password is compromised, it may open many doors. Long and random passwords are more secure but harder to remember, which prompts some users to write them down in accessible locations (e.g., under the keyboard). Strong (difficult to remember) passwords also result in more system help desk calls for forgotten passwords. Cryptographic techniques such as encryption can provide very long passwords that are not required to be remembered but that are in turn protected by simple passwords, thus defeating their purpose. Furthermore, a hacker needs to break the password of only one employee to gain access to a company's Intranet and thus a single weak password compromises the overall security of the system. Therefore, the security of the entire system is only as good as the weakest password (weakest link). Finally, when a password is shared with a colleague, there is no way for the system to know who the actual user is. Similarly, there are many problems with possession-based authentication. For example, keys and tokens can be shared, duplicated, lost, or stolen. However, fingerprints are significantly more difficult to copy, share, and distribute than passwords and tokens. Fingerprints cannot be lost or forgotten and fingerprint-based recognition requires the person to be present at the point of authentication. It is difficult to forge fingerprints and unlikely for a user to repudiate having used the system. All the users of a system will have *relatively* same security level and one fingerprint is not much easier to break than the others (even though some poor quality fingerprints may be slightly more vulnerable). The main advantage of a fingerprint recognition system is the convenience it provides the users while maintaining high accuracy. No other security technology besides biometrics provides such a strong link between a physical person and an action taken by the person (e.g., a logon).

The above-mentioned properties make fingerprints a very attractive choice for person recognition. An application using a fingerprint system would certainly address many of the severe shortcomings of traditional password and token-based systems but may have some of its own vulnerabilities. As a result, a layered approach is often recommended, commonly known as *multifactor authentication*. Still, each security layer should address its own vulnerabilities such that the combined system is even stronger. We first list the ways in which a fingerprint system can fail. Then we discuss how these failures could be triggered by a hacker, followed by a discussion of techniques that have been developed as countermeasures.

9.2 Types of Failures in Fingerprint Systems

There are primarily two types of failures in a fingerprint system:

- *Denial of service (DoS)*: in a denial of service failure, legitimate (authorized) users are "locked out" of the services, goods, or access. In some mission critical applications, such a lock out may be devastating. In other applications, it can cause very poor user experience. The DoS could be complete (everyone, every time) or partial. It could be caused by high intrinsic error rate of fingerprint systems (e.g., failure to acquire or false rejects) or caused by an active adversary (e.g., by sabotaging the power supply or overloading the system with bogus matching or communication requests, or damaging a fingerprint sensor, etc.). One of the reasons why hackers may lunch DoS attack is to force the use of a fallback system (say a password system), which may then be easier for the hacker to intrude (rather than the fingerprint system).

- *Intrusion*: intrusion refers to an adversary gaining illegitimate access to the system. After gaining access, the hacker may either modify some data (e.g., issue a withdrawal of all of the money in a bank account) or simply access privileged data (e.g., customers' private information). One issue peculiar to biometrics and fingerprints is related to "revocation" (Schneier, 1999a). In traditional password/cryptographic systems, if a certain password or key is compromised, it can be put on a "revocation list" to prevent its future use and a new one is issued to the user. If a fingerprint is compromised, although it can be put on a revocation list, a new one cannot be issued (a different finger may still be used but unlike passwords and keys, we have only a limited number of fingers). As a result, if a hacker intrudes a user's account once, he may be able to intrude again and again. Further, since the user may have enrolled the same finger in many different systems, a hacker who successfully intrudes that user's account in one system (say the weakest one) may then be able to intrude her account in a different system. Finally, a successful intrusion may be exploited for *function creep*. For example, by having access to a user's fingerprint data gained through a successful intrusion, a hacker may use it to link the user into another different database (say an anonymous database) thus compromising the user's privacy. For example, an account in an anonymous online social networking website may be linked with a bank account.

There is often a trade-off between preventing denial of service attack and preventing intrusion, i.e., there is a trade-off between security and usability of every countermeasure. Here, we will focus only on intrusion and assume that the trade-off with DoS is always evaluated at each step and appropriate balance between security and usability is maintained.

For a successful intrusion, a hacker needs to first obtain fingerprint data and then inject it into the authentication system. Acquisition and insertion of non-biometric data is beyond the scope of our discussion. We will discuss the different ways by which a hacker can obtain fingerprint data and then inject it into the system. Techniques to prevent the hacker from obtaining and injecting fingerprint data into the system will also be presented. We expect that a number of these techniques will be used simultaneously in an application.

9.3 Methods of Obtaining Fingerprint Data and Countermeasures

Usable fingerprint data is that fingerprint data that a hacker can use to lunch an injection attack. For example, if fingerprint data is encrypted and the hacker cannot decrypt it, it is not usable. Therefore, the hacker would try to get either unencrypted fingerprint data or try to obtain means to decrypt the encrypted data. In some cases, it is not possible to prevent the hacker from obtaining certain type of fingerprint data. In such cases, the burden of security is moved to techniques that prevent the injection of the data into the system. In some cases, there may be tradeoffs between preventing hacker's obtaining of fingerprint data and preventing hacker's insertion of fingerprint data. In such cases, it is more important to prevent injection of fingerprint data into the system because biometric data in general is not private (biometric data is *personal* data but not *private* data). For example, face images and videos of individuals are widely published in all types of media.

Obtaining fingerprint data of a specific user is generally more difficult and expensive for the hacker but also more rewarding. In fact, it is much easier for a hacker to successfully inject the fingerprint data into a system, even a well protected one, if he has fingerprint data of a specific subject. On the contrary, it is much more difficult for the hacker to succeed in injecting fingerprint data that is not of a specific user (i.e., generic fingerprint data) as the hacker will need to make a relatively large number of injection attempts (e.g., to cause a false fingerprint match). However, once the hacker succeeds in an injection of generic fingerprint data, the hacker gains the knowledge that the generic fingerprint data is sufficiently similar to one of the enrollment template. This enables the hacker to turn the generic fingerprint data into fingerprint data of a specific subject and he will now have an easier time intruding against this subject in the future.

9.3.1 Obtaining fingerprint data of a specific user

There are many ways in which a hacker can obtain fingerprint data of a specific user. For example, the hacker can:

- Lift a latent fingerprint left on physical surfaces that the user has touched.
- Obtain the fingerprint with the cooperation of the user.
- Coerce the user to provide her fingerprint data.
- Guess the fingerprint data by *hill climbing*.
- Gain direct access to fingerprint data of the user by breaking another system (or a different part of the system).

We describe these cases below.

Lifting a latent fingerprint

To lift a latent fingerprint of a specific user, the hacker needs to have the knowledge of the whereabouts of that user. The hacker follows the subject, obtains access to surfaces/objects that she has touched, lifts a latent fingerprint from it, and scans it into a fingerprint image. Latent fingerprint impressions can be colored with a dye (e.g., graphite powder) and then "lifted" with adhesive tape or glue. Latent fingerprints are, in most cases, of poor quality because they are incomplete, wrapped around irregular surfaces, or partially smudged by the finger slipping. To lift a latent fingerprint from difficult surfaces, much expertise, and unconventional equipment is needed (see Section 2.2) and even then most of the lifted fingerprints are too poor in quality to be matched successfully by an automatic system. There is also no economy of scale that the hacker can exploit since a single latent fingerprint cannot be used to launch attacks against multiple users. Additionally, the threat of a hacker obtaining such fingerprint data is fairly low in a remote network logon application. So obtaining latent fingerprints is complicated, expensive and of limited use. While there is no specific countermeasure to stop a hacker from lifting a latent fingerprint, the threat is low in most applications but remains a concern in some high security applications.

Obtaining fingerprint data with collusion or coercion

If the hacker has a friend who is an authorized user, he may simply request the authorized user to provide her fingerprint data. The authorized user may cooperate to help the hacker in obtaining a valid fingerprint image. This is in fact the most popular method featured in the media to showcase the ease of breaking a fingerprint system. In reality, such a scenario poses little threat in most applications. After all, instead of cooperating with the hacker to clone his fingerprint data, the authorized user may simply grant the hacker access to his account. A legitimate user may also be coerced by the hacker to hand over his fingerprint data. Again, there is really no specific countermeasure to prevent this attack.

Guessing the fingerprint data by hill climbing

If the hacker can inject a synthetically generated fingerprint image (or feature set) into the fingerprint system and if the matcher returns a matching score, then the hacker can iteratively optimize the process of generating synthetic fingerprint data to increase his chance of intrusion. Soutar (2002) described such a hill climbing strategy in the context of a fingerprint recognition system. Hill climbing can be used to optimize the synthetic generation of fingerprint image or feature set. In this case, while the generated fingerprint data is not identical to the enrollment template, it is sufficiently similar to fool the matcher into yielding a decision of match. The hill climbing software iteratively modifies subsequent synthetically generated fingerprint data such that the matching score is higher than in the previous iteration (i.e., the fingerprint image or feature set being synthesized moves closer to the template).

A countermeasure to hill climbing attack was proposed by Soutar (2002). He proposed increasing the granularity of the fingerprint matching score returned by the fingerprint matcher. He argued that if the matching scores are granular (e.g., reported in steps of 10 for a matching score in the range [0,100]), then the hill climbing method would require a sufficiently large number of attempts before observing a change in score and thus the total number of attempts required for the matching score to exceed the system threshold would become prohibitively large. In the limiting case, the system may not output matching scores at all, only the match/non-match decisions. In this case, the number of required attempts is determined by the FMR.

Gaining access to fingerprint data by breaking another authentication system

A hacker may collude or coerce the system administrator to obtain the enrollment templates of one or all of the users, together with their identifiers. A hacker may also intercept any of the communication channels in a fingerprint system and eavesdrop on the fingerprint data. For example, the hacker may obtain fingerprint images as they are transmitted from the fingerprint scanner to the feature extractor, obtain feature sets as they travel from the feature extractor to the matcher or obtain templates as they travel from system storage to the matcher.

There are a number of countermeasures to secure the communication channels and the stored templates to prevent the hacker from eavesdropping on them. These countermeasures are typically implemented using standard cryptographic techniques such as encryption, digital signatures, time-stamp, challenge-response, etc. (Schneier, 1996). The most straightforward method to protect the templates is to save them in encrypted form using standard (and proven) cryptographic techniques (e.g., Advance Encryption Standard [AES] algorithm). Different encryption keys can be used in different applications such that templates from one application cannot be interchanged with templates of another application. If an encryption key is ever compromised, templates can be re-encrypted with a new cryptographic key. However, there is a critical issue with this approach; unlike password comparison, conventional fingerprint matching cannot be performed in the encrypted domain, and the templates need to be decrypted before the matching stage. This is because standard cryptographic algorithms transform tiny difference in the input space into huge differences in the output space, and since multiple impressions of the same finger can be very different from each other, the encryption will make them impossible to match in the encrypted domain. The necessity to decrypt the template introduces a security weakness, since a hacker can access the memory where the template is decrypted and/or try to steal the decryption key. If the system administrator colludes with the hacker (or is forced by the hacker), the hacker can get access to the cryptographic keys and subsequently gain access to usable fingerprint data. Once a key is compromised and templates are "stolen", the templates cannot be revoked and reissued.

One way to protect the enrollment templates is to store them on tamper-resistant secure hardware (Section 9.6) and do not permit them to leave the secure hardware boundary. There is a lot of interest in these methods and in their practical implementations such as match-on-card and system-on-a-chip systems (Grother et al., 2007). One of the advantages of these techniques is that the template storage is distributed across the system users. For example, a user is always in the possession of his enrollment template residing in the tamper-resistant hardware storage of a smart card. Avoiding a central storage also prevents a hacker to exploit economies of scale. However, storing templates on secure hardware has some drawbacks (e.g., accuracy drop, extra cost, etc.) and is very difficult in applications requiring central management or operating in identification mode. For example, some applications allow users to access their accounts from multiple access points without re-enrollment and this requires centralized template management. Therefore, there is a need for technologies to protect fingerprint templates even if the decryption key is compromised. Neither should the hacker be able to link identities across different applications if he gains access to template storage. A class of techniques, called *template protection techniques*, is being developed to provide such countermeasures. We discuss these techniques in Section 9.7.

9.3.2 Obtaining generic fingerprint data

Generic fingerprint data (fingerprint feature sets, templates, and images) can be synthetically generated, extracted from available fingerprint database or collected with a fingerprint scanner. Let us consider minutiae features; a minutiae feature set consist of a list of triplets $\{x,y,\theta\}$ where x, y are the minutia coordinates and θ is the minutia direction (see Section 4.3.1). A hacker can easily generate millions of such synthetic minutiae feature sets. Stoney and Thornton (1987) have reported that minutiae are distributed more or less uniformly in a fingerprint. So the minutiae can be generated in an oval window based on this model. It is helpful to the hacker not only to know the type of features used but also their representation, quantization, spatial reference, ordering, and so on (Hill, 2001). Synthetic fingerprint images can also be generated quite efficiently. See Chapter 6 for the description of a synthetic fingerprint image generation approach.

Several fingerprint databases are available in the public domain (e.g., FVC databases) or can be purchased (e.g., NIST databases), so instead of synthetically generating the fingerprint data, the hacker can try to use real fingerprint data. The hacker may even conduct a fingerprint collection by using live-scan fingerprint scanners. In some cases, the hacker could pay anonymous volunteers to capture their fingerprint images. An offline feature extraction algorithm can be used by the hacker to extract fingerprint features sets from the collected fingerprint images. The hacker can also exploit any prior knowledge to build a more effective "dictionary". For example, the probability of false accepts is higher for poor quality fingerprints, so a hacker may concentrate on collecting poor quality fingerprints, say from construction workers who typically have worn-out ridges.

There really is no way to prevent a hacker from synthetically generating or obtaining generic fingerprint data. In order to inject fingerprint data into the system a hacker can use the generic fingerprint data. He can use the same generic data to launch injection attacks against all the users in a fingerprint system. If the hacker succeeds in an intrusion, he gains access to the information about the user whose account was broken. The hacker can then use this information, together with the "similar enough" fingerprint data that resulted in the successful intrusion, to repeatedly intrude, with a single injection attempt, this account and all the other accounts of this user that are protected by his fingerprints. Instead of attacking all the users in a fingerprint system, the hacker can also attempt to attack a specific subject in a fingerprint verification system. In this case, if a hacker has only generic fingerprint data, he will need an extremely large number of intrusion attempts to succeed. Suppose a fingerprint matcher is operating at a false match rate (FMR) of 0.001%, then it will take, on an average, 100,000 injections with generic fingerprint data to succeed (see Ratha, Connell, and Bolle (2001a) and Chapter 8 for estimation of theoretical bounds).

9.4 Methods of Injecting Fingerprint Data and Countermeasures

The fingerprint data obtained by the hacker may be a fingerprint feature set, fingerprint template or fingerprint image. If a hacker has access to a fingerprint image, he can convert it to fingerprint feature set or template by using a feature extractor (which does not have to be the same one used by the fingerprint system he intends to intrude; it is sufficient that it uses the same representation). It has been argued that if a system uses fingerprint feature sets and templates in proprietary formats, the system is protected from injection of fingerprint data as the hacker does not know its format. This is in general not true – security by obscurity is never a lasting solution as the secrecy of a proprietary template coding (or interface) could be easily broken by an attacker with adequate resources. In fact, it is becoming customary for fingerprint recognition systems to adopt standard minutiae formats such as ISO/IEC 19794–2 (2005), ANSI/INCITS 378 (2004), and ANSI/NIST-ITL 1 (2007) (see also McCabe, 2004) as well as standard APIs (Soutar, 2004). Given this, it is reasonable to expect that a fingerprint image can be converted to feature set or template irrespective of the coding scheme or format used by the target system. Conversion between feature set and template is also straightforward. On the other hand, when it comes to converting a fingerprint feature set or template back to fingerprint image, some have argued that is it not possible. While it is true that an exact reversal is not possible because some information is surely lost during feature extraction, a "close enough" replication that will fool an automatic fingerprint recognition system, is possible, as shown by Hill (2001), Ross, Shah, and Jain (2005, 2007), Cappelli et al. (2007a, b) and Franco and Maltoni (2007). See Figure 9.3 for examples of fingerprint images reconstructed only from fingerprint minutiae data. Such "close enough" fingerprint images can be used for injecting into the fingerprint system with very high success rate (Yanushkevich et al., 2005). For example, Cappelli et al. (2007a) reconstruction approach, starting from ISO/IEC 19794–2 (2005) minutiae based templates, obtained an average percentage of successful attacks of 81%

against nine fingerprint systems, even when these systems were tuned to operate at a high security level.

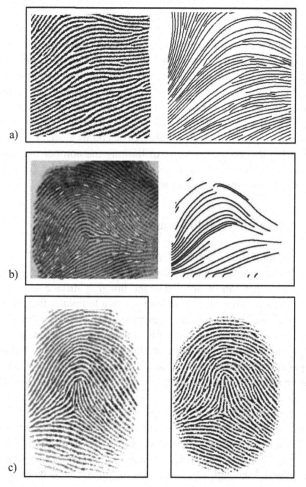

Figure 9.3. Three examples of fingerprint image reversal: the images shown on the right were reversed from the minutiae of the corresponding fingerprint images on the left: a) Hill (2001) method; although the two images do not visually look the same, they are similar enough for an automatic fingerprint recognition system to result in a match decision; b) Ross, Shah, and Jain (2005, 2007) method; c) Cappelli et al. (2007) method produces images that are visually quite realistic; even if these realistic reversals can easily fool an automatic fingerprint recognition system, they cannot fool a human expert. © IEEE. Images courtesy of C. J. Hill.

In case the fingerprint recognition system uses non-minutiae-based representation, the enrollment template (and feature sets) may actually contain the whole fingerprint image, perhaps in compressed form, as specified by the standard finger image data format ISO/IEC 19794-4 (2005). Further, standard finger pattern spectral data formats such ISO/IEC 19794-3 (2006) are specified to contain block-wise wavelet coefficients derived from the fingerprint image and again it is fairly straightforward to reverse a fingerprint image from them.

One of the general countermeasures to prevent injection of fingerprint data against a specific user account is to "lock" the system after a small number of non-match decisions, say three, have occurred within a short period of time. This could help in the case where the hacker is using generic fingerprint data as it is expected that the hacker would need a large number of attempts of injection before success. The hacker may resort to injecting the same generic fingerprint data against a large number of accounts instead of injecting repeatedly against a single user but this countermeasure of limiting the number of attempts still provides some level of protection. We discuss various ways of injecting the fingerprint data into the system and respective countermeasures below.

9.4.1 Injecting a fake finger at the scanner

Injecting fingerprint data at the scanner refers essentially to what is known as "fake finger" attack. An intruder may use a fingerprint image to create a *fake finger* (also known as *dummy finger* or *gummy finger*) that can be applied at the imaging surface of a live-scan fingerprint scanner. In case the hacker intercepted a feature set or a template, these can be first reversed into a "similar enough" fingerprint image as described above and then be used to create a fake finger. The easiest way to create a fake finger is to print the fingerprint image onto a transparency paper or other special paper depending on the fingerprint scanner technology. For example, metallic foil-plated laser printer paper that is electrically conductive may be best suited for solid-state capacitive scanners. A more complicated but more successful method is to create a fake finger that is three dimensional instead of two dimensional. A number of different material types such as silicone, gelatin, moldable plastic, dental material, bubble-gum, Play-Doh, wax, clay, glue and superglue have been proposed to create such a three-dimensional mold (see Figure 9.4). Putte and Keuning (2000) and Matsumoto et al. (2002) documented several methods of creating such molds. Fake fingers made as thin membranes (e.g., made out of silicone or any other material that imitates properties of human skin) worn by the hacker on his own real finger may be most successful in intrusion.

The most natural countermeasure to prevent fake finger injection is to use liveness detection methods. We discuss these methods in Section 9.5. While some of these technologies appear to be quite effective, no proven solution to liveness detection has yet been demonstrated (and verified by third party organizations). Hence in high security applications, fake finger attack remains a concern. If the user authentication is in attended mode (e.g., a border crossing application), the human supervisor can visually inspect the finger surface and detect the presence of an artificial sheet. Otherwise, a multi-biometric system that combines different modalities such as fingerprint and face or a multifactor system that combines different factors such as fingerprint and password raises the bar of security as well as provides sufficient protection against fake biometric attacks.

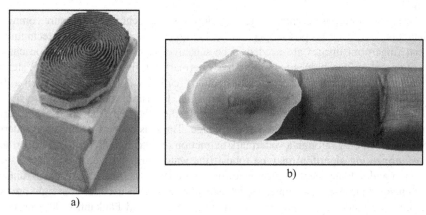

Figure 9.4. Fake finger examples: a) a rubber stamp is made from a fingerprint image; b) a wafer-thin plastic sheet containing a three-dimensional replication of a fingerprint.

It is important to note that in most applications, injection of fake finger is not the most cost effective method of intrusion for a hacker, especially if the hacker has access only to generic fingerprint data. This is because the hacker needs to physically present the fake finger to the scanner, a process that needs to be repeated for every verification attempt. Hackers would rather prefer methods that are fully automated (i.e., computer based), fast, and do not expose their identity.

9.4.2 Injecting fingerprint in a communication channel or in the template storage

Fingerprint images can be injected in the communication channel from the fingerprint scanner to the feature extraction; feature sets can be injected in the channel between the feature extractor and matcher, and templates can be injected in the channel between system storage and matcher. Instead of injecting fingerprint data obtained externally, the hacker could: (i) modify the fingerprint data in the channel itself or (ii) "replay" fingerprint data that he previously obtained by eavesdropping the channel. In general, these kinds of attacks can be prevented by using standard cryptographic techniques (Schneier, 1996).

A hacker may also inject fingerprint data of his choice (for example, his own) into the template storage. Again, injection into the template storage can be prevented using the standard cryptographic techniques (Schneier, 1996). Finally, a hacker may even collude or coerce the system administrator to enroll him as an authorized user; for this case there is no countermeasure except through legislation (e.g., ensuring that the corrupt system administrator will be prosecuted).

Besides general purpose cryptographic techniques, some techniques to secure communication channels have been proposed specifically for fingerprint images. These techniques assume that fingerprint images are needed to be sent over unsecure communication channels. One of the proposed techniques is to digitally watermark the fingerprint images. Watermarking is a technique that hides a secret digital pattern (called a digital watermark) in a digital image. A digital watermark may be visible or invisible. In visible watermarking, a visible pattern or image is embedded in the original image; on the other hand, an invisible watermark does not change the visual appearance of the image. The existence of an invisible watermark can be determined only through a watermark extraction or detection algorithm. Furthermore, a digital watermarking algorithm may be robust (the watermark can withstand attacks such as compression and enhancement of an image) or fragile (the watermark is "broken" under the slightest change to the image). Typically, robust watermarking is used for copyright protection and fragile watermarking is used for data integrity. Yeung and Pankanti (2000) proposed a fragile invisible digital watermarking of fingerprint images that does not affect its recognition accuracy. The fingerprint images acquired by the scanner are watermarked by the scanner itself and any tampering of the image during transmission can be detected by the server. Gunsel, Uludag, and Tekalp (2002) introduced a robust invisible watermarking of fingerprints where the watermark can be verified even if the image is cropped. Ahmed (2007) proposed a composite signature-based digital watermarking technique for fingerprint verification and Zebbiche, Khelifi, and Bouridane (2007) suggested a method to detect watermarks in fingerprint images. Jain and Uludag (2002) and Jain and Uludag (2003) argued that when the fingerprint feature set is transmitted to the matcher over an unsecure link, the feature set should be hidden in a host (i.e., cover) image whose only purpose is to carry the feature set. Some pixels of the host image are modified depending on a secret key and the scheme is robust to cropping of the fingerprint image because of redundancy property. Jain, Uludag, and Hsu (2002) proposed that, in a multi-biometric system, the secret key that is hidden in the fingerprint image could be an image of the user's face. Similarly, Khan, Xie, and Zhang (2007) hide fingerprint data in an audio signal.

Ratha, Connell, and Bolle (2001a, b) introduced a challenge-response mechanism based on an image-based nonce scheme. The nonce sent by the application contains a set of random pixel locations and the scanner returns the values of the pixel intensities at these locations together with the fingerprint image as response. This ensures that the image was acquired by the scanner only after receiving the challenge. Ratha, Connell, and Bolle (2001a, b) also proposed a data hiding method, where the fingerprint scanner returns the nonce sent by the application hidden in a compressed fingerprint image (by Wavelet Scalar Quantization [WSQ]). This technique involves slightly altering certain Discrete Wavelet Transform (DWT) coefficients at the locations specified by the nonce; the approach ensures that there is no degradation in the quality of the fingerprint image when it is uncompressed. In their later work, Ratha et al. (2004) analyzed the security holes in their data hiding approach and proposed some enhancements.

Most of the above approaches are based on the secrecy/obscurity of the algorithms; security based on obscurity is weak and often unsustainable. While standard cryptographic techniques have been proven to be secure in an information-theoretic sense, the security of watermarking, obfuscation, and other similar techniques that have been specifically designed for fingerprint images have not been shown to possess proven security. So it is debatable whether they provide any benefits over standard cryptographic techniques in preventing injection of fingerprint data into the communication channel.

9.4.3 Replacing a system module with malicious software

Another potential attack is where the hacker emulates one of the modules in the fingerprint system. The hacker can then replace the original module(s) in the fingerprint system with this emulator and inject fingerprint data of his choice into the system (see Figure 9.5). For example, the hacker can write a synthetic fingerprint image generation algorithm and package it with other code to make it resemble a fingerprint scanner. This software can then inject desired fingerprint images (synthetically generated or taken from a dictionary of fingerprint images) into the feature extractor. The system may not be able to distinguish whether the fingerprint image is coming from a fingerprint scanner or from the hacker's malicious software (also known as malware). The hacker can similarly write malware to emulate and replace feature extraction module, matching module or system storage module.

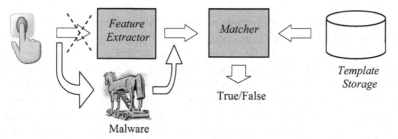

Figure 9.5. A malware emulates the feature extraction module such that neither the fingerprint scanner not the matcher module knows that they are interacting with an emulator. The malware sends fingerprint data of its choice to the matcher instead of the fingerprint data collected by the scanner. In a similar fashion, any of the modules in the fingerprint system could be replaced by malware.

The malware can be delivered through computer viruses and computer worms, which could carry the malicious fingerprint module emulator software as a payload. Phishing attacks on the Internet can also trick users in downloading and running malware. Attackers have been able to exploit the vulnerabilities in the operating system or web browser to intrude into the computers remotely.

A good strategy is to secure the modules such that they are part of a *closed system*. A *closed system* in this context means that the modules trust each other but no one else. We discuss technique to build a closed system in Section 9.6.

9.5 Liveness Detection Techniques

It is customary to use the term *liveness detection* to denote not only methods capable of discriminating live fingers from non-live fingers (e.g., the finger of a cadaver), but also techniques that discriminate real human fingers (live or non-live) from fake fingers. A pattern classifier that distinguishes a dead finger from a live finger can exploit one or more of the vitality signs of a finger such as the blood flow, pulse, blood pressure, or sweating process. A pattern classifier can distinguish between the human epidermis and other synthetic material by measuring thermal, electric, optical or other physical properties of the material presented to the fingerprint scanner.

9.5.1 Finger skin properties and finger vitality signs

Thermal properties

At normal room temperatures (~20°C), the temperature of the epidermis is typically a few degrees higher than the ambient room temperature. A fake finger made of synthetic material is expected to be cooler. In fact, a fake finger made of silicone rubber is about 2 degrees centigrade cooler than a live finger. This temperature difference could be used as a feature to distinguish between live human epidermis and a fake finger. Measurements of the thermal conductivity or thermal capacity could be employed as well. However, due to the temperature variations in operating environments (e.g., air-conditioning or a person holding a cold soda can), and the possibility of artificially heating the fake finger, thermal measurements are not very reliable.

Electrical properties

The electrical conductivity of human tissue differs from conductivity of many other synthetic materials such as silicone rubber and gelatin. The conductivity of the material presented to the fingerprint scanner can be measured to differentiate a live finger from a fake finger. However, the conductivity of live fingers varies substantially depending on weather conditions such as humidity and temperature. If a fake finger is dipped in water, for example, its conductivity may be indistinguishable from that of a live finger. Relative Dielectric Constant (RDC) is also influenced by the humidity of the finger and thus will not be very effective in distinguishing a live finger from a fake. Moreover, simply applying alcohol on a fake finger changes its RDC significantly and thus can make it indistinguishable from live fingers.

Biomedical properties

These methods for finger vitality determination are based on measurements of pulse and blood pressure in the fingers. However, the pulse rate of the finger varies significantly from one person to another. In addition, pulse rate also varies depending on physical activity and emotional state of the person at the time of acquisition. Furthermore, finger pressure on the sensor surface can change the pulse value quite dramatically and a single pulse measurement may take up to 5 s. Finally, if a wafer-thin silicone rubber is glued to a real finger, the heartbeat of the underlying finger will result in the detection of a pulse. Blood pressure and electrocardiogram sensors also have similar limitations.

Odor

Skin odor is different from odor of synthetic materials such as gelatin, latex, silicone, etc. Odor can be detected by using a "chemical sensor" such as those based on metal-oxide technology. Such sensors detect the odorants by detecting the tiny amounts of molecules that are evaporated from materials that have odor. An odor scanner (i.e., an electronic nose) contains an array of such odor sensors. Baldisserra et al. (2006) and Franco and Maltoni (2007) built a liveness detection method based on the use of such an electronic nose. The authors reported an equal error rate of ~8% on fake fingers created using silicone, gelatin, and latex.

Optical properties

FTIR-based optical fingerprint sensors typically have the inherent capability to reject any two-dimensional reproductions of a fingerprint. Human skin has different optical properties than many other synthetic materials and optical fingerprint sensors may incorporate mechanisms to measure the optical properties of the material presented to the sensor. The optical properties of interest include absorption, reflection, scattering and refraction properties under different lighting conditions (such as wavelength, polarization, coherence). However, it is not difficult to find a material (e.g. gelatin) whose optical properties are close to those of a live finger. A thin layer of material, like silicone, on top of a real finger allows reproducing most of the optical properties of the real finger. Color that is similar to human tissue can be added to the synthetic material such as Play-Doh.

One of the most successful methods of liveness detection based on optical properties is reported in Nixon et al. (2004), Nixon and Rowe (2005) and Rowe, Nixon, and Butler (2007). Their approach bears resemblance to pulse oximetry and spectroscopy. Instead of capturing a single property of the surface of a finger, the authors use a multispectral optical sensor to sense optical properties under different wavelengths, illumination orientation, and polarizations of light. The captured data contains information about both the surface properties as well as sub-surface properties of finger since components of blood (oxygenated and deoxygenated hemoglobin) absorb different wavelengths of light. Based on this information, the authors built a liveness detection method that is able to distinguish between live fingers and most types of fake fingers. For the wafer-thin artificial fingerprint glued over a real live finger, the surface and subsurface fingerprints produce a texture of ridge interferences, which is detected by their algorithm. The authors report ~99% accuracy using a database of fake fingers made from latex, silicone, Play-Doh, clay, rubber, glue, resin, gelatin, and tape. Another interesting optic-based method is proposed by Tai et al. (2006) and Tai, Kurita, and Fujieda (2006), who argued that a live finger changes color as it is pressed onto a surface while the color change is not observed in fake fingers. As the blood in a live finger drains out as it is pressed onto a surface, it results in a color change. The authors detect this difference in the change of color between live and fake fingers by measuring scattering properties of (quasi-white) light as the finger is pressed onto the fingerprint scanner surface. The authors report 100% accuracy in a small test demonstrating the usefulness of their approach. To further improve the reliability, the authors later used dual light sources (530 and 630 nm LEDs). A very similar idea was independently proposed by Yau et al. (2007). Finally, Reddy et al. (2007) proposed pulse oxiometry-based method using light at two different wavelengths. The percentage of oxygen in the saturated blood, along with heart pulse rate, determines the liveness of the finger.

Sub-surface properties

Since sub-surface characteristics are not directly visible and are not present in latent fingerprints, they cannot be obtained by a hacker (except in the case the finger owner colludes with the hacker). So liveness detection techniques based on these characteristics are inherently strong against fake finger attacks.

We already discussed some techniques that exploit sub-surface properties in the above Section. However, the best know noninvasive technique to image sub-surface details is based on ultrasonic waves. As discussed in Section 2.3.3, ultrasonic scanners can image the pattern underneath the epidermis based on the reflection/absorption of acoustic waves. Certain solid-state fingerprint sensors can also detect the pattern of ridges and valleys underneath the epidermis; for example electric field sensors (see Section 2.3.2) can image such patterns based on the property that the layer under the epidermis has a higher electric conductivity than the epidermis. Cheng and Larin (2006) and Larin and Cheng (2008) built a liveness detection system based on Optical Coherence Tomography (OCT). The OCT technology is capable of noninvasive in-depth imaging of human tissue with high resolution. The author's preliminary experiments demonstrate that this method is highly accurate in distinguishing fake materials from live tissue. However, the drawback of their prototype is that OCT scanners are still fairly large and expensive.

It is claimed that fingerprint sensors looking beyond the epidermis cannot be fooled by fake fingers (Putte and Keuning (2000); Putte (2001)). However, once it is known which features a sensor is using to detect fake fingers, a multi-layer fake finger could be created to reproduce a real finger. Further independent analysis and testing should be carried out to validate these emerging technologies.

Skin details

One of the most common methods of preventing paper currency counterfeiting is to design the currency with complicated patterns and very fine details. Similarly, if a fingerprint sensor images a finger at a very high resolution, then it may be able to capture certain details (such as the sweat pores) that may be difficult to reproduce with high accuracy in a synthetically made fake finger. By simply checking for the existence of fingerprint sweat pores, it may be possible to reject those replications that do not explicitly duplicate the fingerprint pores in the fake finger as well. Actually, experiments performed by Matsumoto et al. (2002) showed that a coarse reproduction of intra-ridge pores is feasible with gummy fingers and therefore, very high-quality scanners would be needed to capture pore positions and shape. Moon et al. (2005) used surface coarseness-based texture features (extracted through a wavelet analysis of fingerprint image) for detecting fake fingers. Choi et al. (2007b) built liveness classifiers based on frequency shapes and powers of ridge signals that capture properties of pores (including pore distance), residual noise, and first order grayscale statistics such as energy, entropy, median, variance, skew, kurtosis, and coefficients of variance. They reported a correct classification rate of 85%.

Skin distortion

A skin distortion model can be learnt by observing the specific ways in which the finger skin distorts when a finger is pressed on a sensor surface. It is unlikely that fake fingers made of synthetic material fit the natural skin deformation model. In fact, skin is usually more elastic than most materials that are used to create replicas; furthermore, finger skin deforms in a specific way because it is anchored to the underlying derma and the deformation is influenced by the position and shape of the finger bone. Edwards, Torrens, and Bhamra (2006) argue that properties of finger such as elasticity and viscosity can be modeled and used to predict the manner in which the fingertip deforms. Chen, Jain, and Dass (2005) used Thin-Plate Splines (TPS) (see also Section 4.5.2) to estimate the deformation between the enrollment template and the recognition feature set and trained an SVM classifier to distinguish between live fingers and fake fingers made of gelatin. They reported a correct classification rate of 82% on a small dataset. Jia et al. (2007a) measured skin elasticity for liveness detection. They extract two elasticity measures from a fingerprint acquisition sequence: (i) correlation between fingerprint foreground area and average signal intensity; positive correlation is observed for real fingers and no correlation is observed for fake fingers, and (ii) the standard deviation of the fingerprint area extension along x and y axes between successive frames. Based on these features, they designed a liveness detection classifier using linear discriminant analysis (LDA). Zhang et al. (2007a) measure the bending energy of TPS to determine if the template and feature set fingerprints being compared are both from a live finger or not. Antonelli et al. (2006a, b) argue that to produce a relevant (measurable) distortion, the user could apply a firm pressure on the scanner while simultaneously rotating the finger deliberately. Given several frames (at a frame rate of 10–15 frames per second), a feature vector from pairs of successive frames, known as DistortionCode was computed. User specific DistortionCodes can be learnt during enrollment and compared with distortion measured at verification time. A user independent DistorionCode can also be consolidated based on average finger distortion. The authors achieved an equal error rate of ~11% on a database of live fingers from 45 subjects and 40 thin-layer fake fingers made of silicone, gelatin, latex, and wood glue. This method requires the user to perform a specific deliberate task which is hard for most users to learn and replicate. Further, this technique needs a high frame rate that is not available in many commercial fingerprint scanners.

Perspiration

Derakhshani et al. (2003), Schuckers et al. (2004) and Parthasaradhi et al. (2004, 2005) proposed methods based on measurements of the sweating process of a live finger in a video sequence. Live fingers exhibit sweating over a period of time whereas fake fingers do not. In live fingers, the perspiration phenomenon starts at the sweat pores and spreads along the ridge lines. The regions around sweat pores progressively enlarge over time. To observe the sweating process, the finger needs to be kept on the scanner for a few seconds (e.g., 5 s). The authors take one frame (image) at the beginning of the capture and one frame after a few seconds and quantify the sweating process by measuring the changes in pixel intensities along the ridges. Abhyankar and Schuckers (2004, 2006), Schuckers and Abhyankar (2004), Parthasaradhi et al. (2005), Tan and Schuckers, (2006a, b) and Tan and Schuckers (2006) analyzed the ridge signal (using multi-resolution texture analysis and wavelet analysis) extracted along the ridges (using a ridge mask) to detect perspiration phenomenon from a single fingerprint image. A correct classification rate in the range of 84–100% was reported for three different fingerprint scanners. The limitations of perspiration-based methods are caused by varying amounts of moisture content in a finger and different finger pressure on the scanner surface.

Texture-based properties

Tan and Schuckers (2008) analyzed the valleys in fingerprint images instead of the ridges. By training a classifier on the multi-resolution wavelet features extracted from fingerprint valleys, the authors quantify the noise in the fingerprint valleys. Authors were able to achieve 91–100% detection rate between live and fake fingers for three different fingerprint scanners. Because the method is based on a measurement of noise, to achieve a low false rejection rate of live fingers, the scanner needs to be cleaned and finger needs to be wiped before acquisition. Further, the noise characteristic of different scanners is different. Coli, Marcialis, and Roli (2007a, b) propose a method based on power spectrum of fingerprint images. Texture properties are also used in the method proposed by Choi et al. (2007b) described earlier.

9.5.2 Effectiveness of liveness detection techniques

Developments in cryptographic systems have demonstrated that any security solution based on the secrecy of an algorithm (security through obscurity) does not provide satisfactory results over a period of time. This is because the secret needs to be broken only by a single person and once this happens (it eventually always does), the entire solution immediately falls apart (such attempts are often posted on the Internet). Therefore, we should assume that the vitality detection approach being used by a fingerprint scanner is available in the public domain. Based on this knowledge, it is easy to envision the design of a fake finger that will circumvent a specific fingerprint scanner. For example, if it is known that a scanner measures the pulse to check finger vitality, one could design a three-dimensional mold of a finger that has a fingerprint on its outer surface and a pulse generating device inside it. Some characteristics may be easier to simulate (such as thermal or optical property of human skin) than others (such as the sweating process, or the sub-surface features).

Matsumoto et al. (2002) argued that many scanners could be fooled by flashing a light against the fingerprint scanner, or by heating up, cooling down, humidifying, impacting on, or vibrating the scanner outside its environmental tolerances. The feasibility of successfully attacking fingerprint systems with high quality fake fingers was first reported by Putte and Keuning (2000) and Matsumoto et al. (2002a). After these earlier studies several new ideas and technologies on liveness detection have been introduced (as reported in Section 9.5.1). However, no large-scale independent evaluations have been carried out to validate their effectiveness and the resulting trade-off between security and convenience. Note that almost all the solutions to fake finger detection come at the additional cost of increasing scanner hardware price, higher false reject rate (see Antonelli et al. (2006a) for a precise formulation of liveness detection errors), and/or longer fingerprint acquisition time.

9.6 Building a Closed Fingerprint System

To understand the necessity and design of building a closed system, one must consider the different scenarios where modules of a fingerprint system (see Section 1.3) reside at different locations. We discuss two of the most common scenarios:

1. All the modules are located on a single computer (i.e., on the personal computer of an end-user, sometimes known as client). The end-user may protect the fingerprint system by carefully monitoring its security with anti-virus and anti-malware software, so that a remote hacker cannot take control of the local operating system. However, the user still needs to consider the case when the computer becomes physically accessible to the hacker (e.g., a stolen laptop). In a variation of this scenario, all the modules are still located on a single computer even though the computer is shared by many end-users such as employees at a pharmacy (such computers are sometimes known as interactive kiosks). Here too, a hacker (say, a malicious pharmacy employee) can have physical access to the computer (before or after it has been used by an honest employee).

2. In a client-server application, some modules are located on the client side and some modules are located on the server side. The server is usually operated and managed by an entity that does not trust the client side (personal computer of the end-user) as the end-user may be malicious or may collude with a hacker (or be coerced by a hacker).

In both the above scenarios the security can be enforced by moving as many modules as possible on secure (i.e., tamper-resistant) hardware that cannot be accessed by a hacker even if he has physical or remote access to the computer. There are some popular approaches that have lead to commercially viable solutions:

- Move only the storage module (that contains the enrollment templates) and the matching module onto a smart card that can be in the possession of the end-user; this technique is known as *Match-on-Card* (MoC).

- Move all the modules (including feature extraction as well as the acquisition sensor) on the secure hardware platforms. Depending on the hardware platform, different solutions have been proposed.

  - *System-on-Device* (SoD): denotes solutions where feature extraction and matching modules are embedded into the fingerprint scanner hardware board; these solutions are also commercially available under the names MoD (Match-on-Device) or MoB (Match-on-Board).

  - *System-on-Card* or *System-on-a-Chip* (SoC): refers to solutions where all the modules are implemented on a compact platform such as a special smart card or a secure chip. Here, the platform is usually released to the users.

In a secure hardware platform the "critical" processing occurs within a secure environment which is isolated from the operating system of the client system (i.e., the host operating system running on PC, laptop, mobile phone, PDA, etc.). Besides the security advantage (resilience to denial-of-service and intrusion attacks), MoC and SoC solutions also have privacy advantages. In fact, the platform is usually released to the users having full control of their own biometric data.

A secure hardware platform includes a processor (typically an embedded-class processor such as an ARM core), workspace memory (e.g., RAM), code space memory (e.g., ROM/ EEPROM/FLASH), persistent storage (e.g., FLASH) and runs a "light" operating system. See Table 9.1 for a comparison of resources available on typical hardware platforms. It is worth noting the huge difference between the processing powers of a smart card with respect to a modern PC. As a consequence, the complexity of algorithms running on secure hardware platforms need to be substantially reduced, resulting in some performance drop.

	MoC	SoD/SoC	PC
Word-length	8 or 16 bits	32 bits	32 or 64 bits
CPU frequency	24 MHz	200 MHz	3.4 GHz
MIPS[1]	20	200	20,000
Storage	32 KB	1 to 16 MB	200 GB
Floating point support	No	No (usually)	Yes
Memory (RAM)	8 KB	1 to 16 MB	1 GB

Table 9.1. A comparison of typical resources available on different hardware platforms.

9.6.1 Match-on-card techniques

One of the most popular secure hardware platforms for fingerprint verification is the smart card, also known as chip card, or integrated circuit card. A smart card is typically credit card sized or smaller and contains a tamper-proof processor that can usually perform cryptographic functions. Although the smart card storage is very limited, the applications do not envision sharing of smart cards and therefore there is no need to store many templates in them. The on-card fingerprint matcher performs a comparison between the template(s) stored on the card and the feature set sent to it from the host computer (see Figure 9.6).

The advantage of this approach is that the matcher module and the template storage are fully secure. The templates can neither be modified by malicious hackers nor can they be snooped by a hacker. Once the template is transferred to smartcard, there is no need to ever release the templates to the host. Only the matching result of the fingerprint comparison process needs to be released to the host. Finally, cryptographic keys are also stored on the smart

---
[1] Millions of (integer) Instructions Per Second

card and hence the key management is much simplified and secured, further enhancing the system security significantly. Match-on-Card solutions are sometimes claimed to be more secure than System-on-Device solutions because of the stronger isolation of the template. However, it should be noted that even if the enrolled template cannot be obtained by a hacker, a "similar enough" template can be obtained by eavesdropping at the feature extraction module running on the non-secure host of the MoC system. The risk of such an attack should not be underestimated because eavesdropping on the host is not difficult.

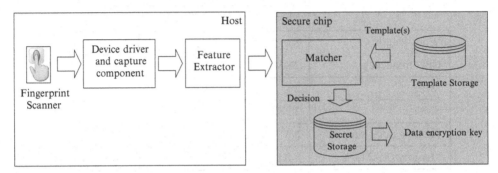

Figure 9.6. Match-on-Card architecture; the enrolled template(s) never leave the confines of the secure hardware platform.

Match-on-Card (MoC) fingerprint comparison algorithms were tested within the recent MINEX II campaign – an Assessment of Match-on-Card technology, organized by NIST (Grother et al., 2007). The results demonstrate that match-on-card algorithms are not as accurate as match-off-card (i.e., match on PC) algorithms; in particular, the best MoC algorithm exhibited a 20–40% drop in FNMR with respect to the same vendor's implementation running on PC (at the same FMR). This is due to the simplification necessary to run them on resource limited hardware (the smart card used in MINEX II mounted a processor/microcontroller running at 8 MHz).

It is indeed quite challenging to develop fingerprint comparison algorithms that can execute under constrained resources of a smart card and still provide acceptable accuracy and execution speed. To overcome the computational complexity of the fingerprint alignment, Reisman, Uludag, and Ross (2005) proposed that minutiae in the stored templates be represented as local triplet structures. The minutiae triplets of the enrollment template are released to the host computer without identifying the relative positioning of the triplets with respect to each other. The host conveys the matching triplets back to the smart card. The smart card then computes the alignment that is sent to the host. The host transforms the verification fingerprint image, computes pre-aligned ridge-based feature map and sends it to the smart card which computes the matching score. Since the template triplets are released to the host (even though weakly obfuscated by withholding the information about their relative positions), this method is not very secure although it has fairly good matching accuracy. For higher security, the fingerprint template information should not be released to the host in any form. Somewhat similar approach is proposed in Barral, Coron, and Naccache (2004). They propose that random minutiae be added into the enrollment template stored on the smartcard and sent to the host for matching. The smartcard stores the information on which minutiae are genuine and which are random but never releases this information. The host is responsible for alignment and matching and conveys the matching minutiae back to the smartcard. The smartcard simply computes a Hamming distance between the genuine minutiae identified by the host and the actual genuine minutiae stored on the smartcard and declares a match if the Hamming distance exceeds a threshold.

Moon et al. (2000) recognized the complexity of alignment establishment but did not wish to off-load the alignment to host. So they pre-align the templates before storing them on the card. They compute the pre-alignment as an average of minutiae locations and minutiae orientations. Such crude pre-alignment is not expected to perform very well in practice. In their later work, Moon, Fong, and Chan (2005) recognize this limitation and use a more robust reference point detection method to pre-align the template. The authors use the point of maximum change of fingerprint orientation or point of discontinuity in the orientation field image as the reference point (see Section 3.5.5).

Ishida, Mimura, and Seta (2001) describe the feasibility of a non-minutiae-based fingerprint matching algorithm for smartcards. They propose that the smartcard store the enrollment fingerprint image together with its core point. The smartcard requests the host to send it a sequence of certain image patches of the verification fingerprint images with respect to the core point. The smartcard then compares these pre-aligned image patches with the corresponding image patches in the enrollment template using correlation.

Pan et al. (2003) realized that alignment is the most memory demanding part of fingerprint comparison but instead of using pre-alignment they perform alignment in an iterative coarse-to-fine fashion. They use an accumulator array to find the alignment; the discretization of the accumulator array is successively refined iteratively as the range becomes smaller.

To avoid global alignment, some authors have proposed minutiae-based local-structure matching techniques, as summarized below.

- Yang and Verbauwhede (2003) propose a fingerprint matching algorithm that has two parts: secure and non-secure. Only the secure part needs to be implemented on the smart card. The non-secure part can be executed on the host. The authors use local minutiae structures that are rotation and translation invariant. Thus, they avoid having to compute a global alignment. Only the secure part of the matching has access to the template and performs the related computation. Remaining computations are performed on the non-secure host.

- Bistarelli, Santini, and Vaccarelli (2005) convert the fingerprint minutiae representation into local minutiae structures, where each structure is translation and rotation invariant. The matching score is computed by aggregating similarities of local structure comparisons. This eliminates global alignment, making the algorithm fast and memory efficient. This algorithm was implemented on a smartcard with 32 KB of EEPROM, 1 KB of RAM, 8-bit CPU running at 7.5 MHz clock frequency and communication capability at 9,600 bits/s. Their match-on-card algorithm takes 1–8 s for most of the genuine matches.

- Govan and Buggy (2007) also propose a very similar minutiae matching algorithm that uses alignment-free local structures.

9.6.2 System-on-device and system-on-a-chip techniques

In the MoC systems described above, even though the template is protected, the fingerprint scanner is attached to a host system, whose security may be weak and untrustworthy. The feature extraction is also performed on the host and thus continues to be susceptible to intrusion and denial-of-service attacks. These vulnerabilities can be addressed by moving the remaining modules, that is, feature extractor and possibly even the fingerprint scanner to a secure hardware platform. When the target hardware platform is the fingerprint scanner, the solution is referred to as System-on-Device (SoD); when the target is a special smart card or a secure chip, the architecture is called System-on-Card or System-on-a-Chip (SoC). As a result, no fingerprint data travels outside the secure space (see Figure 9.7).

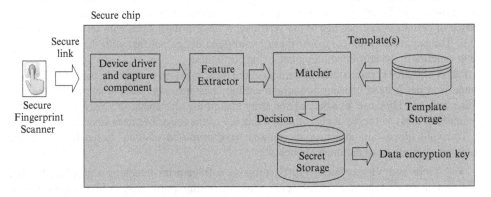

Figure 9.7. In System-on-a-chip architecture, all the processing is done within the confines of a secure chip. Even if the scanner is physically separated from the chip, the communication channel can be protected by embedding the cryptographic keys into both the hardware (the scanner and the chip).

Hence the only remaining potential threat is a fake finger attack on the scanner. The resulting system is expensive because feature extractor requires more powerful processor as well as more workspace and codespace memory than fingerprint matcher. Similar to MoC, the accuracies of SoD or SoC can be lower than PC algorithms; this was demonstrated in FVC campaigns where performance drop was reported for algorithms competing in the resource limited "light" category (Cappelli et al., 2006).

Yang, Moon, and Chan (2004) describe a 32-bit fixed point feature extraction and matching algorithm suitable for resource constrained devices such as a PDA. Yang, Sakiyama, and Verbauwhede (2006) implement a complete fingerprint verification system including the feature extraction and matching on a 50 MHz embedded platform with an execution time of 4 s. They optimize both the algorithm as well as its implementation in order to reduce the computation and memory requirements.

Many authors have proposed efficient implementations to reduce the computation complexity of well known fingerprint feature extraction and matching algorithms. For example, Yeung et al. (2005) optimized all the algorithms used in a fingerprint recognition system for implementation on Intel PXA255 processor, which is typically used in high end PDAs. Su et al. (2005) optimized their fingerprint algorithm for an ARM processor, which is extensively used in mobile phones. Chen, Moon, and Fong (2004) proposed fixed-point arithmetic and other computation optimizations for Gabor-filters based fingerprint enhancements. Xie et al. (2005) proposed using a DSP processor to efficiently compute orientation field in fingerprint images. Lee et al. (2005b) introduced a real-time image selection algorithm for fingerprint recognition on mobile devices with non-contact embedded video camera. Nakajima et al. (2006) designed a phase-only correlation-based fingerprint recognition algorithm for SoC architecture. Wang et al. (2007) investigated the feasibility of implementing a hierarchical correlation-based feature extraction and matching algorithms on mobile devices. They tested their algorithms on a smart phone emulator. Pan et al. (2006) implemented a ridge-line following minutiae extraction algorithm for a special hardware. The proposed system can operate on 32-bit 50 MHz ARM processor.

9.6.3 Mutual and distributed trust techniques

In a client–server application, since the client cannot be trusted, the modules in the client can be protected by taking the client operating system completely out of the security equation. All the modules will now need to reside in secure hardware. The server is considered a trusted secure hardware because it is usually located in a physically secure server room as well as kept up-to-date with the latest anti-virus and anti-malware software. Similarly, fingerprint scanners are also trusted secure hardware since they are issued (and managed) by a central authority. To complete a closed system, a two-way trust must be established between the fingerprint scanner and the server. Then a scanner can trust that it is sending the fingerprint image to a trusted server and the server can trust that the fingerprint it is receiving is coming from a trusted scanner. An architecture where all the modules (feature extraction, matching, and system storage) reside on the server, with the only outside module being the scanner hardware (which is trusted through establishment of mutual trust), is a closed system. To establish mutual trust, standard cryptographic techniques can be used but this means that the scanner needs to have cryptographic capabilities; in this case, the untrusted client acts only as a medium that passes the encrypted fingerprint image from the scanner to the server. Maio and Maltoni (1999) argue that if the client does not trust the server, the two sides can use a third-party "certifier" that can be trusted by both parties to establish mutual trust. They illustrate this through an electronic commerce system where the buyer and the seller do not trust each other. So they propose that the fingerprint matching be performed by a trusted third party which also manages the fingerprint template storage. If the seller can be trusted, it can perform the fingerprint matching and store the templates on its server. Protocols and analysis for trust establishment are also presented in Lee, Ryu, and Yoo (2002), Ku, Chang, and Chiang (2005) and Scheirer and Boult (2008).

Establishing trust between fingerprint scanner on the client side and the server is actually quite difficult in practice. This is primarily due to issues related to cryptographic key management. Although the standard cryptographic algorithms are strong and fairly well established, they require some secret cryptographic keys to be managed. Often the keys need to be exchanged securely to establish the mutual trust. If any of the keys is compromised, then the key management process is required to move the compromised key on a revocation list. Thus prior to each transaction involving a cryptographic key, the revocation list must be checked. Such key management issues (and the cost associated with it) make this approach difficult in practice. Further, not all fingerprint scanners may have cryptographic capabilities. And finally, the end-user may feel uncomfortable in entrusting the corporate system administrator with his fingerprint template. An alternative solution is to use MoC or SoC approach as described above with the added feature of central management being provided by the corporate server (e.g., maintaining a revocation list). Such central management offers another advantage, which we call *roaming*. By roaming, we mean that the same end-user, say, a corporate employee, uses several different access points (e.g., a desktop, a laptop, a PDA, etc.) and would like to use fingerprint scanners embedded in these multiple access point devices without having to re-enroll on each one of them separately. Thus, MoC or SoC combined with central management tools would offer a good balance of security and manageability in a client–server application.

9.7 Template Protection Techniques

In this section, we will use the term *protected template* and *unprotected template* to denote an enrollment template subject to specific protection techniques or in its native form, respectively. The template protection techniques are aimed at providing the following properties:

1. *Non-reversibility*: it should be computationally infeasible to obtain the unprotected fingerprint template from the protected fingerprint template. One of the consequences of this requirement is that the fingerprint matching needs to be performed in the transformed space of the protected template, which may be very difficult to achieve with high accuracy.

2. *Accuracy*: accuracy of fingerprint recognition when using protected templates should be preserved (or degrade smoothly). This is because if the accuracy of fingerprint recognition degrades substantially, it will constitute the weakest link in the security equation. For example, instead of reversing the enrollment template, the hacker may try a "dictionary of fingerprints" attack to cause a false accept. Thus, it is important that the protection technique does not substantially degrade the matching accuracy.

3. *Diversity*: it should not be possible to match protected templates from different applications. Furthermore, it should be possible to produce a very large number of protected templates (to be used in different applications) from the same unprotected fingerprint template.

It should be possible to put an enrollment template on a "revocation list" and issue a new template to replace the compromised one. This property, known as *revocability*, is a direct result of the diversity property in that a new template can be generated from the same finger to replace the old one only if the technique offers the diversity property. Diversity not only secures the protected templates from function creep but also provides a method of recovering from a prior successful intrusion. After an intrusion, new protected templates can be generated from the same finger of a user for future use with the old compromised protected template being placed in the revocation list. Templates with such a property are usually referred to as *cancelable* or *private* or *renewable* templates.

Note that all the above properties are required to be satisfied simultaneously in order to effectively protect the template. For example, a hacker must not be able to use multiple protected templates of the same finger to reverse the protected template. Designing methods to provide all of the above mentioned properties to the protected templates is a very challenging task due to the large intra-class variations in multiple impressions of the same finger (see Section 4.1). This is currently an area of substantial research. Jain, Nandakumar, and Nagar (2008) reviewed the available template protection methods and categorized them into two major categories (see Figure 9.8 and Table 9.2):

1. *Feature transformation*: in these approaches, the unprotected enrollment template is transformed into a protected template with the help of a transformation function. The transformation function may have different characteristics and use certain parameters (including the use of a key or password as a parameter). During verification, the verification feature set is also transformed in the same fashion (using the same transformation and its parameters) as the enrollment template and the fingerprint comparison occurs in the transformed space. Depending on the characteristics of the transforma-

tion function, the approaches can be further divided into two categories: (i) *non-invertible transforms* and (ii) *salting*. The non-invertible transforms typically apply a one-way function (e.g., a hash function) to the unprotected template such that it is computationally hard to revert the protected template even if any of the parameters of the transforms are known or revealed. Salting transforms make use of a password such that the protected template is not invertible without the knowledge of the password. However, if both the password and the protected template are available, the unprotected template (or at least a close approximation of it) can be obtained (Jain, Nandakumar, and Nagar, 2008). Note that salting approaches are two-factor authentication approaches by definition.

2. *Biometric cryptosystem*: biometric cryptosystems (Uludag et al., 2004), also see Soutar et al. (1998a, b), were developed to either generate a cryptographic key from the fingerprint or securing a cryptographic key using a fingerprint. In these approaches, some public information known as *helper data* is stored and used to set up protected transmission. Typically, the helper data consists of a key bounded with a template and some additional information. The helper data is not required to be secret, that is, it is not expected to reveal any significant information about the fingerprint template (non-reversibility), nor is it expected to assist in cross-linking (diversity). Further, it is not expected to reveal the cryptographic key. The fingerprint comparison is implicit, that is, if the correct key is retrieved, the fingerprint comparison is assumed to have resulted in a match decision and if the correct key is not retrieved, the comparison is assumed to have resulted in a non-match decision. Error correction techniques are often used to provide tolerance in order to compensate for intra-class variations in fingerprints. Biometric cryptosystems can be further divided into two categories: (i) *key-generation* and (ii) *key-binding* depending on how the helper data is formed (Uludag et al., 2004). If the helper data is derived from the unprotected enrollment template and the cryptographic key is generated from the helper data and the verification feature set, the methods are known as *key-generation biometric cryptosystems*. If the helper data is obtained by binding an independent external key (independent of the enrollment template) with the template, the method is referred to as *key-binding biometric cryptosystems* (Jain, Nandakumar, and Nagar, 2008). Fingerprint comparison in the key-binding methods involves recovery of the key from the helper data using the verification feature set.

The above classification (see Table 9.2) is not exclusive. When a method for template protection draws upon more than one of the four basic approaches described above, it is called a *hybrid approach* (Jain, Nandakumar, and Nagar, 2008).

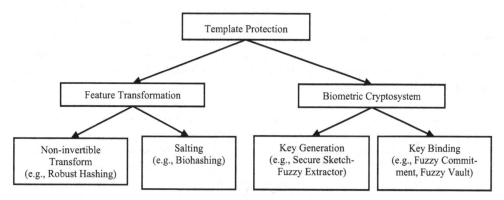

Figure 9.8. Categorization of template protection schemes (Jain, Nandakumar, and Nagar, 2008).

Approach	What imparts security to the template?	What entities are stored?	How is intra-class variations handled?
Salting	Secrecy of key K	*Public domain*: transformed template F(T, K) *Secret*: key K	Quantization and matching in transformed space $M(F(T,K), F(Q,K))$
Non-invertible transform	Non-invertibility of the transformation function F	*Public domain*: transformed template F(T, K), key K	Matching in transformed space $M(F(T,K), F(Q,K))$
Key binding biometric cryptosystems	Level of security depends on the amount of information revealed by the helper data H	*Public domain*: helper data H = F(T, K)	Error correction and user-specific quantization $K = M(F(T,K),Q)$
Key-generating biometric cryptosystems	Level of security depends on the amount of information revealed by the helper data H	*Public domain*: helper data H = F(T)	Error correction and user-specific quantization $K = M(F(T),Q)$

Table 9.2. Characteristics of template protection schemes (Jain, Nandakumar, and Nagar, 2008). Here, T represents the unprotected enrollment template, Q represents the query (verification feature set) and K is the key used to protect the template. In salting and non-invertible feature transform, F represents the transformation function, and M denotes the matcher operating in the transformed domain. In biometric cryptosystems, H is the helper data, F is the helper data extraction scheme and M is the error correction scheme that allows reconstruction of the key K.

Traditional fingerprint verification systems output a binary (yes/no) decision, which could be trapped and altered by a malicious program. Hence, in certain applications, it is beneficial that the fingerprint verification release a stronger secret (e.g., cryptographic key) instead of the simple "yes" output upon a successful fingerprint match. An application can then use this released secret as a cryptographic key, thus alleviating the hard problem of key management (see Figure 9.9).

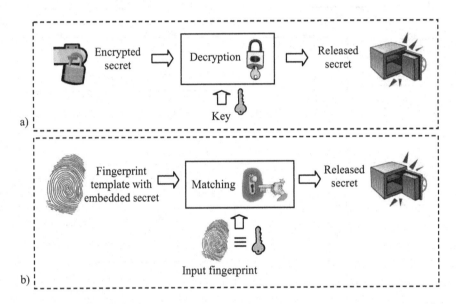

Figure 9.9. a) Password and b) fingerprint-based verification through the release of a secret instead of the traditional true/false answer.

In its most simple form, a biometric cryptosystem can be built by storing a key as part of a user's database record, together with the user name, fingerprint template, access privileges, and the like, which may be released upon a successful match. This provides convenience in key management, however, it is secure only when the database record is located and the matching is performed at a secure location. A more flexible solution is to hide a cryptographic key within the enrollment template itself (e.g., via a trusted and secret bit-replacement algorithm that can replace the least significant bits of the pixel values/features with bits from the key). Upon a successful fingerprint match, the correct secret is extracted from the fingerprint database template and released into the system. The security of this method is dependent on the secrecy of the key hiding and retrieval algorithms. If the key hiding and retrieval algorithms are deterministic (e.g., they always hide the key at the same location), they can be easily compromised. For example, an attacker may enroll several people in the system using identical keys and locate the bits with common information across the enrolled templates. Therefore, it is useful that the secret be bound to the fingerprint template in the stored database in such a way that it cannot be revealed without a successful fingerprint match. This binding is required to have properties similar to encryption, where the fingerprint is used as a key to lock the secret. Biometric cryptosystems provide an elegant solution to this problem while still being effective for template protection.

9.7.1 Non-invertible transforms

Conceptually, a template can be protected by transforming the unprotected template into another representation space through a *non-invertible transform*. The most popular non-invertible transform is a one-way hash function, $H(x) = c$ which is used together with a verification function $V(x,c) \Rightarrow \{True, False\}$. The pair must have the following properties:

- *Collision avoidance*: $V(x,c)$ and $V(y,c)$ cannot both be *True* if $x \neq y$.

- *Information hiding*: if an adversary has access to a hashed code c^* and knows the hashing function $H(x)$, the only way to determine the data x^* corresponding to the hashed code c^* (i.e., $H(x^*) = c^*$) is to exhaustively search over x (brute force attack).

Thus the security (cryptographic strength) provided by the one-way hash function is largely dependent on the information content of the data x.

Hashing techniques are extensively used in password-based authentication systems; passwords are hashed and stored in the password database during user enrollment (see Figure 9.10a). When an input password is entered, it is also hashed and compared with the stored hashed password. Since the transformation is non-invertible in the cryptographic sense, the original password cannot be recovered even if the exact transformations as well as the transformed password are known. A different transform (or a differently parameterized transform) is used for a different application thus avoiding cross-use of the passwords.

The same concept could in principle be applied to fingerprints. Instead of maintaining a database of fingerprint templates, the hashes of the templates can be stored; at each recognition attempt, the verification feature set is also hashed and the fingerprint comparison is performed in the non-invertible transformed space (Figure 9.10b). Although there is an analogy between password and fingerprint hashing, a significant difference exists between the two cases. Passwords are exactly the same during different authentication attempts, but fingerprint images at different acquisitions (different verification attempts) are never identical, and this prevents the same hash to be obtained. Therefore, matching in the non-invertible transformed space needs to be invariant to intra-class variation, which is a difficult problem.

Password enrollment

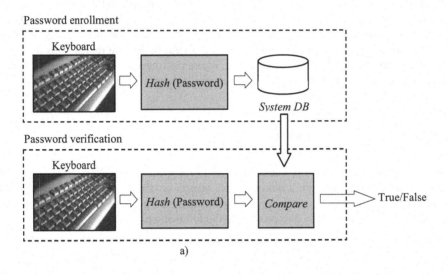

a)

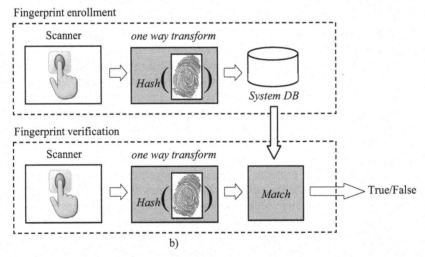

b)

Figure 9.10. Hashing techniques. a) Passwords are typically stored in the database after they are hashed; when a new password is received, it is hashed and compared with the hashed enrollment. If a person has access to the database of hashed passwords, a password is not compromised. In b), a similar analogy is applied to fingerprint recognition. Only one-way transformed representation is stored and thus, if an adversary has access to the database, the biometric information is not compromised.

A major problem in comparing hashed fingerprint templates is recovering the correct alignment between the two fingerprints, namely the template and the query feature set. One method to alleviate this difficulty is to pre-align the fingerprint images or feature sets before the transformation is applied (e.g., by registering them with respect to the core point). Another method is to design the transformation in such a way that it results in an alignment invariant representation. The security provided by non-invertible transform also depends on the system module where the transformation is applied (e.g., fingerprint scanner, client, server, or third party certifier) and the location where the fingerprint template resides (e.g., client, server, third party certifier, or smartcard). Diversity (and hence cancellation or revocation) can be obtained by re-enrolling the same user by applying a different transform (or different parameters of the same transform function) to his fingerprints. Non-invertibility is guaranteed by the construction of the hash function itself. So in principle, this method is very attractive. However, in practice it is quite difficult to find non-invertible transforms that are both secure from a cryptographic point of view and accurate from a biometric point of view.

Ratha, Connell, and Bolle (2001b) pioneered the concept of non-invertible transforms for template protection. In Ratha et al. (2006, 2007), the authors extend their conceptual work by providing three specific non-invertible transforms. Their approach first locates singular points (cores and deltas) in fingerprint images. The minutiae points are transformed with respect to the core point using three different transforms: (i) Cartesian, (ii) polar, and (iii) functional surface folding. These transforms were chosen such that the resulting minutiae (in the transformed space) are still two-dimensional arrangements of points. Hence, existing fingerprint comparison algorithms can be used to match a protected template against a protected feature set. The Cartesian and polar transforms have the limitations that they can convert small differences in relative locations of two minutiae in the original space into large differences in the transformed space, leading to large number of false rejects. As a result, the authors recommend the use of a transform that is locally smooth. However, to be cryptographically secure the transform should not be globally smooth, otherwise it would be easy to invert it. The functional surface folding transform that the authors propose is locally smooth but is not globally smooth (Figure 9.11); the function has "folds", that is, multiple locations in the original space are mapped to the same location in the transformed space. Conceptually, this is the same property that gives non-invertibility to standard hash functions; in fact, this produces ambiguity in reversing the transform and thus provides the desired non-invertibility. However, the proposed transform has fairly low "degree of folding". In fact, the authors found that only 8% of minutiae have their neighbors perturbed after this transformation. As a result, in spite of the high matching accuracy, the non-invertibility provided by the proposed approach is not strong.

Some authors have proposed methods which do not need global alignment. The basic idea is to use local features similar to those introduced in Section 4.4:

- Chikkerur et al. (2008) encode appearance of individual minutia points by extracting a texture-based feature vector called "signature" from the grayscale neighborhood of each minutia. Each individual signature can be transformed using a non-invertible function that uses a random key (or a password) as a parameter. The use of the key makes this a two-factor approach (fingerprint + password). While the approach is promising, theoretical security proofs are not provided and the accuracy even on a proprietary database is not high.

- Lee et al. (2007) compute, for each minutia, a rotation and translation invariant value from the orientation information in its neighborhood. The cancelable template is built by transforming minutiae according to certain changing functions that output two invariant values for the translation and rotation movements of the original minutiae. When a template is compromised, it is replaced by a new one generated by different changing functions.

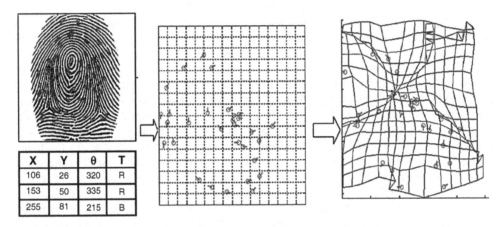

Figure 9.11. In a surface folding transformation, both the position and the orientation of the minutiae are changed by a mapping function. Conceptually, the minutiae are embedded in a sheet which is then crumpled. This function is locally smooth, but is not globally smooth. © IEEE.

Other interesting techniques in this category are presented by Savvides, Kumar, and Khosla (2004), Farooq et al. (2007), Tulyakov et al. (2007), and Sutcu, Sencar, and Memon (2005, 2007). Sutcu, Sencar, and Memon (2007) map the minutiae points onto a circle via a one-to-many transformation. Tulyakov et al. (2007) use symmetric hash functions. Sutcu, Sencar, and Memon (2005) make use of robust hash functions, i.e., hash functions that are tolerant to small changes in the fingerprint data. Overall, non-invertible transform based approaches continue to be conceptually attractive but difficult to implement (i.e., striking the right balance between biometric accuracy, non-invertibility and diversity has been difficult in practice).

9.7.2 Salting

Fingerprint *salting* (also called *biohashing*) (Jin, Ling, and Goh, 2004; Teoh, Goh, and Ngo, 2006) is inherently a two-factor approach where the fingerprint template is transformed by using a function whose parameters are defined by an external key. The approach involves use of the so called Random Multispace Quantization (RMQ) that includes the following three stages:

1. Projection of fingerprint feature vector into a lower dimensional space using linear dimensionality reduction transforms (such as principal component analysis or Fisher discrimination analysis).
2. Projection onto a set of random orthogonal vectors derived from the external key.
3. Quantization of the individual maps.

See Figure 9.12 for a depiction of the enrollment and verification processes using the biohashing method. While the original approach is demonstrated by the authors for face recognition, it is applicable to any alignment-invariant feature vectors, such as the FingerCode (Jain et al., 2000) representation of fingerprints.

In biohashing the protected templates are not reversible unless both the template and the key are known simultaneously. However, if the key is known (or is weak enough that it can be cracked by a simple dictionary attack), the "randomness" fades out (Kong et al., 2006) and the quantization does not sufficiently preserve the protected template. Even if a small amount of information is lost due to quantization, a fairly good approximation of the template can be recovered (Jain, Nandakumar, and Nagar, 2008). To improve the security of biohashing approaches, it is recommended that the key be not stored but rather remembered by the user, but this reintroduces the weakness of password-based schemes that we are trying to circumvent.

A nice property of biohashing is that the external key not only provides the non-invertibility property, but also improves the matching accuracy, which is not surprising given the two-factor nature of the approach. By changing the key, diversity (and thus cancelability/revocability) can be easily achieved.

The challenge in designing a practical implementation of biohashing is in finding a salting mechanism that works with "public" key or with the key shared by all users but does not degrade the matching accuracy. Another interesting technique in this category is presented by Sakata et al. (2006).

9.7.3 Key-generation biometric cryptosystems

The objective here is to generate a cryptographic key directly from the biometric data. Dodis, Reyzin, and Smith (2004) and Dodis et al. (2008) propose two approaches to turn biometric data into keys usable for general purpose cryptographic application: (i) *secure sketch* and (ii) *fuzzy extractor*.

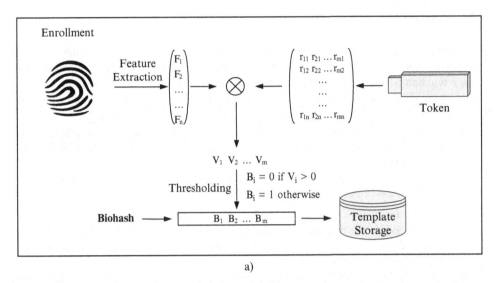

a)

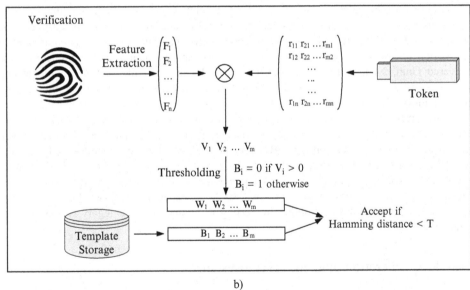

b)

Figure 9.12. The processes for the biohashing technique; a) enrollment and b) verification.

- The secure sketch addresses the intra-class variability in the fingerprint. A protected template generated through this approach is called "sketch of the unprotected template". The sketch does not reveal any significant information about the corresponding unprotected template and thus can be made public. The unprotected template can be exactly reconstructed only starting from a feature set that is close enough to the original unprotected template.
- The fuzzy extractor addresses both the intra-class variability in the fingerprint as well as nonuniformity, that is, it extracts a uniform random string (key) from its input in an error tolerant way. If the fingerprint input changes somewhat, the extracted key remains the same. In a modification of this approach, the fuzzy extractors (such as strong hash function) can be chosen randomly at each enrollment such that the same fingerprint would generate different keys and hash values during multiple enrollments, thus providing diversity. This modification makes this approach more similar to the key binding cryptosystems that we will explain in the next section.

Vielhauer, Steinmetz, and Mayerhofer (2002) and Chang, Zhang, and Chen (2004) proposed key generation methods that used user-specific quantization schemes. Information on quantization boundaries is stored as secure sketch (helper data) which is used during recognition to account for intra-class variations. While Dodis et al. (2008)'s method used single-level quantization, Li and Chang (2006) used two-level quantization to convert the fingerprint features into binary representation. Buhan et al. (2007a) studied the problem of generating fuzzy extractors from continuous distributions and showed that the maximum length of the key extracted is directly related to the intrinsic error rates of the fingerprint recognition system.

Arakala, Jeffers, and Horadam (2007) proposed a way to quantize and represent fingerprint minutiae in order to build a secure sketch for a fingerprint system. Chang and Roy (2007) propose locality preserving hash for secure sketch construction in minutiae-based fingerprint systems. An implementation for 3D face has been proposed in Zhou (2007). Sutcu, Li, and Memon (2007a) introduced a specific implementation for a multi-biometric system involving fingerprint and face. Boyen et al. (2005) discuss the use of secure sketch methods in a protocol that enables unidirectional authentication (of a user to a server) when a reliable/secure communication channel is not available. Buhan et al. (2007b) proposed a method to achieve mutual authentication over a completely insecure channel.

Sutcu, Li, and Memon (2007b) analyzed the secure sketch methods and identified a number of practical implementation issues. They caution that the entropy loss may not be a sufficient measurement of security and that entropy loss alone may be very large. Key generating fingerprint cryptosystems in general must balance between *key stability* and *key entropy*. Key stability denotes the extent to which the key generated from the fingerprint data is repeatable. Key entropy relates to the number of possible keys that can be generated. If a method generates the same key for all the fingers, then the stability is high but the entropy is zero, leading to high false match rate. On the other extreme, if a method generates different keys for different impressions of the same finger, the scheme has high entropy but no stability, leading to high false non-match rate. In practice, it is difficult to simultaneously achieve high key entropy and high key stability from the existing key generation methods (Jain, Nandakumar, and Nagar, 2008).

9.7.4 Key-binding biometric cryptosystems

In a key-binding biometric cryptosystem, a cryptographic key and an unprotected fingerprint template are monolithically bounded together within a cryptographic framework to generate the helper data. The helper data is essentially a publicly available protected template which does not reveal any significant information neither about the key nor about the fingerprint template. In other words, it is computationally hard to decode the key or the template from the helper data without any knowledge of the user's fingerprint data. The helper data is usually obtained by associating the enrollment template with codeword obtained from an error correcting code using the key as the message. A codeword recovered from a feature set that is similar but not identical to a template is affected by a certain amount of error. By exploiting error correction codes, the exact key is recovered from the codeword that contains some errors. If the correct key is recovered, it implies that the feature set and the protected template resulted in a match. The error correction capability of this approach provides tolerance to intra-class variations in fingerprints. However, unlike Ratha et al. (2007)'s non-invertible transform-based approach that can use existing fingerprint matching algorithms, the key-binding approach requires a new algorithm to be designed to match the feature set with the helper data in the encrypted domain. While non-invertible transform-based approaches were designed to provide diversity of template as their main feature, the original key-binding constructs were not designed to provide diversity (and thus revocability). However, modification can be made to key-binding approaches to obtain diversity.

Some of the earliest works in key-binding based cryptosystems are described in Soutar and Tomko (1996), Soutar et al. (1998a, b), Johnson et al. (1998), Davida, Frankel, and Matt (1998), Davida et al. (1999), Monrose, Reiter, and Wetzel (1999) and Monrose et al. (2001). These early approaches, all using error correcting codes, described the basic concepts very well and inspired much of the later research on key-binding methods; however, they did not provide rigorous security analysis, convincing experimental results and did not discussed implications related to practical implementations.

Juels and Wattenberg (1999), motivated by the Monrose, Reiter, and Wetzel (1999) work, proposed an approach called *fuzzy commitment*. The user chooses a random codeword C of an error correcting code. Then the hash of C (i.e., *hash*(C)) is stored, and the difference between the unprotected template T and C, is also stored as helper data (i.e., $H = T - C$). It is the binary difference vector $(T - C)$, which binds the codeword C to the template T. At verification time, the feature set denoted by I, is used to compute the vector $C' = I - (T - C)$; if I is similar to T, C' is expected to be similar to C. Error correction is then applied to C' to get C''. Finally, the stored *hash*(C) is compared to *hash*(C''); the comparison is successful if I is sufficiently close to T such that the correct codeword can be exactly recovered (i.e., $C'' = C$). Concrete implementations or experimental results were, however, not reported in Juels and Wattenberg (1999). The fuzzy commitment scheme requires the biometric representation to be alignment-free and ordered (i.e., there should exist a way to order single features within the feature set). This is relatively simple for some modalities such as iris; for example in the IrisCode approach (Daugman, 1999), the iris representation is a texture-based fixed-length feature vector invariant with respect to translation and rotation. Hao, Anderson, and Daugman (2006) implemented the basic idea of fuzzy commitment for IrisCode features by using Reed-Solomon code to correct errors at the block level and Hadamard code to correct random errors at the binary level. This implementation actually adds a second authentication factor (e.g., a password or a token) and leads to promising experimental results. Teoh and Kim (2007) suggested Randomized Dynamic Quantization Transformation to binarize data such that the resulting binary string is uniformly random and distinctive. Tong et al. (2007) proposed an implementation based on FingerCode features of fingerprints.

Juels and Sudan (2002)'s *fuzzy vault* method can be thought of as an order-invariant version of the Juels and Wattenberg (1999) method, that is, the fuzzy vault method does not require the biometric features to be ordered set of elements. This bodes very well for fingerprint recognition since the most popular fingerprint features (i.e., the minutiae) are not characterized by a natural ordering, and any attempt to sort them could lead to robustness issues. In the fuzzy vault method, a user, say Alice, places a secret value K (e.g., her private cryptographic key) in a vault and locks (secures) the vault by using an unordered set T_A (e.g., a list of minutiae points extracted from her fingerprint). Another user, say Bob, using another unordered set I_B, cannot unlock the vault (and thus cannot access the secret K) unless I_B is similar enough to T_A. To construct the vault, Alice performs following operations:

- Selects a polynomial p that encodes K (e.g., by fixing the coefficients of p according to K).
- Computes the polynomial projections, $p(T)$, for the elements of T.
- Adds some noise (i.e., randomly generated chaff points having projection values different from that corresponding to p) to derive the final point set V (that corresponds to the helper data for the fuzzy vault approach).

When Bob tries to learn K (e.g., by finding p), he uses his own unordered set I_B. If I_B is not sufficiently similar to T (which is expected since Bob's fingerprint will be very different from Alice's) he will be unable to locate many points in V that lie on p, especially in light of the chaff points that will mislead Bob's efforts. Thus, Bob will not be able to obtain K. On the other hand, when Alice needs to retrieve K from the vault, she will provide a new unordered set I_A derived from a different impression of her finger. Now, since I_A is expected to be sufficiently similar to T_A, by using error correcting codes (e.g., Reed Solomon codes), Alice will be able to reconstruct p, and hence her secret key K. See Figure 9.13 for examples of the enrolment and the verification processes using the fuzzy vault technique.

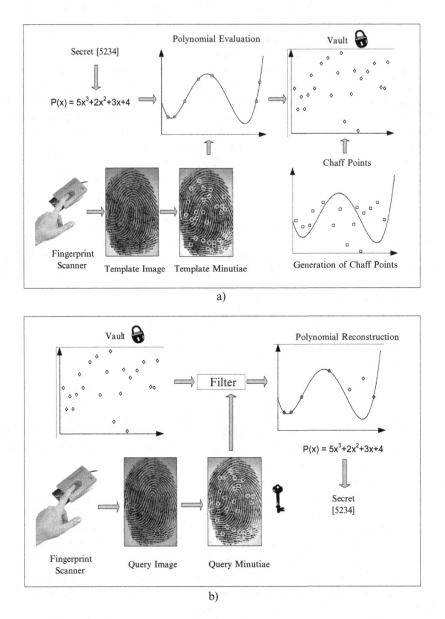

Figure 9.13. The fuzzy vault technique; a) enrollment and b) verification.

The security of this method is based on the infeasibility of the polynomial reconstruction problem: in particular, if Bob does not know many points that lie on p, it is not feasible for him to find the parameters of p. Hence he will not be able to learn K. Three parameters control the trade off between security and convenience: (i) the number of points in the vault that lie on the polynomial which in turn depends upon the number of minutiae extracted from a fingerprint image; (ii) the number of chaff points (random noise) that are added, and (iii) the degree of the encoding polynomial. For example, large number of chaff points increases the security but decrease the robustness.

While Juels and Sudan (2002) developed a sound framework for securing a secret with biometric data, they did not provide a practical implementation of their method. Clancy, Kiyavash, and Lin (2003) realized an implementation of the fuzzy vault method for fingerprints based on minutiae locations. They noted that the number of chaff points that can be added is limited by the variance in the minutiae configurations among multiple impressions of the same finger (intra-class variability). In their experiments, they added only 313 chaff points and used a 14 degree polynomial. Their implementation resulted in a high FNMR of 20–30% (the authors did not report the FMR) even though they used multiple impression of each finger to determine stable minutiae and assumed that feature sets and templates can be properly pre-aligned.

Uludag, Pankanti, and Jain (2005), while setting the alignment problem aside (they assumed that the true alignment is known), focused on an actual implementation of fuzzy fingerprint vault. Since Reed Solomon error correction has serious difficulty on noisy fingerprint data, they used multiple point combinations to reconstruct the correct polynomial using cyclic redundancy check instead of the Reed Solomon code. The method is promising in terms of accuracy and security even though it has a very high computational complexity. So, while other implementation issues are easier to deal with, the most difficult problem, namely the alignment remains open.

Uludag and Jain (2004) recognized that fingerprint alignment is one of the biggest barriers in fingerprint vault implementation. The authors proposed to use minutiae pair representation of fingerprints. Each pair of minutiae is described by the distance between the two minutiae and the relative directions of the two minutiae with respect to the line joining them. Thus, the pair representation is translation and rotation invariant. The representation is further quantized to handle non-linear distortions as well. A voting/consensus-based alignment is used where the correspondence between each minutiae pair from the feature set and the template generates a vote for the relative alignment. The voting space is then examined to generate alignment hypothesis. Yang and Verbauwhede (2005) proposed an implementation to solve the alignment problem in a slightly different way. First they consider a pair-based representation of minutiae points such that each feature is translation and rotation invariant. Then they conduct a search for the "most reliable pair" in three impressions of the same finger collected during enrollment. The most reliable pair is the one that maximizes the similarity when each of the three fingerprints is matched with the other two. Once the most reliable pair is established, it is used as a reference point and all the minutiae are transformed into a polar coordinate system with respect to the reference point. The local structure of the reference minutiae is saved together with the vault in order to assist in the alignment. However, the authors were not able to achieve a FNMR lower than 17% (FMR is not reported). Chung et al. (2005) proposed a geometric hashing technique to perform alignment in a minutiae-based fingerprint fuzzy vault. Jeffers and Arakala (2006, 2007) use minutiae local structures for pre-alignment. Nagar and Chaudhury (2006) based their pre-alignment on the core location.

Uludag and Jain (2006) compute orientation field flow curves from orientation map of fingerprint images, find curvatures of the flow curves and then choose points of maximum curvature on each flow curve. This information constitutes the helper data (see Figure 9.14) and is used for alignment. By using 24 minutiae and 200 chaff points, the authors achieved a FNMR of 27.4% on FVC2002 DB2 at 0% FMR. Nandakumar, Jain, and Pankanti (2007) rely on helper data derived from orientation field for alignment, chaff point filtering and selection of the most reliable minutiae based on quality estimation. The authors report a reasonable accuracy but indicate that multi-biometrics may be necessary for desired accuracy. Nagar, Nandakumar, and Jain (2008) associate a discriminative descriptors with each minutia (a feature vectors computed from the orientation and frequency estimates in the neighborhood of each minutia), to improve the accuracy of the fingerprint fuzzy vault. Finally, Nandakumar and Jain (2008) combine fingerprint and iris in a single fuzzy vault to achieve a good balance between security (i.e., low FMR and high cryptographic security) and usability (low FNMR).

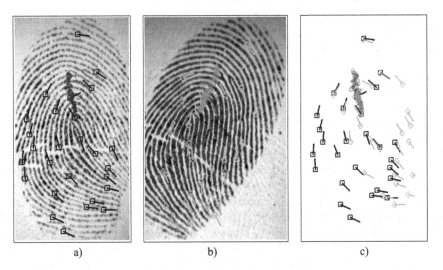

Figure 9.14. Use of helper data. a) Enrolled fingerprint showing the minutiae and helper data, b) query fingerprint, and c) two minutiae sets aligned using helper data.

Scheirer and Boult (2007) discussed three potential attacks that can be launched against fuzzy vaults: (i) attack via record multiplicity, (ii) stolen key inversion attack, and (iii) blended substitution attack. If multiple vaults of the same fingerprint (e.g., from two different applications) become available to a hacker, he can identify the common minutiae points in the two vaults (since the chaff points are different) and thereby decode the vault. Also, if the hacker gains access to the key embedded in a vault (say through snooping), he can decode the vault and obtain the original unprotected template. Finally, if the hacker is able to modify the vault, he can substitute some of the chaff points with minutiae points from her own finger and blend it into the vault; this will make the modified vault to be successfully matched with her own fingerprint. To protect against these vulnerabilities, Nandakumar, Nagar, and Jain (2007) proposed blending a password as a "salt" with the minutiae points for vault construction. The password is used again to derive an encryption key and encrypt the vault with this key. The salting prevents multiple vaults to be linked and thus provides diversity (and thus revocability). The encryption of the vault provides resistance against blended substitution and stolen key inversion attacks. However, this is a two-factor authentication approach that reintroduces problems inherent to passwords.

Syndrome approaches proposed by Martinian, Yekhanin, and Yedidia (2005) and Draper et al. (2007a, b) also fall in the group of key-binding cryptosystems. Instead of using error correcting code, these methods are based on low density syndrome codes and employ iterative belief propagation decoding for template protection. Fewer syndrome bits mean greater security but less robustness, and vice-versa. Further, instead of using simple quantization (binarization), they use random projection and thresholding.

Other interesting approaches are by Linnartz and Tuyls (2003), Tuyls and Goseling (2004), Tuyls et al. (2005), Sahai and Waters (2005), Kelkboom et al. (2007) and Kerschbaum et al. (2004). Hybrid approaches that do not fall in any of the categories in Figure 9.8 have also been proposed, such as Boult, Scheirer, and Woodworth (2007) and Boult and Woodworth (2007)'s "biotokens" approach. Scheirer and Boult (2008) further extend the biotokens method to incorporate nesting properties and developed a cryptographic protocol for electronic transactions and digital signatures. A biometric version of Kerberos is also discussed, where both the parties involved can mutually validate the transactions.

Many of the practical implementations proposed in the literature blend password or token with fingerprint to form the protected template, which makes them two-factor authentication approaches. Such an approach not only reintroduces some of the problems associated with passwords, it also does not allow it to operate in identification mode. Jain, Nandakumar, and Nagar (2008) compared and contrasted several template protection schemes for fingerprints and concluded that each family of method has its own advantages and disadvantages with respect to non-invertibility, diversity and accuracy. In general, template protection remains a challenging research problem and, to the best of our knowledge, techniques presented here have not yet been practically deployed in any large scale application. However, it continues to draw a significant amount of attention from researchers, policy makers and user community. A consortium of academics and industry has been funded by European Commission to actively work on this topic (Delvaux et al., 2008).

9.8 Summary

With increasing deployments of fingerprint systems in various commercial and government applications, security of biometric systems itself is of growing concern to system developers, organizations deploying these systems and the general public. Fingerprint vendors are rapidly adopting various technologies to address some of these vulnerabilities. Techniques for liveness detection, match-on-card, system-on-a-chip, and template protection, are active areas of research. In particular, template protection techniques address crucial security issues such as revocability of compromised templates and preventing the use of the same fingerprint data across different authentication systems. If a hacker is successful in intruding into a fingerprint system, it is essential to have a recovery mechanism that prevents the hacker from intruding again. It is also critical that a single breach into one system does not make it easier for a hacker to breach another system. We expect substantial progress in research in this area and in particular in the design of template protection methods that provide not only good security but also high recognition accuracy.

Match-on-card, system-on-device and system-on-a-chip technologies are generating a lot of interest because they support decentralized operation and users feel secure that their fingerprint templates are always in their own possession on a tamper resistant hardware. Most of the credentialing programs (e.g., transportation worker identification credential in the US) use smart card for the storage of fingerprint templates, even if the feature extraction (and often even the matching) is currently being performed outside the card (e.g., on a host). Independent evaluations of these technologies, such as MINEX II (Grother et al., 2007) have shown that the matching performance of these smart card technologies is inferior to the performance of PC-based fingerprint systems. We expect that the improvement in fingerprint algorithms and the availability of secure chips (for system-on-a-chip systems) with increased computing capabilities will reduce this performance gap. We expect that system-on-a-chip will be more popular than match-on-card techniques.

It is important to recognize that foolproof fingerprint recognition systems simply may not exist. Security is a risk management strategy to identify, control, eliminate, or minimize uncertain events that may adversely affect system resources and information assets. The security requirements of a fingerprint system will depend on the threat model of the application where it would be deployed and the related cost–benefit analysis.

Bibliography

Abdelmalek et al. (1984). Abdelmalek N., Kasvand T., Goupil D. and Otsu N., "Fingerprint data compression," in *Proc. Int. Conf. on Pattern Recognition (7th)*, pp. 834–836, 1984.

Abhyankar and Schuckers (2004). Abhyankar A.S. and Schuckers S.C., "A Wavelet-Based Approach to Detecting Liveness in Fingerprint Scanners," in *Proc. SPIE Conf. on Biometric Technology for Human Identification I*, 2004.

Abhyankar and Schuckers (2006). Abhyankar A.S. and Schuckers S.C., "Fingerprint Liveness Detection Using Local Ridge Frequencies and Multiresolution Texture Analysis Techniques," in *Proc. Int. Conf. on Image Processing*, pp. 321–324, 2006.

Abutaleb and Kamel (1999). Abutaleb A.S. and Kamel M., "A genetic algorithm for the estimation of ridges in fingerprints," *IEEE Transactions on Image Processing*, vol. 8, no. 8, p. 1134, 1999.

Adler (2005). Adler A., "Vulnerabilities in Biometric Encryption Systems," in *Proc. Int. Conf. on Audio- and Video-Based Biometric Person Authentication (5th)*, 2005.

Ahmed (2007). Ahmed F., "Integrated fingerprint verification method using a composite signature-based watermarking technique," *Optical Engineering*, vol. 46, no. 8, 2007.

Ahuja, Magnanti and Orlin (1993). Ahuja R., Magnanti T. and Orlin J., *Network Flows*, Prentice-Hall, Upper Saddle River, NJ, 1993.

Ailisto et al. (2006). Ailisto H., Vildjiounaite E., Lindholm M., Mäkelä S.M. and Peltola J., "Soft biometrics-combining body weight and fat measurements with fingerprint biometrics," *Pattern Recognition Letters*, vol. 27, no. 5, pp. 325–334, 2006.

Alessandroni et al. (2008). Alessandroni A., Cappelli R., Ferrara M. and Maltoni D., "Definition of Fingerprint Scanner Image Quality Specifications by Operational Quality," in *Proc. European workshop on Biometrics and Identity Management*, 2008.

Allinson et al. (2007). Allinson N.M., Sivarajah J., Gledhill I., Carling M. and Allinson L.J., "Robust Wireless Transmission of Compressed Latent Fingerprint Images," *IEEE Transactions on Information Forensics and Security*, vol. 2, no. 3, pp. 331–340, 2007.

Almansa and Cohen (2000). Almansa A. and Cohen L., "Fingerprint Image Matching by Minimization of a Thin-Plate Energy Using a Two-Step Iterative Algorithm with Auxiliary Variables," in *Proc. Workshop on Applications of Computer Vision*, pp. 35–40, 2000.

Almansa and Lindeberg (1997). Almansa A. and Lindeberg T., "Enhancement of fingerprint images using shape-adapted scale-space operators," in *Gaussian Scale-Space Theory*, J. Sporring, M. Nielsen, L. Florack and P. Johansen (Eds.), Kluwer, New York, pp. 21–30, 1997.

Almansa and Lindeberg (2000). Almansa A. and Lindeberg T., "Fingerprint enhancement by shape adaptation of scale-space operators with automatic scale selection," *IEEE Transactions on Image Processing*, vol. 9, no. 12, pp. 2027–2042, 2000.

Alonso-Fernandez et al. (2007). Alonso-Fernandez F., Fierrez J., Ortega-Garcia J., Gonzalez-Rodriguez J., Fronthaler H., Kollreider K. and Bigun J., "A comparative study of fingerprint image-quality estimation methods," *IEEE Transactions on Information Forensics and Security*, vol. 2, no. 4, pp. 734–743, 2007.

Alonso-Fernandez, Fierrez-Aguilar and Ortega-Garcia (2005). Alonso-Fernandez F., Fierrez-Aguilar J. and Ortega-Garcia J., "An Enhanced Gabor Filter-Based Segmentation Algorithm for Fingerprint Recognition Systems," in *Proc. Int. Symp. on Image and Signal Processing and Analysis*, 2005.

Amornraksa and Tachaphetpiboon (2006). Amornraksa T. and Tachaphetpiboon S., "Fingerprint recognition using DCT features," *Electronics Letters*, vol. 42, no. 9, pp. 522–523, 2006.

Amy (1948). Amy L., "Recherches Sur L'identification des Traces Papillaries," *Annales de Medecine Legale*, vol. 28, no. 2, pp. 96–101, 1948.

Anderson (1994). Anderson R.J., "Why cryptosystems fail," *Communications of the ACM*, vol. 37, no. 11, pp. 32–40, 1994.

Anderson et al. (1991). Anderson S., Bruce W., Denyer P., Renshaw D. and Wang G., "A Single Chip Sensor & Image Processor for Fingerprint Verification," in *Proc. IEEE Custom Integrated Circuits Conf.*, 1991.

Ansari, Chen and Hou (1992). Ansari N., Chen M.H. and Hou E.S.H., "A genetic algorithm for point pattern matching," in *Dynamic Genetic and Chaotic Programming*, B. Souckec and IRIS group (Eds.), Wiley, New York, 1992.

ANSI/INCITS 378 (2004). ANSI/INCITS, "INCITS 378-2004 – Finger Minutiae Format for Data Interchange," ANSI/INCITS standard, 2004.

ANSI/NIST–ITL 1 (2007). ANSI/NIST, "Data Format for the Interchange of Fingerprint Facial, & Other Biometric Information (revision of ANSI/NIST–ITL 1–2000)," ANSI/NIST–ITL 1–2007; NIST Special Public Report: 500–271, American National Standards Institute, 2007.

Antonelli et al. (2001). Antonelli K., Vanderkooy G., Vlaar T. and Immega G., "Fingerprint Image Optical Input Apparatus," US Patent 6259108 B1, 2001.

Antonelli et al. (2006a). Antonelli A., Cappelli R., Maio D. and Maltoni D., "Fake finger detection by skin distortion analysis," *IEEE Transactions on Information Forensics and Security*, vol. 1, no. 3, pp. 360–373, 2006a.

Antonelli et al. (2006b). Antonelli A., Cappelli R., Maio D. and Maltoni D., "A New Approach to Fake Finger Detection Based on Skin Distortion," in *Proc. Int. Conf. on Biometrics*, LNCS 3832, pp. 221–228, 2006b.

Arakala, Jeffers and Horadam (2007). Arakala A., Jeffers J. and Horadam K.J., "Fuzzy Extractors for Minutiae-Based Fingerprint Authentication," in *Proc. Int. Conf. on Biometrics*, LNCS 4642, pp. 760–769, 2007.

Araque et al. (2002). Araque J.L., Baena M., Chalela B.E., Navarro D. and Vizcaya P.R., "Synthesis of Fingerprint Images," in *Proc. Int. Conf. on Pattern Recognition (16th)*, vol. 2, pp. 442–445, 2002.

Arcelli and Baja (1984). Arcelli C. and Baja G.S.D., "A width independent fast thinning algorithm," *IEEE Transactions on Pattern Analysis Machine Intelligence*, vol. 4, no. 7, pp. 463–474, 1984.

Areekul et al. (2005). Areekul V., Watchareeruetai U., Suppasriwasuseth K. and Tantaratana S., "Separable Gabor Filter Realization for Fast Fingerprint Enhancement," in *Proc. Int. Conf. on Image Processing*, vol. 3, pp. 253–256, 2005.

Areekul, Suppasriwasuseth and Jirachawang (2006). Areekul V., Suppasriwasuseth K. and Jirachawang S., "The New Focal Point Localization Algorithm for Fingerprint Registration," in *Proc. Int. Conf. on Pattern Recognition (18th)*, vol. 4, pp. 497–500, 2006.

Asai et al. (1975). Asai K., Hoshino Y., Yamashita N. and Hiratsuka S., "Fingerprint Identification System," in *Proc. Int. Conf. US–Japan Computer (2nd)*, pp. 30–35, 1975.

Ashbaugh (1999). Ashbaugh D.R., *Quantitative–Qualitative Friction Ridge Analysis: An Introduction to Basic and Advanced Ridgeology*, CRC Press, Boca Raton, FL, 1999.

Aushermann et al. (1973). Aushermann D.A., Fairchild R.C., Moyers R.E., Hall W.D and Mitchel R.H., "A Proposed Method for the Analysis of Dermatoglyphics Patterns," *Proc. Society of Photooptic Instrumentation Engineers*, vol. 40, 1973.

Babler (1991). Babler W.J., "Embryologic development of epidermal ridges and their configuration," *Birth Defects Original Article Series*, vol. 27, no. 2, 1991.

Bahuguna and Corboline (1996). Bahuguna R.D. and Corboline T., "Prism fingerprint sensor that uses a holographic element," *Applied Optics*, vol. 35, no. 26, pp. 5242–5245, 1996.

Baird (1984). Baird H., *Model Based Image Matching Using Location*, MIT Press, Cambridge, MA, 1984.

Bal, El-Saba and Alam (2005a). Bal A., El-Saba A.M. and Alam M.S., "Improved fingerprint identification with supervised filtering enhancement," *Applied Optics*, vol. 44, no. 5, pp. 647–654, 2005a.

Bal, El-Saba and Alam (2005b). Bal A., El-Saba A.M. and Alam M.S., "Enhanced fingerprint verification and identification using a Widrow cellular neural network," *Optical Engineering*, vol. 44, no. 3, 2005b.

Baldi and Chauvin (1993). Baldi P. and Chauvin Y., "Neural networks for fingerprint recognition," *Neural Computation*, vol. 5, no. 3, 402–418, 1993.

Baldisserra et al. (2006). Baldisserra D., Franco A., Maio D. and Maltoni D., "Fake Fingerprint Detection by Odor Analysis," in *Proc. Int. Conf. on Biometrics*, LNCS 3832, pp. 265–272, 2006.

Ballan, Sakarya and Evans (1997). Ballan M., Sakarya F.A. and Evans B.L., "A Fingerprint Classification Technique Using Directional Images," in *Proc. Asilomar Conf. on Signals Systems and Computers*, 1997.

Ballard (1981). Ballard D.H., "Generalizing the Hough transform to detect arbitrary shapes," *Pattern Recognition*, vol. 3, no. 2, pp. 110–122, 1981.

Balthazard (1911). Balthazard V., "De l'identification par les empreintes digitales," *Comptes Rendus des Seances de l'Academie des Sciences*, vol. 152, pp. 1862–1864, 1911.

Banner and Stock (1974). Banner C.B. and Stock R.M., "Finder, the FBI's Approach to Automatic Fingerprint Identification," in *Proc. Conf. on Science of Fingerprints*, 1974.

Banner and Stock (1975a). Banner C.B. and Stock R.M., "The FBI's Approach to Automatic Fingerprint Identification (Part I)," U.S. Government Publication, FBI Law Enforcement Bulletin, vol. 44, no. 1, Jan. 1975a.

Banner and Stock (1975b). Banner C.B. and Stock R.M., "The FBI's Approach to Automatic Fingerprint Identification (Part II)," U.S. Government Publication, FBI Law Enforcement Bulletin, vol. 44, no. 2, Feb. 1975b.

Barral, Coron and Naccache (2004). Barral C., Coron J.S. and Naccache D., "Externalized Fingerprint Matching," in *Proc. Int. Conf. on Biometric Authentication (1st)*, LNCS 3072, pp. 309–315, 2004.

Bartels, Beatty and Barsky (1987). Bartels R.H., Beatty J.C. and Barsky B.A., *An Introduction to Splines for Use in Computer Graphics and Geometric Modeling*, Morgan Kauffmann, San Mateo, CA, 1987.

Bartesaghi, Fernández and Gómez (2001). Bartesaghi A., Fernández A. and Gómez A., "Performance Evaluation of an Automatic Fingerprint Classification Algorithm Adapted to a Vucetich Based Classification System," in *Proc. Int. Conf. on Audio- and Video-Based Biometric Person Authentication (3rd)*, pp. 259–265, 2001.

Baruch (1988). Baruch O., "Line thinning by line following," *Pattern Recognition Letters*, vol. 8, no. 4, pp. 271–276, 1988.

Bazen and Gerez (2001a). Bazen A.M. and Gerez S.H., "An Intrinsic Coordinate System for Fingerprint Matching," in *Proc. Int. Conf. on Audio- and Video-Based Biometric Person Authentication (3rd)*, pp. 198–204, 2001a.

Bazen and Gerez (2001b). Bazen A.M. and Gerez S.H., "Segmentation of Fingerprint Images," in *Proc. Workshop on Circuits Systems and Signal Processing (ProRISC 2001)*, 2001b.

Bazen and Gerez (2002). Bazen A.M. and Gerez S.H., "Systematic methods for the computation of the directional fields and singular points of fingerprints," *IEEE Transactions on Pattern Analysis Machine Intelligence*, vol. 24, no. 7, pp. 905–919, 2002.

Bazen and Gerez (2003). Bazen A.M. and Gerez S.H., "Fingerprint matching by thin-plate spline modelling of elastic deformations," *Pattern Recognition*, vol. 36, no. 8, pp. 1859–1867, 2003.

Bazen and Veldhuis (2004). Bazen A.M. and Veldhuis R.N.J., "Likelihood-ratio-based biometric verification," *IEEE Transaction on Circuits and Systems for Video Technology*, vol. 14, no. 1, pp. 86–94, 2004.

Bazen et al. (2000). Bazen A.M., Verwaaijen G.T.B., Gerez S.H., Veelenturf L.P.J. and van der Zwaag B.J., "A Correlation-Based Fingerprint Verification System," in *Proc. Workshop on Circuits Systems and Signal Processing (ProRISC 2000)*, 2000.

Bazin and Mansfield (2007). Bazin A.I. and Mansfield T., "An Investigation of Minutiae Template Interoperability," in *Proc. Workshop on Automatic Identification Advanced Technologies*, pp. 13–18, 2007.

Bebis, Deaconu and Georgiopoulos (1999). Bebis G., Deaconu T. and Georgiopoulos M., "Fingerprint Identification Using Delaunay Triangulation," in *Proc. IEEE International Conference on Intelligence, Information, and Systems (ICIIS)*, pp. 452–459, 1999.

Becker and Potts (2007). Becker G. and Potts M., "Non-Metric Biometric Clustering," in *Proc. Biometric Symposium*, 2007.

Beleznai et al. (2001). Beleznai C., Ramoser H., Wachmann B., Birchbauer J., Bischof H. and Kropatsch W., "Memory-Efficient Fingerprint Verification," in *Proc. Int. Conf. on Image Processing*, 2001.

Benhammadi et al. (2007). Benhammadi F., Amirouche M.N., Hentous H., Beghdad K.B. and Aissani M., "Fingerprint matching from minutiae texture maps," *Pattern Recognition*, vol. 40, no. 1, pp. 189–197, 2007.

Ben-Yacoub (1999). Ben-Yacoub S., "Multi-Modal Data Fusion for Person Verification Using SVM," in *Proc. Int. Conf. on Audio- and-Video-Based Biometric Person Authentication (2nd)*, pp. 25–30, 1999.

Ben-Yacoub et al. (1999). Ben-Yacoub S., Luettin J., Jonsson K., Matas J. and Kittler J., "Audio-Visual Person Verification," in *Proc. Int. Conf. Computer Vision and Pattern Recognition*, vol. 1, pp. 580–585, 1999.

Ben-Yacoub, Abdeljaoued and Mayoraz (1999). Ben-Yacoub S., Abdeljaoued Y. and Mayoraz E., "Fusion of face and speech data for person identity verification," *IEEE Transactions on Neural Networks*, vol. 10, no. 5, pp. 1065–1074, 1999.

Berdan and Chiralo (1978). Berdan L. and Chiralo R., "Adaptive Digital Enhancement of Latent Fingerprints," in *Proc. Int. Carnahan Conf. on Electronic Crime Countermeasures*, pp. 131–135, 1978.

Bergengruen (1994). Bergengruen O., "Preprocessing of Poor Quality Fingerprint Images," in *Proc. Int. Conf. of the Chilean Computer Science Society (14th)*, 1994.

Bernard et al. (2001). Bernard S., Boujemaa N., Vitale D. and Bricot C., "Fingerprint Classification Using Kohonen Topologic Map," in *Proc. Int. Conf. on Image Processing*, 2001.

Bernard et al. (2002). Bernard S., Boujemaa N., Vitale D. and Bricot C., "Fingerprint Segmentation Using the Phase of Multiscale Gabor Wavelets," in *Proc. Asian Conf. Computer Vision*, 2002.

Berry and Stoney (2001). Berry J. and Stoney D.A., "The history and development of fingerprinting," in *Advances in Fingerprint Technology*, 2nd edition, H.C. Lee and R. Gaensslen (Eds.), pp. 1–40, CRC Press, Boca Raton, FL, 2001.

Besl and McKay (1992). Besl P.J. and McKay N.D., "A method for registration of 3-D shapes," *IEEE Transactions on Pattern Analysis Machine Intelligence*, vol. 14, no. 2, pp. 239–256, 1992.

Beyer, Lake and Lougheed (1993). Beyer J., Lake C. and Lougheed R., "Ridge Flow Determination in Fingerprint Images," in *Proc. Conf. Artificial Intelligence Pattern Recognition*, 1993.

Bhanu and Tan (2001a). Bhanu B. and Tan X., "A Triplet Based Approach for Indexing of Fingerprint Database for Identification," in *Proc. Int. Conf. on Audio- and Video-Based Biometric Person Authentication (3rd)*, pp. 205–210, 2001a.

Bhanu and Tan (2001b). Bhanu B. and Tan X., "Learned Templates for Feature Extraction in Fingerprint Images," in *Proc. Conf. Computer Vision and Pattern Recognition*, vol. 2, pp. 591–596, 2001b.

Bhanu and Tan (2003). Bhanu B. and Tan X., "Fingerprint indexing based on novel features of minutiae triplets," *IEEE Transactions on Pattern Analysis Machine Intelligence*, vol. 25, no. 5, pp. 616–622, 2003.

Bhanu and Tan (2004). Bhanu B. and Tan X., *Computational Algorithms for Fingerprint Recognition*, Kluwer, Norwell, MA, 2004.

Bhanu, Boshra and Tan (2000). Bhanu B., Boshra M. and Tan X., "Logical Templates for Feature Extraction in Fingerprint Images," in *Proc. Int. Conf. on Pattern Recognition (15th)*, vol. 2, pp. 850–854, 2000.

Bhatnagar, Kumar and Saggar (2007). Bhatnagar J., Kumar A. and Saggar N., "A Novel Approach to Improve Biometric Recognition Using Rank Level Fusion," in *Proc. Conf. Computer Vision and Pattern Recognition*, pp. 1–6, 2007.

Bhowmick and Bhattacharya (2004). Bhowmick P. and Bhattacharya B.B., "Approximate Fingerprint Matching Using kd-tree," in *Proc. Int. Conf. on Pattern Recognition (17th)*, vol. 1, pp. 544–547, 2004.

Bhowmick et al. (2002). Bhowmick P., Bishnu A., Bhattacharya B.B., Kundu M.K., Murthy C.A. and Acharya T., "Determination of Minutiae Scores for Fingerprint Image Applications," in *Proc. Indian Conf. Computer Vision Graphics Image Processing*, pp. 463–468, 2002.

Bicz (2003). Bicz W., "The Idea of Description (Reconstruction) of Fingerprints with Mathematical Algorithms and History of the Development of this Idea at Optel," available at: http://www.optel.pl/article/english/idea.htm (accessed 27 November 2008).

Bicz et al. (1999). Bicz W., Banasiak D., Bruciak P., Gumienny S., Gumuliński Z., Kosz D., Krysiak A., Kuczyński W., Pluta M. and Rabiej, G., "Fingerprint structure imaging based on an ultrasound camera," *Instrumentation Science and Technology*, vol. 27, pp. 295–303, 1999.

Bigun and Granlund (1987). Bigun J. and Granlund G.H., "Optimal Orientation Detection of Linear Symmetry," in *Proc. Int. Conf. on Computer Vision (1st)*, pp. 433–438, 1987.

Bigun et al. (1997). Bigun E.S., Bigun J., Duc B. and Fischer S., "Expert Conciliation for Multi Modal Person Authentication Systems by Baysian Statistics," in *Proc. Int. Conf. on Audio- and-Video-Based Biometric Personal Authentication (1st)*, pp. 291–300, 1997.

Bigun, Bigun and Nilsson (2004). Bigun J., Bigun T. and Nilsson K., "Recognition by symmetry derivatives and the generalized structure tensor," *IEEE Transactions on Pattern Analysis Machine Intelligence*, vol. 26, no. 12, pp. 1590–1605, 2004.

BioLab (2007). BioLab – University of Bologna, "FVC 2006 Web Site," available at: http://bias.csr.unibo.it/fvc2006 (accessed 27 November 2008).

BioSecure (2008). BioSecure Association, "Biometrics for Secure Authentication," available at: http://www.biosecure.info (accessed 27 November 2008).

Bishnu et al. (2006). Bishnu A., Das S., Nandy S.C. and Bhattacharya B.B., "Simple algorithms for partial point set pattern matching under rigid motion," *Pattern Recognition*, vol. 39, no. 9, pp. 1662–1671, 2006.

Bistarelli, Santini and Vaccarelli (2005). Bistarelli S., Santini F. and Vaccarelli A., "An Asymmetric Fingerprint Matching Algorithm for Java Card," in *Proc. Int. Conf. on Audio- and Video-Based Biometric Person Authentication (5th)*, pp. 279–288, 2005.

Blue et al. (1993). Blue J.L., Candela G.T., Grother P.J., Chellappa R. and Wikinson R. and Wilson C., "Evaluation of Pattern Classifiers for Fingerprint and OCR Applications," Tech. Report: NIST TR 3162, 1993.

Bolle et al. (2002). Bolle R., Serior A.W., Ratha N.K. and Pankanti S., "Fingerprint Minutiae: A Constructive Definition," in *Proc. Workshop on Biometric Authentication (in ECCV 2002)*, LNCS 2359, Springer, pp. 58–66, 2002.

Bolle et al. (2003). Bolle R., Connell J., Pankanti S. and Ratha N., *Guide to Biometrics*, Springer, New York, 2003.

Bolle, Connell and Ratha (2002). Bolle R.M., Connell J.H. and Ratha N.K., "Biometric perils and patches," *Pattern Recognition*, vol. 35, no. 12, pp. 2727–2738, 2002.

Bolle, Ratha and Pankanti (1999). Bolle R.M., Ratha N.K. and Pankanti S., "Evaluating Authentication Systems Using Bootstrap Confidence Intervals," in *Proc. Workshop on Automatic Identification Advanced Technologies*, pp. 9–13, 1999.

Bolle, Ratha and Pankanti (2000). Bolle R.M., Ratha N.K. and Pankanti S., "Evaluation Techniques for Biometrics-Based Authentication Systems," in *Proc. Int. Conf. on Pattern Recognition (15th)*, 2000.

Bolle, Ratha and Pankanti (2004). Bolle R.M., Ratha N.K. and Pankanti S., "Error analysis of pattern recognition systems – The subsets bootstrap," *Computer Vision and Image Understanding*, vol. 93, no. 1, pp. 1–33, 2004.

Bonnevie (1924). Bonnevie K., "Studies on papillary patterns in human fingers," *Journal of Genetics*, vol. 15, pp. 1–111, 1924.

Borgefors (1988). Borgefors G., "Hierarchical chamfer matching: A parametric edge matching algorithm," *IEEE Transactions on Pattern Analysis Machine Intelligence*, vol. 10, no. 8, pp. 849–865, 1988.

Bose (1917). Bose H.C., *Hints on Finger-Prints with a Telegraphic Code for Finger Impressions*, Thacker Spink and Company, Calcutta/Simla, 1917.

Bouchaffra and Amira (2008). Bouchaffra D. and Amira A., "Structural hidden Markov models for biometrics: Fusion of face and fingerprint," *Pattern Recognition*, vol. 41, no. 3, pp. 852–867, 2008.

Boult and Woodworth (2007). Boult T.E. and Woodworth R., "Privacy and Security Enhancements in Biometrics," in *Advances in Biometrics: Sensors, Algorithms and Systems*, N.K. Ratha and V. Govindaraju (Eds.), Springer, Heidelberg, 2007.

Boult, Scheirer and Woodworth (2007). Boult T.E., Scheirer W.J. and Woodworth R., "Revocable Fingerprint Biotokens: Accuracy and Security Analysis," in *Proc. Conf. Computer Vision and Pattern Recognition*, 2007.

Bowen (1992). Bowen J., "The Home Office Automatic Fingerprint Pattern Classification Project," in *Proc. IEE Colloquium on Neural Networks for Image processing Applications*, 1992.

Boyen et al. (2005). Boyen X., Dodis Y., Katz J., Ostrovsky R. and Smith A., "Secure Remote Authentication Using Biometric Data," in *Proc. Int. Conf. on Advances in Cryptology (EUROCRYPT 06)*, LNCS 3494, pp. 147–163, 2005.

Bradley (1981). Bradley R., "Performance Estimates for Personnel Access Control System," in *Proc. Int. Carnahan Conf. on Electronic Crime Countermeasures*, pp. 23–27, 1981.

Bradley, Brislawn and Hopper (1992). Bradley J.N., Brislawn C.M. and Hopper T., "The FBI Wavelet/ Scalar Quantization Standard for Grayscale Fingerprint Image Compression," *Proc. of SPIE (Visual Info. Proc. II)*, pp. 293–304, 1992.

Brass and Knauer (2002). Brass P. and Knauer C., "Testing the congruence of d–dimensional point sets," *International Journal of Computational Geometry and Applications*, vol. 12, pp. 115–124, 2002.

Breiman (1996). Breiman L., "Bagging predictors," *Machine Learning*, vol. 24, no. 2, pp. 123–140, 1996.

Brin (1998). Brin D., *The Transparent Society: Will Technology force us to choose between privacy and freedom?*, Addison-Wesley, Reading, MA, 1998.

Brislawn et al. (1996). Brislawn C.M., Bradley J.N., Onyshczak R.J. and Hopper T., "The FBI Compression Standard for Digitized Fingerprint Images," *Proc. of SPIE (Applications of Digital Image Processing XIX)*, vol. 2847, 1996.

Brooks and Iyengar (1997). Brooks R.R. and Iyengar S.S., *Multi-sensor Fusion: Fundamentals and Applications with Software*, Prentice-Hall, Upper Saddle River, NJ, 1997.

Brown (1992). Brown L.G., "Image registration techniques," *ACM Computing Surveys*, vol. 24, no. 4, pp. 326–376, 1992.

Brunelli and Falavigna (1995). Brunelli R. and Falavigna D., "Personal identification using multiple cues," *IEEE Transactions on Pattern Analysis Machine Intelligence*, vol. 17, no. 10, pp. 955–966, 1995.

Buettner and Orlans (2005). Buettner D.J. and Orlans N.M., "A Taxonomy for Physics Based Synthetic Biometric Models," in *Proc. Workshop on Automatic Identification Advanced Technologies*, pp. 10–14, 2005.

Buhan and Hartel (2005). Buhan I. and Hartel P., "The State of the Art in Abuse of Biometrics," Tech. Report: TR–CTIT–05–41, Centre for Telematics and Information Technology, University of Twente, 2005.

Buhan et al. (2007a). Buhan I., Doumen J., Hartel P. and Veldhuis R., "Fuzzy Extractors for Continuous Distributions," in *Proc. Symp. on Information, Computer and Communications Security (ASIACCS 07)*, pp. 353–355, 2007a.

Buhan et al. (2007b). Buhan I., Doumen J., Hartel P. and Veldhuis R., "Secure Ad-hoc Pairing with Biometrics: SAfE," in *Proc. Workshop on Security for Spontaneous Interaction (IWSSI 07)*, pp. 450–456, 2007b.

Bunke (1993). Bunke H., "Structural and syntactic pattern recognition," in *Handbook of Pattern Recognition & Computer Vision*, C.H. Chen et al. (Eds.), World Scientific, Singapore, 1993.

Campbell (1997). Campbell J., "Speaker recognition: A tutorial," *Proceedings of the IEEE*, vol. 85, no. 9, pp. 1437–1462, 1997.

Candela and Chellappa (1993). Candela G.T. and Chellappa R., "Comparative Performance of Classification Methods for Fingerprints," Tech. Report: NIST TR 5163, Apr. 1993.

Candela et al. (1995). Candela G.T., Grother P.J., Watson C.I., Wilkinson R.A. and Wilson C.L., "PCASYS – A Pattern-Level Classification Automation System for Fingerprints," Tech. Report: NIST TR 5647, Aug. 1995.

Canyellas et al. (2005). Canyellas N., Cantó E., Forte G. and López M., "Hardware–Software Codesign of a Fingerprint Identification Algorithm," in *Proc. Int. Conf. on Audio- and Video-Based Biometric Person Authentication (5th)*, pp. 683–692, 2005.

Cappelli and Maio (2004). Cappelli R. and Maio D., "State-of-the-art in fingerprint classification," in *Automatic Fingerprint Recognition Systems*, N. Ratha and R. Bolle (Eds.), Springer, New York, pp. 183–205, 2004.

Cappelli et al. (1999). Cappelli R., Lumini A., Maio D. and Maltoni D., "Fingerprint classification by directional image partitioning," *IEEE Transactions on Pattern Analysis Machine Intelligence*, vol. 21, no. 5, pp. 402–421, 1999.

Cappelli et al. (2003). Cappelli R., Maio D., Maltoni D. and Nanni L., "A Two-Stage Fingerprint Classification System," in *Proc. ACM SIGMM Multimedia Biometrics Methods and Applications Workshop*, Berkley, pp. 95–99, Nov. 2003.

Cappelli et al. (2006). Cappelli R., Maio D., Maltoni D., Wayman J.L. and Jain A.K., "Performance evaluation of fingerprint verification systems," *IEEE Transactions on Pattern Analysis Machine Intelligence*, vol. 28, no. 1, pp. 3–18, 2006.

Cappelli et al. (2007a). Cappelli R., Lumini A., Maio D., Maltoni D., "Fingerprint image reconstruction from standard templates," *IEEE Transactions on Pattern Analysis Machine Intelligence*, vol. 29, no. 9, pp. 1489–1503, 2007a.

Cappelli et al. (2007b). Cappelli R., Lumini A., Maio D. and Maltoni D., "Evaluating Minutiae Template Vulnerability to Masquerade Attack," in *Proc. Workshop on Automatic Identification Advanced Technologies*, pp. 174–179, 2007b.

Cappelli, Ferrara and Maltoni (2008). Cappelli R., Ferrara M. and Maltoni D., "On the operational quality of fingerprint scanners," *IEEE Transactions on Information Forensics and Security*, vol. 3, no. 2, pp. 192–202, 2008.

Cappelli, Maio and Maltoni (1999). Cappelli R., Maio D. and Maltoni D., "Fingerprint Classification Based on Multi-space KL," in *Proc. Workshop on Automatic Identification Advances Technologies*, pp. 117–120, 1999.

Cappelli, Maio and Maltoni (2000a). Cappelli R., Maio D. and Maltoni D., "Combining Fingerprint Classifiers," in *Proc. Int. Workshop on Multiple Classifier Systems (1st)*, pp. 351–361, 2000a.

Cappelli, Maio and Maltoni (2000b). Cappelli R., Maio D. and Maltoni D., "Synthetic Fingerprint-Image Generation," in *Proc. Int. Conf. on Pattern Recognition (15th)*, vol. 3, pp. 475–478, 2000b.

Cappelli, Maio and Maltoni (2000c). Cappelli R., Maio D. and Maltoni D., "Indexing Fingerprint Databases for Efficient 1:N Matching," in *Proc. Int. Conf. on Control Automation Robotics and Vision (6th)*, 2000c.

Cappelli, Maio and Maltoni (2001a). Cappelli R., Maio D. and Maltoni D., "Modelling Plastic Distortion in Fingerprint Images," in *Proc. Int. Conf. on Advances in Pattern Recognition (2nd)*, pp. 369–376, 2001a.

Cappelli, Maio and Maltoni (2001b). Cappelli R., Maio D. and Maltoni D., "Multi-space KL for pattern representation and classification," *IEEE Transactions on Pattern Analysis Machine Intelligence*, vol. 23, no. 9, pp. 977–996, 2001b.

Cappelli, Maio and Maltoni (2002a). Cappelli R., Maio D. and Maltoni D., "A multi-classifier approach to fingerprint classification," *Pattern Analysis and Applications (special Issue on Fusion of Multiple Classifiers)*, vol. 5, no. 2, pp. 136–144, 2002a.

Cappelli, Maio and Maltoni (2002b). Cappelli R., Maio D. and Maltoni D., "Synthetic Fingerprint-Database Generation," in *Proc. Int. Conf. on Pattern Recognition (16th)*, 2002b.

Cappelli, Maio and Maltoni (2004). Cappelli R., Maio D. and Maltoni D., "An Improved Noise Model for the Generation of Synthetic Fingerprints," in *Proc. Int. Conf. on Control*, Automation, Robotics and Vision (ICARCV2004), Kunming, China, 2004.

Carvalho and Yehia (2004). Carvalho C. and Yehia H., "Fingerprint Alignment Using Line Segments," in *Proc. Int. Conf. on Biometric Authentication (1st)*, LNCS 3072, pp. 380–387, 2004.

CDEFFS (2008). ANSI/NIST – CDEFFS group, "Data Format for the Interchange of Extended Fingerprint and Palmprint Features – Addendum to ANSI/NIST–ITL 1–2007," ANSI/NIST, Working Draft 0.2, 2008, available at: http://fingerprint.nist.gov/standard/cdeffs (accessed 27 November 2008).

Ceguerra and Koprinska (2002a). Ceguerra A. and Koprinska I., "Automatic Fingerprint Verification Using Neural Networks," in *Proc. Int. Conf. on Artificial Neural Networks*, LNCS 2415, pp. 136, 2002a.

Ceguerra and Koprinska (2002b). Ceguerra A.V. and Koprinska I., "Integrating Local and Global Features in Automatic Fingerprint Verification," in *Proc. Int. Conf. on Pattern Recognition (16th)*, vol. 3, pp. 347–350, 2002b.

Champod and Margot (1996). Champod C. and Margot P.A., "Computer assisted analysis of minutiae occurrences on fingerprints," in *Proc. Int. Symposium on Fingerprint Detection and Identification*, J. Almog and E. Spinger (Eds.), Israel National Police, Jerusalem, pp. 305, 1996.

Champod et al. (2004). Champod C., Lennard C.J., Margot P. and Stoilovic M., *Fingerprints and Other Ridge Skin Impressions*, CRC Press, Boca Raton, FL, 2004.

Chan, Moon and Cheng (2004). Chan K.C., Moon Y.S. and Cheng P.S., "Fast fingerprint verification using subregions of fingerprint images," *IEEE Transactions on Circuits and Systems for Video Technology*, vol. 14, no. 1, pp. 95–101, 2004.

Chang (1980). Chang T., "Texture Analisys of Digitized Fingerprints for Singularity Detection," in *Proc. Int. Conf. on Pattern Recognition (5th)*, pp. 478–480, 1980.

Chang and Fan (2001). Chang J.H. and Fan K.C., "Fingerprint ridge allocation in direct gray-scale domain," *Pattern Recognition*, vol. 34, no. 10, pp. 1907–1925, 2001.

Chang and Fan (2002). Chang J.H. and Fan K.C., "A new model for fingerprint classification by ridge distribution sequences," *Pattern Recognition*, vol. 35, no. 6, pp. 1209–1223, 2002.

Chang and Roy (2007). Chang E.C. and Roy S., "Robust Extraction of Secret Bits from Minutiae," in *Proc. Int. Conf. on Biometrics*, LNCS 4642, pp. 750–759, 2007.

Chang et al. (1997). Chang S.H., Cheng F.H., Hsu W.H. and Wu G.Z., "Fast algorithm for point pattern-matching: Invariant to translations, rotations and scale changes," *Pattern Recognition*, vol. 30, pp. 311–320, 1997.

Chang, Zhang and Chen (2004). Chang Y.J., Zhang W. and Chen T., "Biometrics-Based Cryptographic Key Generation," in *Proc. Int. Conf. on Multimedia and Expo (ICME 04)*, vol. 3, pp. 2203–2206, 2004.

Chapel (1971). Chapel C., *Fingerprinting – A Manual of Identification*, Coward McCann, New York, 1971.

Chebira et al. (2007). Chebira A, Coelho L.P., Sandryhaila A., Lin S., Jenkinson W.G., MacSleyne J., Hoffman C., Cuadra P., Jackson C., Puschel M. and Kovacevic J., "An Adaptive Multiresolution Approach to Fingerprint Recognition," in *Proc. Int. Conf. on Image Processing*, vol. 1, pp. 457–460, 2007.

Chen and Dong (2006). Chen H. and Dong G., "Fingerprint Image Enhancement by Diffusion Processes," in *Proc. Int. Conf. on Image Processing*, pp. 297–300, 2006.

Chen and Jain (2007). Chen Y. and Jain A.K., "Dots and Incipients: Extended Features for Partial Fingerprint Matching," in *Proc. Biometric Symposium*, 2007.

Chen and Kuo (1991). Chen Z. and Kuo C.H., "A Topology-Based Matching Algorithm for Fingerprint Authentication," in *Proc. Int. Carnahan Conf. on Security Technology (25th)*, pp. 84–87, 1991.

Chen and Kuo (1995). Chen W.S. and Kuo C.L., "Apparatus for Imaging Fingerprint or Topographic Relief Pattern on the Surface of an Object," US Patent 5448649, 1995.

Chen and Moon (2006). Chen J.S. and Moon Y.S., "A Statistical Evaluation Model for Minutiae-Based Automatic Fingerprint Verification Systems," in *Proc. Int. Conf. on Biometrics*, LNCS 3832, pp. 236–243, 2006.

Chen and Moon (2007). Chen J. and Moon Y.S., "A Minutiae-Based Fingerprint Individuality Model," in *Proc. Conf. Computer Vision and Pattern Recognition*, 2007.

Chen and Moon (2008). Chen J. and Moon Y.S., "The Statistical Modelling of Fingerprint Minutiae Distribution with Implications for Fingerprint Individuality Studies," in *Proc. Int. Conf. on Computer Vision and Pattern Recognition (CVPR08)*, pp. 1–7, 2008.

Chen et al. (2004). Chen X., Tian J., Cheng J. and Yang X., "Segmentation of fingerprint images using linear classifier," *EURASIP Journal on Applied Signal Processing*, vol. 2004, no. 4, pp. 480–494, 2004.

Chen et al. (2006a). Chen X., Tian J., Yang X. and Zhang Y., "An algorithm for distorted fingerprint matching based on local triangle feature set," *IEEE Transactions on Information Forensics and Security*, vol. 1, no. 2, pp. 169–177, 2006a.

Chen et al. (2006b). Chen X., Tian J., Zhang Y. and Yang X., "Enhancement of Low Quality Fingerprints Based on Anisotropic Filtering," in *Proc. Int. Conf. on Biometrics*, LNCS 3832, pp. 302–308, 2006b.

Chen, Chan and Moon (2007). Chen J., Chan F. and Moon Y.S., "Fingerprint Matching with Minutiae Quality Score," in *Proc. Int. Conf. on Biometrics*, LNCS 4642, pp. 663–672, 2007.

Chen, Dass and Jain (2005). Chen Y., Dass S.C. and Jain A.K., "Fingerprint Quality Indices for Predicting Authentication Performance," in *Proc. Int. Conf. on Audio- and Video-Based Biometric Person Authentication (5th)*, pp. 160–170, 2005.

Chen, Jain and Dass (2005). Chen Y., Jain A.K. and Dass S., "Fingerprint Deformation for Spoof Detection," in *Proc. Biometrics Symposium*, 2005.

Chen, Jiang and Yau (2004). Chen T., Jiang X. and Yau W., "Fingerprint Image Quality Analysis," in *Proc. Int. Conf. on Image Processing*, pp. 1253–1256, 2004.

Chen, Moon and Fong (2004). Chen J.S., Moon Y.S. and Fong K.F., "Efficient Fingerprint Image Enhancement for Mobile Embedded Systems," in *Proc. Workshop on Biometric Authentication (in ECCV 2004)*, LNCS 3087, pp. 146–157, 2004.

Chen, Tian and Yang (2003). Chen H., Tian J. and Yang X., "Fingerprint Matching with Registration Pattern Inspection," in *Proc. Int. Conf. on Audio- and Video-Based Biometric Person Authentication (4th)*, pp. 327–334, 2003.

Chen, Tian and Yang (2006). Chen X., Tian J. and Yang X., "A new algorithm for distorted fingerprints matching based on normalized fuzzy similarity measure," *IEEE Transactions on Image Processing*, vol. 15, no. 3, pp. 767–776, 2006.

Cheng and Larin (2006). Cheng Y. and Larin K.V., "Artificial fingerprint recognition by using optical coherence tomography with autocorrelation analysis," *Applied Optics*, vol. 45, no. 36, pp. 9238–9245, 2006.

Cheng and Tian (2004). Cheng J. and Tian J., "Fingerprint enhancement with dyadic scale-space," *Pattern Recognition Letters*, vol. 25, no. 11, pp. 1273–1284, 2004.

Cheng et al. (2003). Cheng J., Tian J., Chen H., Ren Q. and Yang X., "Fingerprint Enhancement Using Oriented Diffusion Filter," in *Proc. Int. Conf. on Audio- and Video-Based Biometric Person Authentication (4th)*, pp. 164–171, 2003.

Cheng, Tian and Chen (2004). Cheng J., Tian J. and Chen H., "Fingerprint Minutiae Matching with Orientation and Ridge," in *Proc. Int. Conf. on Biometric Authentication (1st)*, LNCS 3072, pp. 351–358, 2004.

Cheng, Tian and Zhang (2002). Cheng H., Tian J. and Zhang T., "Fingerprint Enhancement with Dyadic Scale-Space," in *Proc. Int. Conf. on Pattern Recognition (16th)*, vol. 1, pp. 200–203, 2002.

Chikkerur and Ratha (2005). Chikkerur S. and Ratha N., "Impact of Singular Point Detection on Fingerprint Matching Performance," in *Proc. Workshop on Automatic Identification Advanced Technologies*, pp. 207–212, 2005.

Chikkerur et al. (2005). Chikkerur S., Govindaraju V., Pankanti S., Bolle R. and Ratha N., "Novel Approaches for Minutiae Verification in Fingerprint Images," in *Proc. Workshops on Application of Computer Vision*, vol. 1, pp. 111–116, 2005.

Chikkerur et al. (2006). Chikkerur S., Pankanti S., Jea A., Ratha N. and Bolle R., "Fingerprint Representation Using Localized Texture Features," in *Proc. Int. Conf. on Pattern Recognition (18th)*, vol. 4, pp. 521–524, 2006.

Chikkerur et al. (2008). Chikkerur S., Ratha N.K., Connell J.H. and Bolle R.M., "Generating Registration-Free Cancelable Fingerprint Templates," in *Proc. Int. Conf. on Biometrics: Theory, Applications and Systems (BTAS 08)*, 2008.

Chikkerur, Cartwright and Govindaraju (2006). Chikkerur S., Cartwright A.N. and Govindaraju V., "K-plet and Coupled BFS: A Graph Based Fingerprint Representation and Matching Algorithm," in *Proc. Int. Conf. on Biometrics*, LNCS 3832, pp. 309–315, 2006.

Chikkerur, Cartwright and Govindaraju (2007). Chikkerur S., Cartwright A.N. and Govindaraju V., "Fingerprint enhancement using STFT analysis," *Pattern Recognition*, vol. 40, no. 1, pp. 198–211, 2007.

Cho et al. (2000). Cho B.H., Kim J.S., Bae J.H., Bae I.G. and Yoo K.Y., "Core-Based Fingerprint Image Classification," in *Proc. Int. Conf. on Pattern Recognition (15th)*, vol. 2, pp. 863–866, 2000.

Cho, Hong and Cho (2007). Cho U.K., Hong J.H. and Cho S.B., "Automatic Fingerprints Image Generation Using Evolutionary Algorithm," in *Proc. Int. Conf. on Biometrics*, LNCS 4642, pp. 134–143, 2007.

Choi et al. (2003). Choi K., Lee D., Lee S. and Kim J., "An Improved Fingerprint Indexing Algorithm Based on the Triplet Approach," in *Proc. Int. Conf. on Audio- and Video-Based Biometric Person Authentication (4th)*, pp. 584–591, 2003.

Choi et al. (2007a). Choi K., Choi H., Lee S. and Kim J., "Fingerprint image mosaicking by recursive ridge mapping," *IEEE Transaction on Systems, Man, and Cybernetics, Part B*, vol. 37, no. 5, pp. 1191–1203, 2007a.

Choi et al. (2007b). Choi H., Kang R., Choi K. and Kim J., "Aliveness Detection of Fingerprints Using Multiple Static Features," in *Proc. World Academy of Science, Engineering and Technology (WASET 07)*, pp. 157–162, 2007b.

Choi, Choi and Kim (2005). Choi K., Choi H.S. and Kim J., "Fingerprint Mosaicking by Rolling and Sliding," in *Proc. Int. Conf. on Audio- and Video-Based Biometric Person Authentication (5th)*, pp. 260–269, 2005.

Chong et al. (1992). Chong M., Gay R., Tan H. and Liu J., "Automatic representation of fingerprints for data compression by B-spline functions," *Pattern Recognition*, vol. 25, no. 10, pp. 1199–1210, 1992.

Chong et al. (1997). Chong M.M.S., Ngee T.H., Jun L. and Gay R.K.L., "Geometric framework for fingerprint image classification," *Pattern Recognition*, vol. 30, no. 9, pp. 1475–1488, 1997.

Choudhury et al. (1999). Choudhury T., Clarkson B., Jebara T. and Pentland A., "Multimodal Person Recognition Using Unconstrained Audio and Video," in *Proc. Int. Conf. on Audio- and-Video-Based Biometric Person Authentication (2nd)*, pp. 176–181, 1999.

Chung et al. (2005). Chung Y., Moon D., Lee S., Jung S., Kim T. and Ahn D., "Automatic Alignment of Fingerprint Features for Fuzzy Fingerprint Vault," in *Proc. Conf. on Information Security and Cryptology*, pp. 358–369, 2005.

CJIS (1999). FBI – CJIS Division, "Electronic Fingerprint Transmission Specification," Int. Report: CJIS–RS–0010 (V7), 1999, available at: http://www.fbi.gov/hq/cjisd/iafis/efts70/cover.htm (accessed 27 November 2008).

CJIS (2006). FBI – CJIS Division, "Image Quality Specifications for Single Finger Capture Devices," available at: http://www.fbi.gov/hq/cjisd/iafis/piv/pivspec.pdf (accessed 27 November 2008).

Clancy, Kiyavash and Lin (2003). Clancy T., Kiyavash N. and Lin D., "Secure Smartcard-Based Fingerprint Authentication," in *Proc. ACM SIGMM Workshop on Biometric Methods and Applications*, pp. 45–52, 2003.

Clark and Yuille (1990). Clark J. and Yuille A., *Data Fusion for Sensory Information Processing Systems*, Kluwer, Boston, MA, 1990.

Clausen (2007). Clausen S., "A single-line AC capacitive fingerprint swipe sensor," in *Advances in Biometrics: Sensors, Algorithms and Systems*, N.K. Ratha and V. Govindaraju (Eds.), Springer, Heidelberg, pp. 49–62, 2007.

Coetzee and Botha (1990). Coetzee L. and Botha E.C., "Fingerprint Recognition with a Neural-Net Classifier," in *Proc. South African Workshop on Pattern Recognition (1st)*, vol. 1, pp. 33–40, Nov. 1990.

Coetzee and Botha (1993). Coetzee L. and Botha E.C., "Fingerprint recognition in low quality images," *Pattern Recognition*, vol. 26, no. 10, pp. 1441–1460, 1993.

Cole (2001a). Cole S.A., "What counts for identity?" *Fingerprint World*, vol. 27, no. 103, pp. 7–35, 2001a.

Cole (2001b). Cole S.A., *Suspect Identities: A History of Fingerprint and Criminal Identification*, Harvard University Press, Cambridge, MA, May 2001b.

Cole (2004). Cole S.A., "History of fingerprint pattern recognition," in *Automatic Fingerprint Recognition Systems*, N. Ratha and R. Bolle (Eds.), Springer, New York, pp. 1–25, 2004.

Cole (2006). Cole S., "Is fingerprint identification valid? Rhetorics of reliability in fingerprint proponents discourse," *Law & Policy*, vol. 28, no. 1, pp. 109–135, 2006.

Coli, Marcialis and Roli (2007a). Coli P., Marcialis G.L. and Roli F., "Vitality Detection from Fingerprint Images: A Critical Survey," in *Proc. Int. Conf. on Biometrics*, LNCS 4642, pp. 722–731, 2007a.

Coli, Marcialis and Roli (2007b). Coli P., Marcialis G.L. and Roli F., "Power Spectrum-Based Fingerprint Vitality Detection," in *Proc. Workshop on Automatic Identification Advanced Technologies*, pp. 169–173, 2007b.

Colins (1992). Colins M.W., *Realizing the Full Value of Latent Prints*, California Identification Digest, 1992.

Connell, Ratha and Bolle (2002). Connell J.H., Ratha N.K. and Bolle R.M., "Fingerprint Image Enhancement Using Weak Models," in *Proc. Int. Conf. on Image Processing*, vol. 1, pp. 45–48, 2002.

Cormen, Leiserson and Rivest (1990). Cormen T.H., Leiserson C.E. and Rivest R.L., *Introduction to Algorithms*, McGraw-Hill, New York, 1990.

Costello, Gunawardena and Nadiadi (1994). Costello B.D., Gunawardena C.A. and Nadiadi Y.M., "Automated Coincident Sequencing for Fingerprint Verification," in *Proc. IEE Colloquium on Image Processing for Biometric Measurement*, 1994.

Cover (1974). Cover T.M., "The best two independent measurements are not the two best," *IEEE Transactions on Systems Man and Cybernatics*, vol. 4, no. 1, pp. 116–117, 1974.

Cover (1977). Cover T.M., "On the possible ordering in the measurement selection problem," *IEEE Transactions on Systems Man and Cybernatics*, vol. 9, pp. 657–661, 1977.

Cowger (1983). Cowger J., *Friction Ridge Skin: Comparison and Identification of Fingerprints*, Elsevier, New York, 1983.

Crouzil, Massip-Pailhes and Castan (1996). Crouzil A., Massip-Pailhes L. and Castan S., "A New Correlation Criterion Based on Gradient Fields Similarity," in *Proc. Int. Conf. on Pattern Recognition (13th)*, pp. 632–636, 1996.

Cukic and Bartlow (2005). Cukic B. and Bartlow N., "Biometric System Threats and Countermeasures: A Risk Based Approach," in *Proc. Biometric Consortium Conference (BCC 05)*, Crystal City, VA, USA, Sept. 2005.

Cummins (1926). Cummins H., "Epidermal-ridge configurations in developmental defects, with particular reference to the ontogenetic factors which condition ridge direction," *American Journal of Anatomy*, vol. 38, pp. 89–151, 1926.

Cummins and Midlo (1943). Cummins H. and Midlo C., *Fingerprints, Palms and Soles*, Dover, New York, 1943.

Cummins and Midlo (1961). Cummins H. and Midlo C., *Fingerprints, Palms and Soles: An Introduction to Dermatoglyphics*, Dover, New York, 1961.

Cummins, Waits and McQuitty (1941). Cummins H., Waits W.J. and McQuitty J.T., "The breadths of epidermal ridges on the fingertips and palms: A study of variations," *American Journal of Anatomy*, vol. 68, pp. 127–150, 1941.

Da Costa et al. (2001). Da Costa J.P., Le Pouliquen F., Germain C. and Baylou P., "New Operators for Optimized Orientation Estimation," in *Proc. Int. Conf. on Image Processing*, 2001.

Danielsson and Ye (1988). Danielsson P. and Ye Q., "Rotation-Invariant Operators Applied to Enhancement of Fingerprints," in *Proc. Int. Conf. on Pattern Recognition (9th)*, pp. 329–333, 1988.

Dasarathy (1994). Dasarathy B.V., *Decision Fusion*, IEEE Computer Socienty Press, Los Alamitos, CA, 1994.

Dass (2004). Dass S.C., "Markov random field models for directional field and singularity extraction in fingerprint images," *IEEE Transactions on Image Processing*, vol. 13, no. 10, pp. 1358–1367, 2004.

Dass, Nandakumar and Jain (2005). Dass S., Nandakumar K. and Jain A.K., "A Principled Approach to Score Level Fusion in Multimodal Biometric Systems," in *Proc. Int. Conf. on Audio- and Video-Based Biometric Person Authentication (5th)*, pp. 1049–1058, 2005.

Dass, Zhu and Jain (2005). Dass S.C., Zhu Y. and Jain A.K., "Statistical Models for Assessing the Individuality of Fingerprints," in *Proc. Workshop on Automatic Identification Advanced Technologies*, pp. 3–9, 2005.

Dass, Zhu and Jain (2006). Dass S.C, Zhu Y. and Jain A.K, "Validating a biometric authentication system: Sample size requirements," *IEEE Transactions on Pattern Analysis Machine Intelligence*, vol. 28, no. 12, pp. 1302–1319, 2006.

Daugman (1985). Daugman J.G., "Uncertainty relation for resolution in space, spatial-frequency, and orientation optimized by two-dimensional visual cortical filters," *Journal Optical Society American*, vol. 2, pp. 1160–1169, 1985.

Daugman (1999). Daugman J., "Recognizing persons by their iris patterns," in *Biometrics: Personal Identification in a Networked Society*, A.K. Jain, R. Bolle and S. Pankanti (Eds.), Kluwer, Norwell, MA, 1999.

Daugman (2000). Daugman J., "Biometric decision landscapes," Tech. Report: TR482, University of Cambridge, 2000.

Davida et al. (1999). Davida G., Frankel Y., Matt B.J. and Peralta R., "On the Relation of Error Correction and Cryptography to an Offline Biometric Based Identification Scheme," in *Proc. Workshop on Coding and Cryptography*, 1999.

Davida, Frankel and Matt (1998). Davida G.I., Frankel Y. and Matt B.J., "On Enabling Secure Applications Through Off-Line Biometric Identification," in *Proc. Symp. on Privacy and Security*, pp. 148–157, 1998.

De Boer, Bazen and Gerez (2001). De Boer J., Bazen A.M. and Gerez S.H., "Indexing Fingerprint Databases Based on Multiple Features," in *Proc. Workshop on Circuits Systems and Signal Processing (ProRISC 2001)*, 2001.

Delvaux et al. (2008). Delvaux N. et al., "Pseudo Identities Based on Fingerprint Characteristics," in *Proc. Int. Conf on Intelligent Information Hiding and Multimedia Signal Processing (IIH–MSP 2008)*, 2008.

Deng and Huo (2005). Deng H. and Huo Q., "Minutiae Matching Based Fingerprint Verification Using Delaunay Triangulation and Aligned-Edge-Guided Triangle Matching," in *Proc. Int. Conf. on Audio- and Video-Based Biometric Person Authentication (5th)*, pp. 270–278, 2005.

Derakhshani et al. (2003). Derakhshani R., Schuckers S.A.C., Hornak L.A. and O'Gorman L., "Determination of vitality from a non-invasive biomedical measurement for use in fingerprint scanners," *Pattern Recognition*, vol. 36, no. 2, pp. 383–396, 2003.

Deriche, Kasaei and Bouzerdoum (1999). Deriche M., Kasaei S. and Bouzerdoum A., "A Novel Fingerprint Image Compression Technique Using The Wavelet Transform And Piecewise Uniform Pyramid Lattice Vector Quantization," in *Proc. Int. Conf. on Image Processing*, 1999.

Dickinson et al. (2000). Dickinson A., McPherson R., Mendis S. and Ross P.C., "Capacitive Fingerprint Sensor with Adjustable Gain," US Patent 6049620, 2000.

Dieckmann, Plankensteiner and Wagner(1997). Dieckmann U., Plankensteiner P. and Wagner T., "SESAM: A biometric person identification system using sensor fusion," *Pattern Recognition Letters*, vol. 18, pp. 827–833, 1997.

Dimitriadis and Polemi (2004). Dimitriadis C. and Polemi D., "Application of Multi-criteria Analysis for the Creation of a Risk Assessment Knowledgebase for Biometric Systems," in *Proc. Int. Conf. on Biometric Authentication (1st)*, LNCS 3072, pp. 724–730, 2004.

Dinish et al. (2005). Dinish U.S., Chao Z.X., Seah L.K., Singh A. and Murukeshan V.M., "Formulation and implementation of a phase-resolved fluorescence technique for latent-fingerprint imaging: theoretical and experimental analysis," *Applied Optics*, vol. 44, no. 3, pp. 297–304, 2005.

DOD (2007). Department of Defense (US), "Electronic Biometric Transmission Specification," Internal Report, Jan. 2007, available at: http://www.biometrics.dod.mil (accessed 27 November 2008).

Doddington et al. (1998). Doddington G., Ligget W., Martin A., Przybocki M. and Reynolds D., "Sheeps, Goats, Lambs, Wolves: An Analysis of Individual Differences in Speaker Recognition Performance," in *Proc. Int. Conf. on Speech and Language Processing*, 1998.

Dodis et al. (2008). Dodis Y., Ostrovsky R., Reyzin L. and Smith A., "Fuzzy extractors: How to generate strong keys from biometrics and other noisy data," *SIAM Journal on Computing*, vol. 38, no. 1, pp. 97–139, 2008.

Dodis, Reyzin and Smith (2004). Dodis Y., Reyzin L. and Smith A., "Fuzzy Extractors: How to Generate Strong Keys from Biometrics and Other Noisy Data," in *Proc. Int. Conf. on Cryptology (EUROCRYPT 04)*, pp. 523–540, 2004.

Domeniconi, Tari and Liang (1998). Domeniconi C., Tari S., Liang P., "Direct Gray Scale Ridge Reconstruction in Fingerprint Images," in *Proc. Int. Conf. on Acoustic Speech and Signal Processing*, 1998.

Donahue and Rokhlin (1993). Donahue M.L and Rokhlin S.I., "On the use of level curves in image analysis," *CVGIP: Image Understanding*, vol. 57, no. 2, pp. 185–203, 1993.

Dorai, Ratha and Bolle (2000). Dorai C., Ratha N.K. and Bolle R.M., "Detecting Dynamic Behavior in Compressed Fingerprint Videos: Distortion," in *Proc. Conf. Computer Vision and Pattern Recognition*, vol. 2, pp. 320–326, 2000.

Dorai, Ratha and Bolle (2004). Dorai C., Ratha N. and Bolle R.M., "Dynamic behavior in fingerprint videos," in *Automatic Fingerprint Recognition Systems*, N. Ratha and R. Bolle (Eds.), Springer, New York, pp. 67–86, 2004.

Dowling and Knowlton (1988). Dowling Jr. R.F. and Knowlton K.L., "Fingerprint Acquisition System with a Fiber Optic Block," US Patent 4785171, 1988.

Drake, Lidd and Fiddy (1996). Drake M.D., Lidd M.L. and Fiddy M.A., "Waveguide hologram fingerprint entry device," *Optical Engineering*, vol. 35, no. 9, pp. 2499–2505, 1996.

Draper et al. (2007a). Draper S.C., Khisti A., Martinian E., Vetro A. and Yedidia J.S., "Secure Storage of Fingerprint Biometrics Using Slepian–Wolf Codes," in *Proc. Information Theory and Applications Workshop*, 2007a.

Draper et al. (2007b). Draper S.C., Khisti A., Martinian E., Vetro A. and Yedidia J.S., "Using Distributed Source Coding to Secure Fingerprint Biometrics," in *Proc. Int. Conf. on Acoustics, Speech, and Signal Processing*, 2007b.

Drets and Liljenstrom (1998). Drets G. and Liljenstrom H., "Fingerprint sub-classification and singular point detection," *International Journal of Pattern Recognition and Artificial Intelligence*, vol. 12, no. 4, pp. 407–422, 1998.

Duc et al. (1997). Duc B., Bigun E.S., Bigun J., Maitre G. and Fischer S., "Fusion of audio and video information for multi modal person authentication," *Pattern Recognition Letters*, vol. 18, no. 9, pp. 835–843, 1997.

Duda, Hart and Stork (2000). Duda R.O., Hart P.E. and Stork D.G., *Pattern Classification*, 2nd edition, Wiley, New York, 2000.

Edwards (1984). Edwards D.G., "Fingerprint Sensor," US Patent 4429413, 1984.

Edwards, Torrens and Bhamra (2006). Edwards M.B., Torrens G.E. and Bhamra T.A., "The Use of Fingerprint Contact Area for Biometric Identification," in *Proc. Int. Conf. on Biometrics*, LNCS 3832, pp. 341–347, 2006.

Eleccion (1973). Eleccion M., "Automatic fingerprint identification," *IEEE Spectrum*, vol. 10, pp. 36–45, Sept. 1973.

Engel, Pschernig and Uhl (2008). Engel D., Pschernig E. and Uhl A., "An analysis of lightweight encryption schemes for fingerprint images," *IEEE Transactions on Information Forensics and Security*, vol. 3, no. 2, pp. 173–182, 2008.

Erol, Halici and Ongun (1999). Erol A., Halici U. and Ongun G., "Feature selective filtering for ridge extraction," in *Intelligent Biometric Techniques in Fingerprint & Face Recognition*, L.C. Jain, U. Halici, I. Hayashi and S.B. Lee (Eds.), CRC Press, Baco Raton, FL, 1999.

Ersoy, Ercal and Gokmen (1999). Ersoy I., Ercal F. and Gokmen M., "A Model-Based Approach for Compression of Fingerprint Images," in *Proc. Int. Conf. on Image Processing*, 1999.

Fan et al. (2008). Fan L., Wang S., Wang H. and Guo T., "Singular points detection based on zero-pole model in fingerprint images," *IEEE Transactions on Pattern Analysis Machine Intelligence*, vol. 30, no. 6, pp. 929–940, 2008.

Fan, Liu and Wang (2000). Fan K.C., Liu C.W. and Wang Y.K., "A randomized approach with geometric constraints to fingerprint verification," *Pattern Recognition*, vol. 33, no. 11, pp. 1793–1803, 2000.

Fang (1979). Fang G.S., "A note on optimal selection of independent observables," *IEEE Transactions on Systems Man and Cybernatics*, vol. 9, no. 5, pp. 309–311, 1979.

Fang et al. (2007). Fang G., Srihari S.N., Srinivasan H. and Phatak P., "Use of Ridge Points in Partial Fingerprint Matching," in *Proc. SPIE Conf. on Biometric Technology for Human Identification IV*, 2007.

Farina, Kovacs-Vajna and Leone (1999). Farina A., Kovacs-Vajna Z.M. and Leone A., "Fingerprint minutiae extraction from skeletonized binary images," *Pattern Recognition*, vol. 32, no. 5, pp. 877–889, 1999.

Farooq et al. (2007). Farooq F., Bolle R.M., Tsai-Yang J and Ratha N., "Anonymous and Revocable Fingerprint Recognition," in *Proc. Conf. Computer Vision and Pattern Recognition*, 2007.

Fatehpuria et al. (2007). Fatehpuria A., Lau D.L., Yalla V. and Hassebrook L.G., "Performance Analysis of Three-Dimensional Ridge Acquisition from Live Finger and Palm Surface Scans," in *Proc. SPIE Conf. on Biometric Technology for Human Identification IV*, 2007.

Fatehpuria, Lau and Hassebrook (2006). Fatehpuria A., Lau D.L. and Hassebrook L.G., "Acquiring a 2D Rolled Equivalent Fingerprint Image from a Non-contact 3D Finger Scan," in *Proc. SPIE Conf. on Biometric Technology for Human Identification III*, 2006.

FBI (2008). FBI, "Products Certified for Compliance with the FBI's Integrated Automated Fingerprint Identification System Image Quality Specifications," available at: http://www.fbi.gov/hq/cjisd/iafis/cert.htm (accessed 27 November 2008).

Federal Bureau of Investigation (1984). Federal Bureau of Investigation, *The Science of Fingerprints: Classification and Uses*, U.S. Government Publication, Washington, DC, 1984.

Federal Bureau of Investigation (1991). Federal Bureau of Investigation, *The FBI fingerprint identification automation program: issues and options*, U.S. Government Publication/Congress of the U.S., Office of Technology Assessment, Washington, DC, 1991.

Feng (2008). Feng J., "Combining minutiae descriptors for fingerprint matching," *Pattern Recognition*, vol. 41, no. 1, pp. 342–352, 2008.

Feng and Cai (2006a). Feng J. and Cai A., "Fingerprint Representation and Matching in Ridge Coordinate System," in *Proc. Int. Conf. on Pattern Recognition (18th)*, vol. 4, pp. 485–488, 2006a.

Feng and Cai (2006b). Feng J. and Cai A., "Fingerprint Indexing Using Ridge Invariants," in *Proc. Int. Conf. on Pattern Recognition (18th)*, vol. 4, pp. 433–436, 2006b.

Feng et al. (2006). Feng Y., Feng J., Chen X. and Song Z., "A Novel Fingerprint Matching Scheme Based on Local Structure Compatibility," in *Proc. Int. Conf. on Pattern Recognition (18th)*, vol. 4, pp. 374–377, 2006.

Feng, Ouyang and Cai (2006). Feng J., Ouyang Z. and Cai A., "Fingerprint matching using ridges," *Pattern Recognition*, vol. 39, no. 11, pp. 2131–2140, 2006.

Ferrara, Franco and Maltoni (2007). Ferrara M., Franco A. and Maltoni D., "Estimating Image Focusing in Fingerprint Scanners," in *Proc. Workshop on Automatic Identification Advanced Technologies*, pp. 30–34, 2007.

Fielding, Homer and Makekau (1991). Fielding K., Homer J. and Makekau C., "Optical fingerprint identification by binary joint transform correlation," *Optical Engineering*, vol. 30, no. 12, pp. 1958, 1991.

Fierrez-Aguilar et al. (2005a). Fierrez-Aguilar J., Ortega-Garcia J., Gonzalez-Rodriguez J. and Bigun J., "Discriminative multimodal biometric authentication based on quality measures," *Pattern Recognition*, vol. 38, no. 5, pp. 777–779, 2005a.

Fierrez-Aguilar et al. (2005b). Fierrez-Aguilar J., Garcia-Romero D., Ortega-Garcia J. and Gonzalez-Rodriguez J., "Bayesian adaptation for user-dependent multimodal biometric authentication," *Pattern Recognition*, vol. 38, no. 8, pp. 1317–1319, 2005b.

Fierrez-Aguilar et al. (2006). Fierrez-Aguilar J., Chen Y., Ortega-Garcia J. and Jain A.K., "Incorporating Image Quality in Multi-algorithm Fingerprint Verification," in *Proc. Int. Conf. on Biometrics*, LNCS 3832, pp. 213–220, 2006.

Fierrez-Aguilar et al. (2007). Fierrez-Aguilar J., Ortega-Garcia J., Torre-Toledano D. and Gonzalez-Rodriguez J., "BioSec baseline corpus: a multimodal biometric database," *Pattern Recognition*, vol. 40, no. 4, pp. 1389–1392, 2007.

Figueroa-Villanueva, Ratha and Bolle (2003). Figueroa-Villanueva M.A., Ratha N.K. and Bolle R.M., "A Comparative Performance Analysis of JPEG 2000 vs. WSQ for Fingerprint Image Compression," in *Proc. Int. Conf. on Audio- and Video-Based Biometric Person Authentication (4th)*, pp. 385–392, 2003.

Fitz and Green (1996). Fitz A.P. and Green R.J., "Fingerprint classification using hexagonal fast Fourier transform," *Pattern Recognition*, vol. 29, no. 10, pp. 1587–1597, 1996.

Fjetland and Robbins (1989). Fjetland R., Robbins C., "The AFIS advantage: A milestone in fingerprint identification technology," *The Police Chief*, vol. 56, no. 6, pp. 20, 1989.

Forkert et al. (1994). Forkert R.D., Kearnan G.T., Nill N.B. and Topiwala P.N., "Test Procedures for Verifying IAFIS Scanner Image Quality Requirements," MITRE Tech. Report: MP 94B0000039R1, Nov. 1994.

Franco and Maltoni (2007). Franco A. and Maltoni D., "Fingerprint synthesis and spoof detection," in *Advances in Biometrics: Sensors, Algorithms and Systems*, N.K. Ratha and V. Govindaraju (Eds.), Springer, London, pp. 385–406, 2007.

Freeman and Adelson (1991). Freeman W.T. and Adelson E.H., "The design and use of steerable filters," *IEEE Transactions on Pattern Analysis Machine Intelligence*, vol. 13, no. 9, pp. 891–906, 1991.

Freund and Schapire (1996). Freund Y. and Schapire R., "Experiments with a New Boosting Algorithm," in *Proc. Int. Conf. Machine Learning*, pp. 148–156, 1996.

Frischholz and Dieckmann (2000). Frischholz R.W. and Dieckmann U., "BioId: A multimodal biometric identification system," *IEEE Computer*, vol. 33, no. 2, pp. 64–68, Feb. 2000.

Fronthaler et al. (2008). Fronthaler H., Kollreider K., Bigun J., Fierrez J., Alonso-Fernandez F., Ortega-Garcia J. and Gonzalez-Rodriguez J., "Fingerprint image-quality estimation and its application to multialgorithm verification," *IEEE Transactions on Information Forensics and Security*, vol. 3, no. 2, pp. 331–338, 2008.

Fronthaler, Kollreider and Bigun (2006). Fronthaler H., Kollreider K. and Bigun J., "Automatic Image Quality Assessment with Application in Biometrics," in *Proc. Workshop on Biometrcis in assoc. with CVPR* 2006, pp. 30–35, 2006.

Fronthaler, Kollreider and Bigun (2007). Fronthaler H., Kollreider K. and Bigun J., "Pyramid-Based Image Enhancement of Fingerprints," in *Proc. Workshop on Automatic Identification Advanced Technologies*, pp. 45–50, 2007.

Fronthaler, Kollreider and Bigun (2008). Fronthaler H., Kollreider K. and Bigun J., "Local features for enhancement and minutiae extraction in fingerprints," *IEEE Transactions on Image Processing*, vol. 17, no. 3, pp. 354–363, 2008.

Fu and Booth (1986a). Fu K.S. and Booth T.L., "Grammatical inference: Introduction and survey: Part I," *IEEE Transactions on Pattern Analysis Machine Intelligence*, vol. 8, no. 3, pp. 343–360, 1986a.

Fu and Booth (1986b). Fu K.S. and Booth T.L., "Grammatical inference: Introduction and survey: Part II," *IEEE Transactions on Pattern Analysis Machine Intelligence*, vol. 8, no. 3, pp. 360–376, 1986b.

Fujieda, Ono and Sugama (1995). Fujieda I., Ono Y. and Sugama S., "Fingerprint Image Input Device Having an Image Sensor with Openings," US Patent 5446290, 1995.

FVC-onGoing (2009). Maio D., Maltoni D., Cappelli R., Franco A. and Ferrara M., "On-Line Evaluation of Fingerprint Recognition Algorithms," available at: http://bias.csr.unibo.it/FVConGoing/ (accessed 27 November 2008).

Galton (1892). Galton F., *Finger Prints*, Macmillan, London, 1892.

Gamassi, Piuri and Scotti (2005). Gamassi M., Piuri V. and Scotti F., "Fingerprint Local Analysis for High-Performance Minutiae Extraction," in *Proc. Int. Conf. on Image Processing*, vol. 3, pp. 265–268, 2005.

Gamble, Frye and Grieser (1992). Gamble F.T., Frye L.M. and Grieser D.R., "Real-time fingerprint verification system," *Applied Optics*, vol. 31, no. 5, pp. 652–655, 1992.

Garcia-Salicetti et al. (2003). Garcia-Salicetti S., Beumier C., Chollet G., Dorizzi B., Les Jardins J., Lunter J., Ni Y. and Petrovska-Delacretaz D., "BIOMET: A Multimodal Person Authentication Database Including Face, Voice, Fingerprint, Hand and Signature Modalities," in *Proc. Int. Conf. on Audio- and Video-Based Biometric Person Authentication (4th)*, pp. 845–853, 2003.

Garris and McCabe (2000). Garris M.D. and McCabe R.M., "NIST Special Database 27, Fingerprint Minutiae from Latent and Matching Tenprint Images," U.S. National Institute of Standards and Technology, 2000.

Geng and Shen (1997). Geng Z.J. and Shen W.C., "Fingerprint classification using fuzzy cerebellar model arithmetic computer neural networks," *Journal of Electronic Imaging*, vol. 6, no. 3, pp. 311–318, 1997.

Germain, Califano and Colville (1997). Germain R., Califano A. and Colville S., "Fingerprint matching using transformation parameters," *IEEE Computational Science and Engineering*, vol. 4, no. 4, pp. 42–49, 1997.

Ghosal et al. (2000a). Ghosal S., Ratha N.K., Udupa R. and Pankanti S., "Hierarchical Partitioned Least Squares Filter-Bank for Fingerprint Enhancement," in *Proc. Int. Conf. on Pattern Recognition (15th)*, pp. 334–337, 2000a.

Ghosal et al. (2000b). Ghosal S., Udupa R., Pankanti S. and Ratha N.K., "Learning Partitioned Least Squares Filters for Fingerprint Enhancement," in *Proc. Workshop on Applications of Computer Vision*, pp. 2–7, 2000b.

Gokmen and Jain (1997). Gokmen M. and Jain A.K., "$\lambda\tau$-space representation of image and generalized edge detection," *IEEE Transactions on Pattern Analysis Machine Intelligence*, vol. 19, no. 6, pp. 545–563, 1997.

Gokmen, Ersoy and Jain (1996). Gokmen M., Ersoy I. and Jain A.K., "Compression of Fingerprint Images Using Hybrid Image Model," in *Proc. Int. Conf. on Image Processing*, 1996.

Gold and Rangarajan (1996). Gold S. and Rangarajan A., "A graduated assignement algorithm for graph matching," *IEEE Transactions on Pattern Analysis Machine Intelligence*, vol. 18, no. 4, pp. 377–388, 1996.

Goldberg (1989). Goldberg D., *Genetic Algorithms in Search, Optimization and Machine Learning*, Addison-Wesley, Reading, MA, 1989.

Golfarelli, Maio and Maltoni (1997). Golfarelli M., Maio D. and Maltoni D., "On the error-reject tradeoff in biometric verification systems," *IEEE Transactions on Pattern Analysis Machine Intelligence*, vol. 19, no. 7, pp. 786–796, 1997.

Gong (2004). Gong W., "On Optimal Estimate of Directional Maps for Fingerprint Images," in *Proc. Int. Conf. on Biometric Authentication (1st)*, LNCS 3072, pp. 264–271, 2004.

Gonzales and Woods (2007). Gonzales R.C. and Woods R.E., *Digital Image Processing*, 3rd edition, Prentice-Hall, Englewood Cliffs, NJ, 2007.

Govan and Buggy (2007). Govan M. and Buggy T., "A Computationally Efficient Fingerprint Matching Algorithm for Implementation on Smartcards," in *Proc. Int. Conf. on Biometrics: Theory, Applications, and Systems (BTAS 07)*, pp. 1–6, 2007.

Govindaraju, Shi and Schneider (2003). Govindaraju V., Shi Z. and Schneider J., "Feature Extraction Using a Chaincoded Contour Representation of Fingerprint Images," in *Proc. Int. Conf. on Audio- and Video-Based Biometric Person Authentication (4th)*, pp. 268–275, 2003.

Gowrishankar (1989). Gowrishankar T.R., "Fingerprint Identification on a Massively Parallel Architecture," in *Proc. Symp. on Frontiers of Massively Parallel Computation (2nd)*, pp. 331–334, 1989.

Grasselli (1969). Grasselli A., "On the automatic classification of fingerprints," in *Methodologies of Pattern Recognition*, S. Watanabe (Ed.), Academic, New York, 1969.

Greenberg and Kogan (2005). Greenberg S. and Kogan D., "Structure-adaptive anisotropic filter applied to fingerprints," *Optical Engineering*, vol. 44, no. 12, 2005.

Greenberg et al. (2000). Greenberg S., Aladjem M., Kogan D. and Dimitrov I., "Fingerprint Image Enhancement Using Filtering Techniques," in *Proc. Int. Conf. on Pattern Recognition (15th)*, vol. 3, pp. 326–329, 2000.

Grother et al. (2006). Grother P., McCabe M., Watson C., Indovina M., Salamon W., Flanagan P., Tabassi E., Newton E. and Wilson C., "Performance and Interoperability of the INCITS 378 Fingerprint Template," NIST Research Report: NISTIR 7296, Mar. 2006.

Grother et al. (2007). Grother P., Salamon W., Watson C., Indovina M. and Flanagan P., "MINEX II: Performance of Fingerprint Match-on-Card Algorithms," NIST Interagency Report 7477, 2007.

Grycewicz (1995). Grycewicz T.J., "Fingerprint Identification with Joint Transform Correlator Using Multiple Reference Fingerprints," *Proc. of SPIE (Optical Pattern Recognition VI)*, vol. 2237, pp. 249–254, 1995.

Grycewicz (1996). Grycewicz T.J., "Fingerprint recognition using binary nonlinear joint transform correlators," *Optoelectronic Devices and Systems for Processing, Critical Review*, vol. CR65., 1996.

Grycewicz (1999). Grycewicz T.J., "Techniques to improve binary joint transform correlator performance for fingerprint recognition," *Optical Engineering*, vol. 38, no. 1, pp. 114–119, 1999.

Grycewicz and Javidi (1996). Grycewicz T.J. and Javidi B., "Experimental comparison of binary joint transform correlators used for fingerprint identification," *Optical Engineering*, vol. 35, pp. 2519–2525, 1996.

Gu, Zhou and Yang (2006). Gu J., Zhou J. and Yang C., "Fingerprint recognition by combining global structure and local cues," *IEEE Transactions on Image Processing*, vol. 15, no. 7, pp. 1952–1964, 2006.

Gudmundsso, Hammar and Van Kreveld (2002). Gudmundsson J., Hammar M.H. and Van Kreveld M., "Higher order Delaunay triangulations," *Comput. Geom. Theory Appl.*, vol. 23, no. 1, 2002.

Guiasu (1977). Guiasu S., *Information Theory with Applications*, McGraw-Hill, New York, 1977.

Gunawardena and Sagar (1991). Gunawardena C.A. and Sagar V.K., "Fingerprint Verification Using Coincident Sequencing and Thinning," in *Proc. Conf. of the IEEE Industrial Electronics Society (IECON)*, pp. 1917–1922, 1991.

Gunsel, Uludag and Tekalp (2002). Gunsel B., Uludag U. and Tekalp A.M., "Robust watermarking of fingerprint images," *Pattern Recognition*, vol. 35, no. 12, pp. 2739–2747, 2002.

Gupta (1968). Gupta S.R., "Statistical Survey of Ridge Characteristics," *Int. Criminal Police Review*, vol. 218, no. 130, 1968.

Haber and Haber (2004). Haber L. and Haber R.N., "Error rates for human latent fingerprint examiners," in *Automatic Fingerprint Recognition Systems*, N. Ratha and R. Bolle (Eds.), Springer, New York, pp. 339–360, 2004.

Halici and Ongun (1996). Halici U. and Ongun G., "Fingerprint Classification Through SelfOrganizing Feature Maps Modified to Treat Uncertainties," *Proceedings of the IEEE*, vol. 84, no. 10, pp. 1497–1512, 1996.

Hamamoto (1999). Hamamoto Y., "A Gabor Filter-Based Method for Fingerprint Identification," in *Intelligent Biometric Techniques in Fingerprint & Face Recognition*, L.C. Jain, U. Halici, I. Hayashi and S.B. Lee (Eds.), CRC Press, 1999.

Hampel et al. (1986). Hampel F.R., Ronchetti E.M., Rousseeuw P.J. and Stahel W.A., *Robust Statistics. The Approach Based on Influence Functions*, Wiley, New York, 1986.

Han and Koshimoto (2008). Han H. and Koshimoto Y., "Characteristics of Thermal-Type Fingerprint Sensor," in *Proc. SPIE Conf. on Biometric Technology for Human Identification V*, 2008.

Han et al. (2006). Han Y., Nam J., Park N. and Kim H., "Resolution and Distortion Compensation Based on Sensor Evaluation for Interoperable Fingerprint Recognition," in *Proc. Int. Joint Conf. on Neural Networks*, pp. 692–698, 2006.

Hao, Anderson and Daugman (2006). Hao F., Anderson F. and Daugman J., "Combining crypto with biometrics," *IEEE Transactions on Computers*, vol. 55, no. 9, pp. 1081–1088, 2006.

Hao, Tan and Wang (2002). Hao Y., Tan T. and Wang Y., "Fingerprint Matching Based on Error Propagation," in *Proc. Int. Conf. on Image Processing*, vol. 1, pp. 273–276, 2002.

Harris and Stephens (1988). Harris C. and Stephens M., "A Combined Corner and Edge Detector," in *Proc. Alvey Vision Conference*, pp. 147–151, 1988.

Hase and Shimisu (1984). Hase M. and Shimisu A., "Entry method of fingerprint image using a prism," *Trans. Institute Electron. Commum. Eng. Jpn.*, vol. J67–D, pp. 627–628, 1984.

Hashido et al. (2003). Hashido R., Suzuki A., Iwata A., Okamoto T., Satoh Y. and Inoue M., "A capacitive fingerprint sensor chip using low-temperature poly-Si TFTs on a glass substrate and a novel and unique sensing method," *IEEE Journal of Solid-State Circuits*, vol. 38, no. 2, pp. 274–280, 2003.

Hatano et al. (2002). Hatano T., Adachi T., Shigematsu S., Morimura H., Onishi S., Okazaki Y. and Kyuragi H., "A Fingerprint Verification Algorithm Using the Differential Matching Rate," in *Proc. Int. Conf. on Pattern Recognition (16th)*, vol. 3, pp. 799–802, 2002.

He et al. (2003a). He Y., Tian J., Luo X. and Zhang T., "Image enhancement and minutiae matching in fingerprint verification," *Pattern Recognition Letters*, vol. 24, no. 9, pp. 1349–1360, 2003a.

He et al. (2003b). He Y., Tian J., Ren Q. and Yang X., "Maximum-Likelihood Deformation Analysis of Different-Sized Fingerprints," in *Proc. Int. Conf. on Audio- and Video-Based Biometric Person Authentication (4th)*, pp. 421–428, 2003b.

He et al. (2006). He Y., Tian J., Li L., Chen H. and Yang X., "Fingerprint matching based on global comprehensive similarity," *IEEE Transactions on Pattern Analysis Machine Intelligence*, vol. 28, no. 6, pp. 850–862, 2006.

He et al. (2007). He X., Tian J., Li L., He Y. and Yang X., "Modeling and analysis of local comprehensive minutia relation for fingerprint matching," *IEEE Transaction on Systems, Man, and Cybernetics, Part B*, vol. 37, no. 5, pp. 1204–1211, 2007.

He, Kohno and Imai (1993). He Y., Kohno R. and Imai H., "A fast automatic fingerprint identification method based on a weighted-mean of binary image," *IEICE Transactions on Fundamentals of Electronics Communications and Computer Sciences*, vol. E76–A, no. 9, pp. 1469–1482, 1993.

Henry (1900). Henry E., *Classification and Uses of Finger Prints*, Routledge, London, 1900.

Hiew, Teoh and Pang (2007). Hiew B.Y., Teoh A.B.J. and Pang Y.H., "Touch–Less Fingerprint Recognition System," in *Proc. Workshop on Automatic Identification Advanced Technologies*, pp. 24–29, 2007.

Hill (2001). Hill C.J., "Risk of Masquerade Arising from the Storage of Biometrics," Bachelor of Science Thesis, The Department of Computer Science Australian National University, Nov. 2001.

Ho, Hull and Srihari (1994). Ho T.K., Hull J.J. and Srihari S.N., "Decision combination in multiple classifier systems," *IEEE Transactions on Pattern Analysis Machine Intelligence*, vol. 16, no. 1, pp. 66–75, 1994.

Hollingum (1992). Hollingum J., "Automated fingerprint analysis offers fast verification," *Sensor Review*, vol. 12, no. 3, pp. 12–15, 1992.

Hong and Jain (1996). Hong L. and Jain A.K., "On-Line Fingerprint Verification," in *Proc. Int. Conf. on Pattern Recognition (13th)*, pp. 596–600, 1996.

Hong and Jain (1997). Hong L. and Jain L., "Automatic Personal Identification by Integrating Faces and Fingerprints," in *Proc. Workshop on Automatic Identification Advanced Technologies*, pp. 15–18, 1997.

Hong and Jain (1998a). Hong L. and Jain A.K., "Integrating Faces and Fingerprints for Personal Identification," in *Proc. Asian Conf. Computer Vision*, 1998a.

Hong and Jain (1998b). Hong L. and Jain A.K., "Integrating faces and fingerprints for personal identification," *IEEE Transactions on Pattern Analysis Machine Intelligence*, vol. 20, no. 12, pp. 1295–1307, 1998b.

Hong and Jain (1999). Hong L. and Jain A.K., "Classification of Fingerprint Images," in *Proc. Scandinavian Conf. on Image Analysis (11th)*, 1999.

Hong et al. (1996). Hong L., Jain A.K., Pankanti S. and Bolle R., "Fingerprint Enhancement," in *Proc. Workshop on Applications of Computer Vision*, pp. 202–207, 1996.

Hong et al. (1997). Hong L., Jain A.K., Bolle R. and Pankanti S., "Identity Authentication Using Fingerprints," in *Proc. Int. Conf. on Audio- and-Video-Based Biometric Person Authentication (1st)*, pp. 103–110, 1997.

Hong et al. (2008). Hong J.H., Min J.K., Cho U.K. and Cho S.B., "Fingerprint classification using one-vs-all support vector machines dynamically ordered with naive Bayes classifiers," *Pattern Recognition*, vol. 41, no. 2, pp. 662–671, 2008.

Hong, Jain and Pankanti (1999). Hong L., Jain A.K. and Pankanti S., "Can Multibiometrics Improve Performance ?" in *Proc. Workshop on Automatic Identification Advanced Technologies*, pp. 59–64, 1999.

Hong, Wan and Jain (1998). Hong L., Wan Y. and Jain A.K., "Fingerprint image enhancement: Algorithms and performance evaluation," *IEEE Transactions on Pattern Analysis Machine Intelligence*, vol. 20, no. 8, pp. 777–789, 1998.

Hopper and Preston (1991). Hopper T. and Preston F., "Compression of Grey-Scale Fingerprint Images," in *Proc. Data Compression Conf.*, pp. 309–318, 1991.

Hopper, Brislawn and Bradley (1993). Hopper T., Brislawn C. and Bradley J., *WSQ GrayScale Fingerprint Image Compression Specification*, Federal Bureau of Investigation, Washington, DC, Feb., 1993.

Hoshino et al. (1980). Hoshino Y., Asai K., Kato Y. and Kiji K., "Automatic Reading and Matching for Single-Fingerprint Identification," in *Proc. Int. Conf. Association for Identification (65th)*, pp. 1–7, 1980.

Hrechak and McHugh (1990). Hrechak A. and McHugh J., "Automated fingerprint recognition using structural matching," *Pattern Recognition*, vol. 23, no. 8, pp. 893–904, 1990.

Hsieh, Lai and Wang (2003). Hsieh C.T., Lai E. and Wang Y.C., "An effective algorithm for fingerprint image enhancement based on wavelet transform," *Pattern Recognition*, vol. 36, no. 2, pp. 303–312, 2003.

Huang and Aviyente (2004a). Huang K. and Aviyente S., "Choosing Best Basis in Wavelet Packets for Fingerprint Matching," in *Proc. Int. Conf. on Image Processing*, vol. 2, pp. 1249–1252, 2004a.

Huang and Aviyente (2004b). Huang K. and Aviyente S., "Fingerprint Verification Based on Wavelet Subbands," in *Proc. SPIE Conf. on Biometric Technology for Human Identification I*, 2004b.

Huang and Suen (1995). Huang Y.S. and Suen C.Y., "A method of combining multiple experts for the recognition of unconstrained handwritten numerals," *IEEE Transactions on Pattern Analysis Machine Intelligence*, vol. 17, no. 1, pp. 90–94, 1995.

Huang, Liu and Hung (2007). Huang C.Y., Liu L.M. and Hung D.C.D., "Fingerprint analysis and singular point detection," *Pattern Recognition Letters*, vol. 28, no. 15, pp. 1937–1945, 2007.

Huckemann, Hotz and Munk (2008). Huckemann S., Hotz T. and Munk A., "Global models for the orientation field of fingerprints: An approach based on quadratic differentials," *IEEE Transactions on Pattern Analysis Machine Intelligence*, vol. 30, no. 9, 1507–1519, 2008.

Hughes and Green (1991). Hughes P. and Green A., "The Use of Neural Networks for Fingerprint Classification," in *Proc. Int. Conf. on Neural Networks (2nd)*, 1991.

Hui and Li (2004). Hui H. and Li J.H., "Compensatory Algorithm for Fingerprint Recognition," in *Proc. Int. Conf. on Biometric Authentication (1st)*, LNCS 3072, pp. 366–372, 2004.

Hui et al. (2004). Hui H., Song F.J., Widjaja J. and Li J.H., "ANFIS-based fingerprint-matching algorithm," *Optical Engineering*, vol. 43, no. 8, pp. 1815–1819, 2004.

Hung (1993). Hung D.C.D., "Enhancement and feature purification of fingerprint images," *Pattern Recognition*, vol. 26, no. 11, 1661–1671, 1993.

Hung and Huang (1996). Hung. D.C.D. and Huang C., "A Model for Detecting Singular Points of a Fingerprint," in *Proc. Florida Artificial Intelligence Research Symposium (9th)*, pp. 444–448, 1996.

Huvanandana, Kim and Hwang (2000). Huvanandana S., Kim C. and Hwang J.N., "Reliable and Fast Fingerprint Identification for Security Applications," in *Proc. Int. Conf. on Image Processing*, 2000.

Hwang (2004). Hwang K., "Statistical Quality Assessment of a Fingerprint," in *Proc. SPIE Conf. on Biometric Technology for Human Identification I*, 2004.

Igaki et al. (1992). Igaki S., Eguchi S., Yamagishi F., Ikeda H. and Inagaki T., "Real-time fingerprint sensor using a hologram," *Applied Optics*, vol. 31, no. 11, pp. 1794–1802, 1992.

Ikeda et al. (2002). Ikeda N., Nakanishi M., Fujii K., Hatano T., Shigematsu S., Adachi T., Okazaki Y. and Kyuragi H., "Fingerprint Image Enhancement by Pixel-Parallel Processing," in *Proc. Int. Conf. on Pattern Recognition (16th)*, vol. 3, pp. 752–755, 2002.

Indovina et al. (2003). Indovina M., Uludag U., Snelick R., Mink A. and Jain A.K., "Multimodal Biometric Authentication Methods: A COTS Approach," in *Proc. Workshop on Multimodal User Authentication*, pp. 99–106, 2003.

Inglis et al. (1998). Inglis C., Manchanda L., Comizzoll R., Dickinson A., Martin E., Mandis S., Silveman P., Weber G., Ackland B. and O'Gorman L., "A Robust, 1.8V, 250mW, Direct Contact 500dpi Fingerprint Sensor," in *Proc. IEEE Solid-State Circuits Conf.*, 1998.

Isenor and Zaky (1986). Isenor D.K. and Zaky S.G., "Fingerprint identification using graph matching," *Pattern Recognition*, vol. 19, pp. 113–122, 1986.

Ishida, Mimura and Seta (2001). Ishida S., Mimura M. and Seta Y., "Development of personal authentication techniques using fingerprint matching embedded in smart cards," *IEICE Transactions on Information and Systems (special issue on biometrics)*, vol. E84–D, no. 7, pp. 812–818, 2001.

ISO/IEC 19794–2 (2005). ISO/IEC, "ISO/IEC 19794–2:2005 – Biometric data interchange formats – Part 2: Finger minutiae data," ISO/IEC Standard, 2005.

ISO/IEC 19794–3 (2006). ISO/IEC, "ISO/IEC 19794–3:2006 – Biometric data interchange format – Part 3: Finger pattern spectral data," ISO/IEC Standard, 2006.

ISO/IEC 19794–4 (2005). ISO/IEC, "ISO/IEC 19794–4:2005 – Biometric data interchange formats – Part 4: Finger image data," ISO/IEC Standard, 2005.

ISO/IEC 19794–8 (2006). ISO/IEC, "ISO/IEC 19794–8:2006 – Biometric data interchange format – Part 8: Finger pattern skeletal data," ISO/IEC Standard, 2006.

ISO/IEC 19795–1 (2006). ISO/IEC, "ISO/IEC 19795–1:2006 –Biometric performance testing and reporting – Part 1: Principles and framework," ISO/IEC Standard, 2006.

ISO/IEC 19795–2 (2007). ISO/IEC, "ISO/IEC 19795–2:2007 – Biometric performance testing and reporting – Part 2: testing methodologies for technology and scenario evaluation," ISO/IEC Standard, 2007.

ISO/IEC 19795–4 (2008). ISO/IEC, "ISO/IEC 19795–4:2008 – Biometric performance testing and reporting – Performance and Interoperability Testing of Interchange Formats," ISO/IEC Standard, 2008.

ISO/IEC N 2777 (2008). ISO/IEC, "ISO/IEC JTC 1/SC 37 N 2777 Standing Document 2, Harmonized Biometric Vocabulary," available at: http://isotc.iso.org/ (accessed 27 November 2008).

ISO/IEC TR 19795–3 (2007). ISO/IEC, "ISO/IEC TR 19795–3:2007 – Biometric performance testing and reporting – Technical Report – Modality-specific Testing," ISO/IEC Standard, 2007.

Ito et al. (2005). Ito K., Morita A., Aoki T., Higuchi T., Nakajima H. and Kobayashi K., "A Fingerprint Recognition Algorithm Using Phase-Based Image Matching for Low-Quality Fingerprints," in *Proc. Int. Conf. on Image Processing*, vol. 2, pp. 33–36, 2005.

Ito et al. (2006). Ito K., Morita A., Aoki T., Nakajima H., Kobayashi K. and Higuchi T., "A Fingerprint Recognition Algorithm Combining Phase-Based Image Matching and Feature-Based Matching," in *Proc. Int. Conf. on Biometrics*, LNCS 3832, pp. 316–325, 2006.

Jacobs et al. (1991). Jacobs R.A., Jordan M.I., Nowlan S.J. and Hinton G.E., "Adaptive mixtures of local experts," *Neural Computation*, vol. 3, pp. 79–87, 1991.

Jain and Chandrasekaran (1982). Jain A.K. and Chandrasekaran B., "Dimensionality and sample size considerations in pattern recognition practice," in *Handbook of Statistics*, P.R. Krishnaiah and L.N. Kanal (Eds.), North-Holland, Amsterdam, vol. II, pp. 835–855, 1982.

Jain and Farrokhnia (1991). Jain A.K. and Farrokhnia F., "Unsupervised texture segmentation using Gabor filters," *Pattern Recognition*, vol. 24, no. 12, pp. 1167–1186, 1991.

Jain and Minut (2002). Jain A.K. and Minut S., "Hierarchical Kernel Fitting for Fingerprint Classification and Alignment," in *Proc. Int. Conf. on Pattern Recognition (16th)*, 2002.

Jain and Pankanti (2000). Jain A.K. and Pankanti S., "Fingerprint classification and recognition," in *Image and Video Processing Handbook*, A. Bovik (Ed.), Academic, Orlando, FL, Apr. 2000.

Jain and Pankanti (2001a). Jain A.K. and Pankanti S., "Automated fingerprint identification and imaging systems," in *Advances in Fingerprint Technology*, 2nd edition, H.C. Lee and R. Gaensslen (Eds.), CRC Press, Boca Raton, FL, 2001a.

Jain and Pankanti (2001b). Jain A.K. and Pankanti S., "Biometrics systems: Anatomy of performance," *IEICE Transactions on Information and Systems (special issue on biometrics)*, vol. E84–D, no. 7, pp. 788–799, 2001b.

Jain and Pankanti (2006). Jain A.K. and Pankanti S., "A touch of money," *IEEE Spectrum*, vol. 43, no. 7, pp. 22–27, 2006.

Jain and Ross (2002a). Jain A.K. and Ross A., "Learning User-Specific Parameters in a Multibiometric System," in *Proc. Int. Conf. on Image Processing*, 2002a.

Jain and Ross (2002b). Jain A.K. and Ross A., "Fingerprint Mosaicking," in *Proc. Int. Conf. on Acoustic Speech and Signal Processing*, 2002b.

Jain and Uludag (2002). Jain A.K. and Uludag U., "Hiding Fingerprint Minutiae in Images," in *Proc. Workshop on Automatic Identification Advanced Technologies*, pp. 97–102, 2002.

Jain and Uludag (2003). Jain A.K. and Uludag U., "Hiding biometric data," *IEEE Transactions on Pattern Analysis Machine Intelligence*, vol. 25, no. 11, pp. 1494–1498, 2003.

Jain and Uludag (2004). Jain A.K. and Uludag U., "Attacks on Biometric Systems: A Case Study in Fingerprints," in *Proc. Security, Seganography and Watermarking of Multimedia Contents VI (SPIE–EI 2004)*, pp. 622–633, 2004.

Jain et al. (1997). Jain A.K., Hong L., Pankanti S. and Bolle R., "An identity authentication system using fingerprints," *Proceedings of the IEEE*, vol. 85, no. 9, pp. 1365–1388, 1997.

Jain et al. (1999). Jain A.K., Prabhakar S., Hong L. and Pankanti S., "FingerCode: A Filterbank for Fingerprint Representation and Matching," in *Proc. Conf. Computer Vision and Pattern Recognition*, vol. 2, pp. 187–193, 1999.

Jain et al. (2000). Jain A.K., Prabhakar S., Hong L. and Pankanti S., "Filterbank-based fingerprint matching," *IEEE Transactions on Image Processing*, vol. 9, pp. 846–859, 2000.

Jain et al. (2001). Jain A.K., Pankanti S., Prabhakar S. and Ross A., "Recent Advances in Fingerprint Verification," in *Proc. Int. Conf. on Audio- and Video-Based Biometric Person Authentication (3rd)*, pp. 182–191, 2001.

Jain et al. (2004a). Jain A.K., Nandakumar K., Lu X. and Park U., "Integrating Faces, Fingerprints, and Soft Biometric Traits for User Recognition," in *Proc. Workshop on Biometric Authentication (in ECCV 2004)*, LNCS 3087, pp. 259–269, 2004a.

Jain et al. (2004b). Jain A.K., Pankanti S., Prabhakar S., Hong L., Ross A. and Wayman J.L., "Biometrics: A Grand Challenge," in *Proc. Int. Conf. on Pattern Recognition (17th)*, vol. 2, pp. 935–942, 2004b.

Jain et al. (2006). Jain M.D., Pradeep N.S., Prakash C. and Raman B., "Binary Tree Based Linear Time Fingerprint Matching," in *Proc. Int. Conf. on Image Processing*, pp. 309–312, 2006.

Jain L.C. et al. (1999). Jain L.C., Halici U., Hayashi I. and Lee S.B., *Intelligent Biometric Techniques in Fingerprint and Face Recognition*, CRC Press, Boca Raton, FL, 1999.

Jain, Bolle and Pankanti (1999). Jain A.K., Bolle R. and Pankanti S., *Biometrics: Personal Identification in Networked Society*, Kluwer, Norwell, MA, 1999.

Jain, Chen and Demirkus (2007). Jain A.K., Chen Y. and Demirkus M., "Pores and ridges: High-resolution fingerprint matching using Level 3 features," *IEEE Transactions on Pattern Analysis Machine Intelligence*, vol. 29, no. 1, pp. 15–27, 2007.

Jain, Dass and Nandakumar (2004a). Jain A.K., Dass S.C. and Nandakumar K., "Can Soft Biometric Traits Assist User Recognition?" in *Proc. SPIE Conf. on Biometric Technology for Human Identification I*, vol. 5404, pp. 561–572, Apr. 2004a.

Jain, Dass and Nandakumar (2004b). Jain A.K., Dass S.C. and Nandakumar K., "Soft Biometric Traits for Personal Recognition Systems," in *Proc. Int. Conf. on Biometric Authentication (1st)*, LNCS 3072, pp. 731–738, 2004b.

Jain, Duin and Mao (2000). Jain A.K., Duin P.W. and Mao J., "Statistical pattern recognition: A review," *IEEE Transactions on Pattern Analysis Machine Intelligence*, vol. 22, no. 1, pp. 4–37, 2000.

Jain, Flynn and Ross (2007). Jain A.K., Flynn P. and Ross A.A., *Handbook of Biometrics*, Springer, New York, 2007.

Jain, Hong and Bolle (1997). Jain A.K., Hong L. and Bolle R., "On-line fingerprint verification," *IEEE Transactions on Pattern Analysis Machine Intelligence*, vol. 19, no. 4, pp. 302–313, 1997.

Jain, Hong and Kulkarni (1998). Jain A.K., Hong L. and Kulkarni Y., "F2ID: A Personal Identification System Using Faces and Fingerprints," in *Proc. Int. Conf. on Pattern Recognition (14th)*, pp. 1373–1375, 1998.

Jain, Hong and Kulkarni (1999). Jain A.K., Hong L. and Kulkarni Y., "A Multimodal Biometric System Using Fingerprint, Face, and Speech," in *Proc. Int. Conf. on Audio- and-Video-Based Biometric Person Authentication (2nd)*, pp. 182–187, 1999.

Jain, Hong and Pankanti (2000). Jain A.K., Hong L. and Pankanti S., "Biometrics: Promising frontiers for emerging identification market," *Communications of the ACM*, pp. 91–98, Feb. 2000.

Jain, Nandakumar and Nagar (2008). Jain A.K., Nandakumar K. and Nagar A., "Biometric Template Security," *EURASIP Journal on Advances in Signal Processing*, vol. 8, no. 2, pp. 1–17, Jan. 2008.

Jain, Nandakumar and Ross (2005). Jain A.K., Nandakumar K. and Ross A., "Score normalization in multimodal biometric systems," *Pattern Recognition*, vol. 38, no. 12, pp. 2270–2285, 2005.

Jain, Prabhakar and Chen (1999). Jain A.K., Prabhakar S. and Chen S., "Combining multiple matchers for a high security fingerprint verification system," *Pattern Recognition Letters*, vol. 20, no. 11–13, pp. 1371–1379, 1999.

Jain, Prabhakar and Hong (1999). Jain A.K., Prabhakar S. and Hong L., "A multichannel approach to fingerprint classification," *IEEE Transactions on Pattern Analysis Machine Intelligence*, vol. 21, no. 4, pp. 348–359, 1999.

Jain, Prabhakar and Pankanti (2001). Jain A.K., Prabhakar S. and Pankanti S., "Twin Test: On Discriminability of Fingerprints," in *Proc. Int. Conf. on Audio- and Video-Based Biometric Person Authentication (3rd)*, 2001.

Jain, Prabhakar and Pankanti (2002). Jain A.K., Prabhakar S. and Pankanti S., "On the similarity of identical twin fingerprints," *Pattern Recognition*, vol. 35, no. 11, pp. 2653–2663, 2002.

Jain, Prabhakar and Ross (1999). Jain A.K., Prabhakar S. and Ross A., "Fingerprint Matching: Data Acquisition and Performance Evaluation," Tech. Report: MSU TR99–14, 1999.

Jain, Ross and Pankanti (2006). Jain A.K., Ross A. and Pankanti S., "Biometrics: A tool for information security," *IEEE Transactions on Information Forensics and Security*, vol. 1, no. 2, pp. 125–143, 2006.

Jain, Ross and Prabhakar (2001). Jain A.K., Ross A. and Prabhakar S., "Fingerprint Matching Using Minutiae and Texture Features," in *Proc. Int. Conf. on Image Processing*, pp. 282–285, 2001.

Jain, Ross and Uludag (2005). Jain A.K., Ross A. and Uludag U., "Biometric Template Security: Challenges and Solutions," in *Proc. European Signal Processing Conference (EUSIPCO)*, 2005.

Jain, Uludag and Hsu (2002). Jain A.K., Uludag U. and Hsu R.L., "Hiding a Face in a Fingerprint Image," in *Proc. Int. Conf. on Pattern Recognition (16th)*, 2002.

Jain, Uludag and Ross (2003). Jain A.K., Uludag U. and Ross A., "Biometric Template Selection: A Case Study in Fingerprints," in *Proc. Int. Conf. on Audio- and Video-Based Biometric Person Authentication (4th)*, pp. 335–342, 2003.

Jang et al. (2006). Jang W., Park D., Lee D. and Kim S.J., "Fingerprint Image Enhancement Based on a Half Gabor Filter," in *Proc. Int. Conf. on Biometrics*, LNCS 3832, pp. 258–264, 2006.

Jang, Elliott and Kim (2007). Jang J., Elliott S.J. and Kim H., "On Improving Interoperability of Fingerprint Recognition Using Resolution Compensation Based on Sensor Evaluation," in *Proc. Int. Conf. on Biometrics*, LNCS 4642, pp. 455–463, 2007.

Jarosz, Founder and Dupre (2005). Jarosz H., Founder J.C. and Dupre X., "Large-scale identification system design," in *Biometric Systems: Technology, Design and Performance Evaluation*, Wayman J. et al. (Eds.), Springer, New York, pp. 263–287, 2005.

Jea and Govindaraju (2005). Jea T.Y. and Govindaraju V., "A minutia-based partial fingerprint recognition system," *Pattern Recognition*, vol. 38, no. 10, pp. 1672–1684, 2005.

Jea et al. (2004). Jea T.Y., Chavan V.S., Govindaraju V. and Schneider J.K., "Security and Matching of Partial Fingerprint Recognition Systems," in *Proc. SPIE Conf. on Biometric Technology for Human Identification I*, 2004.

Jeffers and Arakala (2006). Jeffers J. and Arakala A., "Minutiae-Based Structures for A Fuzzy Vault," in *Proc. Biometric Symposium*, 2006.

Jeffers and Arakala (2007). Jeffers J. and Arakala A., "Fingerprint Alignment for a Minutiae-Based Fuzzy Vault," in *Proc. Biometric Symposium*, 2007.

Ji and Yi (2008). Ji L. and Yi Z., "Fingerprint orientation field estimation using ridge projection," *Pattern Recognition*, vol. 41, no. 5, pp. 1508–1520, 2008.

Ji et al. (2007). Ji L., Yi Z., Shang L. and Pu X., "Binary fingerprint image thinning using template-based PCNNs," *IEEE Transaction on Systems, Man, and Cybernetics, Part B*, vol. 37, no. 5, pp. 1407–1413, 2007.

Jia et al. (2007a). Jia J., Cai L., Zhang K. and Chen D., "A New Approach to Fake Finger Detection Based on Skin Elasticity Analysis," in *Proc. Int. Conf. on Biometrics*, LNCS 4642, pp. 309–318, 2007a.

Jia et al. (2007b). Jia J., Cai L., Lu P. and Lu X., "Fingerprint matching based on weighting method and the SVM," *Neurocomputing*, vol. 70, no. 4–6, pp. 849–858, 2007b.

Jiang (2000). Jiang X., "Fingerprint Image Ridge Frequency Estimation by Higher Order Spectrum," in *Proc. Int. Conf. on Image Processing*, 2000.

Jiang (2001). Jiang X., "A Study of Fingerprint Image Filtering," in *Proc. Int. Conf. on Image Processing*, 2001.

Jiang and Ser (2002). Jiang X. and Ser W., "Online fingerprint template improvement," *IEEE Transactions on Pattern Analysis Machine Intelligence*, vol. 24, no. 8, pp. 1121–1126, 2002.

Jiang and Yau (2000). Jiang X. and Yau W.Y., "Fingerprint Minutiae Matching Based on the Local and Global Structures," in *Proc. Int. Conf. on Pattern Recognition (15th)*, vol. 2, pp. 1042–1045, 2000.

Jiang, Liu and Kot (2004). Jiang X., Liu M. and Kot A.C., "Reference Point Detection for Fingerprint Recognition," in *Proc. Int. Conf. on Pattern Recognition (17th)*, vol. 1, pp. 540–543, 2004.

Jiang, Liu and Kot (2006). Jiang X., Liu M. and Kot A.C., "Fingerprint retrieval for identification," *IEEE Transactions on Information Forensics and Security*, vol. 1, no. 4, pp. 532–542, 2006.

Jiang, Yau and Ser (1999). Jiang X., Yau W.Y. and Ser W., "Minutiae Extraction by Adaptive Tracing the Gray Level Ridge of the Fingerprint Image," in *Proc. Int. Conf. on Image Processing*, 1999.

Jiang, Yau and Ser (2001). Jiang X., Yau, W.Y. and Ser W., "Detecting the fingerprint minutiae by adaptive tracing the gray-level ridge," *Pattern Recognition*, vol. 34, no. 5, pp. 999–1013, 2001.

Jie et al. (2006). Jie Y., Fang Y.Y., Renjie Z. and Qifa S., "Fingerprint minutiae matching algorithm for real time system," *Pattern Recognition*, vol. 39, no. 1, pp. 143–146, 2006.

Jin, Ling and Goh (2004). Jin A.T.B., Ling D.N.C. and Goh A., "Biohashing: Two factor authentication featuring fingerprint data and tokenised random number," *Pattern Recognition*, vol. 37, no. 11, pp. 2245–2255, 2004.

Jirachaweng and Areekul (2007). Jirachaweng S. and Areekul V., "Fingerprint Enhancement Based on Discrete Cosine Transform," in *Proc. Int. Conf. on Biometrics*, LNCS 4642, pp. 96–105, 2007.

Johannesen et al. (1996). Johannesen F.R., Raaschou S., Larsen O.V. and Jurgensen P., "Using Weighted Minutiae for Fingerprint Identification," in *Proc. Advances in Structural and Syntactical Pattern Recognition*, pp. 289–299, 1996.

Johnson et al. (1998). Johnson E.G., Brasher J.D., Gregory D., Erbach P., Duignan M., Behrmann G., Lee S.H., Daschner W. and Long P., "Optical recognition of phase-encrypted biometrics," *Optical Engineering*, vol. 37, no. 1, pp. 18–26, 1998.

Jolliffe (1986). Jolliffe I.T., *Principle Component Analysis*, Springer, New York, 1986.

Jones (2000). Jones G.W., *Introduction to Fingerprint Comparison*, Staggs Publishing, Temecula, CA, 2000.

Jordan and Jacobs (1994). Jordan M.I. and Jacobs R.A., "Hierarchical mixtures of experts and the EM algorithm," *Neural Computation*, vol. 6, pp. 181–214, 1994.

Juels and Sudan (2002). Jules A. and Sudan M., "A Fuzzy Vault Scheme," in *Proc. Int. Symp. on Information Theory*, 2002.

Juels and Wattenberg (1999). Juels A. and Wattenberg M., "A Fuzzy Commitment Scheme," in *Proc. ACM Conf. on Computer and Communications Security*, pp. 28–36, 1999.

Jung et al. (1999). Jung S., Thewes R., Scheiter T., Goser K.F. and Weber W., "A low-power and high-performance CMOS fingerprint sensing and encoding architecture," *IEEE Journal of Solid-State Circuits*, vol. 34, no. 7, pp. 978–984, 1999.

Jung et al. (2005). Jung S.M., Nam J.M., Yang D.H. and Lee M.K., "A CMOS integrated capacitive fingerprint sensor with 32-bit RISC microcontroller," *IEEE Journal of Solid-State Circuits*, vol. 40, no. 8, pp. 1745–1750, 2005.

Kamei (2004a). Kamei T., "Image filter design for fingerprint enhancement," in *Automatic Fingerprint Recognition Systems*, N. Ratha and R. Bolle (Eds.), Springer, New York, pp. 113–126, 2004a.

Kamei (2004b). Kamei T., "Fingerprint preselection using eigenfeatures for large-size database," in *Automatic Fingerprint Recognition Systems*, N. Ratha and R. Bolle (Eds.), Springer, New York, pp. 263–282, 2004b.

Kamei and Mizoguchi (1995). Kamei T. and Mizoguchi M., "Image Filter Design for Fingerprint Enhancement," in *Proc. Int. Symp. on Computer Vision*, pp. 109–114, 1995.

Kamei and Mizoguchi (1998). Kamei T. and Mizoguchi M., "Fingerprint Preselection Using Eigenfeatures," in *Proc. Conf. Computer Vision and Pattern Recognition*, pp. 918–923, 1998.

Kamijo (1993). Kamijo M., "Classifying Fingerprint Images Using Neural Network: Deriving the Classification State," in *Proc. Int. Conf. on Neural Networks*, 1993.

Kamijo, Mieno and Kojima (1992). Kamijo M., Mieno H. and Kojima K., "Classification of fingerprint images using a neural network," *Systems and Computers in Japan*, vol. 23, pp. 89–101, 1992.

Kang et al. (2003). Kang H., Lee B., Kim H., Shin D. and Kim J., "A Study on Performance Evaluation of Fingerprint Sensors," in *Proc. Int. Conf. on Audio- and Video-Based Biometric Person Authentication (4th)*, pp. 574–583, 2003.

Karen (1989). Karen F., "Encryption, smart cards, and fingerprint readers," *IEEE Spectrum*, vol. 26, no. 8, pp. 22, 1989.

Karu and Jain (1996). Karu K. and Jain A.K., "Fingerprint classification," *Pattern Recognition*, vol. 29, no. 3, pp. 389–404, 1996.

Kasaei, Deriche and Boashash (1997). Kasaei S., Deriche M. and Boashash B., "An efficient quantization technique for wavelet coefficients of fingerprint images," *Signal Processing*, vol. 62, no. 3, pp. 361–366, 1997.

Kasaei, Deriche and Boashash (2002). Kasaei S., Deriche M. and Boashash B., "A novel fingerprint image compression technique using wavelets packets and pyramid lattice vector quantization," *IEEE Transactions on Image Processing*, vol. 11, no. 12, pp. 1365–1378, 2002.

Kass and Witkin (1987). Kass M. and Witkin A., "Analyzing oriented patterns," *Computer Vision Graphics and Image Processing*, vol. 37, no. 3, pp. 362–385, 1987.

Kawagoe and Tojo (1984). Kawagoe M. and Tojo A., "Fingerprint pattern classification," *Pattern Recognition*, vol. 17, pp. 295–303, 1984.

Kaymaz and Mitra (1992). Kaymaz E. and Mitra S., "Analysis and Matching of Degraded and Noisy Fingerprints," in *Proc. of SPIE (Applications of Digital Image Processing XV)*, vol. 1771, pp. 498–508, 1992.

Kaymaz and Mitra (1993). Kaymaz E. and Mitra S., "A novel approach to Fourier spectral enhancement of laser-luminescent fingerprint images," *Journal of Forensic Sciences*, vol. 38, no. 3, pp. 530, 1993.

Kelkboom et al. (2007). Kelkboom E.J.C., Gökberk B., Kevenaar T.A.M., Akkermans A.H.M. and Van Der Veen M., "3D Face: Biometric Template Protection for 3D Face Recognition," in *Int. Conf. on Biometrics*, LNCS 4642, pp. 566–573, 2007.

Kerschbaum et al. (2004). Kerschbaum F., Atallah M.J., M'Raïhi D. and Rice J.R., "Private Fingerprint Verification Without Local Storage," in *Proc. Int. Conf. on Biometric Authentication (1st)*, LNCS 3072, pp. 387–394, 2004.

Khan, Xie and Zhang (2007). Khan M.K., Xie L. and Zhang J., "Robust Hiding of Fingerprint-Biometric Data into Audio Signals," in *Proc. Int. Conf. on Biometrics*, LNCS 4642, pp. 702–712, 2007.

Khanna (2004). Khanna R., "Systems engineering for large-scale fingerprint systems," in *Automatic Fingerprint Recognition Systems*, N. Ratha and R. Bolle (Eds.), Springer, New York, pp. 283–304, 2004.

Kim (2005). Kim D.H., "Minutiae Quality Scoring and Filtering Using a Neighboring Ridge Structural Analysis on a Thinned Fingerprint Image," in *Proc. Int. Conf. on Audio- and Video-Based Biometric Person Authentication (5th)*, pp. 674–682, 2005.

Kim and Park (2002). Kim B.G. and Park D.J., "Adaptive image normalisation based on block processing for enhancement of fingerprint image," *Electronics Letters*, vol. 38, no. 14, pp. 696–698, 2002.

Kim and Yoo (2005). Kim W.S. and Yoo W.H., "A Layered Fingerprint Recognition Method," in *Proc. Int. Conf. on Audio- and Video-Based Biometric Person Authentication (5th)*, pp. 702–709, 2005.

Kim, Kim and Park (2002). Kim B.G., Kim H.J. and Park D.J., "New Enhancement Algorithm for Fingerprint Images," in *Proc. Int. Conf. on Pattern Recognition (16th)*, vol. 3, pp. 879–882, 2002.

Kim, Lee and Kim (2001). Kim S., Lee D. and Kim J., "Algorithm for Detection and Elimination of False Minutiae in Fingerprint Images," in *Proc. Int. Conf. on Audio- and Video-Based Biometric Person Authentication (3rd)*, pp. 235–240, 2001.

Kingston (1964). C. Kingston C., "Probabilistic Analysis of Partial Fingerprint Patterns," Ph.D. thesis, University of California, 1964.

Kittler et al. (1998). Kittler J., Hataf M., Duin R.P.W. and Matas J., "On combining classifiers," *IEEE Transactions on Pattern Analysis Machine Intelligence*, vol. 20, no. 3, pp. 226–238, 1998.

Kittler et al. (2001). Kittler J., Messer K. and Sadeghi M., "Model Validation for Model Selection," in *Proc. Int. Conf. on Advances in Pattern Recognition (2nd)*, 2001.

Klimanee and Nguyen (2004). Klimanee C. and Nguyen D.T., "Classification of Fingerprints Using Singular Points and Their Principal Axes," in *Proc. Int. Conf. on Image Processing*, vol. 2, pp. 849–852, 2004.

Knapp (1994). Knapp A.G., "Fingerprint Sensing Device and Recognition System Having Predetermined Electrode Activation," US Patent 5325442, 1994.

Kobayashi (1992). Kobayashi T., "A Fingerprint Image Recognition Method for Network User Identification," in *Proc. Int. Conf. on Computing and Information (4th)*, pp. 369–372, 1992.

Kobayashi and Toyoda (1999). Kobayashi Y. and Toyoda H., "Development of an optical joint transform correlation system for fingerprint recognition," *Optical Engineering*, vol. 38, no. 7, pp. 1205–1210, 1999.

Kohonen et al. (1992). Kohonen T., Kangas J., Laaksonen J., Torkkola K., "LVQ_PAQ: A Program Package for the Correct Application of Learning Vector Quantization Algorithms," in *Proc. Int. Joint Conf. On Neural Network*, pp. 1725–1730, 1992.

Komarinski (2005). Komarinski P., *Automated Fingerprint Identification Systems (AFIS)*, Elsevier/ Academic, Burlington, MA, 2005.

Kong et al. (2006). Kong A., Cheung K., Zhang D., Kamel M. and You J., "An analysis of BioHashing and its variants," *Pattern Recognition*, vol. 39, no. 7, pp. 1359–1368, 2006.

Koo and Kot (2001). Koo W.M. and Kot A., "Curvature-Based Singular Points Detection," in *Proc. Int. Conf. on Audio- and Video-Based Biometric Person Authentication (3rd)*, pp. 229–234, 2001.

Kosz (1999). Kosz D., "New numerical methods of fingerprint recognition based on mathematical description of arrangement of dermatoglyphics and creation of minutiae," Biometrics in Human Service User Group Newsletter, D. Mintie (Ed.), 1999.

Kovacs-Vajna (2000). Kovacs-Vajna Z.M., "A fingerprint verification system based on triangular matching and dynamic time warping," *IEEE Transactions on Pattern Analysis Machine Intelligence*, vol. 22, pp. 1266–1276, 2000.

Kovacs-Vajna, Rovatti and Frazzoni (2000). Kovacs-Vajna Z.M., Rovatti R. and Frazzoni M., "Fingerprint ridge distance computation methodologies," *Pattern Recognition*, vol. 33, no. 1, pp. 69–80, 2000.

Kristensen, Borthen and Fyllingsnes (2007). Kristensen T., Borthen J. and Fyllingsnes K., "Comparison of Neural Network Based Fingerprint Classification Techniques," in *Proc. Int. Joint Conf. on Neural Networks*, pp. 1043–1048, 2007.

Kryszczuk and Drygajlo (2006). Kryszczuk K. and Drygajlo A., "Singular Point Detection in Fingerprints Using Quadrant Change Information," in *Proc. Int. Conf. on Pattern Recognition (18th)*, vol. 4, pp. 594–597, 2006.

Kryszczuk, Morier and Drygajlo (2004). Kryszczuk K.M., Morier P. and Drygajlo A., "Study of the Distinctiveness of Level 2 and Level 3 Features in Fragmentary Fingerprint Comparison," in *Proc. Workshop on Biometric Authentication (in ECCV 2004)*, LNCS 3087, pp. 124–133, 2004.

Ku, Chang and Chiang (2005). Ku W.C., Chang S.T. and Chiang M.H., "Further cryptanalysis of fingerprint-based remote user authentication scheme using smartcards," *Electronics Letters*, vol. 41, no. 5, pp. 240–241, 2005.

Kücken (2007). Kücken M., "Models for fingerprint pattern formation," *Forensic Science International*, vol. 171, no. 2–3, pp. 85–96, 2007.

Kücken and Newell (2004). Kücken M. and Newell A.C., "A model for fingerprint formation," *Europhysics Letters*, vol. 68, no. 1, pp. 141, 2004.

Kulkarni, Patil and Holambe (2006). Kulkarni J.V., Patil B.D. and Holambe R.S., "Orientation feature for fingerprint matching," *Pattern Recognition*, vol. 39, no. 8, pp. 1551–1554, 2006.

Kumar and Zhang (2006). Kumar A. and Zhang D., "Combining Fingerprint, Palmprint and Hand-Shape for User Authentication," in *Proc. Int. Conf. on Pattern Recognition (18th)*, vol. 4, pp. 549–552, 2006.

Kumar et al. (2004). Kumar B.V.K.V., Savvides M., Xie C., Venkataramani K., Thornton J. and Mahalanobis A., "Biometric verification with correlation filters," *Applied Optics*, vol. 43, no. 2, pp. 391–402, 2004.

Kuncheva (2004). Kuncheva L.I., "Classifier Ensembles for Changing Environments," in *Proc. Multiple Classifier Systems*, pp. 1–15, 2004.

Kuncheva and Whitaker (2003). Kuncheva L.I., Whitaker C.J., "Measures of diversity in classifier ensembles and their relationship with the ensemble accuracy," *Machine Learning*, vol. 51, no. 2, pp. 181–207, 2003.

Kuncheva et al. (2000). Kuncheva L.I., Whitaker C.J., Shipp C.A. and Duin R.P.W., "Is Independence Good for Combining Classifiers," in *Proc. Int. Conf. on Pattern Recognition (15th)*, vol. 2, pp. 168–171, 2000.

Kwon et al. (2006). Kwon D., Yun I.D., Kim D.H. and Lee S.U., "Fingerprint Matching Method Using Minutiae Clustering and Warping," in *Proc. Int. Conf. on Pattern Recognition (18th)*, vol. 4, pp. 525–528, 2006.

Kwon, Yun and Lee (2007). Kwon D., Yun I.D. and Lee S.U., "A Robust Warping Method for Fingerprint Matching," in *Proc. Conf. Computer Vision and Pattern Recognition*, 2007.

Lal, Zang and Millerd (1999). Lal A., Zang D.Y. and Millerd J., "Laser-diode-based joint transform correlator for fingerprint identification," *Optical Engineering*, vol. 38, no. 1, pp. 69–75, 1999.

Lam and Suen (1997). Lam L. and Suen C.Y., "Application of majority voting to pattern recognition: An analysis of its behavior and performance," *IEEE Transactions on Systems Man and Cybernetics*, vol. 27, no. 5, pp. 553–568, 1997.

Lam, Lee and Suen (1992). Lam L., Lee S.W. and Suen C.Y., "Thinning methodologies: A comprehensive survey," *IEEE Transactions on Pattern Analysis Machine Intelligence*, vol. 14, no. 9, pp. 869–885, 1992.

Landy, Cohen and Sperling (1984). Landy M.S., Cohen Y. and Sperling G., "Hips: A Unix-based image processing system," *Computer Vision, Graphics and Image Processing*, vol. 25, no. 3, pp. 331–347, 1984.

Larin and Cheng (2008). Larin K.V. and Cheng Y., "Three-Dimensional Imaging of Artificial Fingerprint by Optical Coherence Tomography," in *Proc. SPIE Conf. on Biometric Technology for Human Identification V*, 2008.

Larkin (2005). Larkin K.G., "Uniform estimation of orientation using local and nonlocal 2-D energy operators," *Optics Express*, vol. 13, no. 20, 2005.

Larkin and Fletcher (2007). Larkin K.G. and Fletcher P.A., "A coherent framework for fingerprint analysis: Are fingerprints holograms?" *Optics Express*, vol. 15, no. 14, pp. 8667–8677, 2007.

Le, Cheung and Nguyen (2001). Le T.V., Cheung K.Y. and Nguyen M.H., "A Fingerprint Recognizer Using Fuzzy Evolutionary Programming," in *Proc. Int. Conf. on System Sciences*, 2001.

Lee and Gaensslen (2001). Lee H.C. and Gaensslen R.E., *Advances in Fingerprint Technology*, 2nd edition, Elsevier, New York, 2001.

Lee and Prabhakar (2008). Lee K. and Prabhakar S., "Probabilistic Orientation Field Estimation for Fingerprint Enhancement and Verification," in *Proc. Biometric Symposium*, 2008.

Lee and Wang (1999). Lee C.J. and Wang S.D., "Fingerprint feature extraction using Gabor filters," *Electronics Letters*, vol. 35, no. 4, pp. 288–290, 1999.

Lee and Wang (2001). Lee C.J. and Wang S.D., "Fingerprint feature reduction by principal Gabor basis function," *Pattern Recognition*, vol. 34, no. 11, pp. 2245–2248, 2001.

Lee et al. (1999). Lee J.W., Min D.J., Kim J. and Kim W., "A 600 dpi capacitive fingerprint sensor chip and image synthesis technique," *IEEE Journal of Solid-State Circuits*, vol. 34, no. 4, pp. 469–475, 1999.

Lee et al. (2003). Lee D., Choi K., Lee S. and Kim J., "Fingerprint Fusion Based on Minutiae and Ridge for Enrollment," in *Proc. Int. Conf. on Audio- and Video-Based Biometric Person Authentication (4th)*, pp. 478–485, 2003.

Lee et al. (2004). Lee K., Park K.R., Lee S. and Kim J., "Multi-unit Biometric Fusion in Fingerprint Verification," in *Proc. Int. Conf. on Biometric Authentication (1st)*, LNCS 3072, pp. 395–402, 2004.

Lee et al. (2005a). Lee K., Park K.R., Jang J., Lee S. and Kim J., "A Study on Multi-unit Fingerprint Verification," in *Proc. Int. Conf. on Audio- and Video-Based Biometric Person Authentication (5th)*, pp. 141–150, 2005a.

Lee et al. (2005b). Lee D., Jang W., Park D., Kim S.J. and Kim J., "A Real-Time Image Selection Algorithm: Fingerprint Recognition Using Mobile Devices with Embedded Camera," in *Proc. Workshop on Automatic Identification Advanced Technologies*, pp. 166–170, 2005b.

Lee et al. (2005c). Lee Y.J., Lee K.H., Jee H.K., Gil Y.H., Choi W.Y., Ahn D. and Pan S.B., "Fusion for Multimodal Biometric Identification," in *Proc. Int. Conf. on Audio- and Video-Based Biometric Person Authentication (5th)*, pp. 1071–1079, 2005c.

Lee et al. (2006). Lee C., Lee S., Kim J. and Kim S.J., "Preprocessing of a Fingerprint Image Captured with a Mobile Camera," in *Proc. Int. Conf. on Biometrics*, LNCS 3832, pp. 348–355, 2006.

Lee et al. (2007). Lee C., Choi J.Y., Toh K.A. and Lee S., "Alignment-free cancelable fingerprint templates based on local minutiae information," *IEEE Transaction on Systems, Man, and Cybernetics, Part B*, vol. 37, no. 4, pp. 980–992, 2007.

Lee et al. (2008). Lee D., Choi K., Choi H. and Kim J., "Recognizable-image selection for fingerprint recognition with a mobile-device camera," *IEEE Transaction on Systems, Man, and Cybernetics, Part B*, vol. 38, no. 1, pp. 233–243, 2008.

Lee, Choi and Kim (2002). Lee D., Choi K. and Kim J., "A Robust Fingerprint Matching Algorithm Using Local Alignment," in *Proc. Int. Conf. on Pattern Recognition (16th)*, vol. 3, pp. 803–806, 2002.

Lee, Kim and Park (2005). Lee S.O., Kim Y.G. and Park G.T., "A Feature Map Consisting of Orientation and Inter-ridge Spacing for Fingerprint Retrieval," in *Proc. Int. Conf. on Audio- and Video-Based Biometric Person Authentication (5th)*, pp. 184–190, 2005.

Lee, Lee and Kim (2006). Lee S., Lee C. and Kim J., "Model-Based Quality Estimation of Fingerprint Images," in *Proc. Int. Conf. on Biometrics*, LNCS 3832, pp. 229–235, 2006.

Lee, Moon and Kim (2005). Lee B., Moon J. and Kim H., "A Novel Measure of Fingerprint Image Quality Using the Fourier Spectrum," in *Proc. SPIE Conf. on Biometric Technology for Human Identification II*, 2005.

Lee, Ryu and Yoo (2002). Lee J.K., Ryu S.R. and Yoo K.Y., "Fingerprint-based remote user authentication scheme using smart cards," *Electronics Letters*, vol. 38, no. 12, pp. 554–555, 2002.

Lepley (2001). Lepley M.A., "JPEG 2000 and WSQ Image Compression Interoperability," MITRE Tech. Report: MTR 00B0000063, 2001.

Leung et al. (1991). Leung W.F., Leung S.H., Lau W.H. and Luk A., "Fingerprint Recognition Using Neural Network," in *Proc. Workshop Neural Network for Signal Processing*, 1991.

Leung, Engeler and Frank (1990). Leung M, Engeler W. and Frank P., "Fingerprint Image Processing Using Neural Network," in *Proc. IEEE Region 10 Conf. on Computer and Communications Systems*, 1990.

Levi and Sirovich (1972). Levi G. and Sirovich F., "Structural description of fingerprint images," *Information Sciences*, pp. 327–355, 1972.

Li and Chang (2006). Li Q. and Chang E.C., "Robust, Short and Sensitive Authentication Tags Using Secure Sketch," in *Proc. Multimedia and Security Workshop (MM and Sec 06)*, pp. 56–61, 2006.

Li and Jain (2005). Li S.Z. and Jain A.K., *Handbook of Face Recognition*, Springer, New York, 2005.

Li and Yau (2004). Li J. and Yau W.Y., "Prediction of Fingerprint Orientation," in *Proc. Int. Conf. on Pattern Recognition (17th)*, vol. 4, pp. 436–439, 2004.

Li and Zhang (1984). Li Z. and Zhang D., "A Fingerprint Recognition System with Micro-computer," in *Proc. Int. Conf. on Pattern Recognition (7th)*, pp. 939–941, 1984.Li et al. (2007). Li J., Yau W.Y., Wang J. and Ser W., "Stability Analysis of Constrained Nonlinear Phase Portrait Models of Fingerprint Orientation Images," in *Proc. Int. Conf. on Biometrics*, LNCS 4642, pp. 493–502, 2007.

Li, Yau and Wang (2006a). Li J., Yau W.Y. and Wang H., "Constrained nonlinear models of fingerprint orientations with prediction," *Pattern Recognition*, vol. 39, no. 1, pp. 102–114, 2006a.

Li, Yau and Wang (2006b). Li J., Yau W.Y. and Wang H., "Fingerprint Indexing Based on Symmetrical Measurement," in *Proc. Int. Conf. on Pattern Recognition (18th)*, vol. 1, pp. 1038–1041, 2006b.

Li, Yau and Wang (2008). Li J., Yau W.Y. and Wang H., "Combining singular points and orientation image information for fingerprint classification," *Pattern Recognition*, vol. 41, no. 1, pp. 353–366, 2008.

Liang and Asano (2006a). Liang X. and Asano T., "A linear time algorithm for binary fingerprint image denoising using distance transform," *IEICE Transactions on Information and Systems*, vol. 89, no. 4, pp. 1534–1542, 2006a.

Liang and Asano (2006b). Liang X. and Asano T., "Fingerprint Matching Using Minutia Polygons," in *Proc. Int. Conf. on Pattern Recognition (18th)*, vol. 1, pp. 1046–1049, 2006b.

Liang, Bishnu and Asano (2007). Liang X., Bishnu A. and Asano T., "A robust fingerprint indexing scheme using minutia neighborhood structure and low-order delaunay triangles," *IEEE Transactions on Information Forensics and Security*, vol. 2, no. 4, pp. 721–733, 2007.

Lim et al. (2004). Lim E., Toh K.A., Suganthan P.N., Jiang X. and Yau W.Y., "Fingerprint Image Quality Analysis," in *Proc. Int. Conf. on Image Processing*, vol. 2, pp. 1241–1244, 2004.

Lim, Jiang and Yau (2002). Lim E., Jiang X. and Yau W., "Fingerprint Quality and Validity Analysis," in *Proc. Int. Conf. on Image Processing*, vol. 1, pp. 469–472, 2002.

Lin and Dubes (1983). Lin W. and Dubes R., "A review of ridge counting in dermatoglyphics," *Pattern Recognition*, vol. 16, pp. 1–8, 1983.

Lin et al. (1982). Lin C.H., Liu J.H., Ostenberg J.W. and Nicol J.D., "Fingerprint comparison I: Similarity of fingerprints," *Journal of Forensic Sciences*, vol. 27, no. 2, pp. 290–304, 1982.

Lindh, Ford and Boudreaux (1981). Lindh T.K., Ford F.A. and Boudreaux N.A., "An automated fingerprint retrieval system," in *Proc. Int. Carnahan Conf. on Electronic Crime Countermeasures*, pp. 71–75, 1981.

Lindoso et al. (2007). Lindoso A., Entrena L., Liu-Jimenez J. and San Millan E., "Correlation-Based Fingerprint Matching with Orientation Field Alignment," in *Proc. Int. Conf. on Biometrics*, LNCS 4642, pp. 713–721, 2007.

Linnartz and Tuyls (2003). Linnartz J.P. and Tuyls P., "New Shielding Functions to Enhance Privacy and Prevent Misuse of Biometric Templates," in *Proc. Int. Conf. on Audio- and Video-Based Biometric Person Authentication (4th)*, pp. 393–402, 2003.

Liu et al. (1982). Liu J.H., Lin C.H., Osterburg J.W. and Nichol J.D., "Fingerprint comparison II: On the development of a single fingerprint filing and searching system," *Journal of Forensic Sciences*, vol. 27, no. 2, pp. 305–317, 1982.

Liu et al. (2005). Liu T., Zhu G., Zhang C. and Hao P., "Fingerprint Indexing Based on Singular Point Correlation," in *Proc. Int. Conf. on Image Processing*, vol. 2, pp. 293–296, 2005.

Liu et al. (2006). Liu L., Jiang T., Yang J. and Zhu C., "Fingerprint registration by maximization of mutual information," *IEEE Transactions on Image Processing*, vol. 15, no. 5, pp. 1100–1110, 2006.

Liu, Hao and Zhang (2005). Liu T., Hao P. and Zhang C., "Fingerprint Singular Points Detection and Direction Estimation with a "T" Shape Model," in *Proc. Int. Conf. on Audio- and Video-Based Biometric Person Authentication (5th)*, pp. 201–207, 2005.

Liu, Huang and Chan (2000). Liu J., Huang Z. and Chan K., "Direct Minutiae Extraction from Gray-Level Fingerprint Image by Relationship Examination," in *Proc. Int. Conf. on Image Processing*, 2000.

Liu, Jiang and Kot (2004). Liu M., Jiang X. and Kot A.C., "Fingerprint Reference Point Detection," in *Proc. Int. Conf. on Biometric Authentication (1st)*, LNCS 3072, pp. 272–279, 2004.

Liu, Jiang and Kot (2006). Liu M., Jiang X. and Kot A.C., "Fingerprint Retrieval by Complex Filter Responses," in *Proc. Int. Conf. on Pattern Recognition (18th)*, vol. 1, pp. 1042–1045, 2006.

Liu, Jiang and Kot (2007). Liu M., Jiang X. and Kot A.C., "Efficient fingerprint search based on database clustering," *Pattern Recognition*, vol. 40, no. 6, pp. 1793–1803, 2007.

Liu, Xia and Li (2004). Liu C., Xia T. and Li H., "A Hierarchical Hough Transform for Fingerprint Matching," in *Proc. Int. Conf. on Biometric Authentication (1st)*, LNCS 3072, pp. 373–379, 2004.

Liu, Zhang and Hao (2006a). Liu T., Zhang C. and Hao P., "Fingerprint Indexing Based on LAS Registration," in *Proc. Int. Conf. on Image Processing*, pp. 301–304, 2006a.

Liu, Zhang and Hao (2006b). Liu T., Zhang C. and Hao P., "Fingerprint Reference Point Detection Based on Local Axial Symmetry," in *Proc. Int. Conf. on Pattern Recognition (18th)*, vol. 1, pp. 1050–1053, 2006b.

Lorch, Morguet and Schroder (2004). Lorch H., Morguet P. and Schroder H., "Fingerprint Distortion Measurement," in *Proc. Workshop on Biometric Authentication (in ECCV 2004)*, LNCS 3087, pp. 111–123, 2004.

Lumini and Nanni (2006). Lumini A. and Nanni L., "Two-class fingerprint matcher," *Pattern Recognition*, vol. 39, no. 4, pp. 714–716, 2006.

Lumini and Nanni (2008). Lumini A. and Nanni L., "Advanced methods for two-class pattern recognition problem formulation for minutiae-based fingerprint verification," *Pattern Recognition Letters*, vol. 29, no. 2, pp. 142–148, 2008.

Lumini, Maio and Maltoni (1997). Lumini A., Maio D. and Maltoni D., "Continuous vs exclusive classification for fingerprint retrieval," *Pattern Recognition Letters*, vol. 18, no. 10, pp. 1027–1034, 1997.

Lumini, Maio and Maltoni (1999). Lumini A., Maio D. and Maltoni D., "Inexact graph matching for fingerprint classification," *Machine Graphics & Vision (special Issue on Graph Trasformations in Pattern Generation and CAD)*, vol. 8, no. 2, pp. 231–248, 1999.

Luo and Tian (2000). Luo X. and Tian J., "Knowledge Based Fingerprint Image Enhancement," in *Proc. Int. Conf. on Pattern Recognition (15th)*, vol. 4, pp. 783–786, 2000.

Luo, Tian and Wu (2000). Luo X., Tian J. and Wu Y., "A Minutia Matching Algorithm in Fingerprint Verification," in *Proc. Int. Conf. on Pattern Recognition (15th)*, vol. 4, pp. 833–836, 2000.

Maeda, Matsushita and Sasakawa (2001). Maeda T., Matsushita M. and Sasakawa K., "Identification algorithm using a matching score matrix," *IEICE Transactions on Information and Systems (special issue on biometrics)*, vol. E84–D, no. 7, pp. 819–824, 2001.

Mainguet, Gong and Wang (2004). Mainguet J.F., Gong W. and Wang A., "Reducing Silicon Fingerprint Sensor Area," in *Proc. Int. Conf. on Biometric Authentication (1st)*, LNCS 3072, pp. 301–308, 2004.

Mainguet, Pegulu and Harris (1999). Mainguet J.G., Pegulu M. and Harris J.B., "Fingerchip: Thermal Imaging and Finger Sweeping in a Silicon Fingerprint Sensor," in *Proc. Workshop on Automatic Identification Advances Technologies*, pp. 91–94, 1999.

Maio and Maltoni (1995). Maio D. and Maltoni D., "An Efficient Approach to On-Line Fingerprint Verification," in *Proc. Int. Symp. on Artificial Intelligence (8th)*, pp. 132–138, 1995.

Maio and Maltoni (1996). Maio D. and Maltoni D., "A Structural Approach to Fingerprint Classification," in *Proc. Int. Conf. on Pattern Recognition (13th)*, 1996.

Maio and Maltoni (1997). Maio D. and Maltoni D., "Direct gray-scale minutiae detection in fingerprints," *IEEE Transactions on Pattern Analysis Machine Intelligence*, vol. 19, no. 1, 1997.

Maio and Maltoni (1998a). Maio D. and Maltoni D., "Ridge-Line Density Estimation in Digital Images," in *Proc. Int. Conf. on Pattern Recognition (14th)*, pp. 1654–1658, 1998a.

Maio and Maltoni (1998b). Maio D. and Maltoni D., "Neural Network Based Minutiae Filtering in Fingerprints," in *Proc. Int. Conf. on Pattern Recognition (14th)*, pp. 1654–1658, 1998b.

Maio and Maltoni (1999). Maio D. and Maltoni D., "A Secure Protocol for Electronic Commerce Based on Fingerprints and Encryption," in *Proc. World Conf. on Systems Cybernetics and Informatics*, vol. 4, pp. 519–525, 1999.

Maio et al. (2000). Maio D., Maltoni D., Cappelli R., Wayman J.L. and Jain A.K., "FVC2000: Fingerprint Verification Competition," Tech. Report: DEIS, University of Bologna, Sept. 2000.

Maio et al. (2002a). Maio D., Maltoni D., Cappelli R., Wayman J.L. and Jain A.K., "FVC2000: Fingerprint verification competition," *IEEE Transactions on Pattern Analysis Machine Intelligence*, vol. 24, no. 3, pp. 402–412, 2002a.

Maio et al. (2002b). Maio D., Maltoni D., Cappelli R., Wayman J.L. and Jain A.K., "FVC2002: Second Fingerprint Verification Competition," in *Proc. Int. Conf. on Pattern Recognition (16th)*, 2002b.

Maio et al. (2004). Maio D., Maltoni D., Cappelli R., Wayman J.L. and Jain A.K., "FVC2004: Third Fingerprint Verification Competition," in *Proc. Int. Conf. on Biometric Authentication (1st)*, LNCS 3072, pp. 1–7, 2004.

Mallat (1989). Mallat S.G., "A theory for multiresolution signal decomposition: The wavelet representation," *IEEE Transactions on Pattern Analysis Machine Intelligence*, vol. 11, no. 7, pp. 674–693, 1989.

Maltoni (2004). Maltoni D., "Generation of synthetic fingerprint image databases," in *Automatic Fingerprint Recognition Systems*, N. Ratha and R. Bolle (Eds.), Springer, New York, pp. 361–384, 2004.

Mansukhani and Govindaraju (2008). Mansukhani P. and Govindaraju V., "Selecting Optimal Classification Features for SVM-Based Elimination of Incorrectly Matched Minutiae," in *Proc. SPIE Conf. on Biometric Technology for Human Identification V*, 2008.

Mansukhani, Tulyakov and Govindaraju (2007). Mansukhani P., Tulyakov S. and Govindaraju V., "Using Support Vector Machines to Eliminate False Minutiae Matches During Fingerprint Verification," in *Proc. SPIE Conf. on Biometric Technology for Human Identification IV*, 2007.

Marcialis and Roli (2003). Marcialis G.L. and Roli F., "Experimental Results on Fusion of Multiple Fingerprint Matchers," in *Proc. Int. Conf. on Audio- and Video-Based Biometric Person Authentication (4th)*, pp. 814–820, 2003.

Marcialis and Roli (2004a). Marcialis G.L. and Roli F., "Fingerprint verification by fusion of optical and capacitive sensors," *Pattern Recognition Letters*, vol. 25, no. 11, pp. 1315–1322, 2004a.

Marcialis and Roli (2004b). Marcialis G.L. and Roli F., "Fingerprint Verification by Decision-Level Fusion of Optical and Capacitive Sensors," in *Proc. Workshop on Biometric Authentication (in ECCV 2004)*, LNCS 3087, pp. 307–317, 2004b.

Marcialis and Roli (2005). Marcialis G.L. and Roli F., "Fusion of multiple fingerprint matchers by single-layer perceptron with class-separation loss function," *Pattern Recognition Letters*, vol. 26, no. 12, pp. 1830–1839, 2005.

Marcialis, Roli and Frasconi (2001). Marcialis G.L., Roli F. and Frasconi P., "Fingerprint Classification by Combination of Flat and Structural Approaches," in *Proc. Int. Conf. on Audio- and Video-Based Biometric Person Authentication (3rd)*, pp. 241–246, 2001.

Marcialis, Roli and Serrau (2003). Marcialis G.L., Roli F. and Serrau A., "Fusion of Statistical and Structural Fingerprint Classifiers," in *Proc. Int. Conf. on Audio- and Video-Based Biometric Person Authentication (4th)*, pp. 310–317, 2003.

Mardia (1972). Mardia K.V., *Statistics of Directional Data*, Academic, London, 1972.

Mardia et al. (1997). Mardia K.V., Baczkowski A.J., Feng X. and Hainsworth T.J., "Statistical methods for automatic interpretation of digitally scanned finger prints," *Pattern Recognition Letters*, vol. 18, no. 11–13, pp. 1197–1203, 1997.

Mardia, Li and Hainsworth (1992). Mardia K.V., Li Q. and Hainsworth T.J., "On the Penrose hypothesis on fingerprint patterns," *IMA journal of mathematics applied in medicine*, vol. 9, no. 4, p. 289, 1992.

Marr and Hildreth (1980). Marr D. and Hildreth E.C., "Theory of edge detection," *Proceedings of the Royal Society London*, B 207, pp. 187–217, 1980.

Martinian, Yekhanin and Yedidia (2005). Martinian E., Yekhanin S. and Yedidia J.S., "Secure Biometrics Via Syndromes," in *Proc. Conf. on Communications*, Control, and Computing, 2005.

Matsumoto et al. (2002). Matsumoto T., Matsumoto H., Yamada K. and Hoshino S., "Impact of Artificial "Gummy" Fingers on Fingerprint Systems," in *Proc. of SPIE*, vol. 4677, pp. 275–289, Feb 2002.

McCabe (2004). McCabe R.M., "Fingerprint interoperability standards," in *Automatic Fingerprint Recognition Systems*, N. Ratha and R. Bolle (Eds.), Springer, New York, pp. 433–451, 2004.

McGinity (2000). McGinity M., "Body of technology," *Communications of the ACM*, vol. 43, pp. 17–19, Sept. 2000.

McMahon et al. (1975). McMahon D., Johnson G.L., Teeter S.L. and Whitney C.G., "A hybrid optical computer processing technique for fingerprint identification," *IEEE Transaction Computer*, vol. C–24, no. 4, pp. 358–369, 1975.

Meagher et al. (1999). S.B. Meagher S.B., Buldowle B. and Ziesig D., "50K Fingerprint Comparison Test," United States of America vs. Byron Mitchell – U.S. District Court Eastern District of Philadelphia. Government Exhibits 6–8 and 6–9 in Daubert Hearing before Judge J. Curtis Joyner, July 8–9, 1999.

Meenen, Ashrafi and Adhami (2006). Meenen P., Ashrafi A. and Adhami R., "The utilization of a Taylor series-based transformation in fingerprint verification," *Pattern Recognition Letters*, vol. 27, no. 14, pp. 1606–1618, 2006.

Mehtre (1993). Mehtre B.M., "Fingerprint image analysis for automatic identification," *Machine Vision and Applications*, vol. 6, no. 2–3, pp. 124–139, 1993.

Mehtre and Chatterjee (1989). Mehtre B.M. and Chatterjee B., "Segmentation of fingerprint images – A composite method," *Pattern Recognition*, vol. 22, no. 4, pp. 381–385, 1989.

Mehtre and Chatterjee (1991). Mehtre B.M. and Chatterjee B., "Automatic fingerprint identification," *Journal of the Institution of Electronics and Telecommunication Engineers (special issue on Pattern Recognition)*, vol. 37, no. 5–6, pp. 493–499, 1991.

Mehtre and Murthy (1986). Mehtre B.M. and Murthy N.N., "A Minutia Based Fingerprint Identification System," in *Proc. Int. Conf. on Avances in Pattern Recognition and Digital Techniques (2nd)*, 1986.

Mehtre et al. (1987). Mehtre B.M., Murthy N.N., Kapoor S. and Chatterjee B., "Segmentation of fingerprint images using the directional image," *Pattern Recognition*, vol. 20, no. 4, pp. 429–435, 1987.

Melin, Bravo and Castillo (2005). Melin P., Bravo D. and Castillo O., "Fingerprint Recognition Using Modular Neural Networks and Fuzzy Integrals for Response Integration," in *Proc. Int. Joint Conf. on Neural Networks*, vol. 4, pp. 2589–2594, 2005.

Melnik, Vardi and Zhang (2004). Melnik O., Vardi Y. and Zhang C.H., "Mixed group ranks: Preference and confidence in classifier combination," *IEEE Transactions on Pattern Analysis Machine Intelligence*, vol. 26, no. 8, pp. 973–981, 2004.

Menzel (2001). Menzel E.R., "Recent advances in photoluminescence detection of fingerprints," *Scientific World Journal*, vol. 1, pp. 498–509, 2001.

Miao, Tang and Fu (2007). Miao D., Tang Q. and Fu W., "Fingerprint minutiae extraction based on principal curves," *Pattern Recognition Letters*, vol. 28, no. 16, pp. 2184–2189, 2007.

Mieloch, Mihailescu and Munk (2005). Mieloch K., Mihailescu P. and Munk A., "Dynamic Threshold Using Polynomial Surface Regression with Application to the Binarization of Fingerprints," in *Proc. SPIE Conf. on Biometric Technology for Human Identification II*, 2005.

Millard (1975). Millard K., "An Approach to Automatic Retrieval of Latent Fingerprints," in *Proc. Int. Carnahan Conf. on Electronic Crime Countermeasures*, pp. 45–51, 1975.

Millard (1983). Millard K., "Developments on Automatic Fingerprint Recognition," in *Proc. Int. Carnahan Conf. on Security Technology (17th)*, pp. 173–178, 1983.

Miller (1994). Miller B., "Vital signs of identity," *IEEE Spectrum*, vol. 31, no. 2, pp. 22–30, Feb. 1994.

Min, Hong and Cho (2006). Min J.K., Hong J.H. and Cho S.B., "Effective Fingerprint Classification by Localized Models of Support Vector Machines," in *Proc. Int. Conf. on Biometrics*, LNCS 3832, pp. 287–293, 2006.

Misao and Kazuo (1984). Misao K. and Kazuo K., "Personal identification by fingerprint or Palm-print," *Information Processing*, vol. 25, pp. 599–605, 1984.

Moayer and Fu (1973). Moayer B. and Fu K., "A Syntactic Approach to Fingerprint Pattern Recognition," in *Proc. Int. Joint Conf. on Pattern Recognition*, 1973.

Moayer and Fu (1975). Moayer B. and Fu K., "A syntactic approach to fingerprint pattern recognition," *Pattern Recognition*, vol. 7, pp. 1–23, 1975.

Moayer and Fu (1976). Moayer B. and Fu K., "An application of stochastic languages to fingerprint pattern recognition," *Pattern Recognition*, vol. 8, pp. 173–179, 1976.

Moayer and Fu (1986). Moayer B. and Fu K., "A tree system approach for fingerprint pattern recognition," *IEEE Transactions on Pattern Analysis Machine Intelligence*, vol. 8, no. 3, pp. 376–388, 1986.

Modi et al. (2007). Modi S.K., Elliott S.J., Whetsone J. and Kim H., "Impact of Age Groups on Fingerprint Recognition Performance," in *Proc. Workshop on Automatic Identification Advanced Technologies*, pp. 19–23, 2007.

Moenssens (1971). Moenssens A., *Fingerprint Techniques*, Chilton Book Company, London, 1971.

Monrose et al. (2001). Monrose F., Reiter M.K., Li Q. and Wetzel S., "Cryptographic Key Generation from Voice," in *Proc. Symp. on Security and Privacy*, 2001.

Monrose, Reiter and Wetzel (1999). Monrose F., Reiter M.K. and Wetzel S., "Password Hardening Based on Keystroke Dynamics," in *Proc. Computer and Communications Security Conf. (6th)*, 1999.

Moon et al. (2000). Moon Y.S., Ho H.C., Ng K.L., Wan S.F. and Wong S.T., "Collaborative Fingerprint Authentication by Smart Card and a Trusted Host," in *Proc. Canadian Conf. Electrical & Computer Engineering*, pp. 108–112, 2000.

Moon et al. (2004). Moon Y.S., Yeung H.W., Chan K.C. and Chan S.O., "Template Synthesis and Image Mosaicking for Fingerprint Registration: An Experimental Study," in *Proc. Int. Conf. on Acoustics, Speech, and Signal Processing (ICASSP)*, vol. 5, pp. 409–412, 2004.

Moon et al. (2005). Moon Y.S., Chen J.S., Chan K.C., So K. and Woo K.C., "Wavelet based fingerprint liveness detection," *Electronics Letters*, vol. 41, no. 20, pp. 1112–1113, 2005.

Moon, Fong and Chan (2005). Moon Y.S., Fong K.F. and Chan K.C., "Secure and Fast Fingerprint Authentication on Smart Card," in *Proc. Int. Conf. on Science of Electronics*, Technologies of Information and Telecommunications, 2005.

Morguet et al. (2004). Morguet P., Narr C., Lorch H., Wallhoff F. and Rigoll G., "Reconstruction-Free Matching for Fingerprint Sweep Sensors," in *Proc. Int. Conf. on Image Processing*, vol. 2, pp. 1257–1260, 2004.

Morimura, Shigematsu and Machida (2000). Morimura H., Shigematsu S. and Machida K., "A novel sensor cell architecture and sensing circuit scheme for capacitive fingerprint sensors," *IEEE Journal of Solid-State Circuits*, vol. 37, no. 10, pp. 1300–1306, 2000.

Moscinska and Tyma (1993). Moscinska K. and Tyma G., "Neural Network Based Fingerprint Classification," in *Proc. Int. Conf. on Artificial Neural Networks (3rd)*, 1993.

Mulvhill (1969). Mulvhill J.J., "The genesis of dematoglyphics," *The Journal of Pediatrics*, vol. 75, no. 4, pp. 579–589, 1969.

Murty (1992). Murty K.G., *Network programming*, Prentice-Hall, Englewood Cliffs, NJ, 1992.

Nagar and Chaudhury (2006). Nagar A. and Chaudhury S., "Biometrics Based Asymmetric Cryptosystem Design Using Modified Fuzzy Vault Scheme," in *Proc. Int. Conf. on Pattern Recognition (18th)*, vol. 4, pp. 537–540, 2006.

Nagar, Nandakumar and Jain (2008). Nagar A., Nandakumar K. and Jain A.K., "Securing Fingerprint Template: Fuzzy Vault with Minutiae Descriptors," in *Proc. Int. Conf. on Pattern Recognition (19th)*, 2008.

Nagaty (2003). Nagaty K.A., "On learning to estimate the block directional image of a fingerprint using a hierarchical neural network," *Neural Networks*, vol. 16, no. 1, pp. 133–144, 2003.

Nakajima et al. (2006). Nakajima H., Kobayashi K., Morikawa M., Katsumata A., Ito K., Aoki T. and Higuchi T., "Fast and Robust Fingerprint Identification Algorithm and Its Application to Residential Access Controller," in *Proc. Int. Conf. on Biometrics*, LNCS 3832, pp. 326–333, 2006.

Nakamura et al. (2004). Nakamura T., Hirooka M., Fujiwara H. and Sumi K., "Fingerprint Image Enhancement Using a Parallel Ridge Filter," in *Proc. Int. Conf. on Pattern Recognition (17th)*, vol. 1, pp. 536–539, 2004.

Nakamura, Goto and Minami (1982). Nakamura O., Goto K. and Minami T., "Fingerprint classification by directional distribution patterns," *System Computer Controls*, vol. 13, pp. 81–89, 1982.

Nakamura, Nagaoka and Minami (1986). Nakamura O., Nagaoka Y. and Minami T., "A restoration algorithm of fingerprint images," *Systems and Computers in Japan*, vol. 17, no. 6, p. 31, 1986.

Nandakumar (2008). Nandakumar K., "Multibiometric Systems: Fusion Strategies and Template Security," Ph.D. thesis, Michigan State University, 2008.

Nandakumar and Jain (2008). Nandakumar K. and Jain A.K., "Multibiometric Template Security Using Fuzzy Vault," in *Proc. Int Conf. on Biometrics: Theory, Applications and Systems (BTAS 08)*, 2008.

Nandakumar et al. (2008). Nandakumar K., Chen Y., Dass S.C. and Jain A.K., "Likelihood ratio based biometric score fusion," *IEEE Transactions on Pattern Analysis and Machine Intelligence*, vol. 30, no. 2, pp. 342–347, 2008.

Nandakumar, Jain and Pankanti (2007). Nandakumar K., Jain A.K. and Pankanti S., "Fingerprint-based fuzzy vault: Implementation and performance," *IEEE Transactions on Information Forensics and Security*, vol. 2, no. 4, pp. 744–757, 2007.

Nandakumar, Nagar and Jain (2007). Nandakumar K., Nagar A. and Jain A.K., "Hardening Fingerprint Fuzzy Vault Using Password," in *Proc. Int. Conf. on Biometrics*, LNCS 4642, pp. 927–937, 2007.

Nanni and Lumini (2007). Nanni L. and Lumini A., "A hybrid wavelet-based fingerprint matcher," *Pattern Recognition*, vol. 40, no. 11, pp. 3146–3151, 2007.

Nanni and Lumini (2008a). Nanni L. and Lumini A., "Local binary patterns for a hybrid fingerprint matcher," *Pattern Recognition*, vol. 41, no. 11, pp. 3461–3466, 2008a.

Nanni and Lumini (2008b). Nanni L. and Lumini A., "A multi-modal method based on the competitors of FVC2004 and on palm data combined with tokenised random numbers," *Pattern Recognition Letters*, vol. 29, no. 9, pp. 1344–1350, 2008b.

Neuhaus and Bunke (2005). Neuhaus M. and Bunke H., "A Graph Matching Based Approach to Fingerprint Classification Using Directional Variance," in *Proc. Int. Conf. on Audio- and Video-Based Biometric Person Authentication (5th)*, pp. 191–200, 2005.

Neumann et al. (2006). Neumann C., Champod C., Puch-Solis R., Egli N., Anthonioz A., Meuwly D. and Bromage-Griffiths A., "Computation of Likelihood Ratios in Fingerprint Identification for Configurations of Three Minutiae," in *Proc. Journal of Forensic Sciences*, vol. 51, no. 6, pp. 1255–1266, 2006.

Neumann et al. (2007). Neumann C., Champod C., Puch-Solis R., Egli N., Anthonioz A. and Bromage-Griffiths A., "Computation of likelihood ratios in fingerprint identification for configurations of any number of minutiae," *Journal of Forensic Sciences*, vol. 52, no. 1, pp. 54–64, 2007.

Newman (2001). Newman A., "Fingerprinting's Reliability Draws Growing Court Challenges," The New York Times, Apr. 7, 2001.

Ng et al. (2004). Ng G.S., Tong X., Tang X. and Shi D., "Adjacent Orientation Vector Based Fingerprint Minutiae Matching System," in *Proc. Int. Conf. on Pattern Recognition (17th)*, vol. 1, pp. 528–531, 2004.

Nill (2005). Nill N.B., "Test Procedures for Verifying IAFIS Image Quality Requirements for Fingerprint Scanners and Printers," MITRE Tech. Report: MTR 05B0000016, Apr. 2005.

Nill (2006). Nill N.B., "Test Procedures for Verifying Image Quality Requirements for Personal Identity Verification (PIV) Single Finger Capture Devices," MITRE Tech. Report: MTR 060170, Dec. 2006.

Nilsson and Bigun (2001). Nilsson K. and Bigun J., "Using Linear Symmetry Features as a Pre-processing Step for Fingerprint Images," in *Proc. Int. Conf. on Audio- and Video-Based Biometric Person Authentication (3rd)*, pp. 247–252, 2001.

Nilsson and Bigun (2002a). Nilsson K. and Bigun J., "Complex Filters Applied to Fingerprint Images Detecting Prominent Points Used Alignment," in *Proc. Workshop on Biometric Authentication (in ECCV 2002)*, LNCS 2359, Springer, pp. 39–47, 2002a.

Nilsson and Bigun (2002b). Nilsson K. and Bigun J., "Prominent Symmetry Points as Landmarks in Fingerprint Images for Alignment," in *Proc. Int. Conf. on Pattern Recognition (16th)*, vol. 3, pp. 395–398, 2002b.

Nilsson and Bigun (2003). Nilsson K. and Bigun J., "Localization of corresponding points in fingerprints by complex filtering," *Pattern Recognition Letters*, vol. 24, no. 13, pp. 2135–2144, 2003.

Nilsson and Bigun (2005). Nilsson K. and Bigun J., "Registration of Fingerprints by Complex Filtering and by 1D Projections of Orientation Images," in *Proc. Int. Conf. on Audio- and Video-Based Biometric Person Authentication (5th)*, pp. 171–183, 2005.

Nissenbaum (2001). Nissenbaum H., "New computer system embody values.," *IEEE Computer Magazine*, pp. 120, Mar. 2001.

NIST (1994). National Institute of Standards and Technology, "Guideline for The Use of Advanced Authentication Technology Alternatives," Federal Information Processing Standards Publication 190, 1994.

NIST (2004). National Institute of Standards and Technology, "Biometric Scores Set - Release 1," available at: http://www.itl.nist.gov/iad/894.03/biometricscores (accessed 27 November 2008).

NIST (2007). National Institute of Standards and Technology, "PIV Program Web Site," available at: http://csrc.nist.gov/piv–program (accessed 27 November 2008).

NIST (2008). National Institute of Standards and Technology, "NIST Proprietary Fingerprint Template (PFT) Testing," available at: http://fingerprint.nist.gov/PFT (accessed 27 November 2008).

Nixon and Rowe (2005). Nixon K.A. and Rowe R.K., "Multispectral Fingerprint Imaging for Spoof Detection," in *Proc. SPIE Conf. on Biometric Technology for Human Identification II*, 2005.

Nixon et al. (2004). Nixon K.A., Rowe R.K., Allen J., Corcoran S., Fang L., Gabel D., Gonzales D., Harbour R., Love S., McCaskill R., Ostrom B., Sidlauskas D. and Unruh K., "Novel Spectroscopy-Based Technology for Biometric and Liveness Verification," in *Proc. SPIE Conf. on Biometric Technology for Human Identification I*, 2004.

Novikov and Glushchenko (1998). Novikov S.O. and Glushchenko G.N., "Fingerprint Ridges Structure Generation Models," in *Proc. of SPIE (Int. Workshop on Digital Image Processing and Computer Graphics (6th): Applications in Humanities and Natural Sciences)*, vol. 3346, pp. 270–274, 1998.

Novikov and Kot (1998). Novikov S.O. and Kot V.S., "Singular Feature Detection and Classification of Fingerprints Using Hough Transform," in *Proc. of SPIE (Int. Workshop on Digital Image Processing and Computer Graphics (6th): Applications in Humanities and Natural Sciences)*, vol. 3346, pp. 259–269, 1998.

Novikov and Ushmaev (2004). Novikov S. and Ushmaev O., "Registration and Modeling of Elastic Deformations of Fingerprints," in *Proc. Workshop on Biometric Authentication (in ECCV 2004)*, LNCS 3087, pp. 80–88, 2004.

Novikov and Ushmaev (2005). Novikov S. and Ushmaev O., "Principal Deformations of Fingerprints," in *Proc. Int. Conf. on Audio- and Video-Based Biometric Person Authentication (5th)*, pp. 250–259, 2005.

O'Gorman (1999). O'Gorman L., "Fingerprint verification," in *Biometrics: Personal Identification in a Networked Society*, A.K. Jain, R. Bolle and S. Pankanti (Eds.), Kluwer, Norwell, MA, 1999.

O'Gorman and Nickerson (1988). O'Gorman L. and Nickerson J., "Matched Filter Design for Fingerprint Image Enhancement," in *Proc. Int. Conf. on Acoustic Speech and Signal Processing*, pp. 916–919, 1988.

O'Gorman and Nickerson (1989). O'Gorman L. and Nickerson J.V., "An approach to fingerprint filter design," *Pattern Recognition*, vol. 22, no. 1, pp. 29–38, 1989.

Oh and Ryu (2004). Oh C. and Ryu Y.K., "Study on the center of rotation method based on minimum spanning tree matching algorithm for fingerprint recognition," *Optical Engineering*, vol. 43, no. 4, pp. 822–829, 2004.

Oh, Lee and Suen (1999). Oh I.S., Lee J.S. and Suen C.Y., "Analysis of class separation and combination of class-dependent features for handwriting recognition," *IEEE Transactions on Pattern Analysis Machine Intelligence*, vol. 21, no. 10, pp. 1089–1094, 1999.

Ohtsuka and Kondo (2005). Ohtsuka T. and Kondo A., "A New Approach to Detect Core and Delta of the Fingerprint Using Extended Relational Graph," in *Proc. Int. Conf. on Image Processing*, vol. 3, pp. 249–252, 2005.

Ohtsuka and Takahashi (2005). Ohtsuka T. and Takahashi T., "A new detection approach for the fingerprint core location using extended relation graph," *IEICE Transactions on Information and Systems*, vol. 88, no. 10, pp. 2308–2312, 2005.

Oliveira and Leite (2008). Oliveira M.A. and Leite N.J., "A multiscale directional operator and morphological tools for reconnecting broken ridges in fingerprint images," *Pattern Recognition*, vol. 41, no. 1, pp. 367–377, 2008.

Omidvar, Blue and Wilson (1995). Omidvar O.M., Blue J.L. and Wilson C.L., "Improving Neural Network Performance for Character and Fingerprint Classification by Altering Network Dynamics," in *Proc. World Congress on Neural Networks*, 1995.

Onyshczak and Youssef (2004). Onyshczak R. and Youssef A., "Fingerprint image compression and the wavelet scalar quantization specification," in *Automatic Fingerprint Recognition Systems*, N. Ratha and R. Bolle (Eds.), Springer, New York, pp. 385–413, 2004.

Ortega-Garcia et al. (2003). Ortega-Garcia J., Fierrez-Aguilar J., Simon D., Gonzalez J., Faundez-Zanuy M., Espinosa V., Satue A., Hernaez I., Igarza J., Vivaracho C., Escudero D. and Moro Q., "MCYT Baseline Corpus: A Bimodal Biometric Database," *IEE Proceedings on Vision, Image and Signal Processing*, vol. 150, no. 6, pp. 395–401, 2003.

Osterburg (1964). Osterburg J.W., "An inquiry into the nature of proof: The identity of fingerprints," *Journal of Forensic Sciences*, vol. 9, pp. 413–427, 1964.

Osterburg et al. (1977). Osterburg J., Parthasarathy T., Raghaven T. and Sclove S., "Development of a mathematical formula for the calculation of fingerprint probabilities based on individual characteristic.," *Journal American Statistic Association*, vol. 72, pp. 772–778, 1977.

Ouyang et al. (2006). Ouyang Z., Feng J., Su F. and Cai A., "Fingerprint Matching with Rotation-Descriptor Texture Features," in *Proc. Int. Conf. on Pattern Recognition (18th)*, vol. 4, pp. 417–420, 2006.

Overton and Richardson (1991). Overton W. and Richardson M., "The Key to Capture. Automated fingerprint identification systems (AFISs) are revolutionizing the way fingerprints are processed identifying and apprehending criminals," *Security management*, vol. 35, no. 1, pp. 54, 1991.

Pais Barreto Marques and Gay Thome (2005). Pais Barreto Marques A.C. and Gay Thome A.C., "A Neural Network Fingerprint Segmentation Method," in *Proc. Int. Conf. on Hybrid Intelligent Systems*, 2005.

Pal and Mitra (1996). Pal S.K. and Mitra S., "Noisy fingerprint classification using multilayer perceptron with fuzzy geometrical and textural features," *Fuzzy Sets and Systems*, vol. 80, no. 2, pp. 121–132, 1996.

Pal and Pal (1993). Pal N.R. and Pal S.K., "A review on image segmentation techniques," *Pattern Recognition*, vol. 26, no. 9, pp. 1277–1294, 1993.

Pan et al. (2003). Pan S.B., Moon D., Gil Y., Ahn D. and Chung Y., "An ultra low memory fingerprint matching algorithm and its implementation on a 32-bit smart card," *IEEE Transaction on Consumer Electronics*, vol. 49, no. 2, pp. 453–459, 2003.

Pan et al. (2006). Pan S.B., Moon D., Kim K. and Chung Y., "A VLSI implementation of Minutiae Extraction for Secure Fingerprint Authentication," in *Proc. Int. Conf. on Computational Intelligence and Security*, vol. 2, pp. 1217–1220, 2006.

Pankanti, Bolle and Jain (2000). Pankanti S., Bolle R. and Jain A.K., *Special Issue on Biometrics, IEEE Computer Magazine*, Feb. 2000.

Pankanti, Prabhakar and Jain (2001). Pankanti S., Prabhakar S. and Jain A.K., "On the Individuality of Fingerprints," in *Proc. Conf. Computer Vision and Pattern Recognition*, pp. 805–812, 2001.

Pankanti, Prabhakar and Jain (2002). Pankanti S., Prabhakar S. and Jain A.K., "On the individuality of fingerprints," *IEEE Transactions on Pattern Analysis Machine Intelligence*, vol. 24, no. 8, pp. 1010–1025, 2002.

Pankanti, Ratha and Bolle (2002). Pankanti S., Ratha N.K. and Bolle R.M., "Structure in Errors: A Case Study in Fingerprint Verification," in *Proc. Int. Conf. on Pattern Recognition (16th)*, vol. 3, pp. 440–443, 2002.

Park and Park (2005). Park C.H. and Park H., "Fingerprint classification using fast Fourier transform and nonlinear discriminant analysis," *Pattern Recognition*, vol. 38, no. 4, pp. 495–503, 2005.

Park and Smith (2000). Park S.I. and Smith M., "Fingerprint Enhancement Based on the Directional Filter Bank," in *Proc. Int. Conf. on Image Processing*, 2000.

Park et al. (2005). Park C.H., Smith M.J.T., Boutin M. and Lee J.J., "Fingerprint Matching Using the Distribution of the Pairwise Distances Between Minutiae," in *Proc. Int. Conf. on Audio- and Video-Based Biometric Person Authentication (5th)*, pp. 693–701, 2005.

Park et al. (2006). Park C.H., Lee J.J, Smith M.J.T. and Park K.H., "Singular point detection by shape analysis of directional fields in fingerprints," *Pattern Recognition*, vol. 39, no. 5, pp. 839–855, 2006.

Park, Pankanti and Jain (2008). Park U., Pankanti S. and Jain A.K., "Novel Fingerprint Verification System Using SIFT," in *Proc. SPIE Conf. on Biometric Technology for Human Identification V*, 2008.

Parthasaradhi et al. (2004). Parthasaradhi S.T., Derakhshani R., Hornak L.A. and Schuckers S.C., "Improvement of an Algorithm for Recognition of Liveness Using Perspiration in Fingerprint Devices," in *Proc. SPIE Conf. on Biometric Technology for Human Identification I*, 2004.

Parthasaradhi et al. (2005). Parthasaradhi S.T.V., Derakhshani R., Hornak L.A. and Schuckers S.A.C., "Time-series detection of perspiration as a liveness test in fingerprint devices," *IEEE Transaction on Systems, Man, and Cybernetics, Part C*, vol. 35, no. 3, pp. 335–343, 2005.

Parziale (2007). Parziale G., "Touchless fingerprinting technology," in *Advances in Biometrics: Sensors, Algorithms and Systems*, N.K. Ratha and V. Govindaraju (Eds.), Springer, Heidelberg, pp. 25–48, 2007.

Parziale and Niel (2004). Parziale G. and Niel A., "A Fingerprint Matching Using Minutiae Triangulation," in *Proc. Int. Conf. on Biometric Authentication (1st)*, LNCS 3072, pp. 241–248, 2004.

Parziale, Diaz-Santana and Hauke (2006). Parziale G., Diaz-Santana E. and Hauke R., "The Surround ImagerTM: A Multi-camera Touchless Device to Acquire 3D Rolled-Equivalent Fingerprints," in *Proc. Int. Conf. on Biometrics*, LNCS 3832, pp. 244–250, 2006.

Patra and Das (2008). Patra A. and Das S., "Enhancing decision combination of face and fingerprint by exploitation of individual classifier space: An approach to multi-modal biometry," *Pattern Recognition*, vol. 41, no. 7, pp. 2298–2308, 2008.

Pattichis and Bovik (2004). Pattichis M. and Bovik A., "Latent fingerprint analysis using an AM/FM model," in *Automatic Fingerprint Recognition Systems*, N. Ratha and R. Bolle (Eds.), Springer, New York, pp. 317–338, 2004.

Pattichis et al. (2001). Pattichis M.S., Panayi G., Bovik A.C. and Hsu S.P., "Fingerprint classification using an AM–FM model," *IEEE Transactions on Image Processing*, vol. 10, no. 6, pp. 951–954, 2001.

Pearson (1930). K. Pearson K., *The Life and Letters of Francis Galton*, vol. IIIA, Cambridge University Press, Cambridge, 1930.

Pearson (1933). Pearson K., "Galton's work on evidential value of fingerprints," *Sankhya: Indian Journal of Statistics*, vol. 1, no. 50, 1933.

Penrose (1965). Penrose L.S., "Dermatoglyphic topology," *Nature*, vol. 205, pp. 545–546, 1965.

Perlin (1985). Perlin K., "An image synthesizer," *Computer Graphics*, vol. 19, no. 3, pp 287–296, 1985.

Pernus, Kovacic and Gyergyek (1980). Pernus F., Kovacic S. and Gyergyek L., "Minutiae Based Fingerprint Recognition," in *Proc. Int. Conf. on Pattern Recognition (5th)*, pp. 1380–1382, 1980.

Perona (1998). Perona P., "Orientation diffusions," *IEEE Transactions on Image Processing*, vol. 7, no. 3, pp. 457–467, 1998.

Petillot, Guibert and De Bougrenet (1996). Petillot Y., Guibert L. and de Bougrenet J.L., "Fingerprint recognition using a partially rotation invariant composite filter in a FLC joint transform correlator," *Optics Communications*, vol. 126, pp. 213–219, 1996.

Phillips et al. (2000). Phillips P.J., Martin A., Wilson C.L. and Przybocki M., "An introduction to evaluating biometric systems," *IEEE Computer Magazine*, Feb. 2000.

Phillips (2008). Phillips P.J., "Multiple Biometric Grand Challenge Web Site," available at: http://face.nist.gov/mbgc/ (accessed 27 November 2008).

Polikarpova (1996). Polikarpova N., "On The Fractal Features in Fingerprint Analysis," in *Proc. Int. Conf. on Pattern Recognition (13th)*, 1996.

Prabhakar and Jain (2002). Prabhakar S. and Jain A.K., "Decision-level fusion in fingerprint verification," *Pattern Recognition*, vol. 35, no. 4, pp. 861–874, 2002.

Prabhakar and Jain (2004). Prabhakar S. and Jain A.K., "Fingerprint matching," in *Automatic Fingerprint Recognition Systems*, N. Ratha and R. Bolle (Eds.), Springer, New York, pp. 229–248, 2004.

Prabhakar and Rao (1989). Prabhakar R.V.S.N. and Rao K., "A Parallel Algorithm for Fingerprint Matching," in *Proc. Tencon Conf.*, pp. 373–376, 1989.

Prabhakar, Jain and Pankanti (2003). Prabhakar S., Jain A.K. and Pankanti S., "Learning fingerprint minutiae location and type," *Pattern Recognition*, vol. 36, no. 8, pp. 1847–1857, 2003.

Pradenas (1997). Pradenas R., "Directional Enhancement in the Frequency Domain of Fingerprint Images," in *Proc. of SPIE*, vol. 2932, pp. 150–160, 1997.

Press et al. (1992). Press W.H., Teukolsky S.A., Vetterling W.T. and Flannery B.P., *Numerical Recipes in C*, Cambridge University Press, Cambridge, 1992.

Putte (2001). Putte T.v.d., "Forging ahead," *Biometric Technology Today*, vol. 10, pp. 9–1, 2001.

Putte and Keuning (2000). Putte T.v.d. and Keuning J., "Biometrical Fingerprint Recognition: Don't Get Your Fingers Burned," in *Proc. Working Conf. on Smart Card Research and Advanced Applications (4th)*, Proc. IFIP TC8/WG8.8, pp. 289–303, 2000.

Qi and Wang (2005). Qi J. and Wang Y., "A robust fingerprint matching method," *Pattern Recognition*, vol. 38, no. 10, pp. 1665–1671, 2005.

Qi et al. (2005a). Qi J., Shi Z., Zhao X. and Wang Y., "Measuring Fingerprint Image Quality Using Gradient," in *Proc. SPIE Conf. on Biometric Technology for Human Identification II*, 2005a.

Qi et al. (2005b). Qi J., Abdurrachim D., Li D. and Kunieda H., "A Hybrid Method for Fingerprint Image Quality Calculation," in *Proc. Workshop on Automatic Identification Advanced Technologies*, pp. 124–129, 2005b.

Quek, Tan and Sagar (2001). Quek C., Tan K.B. and Sagar V.K., "Pseudo-outer product based neural network fingerprint verification system," *Neural Networks*, vol. 14, pp. 305–323, 2001.

Rabinowitz (1980). Rabinowitz A., "Fingerprint Card Search Result with Ridge-Contour Based Classification," in *Proc. Int. Conf. on Pattern Recognition (5th)*, pp. 475–477, 1980.

Rahmes et al. (2007). Rahmes M., Allen J.D., Elharti A. and Tenali G.B., "Fingerprint Reconstruction Method Using Partial Differential Equation and Exemplar-Based Inpainting Methods," in *Proc. Biometric Symposium*, 2007.

Rämö et al. (2001). Rämö P., Tico M., Onnia V. and Saarinen J., "Optimized Singular Point Detection Algorithm for Fingerprint Images," in *Proc. Int. Conf. on Image Processing*, 2001.

Ramoser, Wachmann and Bischof (2002). Ramoser H., Wachmann B. and Bischof H., "Efficient Alignment of Fingerprint Images," in *Proc. Int. Conf. on Pattern Recognition (16th)*, vol. 3, pp. 748–751, 2002.

Ranade and Rosenfeld (1993). Ranade A. and Rosenfeld A., "Point pattern matching by relaxation," *Pattern Recognition*, vol. 12, no. 2, pp. 269–275, 1993.

Rao (1976). Rao M., "Feature extraction for fingerprint classification," *Pattern Recognition*, vol. 8, pp. 599–605, 1976.

Rao (1978). Rao C.V.K., "On fingerprint pattern recognition," *Pattern Recognition*, vol. 10, pp. 15–18, 1978.

Rao (1990). Rao A.R., *A Taxonomy forTexture Description and Identification*, Springer, New York, 1990.

Rao (2008). Rao S.M., "Method for producing correct fingerprints," *Applied Optics*, vol. 47, no. 1, pp. 25–29, 2008.

Rao and Balck (1978). Rao K. and Balck K., "Finding the core point in a fingerprint," *IEEE Transaction Computer*, vol. C–27, pp. 78–81, 1978.

Rao and Balck (1980). Rao K. and Balck K., "Type classification of fingerprints: A syntactic approach," *IEEE Transactions on Pattern Analysis Machine Intelligence*, vol. 2, no. 3, pp. 223–231, 1980.

Rao, Prasad and Sharma (1974). Rao K., Prasad B. and Sharma K., "Automatic Fingerprint Classification System," in *Proc. Int. Conf. on Pattern Recognition (2nd)*, pp. 180–184, 1974.

Ratha and Bolle (1998). Ratha N.K. and Bolle R.M., "Effect of Controlled Image Acquisition of Fingerprint Matching," in *Proc. Int. Conf. on Pattern Recognition (14th)*, 1998.

Ratha and Bolle (2004). Ratha N.K. and Bolle R.M., *Automatic Fingerprint Recognition Systems*, Springer, New York, 2004.

Ratha and Govindaraju (2007). Ratha N.K. and Govindaraju V., *Advances in Biometrics: Sensors, Algorithms and Systems*, Springer, Heidelberg, 2007.

Ratha et al. (1996). Ratha N.K., Karu K., Chen S. and Jain A.K., "A real-time matching system for large fingerprint databases," *IEEE Transactions on Pattern Analysis Machine Intelligence*, vol. 18, no. 8, pp. 799–813, 1996.

Ratha et al. (2000). Ratha N.K., Pandit V.D., Bolle R.M. and Vaish, V., "Robust Fingerprint Authentication Using Local Structural Similarity," in *Proc. Workshop on Applications of Computer Vision*, pp. 29–34, 2000.

Ratha et al. (2004). Ratha N.K., Figueroa-Villanueva M.A., Connell J.H. and Bolle R.M., "A Secure Protocol for Data Hiding in Compressed Fingerprint Images," in *Proc. Workshop on Biometric Authentication (in ECCV 2004)*, LNCS 3087, pp. 205–216, 2004.

Ratha et al. (2006). Ratha N., Connell J., Bolle R.M. and Chikkerur S., "Cancelable Biometrics: A Case Study in Fingerprints," in *Proc. Int. Conf. on Pattern Recognition (18th)*, vol. 4, pp. 370–373, 2006.

Ratha et al. (2007). Ratha N.K., Chikkerur S., Connell J.H. and Bolle R.M., "Generating cancelable fingerprint templates," *IEEE Transactions on Pattern Analysis Machine Intelligence*, vol. 29, no. 4, pp. 561–572, 2007.

Ratha, Chen and Jain (1995). Ratha N.K., Chen S.Y. and Jain A.K., "Adaptive flow orientation-based feature extraction in fingerprint images," *Pattern Recognition*, vol. 28, no. 11, pp. 1657–1672, 1995.

Ratha, Connell and Bolle (1998). Ratha N.K., Connell J. and Bolle R.M., "Image Mosaicing for Rolled Fingerprint Construction," in *Proc. Int. Conf. on Pattern Recognition (14th)*, vol. 2, pp. 1651–1653, 1998.

Ratha, Connell and Bolle (1999). Ratha N.K., Connell J. and Bolle R.M., "A Biometrics-Based Secure Authentication System," in *Proc. Workshop on Automatic Identification Advances Technologies*, 1999.

Ratha, Connell and Bolle (2001a). Ratha N.K., Connell J.H. and Bolle R.M., "An Analysis of Minutiae Matching Strength," in *Proc. Int. Conf. on Audio- and Video-Based Biometric Person Authentication (3rd)*, pp. 223–228, 2001a.

Ratha, Connell and Bolle (2001b). Ratha N.K., Connell J. and Bolle R., "Enhancing security and privacy in biometrics-based authentication systems," *IBM Systems Journal*, vol. 40, no. 3, pp. 614–634, 2001b.

Ratha, Connell and Bolle (2003). Ratha N.K., Connell J.H. and Bolle R.M., "Biometrics break-ins and band-aids," *Pattern Recognition Letters*, vol. 24, no. 13, pp. 2105–2113, 2003.

Ratha, Rover and Jain (1995). Ratha N.K., Rover D. and Jain A.K., "An FPGA-Based Point Pattern Matching Processor with Application to Fingerprint Matching," in *Proc. Conf. Computer Architectures for Machine Perception*, Italy, pp. 394–401, 1995.

Ratha, Rover and Jain (1996). Ratha N.K., Rover D. and Jain A.K., "Fingerprint Matching on Splash 2," in *Splash 2: FPGAS in a Custom Computing Machine*, D. Buell, J. Arnold and W. Kleinfolder (Eds.), IEEE Computer Society Press, Los Alamitos, CA, pp. 117–140, 1996.

Rattani et al. (2007). Rattani A., Kisku D.R., Bicego M. and Tistarelli M., "Feature Level Fusion of Face and Fingerprint Biometrics," in *Proc. Int. Conf. on Biometrics: Theory, Applications and Systems (BTAS07)*, 2007.

Raudys and Jain (1991). Raudys S. and Jain A.K., "Small sample size effects in statistical pattern recognition: Recommendations for practitioners," *IEEE Transactions on Pattern Analysis Machine Intelligence*, vol. 13, no. 3, pp. 252–264, 1991.

Reddy et al. (2007). Reddy P.V., Kumar A., Rahman S.M.K. and Mundra T.S., "A New Method for Fingerprint Antispoofing Using Pulse Oximetry," in *Proc. Int. Conf. on Biometrics: Theory, Applications, and Systems (BTAS 07)*, pp. 1–6, 2007.

Reed and Meier (1990). Reed T. and Meier R., "Taking dermatogyphic prints: A self-instruction manual," *American Dermatoglyphics Association Newsletter: Supplement*, vol. 9, pp. 18, 1990.

Reisman, Uludag and Ross (2005). Reisman J., Uludag U. and Ross A., "Secure Fingerprint Matching with External Registration," in *Proc. Int. Conf. on Audio- and Video-Based Biometric Person Authentication (5th)*, pp. 720–729, 2005.

Ren et al. (2002). Ren Q., Tian J., He Y. and Cheng J., "Automatic Fingerprint Identification Using Cluster Algorithm," in *Proc. Int. Conf. on Pattern Recognition (16th)*, vol. 2, pp. 398–401, 2002.

Rerkrai and Areekul (2000). Rerkrai K. and Areekul V., "A New Reference Point for Fingerprint Recognition," in *Proc. Int. Conf. on Image Processing*, 2000.

Rhodes (1956). Rhodes H.T.F., *Alphonse Bertillon: Father of Scientific Detection*, Abelard-Schuman, New York, 1956.

Ribaric and Fratric (2005). Ribaric S. and Fratric I., "A biometric identification system based on eigenpalm and eigenfinger features," *IEEE Transactions on Pattern Analysis Machine Intelligence*, vol. 27, no. 11, pp. 1698–1709, 2005.

Rice (1995). Rice J.A., *Mathematical Statistics and Data Analysis*, 2nd edition, Duxbury Press, Belmont, CA, 1995.

Riganati (1977). Riganati J., "An Overview of Algorithms Employed in Automated Fingerprint Processing," in *Proc. Int. Carnahan Conf. on Electronic Crime Countermeasures*, pp. 125–131, 1977.

Roberge, Soutar and Kumar (1999). Roberge D., Soutar C. and Kumar B.V.K.V., "Optimal trade-off filter for the correlation of fingerprints," *Optical Engineering*, vol. 38, no. 1, pp. 108–113, 1999.

Roberts (2007). Roberts C., "Biometric attack vectors and defenses," *Computers and Security*, vol. 26, no. 1, pp. 14–25, 2007.

Roddy and Stosz (1997). Roddy A. and Stosz J., "Fingerprint features: Statistical-analysis and system performance estimates," *Proceedings of the IEEE*, vol. 85, no. 9, pp. 1390–1421, 1997.

Rodolfo, Rajbenbach and Huignard (1995). Rodolfo J., Rajbenbach H. and Huignard J., "Performance of a photo-refractive joint transform correlator for fingerprint identification," *Optical Engineering*, vol. 34, no. 4, pp. 1166–1171, 1995.

Rosenfeld and Kak (1976). Rosenfeld A. and Kak A., *Digital Picture Processing*, Academic, New York, 1976.

Ross and Govindarajan (2005). Ross A. and Govindarajan R., "Feature Level Fusion Using Hand and Face Biometrics," in *Proc. SPIE Conf. on Biometric Technology for Human Identification II*, vol. 5404, pp. 196–204, Mar. 2005.

Ross and Jain (2003). Ross A. and Jain A.K., "Information fusion in biometrics," *Pattern Recognition Letters*, vol. 24, no. 13, pp. 2115–2125, 2003.

Ross and Jain (2004). Ross A. and Jain A.K., "Biometric Sensor Interoperability: A Case Study in Fingerprints," in *Proc. Workshop on Biometric Authentication (in ECCV 2004)*, LNCS 3087, pp. 134–145, 2004.

Ross and Mukherjee (2007). Ross A. and Mukherjee R., "Augmenting Ridge Curves with Minutiae Triplets for Fingerprint Indexing," in *Proc. SPIE Conf. on Biometric Technology for Human Identification IV*, 2007.

Ross and Nadgir (2006). Ross A. and Nadgir R., "A Calibration Model for Fingerprint Sensor Interoperability," in *Proc. SPIE Conf. on Biometric Technology for Human Identification III*, 2006.

Ross and Nadgir (2008). Ross A. and Nadgir R., "A thin-plate spline calibration model For fingerprint sensor interoperability," *IEEE Transaction Data and Knowledge Engineering*, vol. 20, no. 8, pp. 1097–1110, 2008.

Ross, Dass and Jain (2005). Ross A., Dass S.C. and Jain A.K., "A deformable model for fingerprint matching," *Pattern Recognition*, vol. 38, no. 1, pp. 95–103, 2005.

Ross, Dass and Jain (2006). Ross A., Dass S.C. and Jain A.K., "Fingerprint warping using ridge curve correspondences," *IEEE Transactions on Pattern Analysis Machine Intelligence*, vol. 28, no. 1, pp. 19–30, 2006.

Ross, Jain and Qian (2001). Ross A., Jain A.K. and Qian J., "Information Fusion in Biometrics," in *Proc. Int. Conf. on Audio- and Video-Based Biometric Person Authentication (3rd)*, 2001.

Ross, Jain and Reisman (2003). Ross A., Jain A.K. and Reisman J., "A hybrid fingerprint matcher," *Pattern Recognition*, vol. 36, no. 7, pp. 1661–1673, 2003.

Ross, Nandakumar and Jain (2006). Ross A.A., Nandakumar K. and Jain A.K., *Handbook of Multibiometrics*, Springer, New York, 2006.

Ross, Reisman and Jain (2002). Ross A., Reisman J. and Jain A.K., "Fingerprint Matching Using Feature Space Correlation," in *Proc. Workshop on Biometric Authentication (in ECCV 2002)*, LNCS 2359, Springer, pp. 48–57, 2002.

Ross, Shah and Jain (2005). Ross A.A., Shah J. and Jain A.K., "Toward Reconstructing Fingerprints from Minutiae Points," in *Proc. SPIE Conf. on Biometric Technology for Human Identification II*, 2005.

Ross, Shah and Jain (2007). Ross A., Shah J. and Jain A.K., "From template to image: Reconstructing fingerprints from minutiae points," *IEEE Transactions on Pattern Analysis Machine Intelligence*, vol. 29, no. 4, pp. 544–560, 2007.

Ross, Shah and Shah (2006). Ross A., Shah S. and Shah J., "Image Versus Feature Mosaicing: A Case Study in Fingerprints," in *Proc. SPIE Conf. on Biometric Technology for Human Identification III*, 2006.

Rowe (2007). Rowe R.K., "Biometrics Based on Multispectral Skin Texture," in *Proc. Int. Conf. on Biometrics*, LNCS 4642, pp. 1144–1153, 2007.

Rowe and Nixon (2005). Rowe R.K. and Nixon K.A., "Fingerprint Enhancement Using a Multispectral Sensor," in *Proc. SPIE Conf. on Biometric Technology for Human Identification II*, 2005.

Rowe et al. (2007a). Rowe R.K., Nixon K.A., Parthasaradhi S. and Uludag U., "Robust Fingerprint Acquisition: A Comparative Performance Study," in *Proc. SPIE Conf. on Biometric Technology for Human Identification IV*, 2007a.

Rowe et al. (2007b). Rowe R.K., Uludag U., Demirkus M., Parthasaradhi S. and Jain A.K., "A Multispectral Whole-Hand Biometric Authentication System," in *Proc. Biometric Symposium*, 2007b.

Rowe, Nixon and Butler (2007). Rowe R.K., Nixon K.A. and Butler P.W., "Multispectral fingerprint image acquisition," in *Advances in Biometrics: Sensors, Algorithms and Systems*, N.K. Ratha and V. Govindaraju (Eds.), Springer, London, pp. 3–24, 2007.

Roxburgh (1933). Roxburgh T., "On evidential value of fingerprints," *Sankhya: Indian Journal of Statistics*, vol. 1, pp. 189–214, 1933.

Ryu, Han and Kim (2005). Ryu C., Han Y. and Kim H., "Super-template Generation Using Successive Bayesian Estimation for Fingerprint Enrollment," in *Proc. Int. Conf. on Audio- and Video-Based Biometric Person Authentication (5th)*, pp. 710–719, 2005.

Ryu, Kim and Jain (2006). Ryu C., Kim H. and Jain A.K., "Template Adaptation based Fingerprint Verification," in *Proc. Int. Conf. on Pattern Recognition (18th)*, vol. 4, pp. 582–585, 2006.

Sahai and Waters (2005). Sahai A. and Waters B., "Fuzzy Identity-Based Encryption," in *Proc. Advances in Cryptology (EUROCRYPT 05)*, 2005.

Sakata et al. (2006). Sakata K., Maeda T., Matsushita M., Sasakawa K. and Tamaki H., "Fingerprint Authentication Based on Matching Scores with Other Data," in *Proc. Int. Conf. on Biometrics*, LNCS 3832, pp. 280–286, 2006.

Saks and Koehler (2005). Saks M.J. and Koehler J.J., "The coming paradigm shift in forensic identification science," *Science*, vol. 309, no. 5736, pp. 892–895, 2005.

Saltzman (2005a). Saltzman J., "SJC bars a type of prints at trial," *The Boston Globe*, Dec. 28, 2005a.

Saltzman (2005b). Saltzman J., "Massachusetts Supreme Judicial Court to hear arguments on banning fingerprint evidence," *The Boston Globe*, Sept. 5, 2005b.

Samet (1990). Samet H., *The Design and Analysis of Spatial Data Structures*, Addison-Wesley, Reading, MA, 1990.

Sarbadhikari et al. (1998). Sarbadhikari S.N., Basak J., Pal S.K. and Kundu M.K., "Noisy fingerprints classification with directional FFT based features using Mlp," *Neural Computing and Applications*, vol. 7, no. 2, pp. 180–191, 1998.

Sasakawa, Isogai and Ikebata (1990). Sasakawa K., Isogai F. and Ikebata S., "Personal Verification System with High Tolerance of Poor Quality Fingerprints," in *Proc. of SPIE*, vol. 1386, pp. 265–272, 1990.

Saviers (1987). Saviers K., *Friction Skin Characteristics: A Study and Comparison of Proposed Standards*, California Police Department, Garden Grove, CA, 1987.

Savvides, Kumar and Khosla (2004). Savvides M., Kumar B.V. and Khosla P., "Cancelable Biometric Filters for Face Recognition," in *Proc. Int. Conf. on Pattern Recognition (17th)*, vol. 3, pp. 922–925, 2004.

Schapire (1990). Schapire R.E., "The strength of weak learnability," *Machine Learning*, vol. 5, pp. 197–227, 1990.

Scheirer and Boult (2007). Scheirer W.J. and Boult T.E., "Cracking Fuzzy Vaults and Biometric Encryption," in *Proc. Biometrics Symposium*, 2007.

Scheirer and Boult (2008). Scheirer W.J. and Boult T.E., "Bio-Cryptographic Protocols with Bipartite Biotokens," in *Proc. Biometric Symposium*, 2008.

Schneider (2007). Schneider J.K., "Ultrasonic fingerprint sensors," in *Advances in Biometrics: Sensors, Algorithms and Systems*, N.K. Ratha and V. Govindaraju (Eds.), Springer, London, pp. 63–74, 2007.

Schneider and Wobschall (1991). Schneider J. and Wobschall D., "Live Scan Fingerprint Imagery Using High Resolution C–SCAN ultrasonography.," in *Proc. Int. Carnahan Conf. on Security Technology (25th)*, pp. 88–95, 1991.

Schneider et al. (2003). Schneider J.K., Richardson C.E., Kiefer F.W. and Govindaraju V., "On the Correlation of Image Size to System Accuracy in Automatic Fingerprint Identification Systems," in *Proc. Int. Conf. on Audio- and Video-Based Biometric Person Authentication (4th)*, pp. 895–902, 2003.

Schneier (1996). Schneier B., *Applied Cryptography*, Wiley, New York, 1996.

Schneier (1998a). Schneier B., "Security Pitfalls in Cryptography," in *Proc. CardTech/SecueTech Conf.*, pp. 621–626, 1998a.

Schneier (1998b). Schneier B., "Cryptographic design vulnerabilities," *Computer*, vol. 31, no. 9, pp. 29–33, 1998b.

Schneier (1999a). Schneier B., "Inside risks: The uses and abuses of biometrics," *Communications of the ACM*, vol. 42, pp. 136, Aug. 1999a.

Schneier (1999b). Schneier B., "Attack trees," *Dr. Dobb's Journal*, vol. 24, no. 12, pp. 21–29, 1999b.

Schuckers and Abhyankar (2004). Schuckers S. and Abhyankar A., "Detecting Liveness in Fingerprint Scanners Using Wavelets: Results of the Test Dataset," in *Proc. Workshop on Biometric Authentication (in ECCV 2004)*, LNCS 3087, pp. 100–110, 2004.

Schuckers et al. (2004). Schuckers S.A.C., Parthasaradhi S.T.V., Derakshani R. and Hornak L.A., "Comparison of Classification Methods for Time-Series Detection of Perspiration as a Liveness Test in Fingerprint Devices," in *Proc. Int. Conf. on Biometric Authentication (1st)*, LNCS 3072, pp. 256–263, 2004.

Sclove (1979). Sclove S.L., "The occurrence of fingerprint characteristics as a two dimensional process," *Journal of American Statistical Association*, vol. 74, no. 367, pp. 588–595, 1979.

Scott (1951). Scott W., *Fingerprint Mechanics – A Handbook*, C. Thomas, Springfield, IL, 1951.

Seigo, Shin and Takashi (1989). Seigo I., Shin E. and Takashi S., "Holographic fingerprint sensor," *Fujitsu Scientific & Technical Journal*, vol. 25, no. 4, pp. 287, 1989.

Senior (1997). Senior A., "A Hidden Markov Model Fingerprint Classifier," in *Proc. Asilomar Conf. on Signals Systems and Computers (31st)*, pp. 306–310, 1997.

Senior (2001). Senior A., "A combination fingerprint classifier," *IEEE Transactions on Pattern Analysis Machine Intelligence*, vol. 23, no. 10, pp. 1165–1174, 2001.

Senior and Bolle (2001). Senior A.W. and Bolle R., "Improved fingerprint matching by distortion removal," *IEICE Transactions on Information and Systems (special issue on biometrics)*, vol. E84–D, no. 7, pp. 825–832, 2001.

Senior and Bolle (2004). Senior A.W. and Bolle R., "Fingerprint classification by decision fusion," in *Automatic Fingerprint Recognition Systems*, N. Ratha and R. Bolle (Eds.), Springer, New York, pp. 207–227, 2004.

Setlak (1999). Setlak D.R., "Electric Field Fingerprint Sensor Apparatus and Related Methods," US Patent 5963679, 1999.

Setlak (2004). Setlak D.S., "Advances in fingerprint sensors using RF imaging techniques," in *Automatic Fingerprint Recognition Systems*, N. Ratha and R. Bolle (Eds.), Springer, New York, pp. 27–53, 2004.

Setlak et al. (2000). Setlak D.R., VanVonno N.W., Newton M. and Salatino M.M., "Fingerprint Sensor Including an Anisotropic Dielectric Coating and Associated Methods," US Patent 6088471, 2000.

Sha and Tang (2004a). Sha L. and Tang X., "Combining Exclusive and Continuous Fingerprint Classification," in *Proc. Int. Conf. on Image Processing*, vol. 2, pp. 1245–1248, 2004a.

Sha and Tang (2004b). Sha L. and Tang X., "Orientation-Improved Minutiae for Fingerprint Matching," in *Proc. Int. Conf. on Pattern Recognition (17th)*, vol. 4, pp. 432–435, 2004b.

Sha, Zhao and Tang (2003). Sha L., Zhao F. and Tang X., "Improved Fingercode for Filterbank-Based Fingerprint Matching," in *Proc. Int. Conf. on Image Processing*, vol. 3, pp. 895–898, 2003.

Sha, Zhao and Tang (2005). Sha L., Zhao F. and Tang X., "Fingerprint Matching Using Minutiae and Interpolation-Based Square Tessellation Fingercode," in *Proc. Int. Conf. on Image Processing*, vol. 2, pp. 41–44, 2005.

Sha, Zhao and Tang (2006). Sha L., Zhao F. and Tang X., "Minutiae-based Fingerprint Matching Using Subset Combination," in *Proc. Int. Conf. on Pattern Recognition (18th)*, vol. 4, pp. 566–569, 2006.

Sha, Zhao and Tang (2007). Sha L., Zhao F. and Tang X., "A Two-Stage Fusion Scheme using Multiple Fingerprint Impressions," in *Proc. Int. Conf. on Image Processing*, vol. 2, pp. 385–388, 2007.

Shah and Sastry (2004). Shah S. and Sastry P.S., "Fingerprint classification using a feedback-based line detector," *IEEE Transaction on Systems, Man, and Cybernetics, Part B*, vol. 34, no. 1, pp. 85–94, 2004.

Shan, Shi and Li (1994). Shan Y., Shi P. and Li J., "Fingerprint Preclassification Using Key-Points," in *Proc. International Symp. on Speech Image Proc. and Neural Network*, 1994.

Shelman (1976). Shelman C., "Fingerprint Classification – Theory and Application," in *Proc. Int. Carnahan Conf. on Electronic Crime Countermeasures*, pp. 131–138, 1976.

Shelman and Hodges (1973). Shelman C.B. and Hodges D., "A Decimal Henry System," in *Proc. Int. Carnahan Conf. on Electronic Crime Countermeasures*, pp. 213–220, 1973.

Shen and Eshera (2004). Shen W. and Eshera M.A., "Feature extraction in fingerprint images," in *Automatic Fingerprint Recognition Systems*, N. Ratha and R. Bolle (Eds.), Springer, New York, pp. 145–181, 2004.

Shen and Khanna (1994). Shen W. and Khanna R., "Automated Fingerprint Identification System (AFIS) Benchmarking Using the National Institute of Standards and Technology (NIST) Special Database 4.," in *Proc. Int. Carnahan Conf. on Security Technology (28th)*, pp. 88–95, 1994.

Shen and Khanna (1997). Shen W. and Khanna R., "Special Issue on Biometrics," *Proceedings of the IEEE*, vol. 85, no. 9, 1997.

Shen, Kot and Koo (2001). Shen L., Kot A. and Koo W.M., "Quality Measures of Fingerprint Images," in *Proc. Int. Conf. on Audio- and Video-Based Biometric Person Authentication (3rd)*, pp. 266–271, 2001.

Sheng et al. (2007). Sheng W., Howells G., Fairhurst M.C. and Deravi F., "A memetic fingerprint matching algorithm," *IEEE Transactions on Information Forensics and Security*, vol. 2, no. 3, pp. 402–412, 2007.

Sherlock (2004). Sherlock B.G., "Computer enhancement and modeling of fingerprint images," in *Automatic Fingerprint Recognition Systems*, N. Ratha and R. Bolle (Eds.), Springer, New York, pp. 87–112, 2004.

Sherlock and Monro (1993). Sherlock B.G. and Monro D.M., "A model for interpreting fingerprint topology," *Pattern Recognition*, vol. 26, no. 7, pp. 1047–1055, 1993.

Sherlock, Monro and Millard (1992). Sherlock B.G., Monro D.M. and Millard K., "Algorithm for enhancing fingerprint images," *Electronics Letters*, vol. 28, no. 18, pp. 1720, 1992.

Sherlock, Monro and Millard (1994). Sherlock B.G., Monro D.M. and Millard K., "Fingerprint enhancement by directional Fourier filtering," *IEE Proceedings Vision Image and Signal Processing*, vol. 141, no. 2, pp. 87–94, 1994.

Sherstinsky and Picard (1994). Sherstinsky A. and Picard R.W., "Restoration and Enhancement of Fingerprint Images Using M-Lattice – A Novel Non-linear Dynamical System," in *Proc. Int. Conf. on Pattern Recognition (12th)*, 1994.

Sherstinsky and Picard (1996). Sherstinsky A. and Picard R.W., "M-lattice: From morphogenesis to image processing," *IEEE Transactions on Image Processing*, vol. 5, no. 7, pp. 1137–1150, 1996.

Shi and Govindaraju (2006). Shi Z. and Govindaraju V., "A chaincode based scheme for fingerprint feature extraction," *Pattern Recognition Letters*, vol. 27, no. 5, pp. 462–468, 2006.

Shi et al. (2004). Shi Z., Wang Y., Qi J. and Xu K., "A New Segmentation Algorithm for Low Quality Fingerprint Image," in *Proc. Int. Conf. on Image and Graphics*, pp. 314–317, 2004.

Shigematsu et al. (1999). Shigematsu S., Morimura H., Tanabe Y. and Machida K., "A single-chip fingerprint sensor and identifier," *IEEE Journal of Solid-State Circuits*, vol. 34, no. 12, pp. 1852–1859, 1999.

Shin, Hwang and Chien (2006). Shin J.H., Hwang H.Y. and Chien I.L., "Detecting fingerprint minutiae by run length encoding scheme," *Pattern Recognition*, vol. 39, no. 6, pp. 1140–1154, 2006.

Shizume and Hefner (1978). Shizume P.K. and Hefner C.G., "A Computer Technical Fingerprint Search System," in *Proc. Int. Carnahan Conf. on Electronic Crime Countermeasures*, pp. 121–129, 1978.

Shogenji et al. (2004). Shogenji R., Kitamura Y., Yamada K., Miyatake S. and Tanida J., "Bimodal fingerprint capturing system based on compound-eye imaging module," *Applied Optics*, vol. 43, no. 6, pp. 1355–1359, 2004.

Shuai, Zhang and Hao (2007). Shuai X., Zhang C. and Hao P., "The Optimal ROS-Based Symmetric Phase-Only Filter for Fingerprint Verification," in *Proc. Int. Conf. on Image Processing*, vol. 2, pp. 381–384, 2007.

Shumurun et al. (1994). Shumurun A., Bjorn V., Tam S. and Holler M., "Extraction of Fingerprint Orientation Maps Using Radial Basis Function Recognition Accelerator," in *Proc. Int. Conf. on Neural Networks*, 1994.

Sim et al. (2007). Sim T., Zhang S., Janakiraman R. and Kumar S., "Continuous verification using multimodal biometrics," *IEEE Transactions on Pattern Analysis Machine Intelligence*, vol. 29, no. 4, pp. 687–700, 2007.

Simon-Zorita et al. (2001a). Simon-Zorita D., Ortega-Garcia J., Cruz-Llanas S. and Gonzalez-Rodriguez J., "Minutiae Extraction Scheme for Fingerprint Recognition Systems," in *Proc. Int. Conf. on Image Processing*, 2001a.

Simon-Zorita et al. (2001b). Simon-Zorita D., Ortega-Garcia J., Cruz-Llanas S., Sanchez-Bote J.L. and Glez-Rodriguez J., "An Improved Image Enhancement Scheme for Fingerprint Minutiae Extraction in Biometric Identification," in *Proc. Int. Conf. on Audio- and Video-Based Biometric Person Authentication (3rd)*, pp. 218–223, 2001b.

Simon-Zorita et al. (2003a). Simon-Zorita D., Ortega-Garcia J., Sanchez-Asenjo M. and Gonzalez-Rodriguez J., "Facing Position Variability in Minutiae-Based Fingerprint Verification Through Multiple References and Score Normalization Techniques," in *Proc. Int. Conf. on Audio- and Video-Based Biometric Person Authentication (4th)*, pp. 214–223, 2003a.

Simon-Zorita et al. (2003b). Simon-Zorita D., Ortega-Garcia J., Sanchez-Asenjo M. and Rodriguez J.G., "Minutiae-Based Enhanced Fingerprint Verification Assessment Relaying on Image Quality Factors," in *Proc. Int. Conf. on Image Processing*, vol. 3, pp. 891–894, 2003b.

Singh, Gyergyek and Pavesic (1977). Singh V.K., Gyergyek L. and Pavesic N., "Feature Recognition and Classification in Fingerprint Patterns," in *Proc. Int. Carnahan Conf. on Electronic Crime Countermeasures*, pp. 241–248, 1977.

Sjogaard (1992). Sjogaard S., "Discrete Neural Networks and Fingerprint Identification," in *Proc. Workshop on Signal Processing*, pp. 316–322, 1992.

Skodras, Christopoulos and Ebrahimi (2001). Skodras A., Christopoulos C. and Ebrahimi T., "JPEG 2000 still image compression standard," *IEEE Signal Processing Magazine*, vol. 18, no. 5, pp. 36–58, 2001.

Snelick et al. (2005). Snelick R., Uludag U., Mink A., Indovina M. and Jain A., "Large-scale evaluation of multimodal biometric authentication using state-of-the-art systems," *IEEE Transactions on Pattern Analysis Machine Intelligence*, vol. 27, no. 3, pp. 450–455, 2005.

Soifer et al. (1996). Soifer V., Kotlyar V., Khonina S. and Skidanov R., "Fingerprint Identification Using Directions Fields," in *Proc. Int. Conf. on Pattern Recognition (13th)*, 1996.

Soutar (2002). Soutar C., "Biometric System Security," *Secure – the Silicon Trust Magazine*, vol. 5, 2002.

Soutar (2004). Soutar C., "Security considerations for the implementation of biometric systems," in *Automatic Fingerprint Recognition Systems*, N. Ratha and R. Bolle (Eds.), Springer, New York, pp. 415–431, 2004.

Soutar and Tomko (1996). Soutar C. and Tomko G.J., "Secure Private Key Generation Using a Fingerprint," in *Proc. CardTech/SecurTech Conf.*, vol. I, pp. 245–252, 1996.

Soutar et al. (1998a). Soutar C., Roberge D., Stoianov A., Gilroy R. and Kumar B.V.K.V., "Biometric Encryption using Image Processing," *Proc. of SPIE*, vol. 3314, pp. 178–188, 1998a.

Soutar et al. (1998b). Soutar C., Roberge D., Stoianov A., Gilroy R. and Kumar B.V.K.V., "Biometric Encryption – Enrollement and Verification Precedures," in *Proc. of SPIE*, vol. 3386, pp. 24–35, 1998b.

Sparrow and Sparrow (1985a). Sparrow M. and Sparrow P., "A Topological Approach to the Matching of Single Fingerprints: Development of Algorithms for Use on Latent Fingermarks," U.S. Government Publication/U.S. Department of Commerce, National Bureau of Standards, Gaithersburg, MD/Washington, DC, 1985a.

Sparrow and Sparrow (1985b). Sparrow M. and Sparrow P., "A Topological Approach to the Matching of Single Fingerprints: Development of Algorithms for Use on Rolled Impressions," U.S. Government Publication/U.S. Department of Commerce, National Bureau of Standards, Gaithersburg, MD/Washington, DC, 1985b.

Srihari et al. (2001). Srihari S.N., Cha S.H., Arora H. and Lee S., "Individuality of Handwriting: A Validation Study," in *Proc. Int. Conf. on Document Analysis and Recognition (6th)*, pp. 106–109, 2001.

Srinivasan and Murthy (1992). Srinivasan V.S. and Murthy N.N., "Detection of singular points in fingerprint images," *Pattern Recognition*, vol. 25, no. 2, pp. 139–153, 1992.

Srinivasan et al. (2006). Srinivasan H., Srihari S.N., Beal M.J., Phatak P. and Fang G., "Comparison of ROC-Based and Likelihood Methods for Fingerprint Verification," in *Proc. SPIE Conf. on Biometric Technology for Human Identification III*, 2006.

Starink and Backer (1995). Starink J.P.P. and Backer E., "Finding point correspondence using simulated annealing," *Pattern Recognition*, vol. 28, no. 2, pp. 231–240, 1995.

Stock (1977). Stock R.M., "Automatic Fingerprint Reading," in *Proc. Int. Carnahan Conf. on Electronic Crime Countermeasures*, pp. 16–28, 1977.

Stock and Swonger (1969). Stock R.M. and Swonger C.W., "Development and evalutation of a reader of fingerprint minutiae," Tech. Report: XM–2478–X–1:13–17, Cornell Aeronautical Labaratory, 1969.

Stockman, Kopstein and Benett (1982). Stockman G., Kopstein S. and Benett S., "Matching images to models for registration of and object detection via clustering," *IEEE Transactions on Pattern Analysis Machine Intelligence*, vol. 4, no. 3, pp. 229–241, 1982.

Stoianov, Soutar and Graham (1999). Stoianov A., Soutar C. and Graham A., "High-speed fingerprint verification using an optical correlator," *Optical Engineering*, vol. 38, no. 1, pp. 99–107, 1999.

Stoney (1985). Stoney D.A., "A Quantitative Assessment of Fingerprint Individuality," Ph.D. thesis, University of California, 1985.

Stoney (1988). Stoney D.A., "Distribution of epidermal ridge minutiae," *American Journal of Physical Anthropology*, vol. 77, 367–376, 1988.

Stoney and Thornton (1986). Stoney D.A. and Thornton J.I., "A critical analisys of quantitative fingerprints individuality models," *Journal of Forensic Sciences*, vol. 31, no. 4, pp. 1187–1216, 1986.

Stoney and Thornton (1987). Stoney D.A and Thornton J.I., "A systematic study of epidermal ridge minutiae," *Journal of Forensic Sciences*, vol. 32, no. 5, pp. 1182–1203, 1987.

Stosz and Alyea (1994). Stosz J.D. and Alyea L.A., "Automated System for Fingerprint Authentication Using Pores and Ridge Structure," in *Proc. of SPIE (Automatic Systems for the Identification and Inspection of Humans)*, vol. 2277, pp. 210–223, 1994.

Su et al. (2005). Su Q., Tian J., Chen X. and Yang X., "A Fingerprint Authentication System Based on Mobile Phone," in *Proc. Int. Conf. on Audio- and Video-Based Biometric Person Authentication (5th)*, pp. 151–159, 2005.

Sudiro, Paindavoine and Kusuma (2007). Sudiro S.A., Paindavoine M. and Kusuma T.M., "Simple Fingerprint Minutiae Extraction Algorithm Using Crossing Number on Valley Structure," in *Proc. Workshop on Automatic Identification Advanced Technologies*, pp. 41–44, 2007.

Sujan and Mulqueen (2002). Sujan V.A. and Mulqueen M.P., "Fingerprint identification using space invariant transforms," *Pattern Recognition Letters*, vol. 23, no. 5, pp. 609–619, 2002.

Sutcu, Li and Memon (2007a). Sutcu Y., Li Q. and Memon N., "Secure Biometric Templates from Fingerprint-Face Features," in *Proc. Conf. Computer Vision and Pattern Recognition*, 2007a.

Sutcu, Li and Memon (2007b). Sutcu Y., Li Q. and Memon N., "Protecting biometric templates with sketch: Theory and practice," *IEEE Transactions on Information Forensics and Security*, vol. 2, no. 3, pp. 503–512, 2007b.

Sutcu, Sencar and Memon (2005). Sutcu Y., Sencar T. and Memon N., "A Secure Biometric Authentication Scheme Based on Robust Hashing," in *Proc. ACM Multimedia Security Workshop*, 2005.

Sutcu, Sencar and Memon (2007). Sutcu Y., Sencar H.T. and Memon N., "A Geometric Transformation to Protect Minutiae-Based Fingerprint Templates," in *Proc. SPIE Conf. on Biometric Technology for Human Identification IV*, 2007.

Svigals (1982). Svigals J., "Low cost personal identification verification device based on finger dimensions," *IBM Technical Disclosure Bulletin*, vol. 25, Sept. 1982.

Swonger (1973). Swonger C.W., "Application of Fingerprint Identification Technology to Criminal Identification and Security Systems.," in *Proc. Int. Carnahan Conf. on Electronic Crime Counter-measures*, pp. 190–212, 1973.

Székely and Székely (1993). Székely E. and Székely V., "Image recognition problems of fingerprint identification," *Microprocessors and microsystems*, vol. 17, no. 4, pp. 215–218, 1993.

Szu et al. (1995). Szu H., Hsu C., Garcia J. and Telfer B., "Fingerprint Data Acquisition, De-smearing, Wavelet Feature Extraction and Identification," in *Proc. of SPIE*, vol. 2491, pp. 96–118, 1995.

Tabassi, Wilson and Watson (2004). Tabassi E., Wilson C. and Watson C., "Fingerprint image quality," NIST Research Report: NISTIR 7151, Aug. 2004.

Tai et al. (2006). Tai K., Matsuyama E., Kurita M. and Fujieda I., "Dual-LED imaging for finger liveliness detection and its evaluation with replicas," *Applied Optics*, vol. 45, no. 24, pp. 6263–6269, 2006.

Tai, Kurita and Fujieda (2006). Tai K., Kurita M. and Fujieda I., "Recognition of living fingers with a sensor based on scattered-light detection," *Applied Optics*, vol. 45, no. 3, pp. 419–424, 2006.

Takeda et al. (1990). Takeda M., Uchida S., Hiramatsu K. and Matsunami T., "Finger Image Identification Method for Personal Verification," in *Proc. Int. Conf. on Pattern Recognition (10th)*, 1990.

Tamura (1978). Tamura H., "A Comparison of Line Thinning Algorithms from Digital Topology Viewpoint," in *Proc. Int. Conf. on Pattern Recognition (4th)*, pp. 715–719, 1978.

Tan and Bhanu (2003a). Tan X. and Bhanu B., "A robust two step approach for fingerprint identification," *Pattern Recognition Letters*, vol. 24, no. 13, pp. 2127–2134, 2003a.

Tan and Bhanu (2003b). Tan X. and Bhanu B., "On the Fundamental Performance for Fingerprint Matching," in *Proc. Conf. Computer Vision and Pattern Recognition*, vol. II, pp. 499–504, 2003b.

Tan and Bhanu (2006). Tan X. and Bhanu B., "Fingerprint matching by genetic algorithms," *Pattern Recognition*, vol. 39, no. 3, pp. 465–477, 2006.

Tan and Schuckers (2006a). Tan B. and Schuckers S., "Comparison of Ridge- and Intensity-Based Perspiration Liveness Detection Methods in Fingerprint Scanners," in *Proc. SPIE Conf. on Biometric Technology for Human Identification III*, 2006a.

Tan and Schuckers (2006b). Tan A. and Schuckers S.A.C., "Liveness Detection for Fingerprint Scanners Based on the Statistics of Wavelet Signal Processing," in *Proc. Int. Conf. on Computer Vision and Pattern Recognition (CVPR06)*, 2006b.

Tan and Schuckers (2008). Tan A. and Schuckers S.A.C., "New approach for liveness detection in fingerprint scanners based on valley noise analysis," *Journal of Electronic Imaging*, vol. 17, no. 1, 2008.

Tan, Bhanu and Lin (2005). Tan X., Bhanu B. and Lin Y., "Fingerprint classification based on learned features," *IEEE Transaction on Systems, Man, and Cybernetics, Part C*, vol. 35, no. 3, pp. 287–300, 2005.

Tartagni and Guerrieri (1998). Tartagni M. and Guerrieri R., "A fingerprint sensor based on the feedback capacitive sensing scheme," *IEEE Journal of Solid-State Circuits*, vol. 33, no. 1, pp. 133–142, 1998.

Teoh and Kim (2007). Teoh A.B.J. and Kim J., "Secure biometric template protection in fuzzy commitment scheme," *IEICE Electronics Express*, vol. 4, no. 23, pp. 724–730, 2007.

Teoh, Goh and Ngo (2006). Teoh A., Goh A. and Ngo D., "Random multispace quantization as an analytic mechanism for BioHashing of biometric and random identity inputs," *IEEE Transactions on Pattern Analysis and Machine Intelligence*, vol. 28, no. 12, pp. 1892–1901, 2006.

Tharna, Nilsson and Bigun (2003). Tharna J., Nilsson K. and Bigun J., "Orientation Scanning to Improve Lossless Compression of Fingerprint Images," in *Proc. Int. Conf. on Audio- and Video-Based Biometric Person Authentication (4th)*, pp. 343–350, 2003.

Thomas and Bryant (2000). Thomas D.A. and Bryant F.R., "Electrostatic Discharge Protection for Integrated Circuit Sensor Passivation," US Patent 6091082, 2000.

Tico and Kuosmanen (1999a). Tico M. and Kuosmanen P., "A Topographic Method for Fingerprint Segmentation," in *Proc. Int. Conf. on Image Processing*, 1999a.

Tico and Kuosmanen (1999b). Tico M. and Kuosmanen P., "A Multiresolution Method for Singular Point Detection in Fingerprint Images," in *Proc. Int. Symp. on Circuit Systems*, vol. IV, pp. 183–186, 1999b.

Tico and Kuosmanen (2003). Tico M. and Kuosmanen P., "Fingerprint matching using an orientation-based minutia descriptor," *IEEE Transactions on Pattern Analysis Machine Intelligence*, vol. 25, no. 8, pp. 1009–1014, 2003.

Tico, Kuosmanen and Saarinen (2001). Tico M., Kuosmanen P. and Saarinen J., "Wavelet domain features for fingerprint recognition," *Electronics Letters*, vol. 37, no. 1, pp. 21–22, 2001.

Toh and Yau (2004). Toh K.A. and Yau W.Y., "Combination of hyperbolic functions for multimodal biometrics data fusion," *IEEE Transaction on Systems, Man, and Cybernetics, Part B*, vol. 34, no. 1, pp. 85–94, 2004.

Toh and Yau (2005). Toh K.A. and Yau W.Y., "Fingerprint and speaker verification decisions fusion using a functional link network," *IEEE Transaction on Systems, Man, and Cybernetics, Part C*, vol. 35, no. 3, pp. 357–370, 2005.

Toh et al. (2001). Toh K.A., Yau W.Y., Jiang X., Chen T.P., Lu J. and Lim E., "Minutiae Data Synthesis for Fingerprint Identification Applications," in *Proc. Int. Conf. on Image Processing*, 2001.

Toh et al. (2003). Toh K.A., Xiong W., Yau W.Y. and Jiang X., "Combining Fingerprint and Hand-Geometry Verification Decisions," in *Proc. Int. Conf. on Audio- and Video-Based Biometric Person Authentication (4th)*, pp. 688–696, 2003.

Ton and Jain (1989). Ton J. And Jain A.K., "Registering landsat images by point matching," *IEEE Transaction Geoscience Remote Sensing*, vol. 27, no. 5, pp. 642–651, 1989.

Tong et al. (2005). Tong X., Huang J., Tang X. and Shi D., "Fingerprint minutiae matching using the adjacent feature vector," *Pattern Recognition Letters*, vol. 26, no. 9, pp. 1337–1345, 2005.

Tong et al. (2007). Tong V.V.T., Sibert H., Lecceur J. and Girault M., "Biometric Fuzzy Extractors Made Practical: A Proposal Based on FingerCodes," in *Proc. Int. Conf. on Biometrics*, LNCS 4642, pp. 604–613, 2007.

Tong et al. (2008). Tong X., Liu S., Huang J. and Tang X., "Local relative location error descriptor-based fingerprint minutiae matching," *Pattern Recognition Letters*, vol. 29, no. 3, pp. 286–294, 2008.

Tou and Hankley (1968). Tou J.T. and Hankley W.J., "Automatic fingerprint interpretation and classification via contextual analisys and topological coding", in *Pictorial Pattern Recognition*, Cheng, C., Ledley, S., Pollock, D. and Rosenfeld, A. (Eds.), Thompson Book,Washington, DC, pp. 411–456, 1968.

Toussaint (1971). Toussaint G.T., "Note on optimal selection of independent binary-valued features for pattern recognition," *IEEE Transactions on Information Theory*, vol. IT–17, pp. 618, 1971.

Trauring (1963). Trauring M., "Automatic comparison of finger-ridge patterns," *Nature*, pp. 938–940, 1963.

Tresp and Taniguchi (1995). Tresp V. and Taniguchi M., "Combining estimators using non-constant weighting functions," in *Advances in Neural Information Processing Systems*, G. Tesauro, D.S. Touretzky and T.K. Leen (Eds.), vol. 7, MIT, Cambridge, MA, 1995.

Trier and Jain (1995). Trier O. and Jain A.K., "Goal-directed evaluation of binarization methods," *IEEE Transactions on Pattern Analysis Machine Intelligence*, vol. 17, no. 12, pp. 1191–1201, 1995.

Tsikos (1982). Tsikos C., "Capacitive Fingerprint Sensor," US Patent 4353056, 1982.

Tulyakov et al. (2007). Tulyakov S., Farooq F., Mansukhani P. and Govindaraju V., "Symmetric hash functions for secure fingerprint biometric systems," *Pattern Recognition Letters*, vol. 28, no. 16, pp. 2184–2189, 2007.

Turing (1952). Turing A., "The chemical basis of morphogenesis," first published in *Philosophical Transactions of the Royal Society*, vol. 237, pp. 37–72, 1952.

Turk and Pentland (1991). Turk M. and Pentland A., "Eigenface for recognition," *Journal of Cognitive Neuroscience*, vol. 3, no. 1, pp. 71–86, 1991.

Tuyls and Goseling (2004). Tuyls P. and Goseling J., "Capacity and Examples of Template-Protecting Biometric Authentication Systems," in *Proc. Workshop on Biometric Authentication (in ECCV 2004)*, LNCS 3087, pp. 158–170, 2004.

Tuyls et al. (2005). Tuyls P., Akkermans A.H.M., Kevenaar T.A.M., Schrijen G.J., Bazen A.M. and Veldhuis R.N.J., "Practical Biometric Authentication with Template Protection," in *Proc. Int. Conf. on Audio- and Video-Based Biometric Person Authentication (5th)*, pp. 436–446, 2005.

Uchida (2004). Uchida K., "Image-Based Approach to Fingerprint Acceptability Assessment," in *Proc. Int. Conf. on Biometric Authentication (1st)*, LNCS 3072, pp. 294–300, 2004.

Uchida et al. (1998). Uchida K., Kamei T., Mizoguchi M. and Temma T., "Fingerprint Card Classification with Statistical Feature Integration," in *Proc. Int. Conf. on Pattern Recognition (14th)*, 1998.

Udupa, Garg and Sharma (2001). Udupa R., Garg G. and Sharma P., "Fast and Accurate Fingerprint Verification," in *Proc. Int. Conf. on Audio- and Video-Based Biometric Person Authentication (3rd)*, pp. 192–197, 2001.

UKBWG (2002). United Kingdom Biometric Working Group, "Best Practices in Testing and Reporting Biometric Device Performance," Tech. Report: Version 2.01, Aug. 2002.

Ulery et al. (2005). Ulery B., Hicklin A., Watson C., Indovina M. and Kwong K., "Slap Fingerprint Segmentation Evaluation 2004," NIST Research Report: NISTIR 7209, Mar. 2005.

Ulery et al. (2006). Ulery B., Hicklin A., Watson C., Fellner W. and Hallinan P., "Studies of Biometric Fusion," NIST Research Report: NISTIR 7346, Sept. 2006.

Uludag and Jain (2004). Uludag U. and Jain A.K., "Fuzzy Fingerprint Vault," in *Proc. Workshop on Biometrics: Challenges Arising from Theory to Practice*, pp. 13–16, 2004.

Uludag and Jain (2006). Uludag U. and Jain A.K., "Securing Fingerprint Template: Fuzzy Vault with Helper Data," in *Proc. Workshop on Privacy Research In Vision*, 2006.

Uludag et al. (2004). Uludag U., Pankanti S., Prabhakar S. and Jain A.K., "Biometric cryptosystems: Issues and challenges," *Proc. of the IEEE*, vol. 92, no. 6, pp. 948–960, 2004.

Uludag, Pankanti and Jain (2005). Uludag U., Pankanti S. and Jain A.K., "Fuzzy Vault for Fingerprints," in *Proc. Int. Conf. on Audio- and Video-Based Biometric Person Authentication (5th)*, pp. 310–319, 2005.

Uludag, Ross and Jain (2004). Uludag U., Ross A. and Jain A.K., "Biometric template selection and update: A case study in fingerprints," *Pattern Recognition*, vol. 37, no. 7, pp. 1533–1542, 2004.

Umeyama (1991). Umeyama S., "Least-square estimation of transformation parameters between two point patterns," *IEEE Transactions on Pattern Analysis Machine Intelligence*, vol. 13, no. 4, pp. 376–380, 1991.

Ushmaev and Novikov (2004). Ushmaev O.S. and Novikov S.O., "Integral Criteria for Large-Scale Multiple Fingerprint Solutions," in *Proc. SPIE Conf. on Biometric Technology for Human Identification I*, 2004.

Uz et al. (2007). Uz T., Bebis G., Erol A. and Prabhakar S., "Minutiae-Based Template Synthesis and Matching Using Hierarchical Delaunay Triangulations," in *Proc. Int. Conf. on Biometrics: Theory, Applications, and Systems (BTAS07)*, pp. 1–8, 2007.

Vacca (2007). Vacca J.R., *Biometric Technologies and Verification Systems*, Butterworth–Heinemann/ Elsevier, Burlington, MA, 2007.

Venkataramani and Kumar (2003). Venkataramani K. and Kumar B.V.K.V., "Fingerprint Verification Using Correlation Filters," in *Proc. Int. Conf. on Audio- and Video-Based Biometric Person Authentication (4th)*, pp. 886–894, 2003.

Venkataramani and Kumar (2004). Venkataramani K. and Kumar B.V.K.V., "Performance of composite correlation filters in fingerprint verification," *Optical Engineering*, vol. 43, no. 8, pp. 1820–1827, 2004.

Venkataramani, Keskinoz and Kumar (2005). Venkataramani K., Keskinoz M. and Kumar B.V.K.V., "Soft Information Fusion of Correlation Filter Output Planes Using Support Vector Machines for Improved Fingerprint Verification Performance," in *Proc. SPIE Conf. on Biometric Technology for Human Identification II*, 2005.

Verlinde, Chollet and Acheroy (2000). Verlinde P., Chollet G. and Acheroy M., "Multi-modal identity verification using expert fusion," *Information Fusion*, vol. 1, no. 1, pp. 17–33, July 2000.

Verma and Chatterjee (1989). Verma M.R. and Chatterjee B., "Partial fingerprint pattern classification," *Journal Institute Electronic & Telecom. Engineers*, vol. 3, no. 1, pp. 28–33, 1989.

Verma, Majumdar and Chatterjee (1987). Verma M.R., Majumdar A.K. and Chatterjee B., "Edge detection in fingerprints," *Pattern Recognition*, vol. 20, pp. 513–523, 1987.

Vermesan et al. (2003). Vermesan O., Riisnaes K.H., Le Pailleur L., Nysaether J.B., Bauge M., Rustad H., Clausen S., Blystad L.C., Grindvoll H., Pedersen R., Pezzani, R. and Kaire, D., "A 500-dpi AC capacitive hybrid flip-chip CMOS ASIC/sensor module for fingerprint, navigation, and pointer detection with on-chip data processing," *IEEE Journal of Solid-State Circuits*, vol. 38, no. 12, pp. 2288–2296, 2003.

Vernon (1993). Vernon D.S.G., "Automatic detection of secondary creases in fingerprints," *Optical Engineering*, vol. 32, no. 10, pp. 2616–2623, 1993.

Vielhauer, Steinmetz and Mayerhofer (2002). Vielhauer C., Steinmetz R. and Mayerhofer A., "Biometric Hash Based on Statistical Features of Online Signatures," in *Proc. Int. Conf. on Pattern Recognition (16th)*, vol. 1, pp. 123–126, 2002.

Viola and Jones (2001). Viola P. and Jones M.J., "Rapid Object Detection Using a Boosted Cascade of Simple Features," in *Proc. Int. Conf. on Computer Vision and Pattern Recognition*, vol. 1, pp. 511–518, 2001.

Viterbi (1967). Viterbi A.J., "Error bounds for convolutional codes and an asymptotically optimum decoding algorithm," *IEEE Transactions on Information Theory*, vol. 13, pp. 260–269, 1967.

Viveros, Balasubramanian and Mitas (1984). Viveros R., Balasubramanian K. and Mitas J.A., "Binomial and negative bionomial analogues under correlated bernoulli trials," *Journal of The American Statistician*, vol. 48, no. 3, pp. 243–247, 1984.

Vizcaya and Gerhardt (1996). Vizcaya P.R. and Gerhardt L.A., "A nonlinear orientation model for global description of fingerprints," *Pattern Recognition*, vol. 29, no. 7, pp. 1221–1231, 1996.

Wahab, Chin and Tan (1998). Wahab A., Chin S.H. and Tan E.C., "Novel approach to automated fingerprint recognition," *IEE Proceedings Vision Image and Signal Processing*, vol. 145, no. 3, pp. 160–166, 1998.

Wahab, Tan and Jonatan (2004). Wahab A., Tan E.C. and Jonatan A., "Direct Gray-Scale Minutiae Extraction," in *Proc. Int. Conf. on Biometric Authentication (1st)*, LNCS 3072, pp. 280–286, 2004.

Wan and Zhou (2006). Wan D. and Zhou J., "Fingerprint recognition using model-based density map," *IEEE Transactions on Image Processing*, vol. 15, no. 6, pp. 1690–1696, 2006.

Wang and Bhanu (2007). Wang R. and Bhanu B., "Predicting fingerprint biometrics performance from a small gallery," *Pattern Recognition Letters*, vol. 28, no. 1, pp. 40–48, 2007.

Wang and Dai (2007). Wang L. and Dai M., "Application of a new type of singular points in fingerprint classification," *Pattern Recognition Letters*, vol. 28, no. 13, pp. 1640–1650, 2007.

Wang and Hu (2008). Wang Y. and Hu J., "Estimate Singular Point Rotation by Analytical Models," in *Proc. SPIE Conf. on Biometric Technology for Human Identification V*, 2008.

Wang and Pavlidig (1993). Wang L. and Pavlidis T., "Direct gray-scale extraction of features for character recognition," *IEEE Transactions on Pattern Analysis Machine Intelligence*, vol. 15, no. 10, pp. 1053–1067, 1993.

Wang and Xie (2004). Wang X. and Xie M., "Fingerprint Classification: An Approach Based on Singularities and Analysis of Fingerprint Structure," in *Proc. Int. Conf. on Biometric Authentication (1st)*, LNCS 3072, pp. 324–329, 2004.

Wang et al. (2004). Wang F., Zou X., Luo Y. and Hu J., "A Hierarchy Approach for Singular Point Detection in Fingerprint Images," in *Proc. Int. Conf. on Biometric Authentication (1st)*, LNCS 3072, pp. 359–365, 2004.

Wang et al. (2006). Wang C., Gavrilova M., Luo Y. and Rokne J., "An Efficient Algorithm for Fingerprint Matching," in *Proc. Int. Conf. on Pattern Recognition (18th)*, vol. 1, pp. 1034–1037, 2006.

Wang et al. (2007). Wang Y., Hu J., Xi K. and Bhagavatula V., "Investigating Correlation-Based Fingerprint Authentication Schemes for Mobile Devices Using the J2ME technology," in *Proc. Workshop on Automatic Identification Advanced Technologies*, pp. 35–40, 2007.

Wang et al. (2008). Wang W., Li J., Huang F. and Feng H., "Design and implementation of Log-Gabor filter in fingerprint image enhancement," *Pattern Recognition Letters*, vol. 29, no. 3, pp. 301–308, 2008.

Wang, Hu and Phillips (2007). Wang Y., Hu J. and Phillips D., "A fingerprint orientation model based on 2D Fourier expansion (FOMFE) and its application to singular-point detection and fingerprint indexing," *IEEE Transactions on Pattern Analysis Machine Intelligence*, vol. 29, no. 4, pp. 573–585, 2007.

Wang, Li and Chen (2006). Wang W., Li J. and Chen W., "Fingerprint Minutiae Matching Based on Coordinate System Bank and Global Optimum Alignment," in *Proc. Int. Conf. on Pattern Recognition (18th)*, vol. 4, pp. 401–404, 2006.

Wang, Li and Niu (2007a). Wang X., Li J. and Niu Y., "Fingerprint matching using OrientationCodes and PolyLines," *Pattern Recognition*, vol. 40, no. 11, pp. 3164–3177, 2007a.

Wang, Li and Niu (2007b). Wang X., Li J. and Niu Y., "Definition and extraction of stable points from fingerprint images," *Pattern Recognition*, vol. 40, no. 6, pp. 1804–1815, 2007b.

Wang, Suo and Dai (2005). Wang L., Suo H. and Dai M., "Fingerprint Image Segmentation Based on Gaussian–Hermite Moments," in *Proc. Int. Conf. on Advanced Data Mining and Applications*, 2005.

Wang, Wang and Tan (2004). Wang Y., Wang Y. and Tan T., "Combining Fingerprint and Voiceprint Biometrics for Identity Verification: An Experimental Comparison," in *Proc. Int. Conf. on Biometric Authentication (1st)*, LNCS 3072, pp. 663–670, 2004.

Watson (1993a). Watson C.I., "NIST Special Database 14, Fingerprint Database," U.S. National Institute of Standards and Technology, 1993a.

Watson (1993b). Watson C.I., "NIST Special Database 10, Supplemental Fingerprint Card Data (SFCD) for NIST Special Database 9, Fingerprint Database.," U.S. National Institute of Standards and Technology, 1993b.

Watson (1998). Watson C.I., "NIST Special Database 24, Digital Video of Live-Scan Fingerprint Data," U.S. National Institute of Standards and Technology, 1998.

Watson and Casasent (2004a). Watson C.I. and Casasent D.P., "Recognition of live-scan fingerprints with elastic distortions using correlation filters," *Optical Engineering*, vol. 43, no. 10, pp. 2274–2282, 2004a.

Watson and Casasent (2004b). Watson C.I. and Casasent D.P., "Fingerprint matching using distortion-tolerant filters," in *Automatic Fingerprint Recognition Systems*, N. Ratha and R. Bolle (Eds.), Springer, New York, pp. 249–262, 2004b.

Watson and Wilson (1992a). Watson C.I. and Wilson C.L., "NIST Special Database 4, Fingerprint Database," U.S. National Institute of Standards and Technology, 1992a.

Watson and Wilson (1992b). Watson C.I. and Wilson C.L., "NIST Special Database 9, Fingerprint Database," U.S. National Institute of Standards and Technology, 1992b.

Watson et al. (2005a). Watson C.I., Wilson C., Marshall K., Indovina M. and Snelick R., "Studies of One-to-One Fingerprint Matching with Vendor SDK Matchers," NIST Research Report: NISTIR 7221, Apr. 2005a.

Watson et al. (2005b). Watson C.I., Wilson C., Indovina M. and Cochran B., "Two Finger Matching with Vendor SDK Matchers," NIST Research Report: NISTIR 7249, July 2005b.

Watson, Candela and Grother (1994). Watson C.I., Candela G.I. and Grother P.J., "Comparison of FFT Fingerprint Filtering Methods for Neural Network Classification," Tech. Report: NIST TR 5493, Sept. 1994.

Watson, Grother and Casasent (2000). Watson C.I., Grother P.J. and Casasent D.P., "Distortion-tolerant filter for elastic-distorted Fingerprint Matching," Tech. Report: NIST IR 6489, National Institute of Standards and Technology, Gaithersburg, Maryland, 2000.

Wayman (1999a). Wayman J.L., "Multi-finger Penetration Rate and ROC Variability for Automatic Fingerprint Identification Systems," Tech. Report: San Jose State University, 1999a.

Wayman (1999b). Wayman J.L., Fundamentals of biometric authentication technologies, in *National Biometric Test Center Collected Works*, Wayman J.L. (Ed.), vol. 1, National Biometric Test Center, San Jose, CA, 1999b.

Wayman (1999c). Wayman J.L., "Technical testing and evaluation of biometric identification devices," in *Biometrics: Personal Identification in a Networked Society*, A.K. Jain, R. Bolle and S. Pankanti (Eds.), Kluwer, Norwell, MA, pp. 345–368, 1999c.

Wayman (2001). Wayman J.L., "Confidence interval and test size estimation for biometric data," *Personal Communication*, 2001.

Wayman (2004). Wayman J.L., "Multi-finger penetration rate and ROC variability for automatic fingerprint identification systems," in *Automatic Fingerprint Recognition Systems*, N. Ratha and R. Bolle (Eds.), Springer, New York, pp. 305–316, 2004.

Wayman (2008). Wayman J.L., "Biometrics in identity management systems," *IEEE Security & Privacy*, vol. 6, no. 2, pp. 30–37, 2008.

Wayman et al. (2005). Wayman J., Jain A., Maltoni D. and Maio D., *Biometric Systems: Technology, Design and Performance Evaluation*, Springer, London, 2005.

Weber (1992). Weber D.M., "A Cost Effective Fingerprint Verification Algorithm for Commercial Applications," in *Proc. South African Symp. on Communication and Signal Processing*, 1992.

Wechsler (2007). Wechsler H., *Reliable Face Recognition Methods: System Design, Implementation and Evaluation*, Springer, New York, 2007.

Wegstein (1972). Wegstein J.H., "The M40 Fingerprint Matcher," U.S. Government Publication, National Bureau of Standars, Technical Note 878, U.S Government Printing Office, Washington, DC, 1972.

Wegstein (1982). Wegstein J.H., "An automated fingerprint identification system," U.S. Government Publication, U.S. Department of Commerce, National Bureau of Standards, Washington, DC, 1982.

Wegstein and Rafferty (1978). Wegstein J.H. and Rafferty J.F., "The LX39 latent fingerprint matcher," U.S. Government Publication, National Bureau of Standards, Institute for Computer Sciences and Technology, 1978.

Wei, Guo and Ou (2006). Wei H., Guo M. and Ou Z., "Fingerprint Verification Based on Multistage Minutiae Matching," in *Proc. Int. Conf. on Pattern Recognition (18th)*, vol. 2, pp. 1058–1061, 2006.

Wei, Yuan and Jie (1998). Wei D., Yuan Q. and Jie T., "Fingerprint Classification System with Feedback Mechanism Based on Genetic Algorithm," in *Proc. Int. Conf. on Pattern Recognition (14th)*, 1998.

Wentworth and Wilder (1918). Wentworth B. and H.H. Wilder, *Personal Identification*, R.G. Badger, Boston, MA, 1918.

Willis and Myers (2001). Willis A.J. and Myers L., "A cost–-effective fingerprint recognition system for use with low-quality prints and damaged fingertips," *Pattern Recognition*, vol. 34, no. 2, pp. 255–270, 2001.

Wilson and Woodard (1987). Wilson T. and Woodard P., "Automated fingerprint identification systems: Technology and policy issues," U.S. Government Publication, U.S. Department of Justice, Bureau of Justice Statistics, Washington, DC, 1987.

Wilson et al. (1992). Wilson C.L., Candela G.T., Grother P.J., Watson C.I. and Wilkinson, R.A., "Massively Parallel Network Fingerprint Classification System," Tech. Report: NIST TR 4880, Oct. 1992.

Wilson et al. (2004). Wilson C.L., Hicklin R.A., Korves H., Ulery B., Zoepfl M., Bone M., Grother P., Micheals R., Otto S. and Watson C., "Fingerprint Vendor Technology Evaluation 2003: Summary of Results and Analysis Report," NIST Research Report: 7123, June 2004.

Wilson, Candela and Watson (1994). Wilson C.L., Candela G.T. and Watson C.I., "Neural network fingerprint classification," *Journal of Artificial Neural Networks*, vol. 1, no. 2, pp. 203–228, 1994.

Wilson, Garris and Watson (2004). Wilson C.L., Garris M.D. and Watson C.I., "Matching Performance for the US–VISIT IDENT System Using Flat Fingerprints," NIST Research Report: NISTIR 7110, 2004.

Wilson, Watson and Paek (1997). Wilson C.L., Watson C.I. and Paek E.G., "Combined optical and neural network fingerprint matching," *Proc. of SPIE (Optical Pattern Recognition VIII)*, vol. 3073, pp. 373–382, 1997.

Wilson, Watson and Paek (2000). Wilson C.L., Watson C.I. and Paek E.G., "Effect of resolution and image quality on combined optical and neural network fingerprint matching," *Pattern Recognition*, vol. 33, no. 2, pp. 317–331, 2000.

Wolpert (1992). Wolper D., "Stacked generalization," *Neural Networks*, vol. 5, pp. 241–259, 1992.

Woodward (1999). Woodward J., "Biometrics: Identifying law and policy concerns," in *Biometrics: Personal Identification in a Networked Society*, A.K. Jain, R. Bolle and S. Pankanti (Eds.), Kluwer, Boston, MA, 1999.

Woodward, Orlans and Higgins (2002). Woodward J.D., Orlans N.M. and Higgins P., *Biometrics: Identity Assurance in the Information Age*, McGraw-Hill, New York, 2002.

Wu and Garris (2007). Wu J.C. and Garris M.D., "Nonparametric Statistical Data Analysis of Fingerprint Minutiae Exchange with Two-Finger Fusion," in *Proc. SPIE Conf. on Biometric Technology for Human Identification IV*, 2007.

Wu and Govindaraju (2006). Wu C. and Govindaraju V., "Singularity Preserving Fingerprint Image Adaptive Filtering," in *Proc. Int. Conf. on Image Processing*, pp. 313–316, 2006.

Wu and Wilson (2006). Wu J.C. and Wilson C.L., "An Empirical Study of Sample Size in ROC-Curve Analysis of Fingerprint Data," in *Proc. SPIE Conf. on Biometric Technology for Human Identification III*, 2006.

Wu and Wilson (2007). Wu J.C. and Wilson C.L., "Nonparametric analysis of fingerprint data on large data sets," *Pattern Recognition*, vol. 40, no. 9, pp. 2574–2584, 2007.

Wu and Zhou (2004). Wu N. and Zhou J., "Model Based Algorithm for Singular Point Detection from Fingerprint Images," in *Proc. Int. Conf. on Image Processing*, vol. 2, pp. 885–888, 2004.

Wu et al. (2003). Wu C., Zhou J., Bian Z. and Rong G., "Robust Crease Detection in Fingerprint Images," in *Proc. Conf. Computer Vision and Pattern Recognition*, vol. II, pp. 505–510, 2003.

Wu, Shi and Govindaraju (2004). Wu C., Shi Z. and Govindaraju V., "Fingerprint Image Enhancement Method Using Directional Median Filter," in *Proc. SPIE Conf. on Biometric Technology for Human Identification I*, 2004.

Wu, Tulyakov and Govindaraju (2007). Wu C., Tulyakov S. and Govindaraju V., "Robust Point-Based Feature Fingerprint Segmentation Algorithm," in *Proc. Int. Conf. on Biometrics*, LNCS 4642, pp. 1095–1103, 2007.

Xia and O'Gorman (2003). Xia X. and O'Gorman L., "Innovations in fingerprint capture devices," *Pattern Recognition*, vol. 36, no. 2, pp. 361–369, 2003.

Xiao and Bian (1986). Xiao Q. and Bian Z., "An Approach to Fingerprint Identification by Using the Attributes of Feature Lines of Fingerprint," in *Proc. Int. Conf. on Pattern Recognition (8th)*, pp. 663–665, 1986.

Xiao and Raafat (1991a). Xiao Q. and Raafat H., "Combining statistical and structural information for fingerprint image processing classification and identification," in *Pattern Recognition: Architectures Algorithms and Application*, R. Plamondon and H. Cheng (Eds.), World Scientific, Singapore, pp. 335–354, 1991a.

Xiao and Raafat (1991b). Xiao Q. and Raafat H., "Fingerprint image post-processing: A combined statistical and structural approach," *Pattern Recognition*, vol. 24, no. 10, pp. 985–992, 1991b.

Xie et al. (2004). Xie X., Su F., Cai A. and Sun J., "A Robust Fingerprint Minutiae Matching Algorithm Based on the Support Model," in *Proc. Int. Conf. on Biometric Authentication (1st)*, LNCS 3072, pp. 316–323, 2004.

Xie et al. (2005). Xie W., Tian J., Yang X., Chen H., He Y. and Zhang T., "Embedded Fingerprint Identification System Based on DSP," in *Proc. SPIE Conf. on Biometric Technology for Human Identification II*, 2005.

Xie, Su and Cai (2006). Xie X., Su F. and Cai A., "Ridge-Based Fingerprint Recognition," in *Proc. Int. Conf. on Biometrics*, LNCS 3832, pp. 273–279, 2006.

Xu, Chen and Feng (2007). Xu W., Chen X. and Feng J., "A Robust Fingerprint Matching Approach: Growing and Fusing of Local Structures," in *Proc. Int. Conf. on Biometrics*, LNCS 4642, pp. 134–143, 2007.

Xu, Krzyzac and Suen (1992). Xu L., Krzyzak A. and Suen C.Y., "Methods for combining multiple classifiers and their applications to handwriting recognition," *IEEE Transactions on Systems Man and Cybernatics*, vol. 22, no. 3, pp. 418–435, 1992.

Xuening et al. (1989). Xuening S., Minde C., Qingyun S., Guisheng Q., "A new automated fingerprint identification system," *Computer Science Technology*, vol. 4, no. 4, pp. 289–294, 1989.

Yager and Amin (2004). Yager N. and Amin A., "Evaluation of Fingerprint Orientation Field Registration Algorithms," in *Proc. Int. Conf. on Pattern Recognition (17th)*, vol. 4, pp. 641–644, 2004.

Yager and Amin (2006a). Yager N. and Amin A., "Dynamic registration selection for fingerprint verification," *Pattern Recognition*, vol. 39, no. 11, pp. 2141–2148, 2006a.

Yager and Amin (2006b). Yager N. and Amin A., "Fingerprint alignment using a two stage optimization," *Pattern Recognition Letters*, vol. 27, no. 5, pp. 317–324, 2006b.

Yahagi, Igaki and Yamagishi (1990). Yahagi H., Igaki S. and Yamagishi F., "Moving-Window Algorithm For Fast Verification," in *Proc. Southeastcon Conf.*, pp. 343–348, 1990.

Yamazaki and Komatsu (2001). Yamazaki Y. and Komatsu N., "A secure communication system using biometric identity verification," *IEICE Transactions on Information and Systems*, vol. E84–D, no. 7 pp. 879–884, 2001.

Yang and Verbauwhede (2003). Yang S. and Verbauwhede I.M., "A Secure Fingerprint Matching Technique," in *Proc. SIGMM Workshop on Biometrics Methods and Applications*, pp. 89–94, 2003.

Yang and Verbauwhede (2005). Yang S. and Verbauwhede I.M., "Secure Fingerprint Verification System Based on Fuzzy Vault Scheme," in *Proc. Int. Conf. on Acoustics, Speech, and Signal Processing (ICASSP 05)*, pp. 609–612, 2005.

Yang and Zhou (2006). Yang C. and Zhou J., "A comparative study of combining multiple enrolled samples for fingerprint verification," *Pattern Recognition*, vol. 39, no. 11, pp. 2115–2130, 2006.

Yang et al. (2003). Yang J., Liu L., Jiang T. and Fan Y., "A modified Gabor filter design method for fingerprint image enhancement," *Pattern Recognition Letters*, vol. 24, no. 12, pp. 1805–1817, 2003.

Yang, Moon and Chan (2004). Yang T.Y., Moon Y.S. and Chan K.C., "Efficient Implementation of Fingerprint Verification for Mobile Embedded Systems Using Fixed-Point Arithmetic," in *Proc. ACM Symp. on Applied Computing*, pp. 821–825, 2004.

Yang, Sakiyama and Verbauwhede (2006). Yang S., Sakiyama K. and Verbauwhede I., "Efficient and secure fingerprint verification for embedded devices," *EURASIP Journal on Applied Signal Processing*, vol. 2006, no. 1, pp. 1–11, 2006.

Yanushkevich et al. (2005). Yanushkevich S.N., Stoica A., Shmerko V.P. and Popel D.V., *Biometric Inverse Problems*, Taylor & Francis/CRC Press, Boca Raton, FL, 2005.

Yao et al. (2003). Yao Y., Marcialis G.L., Pontil M., Frasconi P. and Roli F., "Combining flat and structured representations for fingerprint classification with recursive neural networks and support vector machines," *Pattern Recognition*, vol. 36, no. 2, pp. 397–406, 2003.

Yao, Frasconi and Pontil (2001). Yao Y., Frasconi P. and Pontil M., "Fingerprint Classification with Combination of Support Vector Machines," in *Proc. Int. Conf. on Audio- and Video-Based Biometric Person Authentication (3rd)*, pp. 253–258, 2001.

Yao, Pankanti and Hass (2004). Yao M.Y.S, Pankanti S. and Hass N., "Fingerprint quality assessment," in *Automatic Fingerprint Recognition Systems*, N. Ratha and R. Bolle (Eds.), Springer, New York, pp. 55–66, 2004.

Yau et al. (2000). Yau W.Y., Toh K.A, Jiang X, Chen T.P and Lu Juwei, "On Fingerprint Template Synthesis," in *Proc. Int. Conf. on Control Automation Robotics and Vision (6th)*, 2000.

Yau et al. (2007). Yau W.Y., Tran H.T., Teoh E.K. and Wang J.G., "Fake Finger Detection by Finger Color Change Analysis," in *Proc. Int. Conf. on Biometrics*, LNCS 4642, pp. 888–896, 2007.

Yau, Chen and Morguet (2004). Yau W.Y., Chen T.P. and Morguet P., "Benchmarking of Fingerprint Sensors," in *Proc. Workshop on Biometric Authentication (in ECCV 2004)*, LNCS 3087, pp. 89–99, 2004.

Yeung and Pankanti (2000). Yeung M. and Pankanti S., "Verification watermarks on fingerprint recognition and retrieval," *Journal of Electronic Imaging*, vol. 9, no. 4, pp. 468–476, 2000.

Yeung et al. (2005). Yeung H.W., Moon Y.S., Chen J., Chan F., Ng Y.M., Chung H.S. and Pun K.H., "A Comprehensive and Real-Time Fingerprint Verification System for Embedded Devices," in *Proc. SPIE Conf. on Biometric Technology for Human Identification II*, 2005.

Yeung, Moon and Chan (2004). Yeung H.W., Moon Y.S. and Chan K.C., "Fingerprint Registration for Small Fingerprint Sensors," in *Proc. SPIE Conf. on Biometric Technology for Human Identification I*, 2004.

Yi et al. (2006). Yi C., Parziale G., Diaz-Santana E. and Jain A.K., "3D Touchless Fingerprints: Compatibility with Legacy Rolled Images," in *Proc. Biometric Symposium*, 2006.

Yin, Wang and Yang (2005). Yin Y., Wang Y. and Yang X., "Fingerprint Image Segmentation Based on Quadric Surface Model," in *Proc. Int. Conf. on Audio- and Video-Based Biometric Person Authentication (5th)*, pp. 647–655, 2005.

Yin, Zhang and Yang (2005). Yin Y., Zhang H. and Yang X., "A Method Based on Delaunay Triangulation for Fingerprint Matching," in *Proc. SPIE Conf. on Biometric Technology for Human Identification II*, 2005.

Yin, Zhao and Yang (2005). Yin Y., Zhao B. and Yang X., "An On-Line Template Improvement Algorithm," in *Proc. SPIE Conf. on Biometric Technology for Human Identification II*, 2005.

Young and Elliott (2007). Young M.R. and Elliott S.J., "Image Quality and Performance Based on Henry Classification and Finger Location," in *Proc. Workshop on Automatic Identification Advanced Technologies*, pp. 51–56, 2007.

Young et al. (1997). Young N.D., Harkin G., Bunn R.M., McCulloch D.J., Wilks R.W. and Knapp A.G., "Novel fingerprint scanning arrays using polysilicon tft's on glass and polymer substrates," *IEEE Electron Device Letters*, vol. 18, no. 1, pp. 19–20, 1997.

Yu, Na and Choi (2005). Yu K.D., Na S. and Choi T.Y., "A Fingerprint Matching Algorithm Based on Radial Structure and a Structure-Rewarding Scoring Strategy," in *Proc. Int. Conf. on Audio- and Video-Based Biometric Person Authentication (5th)*, pp. 656–664, 2005.

Zebbiche, Khelifi and Bouridane (2007). Zebbiche K., Khelifi F. and Bouridane A., "Optimum Detection of Multiplicative-Multibit Watermarking for Fingerprint Images," in *Proc. Int. Conf. on Biometrics*, LNCS 4642, pp. 732–741, 2007.

Zhan et al. (2006). Zhan X., Sun Z., Yin Y. and Chu Y., "Fingerprint Ridge Distance Estimation: Algorithms and the Performance," in *Proc. Int. Conf. on Biometrics*, LNCS 3832, pp. 294–301, 2006.

Zhang and Wang (2002). Zhang W. and Wang Y., "Core-Based Structure Matching Algorithm of Fingerprint Verification," in *Proc. Int. Conf. on Pattern Recognition (16th)*, vol. 1, pp. 70–74, 2002.

Zhang and Xiao (2006). Zhang Y. and Xiao Q., "An Optimized Approach for Fingerprint Binarization," in *Proc. Int. Joint Conf. on Neural Networks*, pp. 391–395, 2006.

Zhang and Yan (2004). Zhang Q. and Yan H., "Fingerprint classification based on extraction and analysis of singularities and pseudo ridges," *Pattern Recognition*, vol. 37, no. 11, pp. 2233–2243, 2004.

Zhang and Yan (2007). Zhang Q. and Yan H., "Fingerprint orientation field interpolation based on the constrained delaunay triangulation," *International Journal of Information and Systems Sciences*, vol. 3, no. 3, pp. 438–452, 2007.

Zhang et al. (2003). Zhang T., Tian J., He Y. and Yang X., "Fingerprint Alignment Using Similarity Histogram," in *Proc. Int. Conf. on Audio- and Video-Based Biometric Person Authentication (4th)*, pp. 854–861, 2003.

Zhang et al. (2004). Zhang G., Huang X., Li S. and Wang Y., "Boosting Local Binary Pattern (LBP)-Based Face Recognition," *Sinobiometrics* 2004, LNCS 3338, pp. 179–186, 2004.

Zhang et al. (2007a). Zhang Y., Tian J., Chen X., Yang X. and Shi P., "Fake Finger Detection Based on Thin-Plate Spline Distortion Model," in *Proc. Int. Conf. on Biometrics*, LNCS 4642, pp. 742–749, 2007a.

Zhang et al. (2007b). Zhang Y., Yang X., Su Q. and Tian J., "Fingerprint Recognition Based on Combined Features," in *Proc. Int. Conf. on Biometrics*, LNCS 4642, pp. 281–289, 2007b.

Zhang, Xu and Chang (2003). Zhang L.H., Xu W.L. and Chang C., "Genetic algorithm for affine point pattern matching," *Pattern Recognition Letters*, vol. 24, no. 3, pp. 9–19, 2003.

Zhang, Yang and Wu (2005). Zhang Y.L., Yang J. and Wu H.T., "A Hybrid Swipe Fingerprint Mosaicing Scheme," in *Proc. Int. Conf. on Audio- and Video-Based Biometric Person Authentication (5th)*, pp. 131–140, 2005.

Zhang, Yang and Wu (2006a). Zhang Y.L., Yang J. and Wu H.T., "Sweep fingerprint sequence reconstruction for portable devices," *Electronics Letters*, vol. 42, no. 4, pp. 204–205, 2006a.

Zhang, Yang and Wu (2006b). Zhang Y.L., Yang J. and Wu H.T., "Coarse-to-fine image registration for sweep fingerprint sensors," *Optical Engineering*, vol. 45, no. 6, 2006b.

Zhao and Tang (2007). Zhao F. and Tang X., "Preprocessing and postprocessing for skeleton-based fingerprint minutiae extraction," *Pattern Recognition*, vol. 40, no. 4, pp. 1270–1281, 2007.

Zhao, Su and Cai (2006). Zhao D., Su F. and Cai A., "Fingerprint Registration Using Minutia Clusters and Centroid Structure 1," in *Proc. Int. Conf. on Pattern Recognition (18th)*, vol. 4, pp. 413–416, 2006.

Zheng, Wang and Zhao (2007). Zheng X., Wang Y. and Zhao X., "A Robust Matching Method for Distorted Fingerprints," in *Proc. Int. Conf. on Image Processing*, vol. 2, pp. 377–380, 2007.

Zhixin and Govindaraju (2006). Zhixin S. and Govindaraju V., "Fingerprint Image Enhancement Based on Skin Profile Approximation," in *Proc. Int. Conf. on Pattern Recognition (18th)*, vol. 3, pp. 714–717, 2006.

Zhou (2007). Zhou X., "Template Protection and Its Implementation in 3D Face Recognition Systems," in *Proc. SPIE Conf. on Biometric Technology for Human Identification IV*, pp. 214–225, 2007.

Zhou and Gu (2004a). Zhou J. and Gu J., "A model-based method for the computation of fingerprints' orientation field," *IEEE Transactions on Image Processing*, vol. 13, no. 6, pp. 821–835, 2004a.

Zhou and Gu (2004b). Zhou J. and Gu J., "Modeling orientation fields of fingerprints with rational complex functions," *Pattern Recognition*, vol. 37, no. 2, pp. 389–391, 2004b.

Zhou et al. (2001). Zhou J., He D., Rong G. and Qi Bian Z., "Effective algorithm for rolled fingerprint construction," *Electronics Letters*, vol. 37, no. 8, pp. 492–494, 2001.

Zhou et al. (2004). Zhou J., Wu C., Bian Z. and Zhang D., "Improving Fingerprint Recognition Based on Crease Detection," in *Proc. Int. Conf. on Biometric Authentication (1st)*, LNCS 3072, pp. 287–293, 2004.

Zhou, Gu and Zhang (2007). Zhou J., Gu J. and Zhang D., "Singular Points Analysis in Fingerprints Based on Topological Structure and Orientation Field," in *Proc. Int. Conf. on Biometrics*, LNCS 4642, pp. 261–270, 2007.

Zhou, Qiao and Mok (1998). Zhou G., Qiao Y. and Mok F., "Fingerprint Sensing System Using a Sheet Prism," US Patent 5796858, 1998.

Zhu et al. (2005). Zhu E., Yin J., Hu C. and Zhang G., "Quality Estimation of Fingerprint Image Based on Neural Network," in *Proc. Int. Conf. on Natural Computation* 2005, LNCS 3611, pp. 65–70, 2005.

Zhu et al. (2006). Zhu E., Yin J., Hu C. and Zhang G., "A systematic method for fingerprint ridge orientation estimation and image segmentation," *Pattern Recognition*, vol. 39, no. 8, pp. 1452–1472, 2006.

Zhu, Dass and Jain (2006). Zhu Y., Dass S.C. and Jain A.K., "Compound Stochastic Models For Fingerprint Individuality," in *Proc. Int. Conf. on Pattern Recognition (18th)*, vol. 3, pp. 532–535, 2006.

Zhu, Dass and Jain (2007). Zhu Y., Dass S.C. and Jain A.K., "Statistical models for assessing the individuality of fingerprints," *IEEE Transactions on Information Forensics and Security*, vol. 2, no. 3, pp. 391–401, 2007.

Zhu, Yin and Zhang (2004). Zhu E., Yin J. and Zhang G., "Fingerprint Enhancement Using Circular Gabor Filter," in *Proc. Int. Conf. on Image on Analysis and Recognition*, LNCS 3212, pp. 750–758, 2004.

Zhu, Yin and Zhang (2005). Zhu E., Yin J. and Zhang G., "Fingerprint matching based on global alignment of multiple reference minutiae," *Pattern Recognition*, vol. 38, no. 10, pp. 1685–1694, 2005.

Index